# MANAGERIAL ECONOMICS

# MANAGERIAL ECONOMICS
## theory, practice, and problems

EVAN J. DOUGLAS
*Concordia University*

PRENTICE-HALL, INC.
ENGLEWOOD CLIFFS, NEW JERSEY   07632

*Library of Congress Cataloging in Publication Data*

Douglas, Evan J., - (date)
   Managerial economics.

   Includes bibliographies and index.
   1. Managerial economics.   I. Title.
HD30.22.D68      658.4      78-15358
ISBN   0-13-550236-5

Editorial/production supervision and
interior design by Barbara Alexander

Cover design by Edsal Enterprise

Manufacturing buyer: Phil Galea

Printed in the United States of America

10   9   8   7   6   5   4   3   2

PRENTICE-HALL INTERNATIONAL, INC., *London*
PRENTICE-HALL OF AUSTRALIA PTY. LIMITED, *Sydney*
PRENTICE-HALL OF CANADA, LTD., *Toronto*
PRENTICE-HALL OF INDIA PRIVATE LIMITED, *New Delhi*
PRENTICE-HALL OF JAPAN, INC., *Tokyo*
PRENTICE-HALL OF SOUTHEAST ASIA PTE. LTD., *Singapore*
WHITEHALL BOOKS LIMITED, *Wellington, New Zealand*

To Jane,
and our families

# Contents

vii

# part II

# Demand Theory and Analysis

# part III

## Production and Cost Analysis

# part IV

# Pricing Analysis and Decisions

# part V

# Topics in Managerial Economics

## 13

### Linear-Programming Analysis     *389*

## 14

### Advertising and Promotional Decisions     *420*

## 15

### Capital Budgeting and Investment Decisions     *442*

# appendix A

## Present Value Tables

# appendix B

## Short Answers to Odd-Numbered Problems

# Preface

*Managerial Economics* is concerned with the application of economic principles and methodologies to the decision-making process under conditions of uncertainty. The subtitle to this book, *Theory, Practice, and Problems,* is intended to convey three major features of the approach taken here. First, it is my belief that economic theory is useful and can be applied to business decision-making problems to beneficial effect. Economic theory under conditions of certainty establishes important principles for business practice under conditions of uncertainty. Second, business practice must be recognized and incorporated into the discipline of managerial economics. For example, if firms choose to use markup-pricing policies rather than take the marginalist approach, then the task of the managerial economist is to assist the decision maker in finding the optimal level of the markup rather than to harangue for marginalism. Third, the concepts and issues involved in managerial economics must be put into the context of real-world business decision problems in order to demonstrate methods of identifying problems and finding solutions. Thus each chapter incorporates business examples and is followed by provocative discussion questions and case-study problems.

This book is designed for a one-semester course in managerial economics at the undergraduate or MBA level. The level of treatment presupposes a basic microeconomics course, although this is not necessary for the better students, since each concept is developed from basics (usually quite rapidly) on the presumption that most students need refreshing on their micro principles. The approach is intended to present the material in a more cohesive way to improve comprehension and retention. It should "bring it all together" for the student who has taken the prerequisite course, without offering any disadvantage to the new student of economics. Similarly, students may feel more comfortable with this textbook if they have had basic calculus and statistics courses, but the required mathematical or statistical principles are explained in some detail either in the first chapter or in subsequent chapters. Rather than have a lengthy review chapter at the beginning, it was considered preferable to explain or review much of the mathematical and statistical material at the point at which it can be used by the student in solving a decision problem. This philosophy allows the students to get into the managerial economics material more quickly at the start of the term, avoids their having to understand concepts that they do not yet know how to use, and offers the advantages of "learning by doing."

The major difference between this text and others available is that this one caters to the renewed interest in pricing as a marketing strategy, with four separate chapters on the theory and practice of pricing. It incorporates recent developments in this area, including the incorporation of product attribute theory into the consumer behavior and pricing chapters, and discussion of the requirements for static and dynamic optimality of markup pricing. The chapter entitled "Competitive Bids and Price Quotes" focuses on a pricing situation that is more widely applicable than is generally realized, and it brings together all major elements of the course.

The other important areas of managerial economics are not neglected. The two chapters in Part I of the book lay the groundwork necessary for decision making under uncertainty. Chapter 1 introduces the student to the field of managerial economics and the use of models and other analytical concepts and tools in the decision-making process. More complex analytical tools and techniques are introduced in later chapters at the point where each is first required to solve a decision problem. In Chapter 2 the concepts of certainty, risk and uncertainty, probabilities, discounted cash flow, and the choice and application of decision-making criteria are discussed in detail.

Parts II and III examine the demand and cost conditions facing the firm. Each of these parts is introduced by a chapter on the theoretical underpinnings, with the treatment confined to those segments of the micro theory that are important to an understanding of the concepts that are used for decision making, and avoiding the more esoteric frills. The second chapter in each part is concerned with using this understanding to make better decisions. The third chapter in each part deals with estimation and forecasting of cost and demand conditions, in order to provide the information necessary for decision making.

Part IV brings together the analyses of the earlier parts with two chapters on models of pricing behavior and two chapters on pricing decisions using information generated by the demand and cost estimation procedures. Part V, the final part of the book, examines linear programming, advertising and promotion, and capital budgeting, from a managerial economics perspective. In many commerce or business programs these topics are covered in quantitative methods, marketing, and finance courses and hence may be excluded or covered more quickly if the instructor so desires. Other self-contained sections within chapters, such as the analytical tools, regression analysis, and demand forecasting, may be treated similarly if the students' preparation so warrants.

The entire draft of this text has been class-tested and has benefited from feedback from hundreds of students and several professorial reviewers. As a result this text incorporates several pedagogical and learning aids not commonly found. Summary tables, stage-by-stage development of complex figures and concepts, incorporation of examples and business situations in the text, ample discussion questions and case study problems, and short answers to the odd-numbered problems, are provided to assist the learning process. Further readings and alternate sources of material are referenced at the end of each chapter for the inquisitive and higher level students. Throughout the text efforts have been made to enhance the readability and flow of the material.

*Acknowledgments.* For their constructive comments on earlier drafts of the manuscript, my thanks are due to the reviewers at Colorado State University, New York University, University of California (Berkeley) and University of Florida (Gainsville). Invaluable comments and input were received from students in my classes here at Concordia. Although all names used in the text and problems are fictitious, some of you will find a name like yours as President, Marketing Manager, or similar in the case-study problems. I thank you all, and I trust that it is only a matter of time before you achieve your objectives, whatever they may be.

For typing and a variety of work involved in the preparation of the manuscript over the past two years, my thanks are due to a long list of people, whom I will thank individually. I also wish to thank several of my colleagues for comments and assistance on various issues, but in particular Steve Robbins, Joe Kelly and Gary Johns were valuable sources of information and guidance. The late Cliff Lloyd, and Peter Kennedy and Brian Johns, were three of my best teachers. Last, and perhaps most, my thanks are due to the people at Prentice-Hall. My editors, Susan Anderson at first and then David Hildebrand, deserve a sincere vote of appreciation for their efforts in securing high-quality reviews and providing all kinds of support and encouragement. My production editor, Barbara Alexander, is to be commended for her efforts in transforming the manuscript into a book.

I welcome all comments and suggestions from students, instructors, and others for improving the text and the problems. Please address them to me at the Department of Finance, Concordia University, Montreal, Canada, H3G 1M8.

EVAN J. DOUGLAS
*Montreal, Canada*

# MANAGERIAL
# ECONOMICS

# part I

# Introduction

# 1

# Introduction to Managerial Economics

## 1.1 DEFINITION AND SCOPE OF MANAGERIAL ECONOMICS

Managerial economics is concerned with the application of economic principles and methodologies to the decision-making process within the firm or organization. It seeks to establish rules and principles to facilitate the attainment of the desired economic goals of management. These economic goals relate to costs, revenues, and profits and are important within both the business and the nonbusiness institution. Profit-oriented business firms certainly must strive to make optimal decisions with regard to costs and revenues, but so too must nonbusiness organizations, such as hospitals and universities, seek to spend available funds to maximum effect. The decision problems in the business and nonbusiness institutions are essentially similar in many areas. The decision-making principles to be discussed in this textbook, while primarily introduced in the context of a business firm, are thus applicable to a great variety of economic decision problems in the nonbusiness institution as well.

### Theoretical Antecedents of Managerial Economics

The economic principles and methodologies of managerial economics are derived largely from microeconomics, which is that part of the economics discipline concerned with the behavior of individual economic units such as the consumers, the producers, and the suppliers of labor, capital, and organizational services. Unlike the neoclassical microeconomics, however, in which optimal decisions are made in an environment of full information, managerial economics has evolved to provide guidance for decision making in an environment of uncertainty. The existence of uncertainty requires the use of analytical tools, concepts, and notions from other disciplines, such as mathematics, statistics, operations research, finance, accounting, and marketing, in order to allow the managerial economist to choose the optimal solution to particular decision problems.

4

The principles of microeconomics and the elements of the other disciplines mentioned will be discussed in following chapters on the basis of two assumptions: first, that students have previously taken an introductory course in microeconomics and have had some exposure to basic mathematical and statistical concepts; and second, that students may be somewhat rusty on these principles and therefore will benefit from a review of this material. These reviews are usually brief and fairly rigorous, however, and some students may need to go back to their introductory textbooks in these areas in order to get up to par. But since the material is developed from basics, it should present little difficulty to those students who have not had previous exposure to basic courses in microeconomics, mathematics, and statistics.

### Positive vs. Normative Economics

Within the discipline of economics the distinction is made between those areas that are "positive" and those areas that are "normative." Positive economics is concerned with description: it describes how economic agents or economic systems *do operate* within the economy or society. Normative economics, on the other hand, is concerned with prescription: it prescribes how economic agents or systems *should operate* in order to attain desired objectives. In microeconomics, for example, it is assumed that the consumer wishes to maximize utility, and certain principles prescribe the behavior by which this objective may be attained. Similarly, macroeconomics prescribes certain measures for the attainment of objectives such as full employment and price stability.

Managerial economics is primarily "normative," since it seeks to establish rules and principles to be applied in decision making in order that the desired objectives may be attained. But managerial economists must always be mindful of the actual practices in the business or institutional environment. For example, if firms choose their price level by a policy of applying a markup to their direct costs, rather than by equating marginal revenue and marginal costs as implied by microeconomic principles, managerial economics should be concerned with determining the *optimal level* of the markup rather than attempting to persuade decision makers to use the marginalist principles. The approach taken in this textbook is to integrate business practice with economic principles. Thus business practices, even if divergent from the strictures of normative microeconomics, are discussed in terms of the microeconomic principles. By reference to the microeconomic principles the business practice can be evaluated in terms of its efficiency in attaining the desired objectives.

### Outline of This Book

Managerial economics depends upon the use of certain analytical tools and techniques, including symbolic models, for the solution of decision problems. The remainder of this chapter is concerned with a discussion of the use of models in managerial economics and a review of certain mathematical and statistical concepts and techniques. Types of models, the reasons for using models, and methods of evaluating models in the managerial economics context are discussed. The mathematical and statistical material is not especially rigorous and is not intended to be exhaustive, since many of the more complex analytical tools, techniques, and concepts used in managerial economics are introduced in the following chapters at the point where they may be used to solve decision problems. Chapter 2 continues with concepts basic to the study of managerial economics, such as those of certainty, risk, uncertainty, probabilities, discounted cash flow, and decision-making criteria.

Parts 2, 3, and 4 of the text are concerned with demand, cost, and pricing, respectively. Each of these parts is introduced by a chapter on the theoretical underpinnings, but in each case the treatment is confined to those elements of the microeconomics that are important to an understanding of the concepts that are used for decision making, and it avoids the more esoteric frills. The second chapter in each part is concerned with using this understanding to make better decisions. That is, the theoretical material is integrated into practical decision-making problems such that optimal decisions may be made on the basis of the information available. The third chapter in each of the demand and cost sections is concerned with estimation and forecasting of cost and demand conditions. The principles and techniques of generating the cost and demand information are studied. The third chapter in the pricing section examines competitive bidding and price quotes, a topic that ties together elements of these three major parts of the text.

Part 5, "Topics in Managerial Economics," examines linear programming, advertising, and capital budgeting from a managerial economic's perspective. Since these topics are often covered in quantitative methods, marketing, and finance courses in commerce and business programs, the emphasis here is less on technique and more on the economic interpretation and methodology of these areas.

## 1.2   THE USE OF MODELS IN MANAGERIAL ECONOMICS

### Types of Models

In the following chapters we will have cause to use a number of models in the formulation and analysis of decision problems. *Models* may be defined as simplified representations of reality, and as such they have proved very useful in economics and a wide variety of other disciplines. There are three main types of models, and a description of these will serve to indicate the degree of our reliance on models in day-to-day discussions and decision making.[1] *Scale models* are typically miniaturized versions of the real thing, such as airplanes, buildings, ships, and automobiles, where the model is visually similar to the piece of reality it represents. The second type of model consists of those models known as *analogues:* these are models that, although taking a form physically different from that which they represent, have other features in common, and thus inferences can be drawn by reference to the model rather than to the real situation. Examples of analogues include road maps that depict the highways and

[1] Much of the following relies on the excellent discussion in I. M. Grossack and D. D. Martin, *Managerial Economics* (Boston: Little, Brown, 1973), pp. 5-10.

physical features of an actual geographic area, animals that are used for medical testing instead of humans, and wind tunnels that act as an artificial climatic environment.

The third type is the ③*symbolic model.* Symbolic models use words and other symbols to represent reality, and they include descriptive speech or writing, diagrams, and mathematical expressions. *Descriptive speech* usually simplifies or abstracts from reality, such as in the statement "A horse is a four-legged animal with a long brushy tail." Such a statement is a symbolic model of the members of the equine family, giving the general idea of what a horse is without mentioning the complexities involved in the physical or psychological makeup of a horse or the differences between a Thoroughbred and a Percheron. *Diagrams* similarly represent a situation of reality by means of lines, shading, and other features, and they abstract from the finer details. *Mathematical models* are usually further removed from reality and are used because reality is very difficult to depict visually or verbally or because it involves interrelationships that are extremely complex.

You will have guessed by now that the models we will use in managerial economics are primarily those of the third category. Symbolic, and particularly mathematical, models are an efficient means of representing reality and providing a framework for the analysis of problems or decision making in real-world situations. A graph or a mathematical expression states precisely and concisely the assumed relationship between or among two or more variables. There is no ambiguity in such models, as there may be in descriptive speech or writing regarding the relationship that we assume to exist, since we must state it explicitly and precisely. If this assumed relationship is inaccurate, this inaccuracy will be exposed by later testing of the model against the situation of reality. We may then wish to assume a different relationship that is more in accordance with the feedback received from testing.

### Why Use Models?

The value of models in managerial economics and other disciplines may be summarized as follows. First, models have a *pedagogical* function: they are a useful device for teaching individuals about the operation of complex systems. Second, they are an *explanatory* device, since they are a vehicle for relating separate objects and events in a logical fashion. Third, models are valuable for *predictive* purposes, to the extent that past relationships between objects and events can be expected to hold true for future events. Let us discuss each of these three characteristics in some detail.

Models are useful for pedagogical purposes, since they allow the abstraction from the complexity of reality to a framework or structure of manageable proportions. By excluding from consideration the minor details that do not affect the basic features or relationships that are at issue, the model allows us to deal with the central issues of the problem without the added complexity of relatively minor influences. For example, a student may learn about the interrelationships of an economic system in a basic macroeconomics course by using a simple model of four or five equations. Despite its being an extremely simplified version of reality, this model imparts an understanding of the most important variables and relationships which interact to determine the level of economic activity. Yet the major banks and certain federal departments use models of the economy encompassing as many as six hundred equations in order to derive a more accurate representation of the economic system for purposes of predicting price, unemployment, and aggregate economic activity levels. The purpose of the simple model, however, is not to predict but to educate the student in the basic relationship of an economic system. Once the student achieves an understanding of the basic relationships and interactions, the model may be extended by the use of more complex relationships and introduction of new variables and relationships, such that the student's knowledge is increased further.

The use of models as an explanatory device allows us to relate observation of objects and subsequent events in a logical fashion. The assumed link between the objects and the events may be tested for its authenticity by reference to real-world situations. If an observation that contradicts the link is made, then this link is refuted, while the link is supported (although not proved) by the repeated observation of supporting evidence. Models may aid the researcher in discovering relationships that exist between and among variables. If a high correlation is found to exist between two variables, the researcher then may attempt to discover the reasons for this relationship, construct a model incorporating the assumed relationship, and test for this relationship with future observations. Similarly, a model may be used for explanatory purposes when actual testing in the real environment is impossible or too expensive or too dangerous. Examples of such experimentation to find the actual relationships include the testing of aircraft design in wind tunnels, and the use of animals for medical and research purposes. The results of these tests are then generalized to apply to the situation they represent. Such models have explanatory value, since they show the probable reaction of the real situation to a particular stimulus or environment on the basis of the reaction of the model to that stimulus or environment.

The predictive value of a model is usually based upon the ability of that model to explain the past behavior of a system, and it uses this past relationship to predict the future behavior. Thus, if we have found that two events are causally related, such as low winter temperatures and high consumption of heating oil we may predict increased consumption of heating oil the next time we observe temperatures falling. The model should specify the extent to which heating oil consumption is related to the temperature such that we may predict with some degree of accuracy the consumption of heating oil during a particular cold spell. This model will remain a good predictor as long as the relationships it represents stay constant: for example, if many households were to change to electric heating, the model would no longer represent reality as well as it did, and its predictions would be less accurate than before. A new or revised model would then be called for.

### Must Models Be Realistic?

A model need not be realistic, or be based upon reasonable, testable, or logical assumptions, in order that it be a good model for predictive purposes.

Friedman has argued that it is not necessary for predictive purposes that the assumptions underlying a model be valid and testable.[2] Using the example of a pool player who consistently sinks the designated ball into a designated pocket, the Friedman argument suggests that a model to explain this behavior, and to predict the sinking of subsequent balls, is that the pool player has a doctorate in physics and mathematics. He is therefore able to calculate the angles, force of the shot, degrees of side spin, rolling resistance of the felt, impact absorption of the cushion, and other variables necessary for the perfect execution of the shot. Such a theory would predict that the pool player would sink the next ball, and it is supported when in fact the next ball does drop into the pocket. Such a model is most likely based upon specious assumptions, however, since to become an expert pool player, the individual more likely spent his youth in a pool hall than in a library, and being an excellent pool player probably precludes pursuit of such mundane activities as higher education in mathematics and physics. (In fact, there would be no financial incentive to do so!)

A second example of a model that predicts accurately yet is based on demonstrably false assumptions concerns the observation that a sunflower faces the east at sunrise and follows the path of the sun during the day until it is facing the west at sunset. During the night it slowly returns to its eastward-facing position awaiting the rise of the sun on the next morning. Doubtless the correct explanation of this phenomenon concerns the plant's need for direct sunlight for life-serving purposes, but a simple model that would accurately predict this phenomenon for any newly discovered sunflower is that the sunflower swivels at the base in response to a heat sensor located in the petals. This model, although farfetched and simplistic, would nevertheless allow us to predict the direction the sunflower is facing, given our knowledge of the position of the sun.

For predictive purposes such a model could be quite useful, although for pedagogical and explanatory purposes such a model has no virtue. Even for predictive purposes, however, we may be somewhat cautious and skeptical about the model's ability to predict accurately on its *next* test. Since the relationship postulated is obviously false and the real determinants are apparently unknown, the latter could change without our noticing it and our prediction would turn out to be wrong. Thus we need to be more cautious in using such a model to predict, since it may fail as a predictor at any time if the underlying true relationship changes without our knowledge or observation.

### How Do We Evaluate Models?

It should be clear from the above discussion that a model must be evaluated in the light of its purpose. If a model is intended for pedagogic purposes, then it must be evaluated on this basis. Simple models of oligopoly, for example, do little to explain or predict the actual behavior of real firms in the real world, yet they do introduce the students to the problems of mutual interdependence in business situations. Criticisms of such models as being too simplistic or unrealistic are thus unwarranted to the extent that such models best introduce

[2] M. Friedman, "The Methodology of Positive Economics," in his *Essays in Positive Economics* (Chicago: University of Chicago Press, 1953).

these concepts to the student. If an alternate model could allow the student to obtain a better understanding of the complex system being represented, for a similar input of time and mental effort, then we would have to judge that alternate model as being an improved model, since it best achieves the objective set for that model.

Models designed for explanatory purposes must similarly be evaluated on the basis of how well they explain reality. If an observation that is at variance with the model is generated, such as the pool player's failing to sink a particular shot, then that model is refuted as an explanatory device. If there are two or more separate models that purport to explain a sequence of events, the best model is the one that most accurately depicts the important variables and relationships between and among these variables.

Models designed for predictive purposes must be judged by the accuracy of their predictions in subsequent tests. A predictive model is superior to an alternate predictive model if its predictions are more accurate more of the time. As the situation being depicted changes or evolves, we would expect existing models to become less accurate, since they must be modified to represent the evolving or changed situation.

In all cases when evaluating models, it is important to keep in mind the distinction between the model and the situation of reality. The model is a simplified representation of reality and is thus intended to represent the general features of reality rather than the specific features of a particular instance in reality. Due to this abstraction from some of the finer points and details, the predictive or explanatory power of the model will generally not be exact for any particular instance, due to variables and relationships that have been excluded from the model for the sake of simplicity or expedience. For example, a model may predict that firms will increase the size of their inventories of raw materials when the price of those raw-material components is seasonally reduced. If such a model abstracts from the cash-flow situation of the firm, it may imperfectly predict the behavior of certain firms that are facing a liquidity problem at that particular time.

In the following chapters you will note the considerable use of graphical and mathematical models in order to establish a framework for the solution of decision problems. These are not meant to complicate your existence but rather to simplify the presentation, analysis, and solution of decision problems. Some students have a fear of graphical and mathematical presentations to the extent of a virtual mental block. (As an undergraduate student I used to find myself reading the verbal parts of the text and skipping quickly over the equations to the next verbal part, and wondering why the material was not clear to me.) If this type of syndrome applies to you, I urge you to consider graphical and mathematical representations as the efficient means of communication that they are: once you force yourself to come to grips with them you will wonder why you did not do it before. The following sections review the basic mathematical, graphical, and statistical concepts you will need for this course. As you read through it, you will find that there is nothing fearsome about these methodologies: they are simply tools of analysis used to conceptualize, analyze, and solve decision-making problems.

## 1.3   A REVIEW OF CALCULUS AND ANALYTICAL GEOMETRY

The following sections are not intended to be a "mini course" in mathematics and statistics, but rather a review of some of the more basic concepts and techniques that will be used throughout the text. At this point we shall simply discuss functions and graphs, basic calculus, and a number of statistical concepts.[3] A review of this material will facilitate the use of symbolic models throughout the text and will form the basis for discussion of more advanced issues, such as present value analysis (Chapter 2), regression analysis (Chapter 5), and linear programming (Chapter 13). These more specialized and more difficult concepts and techniques are introduced in subsequent chapters at the point at which they may be applied to a particular decision problem or type of problem.

If your background in calculus, analytical geometry, and statistics is both recently acquired and substantial, I recommend that you either skim lightly over these sections or go directly to the end of this chapter and try the problems.

### Functions and Graphs

A *function* is an expression of the dependence of one variable upon one or more other variables. In *general* form we may write

$$\text{DEPENDENT} \quad \overset{\text{FUNCTION}}{Y = f(X)} \quad \text{INDEPENDENT} \tag{1.1}$$

to read the value of $Y$ is a function of, or depends upon, the value of $X$. $Y$ is known as the dependent variable, while $X$ is the independent variable. The value of $Y$ may depend on more than one independent variable, of course, such that we might express in general form the functional relationship as

$$Y = f(X_1, X_2, X_3, \ldots, X_n) \tag{1.2}$$

In this multivariable function the value of Y is seen to depend upon the value of several independent variables, where $n$ is the number of these independent variables. For example, the sales of umbrellas may be a function of the price of umbrellas, the income of consumers, the rainfall levels, the advertising expenditures of umbrella manufacturers, and the price of taxi fares.

The form of the functional dependence of $Y$ upon the independent variables $X_i$, $(i = 1, 2, \ldots, n)$, remains unspecified in the above expressions. To find the exact nature of the dependence we must examine the specific form of the function. This may take a variety of mathematical forms: for example, $Y$ may be a linear, quadratic, cubic, quartic, or higher-order function of $X$ (or the $X$'s) or it may be a power function, an exponential function, a hyperbolic function, or take some other form. Let us examine these in turn.

### LINEAR FUNCTIONS - 1st DEGREE FUNCTIONS

The general form of a linear function is

$$Y = a + bX \tag{1.3}$$

where $a$ is the INTERCEPT and $b$ is the SLOPE.

---

[3] For a more in-depth treatment of these analytical techniques, see W. J. Baumol, *Economic Theory and Operations Analysis,* 4th ed. (Englewood Cliffs, N. J.: Prentice-Hall, 1976).

11

where $a$ and $b$ are constants. If, for example, $a = 4$ and $b = 0.5$, we could array the values for $Y$ given the values for $X$, as shown in Table 1.1. These values indicate the specific dependence of the variable $Y$ upon the variable $X$. When $X$ is zero, the second term in Eq. (1.3) drops out and $Y$ is simply equal to the parameter $a$. Each time the variable $X$ is increased by one unit, the value of $Y$ increases to the extent of the parameter $b$.

**TABLE 1.1**
**Values of $Y$ for various values of $X$**

| Values of $X$ | 0.0 | 1.0 | 2.0 | 3.0 | 4.0 | 5.0 | 6.0 |
|---|---|---|---|---|---|---|---|
| Values of $Y$ | 4.0 | 4.5 | 5.0 | 5.5 | 6.0 | 6.5 | 7.0 |

Let us plot the above values on a graph that has $X$ on the horizontal axis and $Y$ on the vertical axis. Using the pairs of observations for $X$ and $Y$ as coordinates, we are able to plot the equation $Y = 4 + 0.5X$ as shown in Figure 1.1. Strictly, the graph of this equation would extend into three of the four quadrants, but we show only the northeastern quadrant where both variables have positive values, since for most economic applications these are the only meaningful values of the function. Notice that the graph intercepts the $Y$ axis at the value of 4: hence the parameter $a$ is known as the *intercept* parameter. Similarly, the graph slopes upward and to the right at the rate of half one unit of $Y$ for each one-unit increase in $X$. The slope of the line (the vertical rise over the horizontal run) is thus equal to 0.5, precisely the value of the $b$ parameter. Accordingly, $b$ is often called the *slope* parameter. Thus by observing the values of the $a$ and $b$ terms in a simple linear function, we are able to envisage the graphical form of that function.

For multivariable linear functions we simply extend the above analysis for the

**FIGURE 1.1**
**Graph of a linear function with only one independent variable**

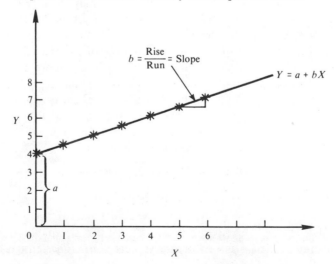

case of additional explanatory variables, such as

$$Y = a + b_1 X_1 + b_2 X_2 + b_3 X_3 + \cdots + b_n X_n \qquad (1.4)$$

*[handwritten: INDEPENDENT VARIABLES]*
*[handwritten: A 1 UNIT Δ IN VALUE OF EACH INDEPENDENT VARIABLE]*

where the $X_i$, $(i = 1, 2, 3, \ldots, n)$, represent several independent variables, and the $b_i$ coefficients represent the influence that a one-unit change in the value of each independent variable would have on the value of $Y$. A simple example of a multivariable linear equation is $Y = 2 - 0.4X_1 + 0.3X_2$. Substituting values for $X_1$ and $X_2$ into this expression allows us to obtain the values for $Y$, as shown in Table 1.2. The values in the body of the table represent the value of $Y$ for the values of $X_1$ and $X_2$ given by the coordinates of that value. Graphing the values of $Y$ against the values of $X_1$ and $X_2$ we obtain Figure 1.2, in which it can be seen that the above equation is that of a plane. Note that the parameter $a$ is again an intercept value, or the value of $Y$ when the values of the independent variables are zero, and that the $b$ coefficients represent the slope of the function as we move one unit in the direction of a particular independent variable. Note too that the sign of $b_1$ is negative, indicating that the value of $Y$ declines as additional units of $X_1$ are added.

*[handwritten: SIGN OF b₁... NEG ⟹ DECLINE OF Y AS X₁... ADDED]*

**TABLE 1.2**
**Values of $Y$ for various values of $X_1$ and $X_2$**

|  |  | *Values of $X_1$* | | | | | |
|---|---|---|---|---|---|---|---|
|  |  | *0* | *1* | *2* | *3* | *4* | *5* |
|  | 0 | 2.0 | 1.6 | 1.2 | 0.8 | 0.4 | 0.0 |
|  | 1 | 2.3 | 1.9 | 1.5 | 1.1 | 0.7 | 0.3 |
| Values of $X_2$ | 2 | 2.6 | 2.2 | 1.8 | 1.4 | 1.1 | 0.7 |
|  | 3 | 2.9 | 2.5 | 2.1 | 1.7 | 1.4 | 1.0 |
|  | 4 | 3.2 | 2.8 | 1.4 | 1.0 | 1.7 | 1.3 |
|  | 5 | 3.5 | 3.1 | 2.7 | 2.3 | 2.0 | 1.6 |

## QUADRATIC FUNCTIONS *[handwritten: - SECOND DEGREE; CURVILINEAR]*

The above linear relationships represent what are known as first-degree functions, since each of the independent variables was raised to the first power only. We move now to quadratic, or second-degree, functions, in which one or more of the independent variables will be squared, or raised to the second power, such as

$$Y = a + bX + cX^2 \qquad (1.5)$$

Hence $Y$ is a function of the constant $a$ plus the constant $b$ times the independent variable $X$, plus the constant $c$ times the square of that independent variable. Suppose we let $a = 5$, $b = 3$, and $c = 2$. We may calculate the values of $Y$ for various values of $X$, as shown in Table 1.3. Plotting these values as a graph, we obtain Figure 1.3, in which it can be seen that the graphical representation of a quadratic function is curvilinear, whereas linear functions are rectilinear. Notice

**FIGURE 1.2**
Graph of a linear function with two independent variables

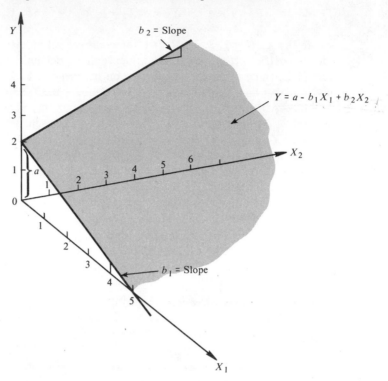

that the parameter $a$ remains the intercept term, but the slope depends not only upon the value of $X$ but also upon the square of the value of $X$. In Figure 1.3 we show a second quadratic function, $Y = 15 + 10X - 2X^2$, and it can be seen that the curvature of this function is concave from below, whereas the curvature of the first function was concave from above. This results from the negative sign in front of the second-degree term in the latter expression.

When there are multiple independent variables, and the relationship between these variables and the independent variable is quadratic, we may express the function as follows:

$$Y = a + bX_1 - cX_1^2 + dX_2 - eX_2^2 \tag{1.6}$$

for the simple case in which there are only two independent variables. This relationship is graphed in Figure 1.4, where it can be seen that the negative signs

**TABLE 1.3**
Values of $Y$ for various values of $X$

| Values of $X$ | 0 | 1 | 2 | 3 | 4 | 5 |
|---|---|---|---|---|---|---|
| Values of $Y$ | 5 | 10 | 19 | 32 | 59 | 70 |

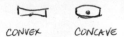
CONVEX      CONCAVE

**FIGURE 1.3**
**Graph of quadratic functions with only one independent variable**

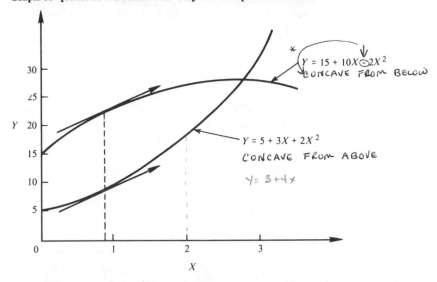

$Y = 15 + 10X - 2X^2$
CONCAVE FROM BELOW

$Y = 5 + 3X + 2X^2$
CONCAVE FROM ABOVE

$Y = 3 + 4X$

preceding the second-degree terms indicate that the surface representing the function will be convex from above. Once again the parameter $a$ is the intercept on the $Y$ axis and takes a positive value. In other cases, of course, the parameter $a$ may be zero or negative, just as the other coefficients may take values positive, zero, or negative.

**FIGURE 1.4**
**Graph of a quadratic function with two independent variables**

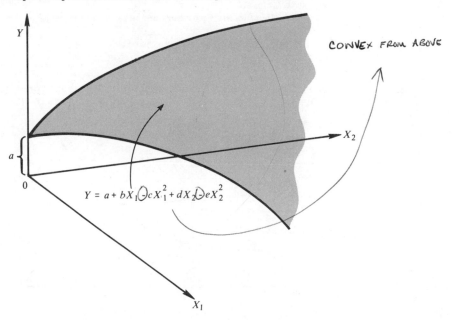

CONVEX FROM ABOVE

$Y = a + bX_1 - cX_1^2 + dX_2 - eX_2^2$

15

- THIRD DEGREE TERM
MAY HAVE PT OF INFLECTION

We turn now to the third-degree terms in the functional relationship. Cubic functions may have first-, second-, and third- degree terms such as the following:

$$Y = a + bX + cX^2 + dX^3 \qquad (1.7)$$

When all the coefficients have positive signs, it is clear that the values of $Y$ will increase by progressively larger increments as the value of $X$ increases. When the signs of the coefficients differ, the graph of $Y$ may display both convex and concave sections, may have hills and valleys, or may simply exhibit a monotonically increasing or decreasing shape, depending upon the values of the coefficients.

As an example, consider the function $Y = 25 + 10X - 5X^2 + 2X^3$. In Table 1.4 we calculate the values of $Y$ for several values of $X$. Plotting the values of $Y$

**TABLE 1.4**
**Values of $Y$ for various values of $X$**

| Values of X | | 0 | 1 | 2 | 3 | 4 | 5 |
|---|---|---|---|---|---|---|---|
| Calculations | $25 =$ | 25 | 25 | 25 | 25 | 25 | 25 |
| | $10X =$ | 0 | 10 | 20 | 30 | 40 | 50 |
| | $-5X^2 =$ | 0 | −5 | −20 | −45 | −80 | −125 |
| | $2X^3 =$ | 0 | 2 | 16 | 54 | 128 | 250 |
| Values of Y | | 25 | 32 | 41 | 64 | 113 | 200 |

MONOTONICALLY INCREASING →

against the value of $X$ as in Figure 1.5, we see that the above function is monotonically increasing yet exhibits convexity from above at first, changing at the

**FIGURE 1.5**
**Graph of cubic functions with only one independent variable**

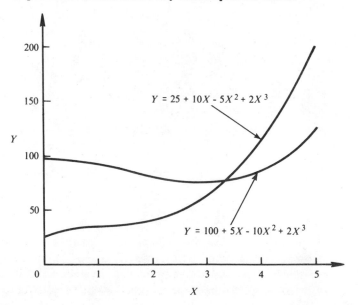

$Y = 25 + 10X - 5X^2 + 2X^3$

$Y = 100 + 5X - 10X^2 + 2X^3$

inflection point to concavity from above. In the same figure we show the graph of the equation $Y = 100 + 5X - 10X^2 + 2X^3$ and note that it has sections of both positive and negative slope. This indicates that the values of the parameters are instrumental in determining the shape of the graphical relationship. The distinguishing feature of a cubic function as compared with a quadratic function is that the former may have an inflection point (where slope changes from convexity in one direction to concavity in that direction, or vice versa), whereas the latter does not.

Cubic functions in two independent variables will produce a three-dimensional surface when graphed, as in Figure 1.6. Again, the value of the parameters

**FIGURE 1.6**
**Graph of a cubic function with two independent variables**

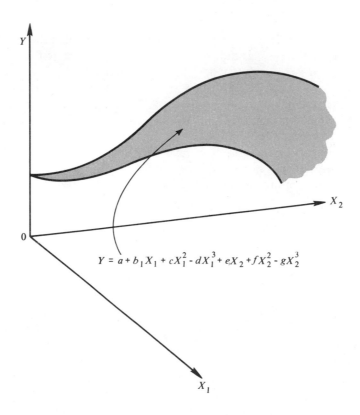

$$Y = a + b_1 X_1 + c X_1^2 - d X_1^3 + e X_2 + f X_2^2 - g X_2^3$$

and the signs of these parameters and coefficients operate to determine the shape and placement of the surface depicting the functional relationship.

We could continue the examination of functional relationships with fourth- and higher-degree terms influencing the value of the variable $Y$, but these are not necessary for an understanding of the remainder of this textbook. Instead we shall turn to some other types of functions that are useful to us.

*Exponential functions* take the form:

$$Y = a + bX \tag{1.8}$$

As you look at this specific form of the functional relationship, you should appreciate that the value of $Y$ will increase monotonically as $X$ increases, since the second term in the function assumes progressively higher degrees. An exponential function is shown in Figure 1.7.

*Power functions* take the form:

$$Y = aX^b \tag{1.9}$$

and can be seen from Figure 1.7 to exhibit the general parabolic shape, as did the exponential and quadratic functions.

*Hyperbolic functions* take the general form:

(POWER FUNCTIONS, b IS NEGATIVE)

$$Y = \frac{a}{X^b} \tag{1.10}$$

In this case, as $X$ grows larger the value of $Y$ diminishes and approaches zero asymptotically, as shown in Figure 1.7. You will note that hyperbolic functions are in fact power functions where the parameter $b$ has a negative sign. A special case of the hyperbolic function is the rectangular hyperbola $Y = a/X$, where the parameter $b$ takes the value unity. Hence $YX = a$ at all points on the curve. In verbal terms the product of the two variables is a constant at all levels of the two variables indicated by points on the curve. The rectangular hyperbola has applications in managerial economics such as the representation of the average-fixed-costs curve, since total fixed costs are a constant equal to the product of the number of output units and the average fixed costs at each output level.

**FIGURE 1.7**
**Graph of other functional relationships between $Y$ and $X$**

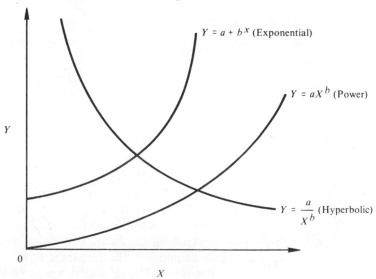

### Derivatives of Functions

Economists make extensive use of the marginal analysis when establishing normative rules for decision making. If $Y$ is to be maximized, for example, the impact on the value of $Y$ for a marginal change in the value of $X$ is sought in order that we may decide to increase, decrease, or hold constant the value of the independent variable $X$. In general terms we would wish to know whether it was worthwhile in terms of the increment to $Y$ to increase or decrease $X$. In terms of the graphical representations above, we are therefore interested in the slopes of the functions.

A mathematical technique that generates the slope of functions is to take the first derivative (or differential) of the function. The derivative of a function shows the change in the value of the dependent variable $Y$ given an infinitesimal change in the variable $X$, and is written as $dY/dX$, where $d$ connotes the increment (or decrement) to each variable. For marginal analysis it is imperative that we consider small increases in the independent variable, since larger increases may incorrectly indicate the extent of change in the dependent variable. In Figure 1.8 we depict a changing marginal relationship between $Y$ and $X$. Suppose that the values of $X$ and $Y$ are as indicated by point $A$ in that figure. The marginal relationship (or the slope of the function) is given by the slope of a tangent to the curve at point $A$. But this is only a correct representation of the slope of the function of an infinitesimal change in the variable $X$. For larger changes such as to $X_2$ or $X_3$, the slopes of the arcs $AB$ and $AC$ are not accurate representations of the slopes of the function over those values of $X$ and $Y$. They are in fact approximations or averages over the wider range of $X$ and $Y$ values. For decision-

**FIGURE 1.8**
**Change in slope as $\triangle X$ is increased**

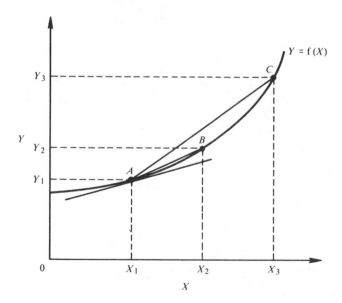

making purposes we are typically concerned with the incremental units of output (or some other variable) and hence require the more accurate marginal relationship between variables. It is therefore important that we understand the rules of derivation for use in optimization procedures.[4]

### Rules of Derivation

*CONSTANTS*

Since the derivative shows the amount by which the dependent variable changes for a change in an independent variable, and since a constant by definition does not change, it is clear that the derivative of a constant must be zero. Therefore,

$$\text{If } Y = a, \text{ then} \frac{dY}{dX} = 0$$

*THE POWER RULE*

When the function includes a term that is raised to the first or higher degree, we use the power rule, which may be stated as follows:

$$\text{If } Y = aX^b, \text{ then} \frac{dY}{dX} = baX^{b-1}$$

To illustrate this, let us begin with a first-degree function such as $Y = aX$. Since $X$ is implicitly equal to $X^1$, it is clear that the application of the power rule reduces the $X$ term to $X^0$. Since $X^0$ equals 1, the derivative of $Y = aX$ is simply the coefficient of the $X$ term. Thus, if $Y = aX$, then

$$\frac{dY}{dX} = 1 \cdot a \cdot X^{1-1}$$

$$= 1 \circ a \cdot X^0$$

$$= 1 \cdot a \cdot 1$$

$$= a$$

For higher-degree terms the power function is applied similarly. Suppose $Y = a + bX^2$, then

$$\frac{dY}{dX} = 2bX^{2-1}$$

$$= 2bX^1$$

$$= 2bX$$

---

[4] These rules are stated without proof. See Baumol, *Economic Theory,* Chap. 4, or any good introductory calculus textbook, for formal proofs.

To demonstrate the power rule in the context of terms of various degrees, consider the function $Y = 5 + 3X + 2X^2 + 5X^3$. Treating one term at a time, $dY/dX = 3 + 4X + 15X^2$. (Is that correct? Confirm it for yourself, using the above steps.)

### THE FUNCTION OF A FUNCTION RULE

In the case where $Y$ and $X$ are related through an intermediate variable $Z$, to find the change in $Y$ due to a variation in $X$ we need first to ascertain the impact on $Z$ of the change in $X$, and then multiply this by the impact of a variation in $Z$ upon $Y$. Thus:

$$\text{If } Y = f(Z) \text{ and } Z = f(X),$$
$$\text{then } \frac{dY}{dX} = \frac{dY}{dZ} \cdot \frac{dZ}{dX}$$

For example, if $Y = 4 + 6Z^2$ and $Z = 8 + 3X^3$ then

$$\frac{dY}{dX} = 12Z \cdot 9X^2$$

$$= 108Z(X^2)$$

### THE CHAIN RULE

Where $Y$ is the product of two variables $X$ and $Z$ which are themselves related, and we wish to find the derivative of $Y$ with respect to $X$, we must consider both the "direct" influence on $Y$ of a change in $X$ and the "indirect" influence on $Y$ of the change in $Z$ that the change in $X$ provokes. Thus:

$$\text{If } Y = ZX \text{ where } X = f(Z),$$
$$\text{then } \frac{dY}{dX} = Z + X\frac{dZ}{dX}$$

$Y = ZX(z)$

### MISCELLANEOUS RULES OF DERIVATION

Some of the additional rules of derivation that may be encountered from time to time include the following:

***Sums.***

$$\text{If } Y = Y_1 + Y_2$$
$$\text{where } Y_1 = f_1(X) \text{ and } Y_2 = f_2(X),$$
$$\text{then } \frac{dY}{dX} = \frac{dY_1}{dX} + \frac{dY_2}{dX}$$

*Products.*

$$\text{If } Y = Y_1 \cdot Y_2$$

$$\text{where } Y_1 = f_1(X) \text{ and } Y_2 = f_2(X),$$

$$\text{then } \frac{dY}{dX} = Y_2\frac{dY_1}{dX} + Y_1\frac{dY_2}{dX}$$

*Division.*

$$\text{If } Y = Y_1/Y_2$$

$$\text{where } Y_1 = f_1(X) \text{ and } Y_2 = f_2(X),$$

$$\text{then } \frac{dY}{dX} = \frac{Y_2\,(dY_1/dX) - Y_1\,(dY_2/dX)}{Y_2^2}$$

*Logarithms.*   Logarithms typically are expressed to the "natural" base (e = 2.7182 . . .) or to base 10.

$$\text{If } Y = a \log_e bX,$$

$$\text{then } \frac{dY}{dX} = \frac{a}{X}$$

$$\text{If } Y = a \log_{10} bX,$$

$$\text{then } \frac{dY}{dX} = \frac{1}{X}(a \log_{10} e)$$

*Exponents.*

$$\text{If } Y = ae^{bX}$$

$$\text{where e is the natural base},$$

$$\text{then } \frac{dY}{dX} = bae^{bX}$$

## PARTIAL DERIVATIVES

When a function has multiple independent variables, and consequently each independent variable is only one of a number of variables that affect the value

22

of the dependent variable $Y$, we take what is known as the partial derivative of the function for each independent variable. This is equivalent to the *ceteris paribus* assumption in economics; that is, we examine the influence of one of the independent variables upon the dependent variable while holding all other variables constant. The partial derivative thus shows the impact upon $Y$ of an infinitesimal change in one of the independent variables while all other independent variables are held constant. By convention, and to distinguish it from the derivative of functions with only one independent variable, we depict the partial derivatives by the lowercase delta ($\delta$), rather than the lowercase $d$ as used above. Thus if $Y$ is a function of several variables such as

$$Y = a + bX + cX^2 + dZ + eZ^2 + fQ^3$$

then $\dfrac{\delta Y}{\delta X} = b + 2cX$

and $\dfrac{\delta Y}{\delta Z} = d + 2eZ$

and $\dfrac{\delta Y}{\delta Q} = 3fQ^2$

Each partial derivative shows the marginal impact of one of the independent variables upon the dependent variable while holding constant the impact of the other independent variables.

### Maximum and Minimum Values of Functions

In the above we have been concerned with "first" derivatives, which show the slope of the function as the independent variable (or *one* of the independent variables) is varied by a small amount. The first derivative thus shows the rate of change of the dependent variable relative to the specified independent variable. With curvilinear functions that rate of change will vary for different starting points in the value of $X$. In Figure 1.9 the quadratic function $Y = -10 + 30X - 3X^2$ is graphed, and it should be appreciated that the derivative of the function is positive initially where the graph is sloping upward and to the right, but it is negative later where the value of $Y$ decreases as additional increments of $X$ are made. It is clear that the derivative is taking progressively declining values, being positive at first, falling to zero, and thereafter becoming increasingly negative. You may confirm this by taking the derivative of the above-mentioned function—viz., $dY/dX = 30 - 6X$—and substituting values for $X$ into this expression. Clearly for values of $X$ less than 5 the derivative is positive, but where $X$ is equal to 5 the derivative is zero, and for values of $X$ greater than 5 the derivative is negative.

The above discussion allows us to establish a simple rule for finding the maximum of a function. To find the value of $X$ for which $Y$ is maximized, we

**FIGURE 1.9**
**Changing value of the first derivative**

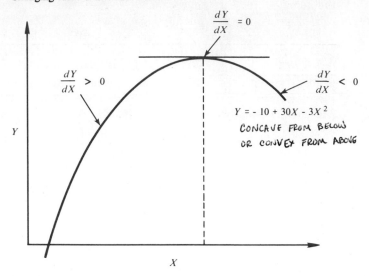

simply set the derivative of the function equal to zero and solve for the value of $X$. Thus where we have

$$\frac{dY}{dX} = 30 - 6X = 0$$

Solving for $X$,

$$6X = 30$$

$$X = 5$$

Thus $Y$ is at a maximum when $X$ takes the value of 5.

But a zero first derivative may indicate a minimum of a function rather than a maximum if the function is concave from above rather than concave from below. Suppose

$$Y = 100 - 16X + 2X^2$$

The first derivative of this function is

$$\frac{dY}{dX} = -16 + 4X$$

and is equal to zero when

$$X = 4.$$

Inspection of the function should indicate to you that it is a parabola that is concave from above, since for small values of $X$ it will be falling, reaching a minimum when $X$ equals 4, and it will rise progressively more steeply for higher values of $X$. In more complex functions, however, the shape of the function may not be obvious from inspection, and thus we must check whether the zero first derivative implies a maximum or a minimum by means of taking the *second* derivative of the function.

### SECOND DERIVATIVES

The second derivative of a function is simply the derivative of the first derivative of that function. Since the first derivative indicated the rate of change of the function, the second derivative indicates the rate of change of the rate of change of the function. If the second derivative is negative, this indicates that the rate of change is falling. Referring to Figure 1.9 we can see that the negative second derivative indicates that the curve is concave from below (or convex from above), since the first derivative at low values of $X$ starts at a relatively high number and progressively falls to zero and then to negative values. Alternatively, if the curve was concave from above, the first derivative would be negative at first, rising to progressively smaller negative values, passing through zero and taking on progressively increasing positive values as $X$ is increased. Thus we can say that the sign of the second derivative will be negative when the first derivative is set equal to zero if the function is concave from below, and that the sign of the second derivative will be positive when the first derivative is set equal to zero when the function is concave from above. Thus we may state the "second-order" condition for a maximum to be that the second derivative must be negative, and the second-order condition for a minimum is that the second derivative must be positive.

+ = MIN
− = MAX

Referring back to the function graphed in Figure 1.9, the first derivative was $dY/dX = 30 - 6X$, we may confirm that the sign of the second derivative is negative. The second derivative is equal to the derivative of the first derivative and is expressed as follows:

$$\frac{d^2 Y}{dX^2} = -6$$

where the squared terms indicate that the value shown is the second derivative of the function. For the other function mentioned above, the first derivative was $dY/dX = -16 + 4X$. The second derivative of this derivative is equal to

$$\frac{d^2 Y}{dX^2} = 4$$

The signs of these second derivatives confirm that the function of $Y$ reaches a *maximum* in the first case when $dY/dX = 0$, and reaches a *minimum* in the second case when the first derivative is set equal to zero.

### Use of Derivatives in Managerial Economics

Since one of the central aims of managerial economics is to establish rules and principles for achieving objectives, it is not surprising that derivatives may be helpful, since in many cases we are interested in maximizing profits or minimizing costs, or optimizing some other variable.

Suppose that a particular firm's cost and revenue functions are of quadratic form as follows:

$$TC = 1500 + 50Q + 2Q^2 \qquad\qquad (1.11)$$

$$TR = 250Q - 3Q^2 \qquad\qquad (1.12)$$

where TC represents total costs, TR represents total revenues, and $Q$ represents the output or sales level. Profits, represented by $\pi$, are the surplus of revenues over costs. Hence

$$\pi = TR - TC$$
$$= 250Q - 3Q^2 - (1500 + 50Q + 2Q^2)$$
$$= 250Q - 3Q^2 - 1500 - 50Q - 2Q^2$$
$$\therefore \quad \pi = -1500 + 200Q - 5Q^2 \qquad\qquad (1.13)$$

represents the profit function. Assuming that the firm wishes to choose the output level that maximizes profits, we may find that output level by setting the first derivative of the profit function equal to zero and solving for $Q$. Thus

$$\frac{d\pi}{dQ} = 200 - 10Q = 0$$

$$10Q = 200$$

$$Q = 20$$

The output level that appears to maximize profits is thus 20 units (where the "units" may represent single units, thousands, or millions, depending upon the initial specification of those units). To ensure that this output level represents the maximum profit rather than the minimum profit, we check the second-order condition. The second derivative of the profit function,

$$\frac{d^2\pi}{d^2Q} = -10$$

is negative, indicating that profits are indeed maximized at the output level of 20 units.

An alternative approach to finding the profit-maximizing output level using derivatives is as follows: We know that profits will be maximized when the difference between revenues and costs is greatest. In terms of Figure 1.10, where

26

the cost and revenue functions are depicted, we wish to find the output level for which the vertical separation of the two curves is greatest.

Observe that the slope (or derivative) of the cost function takes increasingly larger values as output is increased, while the slope of the revenue function takes increasingly reduced values. At some point the slopes of the two functions will be equal, and hence tangents to the two functions at that output level must be parallel lines, as shown in Figure 1.10. Since a property of parallel lines is that they maintain a constant vertical separation, it must be true that as the slope of the cost function continues to increase and as the slope of the revenue function continues to decrease for larger output levels, the vertical distance between the two functions must be decreasing. Thus profits are maximized when the slopes (or first derivatives) of the functions are equal.

To solve for the output level where the slopes (first derivatives) are equal, let us restate the cost and revenue functions:

$$TC = 1500 + 50Q + 2Q^2 \tag{1.11}$$

$$TR = 250Q - 3Q^2 \tag{1.12}$$

Finding the first derivatives of these functions, equating them, and solving for $Q$, we have

$$\frac{dTC}{dQ} = 50 + 4Q$$

$$\frac{dTR}{dQ} = 250 - 6Q$$

**FIGURE 1.10**
**Hypothetical cost and revenue functions**

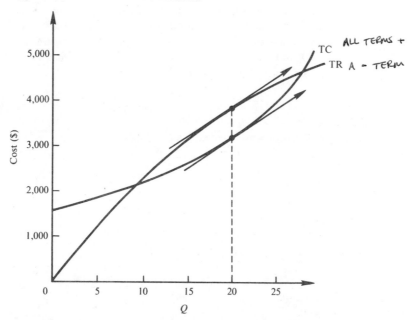

Set $$\frac{d\mathrm{TC}}{dQ} = \frac{d\mathrm{TR}}{dQ}$$

$$50 + 4Q = 250 - 6Q$$

$$10Q = 200$$

$$Q = 20$$

Not surprisingly this alternate approach gives the same profit-maximizing output level as did the initial approach. The latter approach has received some fame (or notoriety) in economics as the "marginalist principle," whereby marginal cost (the increment to total cost for a one-unit change in output level) is set equal to marginal revenue (the increment to total revenue for a one-unit increase in output or sales level). We shall return to this in the context of different market situations in Chapters 9 and 10.

In *every* chapter of this book we will have cause to use some of the above principles of calculus and analytical geometry. Let us turn now to some concepts from the discipline of statistics which similarly will be found throughout the text.

## 1.4   SOME CONCEPTS OF ELEMENTARY STATISTICS

When gathering information in the real world, we would be surprised to find a precise and stable relationship between two or more variables as indicated by the above mathematical expressions. Rather we expect to find a tendency for the observations to approach a particular value, with variability from observation to observation being due to a myriad of real-world factors which influence the observations. For example, the sales of two particular items may vary over time, as shown in Table 1.5. Over the six-week period the sales of each item total 60,000 units, but it can be seen that there is greater variability in the weekly sales of Item B as compared with Item A.

TABLE 1.5
**Variability of sales observations on two items**

| Week No. | Sales per Week (units) | |
| --- | --- | --- |
| | *Item A* | *Item B* |
| 1 | 10,000 | 6,000 |
| 2 | 8,000 | 12,000 |
| 3 | 12,000 | 12,000 |
| 4 | 9,000 | 4,000 |
| 5 | 11,000 | 12,000 |
| 6 | 10,000 | 14,000 |
| Total | 60,000 | 60,000 |

## Measures of Central Tendency

Given the variability of sales for both items, how might we best summarize the weekly level of sales for the six-week observation period? The *mean*, or simple average, of the observations is the total value of the observations divided by the number of observations, or

$$\overline{X} = \frac{\sum\limits_{i=1}^{n} X_i}{n} \tag{1.14}$$

where $\overline{X}$ is the mean of the observations, the sigma ($\Sigma$) notation indicates that the $X$ observation should be summed over $n$ observations beginning with the first observation and ending with the $n$th observation, and $n$ represents the total number of the observations.

Apart from the mean, there are other measures of central tendency that may be useful in describing the distribution of the observation over a range. The *mode* is the term given to the most frequently observed value of the observations. In the case of Item A the mode is equal to the mean at 10,000 units per week, but in the case of Item B the mode is 12,000 units per week.

The distributions of sales for Items A and B are said to be unimodal, since there is only one peak in each distribution when plotted as a frequency distribution, as in Figures 1.11 and 1.12. A frequency distribution shows the frequency with which particular levels of observations are recorded. The peak of a frequency distribution, or the most frequent observation, is the mode of that distribution.

A third measure of central tendency is the *median*. The median is determined by arraying the observations in numerical order and then finding the halfway point of that array. Thus half of the remaining observations will lie below

**FIGURE 1.11**
**Frequency distribution of weekly sales item A**

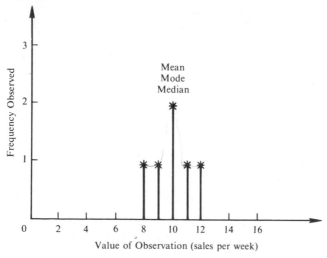

**FIGURE 1.12**
Frequency distribution of weekly sales item B

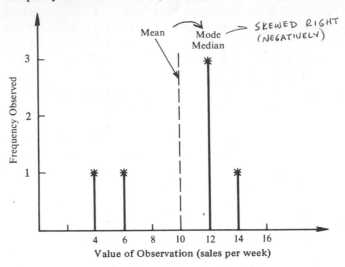

the median, and half will lie above the median observation. In the case of Item A it is clear that the median observation is 10,000 units, equal to the mean and the mode of that distribution, whereas for Item B the median is 12,000 units being greater than the mean, but equal to the mode, in this simple case. In a different example the mean, mode, and median may take on three different values.

## PERCENTILES, DECILES, QUARTILES

When there are many observations we may rank the items in numerical order and divide them in percentiles. A percentile contains one percent of the total number of observations. Thus the median is the 50th percentile observation. The 25th percentile and the 75th percentile are known as the first- and third-quartile observations. The first-quartile observation thus shows that observation below which are ranked 25 percent of the observations, while the third-quartile observation shows that observation below which lie 75 percent of the observations, when they are arrayed in numerical order. Similarly, we may speak of the first-, second-, and higher-order decile observations to indicate the observation below which lie 10 percent, 20 percent, and higher multiples of 10 percent of the observations.

### Symmetric and Skewed Distributions

Where the distribution of values is symmetrical about the mean, we speak of the observations being symmetrically distributed. The weekly sales of Item A are symmetric about the mean and demonstrate that a property of symmetric distributions is that the mean, mode, and median share the same value. Where the distribution is not symmetrically distributed about the mean, we should expect the mode and/or median to take values different from that of the mean. When the mode and/or median lie to the right of the mean, as in Figure 1.12, we say that

30

the distribution is skewed to the right, or that it is negatively skewed. On the other hand, where the mode and/or the median lie to the left of the mean in the frequency distribution, we say that the distribution is skewed to the left, or positively skewed.

### The Standard Deviation of a Distribution

Knowledge of the symmetry or skewedness of a distribution does not, however, convey the *extent* to which observations may diverge from the mean, mode, or median. The standard deviation of a distribution is a measure of the dispersion of the observations around the mean value and may be expressed symbolically as

$$\sigma = \sqrt{\frac{\sum\limits_{i=1}^{n} (X_i - \overline{X})^2}{n}} \qquad (1.15)$$

where the lower-case sigma ($\sigma$) is the symbol conventionally used to connote the standard deviation, the uppercase sigma ($\Sigma$) means "the sum of," $X_i$ represents the observations of the distributed variable ($i = 1, 2, 3, \ldots, n$), $\overline{X}$ is the mean value of the $X_i$, and $n$ is the total number of observations.

The above expression may be interpreted verbally as the square root of the arithmetic mean of the squares of the deviations from the mean. We square the deviations in order to avoid the negative deviations offsetting the positive deviations. By taking the square root of the mean squared deviation (which is itself known as the "variance" of the distribution), we have a measure of dispersion that treats the deviations from the mean in an absolute sense, representing the average absolute deviation from the mean.

Where the observations are a sample from a larger population, it is important that the denominator of Eq. (1.15) be $n - 1$ rather than simply $n$, in order to obtain an unbiased estimate of the standard deviation of the population. Making this change and expressing the numerator differently (but algebraically equivalently), we obtain the most commonly used expression for the standard deviation as follows:

$$(s)\ \sigma = \sqrt{\frac{\Sigma X^2 - \left[(\Sigma X)^2 / n\right]}{n - 1}} \qquad (1.16)$$

This form facilitates calculations, especially when the mean is not a convenient round number. Using Eq. (1.16) to calculate the standard deviations of the distributions of the two items represented in Table 1.5, we find that $\sigma = 1,414.21$ for Item A, and $\sigma = 4,000.00$ for Item B. Thus, as was obvious from Figures 1.11 and 1.12, the distribution of Item B is more widely dispersed about the mean than is that of Item A.[5]

---

[5] You may notice that the standard deviation values are not exactly equal to the average absolute deviation from the mean, which we claimed to be a property of the population standard deviation. This discrepancy is due to our using Eq. (1.16), which has $n - 1$ rather than $n$ as the denominator. With a larger sample size, of course, the standard deviation of a sample distribution would converge upon the value of the average absolute deviation.

The dispersion of a distribution about its mean can be used as a measure of the risk that the mean value will not be attained. In the following chapters we shall use the standard deviation of distributions to evaluate and compare the riskiness associated with those distributions.

### Normal Distributions and Kurtosis

A special case of the symmetric distribution is the "normal" distribution. A normal distribution is bell-shaped, having an inflection point on each side and approaching the axes asymptotically at each extreme. The points of inflection of the curve occur at the values given by one standard deviation above and below the mean. Approximately 68 percent (0.6826) of the observations will fall within these limits. Approximately 95 percent (0.9544) of the observations will fall within the range of plus or minus two standard deviations from the mean, and approximately 100 percent (0.997) of the observations will occur within plus or minus three standard deviations from the mean. We often use these properties to establish "confidence limits." For example, given a normal distribution we can be 95 percent confident that a particular observation will fall within two standard deviations of the mean.

It is clear that a symmetric distribution may be taller or flatter than a normal distribution and thus have more or less than 68 percent of the observations within one standard deviation of the mean. A term to describe this is the *kurtosis* of the distribution. A normal distribution is said to be *mesokurtic.* A distribution that is taller, or more peaked than the normal distribution, is said to be *leptokurtic,* while a distribution that is less peaked than the normal distribution is said to be *platykurtic.* In Figure 1.13 two distributions are indicated. We would say that distribution A is more leptokurtic (or less platykurtic) than distribution

**FIGURE 1.13**
**The kurtosis of a frequency distribution**

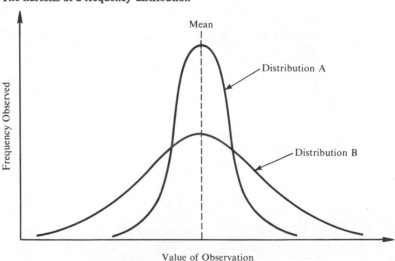

B. The degree of kurtosis can be measured,[6] but we will not have cause to do so. The notion is introduced here simply to warn you that <u>all symmetric distributions are not normal distributions</u>, and that consequently the true "confidence limits" may be wider or narrower than indicated by the properties of the normal distribution.

The above elementary concepts of statistics will serve as a basis for the discussion of various issues throughout the text. Chapters 2, 5, and 8, in particular, will build upon the concepts outlined here.

## 1.5  SUMMARY

Managerial economics seeks to establish rules and principles to aid in the decision-making process of firms and organizations. It is a discipline derived from the microeconomic theory of the firm and the theory of consumer behavior, but it has matured to include concepts and analytical tools from other disciplines. It is primarily normative in approach, although it starts from the positive viewpoint of actual business practices.

Models are used in managerial economics in order to put decision-making problems in a framework that will facilitate analysis and solution. For the most part we confine our interest to symbolic models, which allow the simplification of complex relationships to manageable proportions. We recognize that the function of any particular model may be pedagogical, explanatory, or predictive, and that models should be evaluated in the light of their purpose. Thus an unrealistic model is not necessarily a bad model.

The symbolic models that are used from time to time throughout the text require the understanding of certain basic mathematical and statistical concepts. Thus we reviewed the algebraic and graphical expression of several forms of the functional relationship, the rules of differentiation, and the use of derivatives in optimization procedures. Since much of the decision-making process depends upon collected data, we reviewed the measures of central tendency, measures of dispersion, and other characteristics of distributions. The discussion and content of the analytical tools and techniques section of this chapter were essentially basic, since the more complex concepts and techniques are saved for introduction in later chapters where they are employed in the analysis and solution of more involved decision problems.

## DISCUSSION QUESTIONS

1.1  Why would you expect managerial economics to be a "normative" discipline?

1.2  Can you classify the following as one or the other of the three types of model mentioned in the text?

(a)  a barometer

(b)  fashion models

(c)  topographical charts, and

(d)  Shakespeare's *Othello.*

---

[6] See, for example, G. A. Ferguson, *Statistical Analysis in Psychology and Education,* 2nd ed. (New York: McGraw-Hill, 1966), p. 76.

1.3　How is a model intended for pedagogical purposes likely to differ from a model intended for explanatory purposes?

1.4　Under what circumstances is it acceptable that a model be based on assumptions that are obviously false?

1.5　Under what circumstances is it appropriate that a model be based on extremely simplistic assumptions?

1.6　What advantages are there in the graphical or algebraic representation of a model, as compared with a verbal representation of the same phenomena?

1.7　Define the following terms:

(a)　function

(b)　independent variable

(c)　dependent variable

(d)　slope parameter

(e)　constant

(f)　intercept

(g)　quadratic function, and

(h)　exponent.

1.8　Explain the logic of using the derivatives of a function to find the maximum or minimum of that function.

1.9　If the mode of a distribution exceeds the median but is less than the mean, what can you say about the shape of that distribution?

1.10　If two distributions have a similar mean value over a similar number of observations but one has a larger standard deviation than the other, what can you say about the shape of the two distributions?

## PROBLEMS

1.1　Rewrite $Y = f(X)$ in symbolic form as a function that is

(a)　linear

(b)　quadratic

(c)　cubic

(d)　exponential

(e)　power

(f)　hyperbolic, and

(g)　logarithmic.

1.2　Find the first derivative, with respect to $X$, of the following functions:

(a)　$Y = 36 + 4.5X^3$

(b)　$Y = 8 - 3Z^2$, where $Z = 4 + 3X^3$

(c)　$Y = 7KX$, where $X = 3 - 2K^2$

(d)　$Y = -16 + 4J^2 - 6K^3$, where $J = 8 - 6X^2$ and $K = -3 + 4X^3$

(e)　$Y = 3M(4N^2)$, where $M = -6 + 2X$ and $N = 4 - 2X^2$

(f)　$Y = 4e^{2X}$

(g)　$Y = 6 \log_e 5X$

1.3　Solve for the maximum or minimum value of the following functions, using the second-order condition to specify whether it is a maximum or a minimum:

(a)  $Y = -32 + 6X - 2X^2$

(b)  $Y = 28 - 8X + X^2$

(c)  $A = 4285 - 625B + 5B^2$

(d)  $K = 178 + 40J - 6J^2$

1.4  Suppose the monthly cost of maintaining a certain machine in operating order is a function of the time elapsed between shutdowns for servicing and maintenance as follows: $C = 1400 - 30T + 0.7T^2$ where $C$ represents cost in dollars, and $T$ represents time between services in hours. What is the optimal period between services?

1.5  The number of breakdowns per week in our automobile fleet for the past quarter has been as follows: 4, 6, 3, 2, 5, 6, 1, 4, 5, 5, 3, 4, 5. Find the

(a)  mean

(b)  mode

(c)  median, and

(d)  standard deviation of the above distribution;

(e)  is this distribution positively or negatively skewed?

## SUGGESTED REFERENCES AND FURTHER READING

BAUMOL, W. J., *Economic Theory and Operations Analysis,* 4th ed., Chaps. 2, 3, and 4. Englewood Cliffs, N.J.: Prentice-Hall, 1976.

BRIGHAM, E. F., and J. L. PAPPAS, *Managerial Economics,* 2nd ed., Chaps. 1, 4, and 5. Hinsdale, Ill.: Dryden, 1976.

FERGUSON, G. A., *Statistical Analysis in Psychology and Education,* 2nd ed. New York: McGraw-Hill, 1966.

FRIEDMAN, M., "The Methodology of Positive Economics," in his *Essays in Positive Economics.* Chicago: University of Chicago Press, 1953.

GROSSACK, I. M., and D. D. MARTIN, *Managerial Economics,* Chap. 1. Boston: Little, Brown, 1973.

JOHNSTON, J., *Econometric Methods,* Chaps. 1 and 2. New York: McGraw-Hill, 1963.

KOOROS, A., *Elements of Mathematical Economics,* Chaps. 1, 2, 5, 6, and 7. Boston: Houghton Mifflin, 1965.

McGUIGAN, J. R., and R. C. MOYER, *Managerial Economics,* Chaps. 1, 4, and 5. Hinsdale, Ill.: Dryden, 1975.

NETER, J., W. WASSERMAN, and G. A. WHITMORE, *Fundamental Statistics for Business and Economics,* 4th ed. Boston: Allyn and Bacon, 1973.

PAPPS, I., and W. HENDERSON, *Models and Economic Theory.* Philadelphia: Saunders, 1977.

# 2

# Decision Making under Certainty, Risk, and Uncertainty

## 2.1   INTRODUCTION

The *raison d'être* of a business executive is to make and execute business decisions. One of the reasons that being a business executive pays so well is that making good decisions is not always easy. The main problem is the lack of predictability as to the outcome of the contemplated decision. Without sufficient information to predict *accurately* the outcome of a particular decision, the decision must be made on the basis of the information that *is* available at the time the decision must be made. The amount of information available is commonly characterized under three headings: certainty, risk, and uncertainty.

### Certainty

A *situation of certainty* exists if the outcome of a decision is known in advance. Thus only one possible event will follow a particular act, or decision, in an environment of certainty. In this uncertain world an example is hard to find, but one might regard as a situation of certainty the proposition that if you fall from an aircraft at twenty thousand feet, without a parachute, you *will* be killed (given the virtual certainty of the absence of strong updrafts, passing skydivers with parachutes, or extremely forgiving landing places). In the following chapters you will often encounter similar situations which may appear to represent certainty. Demand curves, for example, purport to show the quantities that *will* be demanded at various price levels, and cost curves similarly show the total or per unit cost that *will* be incurred at various output levels. But if consumer tastes change, or the price of a particular input changes, then neither of these curves will accurately predict the future demand or cost situation. Clearly, these curves must be interpreted as the *expected* demand and cost levels, in the absence of any information that would cause us to form a different expectation. These economic tools are entirely appropriate for decision making, however, since they are based on all the information that is available at the time the decision is taken. If new or different information becomes available at a later point of time, the new cost and demand schedules will reflect this, and a different decision may then need to be taken to obtain the optimal outcome.

### Risk

A *situation of risk* is defined as that in which either of two or more events (outcomes) may follow an act (decision), and where all of these events, and the probability of each occurring, are known to the decision maker. For example, a person playing Russian roulette knows that there are only two outcomes (death or extreme relief) and that the probabilities attached to each, for a six-chamber pistol with only one live shell, are one-sixth and five-sixths, respectively. The *actual* outcome is not known in advance, of course, and even though the "odds are" that the hammer will land on an empty chamber, one should not make expensive plans for the weekend if one expects to enter this particular risk situation. Other examples of risks are found when one flips a coin, throws the dice, or plays a hand of poker. The probability of flipping a coin and having it land "heads" is one-half, since there are only two possible outcomes (ruling out the coin's landing on its edge) and each is equally likely to occur, given an unbiased coin. Similarly, when one throws two dice, the probability that they will turn up "snake eyes" or any other pair of numbers is $\frac{1}{6} \times \frac{1}{6} = \frac{1}{36}$. The probability of drawing a "royal flush" in poker, or any other combination of cards, likewise can be calculated.

In each of the above illustrations the probability of each outcome is known *a priori.* That is, on the basis of known mathematical and physical principles we can deduce, prior to the act, the proportion of the total number of outcomes that should be attained by each outcome. We might wish to confirm this calculation by undertaking a number of trials. Although "heads" might appear three or even four times out of the first four tosses, given a sufficiently large number of trials the proportions will converge upon one-half for each of the two possible outcomes.

A second class of risk situations is that in which probabilities are assigned *a posteriori,* or on the basis of past experience under similar circumstances. The business of insurance is based upon this type of risk situation. The possible outcomes are known: the life assured will or will not expire; alternatively, the building insured will or will not be destroyed by fire. Insurance companies keep extensive data on previous policies and claims and other pertinent information, and from these compile actuarial tables that show the relative incidence of the various outcomes in past situations, or trials. On the presumption that a particular life, or building, is similar in all major respects to those of the data base, they are able to form an expectation (or assign a probability) of the chances of that particular life expiring, or the building burning.

### Uncertainty

A *situation of uncertainty,* as distinct from risk, is defined as one in which one of two or more events will follow an act, but the precise nature of these events may not be known and the probabilities of their occurring cannot be assigned objectively. That is, not all outcomes may be accurately foreseen, and the probabilities cannot be deduced or based on previous empirical data. Instead, the decision maker must use intuition, judgment, and experience, and whatever information is available, to assign the probabilities to the outcomes considered possible in such a situation. Thus the assignment of probabilities in situations of uncertainty proceeds on a *subjective* basis, rather than the objective basis of risk situations.

Most businesses, therefore, operate in a continuing state of uncertainty. For example, a new product may succeed or fail, it may be declared illegal or dangerous, or it may suffer from unforeseen competition or any number of other unexpected circumstances. Yet the decision must be made whether or not to introduce that new product, and the business executive responsible will make the decision on the basis of the outcomes foreseen and the estimated likelihood of each actually occurring. If the product is introduced and proves to be successful, then the firm earns profits. In fact, the willingness to undertake risk and to gamble against uncertainty is a major justification for business profits. Some part of profits must be considered as a compensation for taking on risk and uncertainty, and for making sound decisions in the face of the difficulties posed by the presence of these factors.[1] For the remainder of this chapter we consider decision making under the real-world conditions of risk and uncertainty.

## The Decision-Making Procedure

The procedure for making a decision under conditions of risk and/or uncertainty may be stated as follows:

1. Identify those courses of action (acts) that are available to you. *(DECISIONS THAT MIGHT BE MADE)*
2. Recognize the possible outcomes (events) of each act. *(CONSEQUENCES OF DECISION)*
3. Assign probabilities to each event.
4. Apply the desired decision criterion.

The decision-making procedure is not as easy as might be implied by this simple checklist, however. The first step requires the decision maker to select the possible courses of action, which are, in effect, the decisions that he or she might make, and it therefore requires the identification of all possible courses of action or feasible decisions that might be taken. This set of decisions, or course, includes the decision to do nothing.

The second step requires recognition of all the things that might happen as a consequence of each decision. These specified outcomes or events must be mutually exclusive: we must be able to say that the actual outcome will be either this or that, but not a combination of the specified outcomes. It follows that the specified outcomes must exhaust all possibilities.

The third step in the decision-making procedure is to assign probabilities, and we have seen from the preceding section that this might proceed on either an

[1] Other justifications for profit making include the reward for exceptional organizational ability, the reward for innovation of a product or manufacturing process, and "monopoly" profits that stem from a firm's having certain advantages in resource procurement, marketing, and product differentiation that cannot be duplicated by some or all other firms.

objective or a subjective basis. Objectively, we can apply *a priori* probabilities and/or *a posteriori* probabilities, which will be known to us. Subjectively, the probabilities need to be assigned by the decision maker on the basis of his or her judgment, intuition, and experience in that type of decision-making situation. Three rules need to be followed in the assignment of probabilities: zero probability must be given to events that cannot or will not occur; probabilities must add to unity; and the probability of a subset of the events must equal the sum of the probabilities of each event in the subset.

The fourth step is to apply the desired or appropriate decision criterion. Which decision criterion is appropriate to the particular case is a somewhat difficult issue, since it depends crucially on the type of decision, and just as importantly, on the type of decision maker.

## 2.2   DECISION-MAKING CRITERIA

To introduce the decision criteria and to illustrate the procedure, we shall work with the following simple business problem. Suppose a man has been offered a franchise to sell either hot dogs or ice cream at every home game of his local baseball team. He has to opt for either hot dogs or ice cream because another vendor will be offered the franchise he does not choose. The courses of action or strategies that the decision maker may choose are as follows: he may do nothing; he may take hot dogs; or he may take ice cream. This would seem to exhaust the possibilities. The outcome of these three different decisions depend to a large degree on the number of people at the ball game and the weather on the particular day, since hot dogs are more likely to be in demand by a large number of people on a rainy day, whereas ice cream would be more popular on a sunny day. Let us specify the states of nature that we consider to be possible during the baseball season as rain, cloud, and sun.[2] We exclude snow and other possibilities as being completely unlikely to occur. Table 2.1 expresses, in the form of a payoff matrix, the outcomes possible under the various combinations of actions (or strategies) and states of nature. The payoff matrix demonstrates that if the vendor were to choose hot dogs, and it rains, the payoff would be a net profit to him of $300.[3] If instead it were cloudy, the payoff would be $250. But, if it were sunny, the payoff for hot dogs would be $100. Had he chosen ice cream, however, the payoff would be $75 if it were raining, $150 if it were cloudy, and $400 if it were sunny. The payoff matrix does not demonstrate the payoffs to the strategy of doing nothing, since this would be zero in each of the three states of nature and is quite clearly less preferable to both hot dogs and ice cream, which show a positive profit under all situations.

We must now assign probabilities to each of the three states of nature. Suppose, for the moment, that we have no information at all on the probabilities of

---

[2] Since baseball games are typically postponed if it is raining, for the purposes of this example we shall define *rain* to mean scattered showers throughout the ball game, but not sufficient to cause abandonment of the game.

[3] We will assume that the vendor has deducted from his revenues a salary payment sufficient to compensate for giving up his leisure time or other activities, and that this net profit is on top of that salary payment.

**TABLE 2.1**
**Vendor's payoff matrix**

PAYOFF MATRIX

| | | Strategies | |
|---|---|---|---|
| | | Hot Dogs | Ice Cream |
| States of Nature | Rain | $300 | $ 75 |
| | Cloud | 250 | 150 |
| | Sun | 100 | 400 |

it being rainy or cloudy or sunny at the ball park. In this case we must proceed on a subjective basis, and the most simple method of assignment of probabilities in a zero information case is the "equiprobability of the unknown" method. That is, since we have no information about the relative likelihood of rain, cloud, or sun, we could assign them equal probabilities of occurring. On the other hand, one would expect to have *a posteriori* information about the likelihood of the weather patterns for a particular area during a particular period, and this information should be available from the local meteorological office, radio station, or airport. Suppose that over the past ten years it was raining for 15 percent of the home games, cloudy for 55 percent of the games, and sunny for 30 percent of the games. On the assumption that this season will be like the average of the past ten seasons, we might therefore assign the probabilities of 0.15, 0.55, and 0.30 to the three states of nature.

We are now ready to choose between the two possible acts, and we shall consider first the "expected value" criterion for decision making.

### The Expected Value Criterion

The expected value of an *event* is the payoff, should that event occur, multiplied by the probability that that event will occur. The expected value of an *act* is thus the sum of the expected values of each of the events that may follow that act or decision. The expected value of a decision can therefore be expressed as follows:

$$EV = \Sigma R_i P_i \qquad (2.1)$$

where $\Sigma$ connotes "the sum of"; $R_i$ is the return or payoff of the $i$th event; $i = 1, 2, \ldots, n$, where $n$ is the number of events that could follow the act; and $P_i$ is the probability assigned to the $i$th event.

If we postulate that the vendor wishes to maximize his (expected) profits, he will select the strategy that has the greatest expected value. In Table 2.2 we calculate the expected value of each of the two alternatives. It can be seen that the expected value criterion indicates that the best strategy is to choose ice cream, since this has an expected average payoff of $213.75 each day of the season as compared with the expected average payoff of $212.50 for the strategy of hot dogs. As in the earlier *a posteriori* example of insurance, the validity

41

**TABLE 2.2**
Expected value of strategies

| | Hot Dogs | | | Ice Cream | | |
|---|---|---|---|---|---|---|
| | *Payoff* | *Prob.* | *EV* | *Payoff* | *Prob.* | *EV* |
| Rain | $300 | 0.15 | $ 45.00 | $ 75 | 0.15 | $ 11.25 |
| Cloud | 250 | 0.55 | 137.50 | 150 | 0.55 | 82.50 |
| Sun | 100 | 0.30 | 30.00 | 400 | 0.30 | 120.00 |
| | | | $212.50 | | | $213.75 |

of this calculation depends upon the present case being similar to those constituting the data base. In this example we require the present baseball season to have a weather pattern that resembles the average of previous years. Similarly, the vendor would need to have the franchise over the entire baseball season in order to obtain the distribution of rain, cloud, and sun that is implied by the probabilities. If not, the vendor may find that for the first part of the season it rained continually and the strategy of ice cream would have been a very bad choice. Over the entire season, however, the weather pattern is expected to approximate the proportions indicated by the probabilities.

The expected value criterion, therefore, depends greatly upon the law of averages. But in some cases the law of averages, and hence the expected value criterion, is an inappropriate guide to decision making. Such a case is the "one-shot" decision, in which a decision must be made in a situation that is not likely to be repeated. Using the vendor example, imagine that he is offered the franchise for one specific day of the season, on the Labor Day weekend, for example. The *a posteriori* data are of little use, since they simply indicate the proportion of rainy, cloudy, and sunny days that are expected to be experienced through the entire baseball season, without stating what the weather for a specific day is likely to be. Even if it were possible to obtain a distribution of weather types for that particular day over past years, the one-shot nature of the gamble means that expected value would be a poor decision criterion, since the vendor has only one chance and not the repeated trials necessary to allow the law of averages to work in his favor.

### The Maximin Criterion BEST OF WORST

A decision criterion that is appropriate for the one-shot decision problem, and which reflects a conservative or pessimistic decision maker, is the "maximin" criterion. Using this criterion the decision maker would note the worst outcome associated with each strategy and would choose the strategy that promises the best of these worst outcomes. That is, he would select the maximum of the minimums—hence the name *maximin*. In Table 2.3 we show the vendor's payoff matrix for each of the two strategies under each of the three possible states of nature. For each strategy we indicate the minimum payoff associated with each strategy as the column minima. It is evident that the minimum associated with hot dogs, viz, $100, is larger than the minimum associated with ice cream, viz,

**TABLE 2.3**
Maximin, maximax

|  | Hot Dogs | Ice Cream |
|---|---|---|
| Rain | $300 | $ 75 |
| Cloud | 250 | 150 |
| Sun | 100 | 400 |
| Column minima | $100 | $ 75 |
| Column maxima | 300 | 400 |

$75. The maximum of these minima is $100, and therefore the maximin strategy is to choose hot dogs. In using the maximin decision criterion the decision maker avoids the chance of earning the lowest possible payoff, in this case the $75 associated with ice-cream sales on a rainy day.

The maximin decision criterion carries the implied assumption that whichever strategy the decision maker chooses, the state of nature that eventuates will be the most disadvantageous to that strategy. In this case the decision maker assumes that the weather is malevolent, and if the decision maker were to choose ice cream, it would rain or be cloudy, whereas if he chose hot dogs it would be sunny. With this pessimistic view of life, the decision maker chooses the outcome that will give the best of the worst possible outcomes. Notice that the maximin decision maker ignores all but the worst outcomes for each strategy and takes no account of the probability distribution associated with the outcomes.[4]

### The Maximax Criterion    MOST FAVORABLE WILL OCCUR

At the other extreme is the decision-making criterion that presumes that the best will always happen. The optimistic decision maker using this criterion assumes that the state of nature will turn out to be the most favorable in view of the decision made. This decision-making criterion, known as "maximax," is to choose the strategy that promises the largest of the largest outcomes—hence the name *maximax*. Referring to Table 2.3 it is evident that the maximum outcome for hot dogs is $300, whereas the maximum for ice cream is $400. The maximum of these column maxima is $400, and hence the maximax strategy is to take ice cream to the ball park. The maximax strategy is appropriate for the gambler who has eyes only for the big prize: he ignores all outcomes other than the maximum payoff for each decision.

Both the maximin and the maximax decision criteria represent extreme attitudes to decision making under risk and uncertainty. Neither is appropriate

_= MINIMIZE LOSSES_

[4] A related decision criterion is the *minimax* criterion. This involves choosing the minimum of the maxima associated with each strategy. It is appropriate where all payoffs are losses or are otherwise undesirable, and its use reflects the same pessimistic attitude as does the maximin criterion.

43

in most business situations. Rather, the attitude toward taking profits or losses is likely to be somewhere between the two extremes, and decision makers are likely to consider the probabilities (or riskiness) attached to the possible outcomes. We turn now to some decision criteria that take into account all of the outcomes, and the dispersion of these outcomes.

### The Certainty Equivalent Criterion

The *certainty equivalent* of an act is defined as the amount of money that would make the decision maker indifferent between undertaking the act on the one hand, and receiving that sum of money on the other. In the case of an act that has repeated trials, such as our vendor at the baseball game for the entire baseball season, it is evident that the certainty equivalent should be equal to the expected value of the act. Referring back to Table 2.2 we can see that the expected value of taking hot dogs to the ball park is $212.50 weekly; any sum of money less than this would be considered inferior to taking hot dogs to the ball park, since this is expected to generate an average of $212.50 per game. On the other hand, a sum of money larger than $212.50 per game would be preferred to the act of taking hot dogs to each game, since the vendor expects to gain no more than that amount on average over the entire season. Similarly, for the strategy of taking ice cream to the ball park, the certainty equivalent would be expected to be $213.75 for the case of many trials over the entire baseball season.

For a one-shot deal, however, it is unlikely that the certainty equivalent would be equal to the expected value of the act. Note that the expected value is in effect a weighted average of the various possible outcomes, and it therefore falls between the highest and the lowest possible outcomes of a particular act. Someone desperate for a sum of money greater than the gamble's expected value would probably have a certainty equivalent greater than the expected value. On the other hand, if the decision maker needs a relatively small sum of money badly, his or her certainty equivalent may well be much closer to the gamble's minimum payoff. Not being willing to take the risk of receiving the lower payoff, this decision maker will accept a sum of money that is greater than the minimum payoff but less than the expected value. The certainty equivalent will depend, therefore, upon the decision maker's personal circumstances and willingness to bear uncertainty. If one decision maker's certainty equivalent is higher than another's, this implies that the former requires more money to be bribed into forgoing the gamble and thus is more willing to gamble for the larger payoffs.

Hence, in the case of the vendor's decision on a one-shot basis, the decision will depend upon the vendor's attitude toward the possibility of earning any sum of money from $75 at a minimum to $400 at a maximum. To ascertain the vendor's certainty equivalent of each of the acts, we would offer him progressively increasing sums of money in an effort to induce him to forgo undertaking each of the two possible actions. For the strategy of taking hot dogs to the ball game, it is apparent that the vendor would not accept any sum in cash less than $100, because that is the minimum he expects to earn even if the weather is adverse. Let us suppose that we offer progressively more money until we reach $200, at which point the vendor expresses indifference between the hot-dogs strategy and the certain $200. For the ice-cream strategy it is clear that the vendor would accept no less than $75, since that is the guaranteed minimum he will receive even if the weather is adverse. Let us suppose that the vendor's attitude to uncertainty is such that his certainty equivalent to the strategy of taking ice cream to the ball park is $175. Thus the vendor's certainty equivalent for hot dogs is higher than for ice cream, indicating the vendor's greater preference for the hot-dogs strategy. The vendor apparently prefers the gamble for an income between $100 and $300 to the gamble for an income of somewhere in the larger range of $75 to $400, notwithstanding the higher expected value of the latter strategy.

The certainty equivalent criterion requires an individual to assess the risk or uncertainty involved in a decision and to value this risk and/or uncertainty on the basis of his or her own attitude toward that particular gamble. In the above example it would appear that our decision maker was averse to the ice-cream alternative because of the greater variability in the possible outcomes. We turn now to two decision criteria that explicitly consider the variability of the possible outcomes around the expected values.

### Standard Deviation and the Coefficient of Variation

Variation of the possible payoffs around the mean (or expected value) of the outcomes can be summarized by the standard deviation of the payoffs. The standard deviation of a distribution around its mean is commonly used as a measure of relative risk: the larger the standard deviation, the greater the risk that the actual outcome will lie more distant from the mean or expected value of the distribution. The logic of the standard deviation was discussed in Chapter 1. The formula given there needs to be modified slightly when we are dealing with a probability distribution. After squaring the deviations from the mean, we must multiply each of these squared deviations by its assigned probability. Summing these products we find the variance of the probability distribution, the square root of which is the standard deviation of the probability distribution. Symbolically,

$$\sigma = \sqrt{\Sigma(X_i - \overline{X})^2\, P_i} \qquad (2.2)$$

where $\overline{X}$ represents the mean (expected value) of the $X_i$ outcomes, and $P_i$ is the probability of each occurring.

In Table 2.4 we calculate the standard deviation for the distribution of outcomes associated with the hot-dogs alternative to be 75.62, whereas for ice cream it is 124.62. The greater standard deviation of the ice-cream alternative indicates that the expected outcomes vary over a wider range as compared with the hot-dog outcomes. When evaluating two or more alternatives that have equal or nearly equal expected values, such as in the above example, the standard deviation may be used as a decision criterion. Given equality or near equality of

**TABLE 2.4**
Standard deviation calculations

| | | | | | |
|---|---|---|---|---|---|
| | | | *Hot-Dogs Alternative* | | |
| *Outcome* | *EV* | *Deviation* | *Squared Deviation* | *Prob.* | *Weighted Squared Deviation* |
| $300 | $212.50 | 87.50 | 7,656.25 | 0.15 | 1,148.4375 |
| 250 | 212.50 | 37.50 | 1,406.25 | 0.55 | 773.4375 |
| 100 | 212.50 | −112.50 | 12,656,25 | 0.30 | 3,796.8750 |
| | | | | Variance | 5,718.7500 |

Standard deviation = $\sqrt{\text{Variance}}$ = 75.622

Coefficient of variation = $\dfrac{\text{SD}}{\text{EV}}$ = 0.356

| | | | | | |
|---|---|---|---|---|---|
| | | | *Ice-Cream Alternative* | | |
| *Outcome* | *EV* | *Deviation* | *Squared Deviation* | *Prob.* | *Weighted Squared Deviation* |
| $ 75 | $213.75 | −138.75 | 19,251.5625 | 0.15 | 2,887.7344 |
| 150 | 213.75 | − 63.75 | 4,064.0625 | 0.55 | 2,235.2344 |
| 400 | 213.75 | 186.25 | 34,689.0625 | 0.30 | 10,406.7188 |
| | | | | Variance | 15,529.6876 |

Standard deviation = $\sqrt{\text{Variance}}$ = 124.618

Coefficient of variation = $\dfrac{\text{SD}}{\text{EV}}$ = 0.583

expected values, the distribution with the smaller standard deviation is to be preferred (given a risk-averse decision maker), since this alternative involves less risk of an actual outcome being relatively distant from the expected value.

When the expected values of alternative possibilities are not equal or nearly equal, the coefficient of variation should be used as the decision criterion. *Coefficient of variation* is defined as the standard deviation of the distribution divided by the mean of that distribution. As shown in Table 2.4 the coefficient of variation for the hot-dogs alternative is 0.356, whereas for the ice-cream alternative it is 0.583. The means of the two distributions were very similar, but the greater standard deviation of the ice-cream alternative caused its coefficient of variation to be much higher. The choice criterion when evaluating alternatives that display different expected values, and different degrees of variability around the expected values, is to choose the alternative for which the coefficient of variation is *smallest*. Under this criterion, therefore, the vendor should choose the hot-dogs alternative.

As a general decision criterion, the coefficient of variation is superior to the standard deviation, since the latter is applicable only in cases where the expected values of the strategies are equal or nearly equal. The standard deviation allows a measure of relative risk for comparable returns, while the coefficient of variation criterion considers the absolute size of the expected return as well. Both criteria reflect the trade-off that risk-averse decision makers will have between risk and

46

return: if returns are similar the less risky alternative will be preferred, while additional expected returns will be necessary to induce a risk-averse decision maker to undertake additional risk. Note that if one alternative is more risky than another but has a proportionately greater expected value, the coefficient of variation criterion will indicate selection of the more risky alternative. To illustrate this, suppose that alternative A has EV = 550 and $\sigma$ =100, while alternative B has EV = 480 and $\sigma$ = 90. The coefficient of variation is 100/550 = 0.1818 for A and 90/480 = 0.1875 for B. Alternative A would be selected because its higher expected value more than compensates for its greater riskiness, giving it the smaller coefficient of variation. In other words, the "return-adjusted risk" is lower for alternative A, or inversely the "risk-adjusted return" is greater for alternative A, as compared with alternative B.

Table 2.5 summarizes the results of applying the various decision criteria to the hot-dogs/ice-cream problem.

**TABLE 2.5**
**Comparing decision criteria**

| Criterion | Hot Dogs or Ice Cream? |
| --- | --- |
| Expected value | Ice cream |
| Maximin | Hot dogs |
| Maximax | Ice cream |
| Coefficient of variation | Hot dogs |
| Certainty equivalent | ? |

### Which Criterion Should Be Applied?

The choice among the various decision criteria available depends upon three major factors. First, one must consider the frequency with which one is confronted by the particular decision. Second, the magnitude of the gamble must be considered. Third, the decision maker's attitude toward risk and uncertainty is important. To illustrate each of these factors we shall consider another example, that of insurance. Suppose a firm has two major insurance contracts: one for collision damage to its fleet of automobiles, and the other for fire damage to its plant and buildings. The firm is considering whether it should renew these contracts or carry the risk itself. The risk is known to the firm from insurance company data. The odds are 5 in 100 that each of the company's vehicles will be damaged to a mean value of $5,000. Hence the expected value of the damage is $250 per vehicle. The insurance company, however, charges a premium of $275 per vehicle, since it wishes to contribute to its overhead expenses and profits. The odds are 1 in 1,000 that the company's plant will burn down. The value of the plant is $10 million, and thus the expected value of the possible loss is $10,000. The insurance company's premium for this policy is $11,000. Will the firm carry its own insurance? Let us consider the three factors mentioned above.

First, regarding the frequency with which the company takes the particular gamble, we must remember that risk involves the law of averages. If one runs the risk a large number of times, one might reasonably expect to win and lose in the same proportions as the general population. On the other hand, if one runs the risk only once, then one might be fortunate enough to avoid the unhappy event of an accident or a fire, but on the other hand one might suffer all the bad luck all at once. In the case of the firm deciding to carry its own insurance, the automobiles represent a high frequency of taking the gamble. The company has, say, one hundred vehicles, and this is a sufficiently large number that it might expect the probability of any one being damaged would be similar to the population of vehicles at large. On the other hand, the firm has only one plant and the frequency of this gamble is only once. It does not have one hundred plants; it does not take this gamble at a large number of locations; and therefore it should not expect the average vulnerability to fire damage.

Concerning the second factor, the magnitude of the gamble, the important point to consider here is whether or not the decision maker can afford the worst possible outcomes. That is, can it afford the loss it would sustain if things turned out very badly? In the case of our company considering its insurance, it is possible that it could withstand the (unlikely) loss of all its vehicles for a total loss of $500,000. On the other hand, the loss of the plant and buildings to the tune of $10 million would probably represent a significant setback to that company. Thus the second factor would militate in favor of the company renewing its insurance policy for fire damage to the plant and buildings, but not for the automobile fleet.

The third factor, the decision maker's attitude toward risk and uncertainty, involves the individual's degree of risk preference or aversion. The crucial factor is the willingness of the decision maker to accept risk *and its consequences.* Thus, even though the first two factors above indicate that the firm should perhaps bear the risk on its motor vehicles, the attitude of the decision maker might be such that the policy will be renewed. Alternatively, even though the first two factors above indicate that the firm should probably renew its insurance for fire damage for that plant, a risk-preferring decision maker might decide to cancel that policy.

Tables 2.6 and 2.7 show the payoffs, expected values, standard deviations, and coefficients of variation for each of the two problems confronting the firm. From these data we are able to choose the appropriate decision under each of the five criteria discussed above. Under both the expected value and the maxi-

\* Must have time period attached

**TABLE 2.6**
**Auto fleet insurance problem**

| | Insure | | | Not Insure | | |
|---|---|---|---|---|---|---|
| | Cost | Prob. | EV | Cost | Prob. | EV |
| Accidents | $-27,500 | 0.05 | $- 1,375 | $-500,000 | 0.05 | $ -25,000 |
| No accidents | -27,500 | 0.95 | -26,125 | 0 | 0.95 | 0 |
| Expected value | | | $-27,500 | | | $ -25,000 |
| Standard deviation | | | 0 | | | 112,362.42 |
| Coefficient of variation | | | 0 | | | 4.494 |

for 2 years

ACCIDENT  52,500
NO ACCIDENT  52,500      - 500,000
0

**TABLE 2.7**
**Plant and buildings insurance problem**

| | Insure | | | Not Insure | | |
|---|---|---|---|---|---|---|
| | Cost | Prob. | EV | Cost | Prob. | EV |
| Fire | $-11,000 | 0.001 | $ -11 | $-10,000,000 | 0.001 | $-10,000 |
| No fire | -11,000 | 0.999 | -10,989 | 0 | 0.999 | 0 |
| Expected value | | | $-11,000 | | | $-10,000 |
| Standard deviation | | | 0 | | | 316,543.99 |
| Coefficient of variation | | | 0 | | | 31.65 |

max criteria, the decision maker would insure neither the fleet of automobiles nor the plant and buildings. Under the maximin and coefficient of variation criteria, the decision maker would insure both the fleet and the plant and buildings. Under the certainty equivalent criterion, we are unable to say, since this depends upon the decision maker's individual attitude toward bearing risk and uncertainty. On the basis of the three factors considered above, however, we may hazard a guess that under this criterion a risk-averse decision maker would choose to renew the insurance policy on the plant and buildings, and possibly allow the collision policy on its fleet of cars to lapse. This information is summarized in Table 2.8.

In conclusion, we note an interesting social phenomenon which could cause the probabilities in the above examples to be modified slightly. Actuarial data show that there is a higher probability of a building burning when it is insured, relative to when it is not insured. That is, insured buildings are more likely to burn than noninsured buildings. Reasons for this phenomenon, known as "moral hazard," are largely speculative, but they presumably center on the individual's taking greater care and precautions against fire when he or she bears the risk than when the risk is borne by an insurance company. Of course, there may be a criminal element involved in this phenomenon, due to the intentional destruction of insured buildings for financial gain.

### Noneconomic Factors in Decision Making

Modern business firms are typically complex organizations in which decisions are made at several levels by a variety of decision makers. In such a system it

**TABLE 2.8**
**Comparing decision criteria**

| Criterion | Auto Fleet | Plant and Buildings |
|---|---|---|
| Expected value | Not insure | Not insure |
| Maximin | Insure | Insure |
| Maximax | Not insure | Not insure |
| Coefficient of variation | Insure | Insure |
| Certainty equivalent | (Not insure?) | (Insure?) |

would be surprising if the firm's objectives were completely served by every decision made. Rather we should expect the presence of certain noneconomic factors, such as instances of self-serving political behavior by decision makers, misplaced efforts due to inappropriate reward systems, and a preference for non-monetary objectives in place of some degree of profitability. Let us discuss each of these in turn.

Robbins has defined *organizational politics* as including any behavior by an organizational member that is self-serving.[5] Political behavior by the decision maker may be "functional" in that it operates to enhance the objectives of the organization, or it may be "dysfunctional" in that it hinders the attainment of the firm's objectives. Since in many cases the objectives of the decision maker and the firm may differ, and since the decision maker has the power to make the decision, we should not expect the decision to necessarily reflect single-minded pursuit of the organization's objectives. The personal gains to the decision maker include a wide variety of tangible and intangible benefits, such as power, prestige, comfort, insulation from a competitive environment, job security, promotion, and perhaps even bribes and/or goods and services received in appreciation of a particular decision. These political gains accrue not to the firm but to the decision maker personally. Hence we may see a decision taken that appears irrational, in the sense that company objectives are not being pursued to the limit, but which is rational from the viewpoint of the decision maker.

Reward systems internal to the firm may cause behavior at variance with the firm's objectives. If an executive's salary, annual bonus, power, prestige, or other reward is dependent upon criteria such as maintaining market share or matching actual costs with budgeted costs, these criteria may become de facto objectives and may cause the firm's overall profits or net worth to fall short of what it might have been.[6] On the other hand, rewards for spectacular increases in profitability may induce decisions that although potentially highly profitable are also very risky, with the result that the firm's objectives would have been better served by an alternative project with a lower expected value and a lower risk attached. Similarly, if rewards are primarily associated with short-term profit performance, we might expect to see decisions made that cause immediate cash flow but are inferior to alternative projects in terms of the total cash flow over a number of accounting periods.[7]

The objectives of the firm itself, and/or of the decision makers within the firm, may include certain nonmonetary goals, such as an aesthetic business environment and a lack of anxiety due to competitive pressures from both within and outside the firm. The gratification received from these factors may be expected to have a monetary equivalent that the firm and/or the decision maker is

[5] S. P. Robbins, *The Administrative Process* (Englewood Cliffs, N.J.: Prentice-Hall, 1976), p.64.

[6] See A. R. Cohen, H. Gadon, and G. Miaoulis, "Decision Making in Firms: The Impact of Non-Economic Factors," *Journal of Economic Issues,* 10, No. 2 (June 1976), 242-58.

[7] We mean in present value terms, of course. The concept of present value is introduced later in this chapter, and the issue of shorter payback periods vs. net present value is discussed in the context of capital-budgeting decisions in Chapter 15.

prepared to forgo in order to attain these nonmonetary goals. Accordingly, we might expect that in practice some decisions will be taken that appear inferior in terms of the strictly economic criteria but serve other noneconomic criteria to the overall satisfaction of the firm and/or the decision maker.

## 2.3  THE VALUE OF INFORMATION

Decision making under conditions of risk and uncertainty involves the problem of the lack of certain important information. Given that there are techniques available to obtain additional information, it is of interest to calculate the value of this information to the decision maker. We define *value of information* as the difference between what you can earn with the information already held and what you could earn if you were to know with certainty the outcome prior to making the decision. In some cases it may be found that the *cost* of the information to the decision maker may be greater than the *value* of that information to the decision maker, in which case the decision maker should proceed on the basis of the information already held and should not undertake the cost of obtaining any extra information, since its cost outweighs the benefits derived.

### The Value of Full Information

Let us refer back to the hot-dogs and ice-cream example to illustrate. In that example, we saw that the vendor had an expected average return of $213.75. This is what the vendor expects to earn given the information already held. If the vendor knew for certain the state of nature on each occasion, in advance of having to make the commitment for either hot dogs or ice cream, he would choose the alternative that promised the greater payoff under the particular weather conditions that would occur. Presumably the vendor could obtain the information with certainty by delaying the decision until the day of each game, observing the weather conditions, and at that point deciding which strategy to choose. If it were known for certain that it would rain on a specific day, we know from Table 2.1 that the vendor would choose hot dogs, since this has a higher return under rainy conditions than does ice cream. Alternatively, if it were cloudy, again the vendor would choose hot dogs rather than ice cream, since the return is higher. Lastly, if it were sunny, the vendor would choose ice cream, since the return for ice cream is higher under sunny conditions.

If asked, at the beginning of the season, how much he would be prepared to pay for the right to delay the decision until the day of the game, the vendor would need to know the value of that right, or the information generated, to him. This requires a decision to be made in advance, which must be based on the expected value of knowing the actual weather conditions. In Table 2.9 we show the expected value of the enterprise, given the full information on weather conditions. The probabilities attached are those generated by the *a posteriori* information received earlier. On the basis of past weather patterns, we must expect it to be raining 15 percent of the days when the team plays at home; to be cloudy 55 percent of the games; and to be sunny 30 percent of the games. Multiplying

51

**TABLE 2.9**
Expected value with full information

| State of Nature | Choice | Payoff | Prob. | EV |
|---|---|---|---|---|
| Rain | Hot dogs | $300 | 0.15 | $ 45.00 |
| Cloud | Hot dogs | 250 | 0.55 | 137.50 |
| Sun | Ice cream | 400 | 0.30 | 120.00 |
| | | | | $302.50 |

the payoff in each case by the probability of that state of nature occurring, and summing the results, we arrive at the expected value with full information of $302.50. This figure is larger than the expected value under the state of uncertainty (viz, $213.75) by $88.75. Thus the value of the additional information, or the value of knowing the exact weather conditions on each specific day, is $88.75. If it were to cost the vendor more than that amount to have the right to delay his choice until the morning of the game, then the vendor should not buy such a right, because it would cost more than its expected value to him.

### The Expected Value of Regret

An alternative means of discovering the maximum value of additional information is via the criterion known as *minimax regret*. As you are aware, regret is what one feels when one has made the wrong decision. In this case *regret* is the number of dollars forgone as a result of making the wrong decision. The regret matrix in Table 2.10 shows the amount of revenue forgone under each state of nature for each of the two strategies. Note that when it rains the regret associated with hot dogs is zero, since hot dogs were the best strategy under rainy conditions, and the vendor would regret nothing. For ice cream, however, on a rainy day the vendor would have regret to the extent of $225, since that is the difference between the $300 return for hot dogs and the $75 return for ice cream. Similarly, for cloudy conditions the regret associated with hot dogs is zero, but with ice cream $100. For sunny conditions the regret associated with hot dogs is $300, since the hot-dogs strategy would return $300 less than the ice-cream strategy under sunny conditions.

The minimax regret criterion requires the decision maker to choose the

**TABLE 2.10**
Regret matrix

| | Hot Dogs | Ice Cream |
|---|---|---|
| Rain | $ 0 | $225 |
| Cloud | 0 | 100 |
| Sun | 300 | 0 |
| Column maxima | $300 | 225 |

strategy that promises the smallest of the maximum regret values associated with each strategy. Note that in Table 2.10 the column maxima are $300 for hot dogs and $225 for ice cream. The minimum of these maxima—that is, the minimax—is $225; hence the minimax regret strategy is to choose ice cream.

In Table 2.11 we show the expected value of regret associated with each of the two strategies. Following the hot-dogs strategy, the decision maker expects to have zero regret 15 percent of the time because it is raining, zero regret 55 percent of the time because it is cloudy, and $300 regret 30 percent of the time because it is sunny and under these conditions he is pursuing the wrong strategy. The expected value of this regret is thus 30 percent of $300, or $90. The ice-cream strategy is expected to incur a $225 regret 15 percent of the time, a $100 regret 55 percent of the time, and zero regret 30 percent of the time. Multiplying these regrets by the probabilities and summing the results, we find the expected value of regret associated with the ice-cream strategy to be $88.75. Notice that this figure is exactly the value of information derived earlier. To see why this is so, notice that the expected regret is the expected cost of not knowing exactly what the weather conditions would be. Hence it is equivalent to the value of information.

**TABLE 2.11**
**Expected value of regret**

| State of Nature | Hot Dogs | | | Ice Cream | | |
|---|---|---|---|---|---|---|
| | *Regret* | *Prob.* | *EV* | *Regret* | *Prob.* | *EV* |
| Rain | $ 0 | 0.15 | $ 0 | $225 | 0.15 | $33.75 |
| Cloud | 0 | 0.55 | 0 | 100 | 0.55 | 55.00 |
| Sun | 300 | 0.30 | 90.00 | 0 | 0.30 | 0 |
| Expected regret | | | $90.00 | | | $88.75 |

Thus, by finding the minimax regret strategy and calculating the expected value of regret associated with that strategy, one may determine the value of additional information. If information sources can be purchased at a cost less than this expected value of information, the decision maker is advised to purchase such information and hence improve the decision made. On the other hand, if the information, or the right to delay the decision until the appropriate strategy becomes clear, costs more than the value of that information or right, the decision maker should proceed on the basis of the available information in order to maximize the expected return.

## 2.4 MULTIPERIOD DECISION MAKING

Many decisions involve a flow of revenues extending beyond the present period. In choosing between or among various alternatives, it is important to distinguish between revenues that are received immediately and those that are received at some later date. A dollar received today is worth more than a dollar received next year, which in turn is worth more than a dollar received the following year. The reason for this is that a dollar held today may be deposited in a bank or other interest-earning security, and at the expiry of one year it will be worth the original dollar plus the interest earned on that dollar. Hence, if the interest rate is, say, 10 percent, a dollar today will be worth $1.10 one year from today. Looking at this from the reverse aspect, a dollar earned one year from today is worth less than a dollar that is held today. Thus, the future earnings must be discounted by the interest rate they could have earned had they been held today.

### Present Value Analysis

The general formula[8] for calculating the present value of a sum to be received in the future is

$$PV = \frac{R}{(1+r)^t} \qquad (2.3)$$

where $R$ is the sum of money to be received, $r$ is the appropriate rate of discount, and $t$ is the number of years hence that the money will be received. For example, if one dollar is to be received one year from now, and the discount rate is 10 percent, its present value is

$$PV = \frac{1}{(1+0.1)^1}$$

$$= \frac{1}{(1.1)}$$

$$= 0.90909$$

or almost 91 cents. We can use this present value of one dollar as the *discount factor* for any number of dollars to be received one year from now, when the appropriate discount rate is 10 percent. Thus, if we expect to receive $2,500 in one year, its present value is

$$PV = \$2,500(0.90909)$$

$$= \$2,272.73$$

Table 2.12 shows the discount factors appropriate for sums of money to be received in various years hence and discounted at three different rates. For example, if the appropriate discount rate is 15 percent, a dollar to be received five years from now has a present value of only 49.7 cents, since 49.7 cents invested today at 15 percent interest rate compounded annually would accumulate to $1.00 in five years. Table 2.12 is extracted from Table A.1 in the Present Value Tables that can be found in Appendix A at the end of this book.

[8] W. J. Baumol, *Economic Theory and Operations Analysis,* 3rd ed. (Englewood Cliffs, N.J.: Prentice-Hall, 1972), pp. 446-48.

**TABLE 2.12**
Present value of one dollar earned in future years
calculated at various discount rates

| Discount Rate | Years Hence | | | | | | |
|:---:|:---:|:---:|:---:|:---:|:---:|:---:|:---:|
| | 0 | 1 | 2 | 3 | 4 | 5 | 6 |
| 5% | 1.00 | .952 | .907 | .864 | .823 | .784 | .746 |
| 10 | 1.00 | .909 | .826 | .751 | .683 | .621 | .564 |
| 15 | 1.00 | .870 | .756 | .658 | .572 | .497 | .432 |

### The Opportunity Discount Rate

The decision maker must choose the rate of discount quite carefully, since the "wrong" discount rate could cause a bad decision to be made in cases where the time profiles of future cash flows differ markedly. The "appropriate" discount rate is the rate of interest or return the firm could earn in its best alternative use of the funds that are to be committed by the decision. But other investment opportunities may be more or less risky or uncertain and are thus not strictly comparable with the present proposal. We therefore add the caveat that the appropriate rate of discount is the rate of return on the best alternative use of the funds at the same (or relatively similar) level of risk or uncertainty. We call this equal-risk alternative rate of return the "opportunity" discount rate. To illustrate, suppose a firm intends to invest $10,000 in an expansion of its facilities but might otherwise invest the funds in a bond issue that is considered to be of similar riskiness and would pay 12 percent interest compounded annually. The opportunity discount rate to be used when evaluating the future returns from the project under consideration is therefore 12 percent.

When comparing two or more investment opportunities, a different discount rate may be required for each project under consideration. Since the discount rate is chosen by reference to the riskiness of the project, if the projects have different degrees of riskiness (ie., significantly different standard deviations), then higher discount rates would be applied to the more risky projects to reflect the opportunity being forgone to invest the funds elsewhere at a higher rate of return (for a similar degree of risk). For example, suppose Project A has a standard deviation of expected outcomes similar to that of a 12½ percent bond issue while Project B has a standard deviation similar to that of a 10 percent bond issue. Project A should therefore be discounted at 12½ percent, and Project B should be discounted at 10 percent, in order to compare the present value of their revenue streams on a risk-adjusted basis.

The use of discounted cash flow (or present value) analysis in decision making in the context of the decision tree is illustrated in the following section.

### Decision Diagraming

A technique that is of considerable aid in decision making is that known as the *decision tree,* so called because it illustrates the various consequences that follow from decisions in a chart that resembles the branches of a tree. In the

**TABLE 2.13**
**The decision tree**

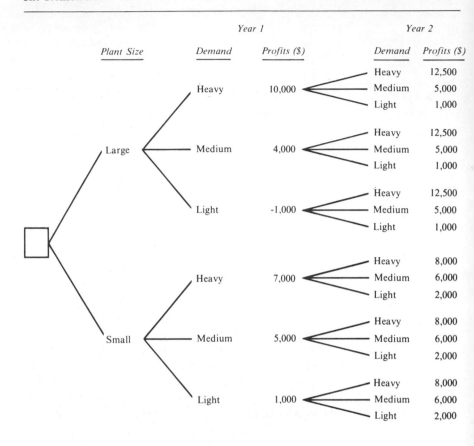

| Plant Size | Year 1 | | | Year 2 | |
| | Demand | Profits ($) | | Demand | Profits ($) |
|---|---|---|---|---|---|
| | | | | Heavy | 12,500 |
| | Heavy | 10,000 | | Medium | 5,000 |
| | | | | Light | 1,000 |
| | | | | Heavy | 12,500 |
| Large | Medium | 4,000 | | Medium | 5,000 |
| | | | | Light | 1,000 |
| | | | | Heavy | 12,500 |
| | Light | -1,000 | | Medium | 5,000 |
| | | | | Light | 1,000 |
| | | | | Heavy | 8,000 |
| | Heavy | 7,000 | | Medium | 6,000 |
| | | | | Light | 2,000 |
| | | | | Heavy | 8,000 |
| Small | Medium | 5,000 | | Medium | 6,000 |
| | | | | Light | 2,000 |
| | | | | Heavy | 8,000 |
| | Light | 1,000 | | Medium | 6,000 |
| | | | | Light | 2,000 |

decision tree illustrated in Table 2.13, a decision maker must choose between a large plant and a small plant for the production of a particular product. The demand condition that will be faced by the product may be "heavy," "medium," or "light" in each of the ensuing two years. The consequences for profits under these various eventualities are indicated in the table.

With the large plant, profits are $10,000, $4,000, and a loss of $1,000, respectively, in the first year. In the second year demand may change as compared with the first year. For example, the demand may be light the first year, yet be either heavy, medium, or remain light in the second year. Profits under each of the possibilities in the second year with both large and small plants are shown in the table. The level of profits that is expected to occur in each of the possible outcome situations apparently reflects the different cost situations of the large and small plants, and the different prices that may be obtained under differing demand conditions. For the purposes of this simple example, we shall assume that the product has a market life of only two years, that the large plant costs $2,000 initially compared with an initial cost of $1,700 for the small plant, that neither plant has any scrap value after two years, and that depreciation expense is not tax deductible.[9]

In order to decide which plant the firm should install, we need to evaluate the expected value of the returns from each of the two possibilities. First, we need to assign probabilities to the possible situations of heavy, medium, and light demand in each of the two years, and we must choose the appropriate discount rate. Let us suppose that the results of market research into the demand for this particular product indicate that in the first year there is a 20 percent chance that demand will be heavy, a 30 percent chance that it will be medium, and a 50 percent chance that it will be light. The same research, however, indicates that in the second year there is a 40 percent chance that demand will be heavy, a 40 percent chance that it will be medium, and a 20 percent chance that it will be only light. On the issue of the appropriate discount rate, we shall suppose that the firm could have earned 10 percent per annum by investing the necessary financial outlay in other assets of comparable risk. Therefore we shall use a 10 percent discount rate in evaluating the future profits from the enterprise. For the purposes of the discounted cash-flow analysis, let us suppose that the first year's profits are received in lump sum at the end of year one, and the second year's profits are received at the end of year two.[10]

The calculation of the expected present value from each of the two plants is shown in Tables 2.14 and 2.15. In each table, column 1 indicates the size and initial cost of the alternatives. Column 2 details the demand possibilities and the probabilities that these demand situations will occur, and column 3 shows the profits expected under each of the demand and plant combinations. Column 4 shows the present value of these profit levels, given a discount rate of 10 percent, which implies a discount factor of 0.909. The demand situations in year two, and the profits derived therefrom, are listed in columns 5 and 6. Column 7 shows the present value of the profits in column 6 using a discount factor of 0.826, since this is the present value of a dollar received two years hence. Column 8 shows the aggregate net present value of the profits of years one and two, minus the initial cost of the plant (which is already in present value terms). Column 9 shows the probability that each of these net present values will be achieved. Note that these probabilities are *joint* probabilities, since being at each particular branch of the tree is conditional upon the preceding year's activity. The appropriate probability, then, is the product of the probability that demand will be heavy in the first year and, for example, also heavy in the second year. Thus the conditional probability of the uppermost branch is 0.08, which is the product of 0.2 times 0.4. In columns 10 and 11 the expected net present value of the alternatives is calculated by summing the weighted net present values. It can be seen that the large plant has an expected net present value of

---

[9] The significance of the latter simplifying assumptions, if not known to you now, will become clear in Chapter 15 where the issue of capital budgeting is treated in more detail.

[10] Later in the text we shall use the more realistic assumption that the funds are received continuously throughout the year. The appropriate discount factors for continuous receipt of funds can be found in Table A.2 in Appendix A at the end of this book.

**TABLE 2.14**
**Calculation of expected present value for the large plant**

| Plant (cost) [1] | Year 1 | | | Year 2 | | | | Calculation of ENPV | | |
|---|---|---|---|---|---|---|---|---|---|---|
| | Demand (prob.) [2] | Profits [3] | PV (DF = .909) [4] | Demand (prob.) [5] | Profits [6] | PV (DF = .826) [7] | Total NPV [8] | Joint Prob. [9] | Weighted NPVs [10] | Sum [11] |
| Large ($2,000) | Heavy (P = 0.2) | $10,000 | $9,090 | Heavy (P = 0.4) | $12,500 | $10,325 | $17,415 | 0.08 | $1,393.20 | $2,607.44 |
| | | | | Medium (P = 0.4) | 5,000 | 4,130 | 11,220 | 0.08 | 897.60 | |
| | | | | Light (P = 0.2) | 1,000 | 826 | 7,916 | 0.04 | 316.64 | |
| | Medium (P = 0.3) | 4,000 | 3,636 | Heavy (P = 0.4) | 12,500 | 10,325 | 11,961 | 0.12 | 1,435.32 | 2,274.96 |
| | | | | Medium (P = 0.4) | 5,000 | 4,130 | 5,766 | 0.12 | 691.92 | |
| | | | | Light (P = 0.2) | 1,000 | 826 | 2,462 | 0.06 | 147.72 | |
| | Light (P = 0.5) | −1,000 | −909 | Heavy (P = 0.4) | 12,500 | 10,325 | 7,416 | 0.20 | 1,483.20 | 1,519.10 |
| | | | | Medium (P = 0.4) | 5,000 | 4,130 | 1,221 | 0.20 | 244.20 | |
| | | | | Light (P = 0.2) | 1,000 | 826 | −2,083 | 0.10 | −208.30 | |
| | | | | | | | | | Expected net present value | $6,401.50 |

**TABLE 2.15**
Calculation of expected present value for the small plant

| Plant (cost) [1] | Demand (prob.) [2] | Profits [3] | PV (DF = .909) [4] | Demand (prob.) [5] | Profits [6] | PV (DF = .826) [7] | Total NPV [8] | Joint Prob. [9] | Weighted NPVs [10] | Sum [11] |
|---|---|---|---|---|---|---|---|---|---|---|
| | | | Year 1 | | Year 2 | | | | Calculation of ENPV | |
| Small ($1,700) | Heavy (P = 0.2) | $ 7,000 | $6,363 | Heavy (P = 0.4) | $ 8,000 | $ 6,608 | $11,271 | 0.08 | $ 901.68 | $1,923.80 |
| | | | | Medium (P = 0.4) | 6,000 | 4,956 | 9,619 | 0.08 | 769.52 | |
| | | | | Light (P = 0.2) | 2,000 | 1,652 | 6,315 | 0.04 | 252.60 | |
| | Medium (P = 0.3) | 5,000 | 4,545 | Heavy (P = 0.4) | 8,000 | 6,608 | 9,453 | 0.12 | 1,134.36 | 2,340.30 |
| | | | | Medium (P = 0.4) | 6,000 | 4,956 | 7,801 | 0.12 | 936.12 | |
| | | | | Light (P = 0.2) | 2,000 | 1,652 | 4,497 | 0.06 | 269.82 | |
| | Light (P = 0.5) | 1,000 | 909 | Heavy (P = 0.4) | 8,000 | 6,608 | 5,817 | 0.20 | 1,163.40 | 2,082.50 |
| | | | | Medium (P = 0.4) | 6,000 | 4,956 | 4,165 | 0.20 | 833.00 | |
| | | | | Light (P = 0.2) | 2,000 | 1,652 | 861 | 0.10 | 86.10 | |
| | | | | | | | | Expected net present value | | $6,346.60 |

**FIGURE 2.1**
**Probability distribution of the outcomes associated with the large plant**

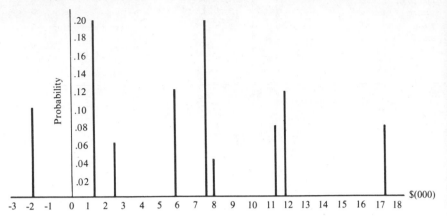

$6,401.50 compared with the small plant's $6,346.60. The expected value criterion would therefore suggest the implementation of the large plant.

As we have noted, however, the expected value criterion does not take into account the riskiness of the possible outcomes. It can be seen from column 8 of the two tables that the outcomes for the large plant vary over a wider range than do the outcomes for the small plant. These outcomes are plotted in Figures 2.1 and 2.2, as a probability distribution. It is apparent that the degree of riskiness associated with the large plant is greater than for the small plant, since the actual outcome may lie quite distant from the expected value; moreover, these distant outcomes have relatively large probabilities of occurring. Although not calculated, it is clear that the standard deviation will be considerably higher for the large plant. Since the expected values are quite similar, the coefficient of

**FIGURE 2.2**
**Probability distribution of the outcomes associated with the small plant**

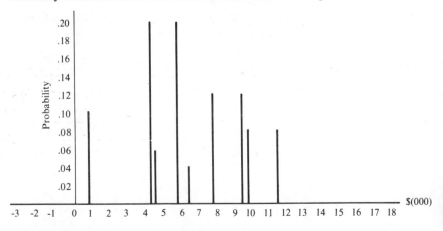

variation will be higher for the large plant, and hence this criterion would suggest the implementation of the small plant.[11]

The maximin criterion, which avoids the lowest possible payoff, would also suggest the small plant, since its worst outcome ($861) is preferable to the large plant's worst outcome ($-2,083). The maximax decision maker, on the other hand, would choose the large plant, since its best outcome ($17,415) is greater than the small plant's best outcome ($11,271). The certainty equivalent criterion depends upon the decision maker's attitude toward risk and uncertainty, the ability of the firm to withstand the worst outcomes, and the frequency of making this type of decision. Not knowing these details in this case we are unable to speculate upon the plant size that will be chosen under this criterion. Table 2.16 summarizes the decision that will be taken under each of the five criteria considered above.

**TABLE 2.16**
**Comparing decision criteria**

| Criterion | Large or Small Plant? |
|---|---|
| Expected value | Large |
| Maximin | Small |
| Maximax | Large |
| Coefficient of variation | Small |
| Certainty equivalent | ? |

## 2.5  SUMMARY

In this chapter we have introduced the concepts of certainty, risk, and uncertainty and examined the decision-making process. We saw that it was necessary to specify the acts that are available to the decision maker, the events that may be expected to follow those acts, the probabilities of each of those events occurring, and the appropriate decision-making criterion.

Five decision criteria were applied to three business problems, and it was seen that the appropriate criterion for a particular decision depends upon both the type of decision problem and the type of decision maker. The *expected value* criterion was essentially neutral with respect to risk, since it did not take into account the variance of the values of the possible events, allowing the law of averages to ensure that the actual returns approximate the expected value. The *maximax* criterion took no account of the range of possible outcomes except to choose the outcome that had the largest possible return. The *maximin*

[11] Since the standard deviations differ, the two alternatives are not equally risky. Thus a higher discount rate is appropriate for the large plant as compared with the small plant. For simplicity we have ignored this here, but this simplification would lead us into a bad decision if we were to use the expected value criterion. Discounting the large plant's revenue stream by a higher rate would cause its expected net present value to fall *below* that of the small plant.

criterion, on the other hand, is for the decision maker who wishes to avoid the worst possible outcome. The *certainty equivalent* criterion requires the decision maker to demonstrate his or her preference for risk and uncertainty by placing a monetary assessment of that risk or uncertainty against the gamble. The *coefficient of variation* criterion is a simple rule of thumb, which takes into account the variability of the possible events and penalizes those events that have larger variance around the expected values.

We saw that information has value and that the value of information could be calculated. By comparing this value with the cost of additional information, the decision maker is able to decide whether or not to undertake market research or other means of obtaining the information that would reduce or eliminate the uncertainty. The *minimax regret* method of ascertaining the value of information was demonstrated.

When the events following a decision occur over an extended period of time, it is necessary to apply discounted cash-flow analysis in order to correctly determine the value of each of the events. It is important that the discount rate that is applied to future cash flows be the "opportunity" discount rate. The decision-tree diagram was used to facilitate solution of a multiperiod decision problem.

Your course in managerial economics could stop right here except for a number of problems. First, what do we mean by the simple term *profits* in the above business examples? We certainly do not mean what is generally understood by accountants or economists as profits. Later chapters will indicate the appropriate way to regard profits in the decision-making problem. Second, where did the underlying cost and revenue figures come from? In later chapters we will examine the principles, or theories, of both cost and demand analysis. Third, the assignment of probabilities in the above examples was a simple matter. In real-life business situations this assignment of probabilities requires a solid understanding not only of the procedures of cost and demand estimation but also of the underlying principles involved. The fourth major problem obscured by the above examples is that the pricing decision is taken for granted. How do we know that the price used is the optimal price? Part 4 of this text considers this issue. Therefore the course does not stop here. We have established a framework within which to make decisions, but we must proceed to examine the issues surrounding the variables that are fundamental to the decision-making process.

## DISCUSSION QUESTIONS

2.1   What are the essential differences between *risk* and *uncertainty* as defined in the text?

2.2   Go through the thought process of determining your own certainty equivalent for a fifty-cent lottery ticket that is one of 100,000 sold for a $10,000 prize.

   (a)   Would you buy such a ticket?

   (b)   How much more or less expensive would the ticket need to be to *just* induce you to buy it?

   (c)   Is that price your certainty equivalent for the gamble?

2.3   A professor I know consistently parks his automobile in a no-parking zone while having his hair cut on the first Monday of every month. He reasons that the police watch that zone only infrequently, and that if he gets a parking fine ($15) it will still be cheaper over the longer term than paying $2 to park in the lot next door.

  (a)  Which decision criterion is the professor using?

  (b)  What is the maximum value of the probability that the professor implicitly places against the outcome of "getting a ticket"?

2.4  The product manager of a large company has had a series of disastrous new-product offerings. He fears that another failure will cost him his job. He is currently trying to make up his mind between two rather different new products for his next new-product launching. Product A has the greater expected value and has both a smaller minimum outcome and a larger maximum outcome as compared with Product B. Which product do you think the product manager will choose, and why?

2.5  *Risk aversion* and *risk preference* were not explicitly defined in the text.

  (a)  Can you deduce a definition for these terms?

  (b)  Will a risk-averse decision maker refuse to take risks?

  (c)  How can we tell if one decision maker is more or less risk-averse than another?

2.6  Why is the expected value criterion not always the appropriate decision criterion for the decision maker who wishes to maximize profits but who is also risk-averse?

2.7  Suppose a decision maker uses the coefficient of variation criterion to make decisions but will accept a maximum value of only 0.5. Can you say what range of outcomes (expressed as a proportion of the expected values) the decision maker is likely to experience?

2.8  Why is the expected value of regret associated with the minimax regret strategy equal to the maximum value of additional information?

2.9  If the opportunity discount rate of one use of funds is 15 percent while for another it is 20 percent, what does this imply about the dispersion of the outcomes associated with each project

  (a)  compared with each other?

  (b)  compared with other possible uses of the funds?

2.10  Why is it methodologically *incorrect* to attempt to find the expected net present value of a multiyear probability distribution by aggregating the expected net present values of *each year,* rather than by the correct procedure of aggregating the total net present values of the terminal branches weighted by the conditional probabilities?

## PROBLEMS

2.1  For the large- and small-plant example given in Tables 2.14 and 2.15 in the text,

  (a)  Calculate the standard deviations of the two distributions (from column 8) around the expected net present values.

  (b)  Calculate the coefficient of variation of the two distributions.

  (c)  State what additional information is needed before you can decide on the appropriate opportunity discount rate for each plant's revenue stream.

2.2    Sounds True, Inc., a small company producing stereo amplifiers, has found that its leading model has suffered substantial market share losses due to the competition from other producers' newer models. The company is considering two alternatives for the coming year: either to give the existing product a minor face-lift or to introduce a totally new model. The success or failure of these strategies will depend ultimately upon the state of the economy, as is evident from the payoff matrix:

|  |  | Strategies ($000) | |
|---|---|---|---|
|  |  | *Minor Face-lift* | *New Model* |
| State of | Downturn | 10 | −20 |
| the | Constant | 30 | 20 |
| Economy | Upturn | 80 | 150 |

The payoffs shown represent thousands of dollars net profit. The company has no idea which state of the economy is more likely to occur and is considering asking a prominent consultant for advice. His fee is $10,000, but he *is* accurate in his predictions on the state of the economy.

(a)    What is the value of the desired information to the stereo company?

(b)    Should it purchase the consultant's advice? Why?

(c)    Which alternative should it choose? (Consider this choice under several different scenarios concerning its attitude to profits, losses, and risk taking and assume that the consultant's advice is not available.)

2.3    The Schasny Paper Company plans to decentralize its customer invoicing and cash collection, a move that is expected to save it $500,000 each year for the next five years. The company is considering two alternative means of acquiring the necessary data-processing equipment. Plan A is to purchase the equipment outright for $1.4 million now, with a maintenance contract (payable yearly in advance) of $1,000 the first year and increasing by $1,000 for each year thereafter. Schasny's present equipment could be sold now for $100,000, and the new equipment would have a salvage value of $250,000 at the end of five years. Plan B is to lease the equipment for five years, for $420,000 yearly payable each year in advance, which includes a maintenance agreement. The leasing company would give Schasny $200,000 credit for the old equipment, and Schasny would have no equity in the leased equipment at the end of the agreement.

(a)    Assuming an opportunity discount rate of 15 percent, calculate the cost of the two alternatives in present value terms (ignore any tax considerations).

(b)    Which plan, if either, should Schasny adopt?

2.4    The Mark U. Cosmetic Company is considering whether or not to develop and market a new men's cologne. Development costs are estimated to be $125,000, and there is a 70 percent probability that development will succeed, based on the company's previous experience. If it does succeed, the product will be marketed at $4 per bottle. Cost of production is expected to be constant at $1.50 per bottle regardless of volume. If the product is "highly" successful (estimated probability 35 percent), it will sell an estimated 95,000 bottles over the year. If it is only "moderately" successful

(45 percent probability), it will sell an estimated 33,000 bottles. If it "fails" (20 percent probability), it will sell only the initial production run of 10,000 bottles.

Should development not be undertaken, the plant capacity could be utilized for an outside contract to produce 20,000 units of a chain-store cologne, which will sell to the retailer for $1.25 profit per bottle.

(a)  Construct the decision tree that reflects the above decision problem.

(b)  Should Mark U. go ahead with the product development, or simply take the contract with the chain store? (Assume all costs and revenues are incurred and received within the first year, so that discounting is not required.)

2.5  Your firm is considering the introduction of a new product, and you are required to set the price. You are considering three price strategies: high ($6), medium ($4), and low ($2.50). Your market research team has indicated that the probability distribution of sales at these prices is as follows:

|  | High Price | | Medium Price | | Low Price | |
| --- | --- | --- | --- | --- | --- | --- |
|  | Sales | Prob. | Sales | Prob. | Sales | Prob. |
| First year | 3,500 | 0.1 | 5,000 | 0.2 | 10,000 | 0.4 |
|  | 2,500 | 0.3 | 4,000 | 0.5 | 7,500 | 0.3 |
|  | 1,500 | 0.6 | 3,000 | 0.3 | 5,000 | 0.3 |
| Second year | 5,000 | 0.2 | 8,000 | 0.3 | 12,000 | 0.3 |
|  | 4,000 | 0.3 | 6,500 | 0.4 | 9,000 | 0.5 |
|  | 3,000 | 0.5 | 5,000 | 0.3 | 7,500 | 0.2 |

The initial investment will be $22,000, and per unit variable costs will be constant at $1 regardless of volume. You are advised by the finance department that the $22,000 could otherwise be invested (at comparable risk) in a forthcoming bond issue at 12.5 percent per annum.

(a)  Using decision-tree analysis, find which pricing strategy promises the greatest net present value over the two-year period.

(b)  Should the investment funds be used to buy the bonds instead? Why?

(c)  Rank the strategies in order of their riskiness. Explain the basis for your ranking.

(d)  Rank the strategies in order of their risk-adjusted expected value.

2.6  A small clothing firm has invested $10,000 in a machine to produce cravats. It is considering the joint decision of the price and quality of the single type of cravat it will market. Three possibilities are considered feasible: (A) lower-quality materials and workmanship, resulting in a per unit direct cost of $5, and priced at $8 per unit; (B) better-quality materials and workmanship, with direct cost of $6 per unit, priced at $11; and (C) top-quality materials and workmanship, with direct cost of $7 per unit, priced at $14. The firm has a planning horizon of two years, after which time the machine will be worthless. The firm considers its opportunity discount rate to be 10 percent.

To help in the decision, the firm employed the Astigmatic Research Company to generate estimates of probable sales for each of the above-mentioned price/quality modes. A.R.C. has produced the following carefully estimated projections of sales volumes for the next two years.

| | Sales Volume | Probabilities | |
| --- | --- | --- | --- |
| | *Each Year* | *Year 1* | *Year 2* |
| *Cravat A* | 2,000 | 0.10 | 0.05 |
| | 4,000 | 0.25 | 0.20 |
| | 6,000 | 0.40 | 0.35 |
| | 8,000 | 0.20 | 0.30 |
| | 10,000 | 0.05 | 0.10 |
| *Cravat B* | 2,000 | 0.15 | 0.10 |
| | 4,000 | 0.30 | 0.25 |
| | 6,000 | 0.25 | 0.30 |
| | 8,000 | 0.20 | 0.25 |
| | 10,000 | 0.10 | 0.10 |
| *Cravat C* | 2,000 | 0.20 | 0.25 |
| | 4,000 | 0.35 | 0.40 |
| | 6,000 | 0.25 | 0.25 |
| | 8,000 | 0.15 | 0.10 |
| | 10,000 | 0.05 | 0.00 |

(a) Apply the expected value, maximin, maximax, and coefficient of variation criteria to these alternatives to find which alternative is indicated under each criterion.

(b) Which price/quality mode should the firm choose, in your judgment?

2.7 Safeguard Stores is a relatively small chain operation in the retail supermarket industry. The area manager for Montreal, Nick Wolkowski, is considering opening a new store in a rapidly expanding suburb. Two sizes of store have been suggested: the regular size of 27,000 square feet, and the superstore size of 40,000 square feet. The initial costs, expected demand situation, profits, and probabilities are as follows:

| | | | Year 1 | | Year 2 | |
| --- | --- | --- | --- | --- | --- | --- |
| *Store Size* | *Initial Cost* | *Demand Situation* | *Profits* | *Prob.* | *Profits* | *Prob.* |
| | $ 000 | | $ 000 | | $ 000 | |
| | | Low | 300 | 0.2 | 500 | 0.2 |
| Regular | 850 | Medium | 500 | 0.5 | 800 | 0.4 |
| | | High | 800 | 0.3 | 1,000 | 0.4 |
| | | Low | 300 | 0.6 | 600 | 0.4 |
| Super | 1,000 | Medium | 600 | 0.3 | 900 | 0.3 |
| | | High | 1,000 | 0.1 | 1,200 | 0.3 |

Mr. Wolkowski is considering only a two-year horizon, since he hopes to be regional manager by then. He feels that the appropriate discount rate is 10 percent. (Treat the profits as though they are received in lump sum at the end of year one and year two. The costs are incurred immediately.)

(a) Which store size promises the larger expected net present value?

(b) Which decision criterion do you think Mr. Wolkowski should apply, given his desire to impress his superiors sufficiently to obtain his promotion?

## SUGGESTED REFERENCES AND FURTHER READING

BAUMOL, W. J., *Economic Theory and Operations Analysis,* 4th ed., Chaps. 18 and 19. Englewood Cliffs, N.J.: Prentice-Hall, 1977.

BRIGHAM, E. F., and J. L. PAPPAS, *Managerial Economics,* 2nd ed., Chap. 3. Hinsdale, Ill.: Dryden, 1976.

CHRISTENSON, C. J., R. F. VANCIL, and P. W. MARSHALL, *Managerial Economics,* rev. ed., Chaps. 4 and 5. Homewood, Ill.: Richard D. Irwin, 1973.

McGUIGAN, J. R., and R. C. MOYER, *Managerial Economics,* Chap. 3. Hinsdale, Ill.: Dryden, 1975.

SIMON, J. L., *Applied Managerial Economics,* Chaps. 2 and 3. Englewood Cliffs, N.J.: Prentice-Hall, 1975.

THOMPSON, A. A., Jr., *Economics of the Firm,* Chap. 2. Englewood Cliffs, N.J.: Prentice-Hall, 1973.

# part II

# Demand Theory and Analysis

# 3

# The Theory of Economic Consumer Behavior

**3.1   Introduction**

**3.2   Indifference Curve Analysis of Choice between Products**

Preference and Indifference.    Indifference Curves.
Assumptions Underlying the Analysis.    The Marginal Rate of Substitution.
The Consumer's Income Constraint.    Utility Maximization.

**3.3   Price, Income, and Substitution Effects**

The Price Effect.    The Law of Demand and the Demand Curve.
The Income Effect.    The Substitution Effect.
Changes in Consumer Tastes and Preferences.
Real Price Changes vs. Nominal Price Changes.

**3.4   The Attribute Approach to Consumer Choice**

Attributes in Products.    Depicting Products in Attribute Space.
The Efficiency Frontier.    Maximizing Utility from Attributes.
The Price Effect.    Changes in Consumer Perception and Tastes.
New Products.    Market Segments.
Problems of Identifying and Measuring Attributes.

**3.5   Aggregation of Individual Demand Curves**

Independent Consumer Preferences.    The Bandwagon Effect.
The Snob Effect.

**3.6   Summary**

## 3.1  INTRODUCTION

Since the first step toward business profits is the demand expressed by consumers, an understanding of the principles underlying and explaining consumer demand is indispensable to the modern business decision maker. We cannot simply assume that demand will always be there, since it is sensitive among other things to changes in prices, changes in consumer incomes, and changes in the prices and availability of substitute products. In this chapter we address ourselves to the consumer's reactions to these economic variables, in order that better decisions may be made, especially in the pricing area.

The next two sections of this chapter review the traditional approach to economic consumer behavior; that is, indifference curve analysis of consumer choice between and among products. This review is at the level of an intermediate microeconomics course. If your previous exposure to microeconomics has been at the intermediate level, you may wish to skim over these sections or bypass them completely (if your memory is perfect!). If your background in microeconomics is restricted to an introductory level course, however, I suggest you read these sections carefully, since they provide the terms and concepts necessary for the following sections and later chapters.

The fourth section of this chapter examines an alternative and relatively new approach to consumer behavior: the attribute approach to consumer choice.[1] Whereas the traditional approach assumes that consumers derive utility from the consumption of products, the attribute approach assumes that consumers derive utility not from the products per se, but from the attributes (or characteristics) embodied in or attached to the products. Using the example of an automobile,

[1] See K. Lancaster, "A New Approach to Consumer Theory," *Journal of Policital Economy,* 84 (April 1966), 132-57; K. Lancaster, *Consumer Demand: A New Approach* (New York: Columbia University Press, 1971); and R. Hendler, "Lancaster's New Approach to Consumer Demand and Its Limitations," *American Economic Review,* 65 (March 1975), 194-99.

the traditional view is that the consumer derives utility from the automobile itself, while the attribute approach is that utility is obtained from the benefits derived from the automobile, such as transportation, comfort, prestige, power, economy, and other features perceived and appreciated by the consumer.

The attribute approach has important implications for managerial economics, especially in the pricing area. Since attributes have utility value to consumers, prices of products should be chosen with regard to the presence, absence, or degree of desirable attributes associated with the product. In fact, the attribute approach provides the bridge between the theory of economic consumer behavior and the pricing practices of marketing managers, as we shall see in Chapters 11 and 12.

## 3.2  INDIFFERENCE CURVE ANALYSIS OF CHOICE BETWEEN PRODUCTS

Economists postulate that consumers derive utility, or psychic satisfaction, from the consumption of goods and services. Consumers purchase products on the expectation that the utility that will be derived, relative to the prices of the products, will be greater for the purchased products than for others. We postulate that consumers are basically hedonists and wish to maximize the utility they are able to derive from their available income or wealth sources. Given a finite supply of income or wealth, the consumer must allocate these funds among the available products such that his or her utility is maximized. A consumer who is pursuing the maximization of utility is said to be acting "rationally."

### Preference and Indifference

The relative amounts of utility expected to be derived from different products, or groups of products, allow the consumer to express either preference or indifference among those products. Suppose there are two products, called A and B. The consumer will regard those two products in one of the following three ways. He will prefer A to B, or he will prefer B to A, or he will have no preference between the two. In the last case we say that the consumer is indifferent between the two products. Extending this analysis to groups of products, we might find, for example, that the consumer prefers three units of A and two units of B, to one unit of A and four units of B, and is indifferent between the latter combination and two units of A and two units of B.

### Indifference Curves

An *indifference curve* is defined as the locus of combinations of two products among which the consumer is indifferent. Similarly, an indifference hyperplane is an *n*-dimensional locus of combinations of *n* goods and services, where the consumer expresses no preference for any one of the combinations of the *n* products over the remaining combinations of the *n* products represented by that hyperplane. For simplicity of exposition and feasibility of graphical treatment, we shall use the simple case of only two products being considered by the consumer. Using algebraic techniques we could extend this analysis to larger numbers of products, but the following two-dimensional model is sufficient to explain and demonstrate the principles involved. By extension, these principles also apply to the *n*-dimensional real-world consumer choice situation.

Let us consider a particular consumer's demand for two particular products. Suppose a female college student buys hamburgers and/or milkshakes for lunch and we wish to know what weekly combination of hamburgers and milkshakes would maximize her utility from those two products. Figure 3.1 shows hamburgers on the vertical axis measured in physical units, and milkshakes on the horizontal axis also measured in physical units. The lines $I_1$ and $I_2$ are two of the student's indifference curves. The combinations of hamburgers and milkshakes represented by indifference curve $I_1$, such as five burgers/one shake and three burgers/two shakes, give her the *same* level of expected utility. Combinations that lie to the right and above indifference curve $I_1$ promise a *higher* level of utility, and combinations that lie to the left and below that curve promise a *lower* level of utility.

For each point in the product space represented by Figure 3.1, there will be a series of other points among which the student is indifferent. Consider point $C$ on indifference curve $I_2$, which represents two burgers/four shakes. Starting from this point we could find the other points on indifference curve $I_2$ by a process of questioning the student about her preference or indifference between other combinations of burgers and shakes.

Suppose we ask the student which would she prefer: two burgers and four shakes (point $C$), or three burgers and three shakes? If she prefers the latter

**FIGURE 3.1**
**Indifference curves between products**

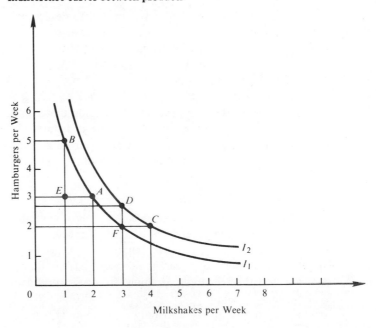

combination, it is evident that the extra burger in the latter combination more than compensates her in terms of utility for the shake that was taken away. If we then offer this consumer the choice of the initial combination $C$, or two-and-a-half burgers and three shakes and she expresses preference for the initial combination, we know that the extra half burger does not compensate her for the loss of the one shake. Continuing this iterative process of questioning, we could find a new combination of burgers and shakes for which the consumer is indifferent when faced with a choice of this combination or the combination represented by point $C$. Suppose this occurs at point $D$, which is 2.75 burgers and three shakes. When confronted with this choice the student says that she has no preference between the two combinations, that either one is as good as the other. Hence points $D$ and $C$ are on the same indifference curve. By the same process we could generate a multitude of combinations that this consumer feels are identical (in terms of utility derived) to points $D$ and $C$, and which therefore also lie on indifference curve $I_2$.

Since we could start this process from any combination of hamburgers and milkshakes, it follows that there is an indifference curve passing through every point in the figure. We have shown simply two of the infinite number of indifference curves that represent this particular consumer's taste and preference pattern between the two products. To the right of those curves shown, there will be curves that depict progressively higher levels of utility; and to the left and below indifference curve $I_1$, there will be curves that depict progressively lower levels of utility.[2]

### Assumptions Underlying the Analysis

We require <u>four</u> simple assumptions to facilitate our analysis of consumer behavior. First, <u>we assume that the consumer is able to rank his or her preferences in the order of utility derived</u>. Notice that we simply require an ordinal ranking and do not expect the consumer to place a value on the amount of utility derived. We simply ask which of two combinations is preferred, but we do not need to know by how much one is preferred to the other.

*ORDINAL*

Second, <u>we require that the consumer's preferences be transitive</u>. Transitivity of preference implies, for example, that if $C$ is preferred to $A$, and $A$ is indifferent to $B$, then $C$ is preferred to $B$. This assumption simply requires that the <u>consumer be consistent in the preferences</u> and indifferences expressed.

Third, <u>we assume that the consumer always prefers more of a commodity to less of that commodity</u>. This assumption of nonsatiation is reasonable in the real world, in view of the wide variety of products a consumer must choose from and the consequent improbability of a rational consumer's consuming any one of those products to the point where the additional utility derived would become zero or negative.

---

[2] It is unlikely that it would ever be feasible for a firm to try to discover the indifference curves of its customers. Such an exercise would be extremely time consuming and expensive. The purpose of the model being employed here is to explain the utility-maximizing responses of consumers to changes in their economic environment. The model has pedagogical and explanatory value without necessarily being economically feasible in the real world.

④ Fourth, we assume that the consumer experiences diminishing marginal utility for all commodities. That is, as the consumer purchases progressively more of any commodity within a particular time period, the additional utility derived from each consecutive unit will diminish. Thus marginal utility monotonically declines from the first unit, approaching but never reaching the value of zero due to the assumption of nonsatiation.

These assumptions allow us to state the following four properties of indifference curves. ① First, points on higher curves are preferred to points on lower curves, due to the assumptions of nonsatiation and transitivity. ② Second, indifference curves have negative slope throughout, due to the assumption of nonsatiation. ③ Third, indifference curves must neither meet nor intersect, due to the transitivity of consumer preferences. ④ Fourth, the indifference curves are convex to the origin, due to the assumption of diminishing marginal utility for all commodities.

### The Marginal Rate of Substitution

To explain the convexity of indifference curves, let us introduce the term *marginal rate of substitution,* abbreviated as MRS. The *MRS* is defined as the amount of one product that the consumer will be willing to give up for an additional unit of another product, in order to remain at the same level of utility. The proviso that the consumer remain at the same level of utility makes it clear that the MRS refers to a movement along a particular indifference curve. By convention we define the MRS between two products for a movement *down* a particular indifference curve. Thus the MRS is the ratio of the amount given up of the product on the vertical axis to the one-unit increment of the product on the horizontal axis.

The MRS is thus equal to the *slope* of an indifference curve at any point on that curve, since it is defined in terms of the vertical rise (or fall) over the horizontal run. Symbolically, and in terms of our example:

$$\text{MRS} = \frac{\Delta H}{\Delta M} \tag{3.1}$$

where $\Delta H$ is the decrement to hamburger consumption necessary to maintain utility at the same level given the one-unit increase in milkshake consumption, $\Delta M$.

Since convexity of an indifference curve means that the slope will be progressively decreasing as we move from left to right along each indifference curve, convexity also means that the MRS will diminish progressively as we move down each indifference curve. In terms of Figure 3.1, the MRS between points $A$ and $B$ on indifference curve $I_1$ is the ratio $BE/EA = 2$. The MRS on indifference curve $I_2$ between points $D$ and $C$ is the ratio $DF/FC = 0.75$.

To appreciate why the assumption of diminishing marginal utility for each product underlies the convexity of indifference curves, let us consider the act of substituting one product for another (such that the consumer stays on the same indifference curve) in two separate steps. Suppose the consumer is about to move from point $D$ in Figure 3.1 to point $C$. We know that this consumer is willing to give up no more than 0.75 hamburgers for the additional (fourth) milkshake. If we simply take away the three-quarters of a hamburger (and do not yet compensate by giving an additional milkshake), the consumer will move from point $D$ to point $F$ on indifference curve $I_1$. This causes a loss of utility equal to the difference between the levels represented by indifference curves $I_2$ and $I_1$, or equal to the marginal utility of the hamburger multiplied by the fraction of a hamburger given up (since <u>marginal utility refers to a one-unit increment or decrement in consumption</u>). Symbolically:

$$I_2 - I_1 = \Delta H \cdot \mathrm{MU}_h \tag{3.2}$$

where $I_2$ and $I_1$ are the levels of utility represented by the indifference curves, $\Delta H$ is the change in consumption of hamburgers, and $\mathrm{MU}_h$ represents the marginal utility of hamburgers at that level of hamburger consumption.

Now let us complete the substitution. To compensate the consumer for the loss of the 0.75 hamburgers, we add an extra milkshake, and so move the consumer from point $F$ to point $C$. The consumer gains utility in this move equal to the difference between indifference curves $I_1$ and $I_2$, or equal to the marginal utility of the extra milkshake. Symbolically:

$$I_2 - I_1 = \Delta M \cdot \mathrm{MU}_m \tag{3.3}$$

where $\Delta M$ is the additional milkshake given to the consumer, and $\mathrm{MU}_m$ is the marginal utility of that milkshake. Notice that the left-hand sides of Eqs. (3.2) and (3.3) are equal in absolute terms, as they must be, since the consumer has been returned to the initial level of utility. Thus the right-hand sides must be equal to each other, that is:

$$\Delta H \cdot \mathrm{MU}_h = \Delta M \cdot \mathrm{MU}_m$$

Rearranging this we have

$$\frac{\Delta H}{\Delta M} = \frac{\mathrm{MU}_m}{\mathrm{MU}_h} \tag{3.4}$$

You will recall from Eq.(3.1) that the left-hand side of Eq.(3.4) is the marginal rate of substitution, so

$$\mathrm{MRS} = \frac{\mathrm{MU}_m}{\mathrm{MU}_h} \tag{3.5}$$

<u>Thus the marginal rate of substitution is equal to the ratio of the marginal utility of the product being acquired to the marginal utility of the product being given up.</u>

Recall that the marginal utility of milkshakes is assumed to fall as additional units are consumed, and the marginal utility of hamburgers is assumed to rise as additional units are given up. The MRS is thus the ratio of a numerator that is falling and a denominator that is rising as we move down along any particular indifference curve. Thus the MRS must diminish as we move down each indifference curve. Hence the assumption of diminishing marginal utilities causes indifference curves to be convex to the origin.

### The Consumer's Income Constraint

Since the consumer prefers higher indifference curves to lower indifference curves, it is evident that to maximize utility he or she would proceed to the highest indifference curve possible. The limits of possibility are defined by the consumer's ability to afford the combinations desired. Were it not for a constraint upon the consumer's income, wealth, and other financial resources, he or she might proceed upward and to the right to a state of infinite euphoria! The income constraint, however, keeps our consumer's feet on the ground, since certain combinations of the two products are simply not affordable. We may express the income (or budget) constraint as

$$B \geqslant \sum_{i=1}^{n} P_i Q_i$$

(3.6)

where $B$ represents the total budget available; $\Sigma$ connotes "the sum of"; $P_i$ represents the price of the $i$th product; $Q_i$ represents the quantity purchased of the $i$th product; and $i = 1, 2, 3, \ldots, n$, where $n$ is the number of products available. Thus the sum of the expenditures on each of the available products must not exceed the total budget available. The assumption of nonsatiation allows us to express the income constraint as an equality rather than the inequality (3.6), since the consumer will derive additional utility from every last cent of the available budget and hence will spend it all in search of maximum utility.[3]

In the simple two-commodity situation discussed above, we can rewrite the budget constraint as

$$B = P_h \cdot H + P_m \cdot M$$

(3.7)

where $B$ is the total dollar budget available to the consumer; $P_h$ and $P_m$ are the prices per physical unit of hamburger and milkshakes; and $H$ and $M$ are the number of physical units of hamburgers and milkshakes purchased by the consumer.

In this equation three symbols represent parameters that will be known to the consumer, namely, the budget available and the prices of hamburgers and milkshakes. The remaining symbols are variables that will take on the values

---

[3] Savings are like any other product in the sense that the consumer expects to derive utility by allocating part of available income to that end. Thus the model does not preclude savings; the consumer is free to "spend" money on savings if this contributes to utility maximization.

necessary to maximize the consumer's utility. Equation(3.7) is actually a linear equation in those two variables. This will be more obvious if we rearrange terms and express the equation in terms of one of the variables. Subtracting $B$ and $P_h \cdot H$ from both sides, we have

$$-P_h \cdot H = -B + P_m \cdot M$$

Dividing both sides by $-P_h$ gives us

$$H = \overset{INTERCEPT}{\frac{B}{P_h}} - \overset{SLOPE}{\frac{P_m}{P_h}} \cdot M \tag{3.8}$$

In this form $H$ is a linear function of the variable $M$ and three parameters, where $B/P_h$ is the intercept term, and the coefficient to $M$ (viz., $-P_m/P_h$) is the slope term. Suppose the parameters take the values $B$ = \$5.00, $P_h$ = \$1.00, and $P_m$ = \$0.50. To solve for the intercept, we set $M = 0$ and find $B/P_h = 5$. Thus, if the consumer spends her entire budget on hamburgers, she will be able to purchase five units weekly. Alternatively, if she spends her total available income on milkshakes, she can purchase ten units weekly.

In Figure 3.2 we show Eq.(3.8) plotted in product space. Note that it intercepts the vertical axis at 5 units and the horizontal axis at 10 units. Starting from the vertical intercept, if milkshake consumption is increased from zero to one, we note from Eq.(3.8) that the value of $H$ is drawn down in the ratio $-P_m/P_h$. This ratio of prices is of course the slope of the line and is constant

**FIGURE 3.2**
**The budget constraint between products**

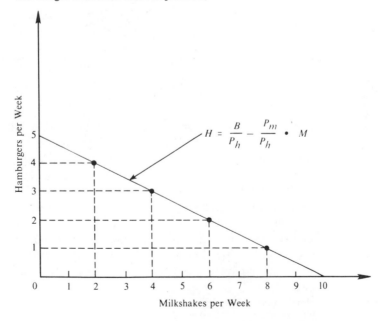

throughout the length of the line, since the price ratio is constant. All combinations of hamburgers and milkshakes that occur on that line cost exactly $5, as may be verified from Figure 3.2. All combinations that lie above and to the right of the income constraint line are unattainable combinations, since they cost more than $5, and all combinations lying below the line cost less than $5.

### Utility Maximization

Let us now superimpose the indifference curves of Figure 3.1 upon the income constraint line of Figure 3.2. This is shown in Figure 3.3. Suppose the consumer is at point $E$, spending all her available income on three hamburgers and

**FIGURE 3.3**
**Maximization of utility from products**

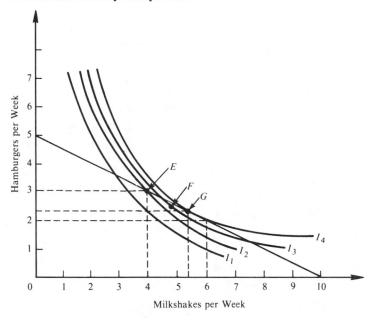

four milkshakes and enjoying a utility level denoted by indifference curve $I_2$. If the consumer shifted to combination $F$, this would allow greater utility but would not use all available income. This shift, while preferable to point $E$, is not yet the utility-maximizing combination. It can be seen that point $G$ is superior to both of the previous two points, and moreover it allows the consumer to attain the highest possible indifference curve. Any higher indifference curve does not touch any of the attainable combinations and therefore is not affordable. The combination of hamburgers and milkshakes that appears to maximize our consumer's utility is thus approximately two and one-third hamburgers and five and one-third milkshakes.[4] By a quick calculation we can

---

[4] These fractional units should not bother us, since we can eliminate them by extending the time period. For example, every three weeks the consumer should purchase seven hamburgers and sixteen milkshakes.

confirm that this combination does not break the consumer's income constraint. The two and one-third hamburgers will cost approximately $2.33, and the five and one-third milkshakes will cost approximately $2.67, making a total expenditure of $5.00.

Utility maximization therefore requires that the consumer chooses the combination on the budget constraint line where this line is tangent to an indifference curve. Tangency between the budget line and an indifference curve requires that their slopes be equal. Recalling that the slope of an indifference curve is the marginal rate of substitution, and the slope of the budget line is the price ratio, we can express the condition for utility maximization as

$$\text{MRS} = \frac{P_m}{P_h} \quad \frac{P_x}{P_y} \tag{3.9}$$

given that all available income is spent. We have previously seen that

$$\text{MRS} = \frac{\text{MU}_m}{\text{MU}_h} \tag{3.5}$$

so we may alternatively express the maximizing condition as

$$\frac{\text{MU}_m}{\text{MU}_h} = \frac{P_m}{P_h} \tag{3.10}$$

Rearranging terms, we have

$$\frac{\text{MU}_m}{P_m} = \frac{\text{MU}_h}{P_h} \tag{3.11}$$

Thus the condition for maximizing utility is to spend the available income such that the ratio of marginal utility to price is the same for all products purchased. In the hamburger/milkshake example it is clear that the consumer must expect to derive twice as much utility from the marginal hamburger compared with the marginal milkshake, since its price is twice as great.[5]

Generalizing to $n$ products, the condition for utility maximization is

$$\frac{\text{MU}_1}{P_1} = \frac{\text{MU}_2}{P_2} = \frac{\text{MU}_3}{P_3} = \cdots = \frac{\text{MU}_n}{P_n} \tag{3.12}$$

given the equality of

$$B = \sum_{i=1}^{n} P_i Q_i \tag{3.13}$$

where the subscripts $i = 1, 2, 3, \ldots, n$ represent the identity of the $n$ products available.

[5] That is, the seventh hamburger in three weeks is expected to generate twice as much utility as the sixteenth milkshake.

The above analysis is concerned with the consumer's utility maximization given a set of available products, their prices, and the consumer's income. We turn now to an analysis of the consumer's utility-maximizing *response* to *changes* in his or her economic environment.

## 3.3 PRICE, INCOME, AND SUBSTITUTION EFFECTS

The economic behavior of the consumer can be categorized under three major headings. These relate to the change or adjustment of an economic variable that influences the consumer's choice between and among products. The economic variables we will consider are changing prices, changing income levels, and changing taste and preference patterns.

### The Price Effect

We define the *price effect* as the change in the quantity demanded of a particular product that results from a change in the price of that product, given *ceteris paribus*.[6] Let us investigate the reaction of a particular consumer to changes in the price level of a particular product. In Figure 3.4 we show the indifference curves of an individual consumer between self-service and full-

**FIGURE 3.4**
**The price consumption curve**

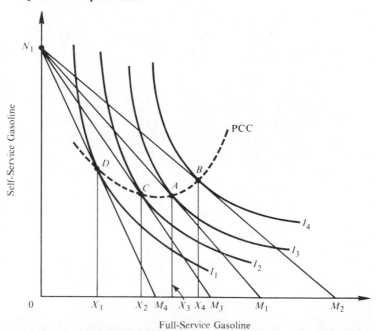

Full-Service Gasoline

[6] In case you have forgotten, *ceteris paribus* means "all other things remaining the same," and in this case requires that the consumer's monetary income and the price of all other available products remain the same. The price effect requires a constant *monetary* income, while the substitution effect, explained on Page 86, requires a constant *real* income.

service gasoline.[7] Suppose the initial prices of self-service gas (SSG) and full-service gas (FSG) and the consumer's income level are such that the appropriate budget line is $N_1M_1$. Thus the consumer maximizes utility at point $A$, at which he purchases $X_3$ units of FSG and the indicated amount of SSG.

Let us now suppose that the price of FSG is reduced. This causes the budget line to swing around to that shown as $N_1M_2$ since its vertical intercept is unchanged while the slope coefficient falls. The consumer responds by moving to point $B$ with a higher level of utility. Notice that consequent to the price reduction for FSG, the consumer's consumption of this product was raised from $X_3$ to $X_4$. Let us now suppose that the price of FSG is *raised* such that the appropriate budget line is $N_1M_3$. The consumer will now maximize utility by attaining the point $C$, where consumption of FSG has fallen to $X_2$ units. If the price of this product were raised still further such that the appropriate budget line was $N_1M_4$, the consumer would select point $D$ on that budget line and would maximize utility by consuming $X_1$ units of FSG and the indicated amount of SSG. If we join the points $A$, $B$, $C$, and $D$, we obtain what is known as the "price consumption curve." This curve is the locus of the points of tangency between the appropriate budget constraint line and the highest attainable indifference curve, at various price levels of the product on the horizontal axis.

### The Law of Demand
### and the Demand Curve

The price consumption curve shows how the consumption of one product (and implicitly of the other as well) changes as the price of that product is varied. Given the validity of the general structure of indifference curves, it is apparent that there is an inverse relationship between the price of a product and the quantity demanded of that product. As price is raised progressively, the consumer demands progressively less of that product; and oppositely, as price is reduced, the consumer demands progressively more of that product. This relationship is known as the "law of demand." It is an empirical law, meaning that it is commonly observed in practice. Expressed graphically, the law of demand is a negatively sloping line relating price to units of quantity demanded. This line is, of course, "the demand curve." The consumer's demand curve for FSG is shown in Figure 3.5.

Notice that the actual data that underlie the demand curve depend upon the individual's reaction to changes in the economic variable of price. This demand curve is thus not likely to be exactly the same as the demand curves of other consumers, who have their own taste and preference patterns and hence their own reactions to changes in the price of the product. These differences in reaction may be traced back to different marginal rates of substitution in their taste and preference patterns reflected in their indifference curves having greater or

[7] We can legitimately regard these as separate products, given that they are composed of different attributes. Full-service gas comes complete with smiling attendant eager to check your oil, fan belt, filters, radiator water and hoses, and tire pressures and wash your windows, headlights and taillights. (This is clearly a *textbook* example.) Self-service gas comes without the above, but with a significant saving per tankful and no anxiety about lost filler caps. Many consumers will demand both types of gas, since they desire the attributes of each at different times.

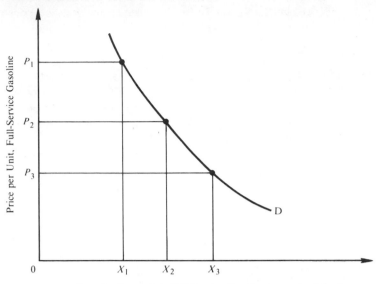

**FIGURE 3.5**
**Demand curve for an individual consumer**

Price per Unit, Full-Service Gasoline

$P_1$
$P_2$
$P_3$

$D$

$0$    $X_1$    $X_2$    $X_3$

Quantity Demanded, Full-Service Gasoline (per unit of time)

lesser degrees of curvature. The above analysis, however, serves to demonstrate that although other consumers may not react to the *same degree* as our present example, they will react in the *same direction* in response to a change in price if they are attempting to maximize their utility from a limited income source. Since consumers in general attempt to get the most out of their money, we expect the law of demand to hold for consumers in general, although some consumers may react to price increases or decreases to a greater or lesser degree than others.

### The Income Effect   MAY BE POSITIVE OR NEGATIVE

We define the *income effect* as the change in the quantity demanded of a particular product when there is a change in the consumer's income, and all other factors, such as the prices of the products and the consumer's tastes, remain unchanged. Whereas the price effect was always negative, the income effect may be either positive or negative. A positive income effect means that the consumer's income level and consumption of Product X move in the same direction. We call products that exhibit a positive income effect "normal" or "superior" goods. Products for which the income effect is negative—that is, for which consumption of the product falls as the income rises, or rises as the income falls—are known as "inferior" goods. For most people, perhaps, products such as housing, automobiles, and travel by air exhibit a positive income effect and hence are known as normal or superior goods. On the other hand, for many people products such as bologna, ground beef, and travel by train exhibit a negative income effect. For these people, therefore, these products are regarded as inferior goods.

84

In Figure 3.6 we show the income effect for a pair of normal goods. A particular consumer's pattern of tastes and preferences is represented by the indifference curves shown in the figure. The income constraint line is moved

**FIGURE 3.6**
**Income consumption curve for normal goods**

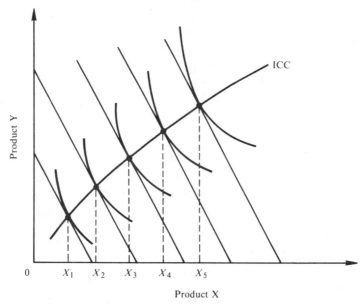

outward and to the right by successive increments, to indicate a progressively increased income for that particular consumer. For each increase in the income constraint, the consumer is able to find an equilibrium (tangency) point on a higher indifference curve and thus enjoy an increased level of utility. The locus of these points of tangency is known as the "income consumption curve" and demonstrates how the consumer will change his or her consumption of the two products in response to successive increases in income. Both Products X and Y are normal goods, since for successive increases in income the demand for each product is successively increased.

In Figure 3.7 we show the income consumption curve where Product X is an inferior good. Note that beyond a certain point, shown as point *A*, the income consumption curve takes a negative slope, indicating that for successive increments of income the consumer chooses to demand successively smaller quantities of Product X.

In this simple two-commodity situation, of course, the consumer is switching away from Product X in favor of Product Y as his or her income increases. Suppose that Product X is ground beef, and Product Y is steak. The income consumption curve indicates that at low-income levels both steak and ground beef exhibit positive income effects, but beyond point *A* ground beef becomes regarded as an inferior good, and the consumer apparently substitutes in favor of

## FIGURE 3.7
Income consumption curve where *X* is an inferior good

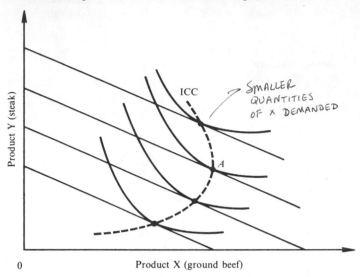

Product Y (steak)

ICC

SMALLER QUANTITIES OF X DEMANDED

A

0                    Product X (ground beef)

steak and away from ground beef as his or her income level rises. It is completely feasible that at still higher levels of income this particular consumer might come to regard ground beef as a normal good again. Suppose this consumer is the proud owner of a purebred Harlequin Great Dane. Being reluctant to feed such an impressive beast ordinary dog food, this consumer may begin to purchase progressively more ground beef (for the dog) as his or her income continues to rise. Hence ground beef exhibits a positive income effect once more.

For any particular product at any particular point of time, it is apparent that some consumers may regard that product as a superior good while others may regard it as an inferior good. This difference in attitude toward a particular product stems from either a difference in income levels or a different pattern of tastes and preferences. Just as the price effect varies between and among consumers, the income effect should also be expected to vary between and among consumers, being high and positive for some, perhaps, while being low or negative for others.

### The Substitution Effect

The *substitution effect* is defined as the change in the quantity demanded of Product X given a change in the price of Product X, with all other factors held constant. These other factors, of course, include the consumer's taste and preference pattern and his or her income level. At this point we must make the distinction between a consumer's "nominal" income and his or her "real" income. Nominal income is, of course, the absolute number of dollars that the consumer has for spending. Given a set of product prices, the consumer can buy certain amounts of various products. Suppose the price of one product is now reduced:

86

the consumer is thus able to buy the same combination of goods and services that he or she was previously buying, for a lesser amount of nominal income. The consumer thus has some amount of money *left over,* which he or she may use in the purchase of more of the commodity whose price has fallen, or for any other product. This increase in purchasing power that follows the reduction of any product price represents an increase in the consumer's *real* income. Real income, or the purchasing power of nominal income, may be expressed as the ratio of nominal income to a price index that represents the prices of all commodities. Hence if the price index is reduced, due to the lowering of any particular price, the consumer's real income is increased. Conversely, if the price of any product is raised, the consumer's real income is reduced.

Since the substitution effect requires *ceteris paribus,* we need to adjust the consumer's nominal income to compensate for the change in real income that follows a price change. In Figure 3.8 we illustrate the isolation of the substitution effect. Suppose the consumer's initial point of equilibrium is point $A$ on the indifference curve $I_1$ and budget line $MN$. At this point the consumer chooses to purchase $X_1$ units of Product X. Suppose now that the price of Product X is reduced such that the income constraint line swings around to the new line $MN'$, allowing the consumer to attain point $B$ on indifference curve $I_2$. The consumer now chooses to purchase $X_2$ units of Product X, and the total effect of the price change is to have increased his or her consumption of Product X by the distance $X_2 - X_1$. It can be seen that this total effect of the price change is what we have called the price effect, since a line joining points $A$ and $B$ would be part of the consumer's price consumption curve. We are now aware, however,

**FIGURE 3.8**
**Income and substitution effects of a price change for a normal good**

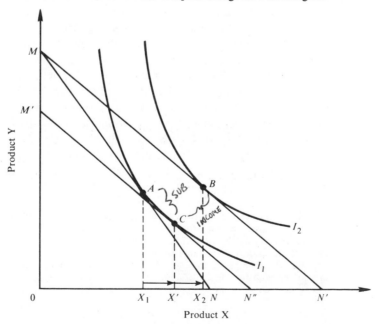

that some part of this price effect is due to an increase in the consumer's real income, which we have called the income effect.

To eliminate the increase in the consumer's real income, we must reduce the consumer to his or her previous level of real income. A means of comparing levels of real income is to compare the utility that may be derived from particular levels of nominal income. Hence if we were to reduce this consumer to the initial level of utility, by a reduction in his or her nominal income, we would in effect have reduced the consumer to the initial level of real income. What we wish to do is to move the consumer from the higher level of utility at point $B$ down to a level of utility that is equivalent to point $A$ and therefore lies on the indifference curve $I_1$. By hypothetically reducing the consumer's nominal income, we begin to move the $MN'$ budget constraint line downward and to the left such that it remains parallel to $MN'$. When this hypothetical budget line is tangent to indifference curve $I_1$, we shall have reduced the consumer to a level of utility, or a level of real income, that is equivalent to that which was previously derived at point $A$. This occurs with budget line $M'N''$, at the tangency point $C$. At the hypothetical point $C$ the consumer would choose to purchase $X'$ units of Product X. The movement from point $B$ to point $C$, or from $X_2$ units to $X'$ units, is what we have called the income effect, since a line joining the points $C$ and $B$ would in fact be part of this consumer's income consumption curve. The remaining part of the total effect of the price change is clearly the substitution effect. The change in consumption of Product X from $X_1$ to $X'$ is simply the result of the differing price ratio exhibited by the different slope of budget line $M'N''$ as compared with the initial budget line $MN$, since all other factors, including the consumer's real income, remain unchanged.

*Inferior Goods.* In Figure 3.9 we show the income and substitution effects of a price change for an inferior good.[8] Again the initial point is a tangency between budget line $MN$ and indifference curve $I_1$ at point $A$. The price of Product X is reduced such that the budget line swings around to $MN'$, allowing the consumer a new higher level of utility at point $B$ on indifference curve $I_2$. The total effect of the price change, or the price effect, is the movement from $A$ to $B$, which in terms of Product X is a change in consumption from $X_1$ to $X_2$. To isolate the income effect, we hypothetically reduce the consumer's income until a budget line with the same slope (that is, with the same price ratio) as budget line $MN'$ is just tangent to the original indifference curve. This occurs at point $C$. The income effect is thus the movement from $C$ to $B$, or in terms of Product X from $X'$ to $X_2$. It is apparent that the income effect is negative, since the increase in real income due to the price reduction was accompanied by a decrease in the quantity demanded of Product X. A line drawn between the points $C$ and

---

[8] The indifference curve map must reflect the inferiority of Product X in order for our graphs to "work out" correctly. When Product X is regarded as being inferior, the indifference curves will not be parallel but will be closer together at the top end than they are at the bottom end, as shown in Figure 3.9. While indifference curves are everywhere dense (meaning that one passes through every point on the graph), they are also infinitely narrow, so that the multitude of indifference curves that exist between the lower parts of curves $I_1$ and $I_2$ have no problem squeezing through the more narrow space at the top end of those curves.

**FIGURE 3.9**
**Income and substitution effects of a price change for an inferior good**

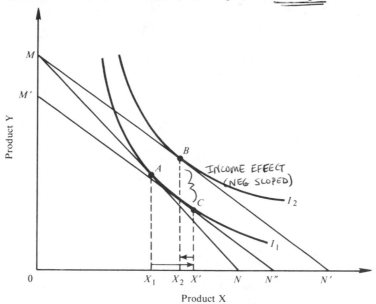

Product Y

Product X

*B*, which is part of the consumer's income consumption curve, would have a negative slope, confirming that Product X is regarded by this consumer as an inferior good. The substitution effect is once again the movement along the initial indifference curve from point *A* to point *C*. This fulfills our definition of the substitution effect, since it is the change in quantity demanded of Product X when the price of Product X changes, with all other factors—including the consumer's real income—held constant. The substitution effect of a price reduction for Product X is thus an increase in the quantity demanded of Product X from level $X_1$ to $X'$. This is partly offset by a negative income effect from $X'$ to $X_2$, such that the total effect (or the price effect) is from $X_1$ to $X_2$.

Notice that in both the normal goods case and the inferior goods case the substitution effect was negative. Given the general validity of the assumptions that underlie the construction of a consumer's indifference curve, the substitution effect is *always* negative; that is, for price reductions corrected for the income effect the consumer will always purchase more of the product, while for price increases corrected for the income effect the consumer will always purchase less of the product. The income effect, however, may be either positive or negative, and, if negative, it offsets part of the substitution effect.

*Giffen Goods.* It is theoretically possible that a negative income effect could be of such magnitude as to more than offset the substitution effect, in which case a price reduction would be followed by a decline in the quantity demanded, or a price increase would be followed by an increase in the quantity demanded. A product that behaved in this way would exhibit a positive price effect and would therefore run counter to the empirical law of demand. Such a product is known as a *Giffen good*, after Sir Robert Giffen, who reported the existence of such perverse price effects in the case of potatoes during the Irish Famine of 1846-49.[9]

A modern-day example of a Giffen good is difficult to find, keeping in mind that we require consumer tastes and preferences to remain unchanged when the price of the product in question is changed. It may be argued that for some products the quantity demanded has been seen to increase when prices were increased, but this is unlikely to indicate that the product is a Giffen good. Suppose a merchant offers hand towels for sale at $0.59 each, and demand for these towels is somewhat less than enthusiastic. If the merchant now raises the price to $0.99 and customers eagerly purchase the towels, does this mean that those hand towels are a Giffen good? The answer is probably no. Consumers tend to make price-quality associations when they are unable to judge quality on any other basis. At the lower price the hand towels were perceived as "low-quality" hand towels, whereas at the higher price they were perceived as "better-quality" hand towels. The consumers' taste and preference patterns between low-quality and high-quality hand towels are probably the same as they were when they were first confronted by the hand towels. The error in calling hand towels a Giffen good rests upon failing to distinguish that consumers regard the higher-priced hand towels as being a different product from the lower-priced hand towels. Our analysis of the income and substitution effects of a price change for a particular good depends upon successive units of that product being identical with the preceding and following units.

Another situation that may seem to indicate a Giffen good is that where a product sells for a while at one price, and later sells more units at a higher price. If and only if *ceteris paribus* prevailed over the entire period of the observations, then the product is a Giffen good. More likely, however, one or more of the underlying factors has changed during the period (such as consumer tastes, incomes, and the prices and availability of other products). If so, the two observations are not on the same demand curve but are on separate demand curves, due to a shift of the demand curve due in turn to a change in an underlying determinant. The two observations are most likely part of two separate negatively sloping demand curves, rather than of one single positively sloping demand curve. "Shifts" versus "movements along" demand curves are discussed in detail in Chapter 4, and the "identification problem," which causes confusion between shifts and movements along demand curves in practice, is discussed in Chapter 5.[10]

---

[9] The Irish peasant was typically so poor that potatoes formed the major part of the family diet, supplemented by meat and other foodstuffs. When the price of potatoes was increased due to a blight affecting the crops the demand for potatoes actually *increased*, since the money left over for meat and other foodstuffs (after buying the same quantity of potatoes) was insufficient to buy enough of these less-bulky items to satisfy the family appetite. Thus more of the more-filling potato was demanded despite its increased price.

[10] Remember that demand curves require *ceteris paribus* to hold for monetary income, consumer tastes and preferences, prices and availability of other products, and any other factor influencing consumer demand except the price of that product. Many marketing textbooks (and some managerial economics textbooks) are replete with examples of confusion over this point. Backwardbending "demand curves" and zigzag "demand curves" are much more likely to be cases of violated *ceteris paribus* (and hence an identification problem) than they are to be examples of a Giffen Good.

### Changes in Consumer Tastes
### and Preferences

In the above analysis consumer tastes and preferences were assumed to remain constant while changes took place in price and income levels. We must recognize, however, that consumer tastes and preferences may change from time to time, either in line with prevailing attitudinal changes in society, in pursuit of the latest fashions or trends, or as the result of actions taken by business firms that supply particular products. We refer of course to the advertising and promotion expenditures of business firms. However induced, changes in consumer tastes and preferences have profound implications for the quantity demanded of particular products. In the following we shall analyze the implications of changes in consumer tastes and preferences on the demand for a product.

Suppose the sellers of Product X institute an advertising campaign to promote the demand for Product X. In the absence of simultaneous new campaigns from the sellers of other products, we would expect this campaign to influence at least some buyers in the direction of Product X. Referring to Figure 3.10, suppose the initial situation is represented by the tangency at point $A$ on indifference curve $I_1$. An advertising campaign that causes Product X to be regarded more favorably than previously would cause that particular level of utility represented by indifference curve $I_1$ to be attained by the consumption of fewer units of Product X, since X is now regarded more highly. Suppose that, whereas the consumer previously required $X_1$ units of Product X to attain the utility level depicted by indifference curve $I_1$, it now takes only $X_1'$ units of Product X to attain the *same level* of utility, in conjunction with $Y_1$ units of Product Y. In effect, then, indifference curve $I_1$ has swung downward and to the

**FIGURE 3.10**

A change in tastes and preferences in favor of product X

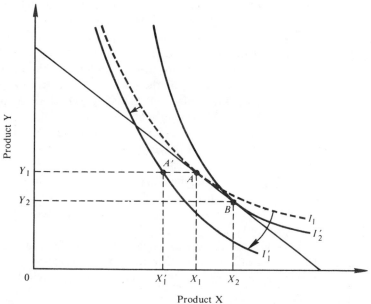

left, since the same level of utility can be obtained with lesser combinations of X and Y due to the new appreciation the consumer has for Product X. Under the new taste and preference conditions, indifference curve $I_1$ is irrelevant, since it refers to a previous pattern of tastes and preferences.

Thus the consumer *could* derive the same level of utility by shifting back from point $A$ to point $A'$. Instead the consumer will wish to reallocate his or her budget such that utility is maximized under the new circumstances. Indifference curve $I_2'$ is the highest attainable indifference curve given the budget constraint facing the consumer, and hence the consumer reallocates his or her income between Products X and Y such that he or she is located at point $B$. Notice that the change of tastes and preferences in favor of Product X has led to the consumption of Product X being increased from $X_1$ to $X_2$, and the consumption of Product Y (the only other alternative product available) being reduced from $Y_1$ to $Y_2$. In this simple two-commodity model the gain of Product X necessarily came at the expense of Product Y, whereas in a multi-commodity system the shift of tastes and preferences in favor of Product X would be at the expense of some, but not necessarily all, of the other products.

It is unlikely that all consumers will be influenced by a particular advertising campaign or by a trend or fashion that is sweeping society, and therefore these consumers will not change their consumption of Product X because neither their taste and preference pattern nor their perception of the product has changed. Moreover, some consumers will be affected more than other consumers, and hence their demand for Product X will be increased to a larger degree.

### Real Price Changes vs.
### Nominal Price Changes

Throughout the above discussion we have been speaking of price changes by a particular nominal amount, with the implied assumption that the real value of the monetary unit remains constant. In the real world, however, we have become accustomed to "inflation," or the depreciation of the monetary unit over time. We should not expect governments to completely eliminate inflation, since an inflation rate of a few percentage points annually is said to be beneficial for business confidence, business investment, and employment, and also, one might argue, for the reelection of the government. Thus we must deal with nominal price changes in a currency unit that is typically slowly depreciating.

To the extent that the price of a particular product increases over a period of time at a rate equal to the rate of inflation, the price increases may be regarded as being adjustments to the depreciating value of the currency unit, and therefore being relatively constant in real, or purchasing power, terms. When the nominal price increases by *more* than the rate of inflation, this amounts to an increase in the real price level. When nominal price increases by less than the rate of inflation, does not change, or is actually reduced, this amounts to a decrease in the real price level.

For most business firms, prices cannot be changed continuously in line with the rate of inflation and therefore must take upward "steps" over time while the general price level continues more smoothly upward. Thus real prices tend to fall progressively, then rise abruptly as nominal prices are adjusted, then fall progressively, and so on. Increasing productivity in the use of resources, expanding markets allowing economics of larger-scale operation, and other factors frequently mean that a firm can allow its prices to increase at a rate slower than that of inflation without suffering a squeeze on profits. On the contrary, the consequent reduction in real prices may allow the firm to make significant gains in sales and market share.

It is important to remember that the entire analysis of consumer behavior presupposes a constant value of the monetary unit. In real-world situations where nominal price changes are observed, we must be careful to evaluate the price change in real terms before concluding that the law of demand is inoperative or that one of the other predictions of consumer behavior theory is inaccurate.

## 3.4 THE ATTRIBUTE APPROACH TO CONSUMER CHOICE

### Attributes in Products

Consumers' preferences between and among products are formed on the basis of their perception of the existence of various desirable features or attributes associated with or embodied in those products. As implied in the "Introduction" to this chapter, an automobile is not viewed simply as an agglomeration of steel, plastic, and rubber, but rather as the means by which the consumer can obtain transportation, comfort, prestige, privacy, performance, economy, and other attributes he or she desires. A meal in a fancy restaurant is not purchased simply to fill one's stomach, but rather to enjoy the attributes of pleasant surroundings, courteous service, exotic food, good company, and no mess to clean up. Skydiving is undertaken not by those wishing to fall out of an airplane but by those in search of danger, exhilaration, solitude, exclusiveness, an outlet for their courage, or something to start conversations with.

If it is the attributes themselves that are desired (rather than the products themselves), it is instructive to examine the consumer's demand for the attributes directly, rather than indirectly as in the product approach. This is particularly useful when a specific attribute (e.g., excitement) is available in a wide variety of products (e.g., automobiles, skydiving, roller coasters, skateboarding on freeways). In such a case the consumer will derive his or her "excitement quota" from some but not necessarily all of the available sources of supply, and the attribute approach allows us to explain this behavior.

Unlike the product approach, which takes the consumer's preferences between and among products as an imponderable fact, the attribute approach looks behind these preferences to explain them in terms of the attributes of those products. The product approach is unable to explain in simple terms why a particular consumer would, for example, never buy a certain type of automobile and never visit some of the nearby restaurants. The attribute approach greatly facilitates the explanation of consumer choice within such groups of substitutes, an area of paramount importance in managerial economics. Moreover, it readily allows us to incorporate new products into the analysis, to identify market segments and to find "gaps" between existing product offerings.

### Depicting Products in Attribute Space

Consumers are unable to purchase the desired attributes directly in most cases. Rather they must purchase the attributes indirectly by purchasing products that embody the desired attributes. Typically, however, different products deliver different amounts and combinations of the desired attributes. To demonstrate how a consumer might choose among products in order to maximize utility derived from the attributes, let us use the example of an aspiring gourmet who dines out frequently and has a choice of six nearby restaurants. The gourmet thus wishes to choose among six products (the meal and its associated attributes at each of six restaurants) such that his utility is maximized.

To treat the problem graphically, we suppose that the gourmet seeks only two attributes—"exotic atmosphere" and "haute cuisine." The six restaurants will provide these attributes in differing proportions and at different prices. Let us suppose that after visiting all six restaurants, our gourmet rates each restaurant on a scale of 100 for both exotic atmosphere and haute cuisine, as shown in Table 3.1

**TABLE 3.1**
**Gourmet's rating of attribute content in six restaurants**

| Restaurant | *Attribute Rating (out of 100)* | | *Ratio of "Atmosphere" to "Cuisine"* |
|---|---|---|---|
| | *Exotic Atmosphere* | *Haute Cuisine* | |
| A | 67 | 30 | 2.23 |
| B | 94 | 50 | 1.88 |
| C | 76 | 86 | 0.88 |
| D | 57 | 90 | 0.63 |
| E | 18 | 72 | 0.25 |
| F | 10 | 77 | 0.13 |

In Figure 3.11 we show the six products depicted in attribute space as rays from the origin. The slope of each ray is determined by the ratio of exotic atmosphere to haute cuisine offered by the six products, as shown in Table 3.1. If the consumer were to visit Restaurant A he would travel out along the steepest ray, absorbing the two attributes in exactly the ratio indicated. The other restaurants (products) are indicated by the lower rays which offer "atmosphere" to "cuisine" in a lower ratio. Notice that a product for which one of the attributes was completely absent, such as home cooking, would be represented by one of the axes. (*You* decide which axis!)

### The Efficiency Frontier

How far along each ray would the gourmet go? That is, how much of Product A, or any other product, is it possible to purchase? The answer of course is up to

**FIGURE 3.11**
**Depicting products in the attribute approach**

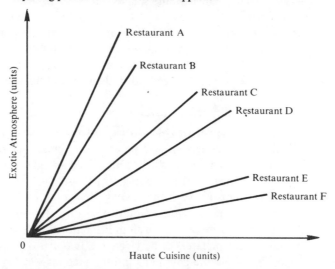

the limit of the gourmet's budget constraint. Suppose our gourmet has examined his finances and has decided to allocate $100 monthly to eating in one or more of the six restaurants. The prices at the six restaurants are similar but not identical. In Figure 3.12 we mark each ray at the point where $100 worth of exotic atmosphere and haute cuisine can be purchased indirectly through visiting and eating at each of the six restaurants, presumably a number of times during

**FIGURE 3.12**
**The efficiency frontier in the attribute approach**

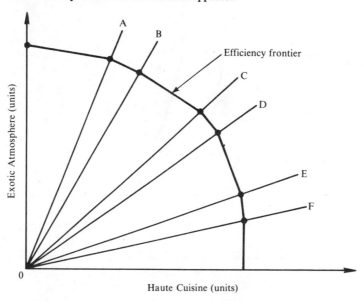

the month. Joining these points on each ray we have what is known as the "efficiency frontier" in attribute space.

The efficiency frontier is the outer boundary of the attainable combinations of the two attributes, given the budget constraint. We shall see presently that any point on the frontier is attainable by consuming combinations of two adjacent products, and that the rational consumer will prefer to choose a combination of attributes on the frontier rather than any combination inside the frontier.

### Maximizing Utility from Attributes

Just as the consumer was able to express preference or indifference between combinations of products, he will be able to express preference or indifference between pairs of combinations of attributes. At any given combination of exotic atmosphere and haute cuisine, our gourmet will be able to express a marginal rate of substitution between the two attributes: an extra unit of haute cuisine will be worth giving up some amount of exotic atmosphere in the consumer's mind. Thus the gourmet will have an indifference map in attribute space expressing his tastes and preferences between the two attributes at all levels of those attributes. We show the gourmet's indifference map in Figure 3.13. As before, higher curves are preferred to lower curves, the curves have negative slopes throughout, they neither meet nor intersect, and they are convex to the origin.

Since both the indifference map and the efficiency frontier are in attribute space, we can superimpose one upon the other to find the combination of attributes that allows the consumer to reach the highest attainable indifference curve. In Figure 3.14 we show indifference curve $I^*$ as tangent to the efficiency

**FIGURE 3.13**
**Indifference curves between attributes**

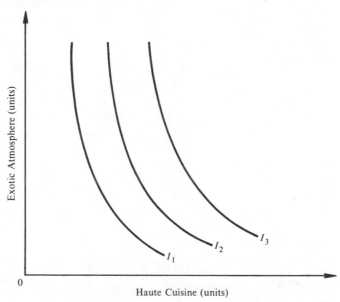

**FIGURE 3.14**
**Maximization of utility from attributes**

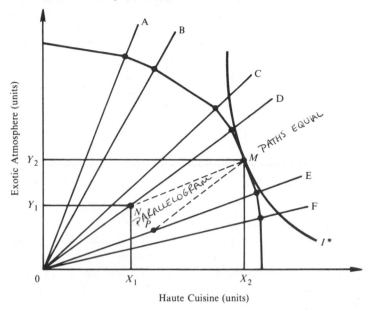

Haute Cuisine (units)

frontier at point $M$. Given the properties of indifference curves, the combination of attributes $Y_2$ of exotic atmosphere and $X_2$ of haute cuisine allows the gourmet to maximize his utility.

Notice that combination $M$ lies *between* the rays representing Restaurant D and Restaurant E. There is no restaurant available that provides the attributes in exactly the ratio represented by point $M$. The gourmet can attain combination $M$, however, by mixing Product D and Product E. That is, by visiting Restaurant D and Restaurant E a number of times each, the consumer can absorb—by aggregating the attributes absorbed at each restaurant over his total number of visits during the month—exactly the combination of attributes represented by point $M$. If the gourmet visits Restaurant D until he reaches point $N$ on that ray, he will accumulate $Y_1$ units of exotic atmosphere and $X_1$ units of haute cuisine. At point $N$ he should then switch to Restaurant E in order to accumulate the attributes in the ratio necessary to achieve point $M$. The line $NM$ in Figure 3.14 has the same slope as the ray representing Restaurant E. By spending the remainder of the \$100 in Restaurant E, the gourmet derives an extra $Y_2 - Y_1$ units of exotic atmosphere and $X_2 - X_1$ units of haute cuisine, bringing his total to $Y_2$ units of the former and $X_2$ units of the latter, and thus maximizing his utility. Alternatively, the gourmet could attain point $M$ by visiting Restaurant E until he had in effect reached point $P$ on the ray representing Restaurant E, and he could then switch to Restaurant D to accumulate the remaining units of the two attributes in the ratio necessary to reach point $M$. The two paths to maximum utility are thus $ONM$ or $OPM$ in Figure 3.14. Since $ONMP$ is a parallelogram, however, the path $OPM$ is equivalent to $ONM$, since $ON = PM$ and $OP = NM$.

The gourmet may visit either restaurant first, or in whatever sequence suits his whims, as long as the attributes accumulate to the combination $M$ without exceeding the $100 budget constraint. It can be shown that the combination of *nonadjacent* products (e.g., F and D) to reach a point on the frontier will cost more than $100 and is therefore inefficient.[11]

If the consumer desires some combination of more than two attributes, let us say $n$ attributes, no more than $n$ products and possibly as few as one product will be required to maximize the consumer's utility within his budget constraint. In the two-dimensional case, if the highest-attainable indifference curve were to touch the frontier at one of its kinks (that is, right on a particular product ray), only one product would be necessary to provide the attributes in the desired combination. In this case there is a single product available that exactly reflects the consumer's tastes and preferences, and which is priced below an acceptable limit.[12]

In the $n$ attribute case as many as $n$ products or as few as one product may be required to maximize the consumer's utility. Let us attempt to visualize the three-attribute case. Suppose our gourmet desired a third attribute, namely, "polite and prompt service," and rated the service at each of the six restaurants. His efficiency frontier will now be three dimensional with flat facets or planes on its surface, with ridges where two facets meet, and triangular points where three facets meet. Since the consumer will now have a marginal rate of substitution between "service" and each of the other two attributes, his indifference "curves" will look like three-dimensional "bowls" or "saucers." The highest-attainable indifference saucer might balance upon one of the flat facets and thus indicate the utility-maximizing combination of *three* of the available products. Alternatively, the highest-attainable indifference saucer might balance on a ridge, requiring only *two* products to provide the desired combination of the three attributes. Finally, if the highest-attainable indifference saucer rests upon one of the triangular points of the efficiency frontier, this means that only *one* product is necessary to provide the optimal combination of the three attributes, since that product provides them in exactly the ratios desired by the consumer.

If the consumer is unable to combine two or more products in order to reach the desired combination of attributes, due to restrictions on the divisibility of products and/or a limited budget, the consumer may have to settle for a suboptimal situation. If the consumer must choose one product or the other (e.g., the purchase of an automobile), he or she is constrained to one of the corners on the efficiency frontier. The consumer will choose the corner that allows the highest indifference curve, although this curve may *cross* the efficiency frontier. The consumer will be unable to combine products to reach any higher indifference curve and thus must be content with the corner situation which is suboptimal compared with the point that could be reached if combinations were possible.

---

[11] See Lancaster, "A New Approach to Consumer Theory," pp. 132-57.

[12] The "acceptable" upper limit on price will be explained in the next subsection.

### The Price Effect

Suppose the price of one of the products embodying the desired attributes is changed. What effect will this have on the demand for this product? What effect will it have on the demand for the other (substitute) products which the consumer also considers purchasing in order to obtain the desired attributes? Let us consider a new example, that of an audiophile who has a cassette tape deck and frequently purchases new tapes. She desires two major attributes in these tapes, namely, "clarity of sound reproduction" and "reliability of tape operation." There are five brands available, and we show the efficiency frontier and two of the audiophile's indifference curves in Figure 3.15.

**FIGURE 3.15**
**The price effect shown by the attribute approach: audiophile #1**

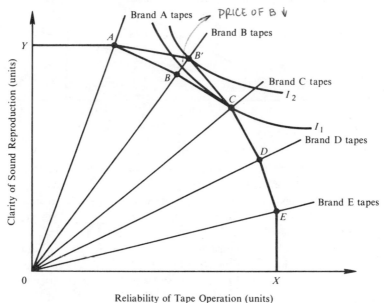

Initially, the prices of the five brands are such that the efficiency frontier is *YABCDEX*, and the consumer is able to maximize utility at point *C*, where indifference curve $I_1$ just touches the frontier. Now suppose that the price of Brand B is reduced, such that the efficiency frontier moves out along the Brand B ray to point *B'* and is now represented by *YAB'CDEX*. The audiophile can now attain a higher indifference curve ($I_2$) by switching to Brand B tapes. Product B offers the attributes in a different ratio to the previously preferred Product C, but the consumer exhibits a marginal rate of substitution between the attributes and is willing to trade off some "reliability" for more "clarity" at the lower price in order to increase her total utility derived.

In Figure 3.16 we show a different case in which a consumer is initially mix-

**FIGURE 3.16**
**The price effect shown by the attribute approach: audiophile #2**

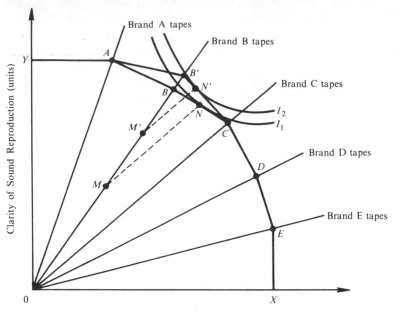

ing two products in order to obtain the desired combination of attributes. Our second consumer has a different taste and preference pattern between the two attributes, as compared with the consumer depicted in Figure 3.15. The second audiophile's indifference map is such that his highest-attainable indifference curve, given the initial efficiency frontier *YABCDEX*, is tangent to the frontier at point *N*. This consumer prefers to purchase both Brand B and Brand C tapes, presumably using the Brand B tapes for applications where "clarity" is relatively more important. Let us suppose his path to the frontier is 0*MN*.

Again we reduce the price of Brand B tapes, and the new efficiency frontier becomes *YAB'CDEX*. Our second audiophile is able to increase utility by moving to point *N'* on indifference curve $I_2$. He still purchases both Brand B and Brand C tapes, but he now will purchase more Brand B tapes and fewer Brand C tapes. Whereas his previous path to the frontier was 0*MN*, it is now 0*M'N'*. The segment 0*M'* exceeds 0*M*, indicating the consumer's greater absorption of the attributes from Product B and hence greater purchases of Product B. The segment *M'N'* is shorter then *MN*, indicating the consumer's reduced purchases of Product C. If the consumer had previously taken the alternate route to the frontier (traveling first along the ray for Product C), you may confirm for your own satisfaction that the price reduction for Product B would cause him to buy more Brand B tapes and fewer Brand C tapes.

Given a consumer's perception of the attributes embodied in a particular product, there is a maximum price that the consumer will pay for that product even if it exactly mirrors his taste and preference pattern. In Figure 3.17 we

**100**

**FIGURE 3.17**
**Pricing a product "out of the market"**

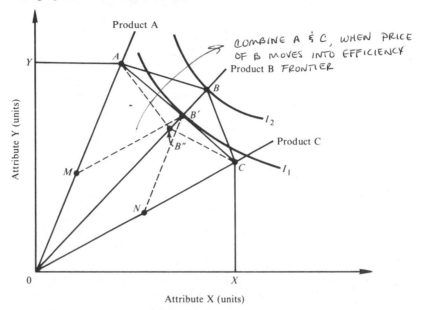

Attribute X (units)

show a simple case where three products offer the two desired attributes X and Y. The initial price situation generates the efficiency frontier *YABCX*, and the consumer maximizes utility on indifference curve $I_2$ by purchasing only Product B. Suppose the price of Product B is now increased such that the efficiency frontier becomes *YAB'CX*. The consumer is now unable to reach indifference curve $I_2$ and must be content with the lower curve $I_1$ at point $B'$, still purchasing only Product B, but necessarily purchasing fewer units of Product B due to its higher price and his unchanged budget.

If the price of Product B is raised still further, such that the consumer's entire budget spent on Product B would purchase only the combination of attributes shown by point $B''$ for example, this consumer will no longer buy any units of Product B. The efficiency frontier remains at *YAB'CX* and Product B has fallen inside the frontier. Purchase of Product B would now be an inefficient use of the consumer's budget, since the other products provide the desired attributes more inexpensively. The consumer is still able to attain point $B'$ on the efficiency frontier and on indifference curve $I_1$, but he will travel via the path O*MB'* or O*NB'* rather than along the ray representing Product B. That is, the consumer will now prefer to combine Products A and C in order to maximize utility from his given budget rather than purchase any of Product B. Thus Product B has been priced out of reach for this consumer, even though it provides the attributes in exactly the preferred ratio. (I feel the same way about Ferraris.)

Other consumers may continue to purchase Product B if they perceive more units of the attributes in each unit of Product B as compared with the perception of the consumer discussed above. Alternatively, some consumers may purchase Product B for a different attribute that is provided by the product but was

101

unimportant to the above consumer. In both cases Product B may remain on the efficiency frontier and be purchased by those consumers who need it to maximize their utility despite its increased price.

Thus we see that the price effect, or the law of demand, still applies to products even though they are purchased as a means of acquiring desired attributes. As price falls, consumers already purchasing the product in question will purchase more units, and other consumers will begin to buy their first units of that product. Alternatively, as price is increased, consumers will buy fewer units or will drop out of the market for that product completely. Substitute products will tend to sell more units when the price of a product on an adjacent ray increases, and sell fewer units when the price of that product is reduced.

### Changes in Consumer Perception and Tastes

Advertising and promotional activity by sellers of particular products, and information from other sources (e.g., word of mouth, published reports by consumer testing agencies), may change the consumer's perception of the quantity of particular attributes embodied in each unit of a particular product. Referring to Figure 3.18, let us suppose that the efficiency frontier is initially *YABCX*. The consumer attains the highest possible indifference curve at point *C* and therefore purchases Product C.

Suppose now that Product B benefits from an advertising campaign such that our consumer now perceives a larger quantity of both attributes Y and X in

**FIGURE 3.18**
**Attribute analysis of a change in consumer perception of a product**

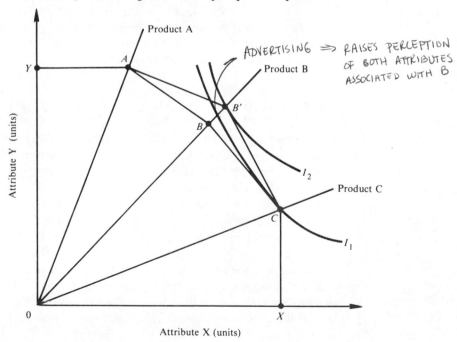

Product B for the same price level. If the consumer perceives the attributes to have increased in the same ratio, the efficiency frontier will move out along the Product B ray from point $B$ to point $B'$. This will allow the consumer to attain a higher indifference curve $(I_2)$ by choosing Product B. Hence this particular consumer is motivated to purchase Product B as a direct result of the advertising campaign. Similarly, other consumers who were previously purchasing either no units of Product B or some units of Product B in combination with adjacent products will now be motivated to purchase more units of Product B, since this will allow each of these consumers to attain higher indifference curves. For some consumers, of course, the changed perception of Product B will not be sufficiently great to cause those consumers to buy any of, or any more of, Product B.

If the advertising were to change the consumer's taste and preference pattern *between* the attributes Y and X, the indifference curves would also shift, causing a new tangency point on the efficiency frontier (unless the highest "new" indifference curve touches the same point on the frontier as did the highest "old" indifference curve). If advertising were to "awaken" the consumer's desire for a particular attribute (e.g., style, status, uniformity), this would add a new dimension to the consumer's choice problem but would not change the nature of the solution. The consumers would seek the highest-attainable indifference hypersurface in the $n$ dimensions of attribute space, given the $n$ dimensional efficiency frontier, where the $n$ attributes now include the newly recognized attribute.

### New Products

The advent of <u>new products</u> presents no difficulty for the attribute approach; a new product <u>can be represented on an existing graph</u> as a new ray. If the ratio of attributes offered by the new product is the same as for an existing product, then it will occupy the same ray as that existing product. If, however, the new product offers more of this combination of attributes per dollar, as compared with the existing product, the new product will push the efficiency frontier outward and will eclipse the existing product in the eyes of rational consumers. Since the new product offers more utility per dollar than the old, no rational consumer would buy the older product. In the case of market entry by a new product that is not identical in its offering of product attributes compared with existing products, there will be a new ray in the figure. If the highest affordable point on that ray (where total income is spent entirely on the new product) occurs outside the existing frontier, then the new product will serve to push the frontier outward at a point where it was previously flat. In both the above cases, where the new product extends the frontier, some consumers will change their consumption in favor of the new product, since the new frontier will now poke through their previously attained indifference curves and allow them to reach a new higher curve. This is illustrated in Figure 3.19, which depicts an initial situation of only three products—A, B, and C. The initial efficiency frontier perceived by the consumer is thus $YABCX$, and he attains indifference curve $I_1$ by purchasing Product B.

We now suppose a new product is launched which competes with Products A, B, and C in the sense that it also offers attributes X and Y. The new product

**FIGURE 3.19**
**Addition of a new product to an existing group of products**

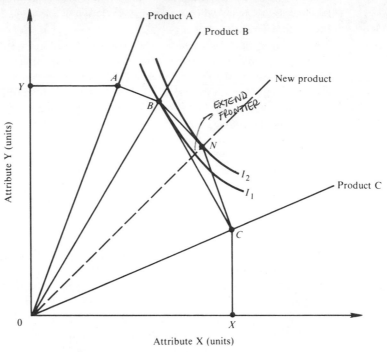

offers these attributes in a different ratio, however, between those of Products B and C. The new product is priced such that the efficiency frontier is extended to *YABNCX*. The consumer is now able to reach indifference curve $I_2$ by switching to the new product. Notice that the new product will steal sales from both B and C but will not affect A unless there are more than two attributes desired by consumers. In the real world, of course, consumers do demand more than two attributes simultaneously, and we should expect the advent of a new product (or new model of an existing product) to affect the sales of a range of other products.

### Market Segments

Attribute analysis allows us a means of determining market "segments" for the products that offer the desired attributes. *Market segments* are groups of consumers who have similar taste and preference patterns and who therefore tend to buy similar products. Groups of consumers with similar marginal rates of substitution, at a particular combination of attributes, will tend to find their highest-attainable indifference curve tangent to the efficiency frontier at similar points. Consumers with relatively *low* MRS between the attributes will tend to buy products with relatively *high* attribute ratio rays, and vice versa. In the case of the cassette tapes discussed earlier, we may be able to identify the "music clarity" segment as consisting of those who will have low marginal rates of substitution between clarity and reliability and who therefore tend to purchase Brands A and B. On the other hand, consumers with relatively high marginal rates of substitution will tend to buy Brands D and E and may be identified as the "reliability" segment.

Knowledge of market segments and competitors' offerings allows firms to design their products in order to incorporate the attributes into the ratio desired by a particular group of consumers. Pricing, promotion, and distribution strategies are then coordinated such that the desired attributes are incorporated and recognized, and the product is competitively priced in that segment. We return to this issue in Chapters 11 and 12.

### Problems of Identifying and Measuring Attributes

Some attributes are readily identifiable and measurable, such as the "power" and "economy" associated with an automobile. Objective measurement of "power" might proceed on the basis of engine horsepower, horsepower divided by vehicle weight, or some similar cardinal measure. Economy likewise can be measured by a standard unit of measure, such as miles per gallon or liters per hundred kilometers. Problems arise, however, with attributes that are measurable only subjectively, such as "modern styling," "prestige," "status," "comfort," and "security." The consumer will typically have an intuitive evaluation of these attributes and will be able to make what appears to that consumer to be an optimal decision in the light of the information held.

The identification and measurability problems really arise when we attempt to explain or predict consumer behavior in real-world situations. As you will appreciate, the implications of attribute analysis for the pricing, promotion, product, and distribution strategies of the business firm are profound. If the firm is able to identify *which* attributes consumers base their choices upon, and on *what basis* they evaluate the attributes, it is in a better position to increase sales and profits by adjusting one or more of its marketing strategies. We return to this issue in the context of pricing policy in Chapter 11.

## 3.5   AGGREGATION OF INDIVIDUAL DEMAND CURVES

### Independent Consumer Preferences

To find the market demand for a particular product, we need to aggregate the demands of all the individual consumers who express demand for the product at each price level. In the simple case in which consumer demands are independent of each other, we simply add (horizontally) the demand curves of all consumers. For each price level there is thus a total market demand which is the simple sum of all individual demands at that price level. Since the individual demand curves are negatively sloping, the aggregate of these will also be negatively sloping. In fact, the law of demand is often more noticeable in aggregate than it is in individual cases. We have all seen instances in which individuals seem to respond to price increases by apparently not reducing consumption much, if at all. Increasing the price of gasoline, for example, does not seem to cause some people to drive their cars less. To explain this we must first be assured that a price increase was real and not simply nominal. Second, we allow that consumer tastes and preferences may differ substantially among consumers, causing the rational response of some to be an extremely slight adjustment in quantity demanded. Third, consumer adjustment often takes time to accomplish. Consumers are unlikely to change immediately to a more economical car on the strength of an increase in gas prices, but when the car is replaced it may well be by a more economical model.

In aggregate the response to changed price levels will be more noticeable and immediate, however, as the sum of many small changes will accumulate to something quite noticeable in terms of a reduction (or increase when price is reduced) in the firm's total demand.

### The Bandwagon Effect

Since individual demand curves are constructed on the basis of *ceteris paribus,* a simple horizontal summation is only valid where consumer demands are independent of each other. For many consumers, however, the quantity they demand of a particular product depends to some degree on the quantity that other people are simultaneously demanding. For example, in the clothing industry a new style becomes fashionable as more and more people adopt that style. An individual's demand for a particular style may depend upon the overall market acceptance of that style. In many cases the widespread market acceptance of a style will cause individuals to demand *more* than they would have demanded had it not been so popular.

The tendency to change one's taste and preference pattern in favor of a particular product (or attribute) in some positive relationship with total demand for that product (or attribute) has been called the "bandwagon" effect.[13] Consumers in effect jump onto the bandwagon so that they can be where the crowd is. They allow their own tastes to be influenced positively by the tastes of the populace, and they might be said to gain utility from the knowledge that their consumption behavior is similar to that of their peer groups or other groups of consumers.

The bandwagon effect will cause the indifference curves to shift in favor of the product that is experiencing the bandwagon effect. Figure 3.10 is appropriate in this case. Rather than advertising, which changes the marginal rate of substitution in favor of Product X, it is an increase in the consumers' appreciation of the virtues of Product X due to its wider social acceptance that causes the movement of the indifference curves.

### The Snob Effect

The opposite relationship of individual consumer demand to total market demand is known as the "snob" effect. In this case individual demands will be

---

[13]H. Leibenstein, "Bandwagon, Snob and Veblen Effects in the Theory of Consumer Demand," *Quarterly Journal of Economics,* May 1950, pp. 183-207.

reduced by the knowledge that a product is gaining wide market acceptance. Whereas under the bandwagon effect it was the attribute of "social conformity" that made the product more desirable, under the snob effect it is the attribute of "exclusivity" that makes the product more desirable. As the product loses this attribute due to widespread market adoption, some consumers will find the product less desirable and will buy fewer units than they would have bought if market demand had been smaller.

Thus, if the bandwagon effect applies, the individual's demand curve will shift outward at all price levels as market demand in total is increased. On the other hand, if the snob effect applies to an individual, his or her demand curve will shift back at all price levels as more and more consumers purchase the product. Thus total market demand will exceed the simple sum of independent individual demands if the bandwagon effect prevails, and it will fall short of the simple sum of individual demands if the snob effect prevails.

If simultaneous purchases by other consumers *are* taken into account when constructing the demand curves of individuals, the market demand curve is again the simple summation of all individual demands at each price level. Each consumer would be asked how much of Product X he or she would buy when market demand is at various levels, in order to determine the presence or absence of either the bandwagon or the snob effect. Some consumers may exhibit bandwagon effects at the same time that others demonstrate snob effects. Market demand is the sum of all individual demands and hence is greater or smaller than the sum of "independent" demands, to the extent that a *net* bandwagon effect, or *net* snob effect, prevails.

## 3.6  SUMMARY

In this chapter we have demonstrated how the rational consumer will adjust to changes in certain economic variables. The price effect gives rise to the individual's demand curve for individual products. In general these demand curves show an inverse relationship between the price of the product and the quantity demanded by a particular consumer. This price effect can be divided into two component parts: the income effect and the substitution effect. The income effect may be either positive or negative, depending upon the taste and preference pattern of the consumer in question and the level of income of each consumer. The substitution effect is always negative; that is, the relationship between price and quantity demanded, with real income constant, is an inverse one. The sum of the income effect and the substitution effect—that is, the price effect—is invariably negative, since the Giffen good seems to be a historical relic. We caution that in the real world the price effect may sometimes be obscured by the effects of inflation or the simultaneous movement of another variable that influences demand.

The attribute approach to consumer behavior was examined for its implications for consumer choice between and among products. This approach gives several valuable insights into consumer choice which are not so readily apparent using the product approach. The attribute approach allows the entire range of substitutes available to the consumer to be depicted on the same graph. It is thus able to explain quite clearly why a consumer buys one brand of a product in preference to the other brands available: the preferred brand offers the consumer the greatest amount of his or her preferred attribute mix per dollar. Moreover, the analysis easily explains why a consumer will purchase combinations of substitute products: this allows the consumer to obtain the desired attribute ratio, even when there is no product that offers the attributes in this ratio. New products are easily handled by the attribute approach, since they are simply added to the existing analysis. The implications for pricing, promotion, product, and distribution policy are more obvious under the attributes approach: the price level determines the degree to which the product extends the efficiency frontier, and the other three policies determine the combination of attributes and hence the product's placement on the frontier.

If tastes and preferences change in favor of a particular product, a larger amount of that product will be demanded by consumers. Tastes and preferences may change due to social phenomena, or as a result of advertising or promotional activities conducted by business firms. Market demand for a product is, in a simple sense, the sum of all individual demand curves. When individual demands are dependent upon what other individuals are demanding, the aggregate market demand can be either greater than or smaller than the simple summation of individual demands determined in isolation from the demands of other consumers. When individual demands are interdependent, the impact of larger or smaller total market demand must be taken into account when constructing individuals' demand curves in order for market demand to be the sum of individual demands at various price levels.

Studying economic consumer behavior is important, for it explains why consumer responses to changes in economic variables are basically predictable, in *direction* if not always in *magnitude.* To the extent that consumers do wish to allocate their available income rationally (i.e., such that they derive the greatest psychic satisfaction from their income), we can expect price reductions to be followed by increases in quantity demanded, and price increases to be followed by reductions in quantity demanded. It is therefore myopic to expect that price changes will go "more or less unnoticed" by consumers, or that the price level is not as important as some of the other instruments available to the decision maker to increase profitability. When price changes are regarded in the real or relative sense and the impact of other variables can be accounted for, we must expect a negative price effect to prevail. The ramifications of this for revenues, profits, and general business decision making are explored in subsequent chapters.

## DISCUSSION QUESTIONS

3.1    Why does the assumption of transitivity of preferences mean that indifference curves do not cross each other? (Hint: Show that a situation of crossed indifference curves violates transitivity of preferences.)

3.2    Explain how the MRS, at a particular combination of the two products, would differ between two consumers—one who "likes" hamburgers and "loves" milkshakes, and another who "loves" hamburgers and merely "likes" milkshakes.

3.3    How does the availability of credit affect the consumer's budget constraint, in the short term and over a longer period?

3.4    In the self-service versus full-service gasoline example used in the text, how would the indifference map of a person who is knowledgeable about preventive maintenance, economy minded, and not lazy compare with that of another person who is the opposite in these respects?

3.5    For a given price change, will the substitution effect be larger or smaller for a consumer whose indifference curves are relatively steep compared with one whose indifference curves are relatively flat? Why?

3.6    How would the indifference map between $X$ and $Y$ look different for a consumer who regards $X$ as a normal good (or attribute) as compared with another who regards $X$ as an inferior product (or attribute)?

3.7    What attributes do you think are being sought by a consumer who chooses to fly somewhere for a holiday, as compared with another consumer who would drive the same distance for the same holiday?

3.8    Why would a consumer not be acting "rationally" in purchasing a product that fell short of the efficiency frontier in attribute space?

3.9    Distinguish between a change in consumer perceptions and a change in consumer tastes.

3.10    How would new-product policy benefit from an analysis of the attributes demanded by consumers in the overall market for several substitute products?

## PROBLEMS

3.1    In the text the income and substitution effects are explained for price reductions only. To indicate that you understand the procedure, separate the income and substitution effects for a price *increase*. (Don't look at any other text!) If that is too easy, separate the income and substitution effects for a price increase of the product on the *vertical* axis.

3.2    Products X and Y are fairly close substitutes. A price increase is contemplated for Product X, but the people at Company X are worried that sales will fall quite steeply as a result of this price increase. The managerial economist suggests that prior to increasing price, a campaign should be undertaken to increase consumer awareness of the special features of Product X, and hence lessen the reduction in sales that will follow the price increase.

Explain the managerial economist's reasoning, using indifference curve analysis of the consumer's choice between Products X and Y. Pay special attention to the substitution effect of the price change.

3.3    Company A sells a Product X which has several close substitutes. At its present price, however, it is not making a sufficient contribution to the firm's profitability. A price rise is contemplated. The marketing manager is adamant that an advertising campaign must be undertaken before the price is raised. The finance department says that this expenditure is unnecessary. Explain the marketing manager's reasoning in terms of the attribute approach to consumer behavior.

3.4    Imagine two consumers—Mr. A, who simply appreciates classical music; and Ms. B, who is wildly enthusiastic about it. Suppose that in a simple two-product situation both buy classical music records in conjunction with some other Product Y.

Using the indifference maps you think are appropriate for each consumer, derive each of their demand curves from their price consumption curves. (Assume that they have the same income and face the same prices.) Aggregate their individual demands to find their total demand for the records at each price.

3.5    In the automobile market, various segments of the market are catered to by the manufacturers. Show graphically how three different consumers might choose three different automobiles in the simple case where they desire only two attributes, "power" and "economy."

3.6    In a western region two brands of beer are sold which between them share almost all the market. Through careful research it has been found that their main differences are perceived to be in the attributes "lightness" and "thirst-quenching." Brand A is perceived to contain 10 "units" of thirst-quench and 5 "units" of lightness, and costs 80¢ per bottle. Brand B is perceived to contain 5 "units" of thirst-quench and 10 "units" of lightness and costs 67¢ per bottle.

Research has also indicated that a significant share of the market would become available if a third beer were introduced, as long as its price was not too high. The Norbert Brewing Company has a new "premium" beer that incorporates 10 "units" of each attribute in each bottle.

For a consumer who has $10 monthly to spend on beer, and who perceives the attributes in the ratios implied above,

(a)    what is the maximum price that may be charged for Norbert's beer such that $10 will buy a combination of the attributes that lies on the efficiency frontier? (An approximate answer derived from your graph will suffice.)

(b)    Supposing that Norbert prices the new beer at $0.72 per bottle, will the above consumer necessarily switch to Norbert's beer or stay with one or the other of the initial brands? Why?

3.7    Richard Poirier has recently graduated from college, and upon receipt of his first pay check he began planning to buy a sports car. He is considering four major attributes: prestige, performance, reliability, resistance to rust. The value he attaches to these attributes varies depending upon whether he will drive the car all year round or in the summer only. The latter decision depends upon whether he is to be transferred fifteen hundred miles north by his employer. If he moves north he will use the car in the summer only.

If he is to drive the car only in the summer, Richard considers performance to be twice as important as reliability, prestige to be three times as important as reliability, and rust resistance to be only half as important as reliability. For year-round driving, he considers rust resistance to be three times as important as reliability, performance half as important as reliability, and prestige twice as important as reliability.

Richard has found three sports cars for sale; each one is secondhand and costs $5,000. All are in good condition and he decides to buy one of the three. After considering the problem and talking with some experts, he has rated each car on a scale of ten for each of the four attributes, as follows:

|                 | Car A | Car B | Car C |
|-----------------|-------|-------|-------|
| Prestige        | 8     | 9     | 6     |
| Performance     | 8     | 8     | 9     |
| Reliability     | 7     | 6     | 9     |
| Rust resistance | 8     | 7     | 6     |

(a) Please advise Richard as to which sports car he should buy to maximize his expected utility if he is in fact transferred fifteen hundred miles north.

(b) Which car should he buy if he is sure that he will not be transferred?

(c) Which car should he buy if the probability of his being transferred north can be reliably estimated at 0.7? (Explain your reasoning in each case.)

3.8    The demand for telephone installation is peaked around the first day of each month, since many subscribers request service on that day due to their moving to a new house or apartment. The Tanguay Telephone Company (T.T.C.) is examining a means to reduce this monthly demand peak, which accounts for 40 percent of all installations. The problem has been aggravated in recent years by the increasing hourly cost of labor, the reluctance of unionized employees to work overtime, the increased "no access" problems due to the greater number of working households, and the decline of profitable auxiliary sales to the subscriber (colored telephones, extension phones, etc.) due to access being given by a third party (landlord, neighbor, etc.).

T.T.C. is considering opening several "Phoneshops" in its area, such that customers could go and obtain their telephone sets which they would install themselves in their own homes. The company would prewire all homes in its territory, installing one or two phone jacks in each room: the installation by the customer would simply involve plugging the sets in where desired. The company would continue to offer home installation for those unable or unwilling to visit the Phoneshops. Two types of Phoneshop are being considered: more conveniently located stores which would offer a moderate saving as compared with the traditional home installation, and less conveniently located stores which would offer a more substantial saving due to the lower overhead costs in the less convenient locations.

A market survey has found that telephone subscribers want two major attributes in their purchase of a new installation—"convenience" and "economy." A "typical" customer has been found who rates the three options on a scale of 100 for "convenience" as Home Installation 100, More Convenient Store 75, and Less Convenient Store 25. The "economy" of the second and third options will be measured by the savings from the $20 it will continue to cost to have home installation. Thus "economy" will be determined by prices that T.T.C. decides to charge for the latter two options.

(a) Supposing initially that T.T.C. prices the More Convenient (MC) Phoneshop service at $16, and the Less Convenient (LC) Phoneshop service at $12, show the consumer's options in attribute space, with "convenience" on the vertical axis and "dollars saved" on the horizontal axis. (Since the consumer wants *one* unit only of *one* of the three services, these options will be represented by points in attribute space, not rays.)

(b) For a consumer who has an MRS = 10 at the point represented by the MC Phoneshop (i.e., who is prepared to give up 10 units of convenience for $1 saved), which of the three options should be selected?

(c) For a person who has an MRS = 15 at the point represented by the MC Phoneshop, which of the three options should be selected?

**SUGGESTED REFERENCES AND FURTHER READINGS**

BAUMOL, W. J. *Economic Theory and Operations Analysis,* 4th ed., Chap. 9. Englewood Cliffs, N.J.: Prentice-Hall, 1977.

HENDLER, R., "Lancaster's New Approach to Consumer Demand and Its Limitations," *American Economic Review,* 65 (March 1975), 194-99.

HIRSHLEIFER, J., *Price Theory and Applications,* Chaps. 3 and 4. Englewood Cliffs, N.J.: Prentice-Hall, 1976.

LANCASTER, K., "A New Approach to Consumer Theory," *Journal of Political Economy,* 84 (April 1966), 132-57.

———., *Consumer Demand: A New Approach.* New York: Columbia University Press, 1971.

LEIBENSTEIN, H., "Bandwagon, Snob and Veblen Effects in the Theory of Consumer Demand," *Quarterly Journal of Economics,* May 1950, pp. 183-207.

# 4

# Demand Concepts
# for
# Decision Making

## 4.1 INTRODUCTION

Whereas the preceding chapter examines the principles underlying the individual consumer's demand, the present chapter is concerned with the aggregate demand for the products produced by the firm. The total demand for a particular product depends upon many variables, and the decision maker will benefit from an awareness of the impact of changes in these variables upon the demand for the product in question. The decision maker should be aware of both the *direction* of the change in total demand and the probable *magnitude* of the change in total demand, which are likely to follow a variation in any of the influencing factors.

In the following sections we examine the major factors likely to influence the total demand for a product, the probable direction of the influence in each case, the relationships among the important revenue concepts, and a means of measuring and summarizing the direction and magnitude of the influence of each variable which impacts upon the total demand for a particular product.

## 4.2 THE DEMAND FUNCTION AND THE DEMAND CURVE

*MATHEMATICAL*

Let us immediately make the following distinction. The demand *function* refers to the relationship that exists between the quantity demanded of a particular product and *all factors* that influence that demand. The demand *curve* refers to the relationship that exists between the quantity demanded of a particular product and the *price* of that product, with all other influencing factors held constant. The demand curve is thus a subset of the demand function in the case where *ceteris paribus* applies to all of the independent variables except price.

CURVE SUBSET OF FUNCTION

114

### The Independent Variables in the Demand Function

Supposing that total quantity demanded of a particular product is a simple linear function of each of the influencing factors, we may express the demand function in terms of its major determinants as follows:

$$Q_x = \alpha - \beta_1 P_x + \beta_2 P_s - \beta_3 P_c + \beta_4 A_x - \beta_5 A_s + \beta_6 A_c + \beta_7 Y + \beta_8 T + \beta_9 E + \beta_{10} N \quad (4.1)$$

where  $Q_x$  is total quantity demanded in physical units of Product X;

$\alpha$  is that part of quantity demanded that is determined exogenously;

$\beta_1, \beta_2, \ldots, \beta_{10}$  are the "coefficients" of the demand function, equal to the first derivative of the demand function with respect to the appropriate independent variable;

$P_x$  is the price of Product X;

$P_s$  is an index of the prices of other products that are regarded as substitutes for Product X;

$P_c$  is an index of the prices of other products that are complementary to Product X;

$A_x$  is the advertising and promotional effort devoted to Product X;

$A_s$  is an index of the advertising effort devoted to the substitutes for Product X;

$A_c$  is an index of the advertising effort devoted to the complementary products;

$Y$  is an index of consumers' disposable income levels;

$T$  is an index of consumer taste and preference patterns;

$E$  is an index of consumers' expectations regarding future prices, availability, or the nature of Product X; and

$N$  is the total market population.

Other variables such as weather conditions, demographic factors, and cultural beliefs may enter the demand function for particular products. Let us examine each of the independent variables in turn.

*Price.* The price of Product X is, of course, the number of currency units to be paid by each buyer. If a discount from list price is to be given, or consumers habitually bargain the price down from list price, the appropriate price is the actual price paid rather than the price that is initially asked for the product. As we have argued in the preceding chapter, the relationship between market demand and the price of a product is almost certain to be an inverse one. For increases in the price of Product X, we expect quantity demanded to fall, and for reductions in the price of Product X, we expect quantity demanded to rise.

*Related Products.* The price of substitute products enters the demand function for Product X because of the willingness of consumers to substitute between and among Product X and its substitutes, given changes in the relative prices of this group of products. If one or more of the prices of substitute products increase, such that the index of these prices increases, we would expect the demand for Product X to increase, since individual consumers will tend to switch away from the substitute products and toward Product X. We expect the converse for reductions in the prices of substitute products.

The prices of complementary goods, on the other hand, are expected to have a negative relation with the quantity demanded of Product X. If the prices of complementary goods rise, such that the index of those prices rises, we expect the quantity demanded of Product X to fall, since the consumption of Product X and its complementary products is now more expensive.

Advertising and other promotional expenditures can be expected to influence the quantity demanded of a product, since they influence the taste and preference patterns of consumers. Advertising related to Product X is expected to be followed by an increase in the quantity demanded of Product X. On the other hand, advertising of rival products is expected to have a negative influence on the quantity demanded of X, since it should be expected to induce consumers to switch their consumption from Product X to one of the substitute products. Advertising of complementary goods is expected to have a positive influence upon the quantity demanded of Product X, since it will make the complementary good more attractive to consumers who, in turn, since they purchased Product X and that complementary good in some proportionate way, will tend to buy more units of Product X.

*Consumer Incomes.* The relationship between consumer income and quantity demanded of Product X can be expected to be either positive or negative, depending upon the product in question and the level of consumer income. We saw in the preceding chapter that for some consumers at some income levels, a particular commodity could have a negative income effect, whereas for other consumers at other income levels, the income effect might be positive. We are clearly interested here in the *aggregate* income effect. Thus, if to most purchasers the product is an inferior good, its demand will be decreased when income levels rise, or increased when income levels fall. On the other hand, if it is a normal or superior product for most purchasers, quantity demanded and income levels will move in the same direction.

*Tastes and Expectations.* The index of tastes and preferences will reflect the extent to which the aggregate preference pattern is moving toward or away from Product X. Since for some consumers tastes will be changing away from Product X, while for others they will be shifting toward Product X, we are clearly interested in the net effect, or the general trend of tastes and preferences toward or away from the product in question. Similarly, the index of expectations is a net figure that indicates the general state of consumer expectations as to the future availability and/or price level, and perhaps other factors such as technological advance, relating to Product X. If, for example, there were a general shift in expectations that the price of Product X would rise in the near future, we would expect a positive impact of this on the quantity demanded of Product X in the current period. Alternatively, if expectations as to the future availability of the product were to become more pessimistic, due for example to the current lack of raw materials for that product, we would expect the market demand of Product X to be increased during the present time period. Finally, if news of a technological improvement were released such that consumers would expect future models of the product to be more efficient, this would be expected to have a negative impact on current demand for the product.

*Other Factors.* Population, or some other indicator of the number of potential consumers for Product X, is expected to be positively related to the demand for Product X. If population were to rise, for example, due to net immigration and/or rising fertility rates, we would expect this to have a positive impact on the quantity demanded of Product X. Where the market for a product is regional rather than national, we must take into account population shifts between and among regions, which will increase or decrease the potential market for the product in question. Other factors include the weather pattern, the cultural milieu, and such demographic variables as the changing composition of the work force, changing median-age levels, and changing retirement levels.

### The Demand Curve Derived
### from the Demand Function

We know that the demand curve is a special case of the demand function in which *ceteris paribus* applies to all independent variables except the price of Product X. From Eq.(4.1) we can express the demand curve as

$$Q_x = A - \beta_1 P_x \tag{4.2}$$

where the parameter $A$ represents all units of quantity demanded that are determined exogenously to Eq.(4.2). It therefore includes $\alpha$ and the influence of all other independent variables (except price) in Eq.(4.1).

Economists traditionally state the demand curve in inverse form. Let us rearrange Eq.(4.2) to express price in terms of quantity demanded. Adding $\beta_1 P_x$ to both sides, subtracting $Q_x$ from both sides, and dividing through by $\beta_1$, we have

$$Q_x + \beta_1 P_x = A$$

$$\beta_1 P_x = A - Q_x \tag{4.3}$$

$$P_x = \frac{A}{\beta_1} - \frac{Q_x}{\beta_1}$$

Letting $\dfrac{A}{\beta_1} = a$ and $\dfrac{1}{\beta_1} = b$, we have

*EXPRESSED AS PRICE
IN TERMS QUAN DEMANDED*

$$P_x = a - bQ_x \tag{4.4}$$

which expresses price as a linear function of quantity demanded, where $a$ is the intercept term and $b$ is the slope term of the traditional demand curve. We expect the slope term to have a negative sign, since the total demand curve is the horizontal summation of individual demand curves,[1] which were argued to be negatively sloped in Chapter 3.

### "Movements along" vs. "Shifts of" the Demand Curve

A "movement along" the demand curve will occur when there is a change in price (and consequently quantity demanded) while all other variables (reflected in the intercept term $a$) remain constant. In Figure 4.1 the price change from $P_1$ to $P_2$ leads to a movement along the demand curve from point $A$ to point $B$ with the associated change in quantity demanded being from $Q_1$ to $Q_2$, given *ceteris paribus.*

A "shift" in the demand curve will occur when *ceteris paribus* does not apply, and thus the value of the intercept term changes. In Figure 4.2 we show shifts in the demand curve which are the result of changes in one or more of the other factors while price is held constant. Suppose that the initial demand curve is that shown as $D$, such that at price $P_1$, quantity demanded is $Q_1$. If, for example, consumer incomes were to increase (or there was an increase in some other variable that has a positive coefficient in Eq.(4.1), or a decrease in a variable that has a negative coefficient), the demand curve would *shift* to the right, as shown by the movement to demand curve $D'$. For the same price level $P_1$ the quantity demanded is now $Q'$; the additional quantity demanded is due to a change in one or more of the other variables. On the other hand, had there been a reduction in consumer incomes (or a shift in consumer tastes away from Product X, or any of a number of other changes in the determining factors), the demand curve would shift to the left to a position such as that shown by demand curve $D''$.

---

[1] Since this aggregate demand curve is the horizontal summation of the individual demand curves for Product X, there is no intrinsic reason that it should be a straight line. However, we are interested in what is known as the "relevant range" of prices and quantities, and through this relevant range it is a sufficient approximation to depict the demand curve as a straight line. Doing so greatly facilitates explanation of the analysis that is to follow. When one considers large price changes, however, it may be an oversimplification to assume that the relationship between price and quantity is a simple rectilinear one.

**FIGURE 4.1**
**Demand curve for product X, with *ceteris paribus***

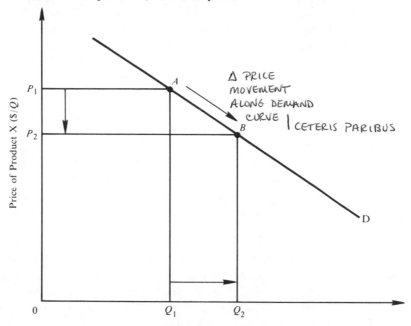

Quantity (*Q*) Demanded of Product X (per unit of time)

**FIGURE 4.2**
**Shifts in the demand curve for product X**

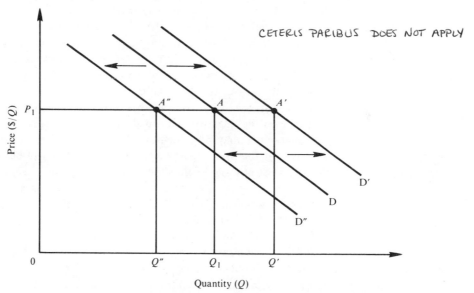

Quantity (*Q*)

Thus changes in price will, *ceteris paribus,* lead to a *movement along* an existing demand curve, whereas changes in any of the other variables cause a *shift* in
the demand curve. Given the new set of the other variables, there will be a new

demand curve that is appropriate, and the initial demand curve will now be inappropriate. Given this new set of the other variables, we may now speak of movements along the new demand curve in response to changes in the price level, *ceteris paribus*. When analyzing the effect on quantity demanded of a change in the price level, it is therefore extremely important to ascertain whether or not any of the other factors have changed, before concluding that there has been a movement along the envisaged demand curve.

### Interrelationships among Price, Total Revenue, and Marginal Revenue

Why are we interested in the variation between price and quantity of a particular commodity? Our concern is to see what happens to total sales revenue when prices and quantities are varied. Whatever the decision maker's objective function, total revenue is likely to play a major role in the optimization of that objective function.

In Table 4.1 we demonstrate the variation of total revenue for the demand curve specified by $P_x = 11 - 0.001/Q_x$. Suppose this represents the demand curve for a carton of twelve cans of dog food at a discount supermarket during a particular month. For this simple demand curve, the intercept on the price axis is thus $11, and the slope is $-0.001$. Thus for every price reduction of one dollar, quantity demanded will increase by 1,000 cartons. Substituting different values of price into this equation, we are able to determine the quantity that will be demanded at all prices, as shown in the second column of Table 4.1. Total revenue at each price is derived by multiplying the price by the quantity demanded at that price, to find the total revenue associated with each price (or quantity) level. It can be seen that total revenue increases progressively as price is lowered from $10 down to $6; the price reduction to $5 leaves the total revenue unchanged; and further price reductions cause total revenue to decline.

Note that high prices are not necessarily the best prices. By progressively lowering the price, we were able to increase total revenue up to a point. Similarly, neither is a very low price necessarily a good strategy, since although it does expand the quantity demanded, it causes a smaller total revenue compared with that which may be earned at a higher price level. Accordingly, statements such as "Set the price at the maximum the market will bear" or "Reduce price to the lowest possible level" should be regarded with suspicion. If taken at face value, they are generally nonsensical. Instead they must be regarded as qualified statements, where the words "will bear" and "lowest possible" carry an implicit reference to the profitability deriving from that price level.

In Table 4.1 the fourth column shows the marginal revenue associated with each price level. *Marginal revenue* is defined as that change in total revenue that results from a one-unit increase in quantity demand. Since quantity demanded increases by blocks of one thousand units in Table 4.1, marginal revenue is calculated here as the row-to-row difference in the total revenue column divided by the change in quantity demanded. It can be seen that marginal revenue falls progressively to zero and becomes negative as price is reduced.

*[Handwritten margin notes:]*

$P_x = 11 - .001 Q_x$

@ $11 ⇒ $Q_x = 0$ ← NOTHING DEMANDED

P↓ to $10

$10 = 11 - .001 Q_x$

SOLVE $Q_x$   $1 = .001 Q_x$

$1000 = Q_x$

**TABLE 4.1**
Revenue implications of the law of demand

| Price ($/unit) | Quantity Demanded (units) | Total Revenue ($) | Marginal Revenue ($/unit) |
|---|---|---|---|
| 10 | 1,000 | 10,000 | — |
| 9 | 2,000 | 18,000 | 8 |
| 8 | 3,000 | 24,000 | 6 |
| 7 | 4,000 | 28,000 | 4 |
| 6 | 5,000 | 30,000 | 2 |
| 5 | 6,000 | 30,000 | 0 |
| 4 | 7,000 | 28,000 | −2 |
| 3 | 8,000 | 24,000 | −4 |
| 2 | 9,000 | 18,000 | −6 |
| 1 | 10,000 | 10,000 | −8 |

In Figure 4.3 we plot the values for the demand curve (given by the price/quantity combinations), and the total revenue and marginal revenue curves, to illustrate the relationships that exist between and among these curves. These relationships hold for any demand curve that is negatively sloped. Total revenue increases at first as prices are lowered, reaches its maximum, and thereafter declines as prices are reduced further. Marginal revenue will always be less than price at each output level; will fall to zero at the point where total revenue reaches its maximum; and takes negative values if price is reduced any further, since this causes an absolute reduction in total revenue.

The price reductions shown in Table 4.1 were made by discrete one-dollar units, and hence the changes in quantity-demanded observations were in blocks of one thousand units. Marginal revenue calculated from these data is strictly the *average* change in total revenue per one-unit change in quantity demanded for each of the 1,000-unit blocks. If we had shown smaller price reductions, we would find that the price generating the highest revenue is $5.50. At this price level, 5,500 units will be demanded and total revenue will be $30,250. Strictly, then, marginal revenue is zero at these price and quantity levels, as shown in Figure 4.3, rather than the more crude approximations shown in Table 4.1.

***Price and Marginal Revenue.*** The relationship between the demand curve and the marginal revenue curve bears further observation. Since both may be derived from the total revenue curve, it is clear that there must be a relationship between them. To find this relationship we begin by expressing the total revenue as the product of price and quantity:

$$TR_x = P_x \cdot Q_x \tag{4.5}$$

Eq.(4.4) gave us the following expression for $P_x$:

$$P_x = a - bQ_x \tag{4.4}$$

DEMAND CURVE =s
AVE REVENUE ⟹
CAN BE DERIVED
FROM TR CURVE

121

### FIGURE 4.3
### Relationships between demand, marginal revenue, and total revenue

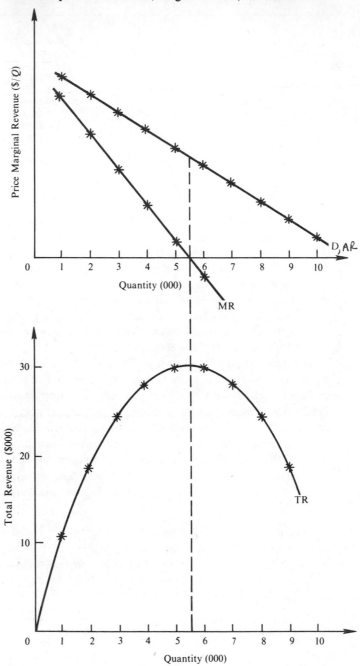

Substituting for $P_x$ in Eq.(4.5), we obtain

$$TR_x = aQ_x - bQ_x^2 \qquad (4.6)$$

Since *marginal revenue* is defined as the change in total revenue for a one-unit change in quantity demanded, it can be expressed as the first derivative of Eq. (4.6) with respect to $Q_x$. Thus

$$P_x = a - bQ_x$$
$$MR_x = a - 2bQ_x \qquad -b = \frac{dP_x}{dQ_x} \qquad (4.7)$$

Now compare the expression for the demand curve, Eq.(4.4), with the expression for the marginal revenue curve, Eq.(4.7). The intercept term of each is $a$, indicating that both curves must emanate from the same point on the vertical axis of the graph, and the slope term in the marginal revenue expression is exactly twice the slope term in the price or demand curve expression. Thus the marginal revenue curve does have a fixed relationship with the demand curve from which it is derived. It begins at the same point on the price axis, and its slope is twice that of the demand curve.

*Curvilinear Demand Curves.* For curvilinear demand curves this relationship still holds, although it must be interpreted a little more carefully. Consider Figure 4.4 in which the demand curve is curvilinear and shown as $DD'$. To find the marginal revenue that would be associated with a price adjustment at point $A$ on that demand curve, we place a tangent against the demand curve at point $A$. This tangent becomes an artificial demand curve for the purposes of ascertaining the level of marginal revenue that is appropriate for point $A$. The marginal revenue curve associated with the artificial demand curve is shown as *mr* in the figure. At output level $Q_1$ it is clear that the level of marginal revenue is indicated by the point $A'$ on the artificial marginal revenue curve, and this must be the appropriate level for point $A$ on the curvilinear demand curve, since $A$ is a point on both the actual and the artificial demand curves.

Suppose we now move to point $B$ on the actual demand curve. A tangent at that point produces another artificial demand curve shown as $d'$. The associated marginal revenue curve is shown as *mr'*. At output level $Q_2$ the level of marginal revenue associated with point $B$ on the demand curve is hence $B'$. Points $A'$ and $B'$ are therefore points on the marginal revenue curve which is associated with the curvilinear demand curve. By continuing we would eventually obtain all the points on the curvilinear MR curve.

Although most market demand curves are curvilinear rather than rectilinear, as mentioned above we typically work with rectilinear demand curves, since the price and quantity adjustments are usually quite small and do not involve the large movement indicated from points $A$ to $B$ in Figure 4.4. A straight-line demand curve is generally a sufficient approximation of the true slope of the demand curve over a small range of price and quantity levels.

*Horizontal Demand Curves.* In some cases the demand curve envisaged by the firm is not negatively sloping but is horizontal at the market price level.

**FIGURE 4.4**
Construction of the marginal revenue curve for curvilinear demand curves

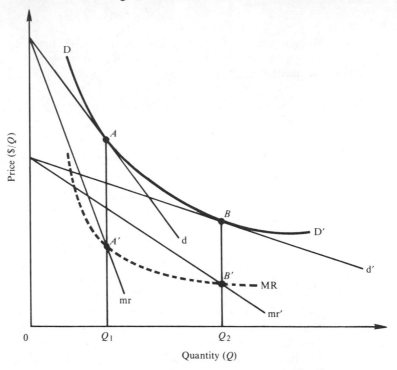

Where competing products are regarded as completely undifferentiated by consumers,[2] a price slightly above the market level would cause zero demand for an individual firm, since consumers would obtain the equivalent product from another supplier at a lower price. Alternatively, a slight price reduction would be greeted by a massive increase in demand as the consumers switch to this firm's product which is now relatively cheaper but identical in all other respects to competitors' products. But there is no gain in such a price reduction because the firm can sell all it wants to at the initial price, and at the slightly lower price the firm will wish to sell slightly *fewer* units, since the marginal units will no longer be profitable.[3]

If the firm's demand curve is horizontal, the total revenue curve will be a straight line, as in Figure 4.5, since total revenue is the product of a constant price and a variable quantity level and is thus directly proportionate to output. The marginal revenue curve must be coincident with the demand curve, since the increments to total revenue as the result of each additional unit sold are equal to the constant price, and all units are sold at the same price.

[2] By completely undifferentiated, or homogeneous, products we mean that all attributes possessed by the products are identical in quantity and quality across products, such that the consumer has no basis for choice except the price level.

[3] That is to say, marginal costs will exceed marginal revenues on the last few units and thus will make marginal profits negative. This is explained in more detail in Chapter 9.

124

FIGURE 4.5

**Total revenue and marginal revenue curves when firm's envisaged demand curve is horizontal**

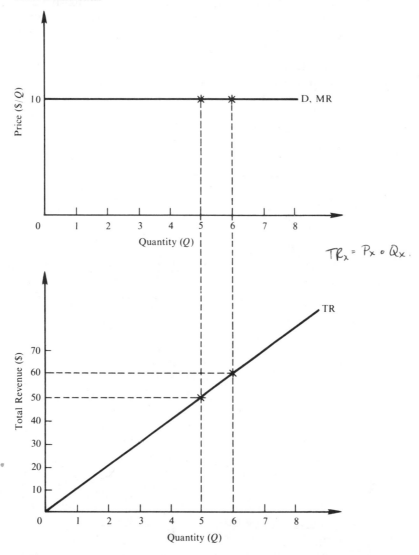

$$TR_x = P_x \circ Q_x.$$

The above relationships between price, quantity demanded, total revenue, and marginal revenue can be summarized in a single number known as the "price elasticity" of demand. The concept of elasticity is used widely in economics and expresses the responsiveness of one variable to a change in another variable. Stated a little more rigorously, an *elasticity* is the percentage change in the dependent variable occasioned by a one percent change in an independent variable. It thus shows the proportionate response of one variable to a change in one of the variables that influence that variable. In the following sections the dependent variable is the quantity demanded, and the independent variables are a selection of the independent variables shown in Eq.(4.1).

## 4.3   PRICE ELASTICITY OF DEMAND

*Price elasticity of demand* is defined as the proportionate change in quantity demanded, divided by the proportionate change in price that induced the change in quantity demanded. Let us immediately make the distinction between "point" price elasticity and "arc" price elasticity. We use point elasticity when the change in price is infinitesimal, since such a small change represents a virtual point on the demand curve. For more substantial price changes we use arc elasticity, since we are considering a discrete movement along, or an arc of, the demand curve. Let us confine our attention first to point price elasticity. In algebraic terms it may be expressed as follows:

$$\epsilon = -\frac{dQ_x/Q_x}{dP_x/P_x} \tag{4.8}$$

where $\epsilon$ (epsilon) is the conventional symbol for price elasticity; $dQ_x/Q_x$ represents the change in the demand for Product X divided by the initial quantity of Product X; and $dP_x/P_x$ is the change in price divided by the initial price. The negative sign in Eq.(4.8) is to convert the elasticity value to a positive number, since either $dQ_x$ or $dP_x$ will have a negative sign. This expression may be restated by rearrangement of terms as follows:

*reciprocal of slope of demand curve*

$$\epsilon = -\frac{dQ_x}{dP_x} \cdot \frac{P_x}{Q_x} \tag{4.9}$$

*Demand (EXPRESSING PRICE AS FUNCTION OF QUANTITY DEMANDED)*

$P_x = a - bQ_x$

$\frac{dP_x}{dQ_x} = -b$ → *SLOPE ⇒ Δ PRICE for a Δ in Q*

In this form it is perhaps intuitively more appealing, since the first part of the expression, $dQ_x/dP_x$, is recognizable as the reciprocal of the slope of the demand curve. On a straight-line demand curve the slope term is constant, and therefore the term $dQ_x/dP_x$ is constant in Eq.(4.9). Note, however, that the second term in the elasticity expression, $P_x/Q_x$, is not constant but varies throughout the length of the demand curve. At points high on the demand curve the ratio $P_x/Q_x$ will be relatively large, whereas for points low on the demand curve the ratio of $P_x$ to $Q_x$ will be relatively low. In fact, this ratio will approach infinity as we move toward the intercept on the price axis, and it will approach zero as we move toward the intercept on the quantity axis. Since elasticity is the product of a constant and a number that varies from infinity to zero, it is apparent that the value for price elasticity must *vary from infinity to zero* as we move from the price intercept down a linear demand curve to the quantity intercept.

### Graphical Method of Determining
### Point Price Elasticity

To determine the price elasticity at any point on the demand curve, the following methodology is quite useful. Refer to Figure 4.6 and assume that we wish to find the price elasticity of demand for price changes in the vicinity of point *A* on that demand curve. Let us identify the point on the quantity axis vertically below point *A* as the point *M*, and the point where the demand curve intercepts

FIGURE 4.6
**Method of calculating the value of price elasticity from the demand curve**

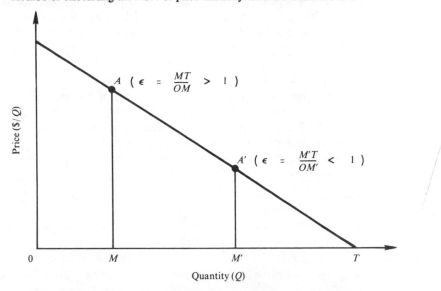

the quantity axis as point $T$. Referring back to Eq.(4.9), we recall that the first term in the elasticity formula is the reciprocal of the slope of the demand curve. In terms of Figure 4.6, the slope of the demand curve can be expressed as the ratio of the distances $AM/MT$. The reciprocal of the slope is thus $MT/AM$. The second term in the elasticity expression is the ratio of the price of Product X to the quantity of Product X at point $A$, and in terms of Figure 4.6 is $AM/0M$. Hence elasticity may be expressed as follows:

$$\epsilon = -\; \frac{-MT}{AM} \cdot \frac{AM}{0M} \qquad\qquad (4.10)$$

The $AM$ terms in Eq.(4.9) will cancel, and the negative signs become positive, such that the elasticity formula may be expressed as follows:

$$\epsilon = \frac{MT}{0M} \qquad\qquad (4.11)$$

Thus the price elasticity of demand for price changes in the vicinity of point $A$ on the demand curve may be expressed as the ratio of the horizontal distance $MT$, over the horizontal distance $0M$.

It is evident that the elasticity value at point $A$ is greater than one, since the distance $MT$ exceeds the distance $0M$. Let us now consider point $A'$ on the demand curve in Figure 4.6. Identifying the point directly below $A'$ as $M'$, and applying the same formula, namely, $M'T/0M'$, we see that the price elasticity at point $A'$ must be less than unity. It is clear that since elasticity at point $A$ exceeds unity, and at point $A'$ is less than unity, and since the value of elasticity varies from infinity down to zero along the demand curve, that at a point somewhere between $A$ and $A'$ the value of elasticity will be exactly unity.

Let us assert that the point at which elasticity will equal unity is the *midpoint* of the demand curve. To prove this assertion we will call upon some high-school geometry, in the form of proof by similar triangles, According to Eq.(4.11), if elasticity is to equal unity, then $MT$ must equal $0M$. In Figure 4.7 we choose point $M$ such that the distance $MT$ is equal to the distance $0M$. Point $A$ is thus the point on the demand curve vertically above point $M$, and point $R$ is the price level represented by point $A$ such that the distance $0R$ is equal to the distance $AM$. Thus we have a pair of triangles, triangle $PAR$ and triangle $ATM$. We know that elasticity is equal to unity at point $A$ and wish to prove that $A$ is the midpoint of the demand curve, or that the distance $PA$ equals the distance $AT$. Since $0M$ equals $MT$, the distance $RA$ also equals $MT$, since $R0$ and $AM$ are parallel lines, and $RA$ and $0M$ are parallel lines. The angles $PAR$ and $ATM$ are equal, since the line $PT$ crosses a pair of parallel lines; and the angles $PRA$ and $AMT$ are equal, since they are formed by the intersection of two pairs of parallel lines. Thus triangle $PAR$ and triangle $ATM$ are similar and congruent triangles, and hence $PA$ equals $AT$. Point $A$ is indeed the midpoint of the demand curve, and the price elasticity is therefore unity at the midpoint of the demand curve.

The midpoint thus divides the demand curve into two major regions of elasticity; above the midpoint elasticity varies from unity to infinity, and below the midpoint it varies from unity to zero. We say that demand is price *elastic* in the upper region and is price *inelastic* in the lower region.

### Price Elasticity, Marginal Revenue, and Total Revenue

Let us now examine the relationship that exists between price elasticity and marginal revenue. Since the marginal revenue curve begins from the same intercept as the demand curve on the price axis but has twice the slope of the demand curve, it must intersect the quantity axis in half the distance from the origin to the demand curve intersection on the quantity axis. Thus, in terms of Figure 4.7, the marginal revenue curve must pass through point $M$. It is therefore apparent that the <u>marginal revenue is zero when elasticity of demand is unity; that marginal revenue is positive when elasticity exceeds unity; and that marginal revenue is negative when elasticity is less than unity.</u>

The specific relationship existing between marginal revenue and elasticity may be derived as follows. Recall that total revenue is price times quantity, as expressed in Eq.(4.5) and restated here:

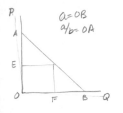

*Q = 0B*
*a/b = 0A*

$Q = a - bP = \text{DEMAND CURVE}$
$Q - a = -bP$
$\frac{1}{b}Q - \frac{a}{b} = -P$
$-\frac{1}{b}Q + \frac{a}{b} = P$
$\frac{a}{b} - \frac{1}{b}Q = P$ ⟵ INVERSE

$\frac{dQ}{dP} = -\frac{1}{b}$

*TR = QP(Q)   (Revenue is function of quantity - not both Q and P since P is*

$$\text{TR}_x = P_x \cdot Q_x \tag{4.5}$$

*a function of Q)*

*functionally related by demand curve* ⟵

Marginal revenue is the first derivative of Eq.(4.5) and can be found using the chain rule (since $P_x$ is a function of $Q_x$):

$$\text{MR}_x = P_x + Q_x \frac{dP_x}{dQ_x} \tag{4.12}$$

*FOR PERF COMP DEMAND CURVE*
*NEGATIVE ⟹ MR = P*

**FIGURE 4.7**
**Elasticity at the midpoint is unity**

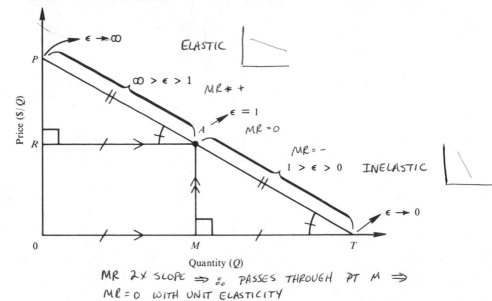

MR 2× SLOPE ⟹ ∴ PASSES THROUGH PT M ⟹
MR = 0 WITH UNIT ELASTICITY

We now perform a manipulation on Eq.(4.12) which will allow a substitution. Multiply and divide the last term by $P_x$ such that we obtain

*same as by 1*

$$MR_x = P_x + \frac{Q_x P_x}{P_x} \cdot \frac{dP_x}{dQ_x} \tag{4.13}$$

Factoring out $P_x$, we obtain

*reciprocal of expression for elasticity*

$$MR_x = P_x \left(1 + \frac{Q_x}{P_x} \cdot \frac{dP_x}{dQ_x}\right) \tag{4.14}$$

Note that the second term in the brackets is in fact the negative of the reciprocal of the expression for elasticity we found in Eq.(4.9), which is restated here:

$$\epsilon = -\frac{dQ_x}{dP_x} \cdot \frac{P_x}{Q_x} \tag{4.9}$$

Substituting from Eq.(4.9) into (4.14), we obtain

$$MR_x = P_x \left(1 - \frac{1}{\epsilon}\right) \qquad \ast \tag{4.15}$$

This expression serves to specify the relationship that exists between marginal revenue, price, and the price elasticity of demand, at any particular price level on a given demand curve.

To check this, let us substitute into Eq.(4.15) a couple of values for which

129

we already know the answers. At the midpoint of the demand curve we know $\epsilon = 1$. Hence

$$MR_x = P_x \left(1 - \frac{1}{1}\right)$$

$$= P_x \left(1 - 1\right)$$

$$= P_x \left(0\right)$$

$$\therefore MR_x = 0$$

as confirmed in Figure 4.7. Second, when the demand curve is horizontal, $\epsilon = \infty$ (since the slope of a horizontal line is zero). Hence

$$MR_x = P_x \left(1 - \frac{1}{\infty}\right)$$

$$= P_x \left(1 - 0\right)$$

$$= P_x \left(1\right)$$

$$\therefore MR_x = P_x$$

as confirmed in Figure 4.5 above.

Let us now look at the relationship between price elasticity of demand and *total* revenue. Referring back to Figure 4.3, you will recall that when marginal revenue is positive (that is, when elasticity exceeds unity), total revenue increases with successive increases in quantity; and when marginal revenue is negative (that is, when elasticity is less than unity), total revenue decreases for successive increases in quantity. These successive increases in quantity, of course, were the result of successive decreases in the price level. In Table 4.2 we summarize what will happen to total revenue when price is either increased or decreased, when elasticity takes values greater than one, equal to one, and less than one.

**TABLE 4.2**
**Relationship between price elasticity and total revenues**

| Elasticity Value | Price Increases | Price Decreases |
|---|---|---|
| $\infty > \epsilon > 1$ | TR falls | TR rises |
| $\epsilon = 1$ | TR constant | TR constant |
| $0 < \epsilon < 1$ | TR rises | TR falls |

The relationship between price changes, price elasticity, and the change in total revenue should be intuitively obvious when one recalls our initial definition of price elasticity. We defined *price elasticity* as the proportionate change in quantity demanded, divided by the proportionate change in the price. Elasticity exceeds unity when the proprotionate change in quantity exceeds the proportionate change in price. Hence it should be obvious that if, for example, price was raised by 10 percent, and quantity demanded fell by 15 percent, that total revenue must fall, since the reduction in quantity demanded was proportionately greater than the increase in the price level. The extra revenue per unit on the quantity actually sold is outweighed by the loss of the revenue from the units that were previously sold but are now not sold.

The above analysis of price elasticity is concerned with what we call *point* price elasticity. That is, at a particular point on the demand curve, the elasticity was calculated. The change in price and the change in quantity at that point were infinitesimal, sufficient only to indicate the slope of the demand curve at that point. In the real world, however, immeasurably small changes in prices are not likely to attract the attention of consumers in the marketplace. Discrete price changes will be necessary to overcome consumer thresholds of price awareness. It would seem therefore that we are unable to generate the data required to calculate point price elasticity in real-market situations, and hence a modification of the elasticity formula becomes necessary. This modified formula allows us to calculate the *arc* price elasticity.

### Arc Price Elasticity

As you know, an *arc* is a line joining two points on a curve. Let us illustrate the arc price elasticity of demand with reference to the following example. Suppose a small store has been selling hanging flowerpots over the last few months at a price of $8 per unit, and sales appear to have stabilized at about 32 units per week. The store now reduces the price of these flowerpots to $7 per unit and after a couple of weeks finds that sales have stabilized at a new level of 44 units per week. If all other factors mentioned in the demand function are thought to have remained constant, then we expect that the two price-quantity combinations above are points on the store's demand curve for those flowerpots. To demonstrate the need for an arc elasticity measure, let us first calculate the point elasticities. Beginning with the initial point on the demand curve, at the coordinates $8 and 32 units, the price elasticity would be calculated as follows:

$$\epsilon = -\frac{dQ}{dP} \cdot \frac{P}{Q}$$

$$= -\frac{Q_1 - Q_2}{P_1 - P_2} \cdot \frac{P_1}{Q_1}$$

$$= -\frac{-12}{1} \cdot \frac{8}{32}$$

$$= \quad 3 \Rightarrow \text{PROPORTIONATE } \Delta \text{ Q IS 3X}$$
$$\qquad\qquad \text{PROPORTIONATE } \Delta \text{ IN PRICE LEVEL}$$

This indicates, of course, that the proportionate change of quantity is three times the proportionate change in the price level, and hence total revenues would be increased by a price reduction in the vicinity of $8. Let us now calculate the point price elasticity at the second pair of coordinates, that is, at $7 and 44 units.

$$\epsilon = -\frac{Q_1 - Q_2}{P_1 - P_2} \cdot \frac{P_2}{Q_2}$$

$$= -\frac{-12}{1} \cdot \frac{7}{44}$$

$$= 1.91$$

It is clear that the point price elasticity is considerably different at the second coordinate on the demand curve. As we should have expected, it is smaller, since it lies farther to the right along the demand curve. The difference arises, of course, with the weights, or the ratio of price to quantity, that are inserted into the elasticity calculation. Both pairs of weights are correct for a particular point but are not applicable to the entire range of points over the length of the arc. While the elasticity value of 3 is appropriate at the price of $8, it is progressively more inappropriate as we move down the demand curve. Similarly, while the elasticity value of 1.91 is correct for the price of $7, it becomes progressively more inappropriate as we move up the demand curve. Clearly, to describe the elasticity of demand in the region of the price change between $7 and $8, or $8 and $7, we need a compromise pair of weights to insert in the elasticity formula.

The values of price and quantity that would minimize the variance from all price and quantity points on an arc of the demand curve are the values at the midpoint of that arc. The values at the midpoint are in turn the *average price and quantity values,* and hence the formula for arc elasticity of demand uses as weights the average price and average quantity:

*＊ AVE FOR ARC*

$$\epsilon = -\frac{Q_1 - Q_2}{P_1 - P_2} \cdot \frac{(P_1 + P_2)/2}{(Q_1 + Q_2)/2}$$

$$= -\frac{Q_1 - Q_2}{P_1 - P_2} \cdot \frac{P_1 + P_2}{Q_1 + Q_2}$$

$$= -\frac{-12}{1} \cdot \frac{15}{76}$$

$$= 2.37$$

It can be seen that the value of the arc price elasticity of demand lies between the two values of the point elasticities calculated above. We should expect this, of course, since the arc elasticity is actually the point elasticity at the midpoint of the arc.[4] It is, however, a better *summary measure* of the elasticity over the

[4] Other formulas have been suggested for arc elasticity, such as using the new price and the old quantity, or the old price and the new quantity. These formulations are inferior, since they base the elasticity calculation on a combination of $P$ and $Q$ which does not lie on the demand curve.

arc than are the point elasticity values at either extreme on that arc. The arc elasticity value becomes progressively less accurate as we move toward the end of the arc, but the degree of inaccuracy is much less than the value given by the point elasticity at the *other* end of the arc.

The second line of the above calculation is the most convenient form of the expression for arc elasticity, so let us now state it formally as Eq. (4.16):

$$\epsilon = -\frac{Q_1 - Q_2}{P_1 - P_2} \cdot \frac{P_1 + P_2}{Q_1 + Q_2} \tag{4.16}$$

### Implications of Price Elasticity
### for Optimal Prices

Suppose we know the current price, output level, and marginal cost per unit for one of the products our firm produces. We should query whether we are in fact charging the profit-maximizing price for that product. This question can be answered given an estimate of the price elasticity at the current price. As an example, suppose that price is $12 per unit, output level is 5,000, and marginal cost per unit is constant at $5. A study[5] reveals that a 10 percent reduction in price would increase sales by 40 percent, and hence price elasticity is estimated at 4.0.

To ascertain whether $12 is the optimal price, we should find marginal revenue and compare it with the marginal cost figure of $5, since the profit-maximizing condition[6] is to expand output or reduce price until MR = MC. From Eq.(4.15) we can find MR, given knowledge of $P$ and $\epsilon$. That is:

$$MR = P\left(1 - \frac{1}{\epsilon}\right) \tag{4.15}$$

$$= 12\,(1 - \tfrac{1}{4})$$

$$= 12\,(1 - 0.25)$$

$$= 12\,(0.75)$$

$$= 9 \qquad MC = 5 \Rightarrow MR > MC$$

Since MR > MC, the current price is *too high* for profit maximization and thus should be reduced until MR = 5. But we cannot "plug in" MR = 5 in Eq.(4.15) and solve for $P$, since $\epsilon$ varies as we move down the demand curve. The value $\epsilon = 4$ would thus be an overstatement of $\epsilon$ for all prices below $12. Instead we need to find an expression for MR that is valid for all values of $P$. We know the MR *curve* is appropriate for all values of $P$ and $Q$, and that it has the same intercept and twice the slope of the demand curve.

[5] In Chapter 5 we examine means of estimating price elasticity of demand.

[6] This should be familiar to you from your basic microeconomics course. In any case it is explained in Chapter 1.

Let us reconstruct the expression for the MR curve from the information already held. The demand curve was expressed earlier as

$$P_x = a - bQ_x \qquad (4.4)$$

for which we know $P_x = 12$ and $Q_x = 5$ (in thousands). We need to find the values of the intercept and slope parameters $a$ and $b$ in order to derive an expression for the MR curve. The slope parameter $b$ $(= dP_x/dQ_x)$ is also involved (in its reciprocal form) in the expression for price elasticity:

$$\epsilon = -\frac{dQ_x}{dP_x} \cdot \frac{P_x}{Q_x} \qquad (4.9)$$

We know $\epsilon = 4$, $P_x = 12$, and $Q_x = 5$. Substituting these values in Eq.(4.9), we solve for $dQ_x/dP_x$ as follows:

$$4 = \frac{dQ_x}{dP_x} \cdot \frac{12}{5}$$

$$\frac{4\,(5)}{12} = \frac{dQ_x}{dP_x}$$

$$\therefore \quad \frac{dQ_x}{dP_x} = 1.667$$

Since $\quad \dfrac{dQ_x}{dP_x} = \dfrac{1}{b}$

$$b = \frac{1}{1.667}$$

$$b = 0.6$$

Substituting for $P_x$, $b$, and $Q_x$ in Eq.(4.4), we can solve for the parameter $a$ as follows:

$$12 = a - 0.6\,(5)$$

$$\therefore \quad a = 12 + 0.6\,(5)$$

$$\therefore \quad a = 15$$

We now have the values of both $a$ and $b$ to insert in the expression for MR derived earlier. That is:

$$MR_x = a - 2bQ_x \qquad (4.7)$$

$$= 15 - 2\,(0.6)\,Q_x$$

$$\therefore \quad MR_x = 15 - 1.2\,Q_x$$

Now, since the profit-maximizing condition is MR = MC, and since MC = 5, we can substitute for MR and solve for the profit-maximizing value of $Q_x$. Thus

$$5 = 15 - 1.2\,Q_x$$

$$1.2\,Q_x = 15 - 5$$

$$Q_x = \frac{10}{1.2}$$

$$\therefore \quad Q_x = 8.333$$

Substituting for $Q_x$, $a$, and $b$ in Eq.(4.4), we can find the price level associated with the profit-maximizing output:

$$P_x = 15 - 0.6\,(8.333)$$

$$= 15 - 5$$

$$\therefore \quad P_x = 10$$

Thus the profit-maximizing price is $10, rather than the present $12, if the estimate of price elasticity is accurate.

In Chapter 11 we shall examine the practice of "markup pricing," in which the firm adds a percentage markup to direct costs in order to determine price. We shall see there that the profit-maximizing markup percentage depends on the value of price elasticity of demand.

### A Priori Guestimation
### of Price Elasticity

What factors would lead us to expect the price elasticity for one product to be greater, or smaller, than for another product? The theory of consumer behavior points to the following two major factors as being determinants of the value of price elasticity:

1. The substitutability of the product
2. The relative expense of the product

We saw in the preceding chapter that the substitution effect of a price change is always negative; that is, a price change in one direction will lead to a quantity demanded response in the opposite direction. This substitution effect is the result of consumers' seeking alternative means of satisfying a particular desire, and they do this by switching to an available substitute product. Thus the greater the number of substitute products, and the more closely substitutable are those products, the more we would expect consumers to switch away from a particular product when its price rose, or toward that product when its price fell. Thus the more substitutes, and the more closely these substitutes resemble the product in question, the greater we expect the price elasticity of demand for that product to be.

A feature of products that is related to this substitutability is their versatility, or the number of uses to which they may be put. A product is more versatile if it can serve two or more purposes than if it serves only one purpose. A *more versatile* product is likely to be *less substitutable*, since it may require two or more other products to serve the purposes of the more versatile product. Hence the more versatile the product, the less sensitive is its demand likely to be to price changes, and vice versa.

Regarding the availability of substitutes, we need to distinguish between substitutability of products from within the same group of products and substitutability from other groups of products. For example, "coffee" is a genus of product in the larger family of beverages; but within the product group of coffee, there are many different brands and types. If we are concerned with the price elasticity of a particular brand of coffee, such as Maxwell House, and the prices of all other coffees and other beverages remain unchanged, we should expect the price elasticity for Maxwell House coffee to be relatively high. On the other hand, if all coffee prices were likely to rise in unison (due to an increase in the price of the imported coffee beans, for example), there would be little or no substitutability between or among coffee brands, but there may be substitutability away from coffee as a class toward other groups of beverages, Therefore, in the case where all close substitutes are expected to follow a similar price strategy, we expect the price elasticity to be somewhat lower, since the substitutability will be toward only the more distant substitutes.

The relative expense of the product as a determinant of price elasticity is related to the income effect of a price change. You will recall from the preceding chapter that for any product, when price is increased for example, the consumer suffers a loss in real income. The consumer is thus able to buy less of all products, including the product for which the price has risen. The larger the fraction of the consumer's budget that the purchase of this product represents, the larger would we expect a given percentage change in price in that product to influence the consumer's real income level. It is clear that a 10 percent change in the price of an automobile, for example, would cause the consumer's real income to be changed considerably, whereas a 10 percent change in the price of bread would have a minimal impact. Alternatively, one might argue that for a given percentage change in a low-priced product as compared with a high-priced product, consumers are less sensitive to the smaller absolute change, and hence price elasticity will tend to be lower when the absolute cost of the item is lower and/ or when the cost, relative to their income level, is lower.

In view of the above factors influencing elasticity, would you expect the price elasticity of demand for kitchen salt to be high or low? With regard to substitutability, it would seem that salt has few close substitutes for its kitchen uses. The relative expense, or proportion of the consumer's income spent on that commodity, is invariably very low. Thus both the substitutability and the relative expense factors militate in favor of salt having a relatively low price elasticity of demand. On the other hand, consider the demand for a particular automobile, such as a Chevrolet Caprice. There are numerous substitute automobiles, many of them quite close substitutes while others are more distant substitutes. The proportion of the consumer's income that is involved in the purchase of an automobile is typically high. Hence both determinants militate in favor of the price elasticity for a particular automobile being quite high. If the price of all automobiles has risen simultaneously, such as at the start of a new model year, the elasticity of demand faced by the Chevrolet Caprice would have been somewhat lower, since the substitutability toward other products is limited to the more distant substitutes such as mass transit, bicycles, and walking.

In some cases the substitutability of a product will indicate high price elasticity, while the relative expense will indicate low price elasticity, or vice versa. Guestimation of the value of price elasticity must then proceed on the basis of judgment as to which factor will be stronger if a decision must be taken immediately. If the decision can be delayed, then research into the nature of the demand function and its elasticities should be undertaken. This, however, is the subject matter of the following chapter. We turn now to some other important elasticity measures.

## 4.4 INCOME ELASTICITY OF DEMAND

The income elasticity of demand measures the responsiveness of quantity demanded of a particular product to changes in consumer income, *ceteris paribus.* It is defined as the proportionate change in quantity demanded, divided by the proportionate change in consumer income. In algebraic terms it may be expressed as follows:

$$\theta = \frac{dQ_x/Q_x}{dY/Y} \tag{4.17}$$

where $\theta$ (theta) is the conventional symbol for income elasticity, $dQ_x/Q_x$ represents the proportionate change in the quantity demanded of Product X, and $dY/Y$ is the proportionate change in the consumer's income level.[7]

### The Engel Curve

Just as the demand curve showed the responsiveness of quantity demanded to the price level, there is a curve that is often constructed to show the responsiveness of quantity demanded to changes in consumers' income levels. This curve is known as the Engel curve and is illustrated in Figure 4.8. The Engel curve shown in the figure is concave from above, indicating that as incomes rise, consumers demand progressively smaller increments of Product X. This information may be obtained through cross-section studies, or in a theoretical sense from the indifference curve analysis of individual consumers as outlined in the preceding chapter.

Suppose we wish to calculate the income elasticity of demand for Product X at point *A* in Figure 4.8. Using the same technique we used above to find the point price elasticity of demand, we begin by placing a tangent against the Engel

[7] The formula is in terms of "point" income elasticity, as is the ensuing discussion. Both are easily modified for "arc" income elasticity (which is appropriate when there is a discrete change in consumer income) by using the average income level and the average quantity demanded.

**FIGURE 4.8**
Engel curve for a <u>necessity good</u>

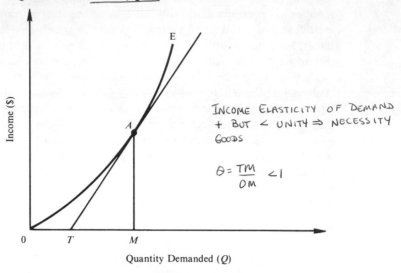

curve at point $A$ and extending it to cut the horizontal axis at point $T$. The point vertically below point $A$, on the quantity axis, is labeled point $M$. Let us now restate Eq.(4.17) as follows:

$$\theta = \frac{dQ_x}{dY} \cdot \frac{Y}{Q_x} \qquad (4.18)$$

It is evident that the $dQ_x/dY$ term on the right-hand side of the equation is related to the slope of the Engel curve; in fact, it is the inverse of the slope, since $dQ_x$ represents the horizontal run, while $dY$ represents the vertical rise. The slope of the Engel curve at point $A$ is given by the slope of the tangent to the Engel curve and hence may be expressed as the ratio $AM/TM$. Thus the reciprocal of the slope is $TM/AM$. The second term in Eq.(4.18) is the level of income divided by the level of quantity demanded at point $A$. In terms of Figure 4.8 this can be expressed as the ratio $AM/OM$. Thus Eq.(4.18) may be restated as follows:

$$\theta = \frac{TM}{AM} \cdot \frac{AM}{OM}$$

which simplifies to

$$\theta = \frac{TM}{OM} \qquad (4.19)$$

### Necessities, Luxuries, and Inferior Goods

*Necessities.*    Calculating the value of the income elasticity allows us to <u>classify products as necessities or luxuries or inferior goods</u>. It is evident in Figure

138

4.8 that the ratio *TM/OM* is less than unity. Products with an income elasticity of demand that is positive but less than unity are known as necessity goods. Examples of so-called necessities are prevalent among foodstuffs and items of apparel for which the quantity demanded increases less than proportionately as income increases.

*Luxuries.* For many products the proportionate change in quantity demanded is greater than the proportionate change in consumer income levels, and hence income elasticity is greater than one. We call such products luxury goods. The Engel curve for a luxury good is illustrated in Figure 4.9. The income elasticity at point *A*, applying the formula given by Eq.(4.19), is clearly greater

**FIGURE 4.9**
**Engel curve for a luxury good**

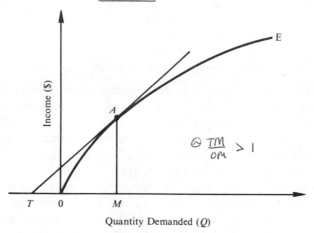

Quantity Demanded (*Q*)

than unity, since the distance *TM* exceeds the distance 0*M*. Examples of luxury goods are items such as fur coats, travel by air, and the use of hotel accommodation.

*Inferior Goods.* A third group of commodities may exhibit an income elasticity that is negative. These products experience a decline in quantity demanded as income levels rise and are known as inferior goods. The Engel curve for an inferior good is illustrated in Figure 4.10. Notice that at lower income levels this particular product behaves like a necessity, since the slope of the Engel curve is initially positive. After a particular income level, however, the Engel curve bends backward and becomes negatively sloping. Calculating the income elasticity at point *A* on the Engel curve using the formula supplied by Eq.(4.19), we derive a negative *TM* distance over the positive distance 0*M*, such that income elasticity takes a negative value. Examples of inferior goods, that is, goods for which consumers tend to reduce their total quantity demanded as their income rises (or increase their total demand as incomes fall), may be items such as potatoes, beans, ground beef, and bologna.

**FIGURE 4.10**
Engel curve for an inferior good

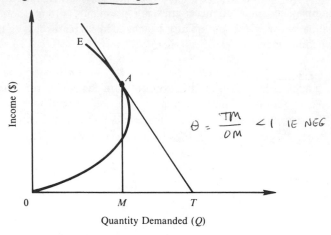

$$\theta = \frac{TM}{OM} < 1 \quad \text{IE NEG}$$

Income ($)

0    M    T

Quantity Demanded ($Q$)

### Business Implications of Income Elasticity

The implications of income elasticity of demand to the business decision maker are considerable. If the income elasticity for your product exceeds unity, then the demand for your product will grow more rapidly than does total consumer income, or it will fall more rapidly than does total consumer income when income levels are generally falling. Hence while income elasticity greater than one in a growing economy indicates a "growth industry," it also indicates a greater susceptibility to fluctuations in the level of aggregate economic activity. On the other hand, if the income elasticity of demand for your product is positive but less than one, the demand for your product will grow more slowly than the gross national product or consumer income but will be relatively "recession proof" in the sense that it will not react in the volatile fashion of luxury goods. Third, if your product is regarded by the market as a whole as an inferior good, you must expect the quantity demanded of your product to decline as the gross national product rises, yet exhibit an anticyclical pattern when the economy is subject to fluctuations in the level of aggregate activity. Good corporate and product planning would therefore indicate the desirability of having all three types of products in your product mix.

## 4.5   CROSS ELASTICITIES AND OTHER ELASTICITIES

### Cross-Price Elasticities

Cross-price elasticity of demand measures the responsiveness of the quantity demanded of Product X to a change in the price of a different product. It is defined as the proportionate change in quantity demanded of X divided by the proportionate change in the price of another product, Y. This can be expressed as follows:

140

$$\eta = \frac{dQ_x/Q_x}{dP_Y/P_Y} \tag{4.20}$$

where $\eta$ (eta) is the conventional symbol for cross elasticity.[8] $dQ_x/Q_x$ is the proportionate change in quantity demanded of Product X, and $dP_Y/P_Y$ is the proportionate change in the price of Product Y. Reorganizing terms, we may restate this as follows:

$$\eta = \frac{dQ_x}{dP_Y} \cdot \frac{P_Y}{Q_x} \tag{4.21}$$

The value of the cross elasticity between two products allows us to specify the relationship between the products as one of either substitutability or complementarity.

### Substitutes and Complements

*Substitutes.* Suppose the price of *Product Y* is reduced from $10 to $9, which induces a change in the quantity demanded of *Product X* from 100 units to 85 units, as shown in Figure 4.11. Inserting these values into Eq.(4.21), we see that the cross elasticity between Product X and Product Y is equal to 1.5.[9]

**FIGURE 4.11**
**Cross elasticity between substitute products**

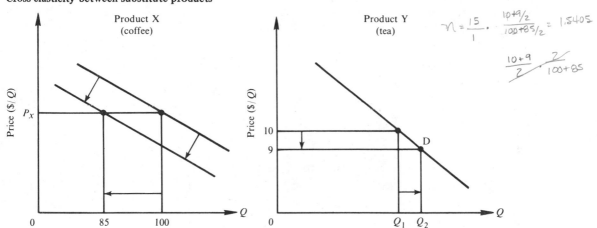

In terms of Figure 4.11 it is clear that Products X and Y must be substitutes for each other, since when the price of Product Y was reduced, the quantity demanded of Product X was reduced from 100 units back to 85 units. Given that

[8] We traditionally shorten the term "cross-price elasticity" to "cross elasticity," by which it is implicit that we mean cross-*price* elasticity, not cross-advertising elasticity or any other cross elasticity.

[9] Strictly we should use the average values of $P_y$ and $Q_x$, since we are discussing an "arc" cross-elasticity situation. The changes in $P_y$ and $Q_x$ were not infinitesimal. Using the average values, the cross elasticity is 1.5405.

*ceteris paribus* prevails, it is clear that the gain of quantity demanded for Product Y came at the expense of the demand for Product X. Recall that the price of Product Y enters the demand function for Product X as a shift parameter; a reduction in the price of Product Y would cause the demand curve for Product X to shift to the left; such that at price $P_x$ the quantity demanded for Product X would be somewhat less. Examples of a pair of substitute products include the product groups of tea and coffee, or pairs of products within either of these groups, such as Maxwell House coffee and Yuban coffee.

*Complements.* On the other hand, suppose a 10 percent price reduction for Product Y leads to a 20 percent *increase* in demand for Product X. Such a situation is illustrated in Figure 4.12. In this case it is clear that the price reduction in Product Y, while being accompanied by an increase in the demand for Product Y, was also accompanied by an increase in the demand for Product X. Given *ceteris paribus*, it is clear that the increase in consumption of Product Y called forth an increase in the consumption of Product X, notwithstanding that the price of Product X did not change. Hence Products X and Y are complementary goods in that they are apparently used jointly in consumption in some predetermined ratio. Notice that in this case the cross elasticity of demand between Product X and Product Y must have a negative sign. Examples of products with negative cross elasticity are coffee and cream, beer and pretzels, and gasoline and tires.

**FIGURE 4.12**
**Cross elasticity between complementary products**

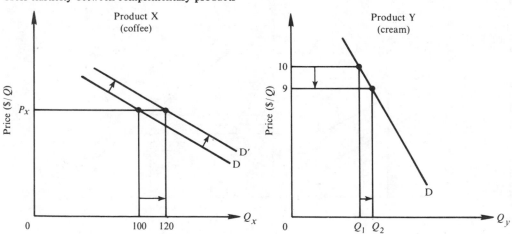

Alternatively, a change in price of Product Y might have zero or minimal impact upon the demand for Product X. In this case we must conclude that Products X and Y are unrelated in consumption. That is, Products X and Y are neither substitutes nor complements. Table 4.3 summarizes the relationships existing between the cross elasticity of demand and the relationship that apparently exists between the two products under examination. As can be seen in the

**TABLE 4.3**
Substitutes, complements, and cross elasticity of demand

| Cross Elasticity | Relationship | Increase in $P_Y$ | Decrease in $P_Y$ |
|---|---|---|---|
| $+$ $\quad \infty > \eta > 0$ | Substitutes | $Q_x$ rises | $Q_x$ falls |
| $\quad \eta \simeq 0$ | Unrelated | $Q_x$ unchanged | $Q_x$ unchanged |
| $-$ $\quad 0 > \eta > -\infty$ | Complements | $Q_x$ falls | $Q_x$ rises |

table, cross elasticity may vary over the range from infinity to minus infinity, and hence the relationship of substitutability or complementarity varies from very strong substitutability or complementarity to quite weak substitutability or complementarity as cross elasticity approaches zero from either the positive or the negative side.

At what level do we define cross elasticity as indicating that we have a pair of "strong" substitutes as compared with "weak" substitutes? Alternatively, how large and negative must the cross-elasticity value be before we decide that the products are "strong" complements rather than simply "weak" complements? In fact, the answer is quite arbitrary. A cross-elasticity value of 2 will mean that a competitor's price adjustment will have a significant impact upon your quantity demanded, but whether we would call this a strong or a weak relationship is essentially a matter of taste. Certainly if another product shared a cross elasticity with your product of 5, for example, we would be able to say that the latter product is a *stronger* substitute for your product than is the former product.

### Advertising and Cross-Advertising Elasticities

We know from the demand function that the quantity demanded of Product X will be responsive to both the advertising in support of Product X and the advertising in support of related products. The advertising elasticity of demand for Product X measures the responsiveness of the change in quantity demanded to a change in advertising budget expended for Product X. We expect a positive relationship between advertising and quantity demanded, but we also expect that the responsiveness of sales to advertising will decline as advertising expenditure continues to increase. Hence advertising elasticity will decline as advertising expenditure increases. There will be a lower limit on the value of the advertising elasticity if advertising expenditure is not to be carried beyond an optimal level. We defer this issue until Chapter 14 where we will see that the critical value of advertising expenditure (and hence advertising elasticity) depends upon the profit contribution expected from each additional unit sold as a result of the advertising.

Cross-advertising elasticity measures the responsiveness of quantity demanded (sales) of Product X to a change in the advertising efforts directed at another product, Y. We expect cross-advertising elasticity to be negative between substitute products and positive between complementary products. For example, increased advertising efforts for a particular movie would be expected to reduce the quantity demanded (sales) of admission tickets to other movies and attractions but increase the sales of the refreshment kiosk in the lobby of that particular movie theatre. In effect, the increased advertising would have shifted the demand curves to the left for all substitute attractions, and shifted the demand curve to the right for the refreshment kiosk.

It is clear that we might calculate the elasticity of demand with respect to any of the independent variables in the demand function. For example, under some conditions, such as high levels of migration or high fertility rates, the population elasticity of demand might be of considerable value to the decision maker. Using the general concept of elasticities, we could construct the appropriate formula and measure population elasticity or any other elasticity useful for decision-making purposes.

### The Value of Elasticities

Many would argue that the various elasticities of demand simply summarize information that is already known to the decision maker, and that if one has the information necessary to calculate the elasticities of demand, then the elasticity value is redundant. (In the case of price elasticity for example, if one knows the two price and quantity coordinates, one can quite simply calculate the change in total revenue that results when moving from one coordinate to the other.) So the question arises, Why calculate elasticities?

Essentially the value of elasticities is twofold. First, they are useful as a summary measure which indicates at a glance the direction of change in total revenue given a price change, or whether products are substitutes, complements, luxury, necessity, or inferior. The magnitude, and in some cases the sign, of the various elasticity measures says in the briefest way possible what there is to know about the relationship between the two variables. Second, by categorizing this relationship in the terms of a single number, we are able to reduce a variety of relationships between products to a common denominator, such that we may rank the values of elasticity for comparison purposes. Hence if Product X is related to a number of other products, we might rank those other products in order of their cross elasticity with Product X. Those with the highest value of cross elasticity would be the stronger substitutes, and those with the largest negative values would be the stronger complements.

Moreover, we shall see in Chapter 11 that the calculation of price elasticity facilitates selection of the optimal markup to be applied to costs in order to determine the profit-maximizing prices of various products. In fact, the value of price elasticity provides the link between the pricing theory of economics and the pricing practice of the marketplace!

## 4.6 SUMMARY

In this chapter we examined the *demand function,* which expresses the dependence of the quantity demanded (or sales) of a particular product upon a variety of independent variables. We examined the impact we would expect changes in these variables to have upon the quantity demanded of a particular product. The *demand curve* was defined as part of the demand function when price is the only variable independent factor. That is to say, all other factors remain constant while price changes *along* a particular demand curve. If any other factor does not remain constant we must expect a *shift* in the demand curve, which will cause a differing quantity to be demanded at the prevailing price level.

The relationship between price, quantity demanded, total revenue, and marginal revenue was examined, and it was determined that for any negatively sloping demand curve, total revenue would increase at first as price is reduced but would later decline. Consequently, marginal revenue would be positive at first, and later negative. Where the demand curve is horizontal, marginal revenue will be constant and equal to the current price level, and hence the total revenue curve will be a proportionate function of quantity demanded.

Several measures of the elasticity of quantity demanded were discussed. Price elasticity of demand is particularly useful for indicating the direction of change in total revenue when there is a particular directional change in price. Moreover, where a firm has several products, the relative price elasticities of these products will indicate which of these products can best sustain a price increase versus those for which a price increase would be a poor strategy. Income elasticity of demand is important for growth and stability considerations in the firm, since the demand for luxury products will tend to be relatively responsive to changes both up and down in the aggregate level of activity. Similarly, necessity goods were argued to be relatively recession proof, and inferior goods are expected to exhibit countercyclical demand patterns.

Cross elasticities of demand allow the summary and classification of the relationships existing between a particular product and all other products. The decision maker should be interested in knowing which of the other products on the market are substitutes for a particular product, and which of these represent the more serious competition to that product. Alternatively, product line considerations require knowledge of the complementarity of other products with a particular product, and negative values of cross elasticity indicate product complementarity, and the relative strength of this complementarity.

The concepts and principles outlined in this chapter will be called upon in subsequent chapters. Pricing of the product requires a strong knowledge of the demand conditions existing in a particular market, and hence an understanding of the responsiveness of demand to the various factors that influence that demand is of considerable importance.

## DISCUSSION QUESTIONS

4.1    Which factors do you think should be held constant while discussing the demand curve for season tickets to the home games of a National Football League team?

4.2    What is the relationship between the coefficient of price in the demand function and the slope term in the demand curve? Explain.

4.3    Set up a matrix with $\epsilon > 1$, $\epsilon = 1$, $\epsilon < 1$ down the left-hand side, and "TR increases" and "TR decreases" along the top. Fill in the six parts of the matrix to indicate whether the coordinates imply an increase or a decrease in the price level.

4.4    Summarize the methodological error and the resultant overestimate or underestimate that is involved when the point elasticity formula is used to calculate elasticity from observations of discrete price and quantity changes.

4.5    Explain how you could calculate the price elasticity at any particular price if you know the parameter values in the mathematical expression for a particular demand curve.

4.6    Classify the probable price elasticity value of the following products as either "relatively high" or "relatively low":

 (a) soft drinks,

 (b) Coca-Cola,

 (c) Diet Pepsi,

 (d) compact automobiles,

 (e) Levi jeans.

(Support each classification with your reasoning.)

4.7    What is the difference between an Engel curve and the income consumption curve discussed in Chapter 3?

4.8    Explain why you would expect the demand for luxury goods such as fur coats and jewelry to be more volatile in periods of fluctuating incomes as compared with items such as groceries and meat.

4.9    How would you explain two products having both a positive cross-price elasticity of demand and a positive cross-advertising elasticity of demand?

4.10    Define the "rainfall elasticity" of demand for umbrellas, using your knowledge of the elasticity concept. What possible usefulness could such an elasticity have?

## PROBLEMS

4.1    The Silverstein Coffee Co. faces the following demand schedule in the relevant price range for one of its products.

| Price (lb) | Quantity demanded (lb/wk) |
|---|---|
| $5.00 | 970 |
| 4.95 | 1,000 |
| 4.90 | 1,026 |
| 4.85 | 1,049 |
| 4.80 | 1,071 |
| 4.75 | 1,085 |
| 4.70 | 1,095 |
| 4.65 | 1,105 |
| 4.60 | 1,114 |
| 4.55 | 1,122 |

 (a) Plot the associated demand curve, marginal revenue curve, and total revenue curve on a graph.

 (b) Calculate the price elasticity for each price change.

 (c) Over what range is demand (1)elastic, (2)inelastic, (3)unitary elastic?

4.2   Billabong Boomerangs Inc. and Swahili Spears are direct competitors in the fast-growing segment of the hunters' equipment market. Due to the recent intense competition, both companies have redeveloped their main product, requiring the users' skills to be less developed than before and thus avoiding extensive field trips for company representatives for on-the-job training. This also reduced the need for costly instruction manuals. Stephen Pesner, president of Billabong Boomerangs, has decided to hire a local market research company to assist his company in planning its strategy. After extensive research in the woods, using new modern methods of data collection and statistical analysis, the researchers came up with Billabong's demand function:

$$Q_B = -1700\,P_B + 750\,Y_H + 350\,A_B - 250\,A_S + 1585\,P_S + 1.05\,\text{Pop} + 7.25\,W$$

where    $Q_B$  is the quantity demanded of boomerangs,

$P_B$  is the price of boomerangs,

$Y_H$  is the average income of hunters (in thousands),

$A_B$  is the advertising budget for Billabong Boomerangs (in thousands),

$A_S$  is the advertising budget for Swahili Spears (in thousands),

$P_S$  is the price of spears,

Pop  is the total population (in millions), and

$W$  is the estimated population of wildlife (in hundreds).

The current values of the independent variables are $P_B$ = 29.95, $Y_H$ = 12.5, $A_B$ = 680, $A_S$ = 525, $P_S$ = 32.25, Pop = 24.68, and $W$ = 8.75.

(a)   What is the current level of demand for Billabong boomerangs?

(b)   Calculate the values of price elasticity, cross-price elasticity, and advertising elasticity.

(c)   Is the price of boomerangs too high or too low in view of Mr. Pesner's desire to maximize profits? Explain.

4.3   Suppose the demand function for a particular firm's Product X has been estimated as

$$Q_x = 5{,}030 - 3806.2\,\overset{8}{P_x} + 458.5\,\overset{9}{P_y} + 256.6\,\overset{168}{A_x} - 32.3\,\overset{182}{A_y} + 0.018\,\overset{9875}{Y}$$

where    $Q_x$ = demand for Product X (in units),

$P_x$ = price of Product X (in dollars),

$P_y$ = price of Product Y (in dollars),

$A_x$ = advertising expenditure for X ($000),

$A_y$ = advertising expenditure for Y ($000), and

$Y$ = per capita disposable income (dollars).

The current values of the independent variables are $P_x$ = 8, $P_y$ = 9, $A_x$ = 168, $A_y$ = 182, and $Y$ = 9,875.

(a)   Calculate the price elasticity of demand for Product X.

(b)   Calculate the advertising elasticity of demand for Product X.

$$\varepsilon = -\frac{dQ_x}{dP_x}\cdot\frac{P_x}{Q_x} \qquad Q_x = 25{,}419.6$$

(c)   If the marginal cost of output is constant at $4 per unit, should the firm change its price? To what extent, and why?

4.4   The Gutowski Grocery Company markets a brand of a particular food item for which there are a number of reasonably similar substitutes. The company has been subject to a series of cost increases recently but feels that the present level of costs is expected to continue in the near future. These recent cost increases have caused the monthly profit to fall below the target of $15,000, and the management feels that this target could be attained if the price were to be reduced to $3.99 unit, presuming that rivals are unlikely to retaliate. Average variable costs are constant up to the maximum output level of 120,000 units. The following data refer to this month's operations.

| | |
|---|---:|
| Variable costs per unit | $2.74 |
| All other costs per unit | 1.57 |
| Price per unit | 4.45 |
| Total profit for month | $11,431.28 |

(a)   What is the price elasticity of demand for the product in the vicinity of the present and contemplated price levels?

(b)   Is $3.99 the profit-maximizing price level? If not, why not?

(c)   Find the profit-maximizing price and the maximum profit level. (Show all calculations and defend your methodology.)

4.5   The Thompson Textile Company has asked you for advice as to the optimality of its pricing policy with respect to one of its products, Product X. The following data are supplied.

| | |
|---|---:|
| Sales (units) | 282,500 |
| Price per unit | $2.00 |
| Marginal cost per unit is constant at | $1.00 |
| Price elasticity of demand | 3.25 |

(a)   Is the present price level optimal if the firm wishes to maximize profits?

(b)   If not, can you say what price it should charge?

4.6   The Bustraen Company manufactures an electric motor that is used in various domestically made washing machines. The washing machine industry purchased its requirements last year as follows:

| *Supplier* | *Quantity* | *Price (unit)* |
|---|---:|---:|
| Bustraen | 108,000 | $15.95 |
| Chernoff | 68,560 | 16.35 |
| Dunham | 240,867 | 14.42 |
| Frohlich | 43,236 | 15.95 |
| Kleiman | 22,481 | 13.95 |

The electric motors from the various suppliers vary in quality, as do the washing machines that use the various motors. The Bustraen Company has a capacity limit of 110,000 units with its present production facilities and is considering increasing its capacity for next year. Total demand for electric motors is expected to remain at approximately the same level next year. A breakdown of cost data for last year is as follows:

| Materials | $421,200 |
| Direct labor | 567,000 |
| Indirect labor | 163,080 |
| Fuel and power | 36,720 |
| Depreciation | 393,120 |

Bustraen has the opportunity to expand its facilities such that it will have a physical capacity limit of 200,000 units. Estimates are that materials cost will be 15 percent lower per unit and direct labor 12½ percent lower per unit with the new facilities. These per unit costs are constant over the entire output range. Indirect labor, fuel and power, and depreciation, none of which vary substantially with output, are expected to be 40 percent, 80 percent, and 70 percent higher, respectively, as compared with the present overhead costs.

To utilize this additional capacity efficiently, a price reduction would appear to be necessary. The cross elasticity of demand between Bustraen's product and that of each of its competitors is estimated to be as follows:

| Chernoff | 1.9 |
| Dunham | 2.8 |
| Frohlich | 2.3 |
| Kleiman | 5.6 |

Price reductions are likely to go unchallenged by each competitor unless their sales volume is reduced by 10 percent or more, in which case they are expected to reduce price by the same absolute amount (as Bustraen's price reduction).

You are consulted as to whether or not to expand, and what price to charge for the coming year. Explain your decisions and state any possible qualifications to those decisions.

4.7  Paul McLaughlin recently purchased the M.F.F. Company, a large company that specializes in the manufacture of minifreezers. Mr. McLaughlin has a reputation for revitalizing companies and reselling them, and he has purchased this company with the intention of holding onto it for a period of two years after which he would sell the entire operation. The management of the M.F.F. Company gave Mr. McLaughlin the following demand function for their product, which they said was based on a number of years of experience:

$$Q = 3000 - 800P + .05A + 2Y$$

where  $Q$ = quantity demanded each quarter,

$P$ = price,

$A$ = advertising expenditures (dollars per quarter), and

$Y$ = personal disposable income per capita (dollars per annum).

As Mr. McLaughlin's special consultant, you are faced with the following problems:

(a)  Mr. McLaughlin wishes to maximize sales revenue. He informs you that he is allocating $23.5 million each quarter for advertising expenditures and that the estimated personal disposable income per capita is $11,000. In order that he might maximize his sales revenue, what price should be charged for his product and how many minifreezers can he expect to sell at this price level? Illustrate this both mathematically and graphically.

(b)   Alternatively, let us assume that Mr. McLaughlin had originally priced his product at $450 and had set as his goal sales of 2 million minifreezers for the four quarters of the first year. Price ($450) and personal disposable income ($11,000) have remained constant throughout the first three quarters and are not expected to change during the fourth quarter. Given that his advertising expenditures were:

| | |
|---|---|
| First quarter | $18,000,000 |
| Second quarter | $15,000,000 |
| Third quarter | $23,000,000 |

what should his advertising expenditures be for the fourth quarter so that he will be able to reach his goal of 2 million products sold?

4.8   The Alpha Beta Company produces and sells toaster ovens. Mr. Learmonth has just been appointed marketing vice-president and is determined to be the first VP to guide the company past the million-dollar sales mark. To do so, A.B.C. must average $84,000 per month for the last nine months of the year.

Mr. Learmonth has been given a free hand to run the marketing side of A.B.C. subject to the following constraints:

1.   Perceived social responsibilities dictate that A.B.C., as the town's largest employer, produce a minimum of 5,800 units per month to avoid layoffs. With overtime, the plant can turn out a maximum of 8,100 units per month.

2.   Budgetary considerations have limited increases in advertising to 15 percent above current monthly levels ($5,000). A.B.C. has already contracted for a minimum of $5,000 per month with local media.

Mr. Learmonth's first move as VP was to have the Con-Sulting Company, a local marketing research firm, do some analytical work, and this company has developed the following normative model based on statistics supplied by Mr. Learmonth:

$$Q = 3000 + 0.3A + 0.4Y - 300P$$

where $Q$ represents the number of ovens demanded, $A$ represents the monthly advertising expenditure, $Y$ represents the per capita income, and $P$ represents the selling price of the ovens. Current selling price is $14, and current values of $A$ and $Y$ are $5,000 and $14,000, respectively. You have been given the assignment of recommending a strategy for the remainder of the year.

(a)   What price level do you recommend?

(b)   What do you recommend with regard to advertising?

(c)   Calculate the income elasticity.

What does this indicate about the nature of the product? (Make any assumptions required for the solution of the problem, indicating why they were made. Show all calculations.)

# SUGGESTED REFERENCES AND FURTHER READING

BRIGHAM, E. F., and J. L. PAPPAS, *Managerial Economics,* 2nd ed., Chap. 4. Hinsdale, Ill.: Dryden, 1976.

HIRSHLEIFER, J., *Price Theory and Applications,* Chap. 5. Englewood Cliffs, N.J.: Prentice-Hall, 1976.

JOHNSON, A. C., Jr., and P. HELMBURGER, "Price Elasticity of Demand as an Element of Market Structure," *American Economic Review,* (December 1967), 1218-21.

McGUIGAN, J. R., and R. C. MOYER, *Managerial Economics,* Chap. 6. Hinsdale, Ill.: Dryden, 1975.

THOMPSON, A. A., Jr., *Economics of the Firm,* Chap. 5. Englewood Cliffs, N.J.: Prentice-Hall, 1973.

5

# Demand Estimation
# and
# Forecasting

**5.1   Introduction**

**5.2   Direct Methods of Estimating the Demand Function**

Direct vs. Indirect Methods.    Interviews and Surveys.
Simulated Market Situations.    Direct Market Experiments.

**5.3   Indirect Demand Estimation: Regression Analysis**

Time-Series vs. Cross-Section Data.    Linearity of the Regression Equation.
Estimating the Regression Parameters.
The Coefficient of Determination and Other Regression Statistics.
Problems in Regression Analysis: Six Major Pitfalls.
Summary of Regression Analysis.

**5.4   Demand Forecasting**

Intention Surveys.    Projection of Established Relationships.
Barometric Indicators: Leading Indicators and Diffusion Indices.

**5.5   Summary**

## 5.1   INTRODUCTION

Much of the discussion in the foregoing chapters was based on the presumption that we could get reliable data concerning the demand situation. Specifically, we presumed to know the quantities of particular products that would be demanded at various price and income levels, and hence we were able to make optimization decisions and calculate the relevant elasticities of demand. It is obvious, however, that this information may not be readily available. Given the prior expectation that the value of the information will exceed the cost of obtaining that information, the managerial economist must generate the data, using a variety of techniques from market research and statistical analysis. This chapter examines the methods by which we might obtain the data for real-world decision problems.

We distinguish between demand estimation and demand forecasting on the basis of the period for which demand data are sought. *Demand estimation* will be taken to mean the process of finding *current* values of demand for various values of price and the other determining variables. *Demand forecasting* will be taken to mean the process of finding values for demand in *future* time periods. Current values are necessary to evaluate the optimality of current pricing and promotional policies, and in order to make day-to-day decisions in these strategy areas. Future values are necessary for planning production, inventories, new-product development, investment, and other situations where the decision to be made has impacts over a prolonged period of time. In the following discussion we shall treat estimation and forecasting separately, although demand estimation often forms the basis for demand forecasting. We shall examine the major methods of both estimation and forecasting and indicate the major problems and pitfalls one may expect to encounter.

In the preceding chapter we considered the demand function in the form

$$Q = \alpha + \beta_1 P + \beta_2 A + \beta_3 Y + \beta_4 T + \ldots + \beta_n N \qquad (5.1)$$

153

where demand (or sales) is expressed as a function of the variables price, advertising, consumer incomes, consumer tastes and preferences, and whatever other variables are thought to be important in determining the demand for a particular product. The $\beta$ coefficients represent the amount by which sales will be increased (or decreased) following a one-unit change in the value of each of the variables. The present level of each of the variables is known, or can be found with some investigation. It is the coefficients of these variables that are the mystery and are important to us for decision making. That is, we wish to know that if we change a particular independent variable by a certain amount, holding all other variables constant, what do we expect would happen to the sales level? Stated alternatively, we wish to know whether or not a change in the value of any of these variables from their present levels would have a beneficial impact on the attainment of our objectives.

Of course, not all of these independent variables are controllable, in the sense that we have the ability to adjust their level. The *controllable* variables are price, promotional efforts, product design, and the place of sale, which are probably known to you as the "4 P's" of marketing. The *uncontrollable* variables in the demand function are those that change independently of the firm's efforts, and they include such variables as consumer incomes, taste and preference patterns, the actions of competitors, population, weather, and political, sporting, and social events or happenings. But even if the firm is unable to influence these variables, knowledge of the probable value of the coefficients is useful, since it reduces the uncertainty of the impact of changes in those variables. Given an expectation of the effect of increased consumer incomes, for example, the firm is able to plan more effectively its production, inventories, and new-product development, in view of expected changes in the affluence of consumers.

## 5.2  DIRECT METHODS OF ESTIMATING THE DEMAND FUNCTION

### Direct vs. Indirect Methods

Methods of estimating the values of these beta coefficients may be classified as either direct or indirect. *Direct* methods are those that directly involve the consumer, and they include interviews and surveys, simulated market situations, and controlled market experiments. Thus the consumer is either asked what his or her reaction would be to a particular change in a determining variable or is observed when actually reacting to a particular change. *Indirect* demand estimation proceeds on the basis of data that have been collected and attempts to find statistical associations between the dependent and the independent variables. The techniques of simple correlation and multiple-regression analysis are employed to find these relationships. Direct methods of demand estimation are covered in detail in marketing research courses, while indirect methods are examined in quantitative methods courses. In the following discussion we confine ourselves to a general overview of these issues and refer the student to the sources cited at the end of the chapter for more theoretical and detailed treatments.

DIRECT
## Interviews and Surveys

The most direct method of demand estimation is simply to ask buyers or potential buyers how much more or how much less they would purchase of a particular product if its price (or advertising, or one of the other independent variables) were varied by a certain amount. Although seemingly simple, this approach is fraught with difficulties. The first problem is that the individuals interviewed or surveyed must represent the market as a whole so that the results will not be biased. Thus a sufficiently large sample, generated by random procedures, must be interviewed in order to form a reasonable estimate of the market's reaction to a proposed change. Apart from biased samples, however, the results may be unreliable because the buyer is being asked a hypothetical question and doubtless will give a hypothetical answer. The answer may not reflect the buyer's true intentions if the buyer feels that the interviewer wants to hear a different response. This problem (of interviewer bias) is also involved in situations where the true answer would suggest some socially deprecating character trait, such as gluttony or hedonism, and to avoid embarrassment the respondent provides a more socially acceptable answer. Furthermore, even if the answer does reflect the buyer's true intentions, the buyer has every right and a considerable likelihood of changing these intentions before actually making such a purchase decision. Finally, the consumer may be unable to answer the question for the simple reason that the answer is unknowable. For example, if asked how you would react to increased advertising on the part of a particular company for its products, can you say that you would buy more or buy less, and how much more or less you might buy? Not knowing the quality of the advertising, nor the actual impact that type of advertising might have upon you, how could you be expected to give an accurate response?

A great deal of research has gone into the problem of questionnaire formulation in order to derive reliable results from interviews and surveys. Rather than asking questions directly, the answers to a specific question may be derived from the respondent's answer to a number of other questions. Reliability of responses to specific questions may be checked by asking the same questions in a different form at a later time during the interview or questionnaire.[1] Thus the types of questions may include direct questions, indirect questions, and questions asked to verify the answers to preceding questions. The form of the question can influence the nature of the results: open-ended questions allow the consumer to express in his or her own words what the response may be, while structured questions, such as multiple-choice questions where the respondent must use one of four or five specific responses, suggest an answer to the consumer and may bias the results toward something the researcher expected to find. The choice of words is an important consideration, since nuances may be involved and some words have different meanings to different people. The questions must be sequenced in a way that creates and holds the subject's interest, provokes accurate

[1] See, for example, P. E. Green and D. S. Tull, *Research for Marketing Decisions,* 3rd ed. (Englewood Cliffs, N.J.: Prentice-Hall, 1975), esp. Chaps. 4 and 5; and D. J. Luck, H. G. Wales, and D. A. Taylor, *Marketing Research,* 4th ed. (Englewood Cliffs, N.J.: Prentice-Hall, 1974), esp. Chaps. 9 and 10.

155

responses, and does not create an emotional reaction that may influence subsequent answers or cause the respondent to refuse to continue.[2]

Thus the interview or survey approach cannot proceed on the basis of a few simple-minded questions if significant results are to be obtained. Considerable care and thought must enter the construction of the questionnaire, and reasoned analysis must be involved in interpreting the results of the survey. In the case of products that have an established marketing history, these results may be compared with previously obtained results of interviews and other methods of demand estimation in order to determine whether they corroborate or contradict earlier findings. With new products, however, interview results may be the only source of information obtainable, and decisions may need to be made without the support of alternate information sources. An example of a possible survey technique to estimate the demand curve for a new product is given in problem 5.1 at the end of this chapter.

### Simulated Market Situations

A means of finding out what consumers would do in response to changes in price or promotion efforts is to construct an artificial market situation and observe the behavior of selected participants. These so-called consumer clinics often involve giving the participants a certain sum of money and asking them to spend this money in an artificial store environment. Different groups of participants may be faced with different price structures between and among competing products, and/or differing promotional display efforts. If the participants are carefully selected to be representative of the market for these products, we may—after observing their reactions to price changes of different magnitudes and to variations in promotional efforts—conclude that the entire market would respond in the same way.

Results of such simulated market test situations must be viewed carefully, however. Participants may spend someone else's money differently from the way they would spend their own money, a phenomenon amply demonstrated by business executives' use of expense accounts! Alternatively, participants may feel that they are expected to choose a particular product when its price is reduced in order to demonstrate that they are thrifty and responsible shoppers. Consumer clinics are likely to be an expensive method of obtaining data, however, since there is a considerable setup cost, participants must be provided with funds, and the process is relatively time consuming. Given these factors it is likely that the samples involved will be quite small, and hence the results may not be representative of the entire market's reaction to the pricing and promotional changes. Nevertheless such experiments may provide useful insight into the price awareness and consciousness of buyers, and their general reaction to changes in specific promotional variables. A hypothetical example of a simulated market experiment to estimate the demand curve for a product is given in problem 5.2 at the end of this chapter.

[2] See P. Kotler, *Marketing Management,* 3rd ed. (Englewood Cliffs, N.J.: Prentice-Hall, 1976), pp. 430-31.

### Direct Market Experiments

The procedures mentioned under the simulated market situations might be implemented in actual market situations, with the use of past information or information from a control market to compare buyers' reactions to changes in specific variables. In a regional market, for example, the firm might reduce the price of its product by 10 percent and compare the reaction of sales in that market over a particular period with previous sales in that market or current sales in a similar but separate regional market. Alternatively, the firm may increase its advertising in a specific area, or introduce a promotional gimmick or campaign in a particular market, to judge the impact of that change before committing itself to the greater expense and risk of instituting this change on a nationwide basis.

With any change in price or other marketing strategy there is likely to be an initial or "impact" effect, followed by a gradual settling of the market into the new longer-term relationship between price (or other controllable variable) and the sales level. In order to observe more than the impact effects of a change, market experiments must be conducted over a reasonably prolonged period of time. During this period, however, one or more of the uncontrollable variables are likely to have changed, and thus the observed change in sales over the period will not be due simply to the change in the controllable variable. To separate the effects of changes in other variables the researcher may use a "control market," which should be chosen to exhibit a similar socioeconomic and cultural profile and be subject to the same climatic, political, and other uncontrollable events. The change in sales in the control market over the period of the experiment will be due solely to the uncontrollable factors. On the assumption that the same change would have occurred in the test market, this magnitude is deducted from (if positive) or added to (if negative) the change in sales in the test market to find the net change in sales due to the manipulation of the controllable variable(s).

To the extent that an uncontrollable variable changes in the test market but remains constant or changes to a different degree in the control market, the results of the market experiment will be less reliable. Even when the control market is nearby, the climatic influence may vary, local politics may intervene, or some other event may cause an impact on the sales level. Competitors may react to the change in the test market by lowering prices or increasing promotional efforts, for example, while maintaining the status quo in the undisturbed control market. Under such circumstances the market experiment could prove to be an expensive exercise in terms of the reliability of the data generated.

Aside from the setup costs of a market experiment and the risk that these costs will be incurred for unreliable results, there are other costs that may be associated with this form of estimating the parameters of the demand function. Customers lost during the experiment may not be regained after the experiment, since they may be satisfied with a newly tried substitute product. An inelastic response to a price reduction may (depending on the cost situation) cause a loss of profits relative to the continuance of the status quo. And if the price is raised to its former level after the experiment, sales may fall below their former level due to the loss of allegiance of some customers who resent being manipulated or who are provoked otherwise at this point to try a substitute. Longer-term damage to sales in the test market may also be inflicted by a distasteful or insensitive promotional campaign.

Thus direct market experiments must be implemented with caution, some luck must be forthcoming such that uncontrollable variables do not distort the results, and the results must be interpreted with care. If the pitfalls are largely anticipated and subsequently avoided such experiments may provide information, the value of which (in terms of the present value of the additional future sales revenue) far exceeds its cost. We turn now to a means of estimating the demand coefficients from secondary data, in contrast to the above reliance on primary data.

## 5.3  INDIRECT DEMAND ESTIMATION: REGRESSION ANALYSIS

*Regression analysis* is a statistical technique used to discover the apparent dependence of one variable upon one or more other variables. It is thus applicable to the problem of determining the coefficients of the demand function, since these express the influence of the independent variables upon the demand for a product. When the statistical relationship between only two variables is studied, we speak of bivariate correlation analysis, whereas regression analysis is applied to situations in which the influence of more than one independent variable is studied. For correlation analysis we require a number of pairs of observations; that is, the $Y$ values plus the $X$ value corresponding to each of those $Y$ values. For regression analysis we require a number of sets of observations, each consisting of the value of the dependent variable $Y$ plus the corresponding values of the independent $X_i$ variables. The technique of correlation or regression analysis allows conclusions to be drawn from the pattern that emerges in the relationships between these pairs or sets of observations.

### ✳ Time-Series vs. Cross-Section Data

Correlation and regression analysis can be applied to either time-series or cross-section data. Time-series analysis uses the pairs or sets of observations that have been recorded *over time in a particular situation.* For example, monthly price and sales levels of a product in a particular firm may have been collected for the past six or twelve months. A problem with time-series analysis, as indicated earlier, is that some of the uncontrollable factors that influence sales tend to change over time, and hence some of the differences in the sales observations will be due to these influences rather than resulting from any changes in the price level. If the changes in the uncontrollable variables are observable and measurable, we may include these variables as explanatory variables in the regression analysis. Actions of competitors and changing consumer income levels, for example, should be readily quantified (either directly or by use of a suitable proxy variable) and incorporated into the analysis.

Changing taste and preference patterns, on the other hand, are difficult to observe and measure, since they are likely to change relatively slowly over time. Using time as an explanatory variable in the regression analysis will pick up the influence of *all* factors (not otherwise included in the analysis) that tend to change over the period. The resulting trend factor may then be extrapolated into future periods as a proxy for changing consumer tastes and whatever other factors may be changing over time.

Cross-section analysis uses the sets or pairs of observations from different firms in the same business environment at the *same point or period of time*. Hence cross-section analysis largely eliminates the problem of uncontrollable variables that change over time, but it introduces other factors that may differ between and among firms at a particular point of time. If factors such as the effectiveness of sales personnel, cash-flow position, level of promotional activity, and objectives of management differ among firms, they should be expected to have differing impacts on the sales level. Again, if these factors can be quantified and data obtained, then they may be entered into the regression analysis to determine their impact upon the dependent variables.

### Linearity of the Regression Equation

Having hypothesized that $Y$ is a function of $X$ or several $X$ variables and having collected data on the variables, we must then specify the form of the dependence of $Y$ upon the $X$ variables. Regression analysis requires that the dependence be expressed in the linear form

$$Y = \alpha + \beta_1 X_1 + \beta_2 X_2 + \ldots + \beta_n X_n + e \qquad (5.2)$$

where the $e$ term is added to represent the error or residual value that will arise as the difference between the *actual* value of each $Y$ that has been observed in association with each set of $X$ values, and the *estimated* value of each $Y$ that the above regression equation would associate with the set of $X$ values. For individual observations we should expect either a positive or a negative residual term, due to the influence of random variations or unspecified influences on the variable $Y$. In aggregate, however, we expect the residuals to occur randomly, be normally distributed, have constant variance, and have an expected value of zero. When the pattern of residuals does not conform to these restrictions several problems arise, as we shall see later in this section.

Although the regression equation must be of the linear form, the hypothesized relationship between the $Y$ and $X$ values need not be linear. Nonlinear forms such as exponential, hyperbolic, and power functions may be used if these best fit the data, since these forms may be converted to linear form by logarithmic transformation. The most commonly used nonlinear form is the power function, such as

$$Z = aG^{\beta_1} H^{\beta_2} u \qquad (5.3)$$

where $G$ and $H$ are independent variables, and $u$ is the error term, and these have a multiplicative (rather than additive) influence on the dependent variable $Z$. Taking logarithms, we may express Eq.(5.3) as

$$\log Z = \log a + \beta_1 \log G + \beta_2 \log H + \log u \qquad (5.4)$$

By defining $Y = \log Z$, $\alpha = \log a$, $X_1 = \log G$, $X_2 = \log H$, and $e = \log u$, Eq.(5.4) can be transformed to look like Eq.(5.2). In this form the coefficients $\beta_1$ and $\beta_2$ of Eq.(5.3) can be found, and the parameter $a$ will be found by reversing the transformation (taking the antilog) of the $\alpha$ parameter.[3]

### Estimating the Regression Parameters

The "method of least squares" is used to find the $\alpha$ and $\beta$ parameters such that the regression equation—for example, Eq.(5.2) or Eq.(5.3)—best represents or summarizes the apparent relationship between the $X_i$ values and the dependent variable $Y$. In the case of correlation analysis, where we have an equation of the form $Y = \alpha + \beta X + e$, we find the parameters $\alpha$ and $\beta$ such that the sum of the squares of the deviations of the actual values of $Y$ from the values of $Y$ estimated by the line is minimized. The resulting correlation equation will be the "line of best fit" to the data. In terms of Figure 5.1, in which some hypothetical

**FIGURE 5.1**
**The line of best fit**

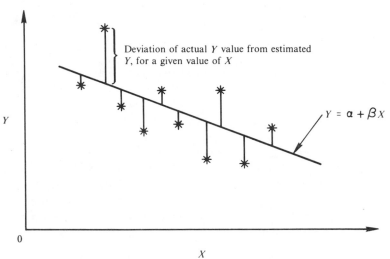

data observations are plotted, the line of best fit is the line that minimizes the total vertical distance between the actual $Y$ observations and the $Y$ values that would be estimated (for each $X$) by the correlation equation. We square these residuals to avoid the positive deviations (those falling above the line) offsetting

[3] For transformation of other nonlinear forms, see J. R. McGuigan and J. C. Moyer, *Managerial Economics* (Hinsdale, Ill.: Dryden, 1975), pp. 137-99.

negative deviations of similar magnitude when these residuals are summed.

Since computer programs (and preprogrammed or programmable hand calculators) for obtaining correlation and regression equations are becoming more readily available, and since the theory underlying regression analysis is typically covered in other courses, we shall not go too deeply into the theory or calculation of regression equations. It is instructive, however, to work through a simple two-variable case to demonstrate some of the issues and problems involved. Without proof, we state the following expressions for $\alpha$ and $\beta$:[4]

$$\beta = \frac{n\Sigma X_i Y_i - \Sigma X_i \Sigma Y_i}{n\Sigma X_i^2 - (\Sigma X_i)^2} \tag{5.5}$$

$$\alpha = \bar{Y} - \beta\bar{X} \tag{5.6}$$

where $n$ is the number of pairs of observations, $\Sigma X_i$ is the sum of the values of the $X$ observations, $\Sigma Y_i$ is the sum of the values of the $Y$ observations, and $i$ equals $1,2,3,..., n$. $\bar{Y}$ ( $= \Sigma Y_i/n$) is the arithmetic mean of the $Y$ observations, and $\bar{X}$ is the arithmetic mean of the $X$ observations. Given a set of $X$ and $Y$ observations, we can solve (preferably using a calculator) for the line of best fit for the relationship that appears to exist between those two variables.

Let us introduce a hypothetical example. Suppose a chain of department stores sells its own brand of frozen broccoli in each of its six stores. The chain is interested in knowing the price elasticity of demand for this product. Its six stores are in similar middle-income suburban neighborhoods, and all are currently selling the item at $0.79 per package. Monthly sales at the six stores average 4,625 units per store, with no store's sales being more than 150 units away from this level. Suppose the management decides to conduct an experiment: it will set the prices at different levels in each of the six stores to observe the reactions of sales to the different price levels. As a control it will maintain the price at $0.79 in the first store. The prices set for the other stores, and the sales levels (in thousands) at each of the six stores over the one-month period of the experiment, are shown in Table 5.1.

The table includes the calculations necessary for the solution of the $\alpha$ and $\beta$ parameters. Using Eq.(5.5), we have

$$\beta = \frac{6(19.506) - 4.96(26.1)}{6(4.5094) - (4.96)^2}$$

$$= \frac{-12.42}{2.4548}$$

$$= -5.0595$$

and from Eq.(5.6), we have

$$\alpha = \bar{Y} - \beta\bar{X}$$

$$= 4.35 - (-5.059)(0.8267)$$

$$= 8.5327$$

[4] See J. Johnston, *Econometric Methods* (New York: McGraw-Hill, 1963), pp. 9-19.

**TABLE 5.1**
Price/sales observations at six stores and calculations
for least-squares analysis

| Store No. | Price $X_i$ ($) | Sales $Y_i$ (000) | $X_iY_i$ | $X_i^2$ | $Y_i^2$ |
|---|---|---|---|---|---|
| 1 | 0.79 | 4.650 | 3.6735 | 0.6241 | 21.6225 |
| 2 | 0.99 | 3.020 | 2.9898 | 0.9801 | 9.1204 |
| 3 | 1.25 | 2.150 | 2.6875 | 1.5625 | 4.6225 |
| 4 | 0.89 | 4.400 | 3.9160 | 0.7921 | 19.3600 |
| 5 | 0.59 | 6.380 | 3.7642 | 0.3481 | 40.1702 |
| 6 | 0.45 | 5.500 | 2.4750 | 0.2025 | 30.2500 |
| | 4.96 ($\Sigma X_i$) | 26.100 ($\Sigma Y_i$) | 19.5060 ($\Sigma X_iY_i$) | 4.5094 ($\Sigma X_i^2$) | 125.1456 ($\Sigma Y_i^2$) |

$$\bar{Y} = \frac{\Sigma Y_i}{n} = \frac{26.1}{6} = 4.35$$

$$\bar{X} = \frac{\Sigma X_i}{n} = \frac{4.96}{6} = 0.8267$$

Thus, $Y = 8.5327 - 5.0595X$ is the "line of best fit" to the data, when sales ($Y$) are measured in thousands of units. As shown in Figure 5.2, the intercept of this line is thus 8,532.7 units on the $Y$ axis and the slope is −5,059.5 units of sales per dollar increase in price (which is to say 50.595 units for each cent the price is increased). The intercept value should not be interpreted as the sales level that would be expected at the price of zero, since the range of price observations is from $0.45 to $1.25, and the values of $\alpha$ and $\beta$ are estimated only for that range. Outside this range a different relationship may hold between $X$ and $Y$. The intercept parameter serves only to locate the line of best fit such that it passes through the observations at the appropriate height. To interpret the inter-

**FIGURE 5.2**
Graphical plot of price/sales observations

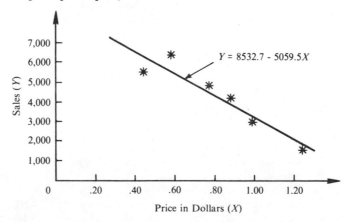

cept as the sales value when price is zero would be an example of the dangerous practice of extrapolation!

Our estimate of the slope of the demand function with respect to changes in the price level is thus 5,059.5 units of sales lost for each additional one-dollar increment in the price level. To calculate elasticity, we must weight this slope by the ratio of the initial price and sales levels as follows:

$$\epsilon = \frac{-dQ}{dP} \cdot \frac{P}{Q}$$

$$= 5059.5 \times \frac{.79}{4625} \qquad \text{USE } Y = 8.5327 - 5.0595 \, (.79)$$

$$4537.25$$

$$= 0.8642$$

The price elasticity of demand in the vicinity of the price level of $0.79 is therefore estimated to be 0.86, indicating an inelastic response to price changes. We should note, however, that the results of this hypothetical experiment may be simply the short-term reaction of consumers to the changes in the price levels. These "impact" effects of a change in a marketing strategy may well differ from the longer-term effects, since buyers in aggregate take time to adjust to changes in their economic environment. If the experiment were to be conducted over a longer time period, with assurances that all other determining factors remained constant, we should expect to find the response of consumers to this price change to be somewhat more elastic than that indicated by the above results.

### The Coefficient of Determination $R^2$ and Other Regression Statistics

How well does this equation explain the relationship between sales and price? Could we confidently use this equation to predict what sales would be at prices of, for example, $0.69 or $1.15? We use the "coefficient of determination" to express the degree of accuracy with which the line of best fit corresponds to the actual observations. Stated without proof, the coefficient of determination may be expressed as

$$R^2 = \left( \frac{n\Sigma X_i Y_i - \Sigma X_i \Sigma Y_i}{\sqrt{[n\Sigma X_i^2 - (\Sigma X_i)^2][n\Sigma Y_i^2 - (\Sigma Y_i)^2]}} \right)^2 \tag{5.7}$$

Inserting the values as calculated in Table 5.1, we have

$$R^2 = \left( \frac{6(19.506) - 4.96(26.1)}{\sqrt{[6(4.5094) - (4.96)^2][6(125.1456) - (26.1)^2]}} \right)^2$$

$$= \left( \frac{-12.42}{\sqrt{171.0102}} \right)^2$$

$$= \left( \frac{-12.42}{13.0771} \right)^2$$

$$= (-0.94975)^2$$

$$= 0.902025$$

It can be demonstrated[5] that the coefficient of determination is equal to the proportion of the variation in $Y$ that is explained by the variation in $X$. Thus we are able to say that slightly more than 90 percent of the variation in the sales observations was due to the influence of the differences in the price levels. The remaining unexplained variance is due to some other influence on sales. This remaining variability could be due to differences in promotional activity, consumer incomes, consumer tastes, or other factors that may differ between and among the six stores.

*Standard Error of Estimate.* A high $R^2$ value alone does not necessarily mean that the regression equation can be used confidently for prediction purposes. Most computer regression programs include as standard output several other statistics which allow the decision maker to evaluate the confidence that may be placed upon certain predictions. The first of these is the *standard error of estimate,* which shows the range within which we can predict the value of the dependent variable and allows us to attach probabilities to the occurrence of the dependent variable within certain parts of this range. Using the properties of a normal distribution, and assuming the error terms are normally distributed about the estimated values, we can say that there is a 68 percent probability that actual observations of the dependent variable will lie within the range given by the estimated value plus or minus one standard error of the estimate. Furthermore, there is a 95 percent probability that the future observations will lie within plus or minus two standard errors of its predicted value, and a 99 percent probability that the observed value will lie within plus or minus three standard errors of the estimated value. Thus, if the standard error of the estimate is relatively small, we can have greater confidence in predicting future values of the dependent variable on the basis of the regression equation.

By adding and subtracting the standard error from the estimated value of $Y$ for each value of $X$, we establish a band within which we can expect the value of $Y$ to fall for a particular value of $X$. A broader band is established when we add or subtract two standard errors of the estimate, and as noted above the probability is raised to 95 percent that the actual observation will lie within this band. The latter band is perhaps the most widely used in decision making, and it establishes what are known as the upper and lower 95 percent confidence limits. That is, we can be 95 percent confident that the actual observation will lie in the band, and that the best and worst outcomes associated with the particular value of the independent varable will be no further than the limits of the band.

The *standard error of the coefficient* provides a measure of the confidence we can place in the coefficient of each independent variable. Again using the features of a normal distribution, we can say that there is a 68 percent probability that the true coefficient will lie in the interval of the estimated coefficient plus

[5] See Johnston, *Econometric Methods,* pp. 30-32, or any introductory statistics textbook.

or minus one standard error of the coefficient; a 95 percent probability that the true coefficient will lie in the interval given by the estimated coefficient plus or minus two standard errors of the coefficient; and a 99 percent probability that the actual relationship will be within plus or minus three standard errors of the coefficient of the estimated marginal relationship. Clearly, the smaller the standard error of the coefficient, the greater the confidence we can put in the regression coefficients generated by the data as being reliable indicators of the true marginal relationships between the $X_i$ values and the $Y$ value.

A simple rule of thumb to test for confidence in the regression coefficient is to take twice the value of the standard error of the coefficient and compare this with the estimated regression coefficient. If the regression coefficient exceeds twice its standard error, we can be 95 percent confident that the estimated coefficient does show the true marginal relationship. Alternatively, if the regression program generates "$t$" statistics for each independent variable, we would require that the $t$ value exceeds 2, since the $t$ statistic is calculated as the correlation (or regression) coefficient divided by its standard error adjusted for the degrees of freedom.[6]

The foregoing discussion in the context of bivariate correlation analysis applies *mutatis mutandis* to the multivariate regression analysis. The formulas for calculating the regression parameters and the coefficient of determination for multivariable situations are not given here.[7] The calculations become increasingly more complex and time consuming as the number of variables is increased and are thus a problem ideally suited to computer solution. The wide availability of computer programs for regression analysis means that essentially we only need to know how to enter the data and interpret the results rather than to know the mechanistic processes of obtaining the results.

### Problems in Regression Analysis: Six Major Pitfalls

Understanding how to enter the data and how to interpret the results nevertheless requires a solid appreciation of the major problem areas likely to be encountered in regression analysis. If one or more of these problems do arise, the mechanistic regression analysis will still turn out regression parameters and statistics, but these results may well be spurious and therefore give misleading explanations and poor predictions. (The computer acts in good faith, presuming that the researcher knows what he or she is doing.) We shall address the major problems in turn.

*Specification Errors.* The first place to create unreliability in the results is in the specification of the relationship that is hypothesized to exist between the dependent variable and the independent variable(s). Two main types of problem occur under this heading. First there is the misspecification of the functional form of the relationship, and second there is the omission of important independent variables. We noted above that the regression equation must be calculated

---

[6] See Johnston, *Econometric Methods,* pp. 19-20.

[7] Ibid., pp. 52-62.

in linear form, but that this could be achieved for nonlinear relationships by logarithmic transformation of the function to linear form. The first specification error is to specify the relationship as being linear when in fact it is nonlinear of some form, or vice versa. How do we know which functional form is the "true" relationship? We find which functional form "best fits" the data, by comparing the coefficient of determination $(R^2)$ for various functional forms. By running the data in both the linear form (Eq.5.2) and, for example, the power form (Eq.5.3), the $R^2$ statistics can be compared to determine which functional form best explains the variance in the dependent variable. For bivariate correlation analysis, of course, a simple plot of the $Y$ values against the $X$ values should allow a visual assurance that the relationship is either linear or nonlinear.

Omission of important explanatory variables leads to probable unreliability in the regression coefficients, and the likely violation of the restrictions that we place upon the error terms. Essentially, since one or more of the explanatory variables are not included in the regression equation, the influence of these variables is attributed to the variables that *are* included, or it shows up as an unexplained residual. To illustrate this problem with a simple example, recall the chain-store problem discussed earlier in which the variability in sales levels was regressed upon the variability of prices in the six stores. Suppose we now learn that *ceteris paribus* did not hold for the period of the experiment: the promotional activity of the six stores differed during the period due to differences in the availability of advertising space in the suburban weekly newspapers and differences in the circulation of these newspapers. Multiplying pages of advertising by circulation in each area, we obtain a proxy measure of advertising exposure for each store as shown in Table 5.2 with the original price and sales data.

**TABLE 5.2**
**Price, sales, and advertising exposure for six stores**
**during the experiment**

| Store No. | Sales $Y$ (000) | Price $X_1$ ($) | Advertising $X_2$ (proxy units) |
|---|---|---|---|
| 1 | 4.650 | 0.79 | 23,000 |
| 2 | 3.020 | 0.99 | 18,500 |
| 3 | 2.150 | 1.25 | 24,600 |
| 4 | 4.400 | 0.89 | 26,200 |
| 5 | 6.380 | 0.59 | 25,100 |
| 6 | 5.500 | 0.45 | 16,800 |

We now hypothesize that $Y = \alpha + \beta_1 X_1 + \beta_2 X_2 + \epsilon$, and call upon the services of a regression program to estimate the $\alpha$ and $\beta$ parameters. The regression equation that "best fits" the data in Table 5.2 is

$$Y = 5718.02 - 5802.62X_1 + 0.153X_2$$
$$(399.746) \quad (0.0298)$$

Standard error of estimate 238.38098
Coefficient of determination $R^2 = 0.986$

where the figures in parentheses under the coefficients to the independent variables are the standard errors of the coefficients. Note that the magnitudes of these standard errors and the standard error of estimate indicate that the independent variables are reliable for predictive purposes, as per the rules of thumb mentioned earlier. The coefficient of determination indicates that the two variables, price and advertising exposure, jointly explain 98.6 percent of the variance of $Y$.

Note that the coefficient to $X_1$ has changed by the addition of the second explanatory variable, and that the $R^2$ value has increased, when compared with our earlier bivariate correlation analysis. Thus the omission of a significant determining factor in the earlier analysis led to a misleading coefficient for the price variable, and a subsequently misleading estimate of the price elasticity of demand. The magnitude of the error in the estimate of the price coefficient might have been greater if the unspecified advertising variables had happened to take systematically greater values for the stores where price was lower, and lower values for the stores where price was higher. In that event, the influence of price and advertising would work in the same direction on sales, but if only price is included as an explanatory variable, the price coefficient would pick up the credit for what was really the influence of an omitted variable. In the case depicted by Table 5.2 the variability in advertising was not systematic in relation to the variability in price, and hence the relatively small change in the price coefficient, when advertising is added, is the result of the balance of the supporting and the opposing effects of the variation in advertising.

A further specification problem arises when there are two closely correlated independent variables, and the wrong one is included in the regression equation. Suppose that, in fact, $Y$ depends on $X,$ and that $X$ and $Z$ both depend on some other variable $W$ and therefore tend to vary together. Suppose the researcher hypothesizes that $Y = f(Z)$ and tests for the explanatory power of $Z$ upon the value of $Y.$ Since $X$ and $Z$ tend to vary together, the regression analysis will indicate the existence of a statistical dependence of $Y$ on $Z.$ Statistical relationships need not indicate causal relationships, however, and the researcher must be satisfied with the logical causality between the independent and the dependent variable before using the results for explanatory purposes. As indicated in Chapter 1, however, the regression equation may be used (with caution) for prediction purposes as long as the underlying relationship does not change significantly.

*Measurement Errors.* Having decided which variables to include in the regression equation, and the appropriate functional form of the relationship, the next pitfall to be avoided is the improper measurement of the variables. In the above chain-store problem, for example, does the proxy measure of advertising exposure *accurately* depict the determining variable we wish to measure? To the extent that some suburban weeklies may have a superior advertising format, or that the newspaper tends to lie neglected on the porches (or under the Porsches!) of some suburbs, the simple measure of advertising exposure may not accurately depict the influence of advertising efforts on sales. If a more accurate measure of a particular variable can be generated, at a cost not exceeding the value of the additional information derived, then this measure should be used in the regression calculations.

The price variable is notorious for its problems of measurement. The most readily available measure of price is usually the "list price" or "manufacturer's suggested price," but in many instances this may not accurately depict the actual price paid. Whenever bargaining, discounts, or trade-ins are involved, the actual money changing hands may be somewhat less than the list price. Researchers are likely to encounter difficulty in determining the actual price paid on each particular sale, since sellers will be reluctant to divulge this information (fearing it will jeopardize their bargaining position in subsequent price negotiations with customers), and the customers are typically so widely dispersed that a survey of them would be prohibitively expensive. Of course, for many products the price displayed on the item will be an accurate measure of the actual price paid if discounts, trade-ins, and customer bargaining are not customary in the purchase of those products. The purpose of the above discussion is largely to stress that if the data used do not accurately measure the level of the variables, the programmer's adage "garbage in, garbage out" is likely to be appropriate.

***Simultaneous Equation Relationships.*** In many situations the single regression equation cannot adequately represent the true relationships existing between and among the variables. The regression analysis proceeds on the assumption that the influence of all other variables remains constant while we investigate for the influence of the specified independent variables. That is, we assume that a single equation explains the entire relationship. One problem with demand estimation arises because the price level is the result of the solution of the simultaneous equations for both demand and supply. Hence if supply is shifting over the period for which the data were collected, some part of the variation in the observations may be due to the influence of this second unspecified relationship.

Consider the following simple situation. Suppose we have three price/quantity observations that have been collected over a period of time and are as shown in Figure 5.3. They seem to indicate a negative relationship between price and quantity and hence may be thought to trace out the demand curve shown in part (a) and be the result of a shifting supply curve that has moved to the right over time, causing progressively lower intersection points on the demand curve. Alternatively, the three observations may be a result of the scenario depicted in part (b) of the figure. The first price/quantity observation may be the result of the intersection of supply and demand curve $S_1$ and $D_1$, while the subsequent price/quantity observations are the result of shifting demand and supply curves as indicated. Regression analysis, however, would conclude that part (a) is the appropriate interpretation of the data and if in error would give a misleading view of the slope and placement of the demand function.

The problem arises because there are insufficient data in the regression analysis to identify the existence of both relationships, and hence this is often called

**FIGURE 5.3**
The identification problem ✗

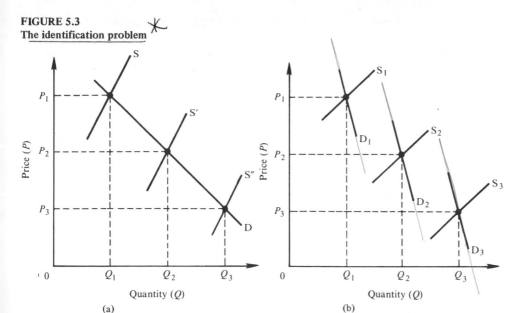

(a)

(b)

the *identification problem.* This problem arises particularly with time-series data in demand estimation, since we cannot expect the supply function to remain constant over time due to changing technology and factor costs, nor can we expect the demand function to remain stable for any extended period of time due to changing influences such as consumer incomes and preference patterns. This problem may be avoided by the use of cross-section data, however, given an appropriate control for comparison with a previous time period (as in the above chain-store example).

*Multicollinearity.* The problem of multicollinearity arises when the independent variables are not independent (of each other) at all. If two or more of the explanatory variables vary together due to their dependence on each other or another variable, the coefficient assigned to each of the variables by the regression solution may have no relationship to the "true" marginal influence of these variables upon the dependent variable. The regression analysis is unable to detect the true relationships and will assign an arbitrary value to the coefficients. Besides reducing the explanatory and predictive power of the regression equation, the presence of multicollinearity is likely to cause the standard error of the coefficient (or *t* test) to be an unreliable indicator of the statistical significance of the coefficients.

The presence of multicollinearity may be uncovered by checking the coefficients of determination between pairs of independent variables. Where variables are highly correlated we may remove all but one from the regression equation, taking care not to fall foul of the specification error of using an independent variable with no logical causal relationship with the dependent variable.[8]

[8] Ibid., pp. 201-6; or see A. S. Goldberger, *Topics in Regression Analysis* (London: Macmillan, 1968), pp. 79-83.

169

RESIDUALS EXHIBIT
SYSTEMATIC
RELATIONSHIP WITH
ONE OR MORE INDEPEN-
DENT VARIABLE

*Heteroscedasticity.* When the error terms do not occur randomly but exhibit a systematic relationship with the magnitude of one or more of the independent variables, we have the condition of heteroscedasticity. This violation of the requirement that observations have uniform variability about the line of best fit (implied by the restrictions placed on the error terms) causes regression analysis to be an inappropriate procedure and thus produces results that are likely to be unreliabile. The presence of heteroscedasticity is likely to cause the standard error of the coefficient to give misleading indications, and cause the coefficient of determination to overstate the explanatory power of the regression equation.

A simple means to discover the presence of heteroscedasticity is to plot the values of the residuals against the values of the independent variable(s), Many regression programs will output these graphs for visual inspection: any systematic relationship that appears will indicate the presence of heteroscedasticity. This problem may be removed by respecifying the independent variables, by changing the functional form of the relationship, by a transformation of the data, or by using a weighted least-squares regression technique.[9]

RESIDUALS FOLLOW
PATTERN OVER
TIME

*Autocorrelation.* Autocorrelation is another problem that arises when the error terms do not conform to the restrictions required for regression analysis. Autocorrelation (also known as serial correlation) is indicated by a sequential pattern in the residuals. If successive values of the error terms exhibit a particular trend or cyclical pattern, this indicates that some other variable is changing systematically and influencing the dependent variable. Autocorrelation may be removed by adding to the regression equation the variable thought to explain the systematic pattern. For example, if the residuals appear to follow a cyclical pattern over time, this may be found to correlate well with the levels of national income over the same period. Alternatively, a continuing upward or downward trend in the residuals could be eliminated by adding time as an explanatory variable.

Most regression programs include as output either a sequence plot of the residuals or the Durbin-Watson statistic, which is calculated to indicate the presence or absence of autocorrelation. A Durbin-Watson statistic around the value of two indicates the absence of autocorrelation, while values significantly greater or less than two indicate that the residuals do not occur randomly, and therefore that the results are likely to be unreliabile.[10]

### Summary of Regression Analysis

Regression analysis is an extremely useful tool for estimating the coefficients of the demand function. But like fire, precautions must be taken with the use of this tool. Most regression programs will produce the various statistics mentioned above and will plot the residuals such that the experienced researcher can readily discover the presence of one or more of the major problems that may occur.

[9] This takes us into the big league. These rectifications are discussed in advanced statistics texts, such as in N. R. Draper and H. Smith, *Applied Regression Analysis* (New York: John Wiley, 1966), pp. 77-81.

[10] See Johnston, *Econometric Methods,* Chap. 7.

Clearly, the greatest care must be taken in the initial steps of specifying the assumed relationship and collecting the data. Once the regression analysis has been conducted, the researcher must carefully interpret the results before concluding that these results are a sufficient basis for decision-making purposes.

## 5.4  DEMAND FORECASTING

The forecasting of sales in future periods has an additional dimension when compared with demand estimation in the current period. In demand estimation we knew or could ascertain the current value of the independent variables, and the problem was to find the level of the coefficients. In demand forecasting the problem is to forecast both the level of the independent variables and the level of the coefficients to those variables. Forecasting the future level of demand is an issue of concern not only to business firms but also to governments, banks, and other institutions. Consequently, there is a considerable amount of forecasting activity at the aggregate, sectoral, and industry levels. Decision makers in firms and institutions have access to the results of much of this forecasting activity and should utilize this material in forming their own forecasts. If the demand for their particular products is closely correlated with GNP or some other measure of aggregate activity, then the published forecasts, such as in the *Monthly Conditions Digest* issued by the U.S. Department of Commerce, will serve as an inexpensive source of data on future demand levels. On the other hand, individual components of the aggregate may move in different directions, and with lags or leads, and the decision maker must modify the forecast for aggregate, sectoral, or industrial activity to suit the specific circumstances of the individual firm.

A full discussion of the methods and techniques of demand forecasting constitutes a course in itself and would take us far beyond the space constraints of this chapter. We shall therefore confine ourselves to a brief discussion of the major methods of demand forecasting and refer the reader who requires more detail to the excellent textbook by Chisholm and Whitaker.[11] In the following section we shall outline the methods of demand forecasting under three broad headings: intention surveys, projection of known relationships, and barometric indicators.

### (i) Intention Surveys

Two main intention surveys are conducted periodically: the survey of consumer intentions and the survey of investor intentions.[12] Both are used to judge the level of confidence the consumer or investor feels concerning the desirability of spending for consumption or investment in the future. If consumers are hesitant about continuing their purchases of consumer durables or semidurables in the near or medium future due to pessimistic expectations about the state of the

[11] R. K. Chisholm and G. R. Whitaker, Jr., *Forecasting Methods* (Homewood, Ill.: Richard D. Irwin, 1971).

[12] Ibid., Chap. 3.

economy (and indirectly the likelihood of their incomes remaining at high levels), we might forecast an attenuation of the demand for these products in future periods. For many purchases, especially nondurables such as food, the consumers' purchases may be expected to continue at a relatively constant level almost regardless of the level of aggregate economic activity. For durables and semidurables, however, the consumer may postpone such purchases if the immediate outlook is less promising. If consumer expectations take a general turn to the pessimistic, we would expect demand for such products to fall in the ensuing period.

Investors' intentions are important not only as an indicator of the future level of aggregate economic activity but also for the implications these intentions have for the demand for a variety of products, such as construction materials, office supplies, and plant and equipment. Decision makers interested in the demand for these products must therefore remain aware of such intentions for the implications these will have for the demand for their own products.

Investors' intentions are similarly highly dependent upon their expectations as to the future levels of aggregate activity. Investors will feel more confident about investing if they expect aggregate activity to remain high or increase from its present level, since this has implications for the degree of idle capacity in future periods. If the investors' expectations are relatively pessimistic, we might expect investment projects to be postponed or canceled, with subsequent impacts upon the level of aggregate economic activity. The ironic feature about both consumers' and investors' expectations is that these expectations tend to become self-fulfilling prophecies. To counter this phenomenon, we often note governments, banks, and business leaders expressing great confidence in the future levels of aggregate economic activity at times when all other indications imply the opposite.

The problems with intention surveys as a forecasting device are similar to those that occur when surveys are used to estimate present levels of the demand parameters, except that some of these problems are increased by our asking the consumers or investors to predict their actions far into the future rather than simply their current actions. A continuing survey of intentions does serve, however, as an ongoing "finger on the pulse" of the people who make the demand decisions. Any change in the expectations of these decision makers, and by association a change in expected future demand levels, should become immediately apparent. Thus decision makers have an advance warning of likely changes and can plan their production, inventories, and other matters more effectively.

### ② Projection of Established Relationships

In the second major category of forecasting, relationships that are assumed to be known are projected into the future. This involves the implicit assumption that the relationship that has held in the immediate past will be a reasonably good predictor of the relationship that will hold in the immediate future. Chisholm and Whitaker speak of "naïve" forecasts as including all simple extrapolations of apparent statistical relationships into the future.[13] In such forecasts no modification is made for any new information that has been received, such as the current state of consumer or investor intentions. Such forecasts are based solely on the presumption that the best indicator of the near future is the experience of the recent past.

③ *Trend Line Projection.* The trend line projection method consists of taking this year's sales level and multiplying it by the trend factor that has become apparent over the past few years, to find the projected level of sales for the next year or the following years. Suppose that from time-series data on sales we have found the correlation equation

$$S_t = \alpha + \beta T_{t\text{-}1969} \qquad (5.8)$$

where $S_t$ is the sales level, $T$ is number of time periods since 1969 (the year in which the observations started), $t$ is the present year, and $\alpha$ and $\beta$ are the parameters of the line of best fit to the time-series data. Suppose that the data used to construct the trend line refer to the ten-year period 1969-78, and that the trend equation is $S = 4{,}585.87 + 175.8T$, where the parameters express thousands of units of sales. This indicates that the intercept of the trend line is 4.58587 million units and that sales increased by 175,800 units per year (on average) over that period. If we wish to estimate the sales level for 1979 and subsequent years, we simply insert in this expression values for $T$ of 11, 12, and higher numbers, since this would be the 11th, 12th and later period from the beginning of the time-series data. We should be very fortunate, however, if the actual sales levels of subsequent years fell right on the trend line, since a multitude of influences may cause actual sales to fall below or above the trend. For longer-term projections, when we can take the good with the bad over a number of periods, trend extrapolation may be a relatively useful method, but it is likely to be a relatively unreliable indicator of the actual year-to-year value of sales.

④ *Constant Growth Rate Projection.* The trend extrapolation model discussed above imputes a constant absolute increase to sales in successive periods. A common feature of the real world, however, is that series tend to grow at a constant rate of change rather than a constant absolute change. Thus if sales grew an average 5 percent each year over the preceding year for a certain period, we could express the sales function as

$$S_t = S_o (1 + k)^t \qquad (5.9)$$

where $S_o$ is the initial year's sales, $k$ is the average rate of growth of sales per annum, and $t$ is the number of periods after the initial period. Thus sales compound at the rate $k$, and we may predict sales in a future period by inserting the appropriate values in the above expression. You will recall that power functions may be transformed to linear form by expressing the relationship in logarithms,

[13] Ibid., Chap. 2.

and hence the parameters of Eq.(5.9) may be estimated using the least-squares regression technique. Given a series of sales levels for previous years, we may fit both the linear expression and the power function to these data and choose for prediction purposes the form that exhibits the higher coefficient of determination.

⑤ *Difference Equations.* A third method of using time-series data from past years to predict the sales level for future periods is that of difference equations, whereby the sales of the current period are found to be a function of the sales of previous periods in the general form

$$S_t = aS_{t\text{-}1} + bS_{t\text{-}2} + cS_{t\text{-}3} + \ldots \tag{5.10}$$

where the subscripts refer to the time period of the sales observations. We should expect the values of the coefficients to decline as we take successively more distant sales observations to explain the current level of sales. One such system is to use exponentially declining weights, which in effect implies that by far the largest influence on the present level of sales is exerted by the immediate-past levels, with successively smaller influences being exerted by more-distant-past sales observations. As did the above trend extrapolation and constant growth rate models, the difference equation approach also neglects any current influence on sales, instead giving full weight to the historical pattern that has emerged over previous years. To predict sales in the next period (period $t$ plus 1), we would insert the weights indicated by the past relationship and express $S_{t+1}$ as a function of $S_t$, $S_{t\text{-}1}$, and so forth.

*Regression Analysis.* The regression analysis of the preceding section can be used for forecasting purposes by assuming that the estimates of the coefficients will reliably indicate the future relationship between each of the independent variables and the dependent variable. The levels of the independent variables in the future periods must then be forecast in order to find the forecast level of demand in future periods. Forecasting the level of the independent variables may proceed on the basis of trend extrapolation, constant growth rate, or difference equations, as indicated above, especially for such factors as consumer incomes, tastes, and price levels. In all cases the naïve forecast should be modified by any information received that would indicate that the historic pattern of events would provide a poor indication of the most likely future pattern of events.

*Econometric Models.* Where a single equation is inadequate to represent the factors that determine sales, we may need to develop a multiple equation model that incorporates a system of equations to explain the interactions that underlie the demand level at any particular point of time. By plugging in the forecast values for the independent variables, and assuming that the coefficients discovered in earlier testing will be reliable indicators of the future relationship, we are able to solve the system of simultaneous equations for the forecast level of demand in future time periods. Suppose that we have found the level of sales to be estimated fairly accurately by the system of equations

$$S_t = a - bP_t + cY_t \tag{5.11}$$

$$P_t = d + e(Y_{t\text{-}1} - Y_{t\text{-}2}) \tag{5.12}$$

$$Y_t = Y_{t\text{-}1}(1 + k) \tag{5.13}$$

In this system current sales are a function of current prices and income levels, but current prices and incomes are in turn a function of past income levels. Since income grows at a constant rate $k$, we are able to project future income levels and future price levels. Hence given the estimates of the parameters $a$, $b$, $c$, $d$, $e$, and $k$, we are able to project the level of sales in future periods.

### Barometric Indicators: Leading Indicators and Diffusion Indices

A *barometer* is a device that predicts changes in one variable (weather) by measuring the change in another variable (air pressure). Since falling air pressure foretells the arrival of relatively inclement weather, and rising air pressure indicates that the weather will begin to improve, the barometer is able to predict tomorrow's weather on the basis of today's air pressure. Barometric indicators in forecasting are named for the same ability: movements in the barometric indicator typically lead movements in the variable that we wish to predict. Thus by observing the level of the barometric time series and its changes, we are able to predict changes in the variable of interest, based on the previous association between these two time series.

*Leading Series Indicators.* The first type of barometric indicator consists of a single leading series. In this case we find a particular time series that tends to consistently lead the performance of the demand for our products. By "lead the performance" we mean that the barometric indicator will experience turning points (the changes in direction from growth to contraction, or from contraction to growth) in advance of the turning points of demand for our products. In addition, a pattern may emerge between the rate of growth or decline of the barometric series and the rate of change of the demand. Examination of time-series data for various industries and sectors should unearth a time series that tends to act as a leading indicator for the sales of our products. We may find, for example, that the shipments of coal and the production of steel vary, as indicated in Table 5.3.

In Table 5.3 it can be seen that reductions in steel production (the negative percentage changes) tend to precede the reductions in coal shipments by two quarters, just as the increases in steel production tend to precede the increases in coal shipments by a period of two quarters. We can rationalize this as the time period it takes for the steel producers to become aware of the reduction in demand for their product and to organize a reduction in their orders for coal. Producers of coal thus have a two-month warning for turning points in the demand for their product, which should aid their production and inventory planning considerably. In this case, then, steel production acts as a barometric indicator of changes in the level of demand for coal.

**TABLE 5.3**
**Steel production as a leading indicator**
**for coal shipments (hypothetical)**

| Year | Quarter | Steel Production— % Changes (qtr. to qtr.) | Coal Shipments— % Changes (qtr. to qtr.) |
|------|---------|---------|---------|
| 1976 | 1 | 2.5 | 1.6 |
| | 2 | 3.1 | 3.2 |
| | 3 | 1.8 | 2.4 |
| | 4 | −0.2 | 1.8 |
| 1977 | 1 | −1.4 | 1.2 |
| | 2 | −1.8 | −0.4 |
| | 3 | 0.6 | −3.8 |
| | 4 | 2.4 | −4.1 |
| 1978 | 1 | 3.0 | 1.6 |
| | 2 | −1.2 | 3.2 |
| | 3 | −2.1 | 3.6 |
| | 4 | 0.8 | −2.5 |

Single-series leading indicators are unlikely to *consistently* lead the series they are intended to and moreover are unlikely to lead by a consistent *lead period*. A multitude of other factors influence the demand for steel in the above example, or the barometric indicator in the general case. It is difficult in practice to find a leading indicator that leads even 90 percent of the time, since random factors intervene to cause the barometric indicator to sometimes indicate continued growth when in fact the dependent time series is already falling, or vice versa.

*Composite Leading Indices.* To avoid the problem of the unreliability of a single indicator, composite barometric indices have been established. Several leading indicators are aggregated to form an index, with the result that the random movements in any one series tend to be offset by opposite movements in one or more of the other series. The result is that the composite index provides a more reliable indication of actual turning points in the series we are attempting to predict. Table 5.4 shows the major leading, coincident, and lagging indicators, as identified by the National Bureau of Economic Research and other sources. The value of the latter two categories for forecasting is to indicate when the peak or trough has in fact passed. Since the coincident indicators are expected to turn at about the same time as GNP or aggregate economic activity and lagging indicators are expected to turn after the GNP has turned, when we observe these series turning we may be confident that GNP has in fact turned as indicated by the leading indicators, without having to wait for actual measurement of GNP to confirm that there has been a turning point.

*The Diffusion Index.* A third category of barometric indicators involves the diffusion index, which shows the proportion of the total number of series in a chosen collection that are rising at any point of time. For prediction of GNP, for example, when the diffusion index exceeds 50 percent we expect that GNP will be rising, and when it is less than 50 percent we expect that GNP will be

**TABLE 5.4**
Selected leading, coincident, and lagging indicators

**Leading Indicators**

1. Average workweek, production workers, manufacturing
2. Nonagricultural placements, BES
3. Index of net business formation
4. New orders, durable goods industries
5. Contracts and orders, plant and equipment
6. New-building permits, private-housing units
7. Change in book value, manufacturing and trade inventories
8. Industrial materials prices
9. Stock prices, 500 common stocks
10. Corporate profits after taxes
11. Ratio, price to unit labor cost, manufacturing
12. Change in consumer debt

**Roughly Coincident Indicators**

1. Employees in nonagricultrual establishments
2. Unemployment rate, total (inverted)
3. GNP in constant dollars, expenditure estimate
4. Industrial production
5. Personal income
6. Manufacturing and trade sales
7. Sales of retail stores

**Lagging Indicators**

1. Unemployment rate (unemployment > 15 weeks, inverted)
2. Business expenditure, new plant and equipment
3. Book value, manufacturing and trade inventories
4. Labor cost per unit of output, manufacturing
5. Commercial and industrial loans outstanding
6. Bank rates on short-term business loans

From Table 2 in J. Shiskin and L. H. Lempert, "Indicator Forecasting," in W. F. Butler et al., *Methods and Techniques of Business Forecasting* (Englewood Cliffs, N.J.: Prentice-Hall, 1974), pp. 48-49.

falling. We could construct a diffusion index to predict the sales of any product by using past data to choose the series to be included in the index such that it will best predict turning points of the sales for that product. In Figure 5.4 we show the relationship between the diffusion index and the variable that we are hoping to predict by the use of the diffusion index. In the ideal situation where the series in the diffusion index are weighted by the exactly appropriate amounts, as the diffusion index rises to 50 percent and above the variable to be predicted reaches its lower turning point and continues to rise. When the diffusion index reaches a maximum the variable to be predicted should exhibit an inflection point, and as the diffusion index drops below 50 percent the variable

**FIGURE 5.4**
**Relationship between a diffusion index and a time series**

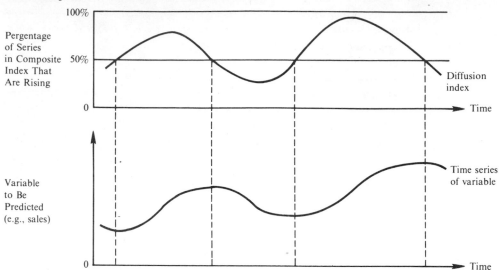

to be predicted will attain a maximum and thereafter fall. There are likely to be random shocks to the diffusion index such that it will not appear smooth, as in Figure 5.4. To better judge the direction of change of the diffusion index, we may need to use a moving average of the past few weeks or months.

The major limitation of barometric indicators generally is that they predict turning points only, and not the magnitudes of the change, such that we must use some other method to find the likely magnitude of the change in the variable to be predicted. Thus barometric indicators, like surveys, are more suited to short-run forecasting, since they require little lead time and indicate turning points rather than the general longer-term direction of sales. Projection techniques, on the other hand, require substantial preparation time in some cases and in all cases generate the general trend of the data and may incorrectly predict the immediate direction and magnitude of the change in the variable.

## 5.5   SUMMARY

*Demand estimation* is concerned with finding the values of the parameters in the demand function that are currently appropriate. This information is important for current decision making and in evaluating whether decisions are optimal in terms of the current demand situation. *Demand forecasting* is concerned with the future values of the parameters and independent variables of the demand function, and it is clearly vital for decision problems where expected sales in future periods must be estimated.

Buyers' reactions to changes in the independent variables in the demand function may be gauged by interviews and surveys, simulated market experiments, or direct market experiments. Regression analysis is a powerful tool, when used correctly, for estimating the parameters of the demand function, on the basis of the statistical association that appears between and among variables in either time-series or cross-section data observations. The pitfalls that may invalidate this technique were outlined in some detail in order that the researcher might better set up the problem for analysis, and better interpret the results of that analysis.

Forecasts of the future demand situation may be constructed with the aid of intention surveys, projections, and barometric indicators. Several of the techniques outlined would allow the researcher to estimate the future level of sales and the probable turning points of sales for the product(s) in question. Considerable forecasting activity is undertaken by governmental and other agencies, and the information generated should be used as input to the individual firm's or organizations's forecasting deliberations. In many cases these public sources may serve as an adequate guide to future demand conditions, but in others it will be necessary to construct surveys, projection models, and barometric indicators for the specific situation to be predicted.

## DISCUSSION QUESTIONS

5.1 Summarize the problems of demand estimation and demand forecasting in terms of the information required.

5.2 Why is it useful to the decision maker to have an estimate of the impact (on the quantity demanded) of variables that are not controllable by the decision maker?

5.3 What is the relationship between direct and indirect demand estimation on the one hand, and primary and secondary data on the other?

5.4 List ten questions you would ask a sample of people in order to estimate their demand function for a specific brand of toothpaste.

5.5 Suppose you were to interview a large number of people, asking each person whether he or she would buy a particular product at a series of prices starting from a relatively low price and then raising the price until each person would *not* buy the product. How would you translate this information into an estimated demand curve?

5.6 Design a simulated market situation intended to ascertain customers' responses to changes in prices, packaging, and point-of-purchase promotion for a particular product.

5.7 What factors must be monitored while conducting a direct market experiment in order to allow confidence that the results obtained give reliable information about the demand function?

5.8 Suppose you had data on the annual quantity demanded of newsprint and the price per ton of newsprint over the past twenty years and found the regression equation relating quantity demanded to price. Why would this be an unreliable estimate of the demand curve?

5.9 Summarize the issues you would need to check before concluding that the results of a regression analysis were a reliable basis for estimating the demand function.

5.10 Outline the methods by which you would obtain a forecast of demand for a particular product group (such as automobiles).

## PROBLEMS

5.1 The Sylvain Leather Products Company intends to introduce a new men's wallet and is confronting the question of probable demand for the new wallet. With the aid of several assistants, Michel Sylvain, the vice-president of marketing, has conducted a questionnaire survey of one thousand people interviewed while shopping for goods of a similar nature. The interviewees were each asked to choose one of six responses as to whether they would actually purchase the new wallet, at each of five price levels. The responses were (a) definitely no, (b) not likely, (c) perhaps, maybe, (d) quite likely, (e) very likely, and (f) definitely yes. The number of people responding in each category at each price level follows.

**Sylvain leather products company**

| Price ($) | Number of People Responding as | | | | | |
|---|---|---|---|---|---|---|
| | (a) | (b) | (c) | (d) | (e) | (f) |
| 9 | 500 | 300 | 125 | 50 | 25 | 0 |
| 8 | 300 | 225 | 175 | 150 | 100 | 50 |
| 7 | 100 | 150 | 250 | 250 | 150 | 100 |
| 6 | 50 | 100 | 100 | 300 | 250 | 200 |
| 5 | 0 | 25 | 50 | 225 | 300 | 400 |

Assume that the probabilities of actually buying the product for each of the six responses above have been reliably estimated as (a) 0.0, (b) 0.2, (c) 0.4, (d) 0.6, (e) 0.8, and (f) 1.0.

(a) Calculate the expected value of quantity demanded at each price level.

(b) Plot the prices and expected values of quantity demanded and sketch in the estimated demand curve.

(c) Suppose the vice-president of marketing chooses the price level of $7 per unit. In order for this to be the profit-maximizing price, what conditions would need to be fulfilled?

5.2 The Brazilian Gold Coffee Company wished to ascertain the responsiveness of consumers to changes in the price of its coffee. Six groups of one hundred shoppers each were organized for a simulated market experiment. The membership of the groups was chosen such that the socioeconomic characteristics of the groups were roughly equal and similar to the market in total. Within one afternoon each group was allowed thirty minutes to shop in a simulated supermarket. Each participant was given $30 in "play money" with which to purchase any items on display in the simulated supermarket. Brazilian Gold coffee was displayed prominently alongside the best-selling brand of coffee. For each of the six groups, Brazilian Gold was priced at different levels while the price of the best-selling brand was held constant. The price levels and the resultant quantities demanded were as follows:

**Simulated market experiment for Brazilian Gold coffee**

| | Brazilian Gold | | Best-Selling Brand | |
| --- | --- | --- | --- | --- |
| Group | Price ($ per lb) | Quantity Demanded (lb) | Price ($ per lb) | Quantity Demanded (lb) |
| 1 | 3.39 | 112 | 3.49 | 150 |
| 2 | 3.29 | 123 | 3.49 | 145 |
| 3 | 3.49 | 94 | 3.49 | 165 |
| 4 | 3.19 | 154 | 3.49 | 134 |
| 5 | 3.69 | 37 | 3.49 | 190 |
| 6 | 3.59 | 71 | 3.49 | 175 |

(a) Estimate the parameters of the demand curve for Brazilian Gold by plotting the price-quantity observations, sketching in the line of best fit, and measuring the approximate intercept and slope of this line.

(b) Calculate the price elasticity of demand for Brazilian Gold at each of the price levels, and comment on the values obtained.

(c) Calculate the cross-price elasticity between Brazilian Gold and the best-selling brand, at each of the price levels, and comment on the values obtained.

(d) Defend your use of either point or arc elasticity measures in parts (b) and (c) above.

5.3 The Leiberman Plastics Company wishes to predict sales for its plastic pails for the coming year. It has recorded data for its past ten years' demand and has obtained data on the number of households within its market area. This information is listed in the accompanying table.

**Leiberman plastics company**

| Year | Sales of Pails (units) | Number of Households (000) |
| --- | --- | --- |
| 1970 | 7,000 | 350 |
| 1971 | 6,750 | 462 |
| 1972 | 7,150 | 548 |
| 1973 | 8,300 | 610 |
| 1974 | 8,000 | 694 |
| 1975 | 9,200 | 830 |
| 1976 | 9,050 | 985 |
| 1977 | 10,100 | 1,080 |
| 1978 | 10,300 | 1,210 |
| 1979 | 10,600 | 1,330 |

(a) Plot the annual sales data against the number of households in the market area, and draw in the "line of best fit" that seems to be visually appropriate.

(b) Measuring the intercept and slope of the above line of best fit, state the approximate functional relationship between the two variables.

(c)  Suppose the number of households is projected as increasing by 165,000 in 1980. Use the above functional relationship to forecast the demand for plastic pails during 1980.

(d)  Comment upon the probable accuracy of your forecast.

5.4  The Karich Electronics Corporation manufactures stereo equipment and has recently developed a distinctly new looking stereo receiver. As a result of surveying several thousand people as to their perceived quality and expected price level, the marketing department of Karich has estimated the probabilities of sales at several levels for each of five price levels (see table).

**Karich electronics corporation**

| Price ($) | Sales (units) | Probability of Sales |
|---|---|---|
| 100 | 7,500 | 0.20 |
|  | 6,000 | 0.25 |
|  | 4,500 | 0.40 |
|  | 3,000 | 0.10 |
|  | 1,500 | 0.05 |
| 125 | 6,000 | 0.10 |
|  | 5,000 | 0.20 |
|  | 4,000 | 0.45 |
|  | 2,500 | 0.20 |
|  | 1,000 | 0.05 |
| 150 | 4,500 | 0.10 |
|  | 4,000 | 0.20 |
|  | 3,000 | 0.40 |
|  | 2,000 | 0.20 |
|  | 750 | 0.10 |
| 175 | 3,500 | 0.05 |
|  | 3,000 | 0.10 |
|  | 2,500 | 0.50 |
|  | 1,000 | 0.20 |
|  | 500 | 0.15 |
| 200 | 3,000 | 0.05 |
|  | 2,500 | 0.15 |
|  | 1,500 | 0.30 |
|  | 1,000 | 0.25 |
|  | 500 | 0.25 |

(a)  Calculate the expected value of quantity demanded at each price level.

(b)  Use these expected values to estimate the demand curve for the new product.

(c)  If the marginal cost of the stereo receivers is $112.50 per unit, regardless of volume, what price would you recommend?

(d)  What qualifications would you add to your recommendation?

5.5  Wido Heck, manager of the Red Baron Flying School, is wondering how many instructional hours will be demanded during the coming season. He needs to have an estimate of demand in order to hire instructors. He has just completed a survey by questionnaire among the students and has summarized the results as shown in the table. He feels that any influx of new students will do no more than balance the attrition of existing students, and that their demands for flying time will be similar to those of the students they replace.

**Demand for flying instruction**

| Price per Flying Hour ($) | Hours per Day Demanded |
|---|---|
| 10 | 64 |
| 15 | 53 |
| 17 | 43 |
| 20 | 37 |
| 27 | 29 |
| 30 | 23 |

(a) Plot prices against quantity demanded and establish an estimate of the demand curve by a freehand smoothing line.

(b) Using regression analysis, calculate and state the demand curve equation, and calculate the coefficient of determination. (Show all workings)

(c) Using the regression equation calculated above, estimate the flying hours per day demanded at a price of $23/hr. Comment on the probable degree of accuracy of this estimate.

(d) If Mr. Heck is now charging $25/hr and his marginal cost is constant at $10/hr, should he raise or lower his price? At what price is his profit maximized?

5.6 The Johnston Raymond Corporation has established a "composite index of demand" which has been relatively accurate in predicting the annual quantity demanded of its cement products. A number of variables are included in the index, such as GNP in current dollars, the Index of Industrial Production, Personal Disposable Income, Manufacturing and Trade Sales, and Industrial Materials Prices. Also included is the average price of JRC's cement products and the prices of substitute products. By trial and error, JRC has adjusted the weights to each of these variables such that composite index has performed very well in predicting sales in the recent past. Historical data for the past twelve years are shown in the table.

**Johnston raymond corporation: historical data**

| Year | Sales (units) (Y) | Demand Index (X) |
|---|---|---|
| 1968 | 1,950 | 500 |
| 1969 | 2,570 | 658 |
| 1970 | 3,140 | 801 |
| 1971 | 3,280 | 843 |
| 1972 | 3,360 | 853 |
| 1973 | 3,570 | 917 |
| 1974 | 3,750 | 953 |
| 1975 | 3,980 | 995 |
| 1976 | 5,800 | 1,485 |
| 1977 | 6,170 | 1,567 |
| 1978 | 6,650 | 1,729 |
| 1979 | 7,130 | 1,854 |

(a) Calculate the regression equation showing the relationship between the quantity demanded and the value of the composite index.

(b) How reliable is the composite index as an explanatory variable?

(c) Form a projection of the value of the composite index over the next five years.

(d) Use this projection in the regression equation to forecast the quantity demanded in each of the next five years.

5.7 A large cosmetics company markets its products directly to customers in eighteen separate campaigns annually. Sales brochures are prepared and printed for each campaign and are sold to the sales representatives, who are paid by commission only. In order to allow time for printing and distribution, and to give the sales representatives sufficient time to utilize the brochures while making their normal rounds to clientele, it is necessary to forecast sales of the brochures three campaigns in advance. The quantity of brochures sold to representatives in a particular territory for each campaign during 1977, 1978, and the first six campaigns of 1979 are shown, in the accompanying table, along with the scheduled printing runs for campaigns 7, 8, and 9.

**Actual brochure sales**

| Campaign | 1977 (000) | 1978 (000) | 1979 (000) |
|---|---|---|---|
| 1 | 1,013 | 865 | 997 |
| 2 | 923 | 811 | 965 |
| 3 | 779 | 712 | 877 |
| 4 | 897 | 712 | 877 |
| 5 | 819 | 774 | 965 |
| 6 | 874 | 831 | 1,051 |
| 7 | 879 | 845 | 1,091* |
| 8 | 885 | 878 | 1,122* |
| 9 | 906 | 840 | 1,100* |
| 10 | 869 | 824 | |
| 11 | 844 | 800 | |
| 12 | 823 | 803 | |
| 13 | 834 | 786 | |
| 14 | 789 | 847 | |
| 15 | 833 | 878 | |
| 16 | 986 | 1,011 | |
| 17 | 1,027 | 1,090 | |
| 18 | 1,024 | 1,141 | |

*Scheduled production based on sales forecasts.

(a) Have you any comments on the levels of the printing runs for the seventh, eighth, and ninth campaigns?

(b) Forecast the sales of brochures for the tenth, eleventh, and twelfth campaigns of 1979, using trend projection.

## SUGGESTED REFERENCES AND FURTHER READING

BAUMOL, W. J., *Economic Theory and Operations Analysis,* 4th ed., Chap. 10. Englewood Cliffs, N.J.: Prentice-Hall, 1977.

BENNETT, S., and J. B. WILKINSON, "Price-Quantity Relationships and Price Elasticity under In-Store Experimentation," *Journal of Business Research,* 2 (January 1974), 27-38.

BUTLER, W. F., R. A. KAVESH, and R. B. PLATT, *Methods and Techniques of Business Forecasting,* esp. Parts 1, 2, and 4. Englewood Cliffs, N.J.: Prentice-Hall, 1974.

CHISHOLM, R. K., and G. R. WHITAKER, Jr., *Forecasting Methods.* Homewood, Ill.: Richard D. Irwin, 1971.

DRAPER, N. R., and H. SMITH, *Applied Regression Analysis.* New York: John Wiley, 1966.

GOLDBERGER, A. S., *Topics in Regression Analysis.* London: Macmillan, 1968.

GREEN, P. E., and D. S. TULL, *Research for Marketing Decisions,* 3rd ed., esp. Chaps. 3-5. Englewood Cliffs, N.J.: Prentice-Hall, 1975.

JOHNSTON, J., *Econometric Methods,* Chaps. 1, 2, 4, 7, and 8. New York: McGraw-Hill, 1963.

KOTLER, P., *Marketing Management,* 3rd ed., Chap. 19. Englewood Cliffs, N.J.: Prentice-Hall, 1976.

LUCK, D. J., H. G. WALES, and D. A. TAYLOR, *Marketing Research*, 4th ed., esp. Chaps. 9, 10, 12, and 14. Englewood Cliffs, N.J.: Prentice-Hall, 1974.

MCGUIGAN, J. R., AND R. C. MOYER, *Managerial Economics,* Chaps. 5, 7, and 8. Hinsdale, Ill.: Dryden, 1975.

PESSEMIER, E. A., "An Experimental Method for Estimating Demand," *Journal of Business,* 33 (October 1960), 373-83.

U.S. DEPARTMENT OF COMMERCE, *Survey of Current Business* and *Business Conditions Digest.* Springfield, Va.: National Technical Information Service, current.

# part III

# Production and Cost Analysis

# 6

# Production
# and
# Cost Theory

**6.1  Introduction**

Short-Run vs. Long-Run Distinction.

**6.2  The Production Function**

General and Specific Forms.    The Output Hill and the Production Surface.

**6.3  The Law of Variable Proportions**

Total Product and Marginal Product Curves.    The Law of Diminishing Returns.

**6.4  Returns to Scale**

Increasing, Constant, and Decreasing Returns to Scale.
Linear Homogeneous Production Functions.

**6.5  Isoquant-Isocost Analysis**

Technical and Economic Efficiency.
The Expansion Path: Long Run and Short Run.
Factor Substitution Due to Changed Relative Factor Prices.

**6.6  Production Theory in Value Terms: Cost Curves**

The Total Variable Cost Curve.    Average Variable and Marginal Costs.
Short-Run Average Costs.    The Long-Run Average Cost Curve.
Economies of Plant Size, Scale, and Firm Size.

**6.7  Summary**

## 6.1  INTRODUCTION

*Production* can be defined in broad economic terms as the transformation of resources into products, or the process whereby inputs are turned into outputs. The efficiency of this process usually depends upon the proportions in which the various inputs are employed, the absolute level of each input, and the productivity of each input at each input level and ratio. Since inputs are generally not free but have a cost attached, the degree of efficiency in production translates into a level of costs per unit of output. Production and costs are thus intimately related. In this chapter the theory of production and costs is presented in a way that both underscores this interrelationship and demonstrates the impact of changing efficiency in production upon the shape and placement of the cost curves. We examine the theory of production and costs in order to lay a sufficient conceptual foundation for the discussion of practical cost concepts and techniques of cost estimation in the two subsequent chapters.[1]

### Short-Run vs. Long-Run Distinction

In production and cost theory the distinction is made between the *short run,* in which the quantities of some inputs are variable while others are in fixed supply, and the *long run,* in which all factors may be varied. Consequently, it is useful to classify the inputs on the basis of whether or not they are variable in the short run. Since labor has traditionally been variable, and capital is typically fixed in the short run, these headings are commonly used to denote, respec-

---

[1] In this chapter we confine our attention to a production process that has a single output. This allows us to demonstrate all the concepts in a relatively simple manner. In Chapter 13 we use the techniques of linear-programming analysis to deal with the problem of choosing the optimal product mix in the multiple output situation.

tively, *all* variable and *all* fixed resources.[2] When using the terms *labor* and *capital* in this sense we should think of one unit of labor as including, say, one hour of a worker's time, plus a "package" of all the necessary raw materials, fuel, and other variable inputs; while capital includes all the plant, equipment, land, buildings, managers' salaries, and other expenses that do not vary with the level of output.

It is important to understand that "the long run" does not refer to a long period of time. It is a peculiarity of the economists' jargon that the term has no direct connection with time at all, and that the firm is likely to be in a long-run situation for relatively short periods of time. When intending to change its scale of production, the firm must continue to operate in a short-run situation until its most-fixed factor becomes variable. At this point of time the firm is in a long-run situation, since it can vary the input levels of all factors. As soon as the firm is committed to new levels of plant, buildings, and other fixed facilities, it is back in a short-run situation, since the input of these factors cannot be varied from their chosen level. Notice that the short run could be a few days for some very simple types of firms (such as a street vendor selling flowers from a wheelbarrow) or as much as five years for large manufacturing concerns (such as steel mills or automobile producers). Thus the phrase "in the long run" should be taken to mean "at the end of the short run" or "when factors that are currently in fixed supply can be increased or decreased." Since the long run may be either a short or a long time coming, we will use the alternate phrase "the long term" to refer to an extended period of time, and reserve "the long run" for its specific connotation in the jargon of economics.

## 6.2   THE PRODUCTION FUNCTION

### General and Specific Forms

The production "function" is a technical specification of the relationship that exists between the inputs and the outputs in the production process. In general form it says simply that output is dependent upon the inputs in an unspecified way. That is:

$$Q = f(K,L) \tag{6.1}$$

where $Q$ is the quantity of output, $f$ represents the functional relationship existing between the inputs and the output, and $K$ and $L$ are the conventional symbols representing the input levels of capital and labor, respectively.

In specific form the functional relationship is stated explicitly, and the functional form of the equation is the one that best expresses the actual relationship between the inputs and the output. Output might be expressed, for example, as a linear additive function of the inputs, or alternatively as a multiplicative

---

[2] Note that with the increasing membership of labor unions, labor is becoming more and more fixed in many production processes. In cases where reductions in the labor supply may be made only through attrition, labor tends to be varied by the use of overtime work for existing employees rather than the hiring and firing of extra workers as volume fluctuates. Whenever labor is hired by contract over a period of time, this labor must be classified as a fixed expense in the sense that it is independent of output levels for the duration of the contract.

**TABLE 6.1**
Motor vehicle assembly production function

| | | Labor Units (hundreds of person-hours) | | | | | | | |
|---|---|---|---|---|---|---|---|---|---|
| | | 1 | 2 | 3 | 4 | 5 | 6 | 7 | 8 |
| Capital | 1 | 1 | 3 | 7 | 10 | 12 | 13 | 13½ | 13 |
| Units (machine- | 2 | 3 | 8 | 14 | 19 | 23 | 26 | 28 | 29 |
| hours, 000) | 3 | 8 | 18 | 29 | 41 | 52 | 62 | 71 | 79 |
| | 4 | 11 | 23 | 36 | 50 | 65 | 78 | 90 | 101 |
| | 5 | 12 | 26 | 42 | 60 | 80 | 98 | 112 | 124 |

power function of the inputs. The exact mathematical specification of the production function depends upon the state of technology, or what may be called the productivity of the input factors at various levels of all inputs. For example, three units of labor and two units of capital may combine to produce fifteen units of output. If technology improves, that is, if either or both labor and capital become more productive, the same combination of labor and capital may then be able to produce, say, eighteen units of output. Thus the state of technology is incorporated into the specification of the production function and is reflected by the precise mathematical form taken by any particular production function.

Given the specific form of the production function, we could insert values for labor and capital and find for every combination of labor and capital the output that would result. A tabular array of the output levels associated with various input levels of all factors for the hypothetical case of automobile assembly by a small company producing sports cars is shown in Table 6.1. The output levels in the body of the table represent the number of vehicles assembled. The table reflects the substitutability of labor and capital: note that particular output levels can be produced using different combinations of capital and labor. For example, twenty-three vehicles can be assembled using either 4,000 machine-hours and 200 person-hours, or 2,000 machine-hours and 500 person-hours. By interpolation between the figures in the table, we could find several combinations of labor and capital that would culminate in the assembly of twenty-three vehicles.

Note that Table 6.1 depicts both the short run and the long run: in the short run the level of capital input would be fixed at a particular level, and output is constrained to that shown in the *row* opposite that level of capital and can only be varied by adding or subtracting labor units. In the long run, that is, when all input quantities are variable, any point in the table may be achieved. Thus if only 3,000 machine-hours were available, output levels would vary as shown along the third row of Table 6.1 as we added or subtracted labor. Given the opportunity to change the scale of operations, the firm could move to any other row of the table to which it would be constrained for the duration of the following short-run period.

The actual values of output shown in the table reflect a number of important concepts in the theory of production which are more easily explained in terms of the "production surface."

**FIGURE 6.1**
The output hill and the production surface

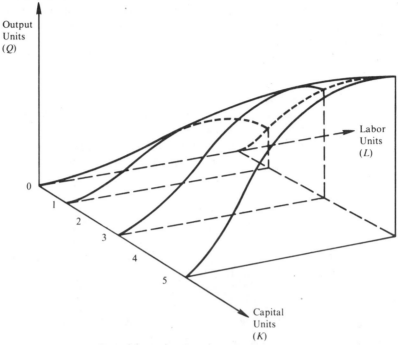

### The Output Hill and the Production Surface

Let us regard the values in the table as being indicators of the elevation of a surface above the base of the grid formed by the labor and capital axes. (As an analogy, think of a hill that has been surveyed for elevation above sea level.) The inputs of labor and capital can be regarded as giving rise to a hill of output, the upper surface of which represents the maximum output that can be attained from the particular combination of labor and capital. A three-dimensional output hill and its production surface is shown in Figure 6.1.

If the production surface is to be smooth, this implies that the input quantities of labor and capital are divisible into infinitesimal pieces. That is, the smooth transition between the figures in the table depends upon fractional units of labor and capital being added or subtracted. This assumption of infinite divisibility of inputs does not contradict a situation in which machines are only available in one size, however. Although it would be impossible to employ one-tenth of a machine, it is possible to employ one machine for one-tenth of the production period, by hiring it, for example. Similarly, one could use overtime labor or employ part-time personnel in order to make up fractional labor units.[3]

[3] If the production technology is available in only a few different processes (using different capital/labor proportions), the analysis proceeds along the lines of the attribute analysis of Chapter 3. The rays from the origin represent the $K/L$ ratio of the available processes, and the efficiency frontier is the locus of points where the budget is exhausted. If the highest attainable isoquant touches a corner of the efficiency frontier, one of the available processes will be optimal. If it touches a facet, a combination of the two adjacent processes will be required.

We can use the production surface to demonstrate a number of important concepts in the theory of production. We do this by slicing the output hill through different planes and observing the shapes of the resultant line cut into the production surface.

## 6.3   THE LAW OF VARIABLE PROPORTIONS

The *law of variable proportions* is concerned with the relative productivity of the marginal units of the variable factor as we progressively add units of the variable factors to the fixed inputs. It states that as more and more of the variable factors are added to a given quantity of all other factors, the increment to output attributable to each of the additional units of the variable factor will increase at first, will later decrease, and will eventually become negative. Notice that this phenomenon relates to the short run, since fixed inputs are involved, and can be witnessed in any row of Table 6.1, where the differences between the adjacent numbers increase at first and later decrease as more labor is added to a particular level of capital. In Table 6.2 we show the increments to output as we move along the third row of the production function exhibited in Table 6.1. Notice that increasing returns prevail up to and including the fourth unit of labor when applied to three units of capital, after which point diminishing returns to the variable factor prevail.

### Total Product and Marginal Product Curves

In terms of the output hill and its surface, the law of variable proportions can be demonstrated by a vertical slice along a baseline representing a constant input of capital. Three such slices are shown in Figure 6.1 for capital inputs of one, three, and five units. The top line of each slice relates total output to the input of labor units, with the capital input constant, and is usually referred to as the "total product" curve. The law of variable proportions is evident from the shape of these total product curves. Each curve is convex from below at first, showing output increasing at an increasing rate as labor units are added. After the point of inflection the curve is concave from below, reflecting diminishing returns to

**TABLE 6.2**
**The law of variable proportions exhibited
by the marginal product of the variable factors**

| Units of the Variable | Units of Output (for K = 3) | Increment to Output over Preceding Row | Returns to the Variable Factor (for K = 3) |
|---|---|---|---|
| 0 | 0 | — | — |
| 1 | 8 | 8 | Increasing |
| 2 | 18 | 10 | Increasing |
| 3 | 29 | 11 | Increasing |
| 4 | 41 | 12 | Increasing |
| 5 | 52 | 11 | Diminishing |
| 6 | 62 | 10 | Diminishing |
| 7 | 71 | 9 | Diminishing |
| 8 | 79 | 8 | Diminishing |

the variable factor. Note that we are talking about the rate of change of total product as the variable factor input is changed. This change in total product, as the result of a one-unit change in input of the variable input, or the rate of change of total product in relation to that of labor, is defined as the "marginal product of labor." In Figure 6.2 we show one of the total product curves in two dimensions (since $K$ is constant), along with the marginal product curve which can be derived from the total product curve.

**FIGURE 6.2**
**The total product and marginal product curves**

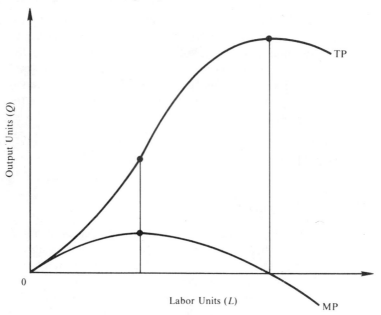

Notice that since *marginal product* is defined as the rate of change of total product as labor is increased, it is equal in mathematical terms to the first derivative of the total product function with respect to labor. This is the same as saying that marginal product is given by the *slope* of the total product curve at every level of labor input. Note that at the point of inflection, where the total product curve changes from being concave upward to concave downward, the total product curve is at its steepest, and marginal product attains its maximum values. Similarly, at the input level where total product reaches its maximum and later falls, marginal product falls to zero and becomes negative. The law of variable proportions can thus be expressed in terms of the behavior of the marginal product of the variable factor: there are increasing returns to the marginal unit of the variable factor while marginal product is rising, and decreasing returns thereafter as the marginal product falls.

The law of variable proportions is an "empirical" law, which is to say it has frequently been observed in actual production situations. This empirical law is not a judicial law, however, and hence there is no compulsion for every production function to exhibit the pattern described above. The range of increasing returns to the variable factors may be quite brief or indeed absent in many production processes. The point of inflection may be extended to exhibit a prolonged range of constant returns to the variable factor. Decreasing returns to the variable factor are a necessary feature of all short-run production situations, however. Sooner or later, as units of the variable factor are added to the fixed supply of capital resources, the marginal product of the variable factor must begin to decrease, due to simple overcrowding if for no other reason.

### The Law of Diminishing Returns

The law of variable proportions is often referred to by another name: the *law of diminishing returns.* The latter law is not as broadly stated as the former, saying simply that as additional units of the variable factor are added to the fixed factor base, *after some point* the increment to total product will decline progressively. Thus the law of diminishing returns refers only to the section of the total product curve that is concave from below, or to the negatively sloped portion of the marginal product curve.

## 6.4    RETURNS TO SCALE

### Increasing, Constant, and Decreasing
### Returns to Scale

The long-run analogy to increasing and decreasing returns to a variable factor in the short run is the increasing and decreasing returns to *all* factors (since all are variable) in the long run. By increasing the inputs of all factors in the same proportion, that is, by increasing the scale of the firm's operation, we expect output to increase by some proportion. If, for example, we double the inputs of both labor and capital, and output more than doubles, we speak of increasing returns to scale. If output increases by a smaller proportion, there are decreasing returns to scale. If output increases by the same proportion as capital and labor were increased, this indicates constant returns to scale.

We demonstrate this in Table 6.3, which is derived from Table 6.1, and by an extension of Table 6.1 to larger scales of operation. Note that capital and labor are combined in the ratio 1:2 in each row of Table 6.3: factor proportions are constant while the *scale* of operations is progressively increased. Returns to scale are determined by the percentage increase in output as compared with the percentage increase in scale of plant. Thus capital and labor *together* become more efficient until the sixth scale of plant (six capital/twelve labor), at which combination there are constant returns to scale followed by decreasing returns for the seventh and subsequent scales of operation.

How can we show the returns to scale on the output hill? Note that we wish to show the impact upon the production surface as all factors are increased in the same proportion. A ray from the origin along the base of the grid will reflect a constant relationship between capital and labor. If we slice the output hill

**TABLE 6.3**
Returns to scale exhibited by the relative increases
in scale and output

| Units of Capital and Labor | Percentage of Preceding Row (%) | Output Level (units) | Percentage of Preceding Row (%) | Returns to Scale |
|---|---|---|---|---|
| 1 and 2 | – | 3 | – | – |
| 2 and 4 | 200 | 19 | 633 | Increasing |
| 3 and 6 | 150 | 62 | 326 | Increasing |
| 4 and 8 | 133.3 | 110 | 177 | Increasing |
| 5 and 10 | 125 | 198 | 180 | Increasing |
| 6 and 12 | 120 | 238 | 120 | Constant |
| 7 and 14 | 116.7 | 273 | 115 | Decreasing |
| 8 and 16 | 114.3 | 300 | 110 | Decreasing |

along such a ray, the shape of the production surface along this slice will provide the information we seek. Two such slices are shown in Figure 6.3. Since returns to scale refer to the rate of change of output (vertical rise) as all inputs are changed in a constant proportion (horizontal run), the slope of the line cut into the production surface indicates whether there are increasing, constant, or de-

**FIGURE 6.3**
Returns to scale exhibited by the production surface

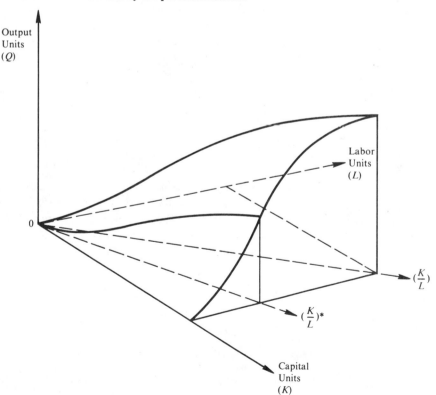

creasing returns to scale. While this line is convex from below, the production process is enjoying increasing returns to scale; and while it is concave from below, there are decreasing returns to scale. If this line is straight over any distance, this represents an area of constant returns to scale.

In the production function shown here, constant returns prevail only momentarily, at the inflection points. The equation that would best fit the hypothetical production function with which we have been dealing would show output as a cubic function of capital and labor. That is,

$$Q = a + bK + cK^2 - dK^3 + eL + fL^2 - gL^3 \qquad (6.2)$$

This specification is intuitively appealing because it incorporates the entire range of possibilities of increasing, constant, and decreasing returns to the factors in both the short- and long-run situations. In empirical applications, however, it is likely that our data base will refer not to the entire spectrum of output possibilities but to a considerably smaller range of observations. Over such a range of observations we may find that a more simple specification of the production function would provide a sufficiently good fit to the data. One such form of the production function that has been widely used in empirical studies is the linear homogeneous production function.

### Linear Homogeneous Production Functions

A linear equation is convenient in research applications because it allows the estimation of the coefficients using the technique of linear-regression analysis. Linear homogeneous equations are even more convenient because of their mathematical tractability. A production function is homogeneous if, when all inputs are augmented by the same proportion, this proportion can be completely factored out. If, when all inputs are augmented by a certain proportion, output increases by the same proportion, we say the production function is homogeneous to degree one, or that it is linear homogeneous. A linear homogeneous production function is, therefore, one that exhibits constant returns to scale over its entire range. As a corollary, the marginal products of the factors depend only upon the ratio in which the inputs are employed, and not upon their absolute amounts. This is a useful result for business applications, since, once the appropriate capital-labor ratio (or more generally the factor proportions ratio) has been established, the firm may change its scale of operations without the necessity of also changing its factor proportions.

The most popular empirical production function[4] is undoubtedly the power function, such as

$$Q = aK^b L^c \qquad (6.3)$$

where $a$, $b$, and $c$ are parameters expressing the relationship between $Q$, $K$, and $L$.

[4] This form of the production function is popularly known as the Cobb-Douglas production function, after two pioneers in the application of this form. See Paul H. Douglas, "Are There Laws of Production?" *American Economic Review*, March 1948, pp. 1-41.

Power functions, although expressing a multiplicative relationship between the inputs, are linear in logarithmic form. That is, Eq.(6.3) may be expressed as

$$\log Q = \log a + b \log K + c \log L \tag{6.4}$$

and linear regression analysis may be used to estimate the values of the parameters. Power functions are homogeneous functions, and the degree of homogeneity is given by the sum of the exponents $b$ and $c$ in Eq.(6.3), or alternatively, by the sum of the regression coefficients $b$ and $c$ in Eq.(6.4). If this sum is unity, the production function exhibits constant returns to scale; if less than unity, there are decreasing returns to scale; and if greater than unity, there are increasing returns to scale.

In terms of the production surface, a linear homogeneous production function means that the top line of a slice along a constant $K/L$ ray must be a straight line from the origin. This is not to deny the possibility of increasing or decreasing marginal product of the variable factor in short-run situations, however. When sliced along a constant capital input level, the total product curve might exhibit the shape shown in Figure 6.2. But if it does, then all higher total product curves must be scale magnifications of that curve in order for this to be a case of constant returns to scale.

## 6.5   ISOQUANT-ISOCOST ANALYSIS

A third dimension in which we may slice the output hill is the horizontal. Any horizontal slice in the output hill will result in a curved line being cut into the production surface. Such a line is known as an *isoquant,* meaning equal quantities, and shows the various combinations of labor and capital that can be used to produce a particular output level. Since the output level is constant for each isoquant curve, we can depict them in two dimensions as in Figure 6.4. Note that isoquant lines are in effect contour lines on the production surface, since all points on a particular line show equal elevation above the base of the output hill.[5]

### Technical and Economic Efficiency

A combination of capital and labor is technically efficient if none of either factor can be subtracted without reducing the output level, given *ceteris paribus.* All combinations on negatively sloped sections of the isoquant curves are technically efficient, since if one factor input is reduced while the other factor input is held constant, output will decline and the new input combination will lie on a lower isoquant curve. On the other hand, all combinations on positively sloped sections of isoquant curves are technically *inefficient,* since some of both factors may be subtracted without output being reduced. In terms of Figure 6.4, output level $Q_1$ can be produced by different combinations of capital and labor at

[5]To stay in accord with the traditional treatment of isoquant curves, we put capital on the vertical axis and labor on the horizontal axis.

FIGURE 6.4
Isoquant curves: contour lines on the output hill

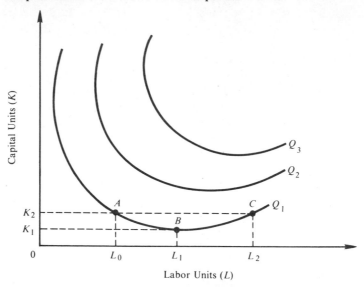

points *A, B,* and *C.* Combination *C* is technically inefficient, however, since the same output level could be produced at combination *A* by subtracting $L_2 - L_0$ units of labor, or at combination *B* by subtracting both $L_2 - L_1$ units of labor and $K_2 - K_1$ units of capital. By the same process of reasoning, *all* points on positively sloped sections of the isoquants are technically inefficient combinations of the inputs.

The slope of an isoquant at any point is the ratio of the amount of capital that can be subtracted from the production process to the amount of labor that is added to the production process, such that output level remains constant. For a one-unit increment in the labor input, this ratio is known as the *marginal rate of technical substitution* of capital for labor. Notice that the marginal rate of technical substitution (MRTS), like the slope, will be negative for all technically efficient combinations of the factors, and positive for all technically inefficient combinations. No rational firm would utilize a combination of capital and labor for which the marginal rate of technical substitution is positive, since this implies the marginal productivity of one factor is negative, and the firm is therefore paying money for an input that causes output to be reduced.[6]

The combinations of capital and labor on the negatively sloped sections of the isoquants represent the range of possibilities open to the rational firm. The actual combination of capital and labor chosen to produce each output level (in the long-run situation where the firm is free to vary all inputs) will depend on the relative prices of the inputs. Only one of the technically efficient ways of

[6] It can be shown, as it was in the context of the marginal rate of substitution between products in Chapter 3, that the MRTS is the negative of the ratio of the marginal products of the two input factors. A positive MRTS at the "upper" end of an isoquant is due to the marginal product of capital being negative, while a positive MRTS at the "lower" end of an isoquant is due to the marginal product of labor being negative.

producing each output level will be *economically* efficient; that is, only one will allow the lowest cost of producing that output level. To show this, we need to introduce isocost lines, which are analogous to the budget lines of consumer behavior theory, and which show combinations of capital and labor that cost the same amount. Let us express the firm's expenditure on inputs as

$$E = K \cdot P_K + L \cdot P_L \tag{6.5}$$

where $E$ is the total dollar expenditure; $P_K$ and $P_L$ are the unit prices of capital and labor, respectively; and $K$ and $L$ are the number of physical units of capital and labor that are to be employed in the production process. This can be re-arranged to appear as

$$K = \frac{E}{P_K} - \frac{P_L}{P_K} \cdot L \tag{6.6}$$

in which form it is perhaps more recognizable as a linear equation explaining $K$ in terms of $L$ and three known values. It can therefore be plotted in the same space as the isoquant curves. The intercept of the isocost line on the capital axis occurs when the labor input is zero, and is therefore simply the total expenditure divided by the price of the capital units, resulting in a certain physical quantity of capital units. As we purchase units of labor it is evident that our purchase of capital units, for the same expenditure (isocost) level, is drawn down in the ratio of the price of labor to the price of capital.

For each output level there will be a minimum-cost combination of the factors necessary to produce that output level. In Figure 6.5 we show three isoquant curves representing 20, 40, and 60 units of output. The cost of produc-

**FIGURE 6.5**
**Isoquant-isocost analysis showing short-run and long-run expansion paths**

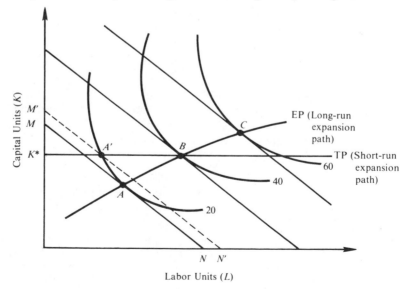

ing 20 units is minimized at point $A$, since any other capital/labor combination producing 20 units, such as at $A'$, will lie to the right of the isocost line $MN$ and would thus require a larger total expenditure to purchase. Recall that the intercept on the capital axis is equal to $E/P_K$, where $P_K$ is presumed to remain unchanged. Hence larger total expenditures are represented by higher intercept points and higher isocost lines. Similarly, the output level of 40 units is produced at least cost at the input combination represented by point $B$, and 60 units are produced at least cost by the input combination at point $C$.

### The Expansion Path:
### Long Run and Short Run

A locus of the tangency points between various isoquants and various isocosts is called the *expansion path,* since it shows the least-cost combinations of labor and capital a firm would choose as it expanded its output level, if it were free to vary both labor and capital and given constant factor prices and a constant state of technology. This expansion path is shown as the line EP in Figure 6.5. Note that this must be the *long-run* expansion path, since all factors must be variable to allow the adjustment in both capital and labor involved in the movement along the line EP.

Suppose the firm wishes to produce 40 units of output and thus selects the combination of factors represented by point $B$ on the long-run expansion path. The firm's capital input will now be fixed at $K^*$ units, and the firm is in a short-run situation. If the firm wishes to vary its output level in the short run, it must simply add or subtract labor to or from the fixed capital input $K^*$. The *short-run expansion path* is therefore a horizontal line at the capital input level $K^*$, and we have shown it as the line TP in Figure 6.5. This short-run expansion path is in fact the total product curve viewed from above the output hill.

Notice that for every output level except the one where TP crosses EP, it costs more to produce the output in the short run than it does in the long run. The isocost line that intersects each isoquant curve on the TP line must lie farther to the right when compared with the isocost line that is *tangent* to each isoquant curve. This is demonstrated in Figure 6.5 for the output level of 20 units. In the long-run situation the optimal input combination is at point $A$, and the lowest attainable isocost line is shown as $MN$. In the short-run situation with capital input of $K^*$, 20 units must be produced by the input combination represented by point $A'$, since the firm is constrained to the "short-run expansion path" TP. The minimum cost of producing 20 units with combination $A'$ is shown by the isocost line $M'N'$, which lies to the right of the line $MN$. The short-run situation costs more than the long-run situation for all except one output level, because the firm is unable in the short run to change the input of capital and is thus forced to have an inappropriate factor combination for all except one output level. In the case shown, only at the output of 40 units does the level of capital ($K^*$) allow the tangency situation of economic efficiency to be attained.[7]

---

[7] The isoquant-isocost analysis can be converted for use in short-run production problems where some of the variable factors are substitutable in production. For example, if more labor means less wastage of raw materials, we could find the optimal input of labor and raw materials for each output level, given the present size of plant, by putting labor on one axis and raw materials on the other and finding the tangency points between those isoquant curves and isocost lines that are appropriate.

### Factor Substitution Due to Changed
### Relative Factor Prices

Economic efficiency depends upon the relative factor prices. If the price of one factor changes, with *ceteris paribus,* the profit-maximizing firm will attempt to substitute away from the factor that has become relatively more expensive and in favor of the factor that has become relatively less expensive. Suppose the initial situation in Figure 6.6 is at point $A$. Output Level $Q_1$ is being produced economically efficiently by the factor combination $K_1$ units of capital and $L_1$ units of labor, and factor prices are such that the lowest-attainable isocost line is $MN$.

Suppose now that labor prices rise, due for example to a new agreement with a labor union or to legislation requiring the firm's contribution to an employee health scheme or similar benefits. Imagine that the increase in the cost of labor is such that the isocost line swings down from $MN$ to $MN'$. If the firm wishes to maintain its output level at $Q_1$, in order to hold its market share for example, it will need to spend more money on the inputs in order to produce $Q_1$. Given a long-run situation the firm will increase capital input to $K_2$ units and reduce labor input to $L_2$ units in order to produce $Q_1$ units of output with economic efficiency at point $B$, given the new factor price ratio. Thus the firm substitutes away from labor and in favor of capital when the price of labor increases relative to that of capital, given time to adjust the input of all factors. History has given us the opportunity to observe this phenomenon, of course: as the price of labor has increased relative to that of capital, we have observed production processes becoming relatively more capital intensive with the introduction of labor-saving equipment such as mobile assembly lines by Henry Ford and the more recent use of computerized production technology.

**FIGURE 6.6**
**Factor substitution due to changed relative factor prices**

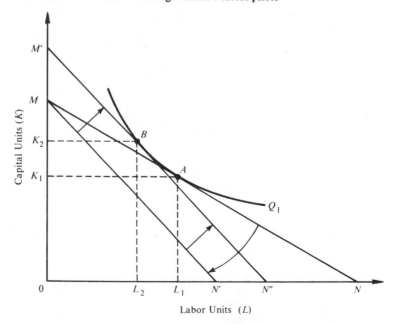

Figure 6.6 also explains why different factor input ratios are appropriate in different economies. Suppose the slope of *MN* reflects the factor price ratio in a relatively underdeveloped economy, for example, while the slope of *M'N''* reflects the factor price ratio in a more developed economy. If a firm in each economy wishes to produce $Q_1$ units, the firm in the first economy should use the more labor-intensive input combination at *A* while the firm in the second economy should use the relatively capital-intensive input combination at *B*, in order that each firm can achieve economic efficiency.

## 6.6 PRODUCTION THEORY IN VALUE TERMS: COST CURVES

In the preceding section we have examined the requirements for technical and economic efficiency in production. It is clear that if we attach factor costs to all levels of factor inputs, we may derive cost levels for all levels of output. Let us begin with the short-run cost curves.

### The Total Variable Cost Curve

In the short run the firm is constrained to a fixed level of capital input and must increase or decrease output along the total product curve. The total variable cost (TVC) curve can be derived from the TP curve simply by multiplying the level of variable inputs by the cost per unit of those inputs and plotting these cost data against the output level. Suppose that the variable factor units cost $10 each, and that the total product curve is as shown on the right-hand side of Figure 6.7. Using the data from the total product curve, and multiplying each unit of the variable factor by $10, we can plot the cost of the variable input against the output, as in the left-hand side of Figure 6.7.

For simplicity we have chosen the scale on the left-hand side of the horizon-

**FIGURE 6.7**
**Relationship between the total product and total variable cost curves**

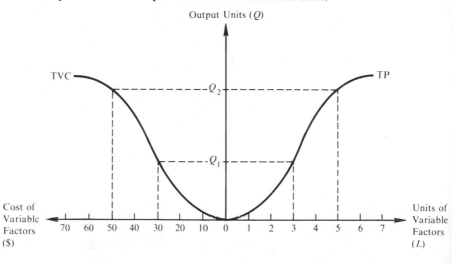

tal axis to be ten times that on the right-hand side, and thus the curve that reflects the total cost of the variable factors for all levels of output is a mirror image of the total product curve. Thus the shape of the total variable cost curve derives directly from the form of the production function and the number of units of capital employed, since these factors underlie the shape of the total product curve.

### Average Variable and Marginal Costs

From the total variable cost curve we can derive the average variable cost (AVC) curve and the marginal cost (MC) curve. In Figure 6.8 we show the TVC curve tipped on its side (by rotating the axes) with the associated average varia-

**FIGURE 6.8**
**Derivation of average variable and marginal cost curves from total variable cost curve**

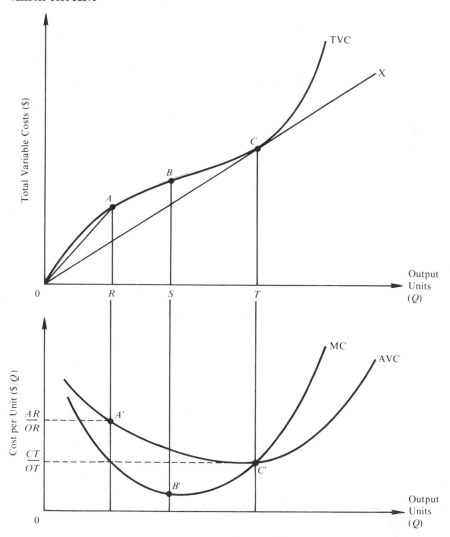

ble and marginal cost curves. Average variable cost is equal to TVC divided by output, $Q$, at every level of $Q$. The AVC at any output level is thus equal to the ratio of the vertical distance from the quantity axis to the TVC curve, to the horizontal distance from the cost axis to the TVC curve. In terms of the graph, this amounts to the vertical rise over the horizontal run, or the *slope of a ray from the origin* that joins the point on the TVC curve. Average variable cost at point $A$ on the TVC curve is equal to the ratio $AR/0R$, or the value of the slope of the line $0A$, and is shown as the point $A'$ on the AVC vertically below.

It can be verified that the slopes of lines between the origin and points on the curve will become progressively flatter as we begin to move up the TVC curve away from the origin. Thus the AVC, which is equal to the value of these slopes, must be falling over this range. A point is reached, however, where the ray from the origin can become no flatter and still touch the TVC curve. Point $C$, where the ray is just tangent to the TVC curve in Figure 6.8, signifies the lowest value for AVC. Since the rays become steeper for points on the TVC to the right of the tangency point, AVC must rise after this output level, as shown in Figure 6.8.

The derivation of marginal cost follows the same procedures as did the derivation of marginal product in Figure 6.2. <u>*Marginal cost* is the change in total variable costs due to a one-unit change in output. It is thus equal to the *slope* of the TVC curve at each output level.</u> If we were to put tangents against the TVC curve at every output level, we would see that the slopes of these tangents would fall at first, up to the point of inflection on the TVC curve, and would then rise. In Figure 6.8 the point of inflection occurs at point $B$, where the TVC curve changes from convexity from above to concavity from above. The slope of the TVC becomes progressively flatter until point $B$, and it becomes progressively steeper after point B as output is increased. This indicates that the marginal cost curve is U shaped, falling to a minimum at the output level where the TVC exhibits its inflection point, and rising thereafter.

It is important to note that while the marginal cost curve lies below the average variable cost curve, the latter is falling. In effect the lower marginal cost is pulling down the average. Conversely, when the MC curve lies above the AVC curve, the latter must be rising, being pulled up by the marginal costs. It follows that when the MC crosses the AVC, the AVC must be at its minimum value. This can be verified in Figure 6.8 at point $C$ on the TVC curve. Marginal costs and average variable costs must be equal, since both are given by the slope of the tangent to the TVC curve at that point.

Marginal costs are the value counterpart of the marginal product of the variable factors. When marginal productivity of labor is falling, marginal cost of output is rising and vice versa. If the efficiency of the marginal units of the variable factor is constant, then output can be produced at a constant level of marginal cost. These relationships can be confirmed by another look at Figures 6.2, 6.7, and 6.8.

### Short-Run Average Costs

To complete the short-run cost picture, we need to add the costs of the fixed factors. The total fixed costs (TFC) will show as a horizontal line when plotted

**FIGURE 6.9**
Derivation of short-run average cost curve

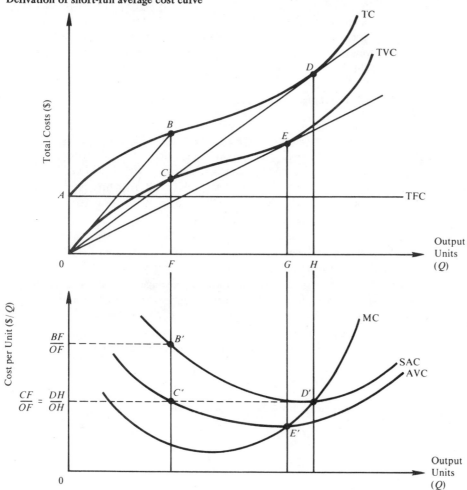

against output, as indicated in Figure 6.9, since these costs are constant what-ever the level of output. To find the total of fixed and variable costs, we add vertically the TFC and TVC curves on the graph. This, in effect, causes the TVC curve to be moved upward a constant distance equal to the total fixed costs. Thus the total cost (TC) curve and the TVC curve have the same shape, as is evident in Figure 6.9. The marginal cost curve could thus have been derived from the TC curve instead of the TVC curve. Since fixed costs are constant, total costs change only because of the change in variable costs, and it is thus legitimate to find MC from either the TC or TVC curve.

Average total costs, or short-run average costs (SAC), may be derived from the TC curve by the same technique as was used to derive the AVC curve. The slope of a ray from the origin to a point on the TC curve gives the value of SAC for each output level. Thus at point $B$ in the upper part of Figure 6.9, SAC is equal to the ratio $BF/OF$, or the slope of the line $0B$. At the same output level

**207**

AVC = $CF/0F$, or the slope of the line $0C$. In the lower part of the figure these values are shown as points $B'$ and $C'$, respectively. Given the shape of the TC curve, SAC must fall at first, reach a minimum, and then rise. Note that at the minimum point, found where the ray from the origin is just tangent to the TC curve, the slope of the ray is equal to that of the TC curve, and hence SAC and MC are equal at that output level.

### The Long-Run Average Cost Curve

To derive the long-run average cost curve, we could proceed by finding the SAC curve that relates to every level of fixed factors. Each level of capital (fixed factor) input will give rise to a TP curve, from which we can derive a TVC curve, and ultimately obtain the appropriate SAC curve as we did above. This procedure would give us a series of SAC curves, each with a slightly larger capital input level as we move from left to right. As shown in Figure 6.10, the long-run average cost (LAC) curve is the "envelope curve" of all these short-run curves. That is, it is made up of the points on the various SAC curves that allow each output level to be produced at the lowest possible cost when the firm is free to vary the input of all resources.

Alternatively, we can derive the long-run average cost curve from the expansion path generated by isoquant-isocost analysis. You will recall that the expansion path is the locus of the points of tangency between a series of isoquant and isocost curves, showing the least-cost (or economically efficient) factor combination for each output level. Since the LAC curve shows the least cost for each

**FIGURE 6.10**
**Long-run average cost curve: envelope curve of all short-run
average cost curves**

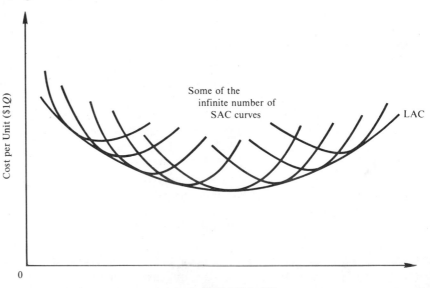

output level when it is possible to vary the input of all factors, we can derive the LAC curve from the data involved in the isoquant-isocost analysis. The level of output is given for each isoquant curve, and the minimum total expenditure necessary to produce each output level can be calculated as the intercept value of the tangent isocost line divided by the price of capital.

Similarly, we could derive the SAC curve from the isoquant-isocost analysis. In Figure 6.5 we showed the capital input fixed at the level $K^*$ and argued that for all output levels other than 40 units, it would cost more to produce those output levels in the short-run situation (constrained to $K^*$) than it would in the long-run situation where the economically efficient combination of both labor and capital could be employed. By finding the intercept value of the isocost lines that cross the intersection of the TP line and each isoquant curve, we could find the (minimum) total cost associated with each output level in the short-run situation. In Figure 6.11 we show the short-run total cost (STC) curve and the

**FIGURE 6.11**

Derivation of short- and long-run average cost curves
from the total cost curves

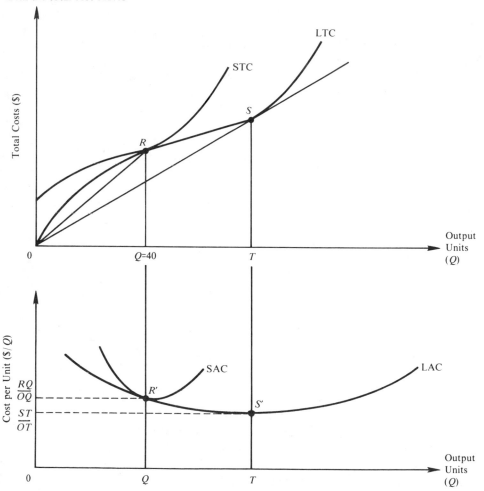

long-run total cost (LTC) curve that would be derived from the isoquant-isocost map in Figure 6.5.

Notice that the STC and LTC curves share the same value at point $R$, where the output level is 40 units, since in Figure 6.5 the TP curve crossed the long-run expansion path at this output level. For all other output levels the STC must lie above the LTC curve. In the lower part of the figure we show the associated SAC and LAC curves. Since SAC = STC/$Q$ and LAC = LTC/$Q$, each can be expressed as the value of the slope of the ray joining the origin and a point on the total cost curve. For $Q = 40$, the SAC = LAC = $RQ/0Q$. For all values of output other than 40, SAC > LAC, hence SAC is tangent to LAC at the output level of 40 units. The minimum value of the LAC curve occurs at point $S'$, since the ray from the origin to a point on the LTC curve reaches its minimum slope at point $S$ on the LTC curve. After the output level designated $T$, the LAC curve must begin to rise, since rays from the origin to points on the LTC curve to the right of point $S$ must have progressively steeper slopes. Thus the LAC curve derived from the cubic production function (See Eq.(6.2)) will fall to a minimum and later rise.

### Economies of Plant Size, Scale, and Firm Size

The U shape of the LAC curve indicates the existence of *economies* and *diseconomies* of plant size. At first, as progressively more capital is employed, the per unit costs of production fall progressively. That is, successive SAC curves lie lower and to the right. These economies arise due to factors such as the output level being large enough to allow the firm to utilize more efficient capital-intensive methods (such as computer-controlled assembly lines) and allows personnel to specialize in the areas of their greatest expertise. After some point, increasing inefficiencies in other areas, due perhaps to the increasing bureaucracy of larger establishments, offset these cost advantages, and the firm will experience diseconomies of plant size.

It is important to make the distinction between economies of *scale,* which are the cost counterpart of increasing returns to scale, and economies of plant *size,* as reflected by the long-run average cost curve. Recall that economies of scale are found when all factors are increased in the same proportion and thus involve an "expansion path" that is a straight line from the origin. Economies of plant size derive from the (least-cost) expansion path, which is not necessarily a straight line, although it does emanate from the origin. That is, firms are unlikely to want to expand all inputs in the same proportion as they increase their output under long-run conditions. In Figure 6.12 the expansion path above $Q_1$ units of output requires a constantly changing capital/labor ratio in order to minimize the costs of each output level. This is the result of differing marginal productivities of the inputs at different input levels and derives from the specific form of the production function underlying those isoquant lines.

In terms of the production surface, the least-cost expansion path is the route taken up the output hill when one always steps in the *steepest* direction, while an increase in scale requires movement up the output hill in a *constant* direction.

Changing factor proportions ratio along the expansion path

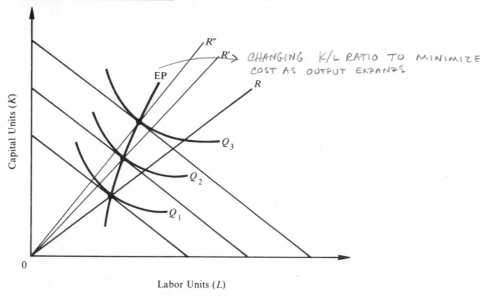

Only in the case of a homogeneous production function would the expansion path be a ray from the origin, as shown in Figure 6.13.

In the homogeneous case the spacing of particular isoquant curves determines the shape of the LAC curve. Where the isoquants are "spaced" such that propor-

FIGURE 6.13
★ Constant factor proportions along the expansion path: the linear homogeneous production function

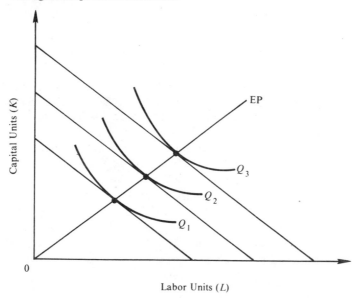

tionate increases in all factors lead to the *same* proportionate increase in output, there are constant returns to both scale and plant size throughout the range. In this case the production function is *linear* homogeneous, and the LAC curve will be a straight line, as in Figure 6.14. The SAC curves will maintain their U shape as long as there are diminishing returns to the variable factors in each short-run situation.

If the production function is not homogeneous to degree one, the LAC curve will be either downward or upward sloping to the right. Recall that if the exponents of the power production function (See Eq.(6.3)) sum to more than one (for the range of output levels under examination), this implies increasing returns to both scale and plant size and consequently a negatively sloping segment of the LAC curve. Conversely, if the exponents sum to less than one, there are decreasing returns to scale and plant size over the range of outputs in question, and the LAC curve will be positively sloping.

**FIGURE 6.14**
Cost curves of the linear homogeneous production function

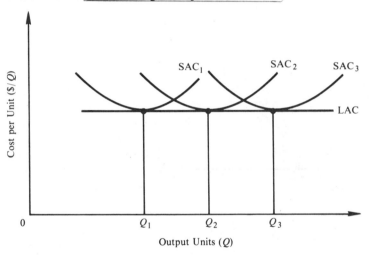

Certain other economies arise as a result of the *absolute size* of the firm. Larger firms are usually able to obtain discounts for bulk purchases of raw materials, for example, which gives them a cost advantage over smaller firms. These cost advantages are often referred to as "pecuniary" economies of plant or firm size and are clearly different from the economies of plant size that are dependent upon increasing efficiency in production. Many large firms derive further pecuniary economies as the result of operating more than one plant. These cost savings are likely to result from the spreading of certain underutilized fixed costs, such as managerial talent, computer rental, and advertising expenditures, over more than one plant. The long-run average cost curve for the first plant would therefore be expected to sink downward to some degree as a result of the opening of a second and subsequent plants. Any short-run average cost

**FIGURE 6.15**
Pecuniary economies causing cost curves to sink downward

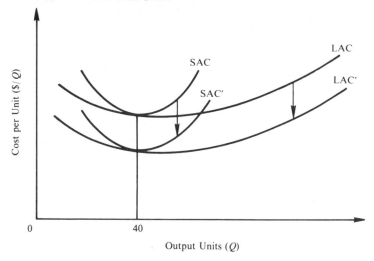

curve would also be lower, as in Figure 6.15, when economies of multiplant operation are experienced. The same effect would be noticed if there was a reduction in factor prices.[8]

## 6.7 SUMMARY

The concepts involved in the theory of production and costs can be explained and demonstrated in terms of the output hill and the production surface. Relating all the concepts back to the production surface serves to emphasize the interdependence of these concepts. The shape of the long-run average cost curve depends upon the various short-run average cost curves. The shapes of the short-run cost curves in turn depend upon the total product curves. The shapes of the total product curves depend upon the production surface. This in turn depends on the specific or mathematical form of the production function. Thus the U-shaped short-run cost curves are the result of the law of variable proportions, and the shape of the long-run average cost curve is due to the economies and diseconomies of plant size. All of this is involved in the underlying production surface. Whenever we draw a particular set of cost curves, we therefore implicitly presume the shape of the underlying production surface. Similarly, whenever a production function is specified, the shape and position of the cost curves is simultaneously implied.

[8] The cost curves would sink *vertically* downward only if there was an equivalent proportionate reduction in the prices of *all* factors. If the prices of variable factors were reduced by a larger proportion than the prices of factors that are fixed in the short run, the cost curves would sink downward *to the left* due to the substitution that would take place between factors where possible. Conversely, if fixed factor prices were reduced by the greater proportion, the curves would sink down toward the right as the firm substitutes in favor of the fixed factors.

213

It is important to emphasize that the long-run average cost curve does not refer to any long period of time, since factor costs and technologies will change over time, causing any particular LAC to become inappropriate. Instead, it refers to the minimum costs for each output level at a point of time, when factor costs and technologies can reasonably be assumed to be constant. When a firm decides what output level to produce, it then chooses its level of capital input, and hence the SAC that produces that output most efficiently. Thus the LAC shows the possibilities (the various plant sizes) that are available to the firm when the firm is free to vary both capital and labor (i.e., at the end of the short run). Once the firm has chosen a particular scale of plant, it is then constrained to that scale for the duration of the following short-run period, that is, until a sufficient period of time has elapsed such that the firm has been able to liquidate its existing plant, renew all its contracts, and employ more or less of the resources that are fixed in the short run.

This chapter provides the reader with a theoretical base for a critical examination of the use of various cost concepts in decision making, which is the subject matter of the following chapter. In decision making we must always be aware of the likelihood that per unit costs will change from their present levels due to changes in the output level. This cost change may be due to the presence of increasing or diminishing returns to the variable factors, or the experience of economies or diseconomies of plant or firm size. Underlying the present cost structure for all output levels is the state of technology and the prices of the input factors. If these change, the entire set of cost curves will shift, requiring a reevaluation of the present output level for its suitability in the light of the firm's objectives.

## DISCUSSION QUESTIONS

6.1   Explain how a tabular representation of a production function represents both the long-run and the short-run situations at the same time.

6.2   Suppose your production process has three inputs—machinery, highly skilled labor, and raw materials. If you wanted a new (larger or smaller) machine, it would take six months to be fabricated, delivered, and installed. Your present workers are all under contract for another eight months. New workers would take three months to acquire, due to the lengthy process of advertising, interviewing, and so forth. Raw-material supplies must be ordered four weeks in advance. How long is your short run? When can you make your long-run decision to expand or contract your plant size?

6.3   How does the law of variable proportions differ from the law of diminishing returns?

6.4   Why is the point of inflection on the total product curve the point where diminishing returns begin?

6.5   Why does a linear homogeneous production function imply constant returns to scale?

6.6   The smooth curve of an isoquant curve implies the ability to substitute continually small amounts of labor for capital. Given that fractions of labor and capital do not exist in a physical sense, how can we achieve the substitutions implied by a smooth isoquant curve?

6.7 Explain why the short-run cost of production exceeds the long-run cost of production for every output level except the one where the total product curve crosses the expansion path.

6.8 Why would you expect the textile industry of some countries to use hand looms (which take, say, two hours of labor per square meter of cloth) while in other countries highly mechanized processes (which take, say, thirty seconds of labor per square meter of cloth) are preferred?

6.9 Explain verbally why the shape of the short-run average variable cost curve depends on the specific form of the production function.

6.10 Distinguish between economies of scale, economies of plant size, and economies of firm size. Under what conditions would a firm's expansion be an example of all three phenomena at once?

## PROBLEMS

6.1 Donald K. Brown and Company operates a pearl-diving operation in the North Pacific Ocean. Mr. Brown owns a large trawler with all the required equipment. He hires local divers from the nearby islands and pays each of them on the basis of the weight of oysters recovered. He sells the pearls and the oyster meat separately. Over the past month he has been out pearling eight times in the same general area, taking all the divers who showed up for each trip. The particulars are as follows:

| Trip Number | Divers Employed | Oysters Recovered (lb) |
|---|---|---|
| 1 | 6 | 38 |
| 2 | 17 | 76 |
| 3 | 9 | 56 |
| 4 | 5 | 32 |
| 5 | 12 | 74 |
| 6 | 3 | 15 |
| 7 | 14 | 80 |
| 8 | 15 | 78 |

(a) Over what ranges do there appear to be increasing, constant, and diminishing returns to the variable factor?

(b) What number of divers appears to be the most efficient in terms of output per diver?

(c) What number of divers appears to be most efficient in terms of the utilization of the trawler and other equipment?

6.2 Taras Panache is the owner-manager of Panache Shirts Enterprises, which manufactures shirts by using rented space and equipment in a large warehouse. Due to the technical aspects of shirt production and the available equipment, separate production centers are used, each consisting of one cutting machine, two sewing machines, and three operators. Six months ago Mr. Panache had only one such production center, but recently he doubled, then tripled, and finally quadrupled the number of production centers by renting more space and equipment and hiring more operators. Throughout the expansion Mr. Panache has personally supervised all the operators and has handled all other aspects of the business. He kept a record of the average daily output from the entire plant for each of the four situations, as follows:

> One production center 20.6 shirts/day
> Two production centers 42.4 shirts/day

Three production centers          60.8 shirts/day
Four production centers           76.3 shirts/day

(a)   Can the expansion of Panache Shirts be regarded as a case of an increase in the *scale* of operations or simply an increase in the *size* of operations? Why?

(b)   Are there economies and/or diseconomies of scale/size evident? Explain.

(c)   Indulge in some speculation as to the probable cause of the economies and diseconomies, if any.

6.3   Given a production function of the form

$$Q = 38.6K + 3.2K^2 - 1.8\,K^3 + 16.3L + 2.8L^2 - 0.85L^3$$

where $K$ represents units of the capital input (in $1,000 units) and L represents units of the labor input (in hundreds of labor hours):

(a)   Construct the total product and marginal product curves for the case of $K = 5$.

(b)   At what level of labor input do diminishing returns become evident?

(c)   If labor were available to you at no cost (students wishing to gain work experience and willing to work without wages), what input level would you choose? Why?

6.4   The Himam Foods Corporation is a relatively small firm producing grocery items. Recently its research department developed a new salad dressing. Production of this new dressing would involve the use of the firm's mixing machine, which combines, shakes, rotates, and warms the ingredients to a specified temperature before pouring the mixture into bottles which are then capped and labeled. Some of the above procedures can be done manually, however, and Himam wants to choose the optimal proportions of machine time and labor time. The production function has been estimated as follows:

**Himam Foods—production function
(output in thousands of units)**

|                |   | Labor-Hours per Year (000) | | | | | |
|----------------|---|-----|-----|-----|-----|-----|-----|
|                |   | *1* | *2* | *3* | *4* | *5* | *6* |
| Machine Hours  | 1 | 25  | 80  | 110 | 120 | 125 | 115 |
| per Year (000) | 2 | 70  | 102 | 120 | 135 | 145 | 150 |
|                | 3 | 86  | 117 | 140 | 160 | 175 | 182 |
|                | 4 | 96  | 125 | 150 | 170 | 185 | 195 |
|                | 5 | 95  | 130 | 155 | 175 | 192 | 205 |
|                | 6 | 90  | 127 | 158 | 178 | 196 | 210 |

Machine-hours cost $25 per hour, and labor costs are $10 per hour. (Raw material costs are constant per bottle and are covered by a separate budget.) Due to the current difficult financial situation, Himam can allocate a budget of only $80,000 for the machine and labor costs of producing the new dressing.

(a)   Using isoquant-isocost analysis, show graphically the technically efficient factor combinations as distinct from the technically inefficient factor combinations.

(b)   Estimate the maximum output level which Himam can produce within its budget constraint, and the factor combination that is required to achieve this level.

(c)    Demonstrate what would happen if the cost of labor hours were to increase to $15 per hour. Estimate the new optimal factor combination and output level.

6.5    The Kolaitis Plastics Company manufactures plastic containers with the use of blow-molding equipment. The variable inputs are labor, plastic pellets, and electricity. The plastic and electricity are used in a fixed proportion with each other, but labor can be substituted for these inputs, since more labor means less wastage of the other two variable inputs. The production manager, Gerry Kolaitis, has a strong background in engineering and has estimated the production function over the relevant range as

$$Q = 10 \, (L^{0.5})^{0.5} \, PE^{0.5}$$

where $Q$ is the hourly output in units, $L$ is labor in hours, and $PE$ represents the combined units of plastic and electricity. Labor costs $6 per hour, and the PE units cost $3 each. Total fixed costs (including depreciation and maintenance on the blow-molding equipment) are $150,000 per annum, or $75 per working hour.

(a)    Derive and plot the isoquant curves for the output levels of 10, 15, 20, 25, and 30 units.

(b)    Estimate (from your graph) the minimum total variable cost of producing each of the above output levels, and show the average variable cost and short run average cost curves over this output range.

(c)    Comment upon the characteristics of this production function and the resultant expansion path and cost curves.

6.6    Gewurz Fabricators Limited manufactures and assembles small aluminum buildings suitable for garden toolsheds, garages, and children's playhouses. Stephen Gewurz, the owner, is considering opening a new plant to diversify into the production of luxury dog kennels for the expanding large dogs' market. He has carefully considered the labor and capital requirements and the substitutability between these inputs at various output levels and has summarized the production function as follows:

**Gewurz Fabricator—Production Function
(output in units per year)**

| | | Labor Inputs (person-years) | | | | | | | |
| | | 1 | 2 | 3 | 4 | 5 | 6 | 7 | 8 |
|---|---|---|---|---|---|---|---|---|---|
| Capital Inputs | 1 | 30 | 52 | 80 | 110 | 130 | 145 | 155 | 162 |
| (machine-years) | 2 | 50 | 80 | 120 | 164 | 200 | 220 | 235 | 248 |
| | 3 | 80 | 124 | 175 | 226 | 260 | 274 | 282 | 287 |
| | 4 | 100 | 160 | 218 | 272 | 302 | 320 | 335 | 345 |

(a)    Supposing that the cost of each unit of capital is $20,000 and the cost of each unit of labor is $10,000, derive the SAC curve for each of the five plant sizes indicated.

(b)    What conclusions can you draw about the returns to increasing plant size in this example?

(c)    Which of the five plants should be selected if demand is expected to be (a) 125 units? (b) 250 units? (c) somewhere within the range of 200-300 units? (Explain and defend your decision fully).

6.7 The newly-formed Beaudry Automobile Corporation plans to produce an expensive sports car and has asked your consulting firm for advice on the size of plant to construct. Due to the union contract and technical features of automobile production, labor must be paid $12,000 per person per annum, and each incremental change in plant size involves $900,000 in annual expenses for depreciation, interest, and other fixed costs. The maximum the firm will have available for expenditure on capital and labor is $9 million per annum. BAC has supplied the following details of its production function, meticulously derived by its chief engineer. (The data in the body of the table represent automobiles produced, in units.) Labor can be varied virtually continuously; the table shows units of 50 persons for convenience. All other variable expenses are constant at $2,500 per vehicle produced.

| Capital (units of $900,000) | Labor (units of 50 persons) | | | | | |
|---|---|---|---|---|---|---|
| | 1 | 2 | 3 | 4 | 5 | 6 |
| 1 | 20 | 40 | 70 | 90 | 100 | 108 |
| 2 | 30 | 50 | 100 | 130 | 140 | 147 |
| 3 | 40 | 90 | 140 | 170 | 180 | 185 |
| 4 | 60 | 120 | 180 | 220 | 230 | 236 |
| 5 | 100 | 170 | 230 | 250 | 260 | 268 |
| 6 | 170 | 200 | 240 | 270 | 280 | 289 |

BAC's market research indicates that the new vehicle should be sold at $35,000 per unit, and that the expected demand situation is as follows:

| Units Demanded (annually) | Probability |
|---|---|
| 0 | 0.05 |
| 50 | 0.05 |
| 100 | 0.25 |
| 150 | 0.35 |
| 200 | 0.25 |
| 250 | 0.05 |

(a) Plot the SAC curves suggested by the production function and input cost figures.

(b) Comment upon the economies and diseconomies of plant size (if any) which are evident in your graph.

(c) Which plant do you suggest that BAC build, and why?

# SUGGESTED REFERENCES AND FURTHER READING

BAUMOL, W. J., *Economic Theory and Operations Analysis,* 4th ed., Chap. 11. Englewood Cliffs, N.J.: Prentice-Hall, 1977.

CHAMBERLIN, E. H., "Proportionality, Divisibility and Economies of Scale," *Quarterly Journal of Economics,* 1948, pp. 229-57.

COLE, C. L., *Microeconomics: A Contemporary Approach,* Chaps. 6 and 7. New York: Harcourt Brace Jovanovich, 1973.

DOUGLAS, P. H., "Are There Laws of Production?" *American Economic Review,* March 1948, pp. 1-41.

LEFTWICH, R. H., *The Price System and Resource Allocation,* 5th ed., Chaps. 8 and 9. Hinsdale, Ill.: Dryden, 1973.

THOMPSON, A. A., Jr., *Economics of the Firm,* Chaps. 6-8. Englewood Cliffs, N.J.: Prentice-Hall, 1973.

# 7

# Cost Concepts
# for
# Decision Making

## 7.1 INTRODUCTION

The cost concepts introduced in this chapter are those that may be used in day-to-day decision making by the business executive. In some cases these are crude when compared with the theoretical nicety of the concepts discussed in the preceding chapter. Real-world business situations, however, seldom provide the data necessary for direct application of the theoretical concepts. Nevertheless, an understanding of the theoretical concepts is important to ensure the proper application of the concepts that will be discussed in this chapter. Decision makers sometimes tend to apply convenient rules of thumb to problems that confront them without first examining the applicability of those rules to the particular problem at hand. The danger of incorrectly applying these shortcuts is perhaps nowhere greater than in the area of costs, since poor decisions here operate directly to erode profitability.

## 7.2 ACCOUNTING VS. ECONOMIC COST CONCEPTS

The data for decision making with respect to costs typically come not from economists but from accountants. In most cases these data are adequate and appropriate, but in some cases, since they were derived for different purposes, they are less suitable for direct insertion into economic decision-making procedures. We shall examine several different economic and accounting cost concepts and the relationships between them.

### Direct and Indirect Costs

In the business firm some costs are incurred that can be directly attributed to the production of a particular unit of a given product. The use of raw materials, labor inputs, and machine time involved in the production of each unit can usually be determined. On the other hand, the cost of fuel for heating, electricity, office and administrative expenses, depreciation of plant and buildings, and other items cannot easily and accurately be separated and attributed to individual units of production (except on an arbitrary basis). Accountants speak of the *direct,* or *prime,* costs per unit when referring to the separable costs of the first category; and *indirect,* or *overhead,* costs when referring to the joint costs of the second category.[1]

Direct and indirect costs are not likely to coincide exactly with the economist's variable- and fixed-cost categories. The criterion used by the economist to divide cost into either fixed or variable is whether or not the cost varies with the level of output, while the criterion used by the accountant is whether or not the cost is separable with respect to the production of individual output units. To bring the accounting costs into line with the economic concepts, we must find that part of the indirect or overhead costs that varies with the output level. Accounting statements often divide overhead expense into "variable overhead" and "fixed overhead" categories, in which case we would add the variable overhead expense per unit to the direct cost per unit to find what economists call *average variable cost.*

*Determining Average Variable Costs.*    In the event that the overhead costs are not subcategorized as variable or fixed, we may be able to discover the variability that exists in the overhead costs by comparison of pairs of output and cost observations. Suppose that production in a metal-casting plant varies from month to month and that we have the data shown in Table 7.1 From the

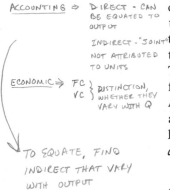

ACCOUNTING ⇒ DIRECT - CAN BE EQUATED TO OUTPUT

INDIRECT - "JOINT" NOT ATTRIBUTED TO UNITS

ECONOMIC ⇒ FC } DISTINCTION, VC } WHETHER THEY VARY WITH Q

TO EQUATE, FIND INDIRECT THAT VARY WITH OUTPUT

**TABLE 7.1**
**Costs of producing metal castings over two months**

| *Output Level (tons)* | June 1,480 | | July 1,620 | |
|---|---|---|---|---|
| *Cost of Production* | *Total* | *Per Unit* | *Total* | *Per Unit* |
| Direct materials | $ 77,700 | $ 52.50 | $ 85,050 | $ 52.50 |
| Direct labor | 36,260 | 24.50 | 42,000 | 25.93 |
| Fuel and plant supplies | 4,280 | 2.89 | 4,800 | 2.96 |
| Other labor | 26,500 | 17.91 | 26,500 | 16.36 |
| Office and administration | 2,700 | 1.82 | 2,700 | 1.67 |
| Utilities | 650 | 0.44 | 800 | 0.49 |
| Depreciation | 1,200 | 0.81 | 1,200 | 0.74 |
| Other overheads | 6,400 | 4.32 | 6,400 | 3.95 |
| Totals | $155,690 | $105.19 | $169,450 | $104.60 |

table it is clear that some cost elements have varied with the level of output while others have not. The direct materials and labor are clearly variable costs. Some part of fuel and plant supplies and utilities expense also appears to vary with the output level. Our estimate of the average variable costs will depend

[1] See, for example, C. T. Horngren, *Introduction to Management Accounting,* 4th ed. (Englewood Cliffs, N.J.: Prentice-Hall, 1978), Chap. 3.

upon how much of these two cost categories we decide to call *variable* and how much we decide to call *fixed*.

There are two extreme assumptions, namely, that they are entirely variable or that they are entirely fixed. These assumptions would generate a high estimate and a low estimate of average variable costs, and the actual figure undoubtedly lies somewhere in-between. The low estimate will include just the direct materials and labor costs and will be $77.00 at 1,480 units and $78.43 at 1,620 units. The high estimate will include the per unit fuel and plant supplies, and utilities costs and will be $80.33 at 1,480 units and $81.88 at 1,620 units. Arbitrarily, or based on better information, we may wish to allocate only some portion of the latter cost categories to variable costs and arrive at our "best estimate" of average variable costs. For decision-making purposes, however, such an exercise is of doubtful value. Decisions made will relate to the *marginal* units, which may or may not be produced as a result of the decision. We should therefore be concerned with the marginal cost per unit of the additional units, rather than the average of the variable costs per unit over the entire output range. A means of estimating the marginal cost per unit over a limited range of output values is known as the gradient method.

**Gradient Method of Determining Marginal Costs.**   *Gradient* means slope, of course, and the gradient of a cost component is the rate at which that cost changes as the output level changes. It is therefore calculated as the change in the cost level divided by the change in the output level, as indicated in Table 7.2.

**TABLE 7.2
Calculation of gradients**

*85,050 - 77,700 = 7350*

*1480 to 1620 = 140*

| Cost Category | Change in Costs | | Change in Output | | Gradient |
|---|---|---|---|---|---|
| Direct materials | $7,350 | ÷ | 140 | = | $52.50 |
| Direct labor | 5,740 | ÷ | 140 | = | 41.00 |
| Fuel and plant supplies | 520 | ÷ | 140 | = | 3.71 |
| Utilities | 150 | ÷ | 140 | = | 1.07 |
| Sum of gradients | | | | | $98.28 |

*DIRECT MATERIALS = AVE PER UNIT COST ⇒ DOES NOT VARY Q*

*DIRECT LABOR = RISING WRT Q (EFFICIENCY ↓)*

*FUEL & PLANT SUPPLIES = ↑ 3.71/TON*

*UTILITY EXPENSE = ↑/TON*

For direct materials the gradient in the table is $52.50, which is—not surprisingly—equal to the average per unit cost of direct materials, since this was the same at both output levels. This indicates that material usage (or wastage) per ton of output is constant. For direct labor the gradient is calculated to be $41.00. When this figure is seen in relation to the per unit cost of direct labor at the two output levels, it can be appreciated that direct labor efficiency is falling dramatically, since the gradient of direct labor costs is substantially above the average direct labor cost per unit of output and is causing the latter to rise. For fuel and plant supplies the gradient is $3.71, indicating that the cost for fuel and plant supplies has increased by the average amount of $3.71 per ton, over the output interval from 1,480 tons to 1,620 tons. Similarly, the gradient for utility expense, or the rate at which this expense increases as output increases by one unit, is calculated to be $1.07. The gradients for all other cost categories are zero.[2]

The approximate marginal cost of a ton of metal castings may be calculated as the sum of the gradients of each cost category. It is approximate because it is the average over the output range of 1,480 to 1,620 tons. Due to the existence of diminishing returns to the variable factors, we should expect an upward trend in marginal costs over this range rather than the constant marginal costs implied by the gradient method. Thus the *actual* marginal cost is probably somewhat below the total of the gradients at the low end of the output range, and somewhat above this figure at the high end.

Decisions with regard to output levels may thus proceed on the basis of the knowledge that the marginal cost is around $98 per unit at these output levels. Use of this figure for output levels beyond 1,620 tons, or below 1,480 tons (that is, extrapolation), is risky, since the apparent trends in some cost components may change outside the range of present observations. For example, the apparent constancy of per unit direct material costs may not hold, due to greater or lesser material wastage rates at other output levels. Alternatively, the apparent increase in inefficiency of direct labor may accelerate for outputs above 1,620 tons, such that per unit direct labor costs may be considerably above $41 per ton on the marginal units. Finally, the gradients calculated for the other cost components (including the zero gradients) cannot be assumed or expected to remain the same at other output levels.

The total per unit costs, or the average total costs of the metal castings, fall from $105.19 at 1,480 tons to $104.60 at 1,620 tons, as shown in Table 7.1. Average total costs decrease as output increases because the marginal costs, although probably rising, are still less than the average total costs over this output range. Stated alternatively, average total costs are falling because average variable costs are rising slower than average fixed costs are falling.

### Explicit and Implicit Costs

The accounting process is predominantly concerned with explicit costs. These are costs that actually involve a transfer of funds from the firm to another party that had previously supplied some materials or services. These are "out-of-pocket" expenses in the current time period, since they are an actual cash outflow in payment for resources. Other cost items, however, are implicit costs, in the sense that they do not involve an actual cash outflow in the current time period. One such cost in the accounting framework is *depreciation,* which seeks to charge against each year's revenue some portion of the cost of acquiring the capital equipment necessary to generate that revenue. The accounting procedures, however, do not include all the implicit costs that economists would like to see included. (There is a good reason for this, as we shall see later.) Let us illustrate with reference to the example of a small-store owner who has $50,000 invested as equity in the store and inventory. As shown in Table 7.3, the annual

---

[2] Beware of "false" gradients. If a change in a cost category might reasonably be expected to be the result of something other than the change in the output level, we should not include it in our calculation of marginal or incremental costs.

**TABLE 7.3**
Accounting income statement for the small-store owner

| | | |
|---|---:|---:|
| Sales | | $200,000 |
| Cost of goods sold | $120,000 | |
| Salaries | 20,000 | |
| Depreciation expense | 5,000 | 145,000 |
| Accounting profit | | $ 55,000 |

sales revenues were $200,000, from which must be deducted the cost of goods sold, salaries of hired labor, and depreciation of equipment and buildings. The accounting profit to the store is thus $55,000.[3]

In Table 7.4 we show the economic statement of profit of the same store. Note that the sales revenues, cost of goods sold, salaries, and depreciation are the same as in the preceding table. The economist, however, would add two

**TABLE 7.4**
Economic statement of profit to small-store owner

| | | |
|---|---:|---:|
| Sales | | $200,000 |
| Cost of goods sold | $120,000 | |
| Salaries | 20,000 | |
| Depreciation expense | 5,000 | |
| Imputed salary to owner-manager | 15,000 | |
| Imputed interest cost on equity  OPPORTUNITY COST  4,000 | | 164,000 |
| Economic profit | | $ 36,000 |

other items relating to the implicit cost of resources that are owned by the manager. Suppose the owner-manager could earn $15,000 as a departmental manager in a large store and this is his best opportunity for salary, then we would add a cost to the business of $15,000 being the imputed salary of the owner-manager. Similarly, the owner-manager has $50,000 equity in the store and inventory, and this sum of money could easily be employed elsewhere for financial gain. Suppose it could be banked or invested elsewhere at comparable risk and would receive 8 percent interest on the principal, or $4,000 per annum. By choosing to invest the $50,000 in the store rather than elsewhere, the owner-manager is therefore forgoing an income of $4,000 per annum, and the economist adds this as an implicit cost on the income statement. Thus the total economic costs, or the costs of all resources used in the production process, are $164,000, and the economic profit of the store is $36,000.

### Opportunity Costs and Historic Costs

We have seen that the accountant's concept of profit differs from that of the economist. Both consider profit as the excess of revenues over costs, but costs

[3] If the owner-manager were to make drawings from the business of cash or goods, these must be accounted for. For simplicity we assume he makes no drawings from the business.

are regarded differently. The accountant subtracts from revenues only those costs that are actually incurred, plus an apportionment of some of the previously incurred lump-sum costs such as the cost of plant and machinery. Profits then represent the net income to the owners of the firm and are their reward for having invested their time and capital in the venture. The economist, on the other hand, is concerned with the wider notion of efficient allocation of resources and is thus concerned that resources are employed where they will earn the maximum for their owners. A means of ensuring this is to consider the "opportunity cost" of each resource.

*Opportunity costs,* or *alternative costs* as they are often called, refer to what the resource could earn in alternative employment. For resources that are actually purchased outright or hired, such as raw-material inputs and labor cost, there is no dispute between economists and accountants. The market price at which they are purchased or hired should reflect their opportunity cost, since the small store must bid for these goods on their respective markets, and if not willing to pay at least what the resources are worth in their best alternative usage the store owner would not be able to purchase the services of these resources. The difference arises with those factors of production that are owned by the firm, such as land and buildings. These are resources that have been acquired in the past and which are not normally depreciated. Thus, although the services of these resources are used in the production process, no charge is made against revenues to reflect this. The economist would either impute a cost of these services on the basis of what the land and buildings might have earned in alternative employment or charge against revenues the interest that the capital tied up in those assets could have earned in an alternative investment, whichever is greater.

Thus the costs of the economist reflect the value of *all* the services provided. If revenues just equal these costs, then all factors are earning the same in that particular employment as they could earn elsewhere, and we say the firm is earning a "normal" profit. If revenues exceed these costs, we say the firm is earning a "pure," or an "economic," profit. Remembering that the owners of the firm are the effective suppliers of the services of the land and buildings mentioned, you will see that an economic profit means that the owners of the firm are earning more profit than they could by investing their capital elsewhere. The accounting profit must be reduced by the opportunity cost of the owned resources (that is, what the firm would have had to pay for the services of those resources if they had to be purchased or hired), before the alternative investment possibilities can be assessed.

This is not to say that either the accountant's or the economist's view of profit is incorrect; each is designed for a different purpose. The accountant's purpose is to find, once the capital has been invested in a particular pursuit, what is the return to the owners of that capital. The economist's purpose is to see that all resources are employed in their most efficient uses, and the existence of economic profit ensures that this is so. Thus the accounting profit may exceed economic profit to the extent that some implicit opportunity costs have not been subtracted from revenues. However, if you were to add the total amount of funds that are at the owner-manager's disposal, including the allowance for depreciation, you would find that it comes to $60,000 in Table 7.3, and it also sums to $60,000 in Table 7.4, the difference being simply the way this return to the owner is classified. Inclusion of the opportunity costs of all factors used in the production process is, however, extremely important for sound decision making. Where there are two or more options for the use of a particular resource, it must be ascertained that the resource is being employed in its most remunerative usage.

The opportunity cost of a resource is sometimes different from the actual cost at which it was purchased. Suppose a firm has in inventory a number of small machines and wishes to value one of these machines for inclusion in its bid price on a particular contract. Suppose the *historic cost* of the machine was $1,000, but the price to buy one now is $1,200. Presumably, then, the firm could sell each of these machines out of its inventory for $1,200. The appropriate cost to be entered in the calculation for the bid price is therefore $1,200, or the opportunity cost of the resource being used. It will, after all, cost $1,200 to replace that item in inventory.

The most common application of the opportunity cost doctrine in decision making concerns the situation where a particular resource has one or more uses at the same point of time. In this case if the resource is used in the production of a particular output, it precludes the production of one or more *other* outputs. Of course, the resource should be used in the production of the most profitable item, but we defer discussion of this until we have defined the cost concept that allows us to determine which is the most profitable item.

### Relevant Costs and Irrelevant Costs

Costs that will be incurred as the result of a decision are the *relevant* costs for decision making. Costs that have been incurred already or which will be incurred in any case are *irrelevant* costs as far as current decision making is concerned. To illustrate the concept of relevant and irrelevant costs, let us consider the following scenario.

The manager of a city pet store buys from a breeding farm a six-week-old St. Bernard puppy, which is to be sold as a pet, since its conformation is not quite good enough for showing or breeding. The puppy costs $50 and the pet-store manager puts it in a cage in the store's window and prices it at $200. The pet store incurs additional costs directly related to this puppy, such as feeding and cleaning the animal and its environs. This cost has been calculated as $5 per week for cleaning, and $1 weekly for food initially, increasing by twenty cents each additional week as the puppy becomes larger and more ravenous. Ten weeks later the puppy is not yet sold. It has grown quite large, lost much of its puppy charm, and barks incessantly (due perhaps to its frustration at spending its puppyhood in a cage). The manager of the pet store wants to get rid of the puppy and decides to price it at "his cost." He calculates this as the initial $50 plus $50 for ten-weeks' cleaning, plus $18 for its food over the period, totaling $118.

Is the \$118 the relevant cost? That is, should the pet-store manager refuse to take less than \$118 for the puppy if he wants to avoid a loss? The answer to the first question is no, and it is probably no to the second question as well. The manager is about to make a decision, and as a result of that decision costs may or may not be incurred, and revenues may or may not be earned. The relevant costs are those that will be incurred as a result of the decision. We might expect few people to be willing to spend \$118 for the puppy in its present form, given the availability of substitute puppies with more endearing personalities and characteristics, albeit at higher prices. Thus the puppy may not sell at \$118 and will remain in the store for subsequent weeks, during which time it will continue to incur feeding and cleaning costs. Given that its marketability is declining it may never sell, and each week the out-of-pocket cost of keeping this item in inventory rises.

Price should be set not in relation to the historic cost level but at some level that will ensure that the dog will be sold very quickly, before future costs are incurred to any great extent. Perhaps the manager should take whatever he is offered for the dog. The costs previously outlaid are irrelevant to the pricing decision to be made here: they are sunk costs which have resulted from the earlier decision to buy the puppy from the breeding farm. To include them in the present decision is to let an earlier bad decision cause another bad decision to be made. In business parlance, the pet-store manager should "cut his losses" and "avoid sending good money after bad."

### Incremental Costs  AGGREGATE Δ COSTS THAT RESULT FROM DECISION

Incremental costs are the most important cost concept for short-term decision making. *Incremental costs* are defined as the change in overall costs that results from a particular decision being made. Incremental costs may therefore be either fixed or variable, since a new decision may require purchase of additional capital facilities plus extra labor and materials. When compared with incremental revenues, that is, with the change in total revenues that occurs as a result of the decision, we can see whether a proposed decision is likely to be profitable or not. Clearly, if incremental revenues exceed incremental costs, then the proposed decision will add to total profits (or reduce losses if the total revenues generated do not cover the total costs incurred).

Incremental costs are not identical with marginal costs. As defined in the preceding chapter, *marginal costs* are the change in total cost for a one-unit change in the output level. Incremental costs, on the other hand, are the aggregate change in costs that results from a decision. This decision may involve a change in the output level of twenty or two thousand units, or it may not involve a change in the output level at all. For example, the decision might be whether or not to introduce a new technology of producing the same output level. Knowledge of marginal costs, however, may be very important for the calculation of the incremental costs.

The incremental costs must be accurately identified. Only those costs that actually change as a result of the decision may be included, but all costs that change as a result of the decision must be included. Factors that have been lying idle, with no alternative use, do not have an incremental cost and therefore may be regarded as being costless for the particular decision at hand. Similarly, costs that have been outlaid in the past for machinery or plant and buildings must be regarded as sunk costs and should not enter the decision-making procedure unless their opportunity cost is positive. That is, unless there is a competing and profitable use for an owned resource, the incremental cost of involving that resource in the present decision will be zero.

## 7.3   CONTRIBUTION ANALYSIS   INCREMENTAL REVENUES LESS INCREMENTAL COSTS

The *contribution* of a decision is defined as the incremental revenues of that decision less the incremental costs of that decision. It should be interpreted as the "contribution made to overhead costs and profits" by the decision. Clearly, only those decisions that have a positive contribution should be undertaken; and where decisions are mutually exclusive, the one with the larger expected contribution is to be preferred. We shall illustrate contribution analysis with three common types of decision problems.

### Project A or Project B?

Suppose a firm is considering adopting either Project A or Project B but cannot adopt both, since they use the same set of machinery and labor. Project A, as shown in Table 7.5, promises sales of 10,000 units at $2 each, with materials, labor, variable overhead, and allocated overhead costs as shown, such that there is an apparent profit of $2,000. Project B promises sales revenues of $18,000, with materials, direct labor, and variable and allocated overhead as shown. The apparent profit from Project B is $4,000, and it would seem that Project B is preferable to Project A by virtue of its higher profitability.

When contribution analysis is applied to the above decision problem, however, the answer may be surprising. Consider Table 7.6, in which the incremental costs are subtracted from the incremental revenues to find the contribution of each project. Since the allocated overheads were not a cost incurred as a result of this particular decision, they are excluded from the contribution analysis, and it can be seen that Project A contributes more to overheads and profits than

**TABLE 7.5**
**Income statements for projects A and B**

| Project A | | | Project B | | |
|---|---|---|---|---|---|
| Revenues (10,000 @ $2) | | $20,000 | Revenues (6,000 @ $3) | | $18,000 |
| Costs | | | Costs | | |
| Materials | $2,000 | | Materials | $5,000 | |
| Direct labor | 6,000 | | Direct labor | 3,000 | |
| Variable overhead | 4,000 | | Variable overhead | 3,000 | |
| Allocated overhead | 6,000 | 18,000 | Allocated overhead | 3,000 | 14,000 |
| Profit | | $ 2,000 | Profit | | $ 4,000 |

TABLE 7.6
Contribution analysis for projects A and B

| | Project A | | | Project B | | |
|---|---|---|---|---|---|---|
| Incremental revenues | | $20,000 | Incremental revenues | | | $18,000 |
| Incremental costs | | | Incremental costs | | | |
|   Materials | $2,000 | |   Materials | $5,000 | | |
|   Direct labor | 6,000 | |   Direct labor | 3,000 | | |
|   Variable overhead | 4,000 | 12,000 |   Variable overhead | 3,000 | | 11,000 |
|     Contribution | | $ 8,000 |     Contribution | | | $ 7,000 |

does Project B. The danger of including arbitrary allocations of fixed overheads is exemplified here. The overheads were allocated on the basis of a particular criterion, in this case as 100 percent of direct labor, and if included as an actual cost would have caused an inferior decision to be taken. Whatever method of overhead allocation is used, the danger is likely to persist. Hence we use contribution analysis, which allows an incisive look at the actual changes in costs and revenues that follow a particular decision.

### Make or Buy?

The Wilson Tool Company manufactures high-quality power tools such as drills, jigsaws, and sanders. All these tools require the same roller-bearing unit, which the company manufactures in its own bearing department. Pertinent cost data for the past year of operations in that department are shown in Table 7.7.

Demand estimates indicate that the company should expand its production of some of the power tools, and that an additional 7,500 bearing units will be required. The company could produce these in its bearing department but is considering having the additional units supplied by a specialist bearing firm. Wilson anticipates that it will require an increase of 15 percent in total direct labor costs, and 12 percent in total materials costs, to produce these additional units in-house. No additional capital expenditure will be necessary, since some machines currently have idle capacity. A specialist bearing producer has been approached, and after considering the specifications has offered to supply the 7,500 bearing units at a total cost of $30,000, or $4 per unit. Should Wilson make or buy the additional bearing units?

TABLE 7.7
Wilson tool company: bearing department costs

| | Total | Per Unit |
|---|---|---|
| Direct materials | $ 38,640 | $ 0.56 |
| Direct labor | 126,390 | 1.81 |
| Allocated overhead | 252,780 | 3.63 |
| | $417,810 | $ 6.00 |
|     Total bearing units produced: | | 69,635 |

We begin by comparing the incremental costs of the two alternatives facing Wilson. The incremental costs of buying them from the specialist come to $30,000, since this is the dollar amount that Wilson must outlay to obtain the additional units. To calculate the incremental costs of making the units in-house, we begin by calculating the increases in materials and direct labor costs that would be occasioned by the manufacture of those units. The 12 percent increase in the total material cost would imply an incremental material cost of $4,637, and a 15 percent increase in total direct labor costs would imply a $18,959 increase in that cost category. As shown in Table 7.8, the total of these two figures is $23,596, which is less than the incremental cost of buying the units from outside. The decision to make, rather than buy, the additional units would thus appear to save the Wilson Tool Company a total of $6,404.[4]

**TABLE 7.8**
**Incremental costs of making the bearing units**

|  |  | *Total* | *Per Unit* |
|---|---|---|---|
| Direct materials | 38640 (.12) = | $ 4,637 | $0.62 |
| Direct labor | 126390 (.15) | 18,959 | 2.53 |
| Allocated overhead |  | – (?) | – (?) |
|  |  | $23,596 | $3.15 |

*Variability of Overheads.* The above analysis, however, does not consider the possibility that some part of overhead expenses may vary with the level of production of the bearing units. It is conceivable that some overhead cost components, such as electricity, office and administration expense, and cafeteria expense, might vary to some degree as a result of producing these units in-house. Rather than make arbitrary assumptions as to the proportion of overheads that will vary, and since we do not have the information necessary to make a reasoned judgment, let us perform a sensitivity analysis on the decision that has been made. That is, we wish to know by how much the overhead expenses might vary before the decision to make the product would be the wrong decision. The answer is obviously that if overheads vary more than $6,404 as a result of this decision, then the best decision would have been to buy the product from the outside supplier. A $6,404 variation in overhead represents slightly more than a 2.5 percent variation in the allocated overhead. It is up to the decision maker to judge whether a variation of this percentage or dollar magnitude is likely to follow the decision to produce the product in-house.

*Longer-Term Incremental Costs.* A number of other considerations should also enter this decision. First, there is the issue of long-term supplier relations. Wilson may need a specialist producer some time in the future when it may be

---

[4] Since the incremental revenue is the same whether Wilson makes or buys the parts, we can do the contribution analysis on the basis of the incremental costs alone. Presuming that the incremental revenues exceed the incremental costs, the "make" alternative would seem to contribute more to overheads and profits than does the "buy" alternative.

unable to produce the bearings in-house due to capacity limitations, and perhaps by giving this contract out at the present time it could establish itself as a customer of the supplier, such that in future situations supply could be assured.

Second, there is the issue of the quality of the bearing units supplied by the outside firm as compared with those produced by Wilson. The decision maker would have to be assured that the units supplied from outside would be at least equal in quality to the standards desired. On the other hand, the specialist producer may be able to produce consistently higher quality bearing units, with subsequent impact upon the quality of Wilson Tools, and long-term buyer goodwill.

Third, the issue of labor relations must be considered. The decision to make the units involves an increase in the labor force, which may lead to crowded working conditions and overtaxed washroom and cafeteria facilities. The data indicate that labor efficiency is decreasing, since the incremental cost per unit to make the additional 7,500 units is $3.15 compared with the total of $2.37 for direct materials and labor per unit shown in Table 7.7. It is conceivable that the hiring of additional labor units and the resultant increased congestion and reduced efficiency could cause a lowering of employee morale, with subsequent longer-term disadvantages to the profitability of the Wilson Tool Company.

In total the decision maker must decide whether or not the expected (present) value of these eventualities, plus the possible variable components in overhead costs, is likely to exceed $6,404. If so, then the decision should be to buy the product from outside.

***Other Considerations.*** Certain additional doubts may be cast upon the above problem. First, the decision maker would need to be assured of the accuracy of the estimations that are involved in his decision. If, for example, demand for the tools does not increase as predicted, and Wilson purchased the roller-bearing units from outside, this would be an irreversible commitment involving considerable expense, whereas the decision to make the units in-house could soon be suspended. The cost estimates are likewise subject to some doubt. These are presumably extrapolations on the estimated marginal costs of producing the units in-house. The decision maker would need to be assured that these were based on the most reasonable assumptions concerning the efficiency of direct labor and material usage, and consequently are the best estimates. To the extent that there is a distribution of both demand and cost estimates, a decision based on the most likely point estimate alone may result in an outcome that is quite different from the one expected.

Another question that arises in the above problem is whether or not the price quotation received is in fact the lowest-cost source of supply of these bearing units. We might assume that tenders were called and the lowest bid was being considered, but if this were not the case then the decision maker should consult alternative sources of supply to confirm that the $30,000 price was in fact the best price at which the units might be bought from outside.

With these qualifications in mind, we turn now to the third category of decision problems in which contribution analysis is an appropriate solution procedure.

## Take It or Leave It?

The Idaho Instruments Company produces a variety of pocket calculators and sells them through a distributing company. The purchasing agent for a large chain of department stores has recently approached Idaho Instruments with an offer to buy 20,000 units of its model X1-9 at the unit price of $8. Idaho's present production level of that model is 160,000 units annually, and it could supply the additional 20,000 units by forgoing production (and sale) of 5,000 of its more sophisticated X2-7 model. Pertinent data relating to these two models are shown in Table 7.9. Due to the highly mechanized production process, the per unit variable costs of each model are believed to be constant over a wide range of outputs. The sales manager for Idaho Instruments is reluctant to sell the X1-9 model for $8 when he normally receives $12 from the distributing company, and he has attempted to negotiate with the purchasing agent. The latter, however, insists that $8 is his only offer. Should Idaho Instruments take it or leave it?

TABLE 7.9
Idaho instruments company: per unit data on calculators

|  | Model X1-9 | Model X2-7 |
|---|---|---|
| Materials | $ 1.65 | $ 1.87 |
| Direct labor | 2.32 | 3.02 |
| Variable overhead | 1.03 | 1.11 |
| Fixed overhead | 5.00 | 6.00 |
| Profits | 2.00 | 2.40 |
| Price to distributor | $12.00 | $14.40 |

Since the average variable cost for both models is expected to be constant over a wide range, we can calculate the incremental cost of this decision on the basis of the average variable cost. The average variable cost is the sum of the first three components in the table, and hence 20,000 additional units of the model X1-9 (with AVC = $5.00) will add $100,000 to the cost levels. This figure is not the total incremental cost, however, since there is an opportunity cost involved. The production of the additional 20,000 units will come partly from the idle capacity that is to be utilized, and partly at the expense of 5,000 units of the model X2-7. The opportunity costs of using the resources that previously produced the X2-7 are the value of those resources in that alternate use. The net value to Idaho Instruments of employing the resources in the production of 5,000 units of the X2-7 is the contribution made by those 5,000 units. From Table 7.9 it can be found that the contribution per unit to overheads and profits is $8.40. Hence the opportunity costs are the total forgone contribution, or $42,000. In Table 7.10 we show the contribution analysis of this problem. The incremental revenues are $160,000, and the incremental costs sum to $142,000. Hence the contribution to overheads and profits that would follow from the decision to take the department store's offer is $18,000. Hence profits

233

**TABLE 7.10**
Contribution analysis of calculator decision problem

| | | |
|---|---:|---:|
| *Incremental revenues* | | |
| 20,000 units of X1-9 @ $8.00 | | $160,000 |
| *Incremental costs* | | |
| Variable costs | | |
| 20,000 units of X1-9 @ $5.00 | $100,000 | |
| Opportunity costs | | |
| 5,000 units of X2-7 @ $8.40 | 42,000 | 142,000 |
| Contribution | | $ 18,000 |

would be $18,000 greater than they would be otherwise, or losses would be $18,000 less.

An alternate method of arriving at the same contribution would be to subtract from the incremental revenues the revenues forgone when the 5,000 units of X2-7 were not sold at $14.40 (that is, $72,000) and subtract from the incremental cost of producing the extra units of the model X1-9 the decremental costs of not producing 5,000 units of the model X2-7 (that is, $30,000). The net adjustment as the result of these manipulations is $72,000 − $30,000, or $42,000, which is exactly the opportunity cost figure we have entered in Table 7.10. The opportunity cost method achieves the same results with some economy of effort, but more importantly, perhaps, it draws the decision maker's attention to the possible alternate uses of resources.

There are some qualifications to the above decision, however. The first issue is that of substitutability between the units sold to the department store and those sold to the distributing company. The above analysis has proceeded upon the implicit assumption that the sale of 20,000 units to the department store will be *in addition to,* and nonsubstitutable with, the 160,000 units sold through the distributing company. To the extent that some customers now buy this product through the department store rather than through the distributing company, Idaho Instruments will be forgoing an amount of $4 per unit, or the difference in the price charged to the two wholesale buyers. If the department stores will tap a totally new market for the calculators, then we can presume that total sales will increase by the entire 20,000 units, and indeed there would be a contribution of $18,000 following this decision. On the other hand, if the sale to the department store reduced normal sales, to what degree could this happen before the decision to take the offer becomes the wrong one? Since the difference in contribution per unit is $4, the number of units that it would take to erode that $18,000 total contribution down to zero is $18,000 ÷ 4 = 4,500. Thus, if in the judgment of the decision maker there are likely to be at least 4,500 units purchased from the department stores which would otherwise have been purchased from the normal distribution channels, then the decision should be reversed.

An additional consideration here is that of customer relations. Doubtless the firms in the normal distributing channels will become aware that the department stores were given a better deal, and these firms may in turn look elsewhere for their supplies. Thus any short-term gain by selling to the department store may be outweighed by longer-term losses due to a deterioration of the relationship currently enjoyed with the distributing company and other firms.[5]

A third area of concern relates to the image of Idaho Instruments' calculators. Presumably the department stores, having purchased at a relatively low cost per unit, will price below the current market price for the model X1-9. This may have a detrimental impact upon the quality image currently held by that model. Since many consumers judge quality on the basis of price when they have no alternate means of discovering quality or durability, the lowering of the price of the X1-9 may reduce the consumer's perception of its quality. Alternatively, this contract with the department store may be the beginning of a long and successful relationship with that particular buyer and may add to rather than detract from the image of the calculators, and total sales.

In summary, then, the decision maker must consider all possible future ramifications of the decision and must calculate the expected present value or loss of each eventuality. The net expected present value or loss must be added to or subtracted from the immediate contribution before the final decision is made.

## 7.4 MULTIPERIOD CONTRIBUTION ANALYSIS

### Present Values of Contributions

Many decisions involve costs that will be incurred or revenues that will be received in future time periods. As discussed in Chapter 2, these costs and revenues must be converted to present value terms in order to make them comparable with cost and revenues incurred or received in the present period. In Chapter 2 we spoke simply of "profits" in the first and subsequent periods which had to be discounted back to present value. We now know that it is the *contribution* in each future period that is important for decision making, and not profits in either the accounting or the economic sense.

Longer-term considerations enter the decision-making problem in multiperiod analysis. First, some fixed expenses may become variable at a point in the future and will need to be replaced or increased or reduced as a result of the decision that has been taken. Those fixed costs that are incurred as a result of the implementation of a current decision must be included as an incremental cost. Second, incremental revenues and incremental costs in future periods will be subject to some uncertainty, and the decision maker may be supplied with a distribution of possible future revenues and costs related to each decision. The decision maker must then calculate the expected value of incremental revenues and incremental costs for each alternative before attempting to calculate the present value of the contribution from the alternative decisions.

Suppose a metal-fabricating firm is considering entry into the metal windows market. The firm must produce either steel windows or aluminum windows. The

---

[5] In fact, if Idaho Instruments continues to favor the department store with a lower price, it may run afoul of legislation concerning price discrimination. Legal constraints on pricing are discussed briefly in Chapter 11.

**TABLE 7.11**
Multiperiod contribution analysis: steel windows

| | Year of Operation | | | |
|---|---|---|---|---|
| | *1* | *2* | *3* | *4* |
| Incremental revenues | $60,000 | $50,000 | $40,000 | $30,000 |
| Incremental costs | | | | |
| Materials | 15,000 | 14,000 | 12,000 | 10,000 |
| Direct labor | 25,000 | 23,000 | 16,000 | 12,000 |
| Indirect labor | 1,000 | – | 1,000 | – |
| Plant and equipment | 6,000 | – | 5,000 | – |
| Contribution | $13,000 | $13,000 | $ 6,000 | $ 8,000 |
| Discount factors (12%) | .9454 | .8441 | .7537 | .6729 |
| Present values | $12,290 | $10,973 | $ 4,522 | $ 5,383 |

Total contribution (undiscounted) $40,000
Present value of total contribution $33,168

initial investment in plant and equipment would be the same whichever market is entered, but the production of steel windows causes the plant and equipment to wear out every two years, whereas aluminum windows are less demanding in that they allow plant and equipment to be used for a period of four years. Suppose that the firm's planning horizon is also four years, and that the projected incremental revenues and costs are as shown in Tables 7.11 and 7.12.

The data in the tables reflect the following features of the production and marketing of the alternate products. Steel windows use cheaper materials but are more expensive in the use of labor and machines. The market price is currently considerably higher for steel windows but is expected to decline progressively over the period of four years due to the growth of competition in this

**TABLE 7.12**
Multiperiod contribution analysis: aluminum windows

| | Year of Operation | | | |
|---|---|---|---|---|
| | *1* | *2* | *3* | *4* |
| Incremental revenues | $ 30,000 | $35,000 | $50,000 | $70,000 |
| Less incremental costs | | | | |
| Materials | 15,000 | 17,000 | 22,000 | 28,000 |
| Direct labor | 10,000 | 11,000 | 15,000 | 18,000 |
| Indirect labor | 1,000 | – | – | – |
| Plant and equipment | 6,000 | – | – | – |
| Contribution | $–2,000 | $ 7,000 | $13,000 | $24,000 |
| Discount factors (12%) | .9454 | .8441 | .7537 | .6729 |
| Present values | $–1,891 | $ 5,909 | $ 9,798 | $16,150 |

Total contribution (undiscounted) $42,000
Present value of total contribution $29,966

236

relatively profitable segment. Aluminum windows, on the other hand, are more expensive in the use of materials but require less labor and equipment cost per unit. The aluminum windows segment is considerably larger than that for steel windows but is characterized by a lower price level and a greater number of competitors. The firm expects, however, to increase its market share over the four-year period, and to progresssively raise its price by small increments as it becomes more firmly established in the market. Note that the incremental cost of indirect labor refers to the cost of installing the plant and equipment, and that for the production of steel windows the purchase and installation of plant and equipment occurs again in year 3.

The total contribution over the four-year period (undiscounted) is higher for the aluminum windows by a margin of $2,000. We must compare the *present values* of these expected returns, however. Suppose the firm's next best investment opportunity for the funds involved (at a similar level of risk) is to put the funds into bond issues with a return of 12 percent per annum. Thus the firm's opportunity discount rate is 12 percent.

### Treatment of Contribution
### Received Continuously

In Chapter 2 we assumed for simplicity that costs and revenues were incurred or received either at the start or at the end of each year, in order to use the discount factors from Table A.1 in Appendix A. In this present case, however, we should expect costs and revenues to be incurred and received more or less *continuously* throughout the year, rather than as a lump sum at the end of each year. Table A.2 in Appendix A gives the appropriate discount factors for continuous cash flows.[6]

In the lower part of Tables 7.11 and 7.12 we calculate the present values of the contributions of each year for each option. Summing these present values of the contributions of each year, we find that the total present value is $3,202 greater for the steel window project than for the aluminum window project, notwithstanding the fact that the total (undiscounted) contribution from the latter is expected to be $2,000 greater. This demonstrates the influence that the conformation of the stream of contributions has upon the present value of that stream. For steel windows the major part of the contribution is to be received in the first two years, whereas for aluminum windows it is expected to be received in the latter two years. Dollars received further into the future are discounted more heavily, and hence the present value of the steel window proposition is expected to be greater. Had the decision been made simply on the basis of total contribution (undiscounted), a suboptimal decision would have been taken.

In the above decision-making problem we must assume that the decision maker has examined all alternative investment possibilities. He or she must be convinced that the two projects under consideration are the two best projects

---

[6] See, for example, E. L. Grant and W. G. Iveson, *Principles of Engineering Economy*, 4th ed. (New York: Ronald Press, 1964), Appendix B, entitled "Continuous Compounding of Interest and the Uniform Flow Convention."

that the firm may become involved in. If the decision maker is not satisfied that this is so, he or she should undertake a review of all possible alternatives, or the opportunity cost of investing the funds in this way. Unforeseen opportunities that may arise during the second or subsequent year of production cannot be evaluated, however. The decision must be made *now* on the basis of information that is currently available. If a lucrative opportunity were to arise during one of the latter years, the decision maker would be faced with the decision problem of whether to continue the involvement in steel windows or to divert resources to the new opportunity. That decision would of course be made at the later point of time on the basis of the information available at that point of time.

## 7.5  BREAKEVEN ANALYSIS

A graphical tool of some value in decision making is the breakeven chart. When applied correctly it allows the decision maker considerable insight into the decision problem and aids in the choice of the optimal price, cost, and output levels for each product. The *breakeven volume* is defined as that sales level for which total revenue equals total cost. Decision makers are concerned with the breakeven volume level, since it is beyond this level that revenues begin to exceed costs and the decision becomes profitable. To the extent that the breakeven point can be surpassed, the decision maker is likely to smile more broadly; the worrisome factor is usually whether or not sales volume will attain the breakeven level.

In Figure 7.1 we show the breakeven charts under three different cost and revenue situations. In part (a) of Figure 7.1 you will notice that total revenue and total cost are equal at two separate output levels. At point *A* total revenue has risen to equality with total costs, and at point *B* total revenue has fallen to equality with the rising total cost. In the interval between point *A* and point *B* the firm is experiencing profits, as shown by the profit curve on the same graph, and to the left of point *A* and to the right of point *B* the firm experiences losses. In part (b) of Figure 7.1 we show a situation where the price level remains constant, while costs are similar to those in part (a). Again there are two breakeven points, and profits are positive in the output range between these two breakeven points. In part (c) of the figure we show the most commonly used form of breakeven analysis, in which both price and average variable cost are constant. Notice that the profit function is therefore a straight line.

The use of linear total costs and total revenue functions, as in part (c) of Figure 7.1, greatly facilitates breakeven analysis. Typically the decision maker will obtain an estimate of expected volume level, and of the cost and price levels at that volume level. Linear extrapolation from those expected cost and price values around the expected volume level obviates the problem of ascertaining the actual variance in average variable costs, and it recognizes that prices are not likely to be variable by small amounts due to the price awareness thresholds of customers.

It is important to recognize, however, that linear revenue and cost functions are generally approximations of the actual form of the cost and revenue func-

## FIGURE 7.1
### Breakeven charts under different cost and revenue conditions

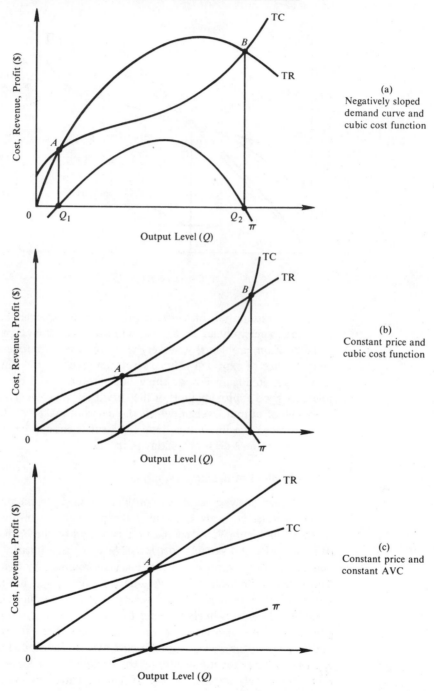

(a)
Negatively sloped demand curve and cubic cost function

(b)
Constant price and cubic cost function

(c)
Constant price and constant AVC

**FIGURE 7.2**
Linear revenue and cost functions in the relevant range

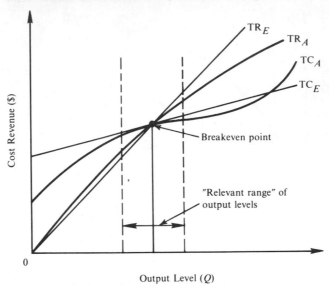

tions. The assumption of constant prices and average variable costs is likely to become progressively less accurate as we move away from expected volume levels. Most decision problems, however, will concern output levels within a fairly limited range of expected volume levels, and we call this limited range the *relevant range*. In Figure 7.2 we show linear revenue and cost functions that are tolerably good approximations of the curvilinear revenue and cost functions over the range of output levels in which the decision maker is interested. Within this relevant range the linear functions are a sufficient approximation of the actual functions for most decision-making purposes.

### Applications of Breakeven Analysis

Breakeven analysis can be of considerable value to the decision maker when decisions must be made concerning the price and quality levels of a proposed product. In Figure 7.3 a comparison is shown of the breakeven points at two different price and variable cost levels. Suppose that initially the decision maker was considering the price and cost levels represented by the curves TR and TC. The indicated breakeven sales volume is shown as $Q_4$. Let us suppose that the decision maker feels that it is unlikely that the product will attain that sales volume and hence is likely to incur losses. The decision maker may rectify this situation in one or a combination of two ways: first, the price may be raised; and/or second, the average variable cost may be lowered. The latter adjustment has implications for the quality of the product, since lowering average variable costs presumably implies the use of lower-quality raw materials, or the use of less labor input per unit of output. It can be seen that at the initial price a reduction in the average variable cost level reduces the breakeven volume to that

**FIGURE 7.3**
**Comparison of breakeven points at different price and variable cost levels**

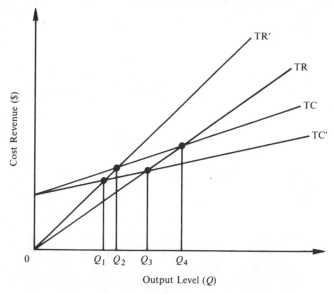

shown as $Q_3$. Alternatively, an increase in the price level with costs per unit remaining unchanged would reduce the breakeven volume to output level $Q_2$. Finally, an increase in the price level and a reduction in the cost level would reduce the breakeven volume to $Q_1$. The decision maker must consider each of these breakeven volume points in conjunction with the estimates of sales volume at those price and quality levels.

Algebraic calculation of the breakeven point is likely to be less time consuming than the graphical procedure. To find the formula for the breakeven volume, recall that it occurs where total revenue equals total costs, which may be expressed as follows:

$$\overset{TR}{P(Q)} = \overset{TC}{AVC(Q) + FC}$$

or $Q(P - AVC) = FC$

or $\qquad Q = \dfrac{FC}{P - AVC} \longrightarrow$ CONTRIBUTION $\qquad$ (7.1)
$\qquad\qquad\qquad\qquad$ INCREMENTAL REV- INCREMENTAL COSTS
$\qquad\qquad\qquad\qquad\qquad$ MARGIN/UNIT

Since $(P - AVC)$ is equal to the contribution margin per unit, we may restate this as

$$Q = \frac{FC}{CM} \quad \frac{\text{TOTAL FIXED COSTS}}{\text{CONT. MARGIN/UNIT}} \qquad (7.2)$$

Thus the breakeven volume may be calculated simply by dividing the total fixed costs by the contribution margin per unit.[7]

[7] Note that this form is applicable only for linear TR and TC functions. If either or both of these are not linear the contribution margin will vary with the level of output, and Eq.(7.1) should be used to find the breakeven point.

241

In multiproduct firms, where each product must attain a particular profit target to maintain its place in the product mix and to withstand being replaced by another profitable product, breakeven analysis can be used to find the sales volume at which this profit target will be attained. Note that a profit target is a constant dollar value, just as fixed costs are a constant dollar value. Hence the profit target may be added to the fixed-cost figure to represent the total dollar amount that must be obtained via contributions from each unit, before fixed costs and the profit target are covered. Algebraically, this may be expressed as follows:

$$Q = \frac{FC + \pi}{CM} \Rightarrow \text{\$ AMOUNT THAT MOST BE OBTAINED VIA CONTRIBUTIONS FROM EACH UNIT} \qquad (7.3)$$

Having calculated the sales volume necessary to cover the fixed costs and attain the desired target profit, the decision maker must then consider whether or not that target sales volume is likely to be achieved. If this appears quite unlikely, the decision maker may wish to revise the target profit, change either price or average variable costs, or delete this product from the product mix in favor of a more profitable product.

A third area in which the breakeven analysis may be useful is that where a particular product may be manufactured under two or more technologies of production. Suppose a firm is considering three alternate means of manufacturing a product for which the market price is established at $4.00 per unit. In Figure 7.4 we show the three technologies under which this product may be manufactured. The total revenue function in each graph is the same, indicating that the firm does not expect to be able to influence market price by its actions. Plant A is characterized by fixed costs of $20,000 and a constant average variable cost of $2.00 per unit of output. Plant B is characterized by fixed costs of $45,000 and a constant average variable cost of $1.00 per unit. Plant C involves the much higher fixed costs of $70,000, but a low and constant average variable cost of $0.50 per unit. Using this information and Eq.(7.2), one may verify that the breakeven points are 10,000, 15,000, and 20,000 units, respectively.

Suppose the decision maker's estimate of sales volume is distributed around a mean of 12,000 units. The breakeven charts of Figure 7.4 would indicate that Plant A would be the most suitable choice, since its breakeven point is at the low end of this distribution, and barring an eventuality at the extreme left-hand tail of the distribution, Plant A will be profitable at the likely sales levels.

In Table 7.13 we show the profitability levels at various expected sales levels for each of the three technologies. Table 7.13 summarizes the information given in Figure 7.4. Plant A remains the most profitable up to the output level of almost 29,000 units, at which point it is overtaken by Plant B. Plant C does not become the most profitable technology until it has an output level greater than 50,000 units. The decision maker must use this information in conjunction with the probability distribution of expected sales levels, before deciding on the scale of plant to implement.

***Operating Leverage.*** The differences in the contribution per unit after the breakeven point are due to the extent to which fixed factors are substituted for

*How did author get most $\pi = 29,000$ and 50,000? See Duen*

## FIGURE 7.4
### Breakeven charts for different production technologies

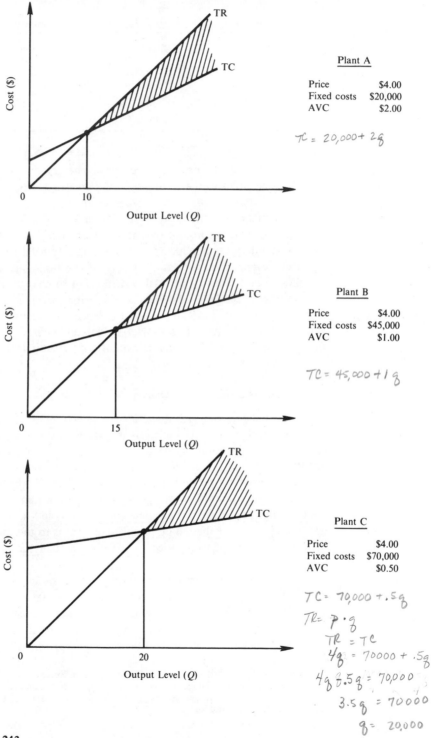

Plant A

| Price | $4.00 |
|---|---|
| Fixed costs | $20,000 |
| AVC | $2.00 |

$TC = 20,000 + 2q$

Plant B

| Price | $4.00 |
|---|---|
| Fixed costs | $45,000 |
| AVC | $1.00 |

$TC = 45,000 + 1q$

Plant C

| Price | $4.00 |
|---|---|
| Fixed costs | $70,000 |
| AVC | $0.50 |

$TC = 70,000 + .5q$

$TR = P \cdot q$

$TR = TC$

$4q = 70000 + .5q$

$4q \, .5q = 70,000$

$3.5q = 70000$

$q = 20,000$

243

**TABLE 7.13**
Profitability at various output levels with differing technologies

| Expected Sales Level | Plant A | Plant B | Plant C |
|---|---|---|---|
| 10,000 | Breakeven | −15,000 | −35,000 |
| 15,000 | 10,000 | Breakeven | −22,500 |
| 20,000 | 20,000 | 15,000 | Breakeven |
| 30,000 | 40,000 | 45,000 | 35,000 |
| 40,000 | 60,000 | 75,000 | 70,000 |
| 50,000 | 80,000 | 105,000 | 105,000 |
| 60,000 | 100,000 | 135,000 | 140,000 |

variable factors in the production process. The greater this substitution, or the more capital intensive the technology, the greater the operating leverage of the production process. *Operating leverage* refers to the extent to which the incremental units sold contribute to overheads and profits. With linear cost and revenue functions, it is constant over the relevant range (equal to the contribution per unit); but with nonlinear total costs and/or total revenue functions, the operating leverage will vary as the slopes of the functions vary. Operating leverage shows the sensitivity of total contribution to changes in volume. Since the difference between total contribution and total profits is a constant (i.e., fixed costs), operating leverage also shows the sensitivity of total profits to changes in volume. When a product is subject to volatile swings in sales in response to fluctuations in general economic conditions, greater leverage involves greater risk of wide variations in profits.[8]

*Handwritten margin note:* TOTAL CONTRIBUTION – $\pi = FC$ (INCREMENTAL REV – COSTS) – $\pi = FC$

### Limitations of Breakeven Analysis

At the beginning of our discussion of breakeven analysis, the cautious note was injected that breakeven analysis is a useful tool *when correctly applied.* It is essential that the form of the total revenue and total cost functions used in breakeven analysis accurately reflect, or at least be a tolerable approximation of, the actual cost and revenue conditions. As indicated, the assumption of linear cost and revenue conditions may be a tolerable approximation within a relatively limited range of outputs but becomes progressively less accurate at higher output levels, due to the likelihood of diminishing returns to the variable factors and/or the necessity of reducing price in order to actually sell those higher output levels.

Second, breakeven analysis must be used in the incremental sense. That is, the total cost function must represent those costs that are incurred as a result of a decision to produce this particular product, and it must not include costs that would be incurred regardless of this decision. In the case of a firm that produces only one product, the total cost function will represent all costs incurred by the

[8] Operating leverage is in fact an elasticity measure. Since it measures the relative responsiveness of profits to a change in quantity demanded, it can be calculated as the percentage change in profits over the percentage change in quantity demanded. It is the "volume elasticity of profit," if you wish.

firm. If implicit costs are included at their opportunity cost value, the breakeven point will be the point of zero economic profits. Similarly, within a multiproduct firm where each department produces a single product, the total overhead costs of a particular department may be included in the total cost function in break-even analysis. Beyond the breakeven point, the profits earned by that department will represent a contribution to the overheads and profits of the entire firm. Otherwise, in multiproduct firms, only the incremental overheads should be included and then profits are the contribution to the joint overheads and profits of the entire firm. Care must be taken, therefore, that the vertical intercept of the total cost function relates to simply the incremental and/or separable fixed costs associated with that particular product.

## 7.6 SUMMARY

The cost concept of prime importance for decision making is that of incremental costs. *Incremental costs* are those that are incurred as a result of the decision under consideration. To calculate incremental costs, however, the decision maker must consider a variety of other cost concepts, such as direct and indirect, explicit and implicit, opportunity and historic, and relevant and sunk costs. Each of these cost concepts was illustrated with reference to a particular business example.

*Contribution analysis* seeks to ascertain the contribution to overheads and profits, or the excess of incremental revenues over incremental costs, which is expected to follow a particular decision. The decision-making criterion outlined in this chapter was that one should choose the alternative that promises the greatest positive contribution to overheads and profits. As shown in some of the examples, however, the relevant incremental costs and revenues included a host of future considerations, some of which are not easily quantifiable. The issues that must be investigated include the following: data accuracy, false leads in the data, opportunity costs, cash-flow considerations, competitor reactions, labor relations, supplier relations, customer relations, and whether or not the decision can be taken in isolation from other decisions. The decision maker must attempt to quantify each of these issues and weigh these against the immediate contribution associated with each alternative.

*Breakeven analysis* is related to contribution analysis and is largely concerned with examining the feasibility of certain cost, price, and output levels. It is a useful aid in the pricing decision, the average variable cost (or quality) decision, the choice of target profit, and the choice of the most suitable scale of plant. It is important, however, that the cost and revenue functions used in breakeven analysis closely approximate the actual conditions and refer only to the incremental costs and revenues associated with the production of that particular product.

## DISCUSSION QUESTIONS

7.1   How might the accountant's calculation of indirect costs differ from the economist's calculation of fixed costs?

7.2    If the indirect cost category "Factory Heat and Light" exhibited an increase over the months of November, December, and January, would you find the gradient of this cost and include it as a component of your estimate of marginal costs? Why or why not?

7.3    Why is the *average* variable cost of production at various output levels less valuable for decision-making purposes than is the *marginal* cost of production at those output levels?

7.4    Suppose the owner-manager of a small grocery store did not draw a salary but took $100 weekly in cash and groceries (at his cost) from the store. If he could alternatively earn $250 weekly managing a chain-store grocery, what is the opportunity cost of his labor and enterprise to his own business? Why?

7.5    Define the *relevant costs* for decision making. When do the relevant costs include some elements of fixed costs?

7.6    Why does contribution analysis ignore the fixed overhead costs that might otherwise be included in the cost analysis of a decision?

7.7    How should future considerations be evaluated and included in contribution analysis?

7.8    In multiperiod contribution analysis, what determines the choice of the appropriate discount factors?

7.9    Discuss the applications of breakeven analysis to business decision making.

7.10    Summarize the limitations involved in the use of breakeven analysis.

## PROBLEMS

7.1    The Muscle-Man Company manufactures forklift tractors and supplies some parts to other manufacturers of forklifts. It fabricates most of the component parts but buys the engines, hydraulic systems, wheels, and tires from suppliers. Demand estimates indicate that Muscle-Man should increase its production level from 60 forklift units monthly to 70 units monthly. Sufficient slack exists in most departments to allow this, except that production of ten extra chassis-assemblies could only be attained by reallocating labor and equipment from fork-assembly manufacture to chassis-assembly manufacture. The fork-assembly department currently produces 90 units monthly, and it supplies the 30 surplus units to other manufacturers at $188 each. With the expanded production level, 70 forks would be required, but the labor and equipment responsible for the remaining 20 units is thought to be just sufficient to produce the 10 extra chassis-assemblies. Alternatively, the extra chassis-assemblies could be purchased from a supplier, and the lowest quote is from Fenton Fabricators, being for $305 per unit. The costs of the chassis and fork departments for a representative month were as follows:

| | Department | |
|---|---|---|
| *Costs* | *Chassis* | *Fork* |
| Direct materials | $ 4,650 | $ 2,070 |
| Direct labor | 6,300 | 4,050 |
| Depreciation | 750 | 500 |
| Allocated burden of fuel, electricity, office, and other overheads (200% of direct labor) | 12,600 | 8,100 |
| Total | $24,300 | $14,720 |
| Production level | 60 | 90 |

(a) Should Muscle-Man make or buy the ten extra chassis-assemblies?

(b) What qualifications would you add to your decision?

7.2 The Crombie Castings Company produces two products, A and B, for which pertinent data are as follows for the past month:

|  | A | B |
|---|---|---|
| Sales (units) | 840,000 | 220,000 |
| Price per unit ($) | 2.50 | 4.25 |
| Materials cost ($) | 386,400 | 105,600 |
| Direct labor ($) | 529,200 | 277,200 |
| Overheads ($) | 567,893 | 297,467 |

C.C.C. is operating at absolute full capacity but is unable to meet the demand for Product A, which is thought to be one million units per month. One way to meet the demand for A would be to reduce the output of Product B and shift resources to the production of A. For each unit reduction in the output of B, the firm could produce two units of A with the labor that is released. Alternatively, C.C.C. could contract out to have Product A manufactured by another firm in the same industry and sold as if this product were from the C.C.C. plant. Donald, Dodge, and Draper, a firm that holds a minor share of the same markets and has considerable excess capacity, was approached on this issue. D.D.D. is willing to sign a contract to supply the extra 160,000 units of A at a price of $2.25 per unit.

How should C.C.C. resolve this problem? Support your answer with discussion of the various issues involved.

7.3 Commodore Candies produces a three-pound box of chocolates which it sells at a price of $6.75 to various retail outlets. Since the product is perishable the company varies its output level with demand, which fluctuates from month to month as indicated in the following table. Commodore's output capacity for this product is 10,000 units per month with a one-shift operation, but it can produce more using overtime labor, which has a premium of 15 percent over regular labor cost. Costs of production for the past three months were as follows:

|  | December | January | February |
|---|---|---|---|
| Output level (units) | 8,000 | 7,500 | 8,500 |
| Raw materials ($) | 9,600 | 8,250 | 11,050 |
| Direct labor | 17,600 | 16,875 | 18,275 |
| Variable overhead ($) | 9,200 | 8,500 | 9,780 |
| Fixed overhead ($) | 14,500 | 14,500 | 15,200 |

Today Commodore is faced with a decision problem. A large retail chain has offered to purchase a bulk order of 4,000 units at $6 per unit, to be delivered at the end of March. Should Commodore take this order? Support your answer with discussion of the issues involved. Defend any assumptions that you make.

7.4 The XYZ Co. produces and sells a product directly to consumers at a price of $6 per unit. Sales have been increasing and this trend is expected to continue. Prices and wages have been, and are expected to remain, constant at the current levels. The company's maximum output capacity is 200,000 with the present investment in plant and equipment.

Following is a summary record of the firm's activities over the past three months:

|                                      | November | December | January |
|--------------------------------------|----------|----------|---------|
| Sales (units)                        | 141,869  | 156,056  | 171,661 |
| Materials ($)                        | 174,500  | 191,950  | 211,143 |
| Direct labor ($)                     | 354,673  | 429,154  | 520,133 |
| Indirect factory labor ($)           | 100,000  | 105,000  | 110,500 |
| Office and administrative salaries ($)| 64,000  | 64,000   | 64,000  |
| Light and heat ($)                   | 9,521    | 10,564   | 12,116  |
| Other fixed expenses ($)             | 24,680   | 24,680   | 24,680  |

A large department store has asked XYZ to consider the following deal: 10,000 units of the product, to be ready at the end of February, at the price of $5 per unit.

Should XYZ accept the order from the large department store? What strategy do you suggest? Support your answer with discussion of the various issues involved.

7.5 A large department store has called for tenders for the following contract: A truck plus its driver must be available, given one day's notice, whenever the store's own trucks are fully utilized, to deliver goods to suburban households. The number of days for which a truck will be required is 20, and the number of miles is expected to be 4,000 for the coming year.

You are the manager of the Clark Renta-Truck Co. and have a number of trucks that you rent out on a day-to-day basis. One truck is a little older than the others, and it is always the last to be rented out because it does less for public relations than the new trucks. In the absence of a contract with the department store, you expect this older truck to be rented out two-thirds of the 300 "rental days" this coming year. Your normal rental charge is $25.00 per day plus $0.35 per mile.

You estimate the costs of operating the older truck to be as follows, assuming 10,000 miles of rental over the coming year.

| Depreciation | $ 800 |
|--------------|-------|
| Interest on investment in truck | 360 |
| License fees and taxes | 125 |
| Insurance | 440 |
| Parking fees (permanently rented space) | 300 |
| Gasoline | 1,367 |
| Oil, grease, and preventive maintenance | 600 |
| Repairs | 1,450 |
| Allocated overheads | 1,650 |

You can hire a driver on one-day's notice for $50 per day. A one-time cost of $400 will be involved in fitting the truck with a special loading ramp required by the contract. This ramp will not interfere with the normal use of the truck.

On the basis of this information, and making whatever assumptions you feel are necessary and reasonable, calculate your incremental costs of undertaking this contract.

7.6 Corcoran Calculators Incorporated is one of the leading manufacturers in the electronic calculator industry. Management is now considering plans for the production of the company's latest development—the minicomputer. The company already manufactures most of the parts, but the design of the new fuse trays would require the additional expenditure of $23,000 for special auxiliary equipment, which has a useful life of only two years and has no scrap value. The marketing department has estimated that sales would require the production of 4,500 fuse trays the first year and 7,000 the following year.

The company has the option of either producing these trays in-house or having them supplied by an outside electronics specialist at a cost of $32.50 per tray. Corcoran would incur additional storage and carrying costs associated with this latter alternative of $26,000 over the first year and $40,000 over the following year.

The breakdown of the in-house manufacturing expenses for the 11,500 units is expected to be as follows:

|  |  | Unit Cost |
|---|---|---|
| Labor |  | $10.00 |
| Raw materials and components |  | 20.00 |
| Variable overhead |  | 4.00 |
| Fixed cost |  |  |
| Existing equipment | $3.50 |  |
| New equipment | 2.00 | 5.50 |
|  |  | $39.50 |

The company's opportunity discount rate is 15 percent. The payments to the supplier would be made in a lump sum at the end of each of the two years. If produced in-house, there would be a continual outflow of funds as the units were produced, although the special equipment must be paid for immediately.

Assuming that the increased production will have a negligible effect on the present operation of the plant, what would your recommendation be on the question of making or buying the fuse trays? (Justify your answer with all supporting calculations and any qualifications you might wish to make.)

7.7　You are the manager of a ski resort, and based on industry projections of this season's demand, your competitive position, and your estimates of costs, you have set the lift ticket price at $8 per day. Due to the variability of demand between weekdays, weekends, and holidays, you hire labor on the basis of the expected demand for each particular day, based on past years' records and on current snow conditions. Extra labor is readily available on a day-to-day basis from the pool of local "ski-bums."

You employ one lift attendant for every 250 tickets sold, on top of a basic staff of four lift attendants. Ski-patrol persons are required at the rate of one for every 400 tickets sold, in addition to the two patrol persons who are required regardless of ticket sales volume. All other labor employees connected with the skiing operation are required regardless of sales volume. Lift attendants are hired at the rate of $25 per day plus a free lift ticket to be used subsequently. Ski-patrol persons receive $30 per day plus a free meal in your restaurant that evening.

Your restaurant serves only one standardized meal, this being an "all you can eat" buffet for $3 per person. Based on expected demand fluctuations, you have hired various people on a full-time and part-time basis for the season. The $3 price represents the average cost of materials and direct labor plus a 50 percent markup to contribute to restaurant overheads and profits. Unexpected fluctuations in demand can be handled, since you keep a large inventory of supplies and can hire temporary labor at short notice. There is, however, an additional $10-per-person cost for this temporary labor, since these people are handled through an employment agency and require transport to the restaurant. To maintain your standard of meals and service, you hire kitchen staff at the rate of one person for every 45 meals expected to be sold, and serving staff at the rate of one person for very 80 meals expected to be sold.

Today you received a phone call from the Students' Association of a nearby university which is asking around various ski resorts for the following deal: Ten busloads of students (500 in total) will come to your resort on Friday of next week if they can get a lift ticket *and* a meal for $4 per person. Your expected sales for that Friday, before this possibility arose, were 1,500 lift tickets and 900 meals.

Should you give the students the deal they are asking for? Explain your decision and state any possible qualifications to that decision.

## SUGGESTED REFERENCES AND FURTHER READING

BRIGHAM, E. F., and J. L. PAPPAS, *Managerial Economics,* 2nd ed., Chap. 8. Hinsdale, Ill.: Dryden, 1976.

GREER, H. C., "Anyone for Widgets?" *Journal of Accountancy,* April 1966. (Despite its title, this paper contains an excellent discussion of relevant and irrelevant costs.)

HAYNES, W. W., and W. R. HENRY, *Managerial Economics: Analysis and Cases,* 3rd ed., Chaps. 2 and 5. Dallas, Tex.: Business Publications, 1974.

HORNGREN, C. T., *Cost Accounting: A Managerial Emphasis,* 4th ed., Chaps. 2 and 3. Englewood Cliffs, N.J.: Prentice-Hall, 1977.

——, *Introduction to Management Accounting,* 4th ed., Chaps. 2, 3, 4, 5, and 10. Englewood Cliffs, N.J.: Prentice-Hall, 1978.

SIMON, J. L., *Applied Managerial Economics,* Chaps. 8 and 9. Englewood Cliffs, N.J.: Prentice-Hall, 1975.

WEBB, S. C., *Managerial Economics,* Chap. 5. Boston: Houghton Mifflin, 1976.

# 8

# Cost Estimation and Forecasting

## 8.1 INTRODUCTION

Cost estimation and forecasting for decision making are concerned with finding the shape and placement of the firm's cost curves. Both the short-run cost functions and the long-run cost functions must be estimated, since both sets of information will be required for some decisions. Knowledge of the short-run cost functions allows the decision maker to judge the optimality of present output levels and to solve decision problems using contribution analysis. We saw in the preceding chapter that the concept of incremental cost is fundamental to short-run decision making on cost issues. Incremental costs will include the variable costs, but they will also include any changes in those costs that are normally regarded as fixed costs. In any short-run situation we may experience increases in some of the fixed-cost items, since these particular facilities may meet their full capacity constraints and need to be increased. Incremental cost analysis is concerned with the variability of all cost components and therefore requires an appreciation of the degree of idle capacity in existing fixed-cost categories. When fixed-cost categories are expected to meet their full capacity constraints, such that overtime use and/or additional facilities must be instituted, the decision maker must account for these costs as well as the variable costs when estimating the incremental cost of a contemplated decision.

Knowledge of long-run cost functions is important when considering the expansion or contraction of plant size, and for confirming that the present plant size is optimal for the output level that is being produced. Recall that the long-run cost function shows the alternate sizes of plant available at the *present* point of time and should not be interpreted as showing the cost levels for various plant sizes that will be available in the future, since both technology and the relative factor prices are likely to change in the future, rendering the present long-run cost function inappropriate. To estimate *future* cost levels, we need to forecast changes in the state of technology and changes in the factor price ratios and separate these from the expected effects of inflation in future time periods.

The remainder of this chapter is therefore organized into three main sections: (1) short-run cost estimation, (2) long-run cost estimation, and (3) cost forecasting and inflation.

## 8.2   SHORT-RUN COST ESTIMATION

As implied in the introduction to this chapter, we are concerned here principally with the behavior of variable costs, but we must also be aware of other incremental costs, such as those changes in a fixed-cost category that would be necessitated by a particular decision. We shall discuss short-run cost estimation under four headings: simple extrapolation, gradient analysis, time-series regression analysis, and the engineering technique.

### Simple Extrapolation   FINE IF COSTS CONSTANT (CONSTANT RTS & ABSENCE OF DRTNS) OVER RANGE

The most simple method of cost estimation is probably to ascertain the present level of marginal or average variable costs and extrapolate this backward or forward to other output levels. Firms often express the belief that their marginal and average variable costs are constant over a range of output levels surrounding the current output level. Note that this implies constant returns to the variable factors, and hence the absence of either increasing or diminishing returns in the short-run production process. If this constant efficiency situation actually exists in the production process, then the simple extrapolation method is an adequate method of accurate cost estimation. However, if marginal costs are simply believed to be constant but are in fact increasing with additional output units, the simple extrapolation method may cause poor decisions to be made. It is a common error in business situations to assume that marginal costs are constant, which in effect is assuming the absence of diminishing returns to the variable factors. It should be intuitively obvious that sooner or later diminishing returns will set in, and the decision maker must be constantly aware of the possible insurgency of this phenomenon.

When we have only one cost/output observation (that is, the current levels), adjustment for possible diminishing returns must take place on the basis of judgment, experience, or intuition. For example, the decision maker may feel that the most reasonable presumption is that marginal costs are likely to increase by, say, 2 percent for each additional 1 percent change in the output level. Clearly, with only one set of cost/output observations, such an assumption is quite risky in that it may easily be significantly inaccurate.

### Gradient Analysis

Since output levels typically fluctuate to some degree from period to period, we should be able to find two or more cost/output observations, in which case we can conduct gradient analysis. You will recall from the preceding chapter that the *gradient* of each cost category is the rate at which that cost category changes as the output level changes. The sum of the gradients, excluding any cost changes that are not the result of changes in the output level (e.g., an increase in municipal taxes), allows an estimate to be made of the marginal cost per unit over the output interval under observation. Three or more observations would allow gradient analysis to more accurately estimate the change in marginal costs as output levels change, as will be demonstrated later in this chapter.

If we have a sufficient number of cost/output observations we are able to use the technique of regression analysis for short-run cost estimation.

### Time-Series Regression Analysis

Given a collection of cost/output observations, we can apply regression analysis to estimate the dependence of costs upon the output level and thus obtain an estimate of the marginal cost.[1] Since we wish to estimate the cost function of a particular firm, we must use time-series data from that firm. This raises some of the standard problems with time-series data: if over the period of the observations some factors have changed, the results of regression analysis will be less reliable. For example, factor prices may change due to inflation or market forces in the factor markets, and/or factor productivities may change due to changing technology and worker efficiency. To largely eliminate these problems the cost data should be deflated by an appropriate price index, and time should be inserted as an independent variable in the regression equation. Any trend in the relative prices or productivities will then be included in the coefficient of the time variable.

Regression analysis of time-series cost data is quite susceptible to the problems of measurement error. The cost data should include all costs that are *caused* by a particular output level, whether or not they are yet paid for. Maintenance expense, for example, should be expected to vary with the rate of output, but it may be delayed until it is more convenient to close down certain sections of the plant or facilities for maintenance purposes. Hence the cost that is caused in an earlier period is not recorded until a later period and is thus likely to understate the earlier cost level and overstate the later cost level. Ideally, our cost/output observations should be the result of considerable fluctuations of output over a short period of time with no cost/output matching problems.

Suppose the weekly output and total variable costs of an ice-cream plant have been recorded over a three-month period as shown in Table 8.1 Output of the product varies from week to week due to the rather volatile nature of the milk supply from dairies, and the impossibility of holding inventories of the fresh milk for more than a few days.

It is apparent from the data supplied that total variable costs tend to vary positively with the output level in this ice-cream plant. But what is the *form* of the relationship? The specification of the functional form of the regression equation has resounding implications for the estimate of the marginal cost curve which will be indicated by the regression analysis. If we specify total variable costs as a linear function of output, such as $TVC = a + bQ$, the marginal cost estimation generated by the regression analysis will be the parameter $b$,

---

[1] The principles of regression analysis, and the major problems associated with the use and interpretation of the results of this method, were discussed in a self-contained section of Chapter 5. The discussion in this chapter presumes your familiarity with the earlier section.

**TABLE 8.1**
Record of output levels and total variable costs
for an ice-cream plant

| Week ending | Output (gallons) | Total Variable Costs ($) |
|---|---|---|
| Sept. 7 | 7,300 | 5,780 |
| Sept. 14 | 8,450 | 7,010 |
| Sept. 21 | 8,300 | 6,550 |
| Sept. 28 | 9,500 | 7,620 |
| Oct. 5 | 6,700 | 5,650 |
| Oct. 12 | 9,050 | 7,100 |
| Oct. 19 | 5,450 | 5,060 |
| Oct. 26 | 5,950 | 5,250 |
| Nov. 2 | 5,150 | 4,490 |
| Nov. 9 | 10,050 | 7,520 |
| Nov. 16 | 10,300 | 8,030 |
| Nov. 23 | 7,750 | 6,350 |

**FIGURE 8.1**
Linear variable cost function

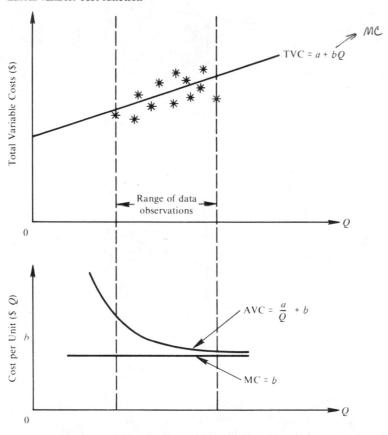

since marginal cost is equivalent to the derivative of the total variable cost function with respect to the output level. In Figure 8.1 we show, for a given collection of data observations, the consequent average variable costs and marginal

255

cost curves that would be generated by regression analysis using a linear specification of the relationship. Since average variable costs are total variable cost divided by output level $Q$, the AVC curve will decline to approach the MC curve asymptotically.

Alternatively, for the same group of data observations, if we specify the functional form as a quadratic such as $TVC = a + bQ + cQ^2$, the marginal cost will not be constant but will rise as a constant function of output. In Figure 8.2 we show the hypothesized quadratic relationship superimposed upon the same data observations, with the consequent average variable cost and marginal cost curves illustrated in the lower half of the figure.

**FIGURE 8.2**
**Quadratic variable cost function**

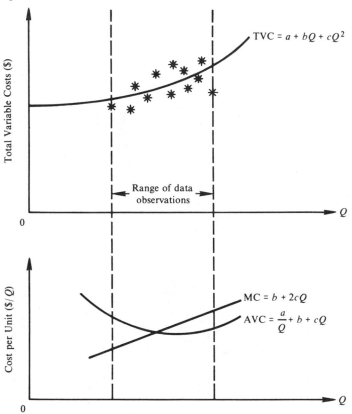

Finally, if we hypothesize that the functional relationship is cubic, such as $TVC = a + bQ - cQ^2 + dQ^3$, the marginal cost estimate generated by regression analysis will be curvilinear and will increase as the square of the output level. Figure 8.3 illustrates the cost curves consequent upon a cubic expression of the cost/output relationship. Alternatively, a power function or other multiplicative relationship may be appropriate.

Which form of the cost function should we specify? Since the results of the regression analysis will be used for decision-making purposes, we must be as-

**FIGURE 8.3**
**Cubic variable cost function**

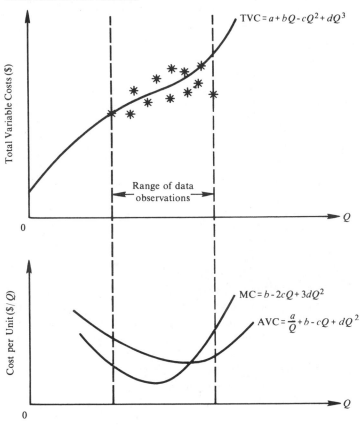

*sured* that the marginal and average cost curves generated are the most accurate representations of the cost/output relationships. By plotting the total variable cost data against output, we may be able to ascertain that one of the above three functional forms best represents the apparent relationship existing between the two variables, and we may thus confidently continue the regression analysis using this particular functional form.

If it is not visually apparent that one particular functional form is the best representation of the apparent relationship, it may be necessary to run the regression analysis first with a linear functional form, and later with one or more of the other functional forms in order to find which equation best fits the data base. You will recall from Chapter 5 that the regression equation that generates the highest coefficient of determination $(R^2)$ is the equation that explains the highest proportion of the variability of the dependent variable, and it can thus be taken to be the best indication of the actual functional relationship that exists between the two variables. Table 8.2 summarizes the results of such an exercise.

Note that the linear equation indicates that 97.614 percent of the variation in TVC is explained by the variation in the output level. The percentage of the

**TABLE 8.2**
Summary of regression equations and comparative explanatory power
for cost/output data, ice-cream plant

| Regression Equation (in symbolic form) | Coefficient of Determination ($R^2$) |
|---|---|
| (1)  TVC $= a + bQ$ (linear) | 0.97614 |
| (2)  TVC $= a + bQ^2$ (quadratic) | 0.96629 |
| (3)  TVC $= a + bQ^3$ (cubic) | 0.94284 |
| (4)  TVC $= a + bQ + cQ^2$ (quadratic) | 0.97632* |
| (5)  TVC $= a + bQ + cQ^2 + dQ^3$ (cubic) | 0.97642* |
| (6)  TVC $= aQ^b$ (power) | 0.97417 |

*Not significant at 95% confidence level.

variation explained declines for both the simple quadratic and the simple cubic specification of the relationship. The proportion of the variation explained increases as additional terms are added in the fourth and fifth specification, but neither of these specifications is significant at the 95 percent confidence level, since the regression coefficients are much less than twice the value of the standard errors of the coefficients.[2] The final specification shown, the power function, was tested to see if a multiplicative relationship would give a better fit than the additive relationships, and although highly significant the proportion of variation explained was slightly less than for the simple linear specification. Thus the linear regression equation "best fits" the observations and should be used for prediction purposes. The computed regression equation was

$$TVC = 1395.29 + 0.6351Q \qquad (8.1)$$

with a standard error of estimate of 182.02 and a standard error of the regression coefficient of 0.0313.

Suppose we now wish to estimate the total variable costs at output levels of 7,000 and 11,000 units. For 7,000 units

$$TVC = 1395.29 + 0.6351 \,(7000)$$

$$= 1395.29 + 4445.70$$

$$= 5840.99$$

Using the standard error of estimate we can be confident at the 68 percent level that the actual TVC will fall within the interval of $5,840.99 plus or minus

[2] Adding extra explanatory variables will inevitably explain more of the variation in the independent variable, even if the extra variables are *not* responsible for variation in the independent variable, since the regression analysis tends to capitalize on chance. We must ensure, therefore, that each additional explanatory variable is a "significant" determinant, and the usual test is to see that its regression coefficient exceeds twice its standard error of the coefficient. Using an insignificant regression equation for predictive purposes is likely to lead us into substantial error.

258

$182.02 (viz., $5,658.97 to $6,023.01) and confident at the 95 percent level that the actual TVC will fall within the interval of $5,840.99 plus or minus two standard errors of estimate (viz., $5,476.95 to $6,205.03).

The estimation of TVC at 11,000 units would proceed in the same way. The result must be viewed with caution, however, because it represents an *extrapolation* from the data base. The regression equation applies over the range of outputs observed and hence could be applied quite confidently for 7,000 units, a case of *interpolation*. Outside the range of the initial observations, the relationship between TVC and $Q$ may not continue to be linear but may instead be curvilinear, exhibiting diminishing returns to the variable factors, for example. Extrapolation may be undertaken, however, if we have no good reason to expect that the relationship should *not* hold outside the range of observations, as long as we are fully cognizant that the relationship may not hold.[3]

### The Engineering Technique of Cost Estimation DEVELOP PROD FUNCTION

An alternate method of cost estimation, known as the *engineering technique,* consists of developing the physical production function that exists between the inputs and the output, and attaching cost values to the inputs in order to obtain a total variable cost figure for each output level. For each output level we must therefore calculate, or test for, the amount of each of the variable factors necessary to produce that output level. Attaching costs to these variable inputs we could subsequently calculate the total variable cost for each output level, and hence the average variable costs and marginal costs at each output level. Let us demonstrate this in the context of a hypothetical example. Suppose a metal-stamping plant has one large machine that can be operated at five different speeds up to a maximum speed of 100 revolutions per minute (rpm). On each revolution it stamps out one unit of the product, and hence output is proportional to the operating speed of the machine. However, the requirements of materials, labor, electric power, and repairs and maintenance need not be proportional to the operating speed of the machine. In Table 8.3 we show the

**TABLE 8.3**
**Physical requirements of a metal-stamping machine
at various operating speeds**

| Operating Speed (rpm) | Output per Hour (units) | Materials Used (lb) | Labor (man-hours) | Power Req'mts. (kwh) | R&M Req'mts. (units) |
|---|---|---|---|---|---|
| 20 | 1,200 | 1,320 | 20 | 2,585 | 10 |
| 40 | 2,400 | 2,880 | 25 | 4,523 | 20 |
| 60 | 3,600 | 4,680 | 27 | 5,262 | 30 |
| 80 | 4,800 | 6,720 | 28 | 6,708 | 35 |
| 100 | 6,000 | 9,000 | 30 | 10,954 | 60 |

[3] Throughout the regression analysis we required *ceteris paribus* to hold. Specifically, the prices of the input factors and the productivities of the factors must reasonably be expected to have remained constant over the period of data collection. The same costs and productivities must be expected to prevail over the prediction period as well.

relationships that supposedly have been found between the output and the inputs of the variable factors, using this machine at each of its five speeds.[4]

By observation of the various input components, you will notice that the ratio of materials used to output per hour increases as the operating speed of the machine is increased. This indicates increased wastage or spoilage as the machine is operated at faster speeds. Labor input, however, increases by different amounts as the operating speed is increased. It apparently requires twenty men to operate the machine at its minimum speed, and this increases at an irregular rate as the operating speed is increased until at maximum speed thirty men are required per hour of operation. Electric power requirements, measured in kilowatt hours, increase rapidly at first and then more slowly, and then more rapidly again as maximum operating speed is attained. Repairs and maintenance requirements are indicated by an index of labor and materials necessary to maintain the machine in operating condition, and they evidently increase quite dramatically as the machine attains its maximum operating speed.

Suppose the variable inputs have the following costs per unit. Materials cost $0.15 per pound, labor cost is $8.00 per hour, power cost is $0.0325 per kilowatt hour, and repairs and maintenance cost is $10.00 per unit. With this information we can calculate the total variable cost of the output at various levels, as shown in Table 8.4. <u>Dividing total variable cost at each output level by that output level, we derive the average variable cost for each output level, and the marginal cost figures are derived by the gradient method and are in effect the *average* marginal costs over each 1,200-unit interval</u>. Note that both average and marginal cost decline at first and later rise.

**TABLE 8.4**
**Costs associated with operating the metal-stamping machine
at various output levels**

| Output Levels (units) | Materials Cost ($) | Labor Cost ($) | Power Cost ($) | R&M Cost ($) | TVC ($) | AVC ($) | MC ($) |
|---|---|---|---|---|---|---|---|
| 1,200 | 198 | 160 | 84 | 100 | 542 | 0.452 | |
| | | | | | | | 0.364 |
| 2,400 | 432 | 200 | 147 | 200 | 979 | 0.408 | |
| | | | | | | | 0.342 |
| 3,600 | 702 | 216 | 171 | 300 | 1,389 | 0.386 | |
| | | | | | | | 0.343 |
| 4,800 | 1,008 | 224 | 218 | 350 | 1,800 | 0.375 | |
| | | | | | | | 0.622 |
| 6,000 | 1,350 | 240 | 356 | 600 | 2,546 | 0.424 | |

In Figure 8.4 we plot these average variable and marginal cost figures against the output level. Interpolating between these observations we are able to sketch in the average variable and marginal cost curves as indicated by the engineering technique. The production process appears to be most efficient in terms of

[4] The figures at any output level should be regarded as the central tendency of the actually observed levels, since we should expect small day-to-day variations in material wastage, labor efficiency, and actual repairs and maintenance requirements.

**FIGURE 8.4**
**Estimated cost curves of metal-stamping plant**

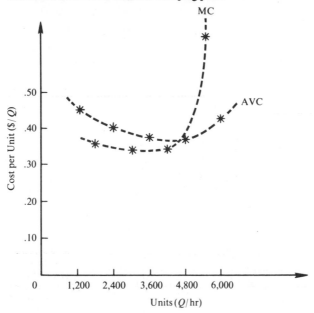

the variable factors at about 4,600 units, where average variable cost appears to reach a minimum at something like $0.37 per unit. If the speed of the machine were infinitely variable, the firm might wish to operate at this output level by running the machine at approximately 77 rpm. If the firm wishes to maximize profits rather than simply minimize costs, it will seek the output level at which marginal revenues from the sale of these output units equal the marginal cost of producing the last unit of output. Note that by multiplying the scale on the horizontal axis in Figure 8.4 by the appropriate factor, the same cost curves will be applicable for output per day, week, or longer period.

Incremental costs associated with any decision to increase or decrease output levels will be determined on the basis of the variable costs as calculated by one or a combination of the above methods, plus an allowance for any opportunity costs that are involved and any incremental fixed costs that may be necessitated. The incremental fixed costs must be calculated on the basis of the knowledge of the production capacity of the fixed factors involved. This in turn may require an engineering-type investigation of the output capacities of particular fixed facilities. Similarly, increased costs associated with overtime use of facilities must be estimated on the basis of known overtime labor costs.

### Studies of Short-Run Cost Behavior

Numerous studies of the short-run cost functions of particular business firms have attempted to ascertain the shape and placement of the cost curves pertaining to those firms. Perhaps the definitive work in the area is the book by Johnston,[5] in which the theoretical and conceptual issues of cost estimation by statistical methods are examined in detail before he summarizes thirty-one separate studies of statistical cost estimation. With regard to short-run cost estimation, the preponderant conclusion is that marginal cost tends to be constant in the operating range of the firms studied. Hence average variable cost is constant at the same level (or is asymptotically approaching that level), and average total costs are declining due to the influence of declining average fixed costs. That is to say, in most cases a linear total variable cost function provided the best fit to the data observations.

In some cases where a curvilinear total variable cost function was hypothesized, the regression analysis generated a high coefficient of determination, but generally the linear equation provided at least as much explanatory power. Thus the general conclusion of the statistical cost studies is that marginal and average variable costs tend to be constant over the output range in which firms tend to operate, or they are sufficiently constant over that range that they may be regarded for decision-making purposes as constant. But constant MC and AVC over the range of recent output levels does not mean that we can expect these unit costs to be constant *outside* this range. For decisions that involve output levels beyond the recent range of output levels, the decision maker must consider the possibility that extrapolation of unit-cost levels is an unreliable procedure due to the possible onset of diminishing returns in the production process. The occurrence of diminishing returns in the incremental units of output should always be suspected, and if these are thought likely to occur the incremental cost figure should be adjusted accordingly.

## 8.3 LONG-RUN COST ESTIMATION

In this section we shall outline methods by which the long-run cost curve, or the alternative short-run cost curves available at a particular point in time, may be ascertained. We shall discuss three methods of long-run cost estimation: cross-section regression analysis, the "survivor principle," and the engineering technique applied to plants of various sizes.

### Cross-Section Regression Analysis

Since long-run cost estimation seeks to find the differing scales of plant available at a particular point of time (while technology and factor prices remain constant), it is clear that we cannot use time-series observations to derive estimates of the long-run cost function. Observations from various plants at a particular point of time (cross-section data) may be analyzed, however, using the technique of regression analysis. Thus we would need to collect pairs of data observations relating the output level to the total cost of obtaining that output level in each plant, for a particular relatively short period of time. Care must be taken to avoid errors of measurement relating either to the actual level or rate of output in that period or to the actual level of costs that should be associated with that level of output in each plant observed.

[5] J. Johnston, *Statistical Cost Analysis* (New York: McGraw-Hill, 1960).

Specification of the functional form of the equation involves the same problems for long-run cost estimation as it did for short-run cost estimation. We must choose the functional form that best fits the data observations subject to each determining variable's being significant at an acceptable level. Since we are interested in whether or not there are likely to be economies of plant size, constant returns to plant size, or diseconomies of plant size, we might initially specify the relationship as being cubic, since this is consistent with the presence of increasing, constant, and decreasing returns to plant size. If a linear function best fits the data, however, we must conclude that increasing returns to plant size prevail over the range of the data observations. If a power function best fits the data, the size of the exponent to the output variable will indicate whether returns to plant size are increasing (if the exponent is less than one), or constant (if equal to one), or decreasing (if exceeding one).

Two major problems exist with cross-section data for estimation of the long-run average cost curve. The first arises because the observations collected may not be points on the long-run average cost curve at all. Let us illustrate this with a simple example. Suppose there are five plants observed, and the current output and cost levels are as shown in Table 8.5. It is clear that economies of plant size exist initially and that diseconomies of plant size prevail for the fourth and fifth largest plants, since the average cost figures decline at first and later rise as we encounter progressively larger plant sizes.

**TABLE 8.5**
**Cross-section estimation of the long-run
average cost curve**

| Plant | Output (Q) | Total Cost ($) | Average Cost ($/Q) |
|---|---|---|---|
| 1 | 1,500 | 7,350 | 4.90 |
| 2 | 3,500 | 12,600 | 3.60 |
| 3 | 6,150 | 18,143 | 2.95 |
| 4 | 8,750 | 26,688 | 3.05 |
| 5 | 11,100 | 43,290 | 3.90 |

Suppose that the *actual* short-run cost curves for each of the five plants are as shown by the $AC_1$, $AC_2$, and other short-run cost curves in Figure 8.5. The observed output/average cost values are shown by the point on each short-run cost curve marked by an asterisk. Given this insight, we can see that the above analysis has overestimated the presence of economies and diseconomies of plant size in this instance due to the fact that the observation points for each plant were not the points of tangency with the actual long-run cost curve. This problem is accentuated if smaller plants are operating beyond the point of tangency with the long-run average cost curve, and large plants are operating to the left of the tangency point, but it occurs whichever side of the "actual" tangency point the firms are operating. Since we cannot expect each firm to be operating at precisely the point of tangency of the short-run average cost curve to the long-run average cost curve, the regression analysis of cross-section data is likely to

FIGURE 8.5
**Estimation of long-run average cost curve from cross-section data**

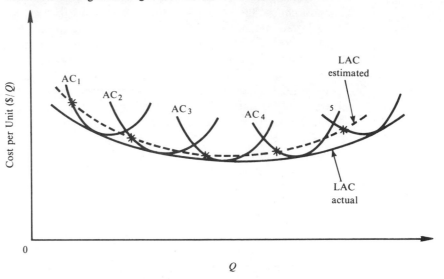

produce a misleading picture of the actual economies and/or diseconomies of plant size that may exist.

The second problem that may arise with cross-section data is that the various plants may not be operating with the benefit of the same factor prices and/or factor productivities. If the plants operate in differing geographical, political, and socioeconomic environments, we may expect both factor prices and productivities of the factors to differ between and among the plants. If this problem exists, regression analysis may indicate economies or diseconomies of plant size where the cost differences are actually due to differences in factor prices and productivities. Alternatively, the differences in these two factors may completely obscure the existence of those economies and diseconomies of plant size that would be seen to occur if the influence of differing factor prices and productivities could be removed from the data. A means of laundering the data to remove these differences is to derive an index for each of the factor price and productivity variables and deflate each observation by the value of the index. Using one plant observation as the base, we might discover that factor prices at a second plant are 10 percent lower, and factor productivities are 15 percent lower. In order to make this second observation comparable with the first observation, we would thus inflate the cost figure by dividing it by the index of 0.9, and inflate the output level by dividing it by the index of 0.85. Continuing this process with the other observations, we would be able to derive an apparent long-run average cost function that would be tolerably appropriate to the plant that was used as the basis for the adjustment process.

### The Survivor Principle

Stigler has devised a test for the presence or absence of economies or diseconomies of plant size in particular industries which is based upon the principle that the more efficient firms will tend to survive and increase their market share, while the less efficient firms will tend to become less important in that industry as time passes.[6] Stigler's procedure was to classify the firms in an industry into size classes and calculate the share of total industry output coming from each class over time. If the share of a particular class declines over time, the inference is made that that size of firm is relatively inefficient and is therefore smaller or larger than the optimal scale of plant. Size categories that maintain or increase their share of industry output over time are considered to be relatively efficient, and therefore likely to have lower per unit average costs. Stigler's test of the United States steel industry for the years 1930 and 1951 indicated that both the smallest firms and the largest firms suffered a decline in their share of total industry output. The firms of intermediate size grew or held their shares over this period and hence appeared to be operating at the optimum sizes of plant. Thus the survivor principle infers a long-run average cost curve that slopes downward at first, is constant over a wide range of outputs, and then slopes upward at relatively large output levels.

An analogous means of inferring the presence of economies and diseconomies of plant size is to compare the Lorenz curve of the firms' outputs from one period with the Lorenz curve of a later period. A Lorenz curve plots the proportion of firms against the proportion of industry output when the firms have been ranked in descending order of their contribution to industry output. In Figure 8.6 we show Lorenz curves constructed from hypothetical 1960 and 1970 data.

**FIGURE 8.6**
**Lorenz curve used to infer economies and diseconomies of plant size**

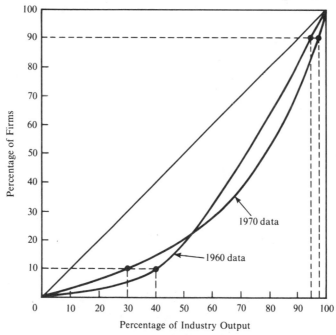

[6]G. J. Stigler, "The Economies of Scale," *Journal of Law and Economics,* Vol. 1, October 1958; reprinted in his *The Organization of Industry* (Homewood, Ill.: Richard D. Irwin, 1968), pp. 71-94.

The fact that each Lorenz curve falls below the diagonal indicates that the output of each firm is not equal, and that a small proportion of relatively large firms account for a relatively large proportion of the output, while a large proportion of relatively small firms account for a relatively small proportion of the output. The 1960 Lorenz curve indicates that 10 percent of the firms account for approximately 40 percent of industry output, and that 90 percent of the firms account for 95 percent of industry output. The 1970 data, however, indicate that the share of the largest 10 percent of the firms has declined to 30 percent of industry output, while the share of the smallest 10 percent of the firms has declined to about 2 percent of the total industry output. Applied to this hypothetical case, the survivor principle would therefore infer that the largest plants and the smallest plants in the industry suffer relatively higher per unit costs than do the intervening-sized firms. Hence the long-run average cost curve applicable to this hypothetical industry could be inferred to have a U shape.

Certain problems arise with the use of the survivor principle to infer the shape of the long-run cost curve. It is obvious that a firm could suffer a decrease in market share for reasons other than its inefficiency in production. Poor management, adverse publicity, low labor productivity due to poor labor-management relations, or a multitude of other factors could cause a particular firm's share of the market to decline over any particular period. If these problems are systematically related to the size of a firm (e.g., occurring in all small firms), the survivor principle would indicate the presence of a cost difference between these particular firms and larger firms. But rather than being inherently due to the size of the firm, these cost differences may be due to other problems of a possibly temporary nature. If the data base is sufficiently large, however, we should expect the influence of these random or temporary factors to cancel, such that a clear tendency can be ascertained as to whether the market shares are increasing or constant or decreasing at particular firm-size levels. If these or other problems are a permanent feature of firms of any particular size, then they are in fact part of the reason for net economies or diseconomies of firm size.[7]

Presuming that it could get the data, a firm might apply the survivor principle to its own industry and find indications of economies and diseconomies of size at various output levels. Relating its own output level to this information, it may then conclude that, for example, expansion of plant facilities will result in reduced average cost levels. Alternatively, the data may indicate that per unit costs will remain relatively constant or decrease as the firm increases its scale of plant.

### Applying the Engineering Technique
### to Several Plants

The engineering technique outlined above in the context of short-run cost estimation can be used to find an estimation of the long-run cost function by

---

[7] Note that there is a problem of firm size versus plant size if some firms operate more than one plant and the data on market share refer to firms, not plants. The resultant economies or diseconomies of size may be the result of both influences in the case of a multiplant firm.

**FIGURE 8.7**
Engineering technique of cost estimation used to derive the long-run
average cost curve

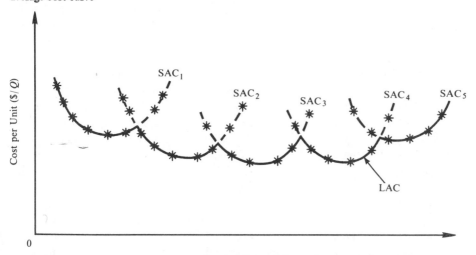

applying the same analysis to a number of plants of differing sizes at a particular point of time. In the short-run cost estimation section, we used the engineering technique to find the cost curves of a particular firm at a particular point of time. If we proceeded in a similar fashion with other plant sizes that are available, we would be able to trace out a series of short-run cost curves that are available to the firm at a particular point of time.

To apply the engineering technique for purposes of long-run cost estimation, we would conduct the analysis as outlined above under short-run cost estimation for each firm. To this we would add the average fixed-cost curve for each plant size, to arrive at the short-run total cost curve for each of the plant sizes. By the shape and placement of the short-run average cost curves, we could infer the presence or absence of economies and diseconomies of plant size. In Figure 8.7 we show a hypothetical case in which five different sizes of plants have been observed, and the short-run average cost curve of each has been derived by the engineering technique. The envelope curve of these short-run curves is the long-run average cost curve. It can be inferred from the figure that there are economies of plant size initially as one moves from the first plant to the second plant, followed by relatively constant returns to plant size as one progresses to the third and fourth plant, and decreasing returns to plant size with the largest plant available.[8]

Note that the construction of the long-run average cost curve by the engineering technique is predicated upon factor productivity and factor prices being at similar levels in each of the available plant sizes. Similarly, the factor prices and productivities depicted by this analysis are applicable only as long as these

[8] Typically we should expect there to be discrete differences in the plant sizes that are available to the firm, rather than the infinite variability of plant sizes that is implied by a smooth long-run average cost curve.

variables do not change. If they do, a new set of short-run average cost curves must be derived, and a new long-run average cost curve will be found.

### Long-Run Cost Estimation Studies

Various studies of the long-run cost function of firms have been undertaken, and a number of these are summarized in the book by Johnston.[9] The most common finding of these studies was that the long-run average cost curve tended to be not so much U-shaped as L-shaped; that is, there were typically significant economies of plant size at relatively low output levels, followed by an extended range of constant returns to plant size with no common tendency for per unit costs to rise at higher output levels. The absence of diseconomies of size in these production processes does not necessarily mean that they would not occur if progressively larger plant sizes were employed. The expectation that per unit costs would increase with a larger plant would presumably cause the firm to operate two smaller plants rather than build one larger plant. Thus the absence of evidence indicating diseconomies of plant size does not mean that they would never occur, it simply means that the data base does not include any plant that is experiencing diseconomies (perhaps due to the foresight of the decision makers.)

## 8.4   COST FORECASTING

Cost forecasting is necessary whenever decisions involve cost levels in future periods, such as in bidding for contracts, make-or-buy problems, or any other decision with cost implications beyond the present period. Forecasting the level of costs for various output levels in future periods requires an assessment of the likely changes in the efficiency in the physical production process, plus changes in the prices of the factors involved in the production process. Changes in the efficiency of factors of production will, as indicated in Chapter 6, change the shape of the production surface and hence the shape of any particular total product curve associated with that production process. If factor prices are expected to change, this will change the relationship between the total product curve and the total variable cost curve which is derived from that total product curve. Hence the change in future costs will be the result of two influences, which we shall consider in turn.

### Changes in Factor Productivities

When considering the physical efficiency of the production process in future periods, we should expect the productivities of at least some of the factors of production to change as time passes. Machines and equipment, for example, should be expected to become progressively more efficient in terms of output per hour (or by some other criterion) due to the incorporation of technological advances into those machines. The increasing use of computer-controlled plant and equipment has allowed the productivity of capital equipment to increase substantially in recent years. Similarly, labor productivity might be expected to

[9] See Johnston, *Statistical Cost Analysis,* Chap. 5.

increase as time progresses due to the workers' higher level of education and increased familiarity with mechanical production processes. On the other hand, changes in the attitude toward work or other sociological factors may lead us to expect reduced labor productivity in the future.

If trends have become apparent in the productivity of the factors of production, we may apply these trends as an estimate of future changes in the efficiency of the physical production process. This extrapolation of productivity trends should be modified by any changes in the productivity of any factor that may be expected to follow foreseen events of an irregular nature.

Labor productivity is typically measured as units of output per labor unit, and hence it takes the credit for increases in the productivity of capital factors such as machines and equipment. Labor productivity figures are therefore an amalgam of labor and capital productivity, and it may be quite difficult to separate the effects of each. Rather than attempt this, we are perhaps better employed searching for trends or patterns in the output per man-hour or some similar index. Data on this measure are frequently available from public sources, and the decision maker may be able to derive estimates of the future productivity of factors based upon these data.

### Changes in Factor Prices

If the costs of all inputs increase over time in the *same proportion*, then the factor combination that is initially optimal for a particular output level will remain optimal, although it will cost more dollars. To explain this, let us recall the isoquant-isocost analysis of Chapter 6. In effect, all isocost curves will shift to the left in a parallel fashion, since the factor price ratio is unchanged. Thus a new (higher-valued) isocost curve will now be tangent to any given isoquant curve at the same combination of the input factors. Costs in a future period will therefore be equal to today's costs plus the expected percentage increase in all costs.

If market forces in the factor markets are expected to be such that the price of one factor will rise *relative* to the prices of other factors, we should expect the firm to wish to substitute away from this factor and toward other factors that become relatively cheaper as a result of that price change. Thus if labor costs are expected to increase faster than capital costs in the future, we should expect the firm to wish to substitute capital for labor in order to minimize the costs of particular output levels. Historically, we have seen this to be the general case, with the increasing automation of production processes. To the extent that this is expected to continue in future periods, the firm should expect to achieve an increasingly capital-intensive production process in the future. You will recall from the isoquant analysis of Chapter 6 that this represents a cost-minimizing response to changing factor prices.

Forecasting factor price changes—or, more generally, forecasting the rate of inflation—requires techniques similar to those introduced in Chapter 5 in the context of demand forecasting. Opinion surveys, trend projections, econometric models, and leading series and other barometric indicators may be used to predict the rate at which costs of production are expected to increase in future periods.[10] Expectations of events likely to influence prices, such as supply short-ages or export embargoes, must be incorporated into the cost forecasts. Given a probability distribution associated with future cost levels, we may proceed on the basis of the "expected value" of cost levels in future periods in order to obtain a point forecast of future cost levels for pricing or other decision problems.[11]

In a socioeconomic system where inflation has become seemingly endemic and relatively low rates of inflation are welcomed for their beneficial impact on business confidence, we should expect a continuing increase in the nominal prices of all factors in future periods. To the extent that the firm is able to pass inflationary cost increases along to its customers, and maintain the ratio of its prices to costs, the *real* cost of the resources to the firm is unchanged. Thus a current decision involving future production and costs can be made on the basis of today's cost levels modified only for expected changes in factor price ratios and any inflationary effects that are not expected to be passed along to the purchaser. We shall see in Chapter 11 that the practice of "markup pricing" ensures that the firm will maintain its *real* contribution margin per unit under inflationary conditions. If the price must be set now but costs will be incurred in future periods, as in competitive bidding and price quotations, the price must include the expected inflation factor in order that the firm's real contribution margin will be preserved.

## 8.5   SUMMARY

*Cost estimation* is concerned with the levels of cost at various output levels of the firm's plant, and with the relative costs of other plant sizes that are currently available to the firm. In the short-run situation we are concerned with the behavior of average variable and marginal costs, plus any other incremental costs that may be required due to the full utilization of some elements of the existing fixed-factor inputs. Long-run cost estimation involves the per unit cost levels of various plant sizes, given the current factor prices and state of technology.

Methods of short-run cost estimation discussed were simple extrapolation, gradient analysis, regression analysis of time-series data, and the engineering technique. Long-run cost possibilities may be estimated using regression analysis of cross-section data, the survivor principle, or the application of the engineering technique to plants of various sizes. Empirical studies of cost estimation have frequently shown marginal costs to be constant in the short run, and the absence of diseconomies of scale in the long run.

*Cost forecasting* requires the estimation of cost levels in future periods, in which factor productivities and prices may be different from today's levels. Trends in factor productivities that have become apparent over recent years may be used to project future changes in cost levels. Factor price changes that are real rather than simply monetary must also be forecast in order to obtain reliable indications of future cost levels for decision-making purposes.

[10] See C. A. Dauten and L. M. Valentine, *Business Cycles and Forecasting,* 4th ed. (Cincinnati, Ohio: South-Western Publishing, 1974), Chap. 18.

[11] Costs to be incurred in the future have a present value that is less than their future value, of course. Decisions to be made now, but which involve both costs and revenues being incurred or received in future periods, should be evaluated in present value terms.

# DISCUSSION QUESTIONS

8.1 Explain the dangers inherent in extrapolation of cost levels beyond the limits of the data base.

8.2 Why are cross-section data likely to be inappropriate for the estimation of short-run cost functions?

8.3 Why is it important to test several specifications of the cost function for their significance and goodness of fit?

8.4 Explain the engineering technique of cost estimation in terms of the production and cost theory of Chapter 6.

8.5 Outline some of the reasons why you might expect raw-material input, labor, and repairs and maintenance not to be simple linear functions of output.

8.6 Discuss the major problems that may arise in regression analysis of cross-section data to estimate the long-run average cost curve.

8.7 Explain why a linear relationship between total costs (of different plants) and output levels (of different plants) means that the data exhibit economies of plant size.

8.8 Outline the "survivor principle" of determining the presence or absence of economies and/or diseconomies of plant size, and state any qualifications you feel are necessary.

8.9 If the productivities of all factors are expected to improve by the same proportion in the coming years, does this mean that there should be no factor substitution in future periods? Why or why not?

8.10 Summarize the issues involved in the forecasting of cost levels in an inflationary situation.

# PROBLEMS

8.1 The Rakita Racquets Company restrings tennis racquets, a business with a highly seasonal demand. The owner-manager, Ian Rakita, has kept a record of the number of racquets restrung and total variable costs for each of the past twelve months, as follows:

| Month | Total Variable Cost ($) | Racquets Restrung (units) |
| --- | --- | --- |
| June | 35,490 | 9,000 |
| July | 42,470 | 11,150 |
| August | 48,980 | 12,600 |
| September | 52,530 | 13,050 |
| October | 37,480 | 10,650 |
| November | 33,510 | 8,100 |
| December | 31,850 | 5,700 |
| January | 27,860 | 4,900 |
| February | 22,160 | 3,050 |
| March | 19,520 | 1,850 |
| April | 25,960 | 3,850 |
| May | 32,980 | 7,000 |

Over the past twelve months Mr. Rakita has experienced a constant price level for all variable factor inputs, and he feels that due to the regular turnover of employees, employee productivity and materials wastage are neither better nor worse than they have ever been.

(a) Plot the total variable cost levels against output. Draw a freehand line through those observations that appear to represent the "line of best fit" to the data.

(b) From your freehand TVC cost function, derive the AVC and MC curves for Mr. Rakita's racquet-stringing operation.

(c) Suppose that demand is expected to move from its present level of 7,000 units (May) to 10,000 units next month (June). What is the incremental cost of meeting this additional demand?

(d) In three months' time (August), demand is expected to reach 13,000 units. What is the incremental cost of meeting the additional units (above June's expected output level)?

(e) Qualify your answers with any implicit or explicit assumptions that are involved in the above analysis.

8.2 The Minical Electronics Company produces pocket calculators which are sold to various retail outlets at a price of $20. Minical feels it can sell all it is able to produce at this price. The following table indicates the physical input requirements for several weekly output levels, as compiled by the production manager, Paula Wald.

| Output (units) | 500 | 650 | 800 | 950 | 1,100 |
|---|---|---|---|---|---|
| Labor hours | 1,000 | 1,200 | 1,400 | 1,600 | 1,800 |
| Component "packages" | 750 | 1,000 | 1,275 | 1,575 | 1,895 |
| Power (kwh) | 225 | 400 | 500 | 650 | 1,000 |
| Maintenance hours | 5 | 15 | 23 | 28 | 42 |
| Machine hours | 20 | 25 | 29 | 32 | 39 |

The hourly wage rate paid for assembly labor is $5.50. The cost of a "package" of components is $5.00 each. (These packages each contain all the components necessary to produce one calculator. Because of imperfections in some components and breakage due to rough handling, more than one package per calculator is typically required.) Power costs $0.038 per kilowatt hour, machine hours are costed at $10 per hour, and maintenance hours cost $25 each.

(a) Using the engineering technique and gradient analysis, construct the AVC and MC curves implied by the physical input/output relationship and the prices of the inputs.

(b) At what output level are the variable inputs (combined) most efficient?

(c) What output level should the firm produce in order to maximize the contribution from this product?

8.3 Beaudet Industries is situated in a relatively small regional center and manufactures cement and related products. Its plant capacity, although small in relation to the larger manufacturers situated near the larger centers, has been adequate to supply local demand. This demand consists mostly of government contracts to furnish materials for road improvement programs and to a lesser degree residential construction. Beaudet has received the contracts on the basis of its ability in the past to reliably and consistently supply the desired quantities, and due to its proximity to the job sites. Beaudet's pricing policy (marking up variable costs by 100 percent) has always been acceptable to its customers. In preparation for the annual corporate-planning session, management hired a team of market researchers to provide an estimate of future demand for the company's product. It was reported that demand in the next five years could go as high as 2 million units per annum, double the present capacity of the Beaudet plant. In view of this, management is studying the feasibility of purchasing new automated equipment which would effectively double the output. A firm of consulting engineers furnished cost figures for a scale of plant that would meet these requirements. Both the existing plant and the proposed plant can be considered to last indefinitely, yet they have no scrap value.

**Probability distribution of annual demand for each of next five years**

| (Units (000) | Probability | Units (000) | Probability |
|---|---|---|---|
| 400 | 0.02 | 1,000 | 0.20 |
| 500 | 0.03 | 1,200 | 0.25 |
| 700 | 0.05 | 1,600 | 0.15 |
| 800 | 0.10 | 2,000 | 0.05 |
| 900 | 0.15 | | 1.00 |

**Cost/output data: proposed plant (all data in thousands)**

| | Output | 2,000 | 1,600 | 1,200 | 800 | 400 |
|---|---|---|---|---|---|---|
| Cost of Inputs ($) | Raw materials | 432 | 224 | 156 | 139.2 | 97.6 |
| | Direct labor | 540 | 280 | 195 | 174 | 122 |
| | Power | 1,080 | 504 | 351 | 313.2 | 219.6 |
| | Variable overhead | 108 | 112 | 78 | 69.6 | 42.8 |
| | Fixed overhead | 750 | 750 | 750 | 750 | 750 |

**Cost/output data: present plant (all data in thousands)**

| | Output | 1,000 | 900 | 700 | 500 | 300 | 100 |
|---|---|---|---|---|---|---|---|
| Cost of Inputs ($) | Raw materials | 351 | 203.75 | 140 | 90 | 57.75 | 26.25 |
| | Direct labor | 351 | 273.6 | 168 | 108 | 69.3 | 31.5 |
| | Power | 409.5 | 256.5 | 196 | 126 | 80.85 | 36.75 |
| | Variable overhead | 58.5 | 68.4 | 56 | 36 | 23.1 | 10.5 |
| | Fixed overhead | 400 | 400 | 400 | 400 | 400 | 400 |

(a)  Derive the average variable and marginal cost curves for both the present and the proposed plant.

(b)  On the basis of the information supplied, should Beaudet invest in the new plant? Explain and defend your answer.

8.4   Your company, King Hi Cards, Inc., is one of twelve small firms producing high-quality greeting cards on the West Coast. At a recent industry-wide conference, you attended a seminar to discuss possible solutions to the cost pressures facing the industry. As a by-product of that inquiry you have obtained the output and total cost levels for each firm for the month of April, as follows:

| Company | Output (000) | Total Costs ($) |
|---|---|---|
| King Hi | 4.92 | 4,872 |
| Man | 5.40 | 5,793 |
| Jamie | 6.75 | 5,422 |
| Dow | 4.20 | 4,367 |
| Jamsheed | 7.80 | 5,316 |
| Khan | 6.55 | 6,050 |
| Julie | 7.15 | 5,658 |
| Krupa | 5.85 | 6,225 |
| John | 3.50 | 4,506 |
| Liddy | 7.40 | 6,488 |
| Nicole | 6.00 | 5,134 |
| Siamas | 4.40 | 5,302 |

Your company is considering expansion to about 7,000 cards monthly. Since this additional output may make it difficult to raise prices in the near future, you wish to know whether per unit costs might be expected to fall, remain constant, or increase as you increase your plant size to the level required.

(a) Using the formulas and method given in Chapter 5, find the linear equation that "best fits" the relationship between the total costs and the output level.

(b) Convert both the cost and the output data to logarithms in order to fit the power function $TC = aQ^b$ (see Chapter 5 for method).

(c) Which of the above functional forms should be used for prediction? Why?

(d) Are there economies and/or constant returns and/or diseconomies of plant size evident over the range of data observations?

(e) Suggest possible reasons to explain the goodness of fit not being especially high.

8.5 The Arato Manufacturing Co. sells small electrical motors to various other manufacturing companies at $10 per unit. It presently operates two plants with different levels of full capacity. The following data have been extracted from the company's operations for the past three months.

| | PLANT A (full capacity = 20,000 units/mo) | | | PLANT B (full capacity = 30,000 units/mo) | | |
|---|---|---|---|---|---|---|
| | Oct. | Nov. | Dec. | Oct. | Nov. | Dec. |
| Units sold | 15,000 | 16,000 | 18,000 | 20,000 | 22,000 | 18,000 |
| Raw materials | $2.40 | $2.46 | $2.58 | $2.60 | $2.66 | $2.54 |
| Direct labor | 3.20 | 3.00 | 2.60 | 2.45 | 2.30 | 2.60 |
| Variable overhead | 1.20 | 1.23 | 1.29 | 1.30 | 1.33 | 1.27 |
| Fixed overhead | .50 | .50 | .60 | .55 | .50 | .55 |
| Average costs | $7.30 | $7.19 | $7.07 | $6.90 | $6.79 | $6.96 |

Both plants operate with a daily eight-hour shift, at times utilizing full capacity if a special order comes in. Since Plant A is the smaller of the two plants, occasionally Plant A will purchase motors from Plant B at a transfer price of $5 per unit so that it can fill an order that would otherwise put it beyond its full capacity. No overtime has been allowed so far. but management may consider it if *both* plants are operating at their full capacities, although per unit cost is expected to take a substantial upward jump under such conditions.

Sales for the next two months have already been booked for both plants as follows:

|          | Jan.   | Feb.   |
|----------|--------|--------|
| Plant A  | 19,000 | 15,000 |
| Plant B  | 21,000 | 23,000 |

On January 10, Gabor Electrical Assemblers offers to purchase 15,000 motors for $6 per unit, to be delivered by the end of February.

(a)  Should the order be accepted? If yes, which plant or combination of plants should be used in making the special order at a maximum benefit to the company as a whole?

(b)  What further information would you like to have before submitting your recommendation?

8.6  The Done Brown Cookie Company produces high-nutrition "Brownie" biscuits which it sells to retailers for $22.55 per carton of 24 packets. While demand for Brownies is not seasonal, it nonetheless fluctuates during the year. Over the past nine months of operations, demand has varied between 6,000 and 10,000 cartons per month, though there is a general growth trend in sales. Done Brown's plant has a monthly one-shift capacity of 12,000 units, and a recently signed two-year labor contract provides for an overtime half-shift (at a 50 percent premium on labor cost) which could produce a further 4,000 units per month. As the forecast for the coming year indicates that monthly sales will not be over 14,000 units, the vice-president of marketing, Mr. White, is quite confident that the plant's total monthly capacity of 16,000 units is adequate to meet all demand for the near future.

The vice-president of corporate planning, Mr. Black, has put forward the proposal that the firm expand its present plant to a capacity of 18,000 units per month. Having investigated the financial situation of Done Brown, he suggests that the cash that the directors are considering paying out as an extra dividend would be put to better use if invested in plant expansion and renovation. Mr. Black contends that it would be more economical to run a larger plant at half-capacity than it is to continue running the present plant.

The vice-president of production, Mr. Green, on the other hand, is vehement in his assertation that the plant is running smoothly, and that sales forecasts in no way indicate that a larger plant is necesssary at this time. Mr. Black, though, seems to have a convincing argument, having procured the cost figures for a competing Brownie manufacturer who has a larger plant than does Done Brown. He suggests that as the two firms are in the same economic milieu, Done Brown should model its plant after that of the competitor.

A task force has been assigned to study the question of expansion. It is to analyze costs for both firms, and the sales forecasts, as shown below, and submit its findings to the board of directors, along with a recommended plan of action. You are the head of the task force. Is Mr. Black correct? Should Done Brown expand its plant? Support your recommendation with discussion of the issues involved. Defend any assumptions that you feel are necessary.

**Sales forecast: average sales per month over the next year**

| Volume | Probability |
|--------|-------------|
| 6,000  | 0.05        |
| 8,000  | 0.20        |
| 10,000 | 0.50        |
| 12,000 | 0.20        |
| 14,000 | 0.05        |

**Done Brown's production costs: past nine months**

| Month | Output Level (cartons) | Materials ($) | Direct Labor ($) | Overhead ($) |
|-------|------------------------|---------------|------------------|--------------|
| April | 6,000 | 88,500 | 21,000 | 15,200 |
| May | 7,500 | 107,250 | 24,000 | 17,450 |
| June | 6,500 | 94,900 | 22,100 | 15,950 |
| July | 8,000 | 113,200 | 24,800 | 18,200 |
| Aug. | 7,000 | 101,150 | 23,100 | 16,700 |
| Sept. | 8,500 | 118,825 | 28,475 | 18,950 |
| Oct. | 10,000 | 148,500 | 45,000 | 21,200 |
| Nov. | 9,000 | 126,850 | 32,400 | 19,700 |
| Dec. | 9,500 | 136,075 | 37,525 | 20,450 |

**Competitor's production costs: past nine months**

| Month | Output Level (cartons) | Materials ($) | Direct Labor ($) | Overhead ($) |
|-------|------------------------|---------------|------------------|--------------|
| April | 10,000 | 140,000 | 30,500 | 24,350 |
| May | 8,500 | 127,075 | 27,025 | 22,175 |
| June | 9,000 | 133,000 | 28,550 | 22,900 |
| July | 10,500 | 144,375 | 32,025 | 25,075 |
| Aug. | 9,500 | 136,565 | 29,875 | 23,625 |
| Sept. | 11,000 | 151,250 | 33,550 | 25,800 |
| Oct. | 12,500 | 173,750 | 47,875 | 27,975 |
| Nov. | 11,500 | 158,125 | 36,675 | 26,525 |
| Dec. | 12,000 | 165,600 | 41,600 | 27,250 |

8.7 The Autoroller Company is situated near Detroit and specializes in producing ball bearings for the automotive industry. Since its inception in 1970, the company has been supplying both the Michigan and the Ohio automobile producers, with increasing sales each year. In 1978 the company sold 600,000 units in Michigan and 200,000 units in Ohio. In 1979 the Ohio customers contracted for 400,000 units, and Michigan demand was expected to increase by 100,000 units. The Ohio customers indicated that they would need 600,000 units in 1980, and Michigan sales were expected to be 750,000 units in that year. The price per unit was increased to $8 effective January 1, 1979, for the whole of 1979. Since the Ohio customers ship other auto parts to their Michigan plant, and return their trucks empty, they purchase at the same price as the Michigan customers at the Detroit plant of Autoroller's.

Autoroller's president, Mr. Blydt-Hansen, was excited about the increasing demand over the years, but was concerned about plant capacity and the effect on profitability. The plant's normal capacity was 600,000 units per year, but with a combination of either overtime or a second shift, both at a 50 percent premium on labor cost, demand has been met so far. A third shift was possible and 1980 demand could have been satisfied from the existing plant, although costs per unit were expected to increase further. Alternatively, Mr. Blydt-Hansen was considering whether or not to build an identical plant in Ohio. This project could have been completed in time for start-up in the beginning of 1980 if a decision was reached immediately. The cost structure of the new plant in Ohio was expected to be identical to that of the existing Michigan plant.

The company accumulated the following data (all figures are thousands):

|  | 1976 | 1977 | 1978 | 1979 (est.) |
|---|---|---|---|---|
| Sales volume | 600 | 700 | 800 | 1,100 |
| Total Revenue | $3,600 | $4,620 | $5,800 | $8,800 |
| Costs: Direct labor | 450 | 620 | 818 | 1,285 |
| Raw materials | 676 | 983 | 1,382 | 2,000 |
| Variable overhead | 900 | 1,240 | 1,636 | 2,400 |
| Fixed overhead | 1,127 | 1,240 | 1,364 | 1,400 |
| Total costs | $3,153 | $4,083 | $5,200 | $7,085 |
| Gross profit | 447 | 537 | 600 | 1,715 |

The company treasurer advises that hourly wages and all other costs have increased by about 10 percent per year for the last few years, and Autorollers have been able to increase their price each year. These price trends are expected to continue through at least 1980.

Advise Mr. Blydt-Hansen whether or not he should build the new plant in Ohio. Support your recommendation with discussion of all issues involved.

## SUGGESTED REFERENCES AND FURTHER READING

DAUTEN, C. A., and L. M. VALENTINE, *Business Cycles and Forecasting,* 4th ed., Chaps. 10 and 18. Cincinnati, Ohio: South-Western Publishing, 1974.

JOHNSTON, J., *Statistical Cost Analysis.* New York: McGraw-Hill, 1960.

McGUIGAN, J. R., and R. C. MOYER, *Managerial Economics,* Chap. 11. Hinsdale, Ill.: Dryden, 1975.

SIMON, J. L., *Applied Managerial Economics,* Chap.13. Englewood Cliffs, N.J.: Prentice-Hall, 1975.

STIGLER, G. J., *The Organization of Industry,* Chap. 7. Homewood, Ill.: Richard D. Irwin, 1968.

# 9
# A Review
# of Basic
# Pricing Theory

## 9.1   INTRODUCTION

In this chapter we examine several simple theories of the firm and the associated models of pricing behavior. In doing so, we lay the foundations for the discussion of more advanced models of pricing behavior in Chapter 10. Although the approach of this chapter may be novel to you, you may have encountered most of the material in an introductory microeconomics course. In this case I suggest that you skim lightly over this chapter and try the discussion questions and problems as a check on your memory before proceeding to Chapter 10.

### The Diversity of Business Situations and the Plethora of Models of Pricing Behavior

Business firms exist in a wide diversity of industries and market situations. Their sizes range from the miniscule to the enormous, their ownership patterns vary from the single owner to widely dispersed shareholdings, and their owner and manager motivations range from "get-rich-quick" to pursuit of the "easy life." It is precisely due to this diversity of situations in which business firms are found that there is no single, universally applicable, theory of the firm. A theory that applies to all situations would be too broad and too general to be of much use in explaining or predicting the behavior of a firm in any particular situation.

Therefore it should not be surprising to find that in the literature of economics there is a proliferation of theories of the firm. Differences in the demand situations, differences in the supply situations, and different patterns of action and reaction have been assumed, such that there is a model of the firm to fit virtually every type of business situation imaginable. This abundance of theories of the firm can be confusing until one realizes that all can be related to a simple basic structure of the theory of the firm. There are seven major assumptions necessary to generate a theory of the firm, and the multiplicity of models differ from each other only to the extent that one or more of these seven assumptions differ.

A theory of the firm requires certain "structural" assumptions to define the supply and demand conditions under which the firm operates, and certain "behavioral" assumptions to define the manner in which the firm will act or react to certain stimuli.

### The Structural Assumptions ℰ ABOUT SUPPLY/DEMAND

There are four structural assumptions, two on the supply side and two on the demand side of the market. First, we must specify the ① *number of sellers* that supply the particular product. For operational purposes it is necessary only to specify whether there are "many" firms or "few" firms, rather than the exact number of firms. "Many" firms is defined as a situation in which there is a sufficiently large number of firms, such that no single firm can directly cause the market price to vary. That is to say, each firm is quite small relative to the market in which it operates. "Few" firms is the converse situation whereby firms are quite large relative to the market and can directly cause the market price to rise or fall as a result of their own pricing or output decisions.

Second, we must make an assumption concerning the ② *cost conditions* under which the product is supplied. That is, we must either explicitly or implicitly specify the production function and resource prices that pertain to the firms in this particular industry. This specification, you will recall from Chapter 6, determines the presence or absence of increasing or diminishing returns to the variable factor in the short run, and economies or diseconomies of plant size in the long run. In effect, we must specify the shape and placement of the cost curves faced by the firm.

Third, we must specify the ③ *number of buyers* who are in the market for this particular product. As in the supply situation, we are content to know whether there are simply "few" or "many" potential buyers. With "many" buyers each will be so small relative to the market that no one buyer will be able to influence the market price directly, whereas with "few" buyers an individual buyer *will* have the power to reduce the market price. Fewness of buyers therefore adds a whole new dimension to the price determination problem of firms.

Fourth, it is necessary to specify the degree to which the competing suppliers' products are perceived as being different, in whatever way, by the buyers in aggregate. That is, the ④ *extent of product differentiation,* or the value of cross elasticity between competing brands, must be assumed. The degree of product differentiation can vary from zero, where all buyers consider the competing brands identical in all respects, to the situation in which buyers consider a particular product as being so different from other available products that it can be regarded as a separate market situation. In between there is the range from very close substitutes (with high cross elasticities) to quite distant substitutes (with relatively low cross elasticities). This assumption is vital for the specification of the demand curve facing the firm, since it determines the extent to which buyers will switch from one product to another when there is a change in the relative prices of the products.

### The Behavioral Assumptions

The firm's pattern of response to its business environment, and to changes in that environment, can be predicted given three behavioral assumptions. The first is the specification of the firm's *objective function*—that is, we must postulate what it is that the firm wishes to achieve as a result of being in business. The traditional assumption is that firms wish to maximize their short-term profits, but alternatively one might assume that the firm strives to maximize sales, growth, or some other objective.

The second behavioral assumption concerns the way in which the firm pursues its objective—that is, what variable does it adjust in order to maximize its profits, sales, or whatever? We call the chosen variable the firm's *strategic variable,* the main candidates for which are the price level, the output level, or the expenditures on promotion and style changes.

The third behavioral assumption concerns the firm's expectations of the reactions of rivals in response to the firm's adjustment of its strategic variable. Where such an adjustment could be expected to have an adverse effect on the profits or sales of its rivals, the firm should expect the outcome of its own actions to be modified to the extent that rivals subsequently adjust their own strategic variables. This expectation concerning the rivals' reaction is called the *conjectural variation*—that is, the firm conjectures that its rivals will, for example, ignore the firm's action, or alternatively adjust their own strategic variables to a greater, lesser, or equivalent degree. This expectation will influence whether or not and to what extent the firm will undertake the contemplated adjustment of its strategic variable.

The above structural and behavioral assumptions form the starting point for any theory of the firm. In the following sections we systematically vary some of the assumptions in order to generate a variety of models of the firm. Each model seeks to show how the firm determines the level(s) of its strategic variable(s) under a particular set of structural and behavioral assumptions.

## 9.3 THE BASIC SPECTRUM OF MARKET FORMS

In basic microeconomic theory of the firm there are four distinctive market forms: pure competition, monopolistic competition, oligopoly, and monopoly. Each of these market forms implies a particular theory of the firm, since the supply and demand conditions that distinguish the market forms enter as structural assumptions in each theory of the firm. These four market types, or models of firm behavior, may be regarded as points along a spectrum, since, by taking any one as a starting point, the other three may be derived simply by varying one or two of the seven underlying assumptions. The two assumptions that vary are both structural: the first one, regarding the number of sellers, and the fourth one, regarding the degree of product differentiation perceived by the buyers. Table 9.1 indicates the market spectrum achieved by variation in these two assumptions.

We shall proceed to examine the theory of the firm pertaining to each of these market forms. For purposes of comparison, we shall assume the same be-

**TABLE 9.1**
**The traditional spectrum of market forms**

|  | Pure Competition | Monopolistic Competition | Oligopoly | Monopoly |
|---|---|---|---|---|
| Number of sellers: | Many | Many | Few | One |
| Product differentiation: | None | Slight | None, to considerable | Complete |

havioral assumptions for the firms in each market situation except for a slight modification under oligopoly. In Chapter 10 we show the impact upon firms' pricing and output behavior of certain variations in the structural and behavioral assumptions.

### Pure Competition

Let us state the theory of the purely competitive firm in terms of the seven assumptions.[1]

| 1. | Number of sellers | : | Many |
|---|---|---|---|
| 2. | Production function | : | Cubic |
| 3. | Number of buyers | : | Many |
| 4. | Product differentiation | : | Zero (i.e., identical products) |
| 5. | Objective function | : | Maximize short-run profits |
| 6. | Strategic variables | : | Price and quantity |
| 7. | Conjectural variation | : | Zero (i.e., no reactions expected) |

Since there are "many" sellers and buyers, and hence no single seller or buyer can directly influence the market price of the product, market price is determined by the interaction of the aggregate market supply and demand curves. These are shown in Figure 9.1. If, at a particular price level, such as $P_1$, supply exceeds demand, there will be downward pressure on prices, due to the desire of firms to reduce inventories to preferred levels. Each firm reduces price in order to clear its excess inventories and thus avoid costs associated with holding those excess inventories. Since many firms will be independently reducing their prices, this causes the market price to fall. One firm alone reducing its price would not cause a reduction in the general price level, since it could sell all it wishes at the lower price without any competing firm suffering a significant loss of sales, due to the assumption that firms are small relative to the market. But the combined effect of many firms reducing their prices is to cause a significant loss of sales to those competitors that have *not* reduced their prices. This in turn causes those firms to suffer excess inventory, and they too will be motivated to reduce price.

Thus excess market supply leads to a reduction in the market price. The lower price causes an increase in the quantity demanded, and at the same time

---

[1] To follow convention we assume a cubic production function, which means U-shaped average variable and marginal cost curves. Pure competition could exist as long as there were diminishing returns to the variable factors, given the other six conditions.

**FIGURE 9.1**
**Determination of price by the interaction of market supply and demand
in pure competition**

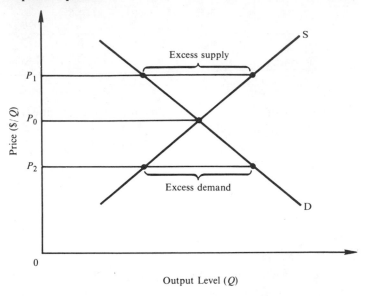

causes the firm to be willing to supply a somewhat reduced amount. Prices will continue to fall until finally supply equals demand, as shown at price $P_0$ in Figure 9.1.

Conversely, if there is excess demand at a particular price level, such as at $P_2$ in Figure 9.1, there will be upward pressure on prices, due to willingness of some buyers to pay more than the market price rather than go without the product. Firms will find they can raise their price slightly yet still sell all they wish to produce, since although other firms may be maintaining their price at $P_2$, those firms are unable to supply the entire complement of buyers willing to purchase at price $P_2$, and some of those unable to purchase are willing to pay more than $P_2$ to obtain the product. The firms setting price $P_2$ then see that they too can ask for a higher price, and the combined effect is for the market price to move upward. As it does, the quantity demanded is reduced as some buyers drop out of the market, and the quantity suppliers are willing to put on sale increases, until finally supply equals demand and no further incentive exists to raise prices. The price $P_0$ in Figure 9.1 is thus the equilibrium price and is determined not by the actions of any one firm but by the combined effects of individual firms' actions.

Given the market price, the purely competitive firm must decide what output level to produce in order to maximize its profits. Profits are maximized when the difference between total revenues and total costs is greatest. Since the firm is small relative to its market, it can sell all it wants to at the market price, and its total revenue curve is a straight line from the origin, as shown in Figure 9.2, because total revenue is a linear function of output. Following our assumption of a cubic production function, the total cost curve takes the shape shown by

286

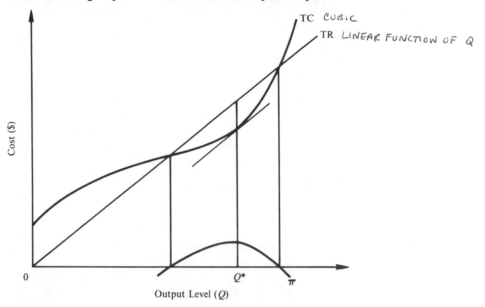

TC in Figure 9.2. Profit, the vertical distance between the curves (where TR lies above TC), is maximized at output level $Q^*$, where a tangent to the TC curve is parallel to the TR curve. A property of parallel lines is that they remain a constant vertical distance apart. The choice of $Q^*$ such that a tangent to the TC curve was parallel to the TR curve ensures that profit is maximized, since output levels to the right or left of $Q^*$ show the TC level moving toward the TR level, and hence away from the tangent that measures the constant vertical distance from the TR curve. The total profit curve can be shown on the same graph, as the curve $\pi$.

The profit-maximizing condition, that the slopes of the TR and TC curves should be equal, is the same as saying that profits are maximized where total revenues and costs are increasing at the same rate. The reader will recall from Chapters 4 and 6 that this in turn can be restated as "profits are maximized when marginal revenue equals marginal costs," since *marginal revenue* and *marginal costs* were defined as the rate of change of total revenues and total costs, respectively. Thus we can show the output decision of the firm in terms of the marginal curves, as in Figure 9.3. The marginal revenue curve will be horizontal at the price level $P_0$, and marginal costs will be U-shaped, as argued in Chapter 6. Note that the MC curve may cut the MR curve twice but that *losses* are maximized where it cuts the MR curve from above, whereas profits are maximized where MC cuts the MR curve from below.

To confirm that profits are maximized at output level $Q^*$ in Figure 9.3, consider an output level slightly to the right of $Q^*$. Here marginal costs exceed marginal revenues. That is, the units to the right of $Q^*$ add more to costs than they add to revenues, and they therefore must cause profits to be reduced.

## FIGURE 9.3
**Output determination in pure competition using the marginal curves**

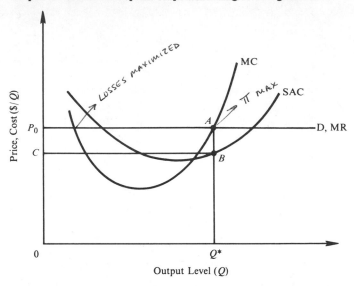

Accordingly, these output units should not be produced. Alternatively, consider the output units to the left of $Q^*$. Here marginal revenues exceed marginal costs, and profits are augmented by the production of each of these units. Hence output should be carried to the level $Q^*$ in order to maximize the firm's profits. Profits can be visualized as the rectangle $P_0ABC$, which is equal to the average profit per unit, $AB$, times the number of units $0Q^*$.

Note that the purely competitive firm has no incentive to either raise or lower its price away from the market price. If it raised its price above $P_0$ it would sell no units at all, since all its buyers would seek the product from other sellers at the market price. If it lowered price this would also lead to reduced profits, since it would sell fewer units (because a lower MR will cut MC at a smaller output level) at a lower price, without a commensurate reduction in per unit costs. Only when there is excess market demand will the firm have a profit incentive to raise price, and only when there is excess market supply (and there is a cost of holding excess inventories) will the firm wish to reduce its price.

Do purely competitive markets exist? Are there any market situations that fulfill the stringent conditions implied by the seven assumptions? In this evolving socioeconomic system there are certainly some markets left that have many buyers and many sellers. The most difficult condition to find is that of identical products. Remember that zero product differentiation requires that all buyers regard all products from the competing suppliers as identical in all respects. Buyers cannot have personal preferences for particular sellers, nor have differing expectations of quality or after-sales service, nor find it more or less convenient to buy from one seller rather than from another. The package of attributes constituting the product must be viewed as identical in all respects. Perhaps the only market in which this condition is fulfilled is the stock exchange, at which hun-

288

dreds of buyers and sellers meet anonymously (through an agent) to buy and sell a company's stock. Each share in the company has the same rights, benefits, and obligations attached (for each class of shares), and no buyer is likely to care about the identity of the previous owner.

Applications of the purely competitive model as an explanatory or predictive device will be inappropriate to the extent that the seven assumptions involved do not accord with the reality of the situation being explained or predicted. The major value of the purely competitive model is probably as a pedagogical device. It allows the theory of the firm to be introduced in a relatively simple context, free of the complications introduced by product differentiation and fewness of buyers and/or sellers. It thus forms a basis upon which we can build an understanding of more complex theories of the firm.

### Monopolistic Competition

Monopolistic competition differs from pure competition in one respect only: products are slightly differentiated rather than completely undifferentiated in the eyes of purchasers. Thus the following seven assumptions are involved:

1. Number of sellers         :    Many
2. Production function     :    Cubic
3. Number of buyers        :    Many
4. Product differentiation :    Slight
5. Objective function       :    Maximize short-run profits
6. Strategic variables      :    Price and quantity
7. Conjectural variation   :    Zero

The relaxation of one assumption leads to a significantly different pattern of pricing behavior, however. Each firm now faces a demand curve that is downward sloping to the right rather than horizontal. That is, the firm can adjust price slightly without experiencing a rush toward or away from its products by buyers. Since products are differentiated, most buyers will still prefer to purchase elsewhere when a particular firm lowers its price. Only some buyers, who now regard the product of this firm as superior value for money, will switch over from various other products and now buy this product. Conversely, for a price increase, most of the firm's customers will stay with the firm, and only some peripheral customers will switch to other firms' products (which they now feel are better value for the money). The extent of this switch depends upon the cross elasticity of demand, which is usually considered to be relatively high in situations of monopolistic competition.

The situation of a representative firm in monopolistic competition is depicted in Figure 9.4. Since the demand curve is negatively sloping, the marginal revenue curve must lie below the demand curve, having twice the slope and the same intercept point, as we saw in Chapter 4. By the same reasoning we used above for the purely competitive firm, the monopolistically competitive firm maximizes its profits at the price and output level where marginal revenue equals marginal costs. In Figure 9.4 price will be set at $P_1$, quantity at $Q_1$, and profits are shown as the area $P_1ABC$.

**FIGURE 9.4**
Price and output determination for a representative firm in monopolistic competition

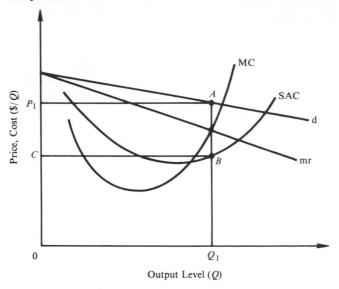

Do monopolistically competitive markets exist? In fact, there are many markets in which the seven assumptions are a reasonable depiction of reality. Small stores, gas stations, and take-out food shops in large city areas, for example, operate in a market that may be characterized as monopolistically competitive. Each firm possesses an element of monopoly power, such as a more favorable location or other product attributes desired by a particular group of customers, yet it must exist in active competition with other firms that have similar small differences in their product offering. These differences might be perceived in the type or quality of the essential product itself, or in the other attributes of a less tangible nature associated with purchase of the product.

The prices set by monopolistic competitors need not be at the same level. In real-world situations we should expect to find slight price differentials between and among monopolistic competitors, with some firms being able to command slightly higher prices and/or larger market shares due to the market's perception of greater value (more attributes per dollar) in the product of some firms as compared with others. Firms with more convenient locations, longer operating hours, and/or quick service, for example, can obtain a premium for what is otherwise the same product (e.g., Brand A bread). Quality differences inherent in the product will also form the basis for price differences.[2]

[2] Price and market share differences arise in the *asymmetric* monopolistic competition model, where both costs and product differentiation are allowed to differ among firms. This is a considerably more complex model than the *symmetric* case outlined above, in which it is implicit that the "representative firm" has the same cost structure and product differentiation advantages as all other firms. The asymmetric model will not be considered here except to note that it allows greater realism, at the expense of greater complexity, by explicitly considering differing cost and product differentiation situations between and among firms

## Oligopoly: The Kinked Demand Curve Model

The word *oligopoly* derives from the Greek *oligos* meaning "few," and the Latin *polis* meaning "seller." Oligopoly is a market situation in which sufficiently few firms compete that the actions of any one firm will have a noticeable impact on the demand for each of the other firms. Products may be identical or differentiated, and product differentiation may range from slight to substantial. Most market situations are oligopolistic, and prominent examples are the automobile, steel, aluminum, and chemical industries. In these market situations, a reduction in the price of one firm, for example, will cause that firm to gain sales and rival firms to suffer a noticeable loss of sales as consumers switch across to the firm that has reduced its price.

The essential difference between oligopoly and monopolistic and pure competition is that the sales gain resulting from the actions of one firm is at the expense of *fewer* firms, rather than the effect being spread imperceptibly over numerous rivals. Oligopolists, therefore, should be expected to react to the actions of their rivals, rather than ignore them as in the other two cases. In turn, this implies that a firm contemplating an adjustment in its strategic variable should anticipate the reaction of its rivals when estimating the impact of that adjustment on its sales and profits.

Several models of oligopoly differ on the basis of the assumption concerning the firm's conjectural variation. In this chapter we shall examine just one simple model, the *kinked demand curve model*.[3] This model assumes that the firm's conjectural variation will be twofold: for price increases the firm expects no reaction from rivals, since the other firms will be content to sit back and receive extra customers who switch away from the firm raising its price; and for price reductions the firm expects rivals to exactly match the price reduction in order to maintain their shares of the market.

The seven assumptions for the kinked demand curve model of oligopoly are as follows:

1. Number of sellers : Few
2. Production function : Cubic
3. Number of buyers : Many
4. Product differentiation : Slight to substantial
5. Objective function : Maximize short-run profits
6. Strategic variables : Price and quantity
7. Conjectural variation : Zero for price increases, unity for price decreases

Since the firm's conjectural variation for price increases is zero, it envisages a *ceteris paribus* demand curve at all prices above the current level, this curve being more or less elastic depending primarily upon the degree of substitutability between its product and rival products. In contemplating price reductions, however, the firm envisages a *mutatis mutandis* demand curve, meaning that it takes

[3] This was initially proposed separately by R. L. Hall and C. J. Hitch, "Price Theory and Business Behavior," *Oxford Economic Papers*, May 1939, pp. 12-45; and by P. M. Sweezy, "Demand under Conditions of Oligopoly," *Journal of Political Economy*, (August 1939), 568-73.

into account all reactions induced by, and/or concurrent with, the firm's price adjustment. In this case the *mutatis mutandis* section of the demand curve represents a constant share of the total market for the product in question.[4]

In Figure 9.5 the firm's current price and output levels are shown as $P$ and $Q$. For prices above $P$, it envisages the relatively elastic *ceteris paribus* demand curve shown by the line $dA$. For prices below $P$, it envisages the relatively inelastic *mutatis mutandis* demand curve shown by the line $AD$. The demand curve facing the firm is therefore $dAD$, being *kinked* at the current price level. The marginal revenue curve appropriate to this demand curve will have two separate sections. The upper section, shown as $dB$ in Figure 9.5, relates to the *ceteris paribus* section of the demand curve and therefore shares the same intercept and has twice the slope of the line $dA$. The lower section, $CMR$, relates to the *mutatis mutandis* section of the demand curve and is positioned such that it has twice the slope of the line $AD$, and if extended up to the price axis would share its intercept point with the line $AD$ similarly extended.

You will note that there is a vertical discontinuity in the marginal revenue curve, shown as the gap $BC$ in Figure 9.5. Given the foregoing, it is apparent that the length of this gap depends upon the relative slopes of the *ceteris paribus* and *mutatis mutandis* demand curves,[5] which in turn are related to the elasticity of demand under the two conjectural variation situations. If the firm is a profit

**FIGURE 9.5**
**The kinked demand curve model of oligopoly**

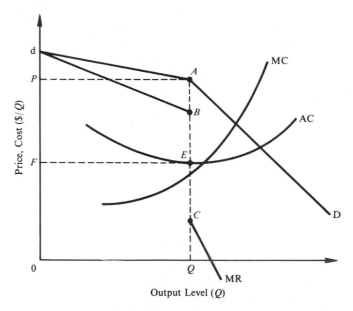

[4] Note that while the *ceteris paribus* demand curve is appropriate for "independent action" by a firm not expecting reactions, the *mutatis mutandis* demand curve is appropriate for "joint action" by firms, taking into account rivals' reactions.

[5] See G. J. Stigler, "The Kinky Oligopoly Demand Curve and Rigid Prices," *Journal of Political Economy*, Vol. 55, October 1947.

maximizer, its marginal cost curve will pass through the gap *BC*. If *P* and *Q* are the profit-maximizing price and output levels, this implies that outputs to the left of *Q* would have marginal revenues exceeding marginal costs, while outputs to the right of *Q* would have marginal costs exceeding marginal revenues. This is only true if the MC curve passes through either of the points *B* or *C*, or through some point in between.[6] The oligopolist's profits are shown by the rectangle *PAEF* in Figure 9.5.

The kinked demand curve analysis is not a theory of price determination, since it starts from the present price and output levels rather than attempting to generate the optimal price and output levels from known cost and demand data. Instead, the kinked demand curve offers an explanation of price rigidity in the

**FIGURE 9.6**
**Price rigidity in oligopoly despite changing cost levels**

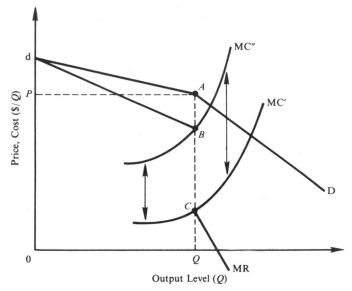

face of changing cost and demand conditions. You will recall that in the market situations of pure competition and monopolistic competition, the firms set price where marginal costs equaled marginal revenue. If either costs or demand conditions changed, one of these marginal curves would shift, and a new price level would become appropriate if the firm were to maximize profits under the new conditions. In the kinked demand curve case, however, the marginal cost and marginal revenue curves may shift to a considerable degree without a new price level becoming appropriate. As shown in Figure 9.6, the MC curve could move up until it passed through point *B*, or down until it passed through point *C*, and *P* would still be the profit-maximizing price.

Similarly, demand at the price *P* could increase or decrease a considerable

[6] See D. S. Smith and W. C. Neale, "The Geometry of Kinky Oligopoly: Marginal Cost, the Gap, and Price Behavior," *Southern Economic Journal*, 37 (January 1971), 276-282.

amount without causing the MC curve to intersect one of the concrete sections of the MR curve. Figure 9.7 shows that sales at price $P$ could increase (due to seasonal influences, increased consumer incomes, or other reasons) out to $Q'$ units and yet leave price $P$ as the profit-maximizing price. Of course, if the cost curve, or demand, shifts more than as indicated in Figures 9.6 and 9.7, there will be a new intersection point between the MC and MR curves, and the firm will change price in order to maximize profits under the new cost or demand conditions.

Under some conditions the firm's conjecture that firms will ignore its price increase may give way to the expectation that other firms will *follow* a price increase rather than ignore it. Such a situation might arise when a cost increase applies to all firms, such as an increase in the basic wage rate or an increase in the cost of an important raw material. In the case of cost increases that apply to all firms, the individual firm might reasonably expect that all firms would like to maintain profit margins by passing the cost on to consumers, and, especially if there is a history of this practice in the industry, the firm's conjectural variation for a price increase, up to the extent necessary to pass on the cost increase, will be unity. Thus the relevant demand curve for this type of price increase is the *mutatis mutandis* demand curve. As indicated in Figure 9.8, the kink in the demand curve moves up the *mutatis mutandis* section to the new price level chosen. It will kink at the level that passes on the cost increase, because the firm expects that any further price increase will not be matched by rivals and therefore expects to experience a more elastic demand response above that price level. The firm's conjectural variation is unity up to the price level that is expected to be agreeable to all firms, and it is zero for price levels above that.

**FIGURE 9.7**
**Price rigidity in oligopoly despite changing demand levels**

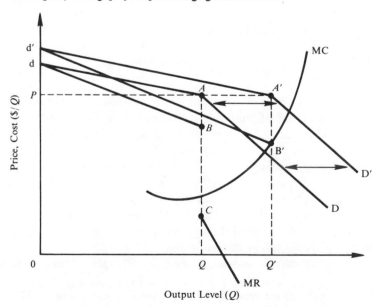

Output Level ($Q$)

**FIGURE 9.8**

**Conscious parallelism in the kinked demand curve model of oligopoly**

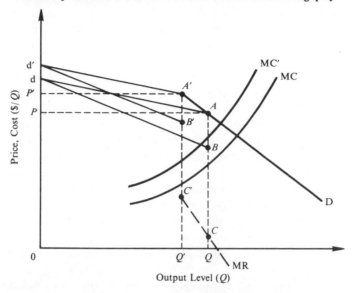

The simultaneous adjustment of prices in response to general cost increases, and with the expectation that rivals will do likewise, has been called "conscious parallelism."[7] This form of coordination among firms in adjusting their prices is similar, in effect, to situations of price leadership, which we examine in Chapter 10.

## Monopoly

*Monopoly* is a market situation in which only one firm faces the entire market demand. In the eyes of consumers, no other firm produces a product that is any more than remotely substitutable for the monopolist's product. We can therefore state the seven assumptions of the monopoly model of pricing behavior as follows:

| | | | |
|---|---|---|---|
| 1. | Number of sellers | : | One |
| 2. | Production function | : | Cubic |
| 3. | Number of buyers | : | Many |
| 4. | Product differentiation | : | Complete |
| 5. | Objective function | : | Maximize short-run profits |
| 6. | Strategic variables | : | Price and quantity |
| 7. | Conjectural variation | : | Zero (no rivals) |

Monopoly situations may arise and persist for a number of reasons. First, a single firm might control the supply of a necessary input factor and deny access to this factor to any potential rivals. Examples include ownership of all known

[7] See W. Hamburger, "Conscious Parallelism and the Kinked Oligopoly Demand Curve," *American Economic Review,* 57 (May 1967), 266-68.

reserves of an input (e.g., Alcoa's early monopoly in the aluminum industry), ownership of the only railroad serving a remote area, or having in your employ the one person who understands a certain phenomenon. As implied above, this type of monopoly tends to become eroded over time as potential entrants overcome these obstacles.

Second, a firm may be given a government mandate to be a monopoly, for reasons of national security, social equity, or economic optimality. The armed forces, post office, and various utilities provide examples of this type of monopoly.

Third, there are what are called "natural" monopolies. These are firms for which economies of plant size are large relative to the size of the market, and it is a natural monopoly in the sense that if there were rivals at first, a monopoly would evolve as time passed, due to the profit incentive for firms to merge with or take over rival firms. Per unit costs of production are minimized in such a market situation when only one firm supplies that market. As implied above, governments often bestow monopoly rights on firms thought to be in this type of situation, but to ensure that at least part of these cost savings are passed on to consumers it is frequently necessary to regulate the pricing and/or output of these firms.

The price and output determination decision for a monopoly (unregulated) is similar to that for a monopolistic competitor. Both face a downward-sloping demand curve, although we should expect the monopolistic competitors demand curve to be more elastic in the relevant range due to the availability of substitutes, while the monopolist's is typically less elastic, since it depends primarily on the income effect. The monopolist, given the market demand curve, calculates the marginal revenue curve and finds the point of equality with marginal costs in order to set the profit-maximizing price and output levels. These are shown as $P_m$ and $Q_m$ in Figure 9.9, and profit is represented by the rectangle $P_mABC$.

This concludes our trip across the basic spectrum of market forms. We turn now to the price and output adjustments we should expect to find when firms are able to change their size of plant.

## 9.4   LONG-RUN ADJUSTMENTS

All of the above models of the firm were discussed in the context of the short run. That is, the cost structure was given and output was constrained at the upper limit due to the presence of fixed factors of production. A further modification of each of the above models is to relax the structural assumption regarding the firm's cost structure. In the long run the firm is able to adjust its size of plant and thus begin production in the subsequent short-run period with a different cost structure and a different upper limit to its output level.

The long-run adjustments to plant size encompass all degrees of expansion and contraction. The ultimate contraction of plant size is to completely liquidate all fixed factors and exit the industry. At the other extreme is new entry to the industry by establishing a plant (increasing plant size from zero to some

**FIGURE 9.9**
**Price and output determination for a monopoly**

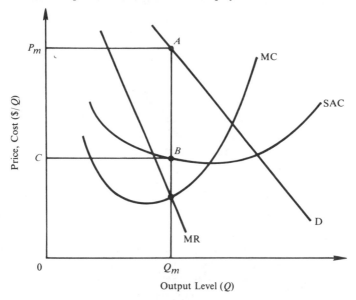

finite level). Why are firms motivated to expand or contract plant size, or to enter or exit the industry? In a nutshell, firms move in the direction of increased profitability (or reduced losses). The expectation of economic profits (or losses) will induce firms to enter (or exit) an industry, and the expectation of larger profits at a different plant size will induce firms to expand (or reduce) their plant size.

In each of the models of pricing behavior examined above, we presented a situation in which the firms were able to earn economic profits in the short run. Whether or not there will be entry of new firms depends upon the presence or absence of "barriers to entry."

### Barriers to the Entry of New Firms

Barriers to entry were absent in the pure competition and monopolistic competition situations and were absolute in the monopoly situation (although we might expect these barriers to break down with the passage of time). In oligopoly, however, barriers to entry will be present to varying degrees, and they may take the form of the limited or nonavailability of such factors as necessary raw materials, technical skills, managerial talent, production and selling locations, or, on the demand side, the product differentiation advantage of existing firms. Some of these barriers to entry may be surmountable, given the application of sufficient funds. But the cost of overcoming the barriers and offsetting any continuing cost disadvantages may cause the entrant firm's cost level to be so high as to make entry and subsequent production insufficiently profitable. On the other hand, a relatively large capital investment required to enter a particular

297

industry, such as automobiles or steel, is not in itself a barrier to entry, since it only precludes those who cannot afford to play the game.[8]

### Adjustment of Plant Size in Pure Competition

Since barriers to entry are absent in pure competition, we should expect the entry of new firms as soon as they can establish a new plant and begin production. The advent of new firms will increase the quantity supplied at each price level, and thus the market supply curve will move to the right. This in turn will cause the market price to fall. At the same time, existing firms will see that they can obtain economies of plant size by moving to the plant size that minimizes per unit costs. The net result is as shown in Figure 9.10.

Let us suppose that in the initial short-run period all firms were producing with the plant size depicted by $SAC_1$. Each firm was making a profit, since price exceeds average total costs. Given an opportunity to adjust the size of their plants each of these firms will move to the plant size depicted by $SAC^*$, since this allows the minimum level of per unit costs.[9] New entrants to the industry, attracted by the existence of "pure" profits, also can be expected to establish the plant size depicted by $SAC^*$. If exactly the right number of new firms enter, the market supply curve will shift across from $S$ to $S'$, and market price will fall from $P_1$ to $P^*$. Given the new market price, all firms will produce output level $Q^*$, price will equal average costs, and all firms can earn only a "normal" profit.

**FIGURE 9.10**
**Long-run plant size adjustment in pure competition**

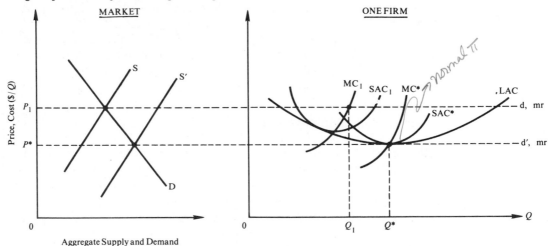

Aggregate Supply and Demand

[8] See J. S. Bain, *Barriers to New Competition* (Cambridge, Mass.: Harvard University Press, 1956).

[9] For this reason it is often referred to as the "optimum" size of plant. This is not to say that firms should always choose the SAC curve that is tangent to the LAC curve at the lowest point of the LAC curve, as we shall see in the context of other market situations.

NORMAL π ⇒ TR = OPPOR. COSTS OF ALL INPUTS
Inputs earning as much as the world in next-best-alt use

You will recall from Chapter 7 that this means that total revenues are equal to the opportunity cost of all inputs, or that inputs are earning as much in this particular usage as they could in their next-best-alternative usage. Hence no firm will wish to leave the industry, and no new firms will wish to enter the industry, since more entry would depress the price below the normal profit level.

Thus the presence of pure or economic profit in the short run leads to the entry of new firms until profits are reduced to the normal level, given the absence of barriers to entry.

### Adjustment of Plant Size in Monopolistic Competition

Long-run plant size adjustment in monopolistic competition proceeds in an essentially similar manner. New firms are motivated to enter by the existence of pure profits, and existing firms are motivated to adjust plant size to that which allows the greatest possible profit.

The entry of new firms, each with a new product slightly differentiated from the other products, causes the total market demand to be shared among more firms. This means that each firm's demand curve shifts to the left, since each firm loses some of its customers to the new entrants. Each firm will be forced to reduce the size of its plant as its share of demand is reduced, until eventually so many firms will have entered that each firm will be earning only a normal profit. This will represent an equilibrium situation, since no more firms will wish to enter and none will wish to leave. The long-run equilibrium situation is shown in Figure 9.11.

**FIGURE 9.11**
**Long-run plant size adjustment in monopolistic competition**

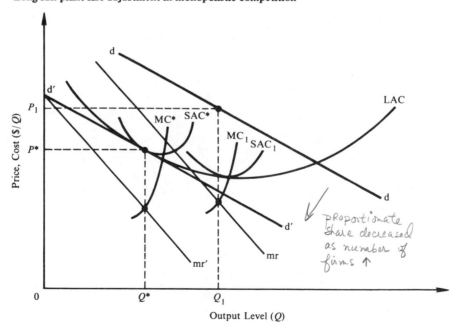

proportionate share decreased as number of firms ↑

In Figure 9.11 we show a representative firm facing the demand curve *dd* in the initial short-run situation. Its plant size is depicted by the $SAC_1$ curve, and it maximized profits at price $P_1$ and output level $Q_1$. The entry of new firms causes this firm's demand curve to shift to the left, eventually reaching that shown as $d'd'$. Given this demand situation, the only way the representative firm can survive is to build the plant represented by $SAC^*$. This is the only plant that allows a normal profit to be made. The firm sets price $P^*$ and produces output level $Q^*$ in order to maximize profits. Note that these normal profits are sufficient to keep the firm in the industry, since they represent at least as much as the resources could earn elsewhere.

Again we see that in the absence of barriers to entry, the entry of new firms tends to reduce the price level to consumers and causes firms to retreat to a position where they are making only normal profits. Let us now examine the case where barriers to entry do exist and prevent the incursion of new competition.

### Adjustment of Plant Size in Monopoly

As long as the barriers to entry restrain new competition, the monopolist is faced with the same demand situation (given that market size is neither increasing nor decreasing). The monopolist's problem is to choose the plant size that allows the greatest profits, given the prevailing demand situation. In Figure 9.12 we show the initial plant size as $SAC_1$, and the monopolist maximizes short-run profits where $MC_1$ = MR at price $P_1$ and quantity $Q_1$. The plant size that allows the *greatest* short-run profit, given the continuation of this demand situation, is shown as $SAC^*$.

The profit-maximizing plant size is found by equating the long-run marginal cost (LMC) curve with the marginal revenue curve. The LMC curve shows the

**FIGURE 9.12**
**Long-run plant size adjustment in monopoly**

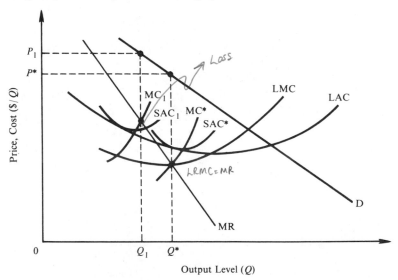

change in total costs as output changes, when all inputs are free to vary (and the firm follows the economically efficient long-run expansion path.) It thus allows us to adjust all inputs to the point where any further input of any factor would cause marginal costs to exceed marginal revenues. The monopolist then builds the plant size (SAC$^*$) that allows the optimal quantity $Q^*$ to be produced at the minimum cost combination shown by the point on the LAC curve. Note that the short-run marginal cost curve associated with the profit-maximizing plant (i.e., MC$^*$) equals marginal revenue at the optimal output level, since short- and long-run average costs are equal at this output level.

### Adjustment of Plant Size in Oligopoly

The oligopoly result is similar to that of monopoly in that the existence of some barriers to entry typically allows the perpetuation of pure profits. In oligopoly situations the barriers are often more accurately described as "hurdles," since they do not necessarily make it impossible to enter an industry—they merely limit the number of firms that are able to enter. Overcoming the hurdles typically involves additional operating costs which means that many potential entrants will *not* enter, since they cannot foresee being able to operate profitably. The firms that now exist in the oligopolistic market may be able to make excess or pure profits in the shelter of these hurdles. This is not to say that either monopolists or oligopolists will always make pure profits. In declining markets, for example, these firms may incur continuing losses, forcing them to eventually exit the industry.

The oligopolist adjusts plant size with an eye to the impact of this upon rival firms and their likely reactions. Given the split conjectural variation of the kinked demand curve model, the oligopolist is likely to adjust to the plant size that produces its current share of the market at minimum cost. In Figure 9.13 we show such an adjustment.

Suppose the firm is now producing $Q_1$ units at price $P_1$ with the plant size depicted by SAC$_1$. Given an opportunity to adjust plant size the firm will adjust to the plant depicted by SAC$^*$, since this produces the profit-maximizing output at the lowest per unit cost. Since the new marginal cost curve (MC$^*$) passes through the vertical discontinuity (BC) of the marginal revenue curve, the present price and output levels remain optimal.[10]

As you will recall from the discussion in Chapter 8, the long-run average cost curve of any firm requires a constant state of factor productivities and factor costs. In the real world, of course, these tend to change over time. The pursuit of long-run equilibrium price and output in any market situation is therefore a lot like shooting at a target that moves just as you pull the trigger. New technology and changed factor prices mean that a new LAC curve (and its associated SAC curves) becomes appropriate, and the firm will select that plant size on the new LAC curve that minimizes the cost of its optimal output level.

The foregoing analysis is nevertheless useful, since it demonstrates the exist-

---

[10] This conclusion depends upon a constant demand situation. If the firm expects the market demand to grow, and/or its share of the market to expand, it may wish to build a larger plant.

**FIGURE 9.13**
Long-run plant size adjustment in oligopoly

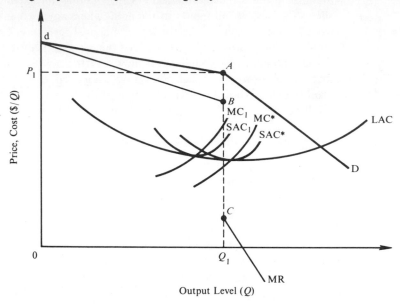

ence of forces that will operate given time for firms to adjust their plant sizes. They will adjust in the direction of the minimum cost of producing their desired output level. To the extent permitted by restriction to entry, new firms will enter the industry. In all cases (including monopoly, since we expect barriers to entry to break down over time) the passage of time should be expected to cause the reduction of excess of pure profits. Prices, in constant purchasing power (or real) terms, are expected to fall as long as the demand situation remains constant. Should market demand increase or decrease over time, prices may rise or fall, depending upon the particular cost and demand situations. These adjustments may be made to the above models without difficulty.

## 9.5 SUMMARY

In this chapter we introduced the notion that models of the firm's pricing behavior can be characterized under seven assumptions. The four structural assumptions relate to number of sellers, cost conditions, number of buyers, and degree of product differentiation. The three behavioral assumptions refer to the firm's objective function, its strategic variables, and its conjectural variation. The models of pricing behavior differ from each other only to the extent that one or more of the seven basic assumptions is different. The difference in one or more of the underlying assumptions, however, leads to a different pattern of behavior of the firm. Thus the price and output levels chosen by a firm depend upon the structural and behavioral conditions under which the firm operates.

The four basic market forms were analyzed for the pricing and output behavior of the firm in each of those market situations. Under conditions of pure competition, monopolistic competition, and monopoly, the pricing and output decision was based on a *ceteris paribus* demand curve due to the expectation that a firm's price or output adjustment would not induce any changes in any other variables. Under oligopoly we introduced the *mutatis mutandis*, or "joint action," demand curve. In the kinked demand curve model of oligopoly the firm envisages no reaction for price increases but expects rivals to match any price reductions. Given these expectations, the oligopolist faces a kinked demand curve, since the *ceteris paribus* section for price increases will be more elastic than the *mutatis mutandis* section for price reductions.

We saw that the pursuit of short-run profit maximization led the firms in all four market situations to choose the price and output level for which marginal revenue equaled marginal cost.[11] Long-run conditions, which allow the entry of new firms (if not prevented by barriers to entry) and the adjustment of plant size, may be expected to cause prices to fall and market supply to increase, as long as total market demand is either constant or increasing. The existence of pure profits will attract potential entrants, while the inability to earn a normal profit will motivate firms to exit the industry, since, by definition of "normal" profits, they could earn more elsewhere.

This chapter has served as a springboard for Chapter 10. Given an understanding of the structure of a theory of pricing behavior, and of the four basic market situations, we are now better equipped for the variety of more complex (and more realistic) models of pricing behavior examined in the following chapter.

## DISCUSSION QUESTIONS

9.1   In what single dimension does monopolistic competition differ from pure competition? In what dimension(s) does oligopoly differ from both of the above?

9.2   Pure competitors are assumed to maximize their short-run profits. In this type of market environment, is it conceivable that firms might wish to pursue sales revenue maximization or any objective function other than short-run profit maximization? Why or why not?

9.3   The pure competitor's marginal cost curve is in effect that firm's supply curve, showing how much it will supply at each price level. Explain this.

9.4   Characterize according to the simple spectrum of market forms the markets in which the following groups of firms operate:

(a)   automobile dealerships in a large city,

(b)   college and universities marketing their degrees to potential students,

(c)   an art dealer who wants to sell a unique painting, such as the Mona Lisa, and

(d)   a grain farmer selling wheat to one of forty or fifty flour-milling companies.

9.5   State why you would intuitively expect a monopolistic competitor

---

[11] In the kinked demand curve model, MC passes through the vertical discontinuity in the MR curve, rather than being strictly equal to the MR value.

with a higher-quality product to command both a higher price and a larger market share, as compared with its rivals.

9.6 Given that an oligopolist envisages a kinked demand curve, explain why it is sometimes profit maximizing to raise prices and incur a loss of market share.

9.7 Under what circumstances will the firms in oligopoly envisage a *mutatis mutandis* demand curve for both price reductions and price increases?

9.8 Why do we expect monopoly situations to be eroded by the passage of time? Under what circumstances might a monopoly be perpetuated?

9.9 In a general sense, and regardless of the type of market situation, explain what motivates the long-run adjustment of plant size.

9.10 Why is it unrealistic to envisage a firm moving along a particular long-run average cost curve over a period of years as it progressively expands its market share, for example? How would you depict this expansion?

## PROBLEMS

9.1 Show graphically the situation in which a purely competitive market suffers a temporary reduction in consumer demand. Summarize what happens to

(a) the price level,

(b) each firm's output level, and

(c) the total number of firms.

9.2 During the 1960s, following the lead of the Beatles and other pop groups, male hairstyles tended toward greater length. Over this decade many barbershops went out of business, and others reduced their size of operation from, say, five or six chairs to one or two chairs.

(a) Characterize this industry in terms of the four basic market forms.

(b) Show graphically the process of adjustment that you think occurred in that industry during the sixties.

9.3 Suppose the automobile producers are confronted with an increase in the negotiated wage for assembly labor of 10 percent, yet prices of their products remain constant.

(a) Explain with the aid of graphs why the firms might not wish to increase their prices.

(b) Why might you expect these firms to raise prices at the start of the next model year, rather than during the present model year?

9.4 Suppose the demand for a monopolist, such as the remaining regional producer of horse-drawn buggies, is slowly but inexorably declining.

(a) Show graphically how this firm might be expected to react to this situation over a period of years.

(b) Does your graph show the price level rising or falling (or both) as the market declines?

(c) Under what conditions would market price (in real terms) increase as the market declined over time?

9.5 The fishing industry, like small farms, is notorious for the periodic influx of new firms followed later by the exit of firms who are unable to continue taking losses. Explain this in terms of the purely competitive model of the firm, using graphs to illustrate your answer.

9.6    The market for digital watches has shown remarkable development over the past decade, from a few firms selling digitals at relatively high prices to dozens of manufacturers selling them today at relatively low prices. Over this period both the cost of production of these watches fell dramatically and the market's appreciation of these watches increased considerably. Using graphical analysis, explain the entry of new firms and the reduction of prices in terms of the profit-maximizing response of oligopolists facing kinked demand curves.

## SUGGESTED REFERENCES AND FURTHER READING

BAIN, J. S., *Barriers to New Competition*. Cambridge, Mass.: Harvard University Press, 1956.

BAUMOL, W. J., *Economic Theory and Operations Analysis*, 4th ed. Englewood Cliffs, N.J.: Prentice-Hall, 1977.

CHAMBERLIN, E. H., *The Theory of Monopolistic Competition*. Cambridge, Mass.: Harvard University Press, 1969.

EFROYMSON, C. W., "The Kinked Oligopoly Curve Reconsidered," *Quarterly Journal of Economics*, 69 (February 1955), 119-36.

HALL, R. L., and C. J. HITCH, "Price Theory and Business Behavior," *Oxford Economic Papers*, May 1939, pp. 12-45.

HAMBURGER, W., "Conscious Parallelism and the Kinked Oligopoly Demand Curve," *American Economic Review*, 57 (May 1967), 266-68.

HAWKINS, C. J., *Theory of the Firm*. London: Macmillan, 1973.

HIRSHLEIFER, J., *Price Theory and Applications*, Chaps. 9-13. Englewood Cliffs, N.J.: Prentice-Hall, 1976.

ROBINSON, J., *The Economics of Imperfect Competition*. London: Macmillan. 1933.

SMITH, D. S., and W. C. NEALE, "The Geometry of Kinky Oligopoly: Marginal Cost, the Gap, and Price Behavior," *Southern Economic Journal*, 37 (January 1971), 276-82.

STIGLER, G. J., "The Kinky Oligopoly Demand Curve and Rigid Prices," *Journal of Political Economy*, 55 (October 1947), 432-49.

SWEEZY, P. M., "Demand under Conditions of Oligopoly," *Journal of Political Economy*, 47 (August 1939), 568-73.

THOMPSON, A. A., Jr., *Economics of the Firm*, Chaps. 9-13. Englewood Cliffs, N.J.: Prentice-Hall, 1973.

# 10

## Advanced Topics
## in
## Pricing Theory

## 10.1 INTRODUCTION

In this chapter we examine several more complex, but at the same time more realistic, pricing models. The models developed here are variants of the basic models introduced in Chapter 9. In that chapter we saw that the basic structure of pricing models consists of seven major assumptions: four structural assumptions and three behavioral assumptions. In the present chapter we shall look first at several models that vary on the basis of the behavioral assumptions, and then turn to some models that vary because of the structural assumptions used.

We confine our attention in this chapter to firms in imperfectly competitive markets, and we are especially concerned with the pricing behavior of oligopolists. The majority of contemporary business activity takes place in oligopolistic market situations, and it is in this type of market that pricing decisions are most crucial, due to the interdependence of the firms' actions. In fact, it is the interdependence, or mutual dependence, of the firms that causes the behavioral assumptions used in Chapter 9 to be inappropriate in many oligopolistic markets.

### The Need for Modified Behavioral Assumptions in Oligopoly Models

The assumption of short-term profit maximization is appropriate enough for cases of pure competition and monopolistic competition, where entry of new firms is unrestricted, and also for pure monopoly, where entry is typically impossible. In oligopoly, however, while entry is not unrestricted, neither are the barriers to entry insurmountable. Hence if oligopolists set too high a price this may induce entry of firms that not only expect to make profits at that price level but will take a share of the market in all future periods. This will in turn dilute future profitability. If the time horizon of oligopolists extends beyond the current time period, we should expect them to wish to prevent this dilution of profits by pricing so as not to attract new competition.

We have considerable reasons *a priori* to expect that oligopolists would be concerned with profitability in future periods. This derives from the form of most oligopolistic firms. By definition, these firms are large relative to their markets, and in most cases this makes them large in absolute terms as well. This in turn favors their taking on corporate form, in order to raise sufficient capital as they expand and to allow individuals to avoid the risk associated with having all their eggs in one basket. The diversity of ownership involved in the firm's being a corporation means that, for operational functionality, the control of the firm will pass to a small group of managers who are responsible only indirectly to the owners. The managers are paid salaries and have a direct interest in profits only to the extent that they are also shareholders and/or that they receive bonuses which depend on profits. But the future of the managers is tied in with the future of the corporation. If the corporation prospers and grows over time, their reputations and salaries would be expected to grow commensurately. If its market share dwindles due to the incursion of new firms, then the reputation and tenure of the managers is placed in jeopardy. It is thus reasonable to expect that, especially where there is separation of ownership and control, oligopolistic firms will tend to forgo short-term profit maximization in favor of their continued existence and profitability over the longer term.

Next, the use of price as a strategic variable is quite appropriate in short-run pure competition, monopolistic competition, and monopoly situations. Under oligopoly, however, price adjustments are likely to cause retaliatory price adjustments, and this could develop into a price-war situation. Price wars, if not actually causing losses for some or all firms, are typically less profitable than the maintenance of the status quo over the same period would have been. While an individual price cut would be profitable if *ceteris paribus* did prevail due to the gain of sales from rival firms, when all firms reduce prices the sales for each firm expand only as a share of the total market's expansion. If the price-war situation is severe and protracted, it could cause the demise of some firms. As a result of this danger, and the expected loss of profits associated with price competition, oligopolists would be expected to look elsewhere for their major strategic variable.

Observation suggests that oligopolists use product differentiation as their major strategic variable, with advertising and other promotional efforts—and product "improvements" (loosely defined!)—as the main means to achieve this. Price is by no means absent as a strategic variable, but price adjustments tend to be used only for temporary sales and/or when the market price is substantially out of line with supply and demand conditions, and price adjustments would be desired by all or most firms, and thus not construed as an offensive marketing strategy. The nonprice areas of competition, referred to above, are regarded as more appropriate areas of competition, since a gain in market share is attained by skill and finesse, rather than by the crude and potentially dangerous means of price competition.

The final behavioral assumption is that concerning the firm's conjectural variation. Under pure competition, monopolistic competition, and monopoly it was appropriate to expect no reaction from rivals, since in the first two cases the impact of a firm's action is spread imperceptibly over many rival firms and in the monopoly case there is no rival to worry about. Under oligopoly, the firm's conjectural variation cannot be assumed to be zero without the implication that the managers of each firm are incredibly myopic in their perception of their business environment.

You will recall that in the kinked demand curve model we modified the conjectural variation assumption to recognize that firms might expect rivals to match their price reductions and ignore their price increases in oligopoly markets. We noted, however, that this model is not a model of price determination but rather explains the frequently observed rigidity of prices in oligopoly. Moreover, it requires modification to incorporate the often observed upward adjustment of prices by all firms acting in "conscious parallelism."

## 10.2 MODIFIED BEHAVIORAL MODELS

Various models have been constructed to incorporate one or more of the "more appropriate" behavioral assumptions mentioned. The first few models examined below are concerned with modifications to the conjectural variation assumption. These are followed by a number of models that utilize differing assumptions as to the objective function of the firms. Models that treat nonprice competition as the strategic variable are deferred until Chapter 14, since this area is quite extensive and in any case is outside the scope of this section on pricing theory and decision making.

### Price Leadership Models

A number of oligopoly models rely upon the notion of price leadership to explain the upward adjustment of prices in oligopoly markets. The major difference between "conscious parallelism" and price leadership is that in the former situation all firms take the initiative in adjusting prices, confident that their rivals will do likewise, whereas in the latter situation one firm will lead the way and will be followed within a relatively short period by all or most of the other firms adjusting their prices to a similar degree. The price leader is the firm willing to take the risk of being the first to adjust price, but, as we shall see, this firm usually has good reason to expect that the other firms will follow suit. The risk involved here relates especially to price increases, since if the firm raises price and is not followed by other firms, it will experience an elastic demand response and a significant loss of profits before it can readjust its price to the original level. Conjectural variation for the price leader is unity, since this firm expects all rivals to adjust prices up or down to the same degree that it does. For the price followers, conjectural variation is zero for self-initiated price increases, since price followers do not expect to have all firms follow their price increases. For price decreases, the price follower might expect all firms to follow suit to protect their market shares, and so the conjectural variation is unity for price reductions. It should be immediately apparent to the reader that the price follower faces a kinked demand curve.

There are three major types of price leaders: the barometric price leader, the low-cost price leader, and the dominant firm price leader.

***The Barometric Price Leader.*** As the name implies, the barometric price leader possesses an ability to accurately predict when the climate is right for a price change. Following a generalized increase in labor or materials costs, or a period of increased demand, the barometric firm judges that all firms are ready for a price change and takes the risk of sales losses by being the first to adjust its price. If the other firms trust that firm's judgment of market conditions, they too will adjust prices to the extent indicated. If they feel the increase is too much, they may adjust prices to a lesser degree and the price leader may bring its price back to the level seemingly endorsed by the other firms. If the other firms fail to ratify the price change, the price leadership role could shift from firm to firm over time and will rest with the firm that has sound knowledge of market supply and demand conditions, the ability to perceive a consensus among the firms, and the willingness to take the risk of sales losses if its judgment on these issues is faulty.

***The Low-Cost Price Leader.*** The low-cost price leader is a firm that has a significant cost advantage over its rivals and inherits the role of price leader largely due to the other firms' reluctance to incur the wrath of the lower-cost firm. In the event of a price war, the other firms would incur greater losses and be more prone to the risk of bankruptcy than would the lower-cost firm. Out of respect for this potential power of the lower-cost firm, the other firms tacitly agree to follow that firm's price adjustments.[1] Alternatively, it might be said that the lower-cost firm is the price leader because it has the least to lose if the other firms refuse to follow its lead.

We can show graphically the determination of price in such a situation, and the most simple situation is the two-firm, identical products case. In Figure 10.1 we show the demand curve $D$ as the curve faced by either firm when each firm sets price at the same level. This curve is thus a *mutatis mutandis* demand curve, being predicated upon the simultaneous adjustment of the other firm's price to the same level.[2] In price leadership situations price adjustments are more or less concurrent, and the demand curve $D$ in this case represents a constant (half) share of the total market at each price level. The marginal cost curves of the two firms are shown as $MC_A$ for the Firm A, the lower-cost firm, and $MC_B$ for Firm B, the higher-cost firm. The lower-cost firm maximizes its profit from its share of the market by setting price $P$ and output level $Q,$ and Firm B follows the lead and also sets price $P.$

Given that it sets price $P,$ what output level should the higher-cost firm produce? Being a profit-maximizing firm, by assumption, it will simply choose the output level that maximizes profits, subject to the (self-imposed) constraint that its price will be the same as the price leader's. The demand curve facing the Firm

---

[1] This agreement is likely to be ruled illegal price fixing if the firms explicitly agree on price levels.

[2] To refresh your memory, *mutatis mutandis* means taking into account all subsequent or induced changes. In the context of oligopoly, the *mutatis mutandis* demand curve is the firm's "share of the market" demand curve when all firms are expected to set the same price levels, or at least maintain the same proportionate price differentials.

**FIGURE 10.1**
Low-cost firm price leadership: simple two-firm, identical products case

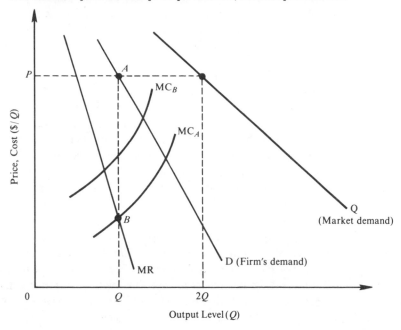

B, in this simple identical products case, is the kinked line *PAD,* since if Firm B sets its price above *P,* all consumers will purchase from Firm A at the lower price. If Firm B sets its price below *P,* the other firm will match this price reduction to avoid having its sales fall dramatically. The marginal revenue curve associated with the demand curve *PAD* is the disjointed line *PAB*MR, with a horizontal section relating to the horizontal part of the demand curve faced by Firm B, and section *B*MR relating to prices below the price *P.* Firm B should therefore choose output level *Q,* since below this output level, marginal revenue exceeds marginal costs, and above this level, marginal costs exceed marginal revenue. The firms thus share the market equally at the price level chosen by the lower-cost firm.

The above simple model allowed us to introduce the low-cost price leadership model. Little difficulty is involved in making the model more realistic by changing the assumptions concerning the degree of product differentiation and the number of sellers. The following verbal treatment should be intuitively clear. When products are differentiated, the price followers will face a kinked demand curve in which the upper section is not horizontal but is nevertheless quite elastic, as in Figure 9.6 in the preceding chapter. Where there are more than two firms, the *mutatis mutandis* section of the demand curve will represent the particular firm's share of the total market when all prices are at a similar level. If product differentiation is symmetric among the products of the various firms, the shares of all firms will be equal, as in the identical products case.[3] If we let

[3] Essentially, *symmetric product differentiation* means that the products are equally differentiated from each other, and so market shares should be equal when prices are equal.

$n$ represent the number of rival firms, then the *mutatis mutandis* demand curve will represent $1/n$ of the total market demand at each price level. If the market divides unequally among the firms when all prices are at a similar level, we say that product differentiation is asymmetric, and the *mutatis mutandis* demand curve will represent a market share that may be greater or less than $1/n$th of the total demand at each price level.

When product differentiation is asymmetric we should expect a range of prices among the rival firms, reflecting the different cost and demand situations facing each firm. Price leadership in this situation requires one slight modification to the above analysis. The price leader may adjust its price by a certain amount, and the price followers will adjust their prices by the *same percentage* as is represented by the price leader's price adjustment. Thus the relative price differentials that prevailed prior to the price changes are unchanged, and no firm expects to gain or lose sales from or to a rival. The price leader simply initiates an upward (or downward) adjustment in the entire price structure of that particular market.

In Figure 10.2 we show a situation in which three firms produce asymmetrically differentiated products. Firm A is the acknowledged price leader and sets price $P_A$, selling $Q_A$ units. Firms B and C are price followers, not wishing to initiate price adjustments in case this might precipitate active competition or a price war in which the lower-cost Firm A would have a definite advantage. Firm B's price is above the price leader's price, and Firm C's price is below the other two prices. Firm B's product may be a higher-quality item desired by a relatively small segment of the market. This firm's higher cost level may well be the result of higher-quality inputs and more hand finishing of the product, for example. Firm C's product is both lower priced and more expensive to produce, as com-

**FIGURE 10.2**
**Low-cost firm price leadership: two or more firms, asymmetric product differentiation and cost conditions**

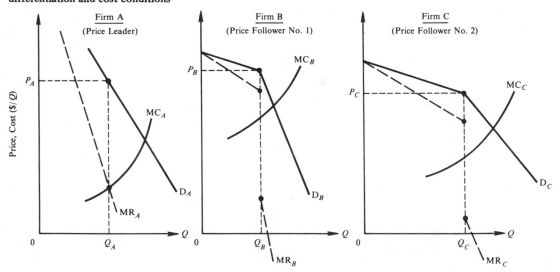

pared with the price leader's. The lower price might be due to the market's perception of inferior after-sales service, an inferior location, or absence of other attributes, while the higher costs may be the result of more expensive sources of the inputs, inefficiencies in production, or a plant size too large or too small in view of the present output level.

The price followers face the kinked demand curves shown because they expect no reaction from rivals for price increases but expect the price leader and the other price follower to match any price reductions. The price leader's demand curve is simply the *mutatis mutandis* demand curve: the price leader expects the other firms to follow both price increases and price reductions. If, for example, the price leader's costs increase, it will adjust price upward along the $D_A$ curve. The price followers, who have probably incurred a similar cost increase, will follow the lead and adjust prices upward. But for this particular price increase they do not expect *ceteris paribus;* they expect that the other firms will be simultaneously adjusting their prices upward (or have seen them do so). As stated earlier, the firms are likely to adjust price upward by a similar *proportion* in order to maintain their relative prices, and hence their market shares. In this case, however, the proportion will be decided by the price leader.

We shall see in Chapter 11 that the common business practice of "markup pricing" allows firms to adjust prices to cost increases by a similar proportion. We turn now to the third type of price leader.

*The Dominant Firm Price Leader.* As the name implies, the dominant firm is large relative to its rivals and its market. The smaller firms accept this firm's price leadership perhaps simply because they are unwilling to risk being the first to change prices, or perhaps out of fear that the dominant firm could drive them out of business, by forcing raw-material suppliers to boycott a particular small firm on pain of losing the order of the larger firm, for example. In such a situation the smaller firms accept the dominant firm's choice of the price level, and they simply adjust output to maximize their profits. In this respect they are similar to pure competitors who can sell as much as they want to at the market price. Like pure competitors, they will want to sell up to the point where their marginal cost equals the price (equals marginal revenue). The dominant firm recognizes that the smaller firms will behave in this manner and that it must therefore choose price to maximize its profits with the knowledge that the smaller firms will sell as much as they want to at that price.

The first task of the dominant firm price leader is, therefore, to ascertain how much the smaller firms will want to supply at each price level. Since each of the smaller firms will want to supply up to the point where MC = MR, and since MR = $P$ in a situation where the individual firm is so small that it does not influence market price, each of the smaller firms will regard its MC curve as its supply curve. Note that a supply curve shows the quantity that will be supplied at each price level. At each price level the firms supply the amount for which marginal cost equals price. The MC curve therefore indicates how much the firm will supply at each price level. It follows that a horizontal aggregation of these curves will indicate the total amount that the smaller firms will supply at each price

## FIGURE 10.3

**Aggregation of small firms' MC curves to find their aggregate supply curve in the dominant firm price leadership model**

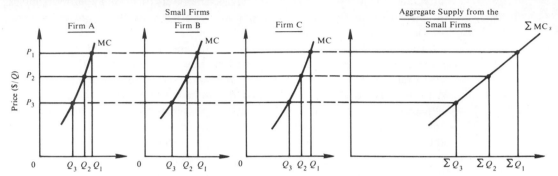

level. In Figure 10.3 we depict this aggregation of the smaller firms' marginal cost curves as the line $\Sigma MC_s$.

In Figure 10.3 we show three small firms and the marginal cost curves of each. Suppose the dominant firm sets price $P_1$. Each of the small firms will expand supply to the point where its MC curve rises to the price level $P_1$, and similarly for lower prices such as $P_2$ and $P_3$. Summing the supply of the three firms at each price level, we obtain the $\Sigma MC_s$ curve in the right-hand part of the figure.

Knowing how much the smaller firms will supply at each price level, the dominant firm can subtract this from the market demand to find how much demand is left over at each price level. This "residual" demand can be measured as the horizontal distance between the $\Sigma MC_s$ and the market demand curve $D$, at

## FIGURE 10.4

**Construction of the dominant firm's residual demand curve**

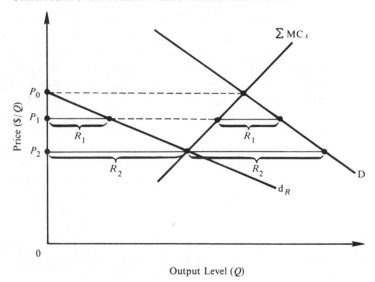

each price level, and is shown as the demand curve $d_R$ in Figure 10.4. Only at prices below $P_0$ is there any demand left for the dominant firm after the smaller firms have supplied their desired amounts. At price $P_1$ there is an excess of market demand over the supply of the smaller firms, shown as the horizontal distance $R_1$ between the $\Sigma MC_s$ curve and the D curve. Similarly, the residual demand at price $P_2$ is shown by the distance $R_2$. Shifting these residual amounts across to the price axis, we find the dominant firm's residual demand curve to be that shown as $d_R$. This residual demand curve is the amount that the dominant firm can be assured of selling at each price level, since the smaller firms will have sold as much as they wanted to and yet there remain buyers willing to purchase at those price levels.

The dominant firm will choose the price level in order to maximize its own profits from this assured or residual demand. The marginal revenue curve associated with the residual demand curve is shown as the curve *mr* in Figure 10.5. The dominant firm's marginal cost curve is depicted by $MC_D$. The dominant firm therefore selects price $P_D$ and output $Q_D$ in order to maximize its profits. Faced with the price $P_D$, each of the smaller firms produces up to the point where its marginal costs equal that price, and hence the smaller firms in aggregate produce the output level $Q_s$. Since the residual demand curve was constructed to reflect the horizontal distance between the $\Sigma MC_s$ and the D curves, the total amount supplied to the market, $\Sigma Q$, is equal to the market demand and an equilibrium situation exists. The dominant firm thus chooses price to maximize its profits under the constraint that the smaller firms will supply the amount at that price level that will maximize their profits.

An interesting long-run implication of the dominant-firm price leadership model is that if the chosen price allows the smaller firms to earn economic

**FIGURE 10.5**
**Price determination by the dominant firm price leader**

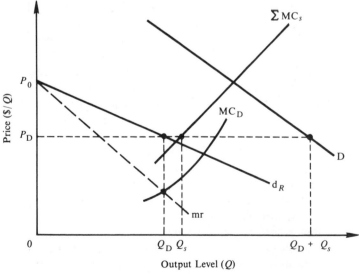

Price ($/$Q$)

Output Level ($Q$)

profits, then the dominance of the large firm will be eroded over time. The reason for this erosion is that in the long run the small firms will expand their plant sizes in search of even greater profitability, and new firms will enter the industry —if the barriers to entry can be overcome—in search of this profitability. In any case the residual demand remaining for the dominant firm, with market demand static, must be reduced, and the price leader will be forced to set a lower price and accept a reduced market share. Eventually, of course, the dominant firm will no longer be dominant, and the above system of market price determination will give way to some other form of price leadership, conscious parallelism, or independent price setting.

We turn now to the modification of the assumption relating to the objective function of the firm.

### Long-Term Profit Maximization

The behavioral assumption of short-run profit maximization, which we have used in all the above models of firm behavior, may be criticized for its realism in oligopolistic markets where short-run profit maximization may induce new firms to overcome the barriers to entry and obtain a share of the market and thus dilute future profits of the existing firms. Earlier in this chapter it was argued briefly that the time horizon envisaged by oligopolists will extend beyond the short-run period, and these firms are likely to forgo immediate profits in order not to attract the entry of new firms.

This suggests, of course, that a more appropriate objective function for the oligopolist is the maximization of long-term profits. To be precise, we would say that the firm might wish to maximize the present value of its future profit stream, since future profits must be discounted to the present at an appropriate discount rate in order to allow comparability of profit amounts from different time periods. In theory, the firm would consider various price levels for each time period up to its time horizon and would form an expectation of demand at each price level for each period. This would need to take into account the loss of sales to new entrants which may occur at some price levels, and the impact of expected changes in other variables, such as population, incomes, consumer preferences, and prices of competing products, which are expected to influence the sales of the firm's products in future periods. On the cost side the firm would need to form expectations of changes in relative factor prices and in the state of technology, such that it could estimate its marginal cost of production at all output levels in each future period. In practice, of course, the above procedure becomes extremely difficult to calculate due to the problems associated with forming reliable expectations on the matters indicated. Even if such predictions could be made, the cost of obtaining the information might far outweigh the extra revenue derived, and thus the firm should not undertake the search procedure necessary.

It is more likely that firms that wish to maximize their long-term profits will adopt a "proxy" objective function. That is, they will pursue a policy that gives approximately the same results but is much more simple and inexpensive to administer. In the following sections we shall examine a number of such proxy policies which, it can be argued, are a short-term means of achieving the long-term objective of profit maximization.

### The Sales Maximization Model

It has been suggested that the appropriate objective function for many firms is the maximization of sales in the short term, subject to the attainment of a certain minimum profit level.[4] First let us consider the minimum profit requirement, which is necessary for two main reasons: (1) a certain minimum profit must be forthcoming to allow payment of dividends sufficient to prevent shareholders from becoming disgruntled and voting for a new board of directors; and (2) the value of the firm's shares on the stock exchange depend, in part, on the current profitability of the firm, since the expectation of dividend payments has a positive influence on the market value of the shares. If, due to low current profits, the shares become undervalued in view of the firm's longer-term prospects, the firm may be subject to a takeover bid by another firm, which again involves the risk that managers may lose their jobs. Hence managers will be motivated to keep profits at a level sufficient to stave off these two possibilities, while at the same time making sure that profits are not so large as to attract the entry of new firms.

Having determined the minimum acceptable level of profits, the firm will wish to maximize its sales subject to this profit constraint. We can show the sales-maximization decision on the same graph as for short-run profit maximization. In Figure 10.6 are displayed the familiar total revenue and total cost

**FIGURE 10.6**
**Sales maximization subject to a minimum profit constraint**

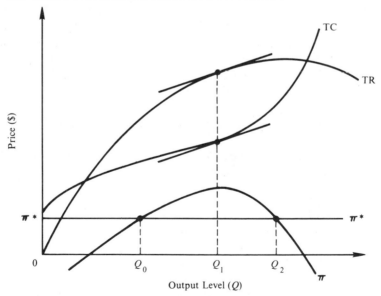

[4] W. J. Baumol, *Business Behavior, Value, and Growth* (New York: Harcourt, Brace and World, 1967).

curves, with the profit curve indicating the excess of total revenue over total costs at each output level. Suppose the minimum profit constraint is the vertical distance indicated by $0\pi^*$. The profit constraint is satisfied anywhere between output (sales) levels $Q_0$ and $Q_2$, but sales are maximized, subject to this constraint, at output level $Q_2$. It is clear that this output level is larger than the short-run profit-maximizing output level $Q_1$ and must be offered at a lower price than the short-run profit-maximizing price, since the firm faces a negatively sloped demand curve.

But why is the maximization of sales in the short run a proxy for the maximization of longer-term profits? The lower price level, as compared with the short-run profit-maximizing price, has three major implications for future profits. First, it will tend to inhibit the entry of new firms whose costs may exceed that price level due to the extra expenses associated with overcoming the barriers to entry. Second, it will introduce more customers to the product now and will thus operate to gain more repeat sales in future periods, due to the goodwill and brand loyalty that will develop over time as customers use the product. This cultivation of consumer loyalty and goodwill acts to raise one of the barriers to entry, since a potential entrant firm would need to spend even more on advertising and promotion of its own product in order to induce customers to try that product. Third, increased sales in the short term provide a larger base for complementary sales in the longer term. This is especially important in the market for some durable consumption goods, such as automobiles and cameras, where apparently quite lucrative markets exist for specialized replacement parts and accessories.

A policy of sales maximization in the short run thus operates to inhibit the entry of new firms and to generate future sales of the firm's product(s). The resultant profit stream probably comes reasonably close to that which could be attained by the present value calculation for long-term profit maximization, given that there are likely to be considerable search costs associated with obtaining the information necessary to make that calculation. Sales maximization is a relatively simple and inexpensive rule-of-thumb procedure which can be applied in each period, and it thus obviates the cost, effort, and uncertainty associated with the continual recalculation of the price that maximizes the present value of the expected profit stream.

### The Limit Pricing Model

A second policy that may be regarded as a proxy for long-term profit maximization is that known as "limit pricing." This involves choosing the price level such that it is *not quite high enough* to induce entry of new firms. In many cases the entrant firm is expected to have higher costs than the existing firms, due both to its probable smaller scale of operation and to the additional product differentiation expense it must incur to offset consumer loyalty to the existing products. Thus the established firms, at the suggestion of a price leader perhaps, choose a price that does not allow the potential entrant to earn even a normal profit at any output level. In Figure 10.7 this price is shown as $P_L$, which is lower than any point on the potential entrant's short-run average cost curve, $SAC_e$.

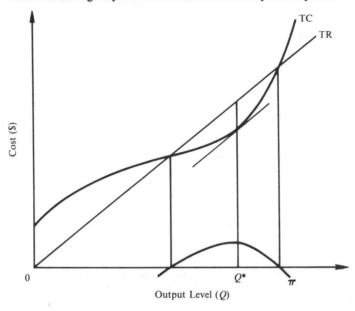

**FIGURE 9.2**
Profit-maximizing output determination for a firm in pure competition

In this chapter we have considered the pricing problem in mature and newly established product markets. Recognizing that firms may lack the information necessary to price by marginalist principles, or that this information may cost more than it is worth, we expect firms to use markup-pricing procedures or to simply follow the price leader(s). We showed, however, that markup pricing can be profit or contribution maximizing if chosen at the level commensurate with the product's price elasticity of demand. If longer-term profit maximization is desired, the markup percentage is likely to be somewhat lower than for short-run profit maximization, since long-term price elasticities tend to be higher than short-term price elasticities. As well as saving decision-making cost, markup pricing acts to pass cost increases along to the customer and maintain the purchasing power or real value of the firm's profits, and it assists in coordinating the pricing behavior of firms in oligopolistic markets.

Choosing the appropriate price level in established product markets requires an evaluation of the attributes perceived to exist in your product vis-à-vis those in competing products. In these markets the general level of prices is established, and the problem is to ensure that each product is positioned in the existing price range such that the firm's objectives are best served. The price chosen should reflect the presence, absence, or degree of desirable attributes in each product, relative to the prices and attributes offered by competing products. Product-line pricing involves essentially the same problem, except that a particular firm produces several of the competing or complementary products and must choose their prices relative to the prices and attributes of products from both its own product line and its competitor's product lines.

New-product pricing is an area of considerable difficulty due largely to the lack of information regarding probable demand and cost conditions, and the number and timing of new entries to this newly established market. To the extent that this information is available with sufficient degrees of accuracy, the decision maker may choose the price that is expected to best serve the relevant objective function. In any case, the cost and demand conditions will be constantly changing and evolving, and considerable price adjustment may be necessary before this market matures and establishes a general price level that is agreeable to all the firms involved.

The decision maker must keep an eye peeled for the legal implications of each pricing strategy. The legal and punitive expenses and customer illwill that may be involved in certain pricing strategies must be considered before each decision is taken.

The pricing problem addressed in this chapter concerned markets in which there are numerous transactions at the chosen price level. The decision maker must choose a price that will be offered to thousands or millions of potential buyers. As time passes, information as to the appropriateness of this price level will be generated, and adjustments may be made for subsequent transactions with subsequent buyers of the essentially similar product. In the following chapter we turn to the market situations in which each transaction is unique in the sense that it may involve different attributes at a different price to a different buyer, and hence the information generated by previous sales may be less valuable for future pricing decisions.

## DISCUSSION QUESTIONS

11.1   Outline the conditions under which it may be profit maximizing to use a rule-of-thumb price determination procedure, rather than to determine price on the basis of estimated marginal cost and marginal revenue curves.

11.2   In using an estimated demand curve to determine price, there is a risk that the actual price/quantity combination (which eventually occurs) is not a point on the estimated demand curve. Does this mean we should not have used that estimated demand curve?

11.3   Under what type of cost and/or demand conditions is the contribution approach the only way to implement the marginalist pricing principle?

11.4   Summarize the relationship between the markup and the contribution margin.

11.5   Express in words the conditions under which the markup price is the profit-maximizing price.

11.6   What forces operate to cause the markups of firms to tend toward the profit-maximizing levels?

11.7   Explain why the presence or absence of desirable attributes in your product influences the optimal price positioning of that product in an established market.

11.8   Summarize the issues involved in product-line pricing strategy.

11.9   Under what conditions would you expect price skimming to be the profit-maximizing strategy for a new product?

11.10   Outline the illegal aspects of pricing of which the price maker must be fully aware before determining prices.

## PROBLEMS

11.1   The Ajzenkopf Company has been in operation for almost fifteen years and has enjoyed considerable success in the manufacture and sale of its glass vases.

The Ajzenkopf plant at present has a capacity of 35,000 units per year, and the facilities at the plant are highly specialized. Sales of vases are currently 29,000 units a year. The selling price is $7.00 per unit. Last month the average costs of production were determined to be: average fixed costs, $1.03; average cost of labor, $1.98; and average cost of materials, $1.05. At those present price and cost levels the Ajzenkopf Company received a profit that management believed was quite acceptable.

This agreeable situation came to an abrupt halt, however, when it was learned that the suppliers of raw materials were raising their prices, and there was a labor dispute which forced negotiations to begin. An agreement was reached, and the final settlement has the effect of increasing the average cost per unit of labor by 20 percent. A new contract has been signed with the suppliers of the raw materials, and the new prices of raw materials had the effect of increasing the average materials cost by 30 percent. This contract had been signed after other suppliers were contacted, but no less-expensive prices of raw materials could be found.

Faced with this situation, a meeting was called to determine what action should be undertaken to maintain an acceptable level of profit. It was agreed that a profit level of $75,000 was the minimum acceptable point. Two alternative suggestions were made. The first suggestion, made by the marketing manager, was to raise prices to $9.00 a unit, since he was fairly certain that this price level would reduce quantity demanded by only 8,500 units per annum. The marketing manager also offered an estimate of the average variable costs, stating that the average labor cost would be $3.10 and the average materials cost would be $1.39 at this level of output.

The plant manager proposed that the price should be reduced to $6.00. The plant manager was also fairly certain about the demand situation, stating that at this price level 32,500 vases would be demanded. He also tendered his estimates of average variable costs, stating that at this level of output the average costs of labor and materials per unit would be $2.85 and $1.24 respectively. The plant manager further supported his proposal by stating that under this alternative, laborers need not be laid off and thus low labor morale would not reduce productivity of the workers.

  (a)  Using the information given above, derive graphical estimates of the firm's revenue and cost functions.

  (b)  Assuming that the firm wishes to maximize sales volume subject to obtaining a minimum profit of $75,000, what price do you suggest they charge? Discuss your answer fully. What qualifications do you wish to add to your analysis?

11.2  Regression analysis of the variations in prices and quantity demanded for our major product (conducted under controlled conditions in a consumer clinic by our marketing research department) provides the following results (where $P$ is in dollars, and $Q$ represents thousands of units):

| | |
|---|---|
| Regression equation | $Q = 49.147 - 2.941P$ |
| Coefficient of determination | $(R^2) = 0.96$ |
| Standard error of estimate | $= 0.958$ |
| Standard error of the coefficient | $= 0.982$ |

Our production department has conducted its own study of the variations of weekly total variable costs and output levels over the past three months. Its results (with TVC in thousands of dollars and $Q$ representing thousands of units) are as follows:

| | |
|---|---|
| Regression equation | $TVC = 102.35 + 0.025Q^2$ |
| Coefficient of determination | $(R^2) = 0.92$ |
| Standard error of estimate | $= 0.785$ |
| Standard error of the coefficient | $= 0.009$ |

You are an executive assistant to the marketing manager, Derek Winton. Mr. Winton feels that the present price of $9.95 is fine. He argues that it positions our product in the upper part of the range of our competitors' prices, and that the current sales level of approximately 20,000 units a week is fine in view of our full capacity limit of only 25,000 units weekly. While he agrees that a price change of a dollar or so either way would go unchallenged by competitors, he does not think such a price change would improve the contribution made by this product.

  (a)  What is the contribution-maximizing price? Is the associated output level feasible?

(b) How confident are you that your prediction will in fact generate a greater contribution than the present price level? Explain in detail with supporting calculations.

(c) Are there any reservations you wish to attach to your recommendation?

11.3 Paul McElligot owns a small movie theatre in the older downtown area of a large city. Its capacity is only 1,500 seats and Mr. McElligot charges $3.75 for admission, which is $0.25 less than that charged by the larger, more luxurious theatres nearby. He shows a major film (plus other short features) twice daily Monday through Thursday, with three showings on Friday, Saturday, and Sunday. Average seats sold per session over the past three months have been as follows:

| Session | Mon. | Tues. | Wed. | Thurs. | Fri. | Sat. | Sun. |
|---------|------|-------|------|--------|------|------|------|
| Matinee | – | – | – | – | 600 | 900 | 900 |
| Early | 600 | 600 | 600 | 600 | 800 | 1,000 | 1,000 |
| Late | 800 | 800 | 800 | 800 | 900 | 1,200 | 1,000 |

Over the same period the average costs and profit per ticket have been as follows:

| | |
|---|---|
| Labor costs | $0.39 |
| Theatre Association dues | 0.07 |
| Film rentals | 0.72 |
| Royalties | 1.43 |
| Selling administrative expenses | 0.32 |
| Depreciation on building and equipment | 0.28 |
| Other overheads | 0.09 |
| Profits before tax | 0.45 |
| | $3.75 |

Other than royalty payments which are strictly proportional to ticket sales, and labor costs which tend to behave in a steplike fashion, most of these costs are indeed fixed. Labor costs for the projectionist, doorman, cashier, security guard, and a few others remain constant regardless of volume. However, such is not the case with ushers or maintenance workers. Ushers are required for both the balcony and the main audience sections of the theatre. Besides a basic staff of two, an additional usher is hired (at $10 per hr.) for every 250 tickets expected to be sold at each show. Ushers are not paid for the time between shows, and shows are typically two hours in length. Only one full-time maintenance worker is employed. On days when ticket sales are expected to exceed 1,500, an additional worker is hired for $40 a day.

The theatre also operates a small snack counter which sells soft drinks, ice cream, popcorn, and various confectionary items. Average weekly sales, sales price, and the costs per item for goods sold at the counter have been as follows:

| Item | Average Weekly Sales (units) | Sales Price | Cost |
|------|------------------------------|-------------|------|
| Popcorn | 2,000 | $0.40 | $0.33 |
| Ice cream | 2,000 | 0.35 | 0.18 |
| Chocolate bars | 1,800 | 0.30 | 0.22 |
| Soda pop | 3,000 | 0.35 | 0.25 |
| Chewing gum | 800 | 0.20 | 0.17 |
| Peppermints | 600 | 0.20 | 0.15 |
| Hard candies | 1,000 | 0.25 | 0.20 |
| Peanuts | 700 | 0.20 | 0.16 |
| Potato chips | 1,500 | 0.25 | 0.21 |

Two people work at the snack counter on a regular basis, and an additional person is hired on weekends, or whenever ticket sales are expected to exceed 1,400 per day at a cost of $35 per day.

Mr. McElligot is considering the implementation of a $33\frac{1}{3}$ percent price discount for older people with a "Golden Age" card, and younger people with a "student" card. Marketing research has shown that these two segments jointly account for an average of 20 percent of current sales. If the price cut is initiated, ticket sales are expected to increase to the following levels:

| Session | Mon. | Tue. | Wed. | Thurs. | Fri. | Sat. | Sun. |
|---------|------|------|------|--------|------|------|------|
| Matinee | – | – | – | – | 900 | 1,200 | 1,200 |
| Early | 900 | 900 | 900 | 900 | 1,000 | 1,400 | 1,400 |
| Late | 1,000 | 1,000 | 1,000 | 1,000 | 1,200 | 1,450 | 1,450 |

The price reduction would also lead to a general increase of 35 percent on all snack-bar sales. As a result, a 10 percent quantity discount would become available on all purchases of popcorn, potato chips, and chewing gum, all of which are currently supplied by the same source.

Should management implement the new pricing policy? Use contribution analysis to explain why, and state any possible qualifications.

11.4 The Pittsburgh Plastics Company introduced a new product in January which received strong initial support and has shown a steady growth of sales in subsequent months. The initial pricing policy was to mark up per unit total costs by 25 percent to arrive at the price level of $6.88 per unit. The company's objective is to maximize the contribution to overheads and profits, and it is now anxious to know whether the $6.88 price is optimal. In light of the continual growth in sales, and changes in certain cost components, it has commissioned a study by Market Researchers Incorporated, who report that the price elasticity of demand is approximately 2.5 at the current (March) price and output level.

The output and cost data for the past three months are as follows:

| | January | February | March |
|---|---|---|---|
| *Sales* (units) | 2,246 | 2,471 | 2,718 |
| Direct materials | $1,415 | $1,557 | $1,712 |
| Direct labor | 3,369 | 4,077 | 4,933 |
| Indirect factory labor | 3,000 | 3,075 | 3,154 |
| Office and administrative salaries | 2,000 | 2,000 | 2,000 |
| Light and heat | 485 | 470 | 320 |
| Other overheads | 2,100 | 2,100 | 2,100 |

(a) Supposing that price can be varied each month, estimate the optimal price for the month of April.

(b) What output level could be sold at the optimal price level in April?

(c) What qualifications and other considerations do you wish to add to the above pricing and output decision?

11.5 The Napper Bag and Canvas Co. Ltd. is a specialist manufacturer of down-filled sleeping bags for sale in the camping equipment market. In this market there are several large companies with annual sales between $25 million and $30 million, and many smaller companies with sales between $1 million and $5 million. Most of these companies have diversified product lines of camping equipment, including tents, cooking equipment, camping furniture, and sleeping bags with various types of filling. Napper's sales of $1.6 million last year came entirely from down-filled sleeping bags, however. Although more expensive than other materials, down has substantially more insulating value by weight and volume and commands the attention of a loyal segment of serious outdoorspeople. Only a few firms produce quality down-filled bags, but these firms face peripheral competition from other firms producing bags filled with other natural and artificial materials.

Last year Napper sold 21,000 bags directly to large department stores, catalog sales companies, and specialty sporting equipment stores. These clients typically require contracts guaranteeing prices for one year. The cost of manufacturing sleeping bags depends on the size of the bag, the materials used, and the amount of fill. A breakdown of Napper's latest manufacturing costs for a typical style follows.

| Item | Cost per Unit |
|---|---|
| Down filling | $30.00 |
| Other raw materials | 14.40 |
| Direct labor | 8.12 |
| Manufacturing overhead | 6.09 |
| Total unit cost | $58.61 |

To the manufacturing cost is added a markup of 30 percent to provide for selling, administration, financial expenses, and profit.

During the past year the cost of down increased by between 80 to 95 percent, depending on the grade and blend. Napper was able to pass this on to its customers without any apparent loss of sales or share of the market. The suppliers of down are forecasting a minimum increase of 80 percent over the next year. For Napper this will mean that the average price of down will increase from the current $12 per pound to $22 per pound. It is anticipated that the cost of other raw materials will rise by 8 percent and labor by 5 percent over the next year.

George Napper, the marketing manager, is concerned about the prospects for the coming year, and you are called upon to advise him.

    (a)    What price level do you advise for Napper's typical style bag?

    (b)    Do you have any other advice for Mr. Napper concerning future marketing strategy?

11.6    The chocolate bar producers in the confectionary industry have been subject to substantial cost increases over the past decade. This industry purchases most of its sugar and cocoa on the international commodities markets, and prices of these products fluctuate sharply in response to supply and demand conditions from year to year. In 1973 the cost of sugar rose dramatically, and together with large increases in packaging and labor costs, this precipitated the disappearance of the ten-cent chocolate bar in late 1973 as all firms raised their prices to twenty cents. The effect of this price increase was largely unexpected by the producing firms. Sales volume dropped by approximately 20 percent during 1974, and by the time the firms reduced output levels, most had built up large inventories of their highly perishable finished product.

One of the firms, Granner Foods Inc., acted to reduce its inventories and increase sales by undertaking a new advertising campaign aimed at convincing the consumer that Granner chocolate bars offered "more bite for your money" than those of its rivals. This strategy proved successful, and Granner's sales and profitability increased satisfactorily. But by mid-1976 profits had been squeezed again to unsatisfactory levels. Packaging and labor costs had been increasing consistently, and then the cost of cocoa rose almost threefold as compared with 1975 levels. This increased average variable costs to $1.70 per box at the 1977 output rate of 900,000 boxes per annum. Each box contains twenty-four chocolate bars and was sold to retailers for $2.40, who in turn marked up this cost by 100 percent in order to set the price for consumers.

After input from the marketing, manufacturing, and sales departments, the president of the company, Howard Granner, was presented with three alternative pricing strategies for 1977: (1) raise the price of chocolate bars to twenty-five cents to consumers, and increase the weight by 10 percent; (2) maintain price at twenty cents, but reduce the weight of the bar by 15 percent; or (3) maintain both price and weight at present levels. Rivals were expected to choose one of these three strategies. The impacts upon Granner's 1977 sales volume for the various strategy combinations were expected to be as follows:

**Strategy Chosen by Granner**

|  |  | 1 | 2 | 3 |
|---|---|---|---|---|
| Strategy | 1 | −5% | +10% | +20% |
| Chosen by | 2 | −10% | −5% | +15% |
| Competitors | 3 | −20% | −10% | − |

The *a priori* probabilities of competitors' employing strategies 1, 2, and 3 were 0.8, 0.15, and 0.05, respectively. Increasing the weight of the bar by 10 percent was expected to add 5 percent to average variable costs, and reducing the weight by 15 percent was expected to reduce average variable costs by 10 percent. For any given weight, the per unit variable cost of producing the bars was virtually constant regardless of output level.

(a)  Which of the three strategies was the profit-maximizing one for 1977?

(b)  Discuss any other matters that you feel should have been considered in this decision.

11.7    The Nguyen Hui Lien Trading Company imports and markets semiprecious jewelry from Southeast Asia. One of its most important items is a small jade pendant which is sold to retail outlets at $5 per unit, at which price these stores currently demand 20,000 units. The owner-manager of the company, Mr. Nguyen, is currently considering his pricing strategy for the next year. Many of his customers issue catalogs and must have a guaranteed price for at least a year in advance.

After extensive inquiries and discussions with his clients, Mr. Nguyen has established the following probabilities associated with the price and demand changes shown:

|  |  | Demand Change (units) | | | | |
|---|---|---|---|---|---|---|
|  |  | −10,000 | −5,000 | 0 | +5,000 | +10,000 |
| Price Change from | +2 | 0.5 | 0.4 | 0.1 | 0.0 | 0.0 |
| Current Level ($) | +1 | 0.3 | 0.2 | 0.3 | 0.2 | 0.0 |
|  | 0 | 0.1 | 0.4 | 0.2 | 0.2 | 0.1 |
|  | −1 | 0.0 | 0.2 | 0.3 | 0.2 | 0.3 |
|  | −2 | 0.0 | 0.0 | 0.1 | 0.4 | 0.5 |

The variable cost structure of the company depends upon how large a shipment Mr. Nguyen brings in from Southeast Asia. As the size of the shipment increases, the per unit cost (for all units in each shipment) changes as follows:

| Amount Supplied (units) | Variable Cost per Unit ($) |
|---|---|
| up to 10,000 | 6.50 |
| 10,001 to 13,000 | 4.50 |
| 13,001 to 15,000 | 4.00 |
| 15,001 to 20,000 | 3.50 |
| 20,001 to 23,000 | 3.00 |
| 23,001 to 25,000 | 2.50 |
| 25,001 to 27,000 | 2.00 |
| 27,001 to 30,000 | 3.00 |

(a) Which price level should be chosen if he wishes to maximize profits?

(b) Which price level should be chosen if he wishes to maximize sales volume subject to the constraint that contribution to overheads and profits exceeds $40,000.

11.8 The refrigerator market is characterized by a wide diversity of product offerings and a price range from under $400 to over $1,200, depending on the features of the specific refrigerator. Within this range, each manufacturer has a product line ranging from the basic no-frills smaller refrigerators to the top-of-the-line luxury units.

A large chain of department stores buys various refrigerators from various manufacturers and sells them under its own brand name "Valhalla." Given the stores' reputation for quality products and after-sales service, this refrigerator line has achieved a substantial market share in the areas where it is sold. The marketing vice-president of the chain has been considering an addition to the Valhalla line. The new refrigerator, designated the GE12456A, is made by General Electric and is similar to several sold by other major manufacturers, but it would fill a gap in the product line offered by the chain stores. The details of the GE12456A are as follows: it is a 12-cubic-foot upright refrigerator/freezer, two door, with freezer at the top and freezer capacity of 3.2 cubic feet, and it has four large aluminum trays for fresh meat and/or vegetables (taking up the lower two shelves), fully compartmentalized inner doors, butter and cheese compartments with individual temperature controls, and "easy-glide" wheels underneath. It comes in four colors and with door hinges on either side.

The refrigerators available that would seem to be most competitive with the GE12456A are as follows (apart from the details shown, they are similar in all other respects to the GE12456A):

| Make/ Model | Price ($) | Total Cubic (cu ft) | Freezer Size | Trays | Wheels |
|---|---|---|---|---|---|
| General Electric GE12456 | 525 | 12.0 | 3.2 | 4 | Yes |
| Westinghouse WH11521 | 505 | 11.5 | 2.3 | 3 | No |
| Store A Housebrand XY-4823 | 485 | 12.0 | 3.0 | 3 | No |

11.8 (continued)

| Make/<br>Model | Price<br>($) | Total<br>Cubic<br>(cu ft) | Freezer<br>Size | Trays | Wheels |
|---|---|---|---|---|---|
| Store B<br>Housebrand<br>BK-7742 | 505 | 12.5 | 3.5 | 4 | No |
| RCA<br>RC-6821 | 515 | 11.8 | 2.8 | 4 | Yes |
| Kelvinator<br>K-7742 | 535 | 12.5 | 3.5 | 4 | No |

You are asked to assist in pricing the new addition to the Valhalla line.

(a) What price level would you recommend?

(b) Explain the basis for your recommendation in detail.

(c) Outline all qualifications you feel should be made to this recommendation.

11.9 The Eastman Paint Company has developed a new paint which is unique in that it allows the user to turn ordinary glass windows and doors into one-way glass. Moreover, it prevents the transmission of ultraviolet rays, a major factor in the fading of furniture fabrics, carpets, and draperies. The production manager, Arthur Eastman, has estimated the following average variable cost levels (per gallon) for the product for this year and for the next two years. Note that costs decline over time as the production process becomes increasingly streamlined.

| | Output Level (gallons/month) | | | | |
| | 2,000 | 4,000 | 6,000 | 8,000 | 10,000 |
|---|---|---|---|---|---|
| Year 1 | $12.61 | $11.82 | $11.74 | $11.84 | $12.07 |
| Year 2 | 10.05 | 9.76 | 9.60 | 9.56 | 9.82 |
| Year 3 | 9.22 | 9.04 | 8.85 | 8.80 | 9.02 |

The advertising manager, Ms. Lois Eastman, is excited about the prospects of the new paint. She believes that the market has long felt the need for such a product, and she has prepared a large campaign to launch the product. Several television advertisements are being prepared and a brochure is in print, all referring to the extensive test results and benefits of the new paint. The focus of the campaign is on the increased privacy afforded by the new paint, with emphasis being given to the protection it provides by filtering out the ultraviolet part of the sun's rays.

The price of the new product is to be determined. Market reasearch suggests that the demand situation will be approximated by $Q = 16 - 0.67P$ in the first year (where $Q$ represents thousands of gallons and $P$ is in dollars); $Q = 20 - 0.77P$ in the second year; and $Q = 17.83 - 0.87P$ in the third year. Indications are that market demand will increase in each of the first three years, but the entry of competitors with substitute paints in Year 3 will cause Eastman's demand curve to shift to the left, as implied by the above specifications.

The marketing manager, Ms. Margaret Turriff, is faced with the problem of plotting price strategy over the next three years. While Year 2 and Year 3 prices can be determined in due time, the president of the company wants to know what type of pricing strategy Ms. Turriff intends to employ, since he is concerned that returns from this product be maximized, given the extensive research and development program that gave rise to the new product.

    (a)    What is the profit-maximizing price in each of the first three years, as estimated from the data given?

    (b)    Under what conditions would you advise the Eastman Paint Company to pursue a penetration-pricing strategy?

## SELECTED REFERENCES AND FURTHER READING

ALPERT, M. I., *Pricing Decisions.* Glenview, Ill.: Scott, Foresman, 1971.

CORR, A. V., "The Role of Cost in Pricing," *Management Accounting,* November 1974, pp. 15-32.

DHALLA, N. K., and S. YUSPEH, "Forget the Product Life Cycle Concept!" *Harvard Business Review,* January-February 1976, pp. 102-12.

DONNELLY, J. H., and M. J. ETZEL, "Degrees of Product Newness and Early Trial," *Journal of Marketing Research,* 10 (August 1973), 295-300.

EARLEY, J. S., "Marginal Policies of 'Excellently Managed' Companies," *American Economic Review,* 46 (March 1956), 46-70.

EICHNER, A. S., "A Theory of the Determination of the Mark-up under Oligopoly," *Economic Journal,* 83 (December 1973), 1184-1200.

FRANKEL, M., "Pricing Decisions under Unknown Demand," *Kyklos,* 26, No. 1 (1973), 1-24.

GABOR, A., and C. W. J. GRANGER, "The Pricing of New Products," *Scientific Business,* August 1965, pp. 141-50.

KOTLER, P., *Marketing Management,* 3rd ed., Chap. 10. Englewood Cliffs, N.J.: Prentice-Hall, 1976.

LIVESEY, F., *Pricing.* London: Macmillan, 1976.

PALDA, K. S., *Pricing Decisions and Marketing Policy,* Englewood Cliffs, N.J.: Prentice-Hall, 1971.

PETERSON, R. A., "The Price-Perceived Quality Relationship: Experimental Evidence," *Journal of Marketing Research,* 7 (November 1970), 525-28.

SABEL, H., "On Pricing New Products," *German Economic Review,* 11, No. 4 (1973), 292-311.

SCHERER, F. M., *Industrial Market Structure and Industrial Performance,* Chaps. 8, 11, and 12. Chicago: Rand McNally, 1970.

SILBERSTON, A., "Price Behavior of Firms," *Economic Journal,* 80 (September 1970), 511-82.

SIMON, J. L., *Applied Managerial Economics*, Chaps. 4-6. Englewood Cliffs, N.J.: Prentice-Hall, 1975.

WESTON, J. F., "Pricing Behavior of Large Firms," *Western Economic Journal,* 10 (March 1972), 1-18.

# 12

# Competitive Bids and Price Quotes

## 12.1 INTRODUCTION

In this chapter we consider the pricing decision that is taken in a certain type of imperfect market; namely, that in which there are a number of sellers who generally cannot or do not communicate with each other, and who seek to provide a product or service to a single buyer. The buyer makes it known that he or she wishes to purchase a particular product or service, and the sellers tender their bids or quotes for the supply of that product or service. If the suppliers are quoting to a particular set of specifications, the buyer would presumably choose the lowest bid, whereas if there are quality differences in the products or services offered by the suppliers, the buyer must decide which of the tenders represents the "best deal," by considering both the price and the quality differences.

This type of pricing decision is found in a great variety of markets. There is a tendency to think of competitive bidding simply in terms of large contracts for bridges, dams, highways, and buildings, but an essentially similar market situation exists for a wide range of industrial and household products. Business firms frequently call for price quotes on a specified volume of a particular product, component part, or raw material. Supplies of everything from office stationery to ball bearings may be purchased in this manner. Similarly, whenever the householder requires someone to fix the refrigerator, unplug the sink, repair the automobile, and perform a variety of other goods and services, he or she might consider two or more price quotes from prospective suppliers. Each supplier should expect the buyer to have obtained price quotes from other suppliers, or at least to have a general awareness of the appropriate price level, and will recognize that if his quote is relatively too high the business will go elsewhere. On the other hand, if the quote is relatively too low, the supplier will get the business but it will be less profitable business than it might have been.

The pricing problem in this type of market is essentially that the seller must choose a price high enough to provide a sufficient contribution to overheads and profits, yet low enough to ensure that a sufficient volume of work is actually obtained. In all the above situations, however, the supplier must choose the price in an environment of considerable uncertainty as to the behavior of the competitors. When compared with the amount of price information generated by established markets, this type of market situation generates very little information, since each transaction is, in effect, a "one-shot" sale with little relationship to previous sales, and little information value for future sales.

To solve this pricing problem, we proceed to find first the absolute minimum bid or quote the supplier should ask, such that obtaining the contract does not cause the supplier to suffer a loss as the result of this pricing decision. We then consider higher price levels to find the optimal bid or quote, trading off the increased profitability of higher quotes against the reduced likelihood of obtaining the contract at those higher prices.

## 12.2   THE INCREMENTAL COST OF THE JOB

The absolute minimum price that the supplier should consider is the incremental cost associated with being awarded the contract and completing production and delivery of the specified goods and services. At this price the incremental revenues would be just equal to the incremental costs, and hence no contribution is earned, but more importantly, perhaps, no loss is incurred as a result of accepting the contract. Finding the level of the minimum bid price thus seems to be the relatively simple matter of calculating and/or estimating the incremental costs associated with the particular contract. In practice, however, the calculation of the incremental costs may be a matter of considerable difficulty, since it includes not only the immediate out-of-pocket costs but also the opportunity costs and the net present value of future costs and revenues which may be expected to vary as a result of this contract. Let us examine each of these factors in turn.

### Immediate Out-of-Pocket Costs

Immediate out-of-pocket costs consist of the direct and explicit costs associated with undertaking and completing the project. Included are such cost categories as direct materials, direct labor, and variable overhead. For each of these cost categories we must be careful to include only those amounts that are expected to be paid for the purchases of materials, labor and supplies, and services required to complete production and delivery of the specified goods and services. These may be estimated on the basis of requirements for similar projects in the past, given present cost levels, plus a trend factor if one is apparent and the production will take an appreciable period of time.

In some cases an item of capital equipment must be purchased for a particular job and will have a useful life remaining after the completion of the present job. Incremental reasoning implies that the whole cost is applied to the present job, and that the machine will not be part of the incremental cost on any subsequent jobs, if these in fact materialize. If ownership of the item will allow a stream of revenues to be earned in the future, the expected net present value of these revenues (or contributions) should enter the present decision, since they are incremental to this decision.[1]

### Opportunity Costs

The opportunity cost of undertaking and completing a specific project is the value of the resources employed (that is, their contribution) in their best alternative usage. Hence if plant, equipment, and personnel are lying idle, the opportunity cost of using them for a particular contract is zero. On the other hand, if these resources are currently employed in a project that will have to be set aside, delayed, or canceled, the contribution that would have been derived from this alternate project must enter the incremental costs as an opportunity cost. A firm might decide to submit a tender on a specific project, and if successful in that tender may choose to defer completion of another project already in process. To the extent provided by the penalty clause in the earlier contract, this decision to defer completion will cost the firm money that is an incremental cost occasioned by receipt of the latter contract. To the extent that a project in process simply is delayed and is completed later, the opportunity cost is the present value of the contribution when the project is finally completed less the present value of the contribution when it otherwise would have been completed.

### Goodwill or Illwill Generated

Decisions made today change the environment for future decisions. On the one hand, successful completion of a project might lead to good publicity in the future from that particular buyer and a continuing stream of sales both to that particular buyer and others over the longer term. Alternatively, delaying other jobs in process or failing to bid on particular jobs could cause the generation of illwill, such that future sales are inhibited. The contribution or loss of contribution expected in the future as a result of the present decision must be converted to present value terms and added to or subtracted from the immediate out-of-pocket and opportunity costs in order to more closely approximate the incremental costs of the project.

### Capacity Utilization Considerations

Another consideration is the capacity utilization rate of the supplier in question. When the firm is at or near full capacity, it must consider the additional incremental costs that will be incurred if it obtains the contract, such as overtime labor rates, outside contracting, penalty charges associated with existing contracts, and any other additional costs, and hence its minimum bid price must be higher to the extent that these costs are incurred. On the other hand, if most of the firm's resources are idle, failure to get this particular job may be followed

---

[1] The practice of apportioning the capital cost of an item over the present and future jobs implies a probability of unity that these future contracts will be gained. This may be an overstatement of the probabilities, of course, and may induce the firm to purchase an item, the cost of which may never be recouped. Moreover, the simple allocation of a cost over future jobs ignores the fact that a dollar received now is worth more than a dollar received in the future.

by layoffs of personnel, with subsequent rehiring and retraining expense. To the extent that these costs are foreseen, their present value should be subtracted from the immediate out-of-pocket and opportunity costs in order to find the total incremental costs of the project.[2]

### Bid Preparation Costs

An expense that one may be tempted to include as an incremental cost associated with obtaining the contract is the cost of bid preparation and submission. These costs include the costs associated with visiting the job site, examining specifications, estimating the labor and materials requirements, computing the strength and other qualitative requirements of the materials, and, finally, costing all elements in order to decide upon the appropriate bid price. For some tenders a cash deposit must accompany the bid to indicate the supplier's "good faith," and the interest forgone on this sum is in effect a cost of bid submission. Typically, however, these costs are not incremental costs.

To see this, note that the bid-pricing decision actually consists of two stages, since the supplier must decide (1) whether or not to bid on the contract and (2) at what price (and quality features) to bid. The first stage is in effect the decision whether or not to incur bid preparation and submission costs. Firms that continually submit bids on various contracts can be expected to maintain some people or a department whose function it is to prepare bid submissions. The cost of these services is not incremental to any specific project but is an overhead cost incurred as a result of being in this type of business. Nevertheless, firms may incur incremental bid preparation and submission costs, for consulting services, outside computer time, and other expenses. In any event, these costs are associated with the decision to bid or not to bid and are not incremental to the subsequent decision as to the exact level of the bid.

The decision to bid or not bid presumably is taken on the basis of such factors as expected profitability, capacity utilization, goodwill considerations, and the personal preferences of the decision maker. If the decision maker feels that there is a "reasonable" chance of obtaining the contract at a "reasonable" price, that capacity will be available to complete the project, and that goodwill and personal preferences will be served by obtaining the contract, then a bid will be prepared. The incremental costs of bid preparation and submission must enter this decision. Once this decision has been taken and these costs have been incurred, however, they are *sunk* costs as far as any subsequent decision is concerned. They become part of the overheads that (it is hoped) will be contributed to by the attainment of this particular contract or by other bids that are subsequently successful. While it would be gratifying to cover these costs in each case, and certainly the firm must cover them over a prolonged period of time if

---

[2] It may be argued that a firm will incur a loss on a contract now in order to gain experience, build up a clientele, or obtain some other benefit. Incremental reasoning requires the expected net present value of these benefits to enter the current decision problem. If the expected present value of all incremental costs exceeds the expected present value of all incremental revenues, and hence an incremental loss would be incurred, the firm should *not* undertake the contract.

it is to stay in business, these costs are not incremental to the *pricing* decision and thus do not enter the calculation of the absolute minimum bid price or quote.

## 12.3   THE OPTIMAL BID PRICE

Once we have ascertained the incremental costs associated with a particular contract, choice of the *actual* bid price amounts to the choice of the contribution we hope to make to overheads and profits. If we ask a higher price, the job will be more lucrative, but we will be less likely to get the contract, since competitive suppliers are more likely to have tendered below this price. On the other hand, if we ask a lower price, this will mean a smaller contribution to overheads and profits, but a greater likelihood of obtaining the contract. The optimal bid price will be the price that is most likely to best serve the decision maker's objectives. In the following sections we shall examine a hypothetical bidding problem under a variety of objectives.

### Expected Value Analysis

You will recall from Chapter 2 that in a situation of uncertainty, the expected value criterion is appropriate for the decision maker who wishes to maximize contribution to overheads and profits and is willing to let the "law of averages" work in his or her favor. Thus the decision maker expects to make this type of decision a relatively large number of times and expects the actual contribution to overheads and profits over a period to approximate the sum of the expected values of the decisions that are made.

To calculate the expected value of each bid price, we need to obtain estimates of the probability of success at each bid price. Later in this chapter we shall examine the factors that underlie the assignment of probabilities to each bid price level, but for the moment let us assume that we have estimated the probabilities of success at each price level, as shown in Table 12.1. In that table we show six bid prices, ranging from the minimum bid price which just covers incremental costs, and increasing by arbitrary intervals of $5,000. The contribution at each bid price is shown, and the expected contribution is the product of the contribution and the probability of success at each bid price level. Note that each bid price has its own distribution of probabilities for success or failure, and hence we should not expect the probabilities over various bid prices to add to unity; rather, the probabilitiy of success plus the probability of failure at a particular bid price should add to unity.

From the table it can be seen that the expected contribution is highest for the bid price of $35,000, and hence we would recommend this price level if the objective function of the decision maker is simply to maximize contribution to overheads and profits over a number of similar decision problems.

Note that the information in Table 12.1 might have been presented alternatively in the form of a decision tree.

**Table 12.1**
Expected value analysis of various bid prices

| Bid Price ($) | Incremental Cost ($) | Contribution ($) | Probability of Success | Expected Contribution ($) |
|---|---|---|---|---|
| 25,000 | 25,000 | – | 0.9 | – |
| 30,000 | 25,000 | 5,000 | 0.7 | 3,500 |
| 35,000 | 25,000 | 10,000 | 0.5 | 5,000 |
| 40,000 | 25,000 | 15,000 | 0.3 | 4,500 |
| 45,000 | 25,000 | 20,000 | 0.2 | 4,000 |
| 50,000 | 25,000 | 25,000 | 0.1 | 2,500 |

### Aesthetic and Political Considerations

It is perhaps unreasonable to expect a decision maker to make his or her choice simply on the basis of quantifiable cost and revenue considerations. In some cases certain aesthetic considerations enter the bidding process. Suppose the project alluded to in Table 12.1 was something other than a straightforward and normal project. On the one hand, it may appeal to the artistic tastes of the decision maker; on the other hand, it may involve considerable amounts of dirty and/or uncomfortable work. In the first case, we might expect a decision maker to choose a bid price somewhat below the expected value, since the nonmonetary gratification received by the decision maker would offset some of the monetary compensation involved in the higher bid price. But if the job is expected to be dirty, uncomfortable, or inconvenient in some nonmonetary way, we might expect the decision maker's bid to be somewhat above the $35,000 indicated by the expected value criterion, since the nonmonetary disutility attached to the job would need to be offset by some additional monetary compensation.

A further consideration that may cause the decision maker to choose a bid price different from the one with the maximum expected contribution is the possibility that the decision maker may see personal gain in bidding at a different price level. We noted in Chapter 2 that individual decision makers within an organization may practice self-serving or political behavior. This may be "functional" political behavior in that it causes certain actions that at the same time promote the organization's objectives, or it may be "dysfunctional" in that it serves the decision maker's purposes but hinders the attainment of the organization's objectives.[3] Since it is not unlikely that the objectives of the decision maker and the organization will differ on occasion, we should not expect all decisions to reflect single-minded pursuit of company goals. Hence if the decision maker feels there is some personal gain likely to follow a bid price above or below that indicated by the expected value criterion, then the actual bid price may well deviate from that standard.

The personal gains to the decision maker may include a wide variety of

[3] See S. P. Robbins, *The Administrative Process* (Englewood Cliffs, N.J.: Prentice-Hall, 1976), p. 64.

367

tangible and intangible benefits which the decision maker may expect to receive as the result of a particular decision's being taken. Hence a relatively low bid price may be chosen when the decision maker feels there is something to gain by winning the contract, and oppositely, a relatively high bid price might be tendered when it is felt that the purchaser owes a favor to the supplier, and the supplier expects the purchaser to settle this debt. Simple friendship between the supplier and the purchaser might also cause a lower bid price to be submitted, and the reduction from the expected value bid price can be ascribed to political motivations; namely, the supplier's recognition of the personal value of the buyer's friendship. Note that these political considerations are separate from the goodwill considerations that we include in the incremental cost calculation.

### The Certainty Equivalent Criterion

You will recall that the certainty equivalent of a gamble is the sum of money that the decision maker regards as equivalent to the value of the gamble. Hence if we were to determine the certainty equivalent of the gamble involved in bidding at each price level, the bid with the highest certainty equivalent would be the one that the decision maker feels is the superior bid price. The certainty equivalent approach is appropriate for decisions that are made on a "one-shot" basis or, at least, are significantly different from decisions that have been taken in the past and are expected to be taken in the future. That is, where the law of averages is not an appropriate guide, we turn to the decision maker's subjective evaluation of the worth of each gamble, rather than the more objective expected value analysis. A further virtue of the certainty equivalent approach is that it will include the aesthetic and political considerations influencing the decision, and in addition it incorporates other nonmonetary or nonquantifiable factors influencing the decision. In determining the certainty equivalent of each bid price, the decision maker would use all information at his or her disposal, and using judgment and experience would decide which bid price level to tender. If a decision maker claims to have chosen the bid price level without any theoretical guidelines, but on the basis of experience or by a "seat-of-the-pants" judgment, we must expect that the highest certainty equivalent would be assigned to the price level tendered. If not, then the decision maker either is not telling us something or has made a suboptimal decision.

In the following section we note that, in practice, firms rarely use the theoretical guidelines outlined above. However, the actual decision taken may not diverge significantly from the one that would be indicated by the factors indicated above. Perhaps the greatest value of these guidelines consists of forcing an evaluation of the decision about to be taken; that is, the decision maker may be able to justify the decision, or revise that decision, after consideration of the theoretical guidelines. If the proposed bid price level is not the one indicated by the expected value analysis, or alternatively if the probabilities (which would need to be attached in order to bring the proposed bid price and the bid price with the highest expected value into agreement) were not reasonable probability values, the decision maker must reevaluate his or her thinking.

## Cost-Plus Bids and Quotes

In practice most firms choose their bidding price or quote on the basis of a markup-pricing procedure. That is, the incremental or full costs of the proposed project are estimated, and to this figure is added a percentage markup to cover overhead and/or profits. This cost-plus pricing policy is not necessarily inferior to the expected value approach, however. Given the information costs and man-power involvement associated with the above theoretical approach, the cost-plus pricing procedure can afford to be wrong to the extent of the cost that would be involved in making a better decision. Where the firm makes many quotes on relatively similar projects, the cost-plus approach allows the decision-making procedure to become routine and simplified, and therefore less expensive.

Let us compare the cost-plus approach with the expected value approach. In Table 12.1 we showed the incremental cost of a particular project as $25,000 and the optimal bid price as $35,000, since at that bid price the expected contribution was maximized. Note that if the firm had applied a 40 percent markup to incremental cost, it would have arrived at the same bid price. Alternatively, suppose the firm had allocated $6,800 of overhead expense to the specific project and had applied a 10 percent markup to the full costs of $31,800. The bid price would be approximately $35,000. The point being made here is that there is a percentage markup, whether applied to incremental or fully allocated costs, which would give the same solution as the expected value analysis. In fact, the two approaches will indicate the same bid price if the percentage markup is determined with an eye to the probability of success at each level of markup. If the decision maker's objective is to maximize the contribution to overheads and profits over a period of time, the judgmental or "seat-of-the-pants" calculation of the markup price should arrive at the same bid price as would the expected value approach. If asked to reconcile the two approaches, the manager would presumably adjust probabilities until the answers match. If this involves an unreasonable assumption of probabilities, the decision maker may wish to change the decision or claim that the objective function being pursued is somewhat different from that of maximization of the contribution to overheads and profits.

What determines the size of the markup in the judgmental approach? Presumably the markup percentage will be adjusted up or down over time so that the firm will obtain the desired degree of capacity utilization. When capacity utilization is low, and hence contracts become relatively more desirable, we would expect lower markups; and when capacity utilization is already quite high, we would expect higher markups. You will note that this is consistent with the expected value approach when incremental costs are calculated as indicated above. The markup percentage applied should also be expected to vary with the longer-term goodwill expected to be associated with a particular contract; if there are expected to be longer-term benefits consequent upon this particular contract, we would expect a lower markup percentage than otherwise. Similarly, the aesthetic and political considerations would be expected to influence the markup percentage (and hence the bid price) up or down in the same manner as indicated in the preceding section.

Thus, if the appropriate markup percentage has been discovered, the firm may continue to apply this markup to its incremental or full costs until industry or market conditions change significantly. That is, the cost-plus pricing procedure, if equivalent to the expected value criterion initially, will continue to serve in its stead while outside conditions do not change. If competitors become more desperate for business, we would expect the probability of success at each bid price to fall, and hence the bid price suggested by the expected value approach is likely to be somewhat lower. Similarly, using the judgmental approach, we would expect the markup percentage to be reduced under these circumstances.

Under inflationary conditions where the costs of materials and labor can be expected to increase over time, the cost-plus pricing procedure preserves the status quo. If it is optimal at first, it remains optimal as long as the relative costs of other bidders and the nature of the buyer do not change. If these conditions do change, the firm will not be getting sufficient business, or may be getting too much business, and will adjust the markup accordingly on future bids.

When there is continuing inflation, and the future rate of inflation is uncertain, firms may wish to bid on the basis of actual cost plus a certain percentage margin for overheads and/or profits. That is, no specific price is stated, and the cost base is that which is actually spent during the completion of the project, presumably subject to the buyer's audit. Insertion of this escalation clause in a price tender will make the firm's bid relatively unattractive if other firms tender bids at similar levels but without the escalation clause. Hence, as in any oligopolistic pricing problem, the simultaneous action of competitors is important in determining the demand response to the pricing strategy of the firm.[4]

## 12.4 ESTIMATING THE PROBABILITY OF SUCCESS

In the above sections we skipped over the problem associated with the assignment of probabilities as to the success or failure of the bid at each price level. Let us now examine this problem in some detail. Since the theoretical approaches and the cost-plus approach may be seen as alternative and possibly equivalent ways of determining the optimal price level, the probability of success at each bid price level is an important underlying factor in both approaches. The probability of a successful bid at a given price level depends upon two major factors: the competition for this particular contract, and the attributes desired by this particular buyer.

### Evaluation of the Competition

We must first ascertain whether or not there are likely to be any other bidders on this particular contract. If not, then the probability of attaining the contract must have a value of one, and we could presumably set the price at the highest

---

[4] In many instances, of course, a company's successful bid will be too low in view of subsequent increases in costs. This is, unfortunately, one of the perils of dealing in an uncertain world, and it emphasizes the importance of careful cost estimation and forecasting.

level that we expect the buyer will accept. More likely there will be other bidders, however. How many other bidders is an important consideration, since the greater the number of bidders in the market, the smaller we should expect the probability of success to be at each price level. The next piece of information is the identities of the other bidders. If we can identify individual firms, this may add information, since we may know something of their current capacity utilization, their attitude toward this type of project, and their previous behavior patterns in this type of bidding situation.

To illustrate the importance of knowing how many and which of the rival firms are submitting bids on a contract, let us consider the following example.[5] Suppose we have calculated our incremental costs to be $50,000 for a particular contract that is similar to dozens of contracts we have tendered for in the last year. Over the past year, four other firms have also been tendering for the same contracts. In Table 12.2 we show the proportion of times that our price level was below each rival's tendered price (or would have been) at each of seven bid prices equal to and above our incremental costs.

Table 12.2
**Success rates against rival firms in previous bidding
on similar contracts**

| Our Bid ($) | Success Rate against Rival | | | | Average Success Rate (ASR) |
| | A | B | C | D | |
|---|---|---|---|---|---|
| 50,000 | 1.00 | 0.98 | 0.95 | 0.99 | 0.9800 |
| 55,000 | 0.92 | 0.88 | 0.84 | 0.94 | 0.8950 |
| 60,000 | 0.80 | 0.76 | 0.72 | 0.79 | 0.7675 |
| 65,000 | 0.61 | 0.55 | 0.49 | 0.60 | 0.5625 |
| 70,000 | 0.43 | 0.37 | 0.32 | 0.41 | 0.3825 |
| 75,000 | 0.24 | 0.18 | 0.15 | 0.21 | 0.1950 |
| 80,000 | 0.10 | 0.03 | 0.00 | 0.09 | 0.0550 |

If past behavior is expected to be the best indicator of present behavior (due to the absence of any significant change in the situation of each of our rivals), we can use the "success ratios" as an estimate of the probability of being successful at each bid price level when any one of the rival firms is expected to bid against us. For example, if we intend to bid $60,000 the probability of success is 0.80 if Firm A is the only other firm bidding, 0.76 if B is the only other bidder, 0.72 if C is the only other bidder, and 0.79 if D is the only other firm bidding on this particular contract.

If we expect two or more firms to submit bids, and we know the identities of those firms, we may estimate the probabilities of success at each price level by finding the *joint* probability of our underbidding those firms on this occasion. For example, if we know that A and B are submitting bids, the probability of

[5] This example is loosely based on a similar example in P. Livesey, *Pricing* (London: Macmillan, 1976), pp. 99-102.

our being successful at a price of $60,000 is 0.80 × 0.76 = 0.608. Similarly, if we expect A, B, and C to submit bids, the probability of success with the $60,000 bid is 0.80 × 0.76 × 0.72 = 0.438. And finally, if all four firms are expected to bid, the probability of success for the $60,000 bid is 0.80 × 0.76 × 0.72 × 0.79 = 0.347. Notice the impact upon the probability as the number of bidding firms increases. As more firms enter the bidding, it is increasingly more likely that any one firm will undercut our bid price, at every price level. If the identities of the firms submitting bids are not known, it will be necessary to calculate probabilities on the basis of the average success rate (ASR). If only one rival, identity unknown, is expected to bid, the ASR will be our best estimate as to the probability of success on this occasion. If two or more rivals, identities unknown, are expected to bid, we must find the joint probability of our bid being the lowest, by finding the square, cubic, or quartic value of the average success rate. These are shown in Table 12.3, which clearly demonstrates the influence that increasing the number of rival firms has upon the probability of success at each bid price level.

We should be wary of naive projections, however. The calculated probabilities are based on past behavior patterns with no input reflecting the present situation. If the present situation is unchanged and we have no other reason to doubt, then these will be our best estimates of the success probabilities. If, on the other hand, we discover that one or more of our rivals are currently experiencing relatively low capacity utilization, we should expect them to bid lower than in the past, and hence we should revise the success probabilities downward. Alternatively, if rivals are at full capacity, we should expect higher bids than usual and accordingly revise the probabilities upward. In fact, all the issues that would cause our own bid price to be higher or lower should be investigated in the context of our rivals in order to discover whether there is any reason to expect their prices to be higher or lower for the current bidding situation. These issues, you will recall, include goodwill considerations, aesthetic and political considerations, and the costs of layoffs, closure, retraining, overtime, and other costs associated with the degree of capacity utilization.

**Table 12.3**
**Calculated probabilities of success with increasing number of competitors, identities unknown**

| Our Bid ($) | Number of Rivals | | | |
|---|---|---|---|---|
| | 1 (ASR) | 2 $(ASR)^2$ | 3 $(ASR)^3$ | 4 $(ASR)^4$ |
| 50,000 | 0.9800 | 0.9604 | 0.9412 | 0.9224 |
| 55,000 | 0.8950 | 0.8010 | 0.7169 | 0.6416 |
| 60,000 | 0.7675 | 0.5891 | 0.4521 | 0.3470 |
| 65,000 | 0.5625 | 0.3164 | 0.1780 | 0.1001 |
| 70,000 | 0.3825 | 0.1463 | 0.0560 | 0.0214 |
| 75,000 | 0.1950 | 0.0380 | 0.0074 | 0.0014 |
| 80,000 | 0.0550 | 0.0030 | 0.0002 | 0.0000 |

## Evaluation of the Buyer

Our first consideration when evaluating the buyer is whether or not that buyer will consider any other factor besides the bid price, presuming that all specifications have been met. If not, then our concern shifts back to the evaluation of competitors and the likely prices they will each bid. If so, we must attempt to evaluate the buyer's appreciation of the attributes involved in our supplying the project. For example, we may use higher-quality materials, take more care in finishing, or have some little artistic flair, and we must attempt to set the price in accordance with the value we estimate that the buyer will place on the additional attributes. Other factors such as our meeting the delivery schedule, having sufficient quality control, and having good labor relations and financial stability will be important to the buyer. Clearly, if we think the buyer doubts the verisimilitude of any of these issues, we must adjust the bid price downward to the extent we feel will put the buyer at ease.

Finding out the buyer's exact wants and needs and then tailoring the qualitative aspects of our bid to suit the buyer's particular preferences will improve our chances of winning the contract at any given price level, *ceteris paribus.* To the extent that we feel we have better catered to the buyer's preferences, as compared with rivals' proposals, we should adjust the success probabilities upward at each price level. Alternatively, if we feel we are bidding from a weak position in a particular case—for example if this buyer had indicated skepticism about our ability to meet the delivery deadlines—we should revise the success probabilities downward. These revisions of the probabilities are likely to shift the maximum expected value to a lower bid level.

To ascertain the value that the buyer is likely to attach to these qualitative and objective considerations, we need to study the buyer's previous purchasing behavior and/or make value judgments based on certain characteristics, such as income, age, and social status. Better still, we could attempt to obtain the information concerning the way in which the buyer chooses among the competing bids. Let us now turn to this issue.

## The Buyer's Problem: Optimal Purchasing

The buyer's problem is to choose the tender that not only has an agreeable price attached to it but also includes the most desirable package of attributes in association with that price. By way of example, let us consider the purchasing decision of a householder who is contemplating having new windows installed in his somewhat older house. He receives three quotes, as shown in Table 12.4, after inviting representatives from each company to quote on the job. Notice that there is a difference not only in the prices quoted but in the qualitative aspects of the offers.

Which quote should the consumer accept? The answer obviously depends upon a variety of considerations, including the consumer's financial liquidity, his aesthetic feelings and misgivings about the different types of materials and construction, the length of time he expects to own the house, and his attitude toward the risk and uncertainty associated with the different warranties. In the

Table 12.4
Details of price quotes on windows

|  | Company A | Company B | Company C |
|---|---|---|---|
| Price | $2,200 | $1,280 | $1,050 |
| Frame | Baked enamel on steel | Baked enamel on aluminum | Anodized aluminum |
| Glass | Two separate 5-mm panes | Double 5-mm "thermopane" | Double 3-mm "thermopane" |
| Warranty | 10 years, complete | 5 years, complete | 3 years, complete |

initial discussions with the buyer, the salesperson should attempt to find out exactly what the consumer wants and is prepared to pay for and should then tailor the bid accordingly. The essential consideration is whether the attributes involved in the different tenders are worth as much (to the consumer) as the suppliers are asking. Clearly we cannot make the decision for this consumer, but we can say that if he chooses the bid made by Company B, this indicates that he values the attributes provided by Company B for that price more highly than he values the attributes provided by the others relative to their prices.

Suppose the consumer telephones Company A to inform its salesperson that he has decided to select the offer from Company B. Suppose then that the Company A salesperson revises his price estimate down to $1,500, deciding to accept a smaller contribution on this job if he can get it. Can we then predict that the consumer will change his patronage to Company A? Again we are unable to say, but it is now more likely that Company A's offer will be preferable to the consumer than it was at the higher price.

### Value Analysis

Industrial purchasers are often required to rationalize their purchasing decisions in some objective manner in order to demonstrate that their purchasing policy is consistent with company objectives. A means of arriving at a purchasing decision (or for *post hoc* rationalization of a purchasing decision) is the technique known as value analysis. Using this approach the decision maker identifies the attributes that are considered desirable and which may be present in each of the tenders, applies weights to those attributes in order of importance to the decision maker, ranks and scales each bidder under each attribute, multiplies the weight by the scale, and chooses the bid that has the highest weighted score.

This procedure might best be illustrated in terms of the following example. Suppose three suppliers have submitted bids on a project that the buyer has put out for tender. In Table 12.5 we indicate that the attributes of interest to this purchaser are price, quality, likelihood of meeting the delivery date, alternative production facilities in case of strike or damage to the original plant, and the longer-term goodwill issues associated with good supplier relations. We presume that the purchaser values these attributes in the proportions shown by the weights. The suppliers are then ranked in terms of their performance on each attribute: the better the performance, the higher the scale. Note that for price

**Table 12.5**
**Value analysis in purchasing**

| Attribute | Weight | Supplier A | | Supplier B | | Supplier C | |
|---|---|---|---|---|---|---|---|
| | | Scale | Score | Scale | Score | Scale | Score |
| Price | 7 | 1 | 7 | 3 | 21 | 4 | 28 |
| Quality | 4 | 5 | 20 | 2 | 8 | 1 | 4 |
| Delivery | 3 | 1 | 3 | 1 | 3 | 2 | 6 |
| Alternatives | 2 | 0 | 0 | 2 | 4 | 1 | 2 |
| Goodwill | 1 | 1 | 1 | 2 | 2 | 3 | 3 |
| Total score | | | 31 | | 38 | | 43 |

Supplier A receives a value of 1, Supplier B is assigned a value of 3, and Supplier C is assigned a value of 4. This indicates the Supplier C has tendered the lowest price, followed somewhat closely by the price of Supplier B, with Supplier A's price being a greater distance above. The scale values given to each of the suppliers need not be consecutive numbers if the attributes are different by different amounts.

Supplier A apparently promises the highest quality, considerably ahead of Supplier B, who in turn offers a slightly higher quality product than Supplier C. In terms of delivery schedule, Supplier C appears to be slightly preferable to Suppliers A and B, who are judged equal in this respect. Supplier B has alternative facilities, which minimizes the risk of problems arising; Supplier C similarly has one production alternative, whereas Supplier A has no alternative sources of supply. Finally, Supplier C is most important with respect to longer-term goodwill considerations, followed by Supplier B and Supplier A. Weighting the scales assigned by the weights for each attribute, we derive each supplier's score on each attribute, and these may be summed to find each supplier's total score over the attributes deemed desirable by the purchaser. Given this system of weighting and scaling the various attributes, it seems that Supplier C has the most desirable tender, since the weighted sum of the scores is greatest.

The choice of the weights assigned to each attribute is essentially arbitrary, depending upon the attitudes and judgment of the decision maker. Similarly, the ranking and then the scaling of the suppliers in terms of these attributes are at the discretion of the decision maker. Finally, other attributes may be included in the analysis, such as the previous experience of suppliers with this type of project, financial stability, quality and reputation of personnel, provision of technical or consulting services, inventory charges, and shipping policy. A different decision maker may score the same three bids differently, such that Supplier A or Supplier B becomes the successful bidder.[6]

The importance of value analysis in purchasing is to force the decision maker to rationalize and scrutinize the purchasing decision. The choice of weights,

[6] The buyer is likely to set some minimum acceptable level or standard for each attribute which must be met in order for the seller's bid to be considered. For example, if the quality or delivery date was unacceptable or was expected to be unacceptable, the seller would be excluded from any further consideration.

value scales, and desirable attributes must be stated explicitly and is thus subject to argumentation by the decision maker's peers and superiors. Out of the discussion should arise a consensus of those weights, scales, and attributes that are considered to be consistent with the firm's objectives. Purchasing decisions may thus be justified on this "relatively objective" basis, rather than as simply being arrived at on the basis of unstated preferences and assumptions.[7]

From the supplier's point of view it would be immeasurably valuable to obtain the criteria upon which the purchasing decision is made. With this information the supplier could tailor the bid price and other features such that the bid would score more highly and/or be more desirable to the buyer. In the previous case of the windows, the supplier should attempt to ascertain the likes and dislikes, willingness to pay for certain features, and other information about the prospective customer. In the industrial purchasing situation the potential supplier should attempt to judge which features the buyer regards as more or less important. In both cases the supplier will then be in a better position to supply exactly what is desired by the purchaser and will thus be more likely to be the successful bidder on the contract.

### Collusive Bidding

In the foregoing we have presumed that the firms bidding for a particular contract do so without benefit of any interaction or direct information flow between and among the potential suppliers. Where a small group of firms continually find themselves bidding against each other, it is not surprising that they will seek better information concerning each other's intended bids. Since retaliatory action cannot remove the immediate gains of a successful low bid, the firms are likely to try to eliminate the possibility of a rival's submitting an unexpectedly low bid. One means of achieving this is to obtain prior agreement among firms as to their bid prices or pricing procedures.

We might expect collusive practices to be more likely to exist in industries in which there is both the ability and the "necessity" to bid collusively. Regarding the ability to collude, where there are relatively few firms we expect firms to be able to communicate with all other firms more easily and effectively. Moreover, the actions of any one firm are more readily visible to the other firms, which assists in the policing of any agreement. Regarding the "necessity" to collude, where contracts are relatively few and far between and are of relatively high value, the incentive will be stronger for each firm to submit a relatively low bid in order to obtain the contract, even if this does not generate a profit above the fully allocated costs of operation. The longer-term result of this could be that all firms are pricing below full costs and that no firm earns a normal profit. As an alternative to some of the firms being forced out of the industry, the firms may see collusive bidding as a necessity to avoid a degeneration of prices to unprofitable levels.

*Identical Bids.*    The competing suppliers for a particular contract may agree to submit identical bid prices at a level that ensures that the business will be

[7] Value analysis is implicit in any purchasing decision. It is done explicitly in many companies for the benefits stated above.

sufficiently profitable to the successful bidder. The purchaser is then forced to select the successful bidder on some criteria other than price level. This situation is akin to nonprice competition in established market situations. The suppliers will attempt to include those attributes in their bid that are desired by the purchaser such that at identical prices their bid appears to be the better deal. Suppliers may consider this nonprice competition to be a "more ethical" form of competition, since the successful bidder is rewarded for the expertise and efficiency involved in supplying a particular bundle of attributes at the given price, rather than for the simple ability to cut prices below what rivals are expected to bid.

*Bid Rotation.* Bid rotation is a method designed to allocate the available business among the competing suppliers in proportions agreeable to all. In effect, the firms take turns in submitting the lowest bid such that the available business is allocated around the industry. It is not necessarily allocated in equal shares among the competing suppliers, but more likely it will be allocated on the basis of historical market shares or current bargaining power.

As noted in Chapter 11, however, collusive price fixing is illegal, and the firm may face prosecution for engaging in this practice. A second factor militating against the longer-term operation of collusive bidding in any particular industry is the profit incentive that individual firms may have to undercut the agreed price. Firms that are not getting sufficient work to obtain their desired degree of capacity utilization may break out of the agreement when an important contract is at stake. If the available business is not shared among the competing suppliers in a manner that is suitable to all, it is likely that a particular supplier will be motivated to undercut the agreed price in order to obtain the additional business.

While the exchange of information involved in collusive bidding operates to reduce the uncertainty involved in the pricing decision, the risk remains that one or more competing suppliers will operate at variance with their stated intentions. Thus it is still important to evaluate and form expectations about the probable behavior of competitors. To the extent that rivals are expected not to maintain their previous behavior pattern, or are expected not to carry through with their stated intent, the decision maker may wish to adjust the bid price accordingly.[8]

### Disclosure of Bids

After the contract is awarded to the successful bidder, the bid prices of other suppliers may be disclosed to all suppliers or to the public in general. The disclosure of the bid prices generates considerable information which may be valuable to the sellers in their future bidding policies. The unsuccessful bidders will obtain information as to the amount they overbid, and the successful bidder will obtain information as to the amount that his bid could have been increased without losing the contract. We should expect, therefore, that disclosure of bid prices would lead to a compression of the range of bids over time,

---

[8] Information concerning rival firms' bidding practices and/or intentions may be gleaned in conversation with rival decision makers at business and social gatherings, or from industry gossip. Some people even believe in industrial espionage!

since the firms would gain an appreciation of the bid levels that are likely to be tendered by the other firms in the industry. Obviously, disclosure of bids provides information useful for the initiation and the policing of collusive bidding.

From the purchaser's point of view it may be a poor strategy to disclose the bid prices after the contract is awarded, since this may lead to a compression of the bid prices nearer the center of the range of bids and may facilitate collusive bidding. This is likely to lead to an increased level of the lowest bid over time. From the purchaser's point of view it is surely better to keep the suppliers in the dark, since they are more likely to submit lower bids when they are in a greater state of uncertainty as to the bids of the other firms. We should thus expect that purchasers would not wish to disclose the bids, and in some industries bid disclosure is considered an unethical procedure. Governments, which frequently purchase goods and services in this type of market, may be required to disclose bid prices, however, in order to show their constituents that the public funds involved have been spent wisely and without corruption.

## 12.5  SUMMARY

In this chapter we have applied the incremental cost or contribution approach to competitive bids and price quotes. The relevant cost concept is the incremental cost associated with the work involved in undertaking and completing the contract, and as long as the bid price exceeds this incremental cost, some contribution will be made to overheads and profits by obtaining the contract. We considered the optimal bid price from the point of view of expected value analysis, modifying this to the extent that aesthetic, political, and other unquantifiable considerations were involved.

In practice many firms use cost-plus pricing procedures in their competitive bids and price quotes. This can be equivalent to the expected value approach, and it saves time and expense in the decision-making procedure. However, it is important that the decision maker attempt to justify the bid price in terms of the theoretical procedures to ensure that the objectives of the company (or the individual decision maker) are being served. In Table 12.6 we summarize the bidding procedure under the two alternative methodologies.

Both the expected value approach and the cost-plus approach involve an implicit or explicit estimation of the probability of success at each bid price level. The major factors involved in estimating these probabilities are the likelihood of competitors' bidding at various price levels, and the appreciation that the buyer will have for price and quality differences. This latter aspect was examined from the buyer's side to show the factors likely to be considered in choosing the successful bid. Potential suppliers would most certainly benefit by an appreciation of the factors considered important by the buyer. The probable bid prices of rivals may be estimated on the basis of information obtained through a collusive exchange of pricing plans, by the disclosure of price levels on previous bid prices, or by knowledge of rival suppliers' capacity utilization levels and other factors.

We should expect there to be a tendency for firms in some industries to bid collusively, either overtly or covertly, but the existence of collusive behavior in

**Table 12.6**
**Summary of bidding procedure**

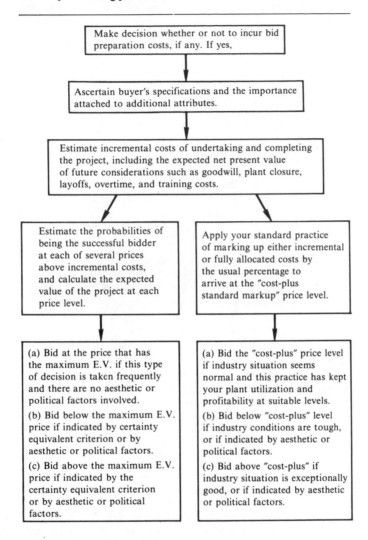

Make decision whether or not to incur bid preparation costs, if any. If yes,

Ascertain buyer's specifications and the importance attached to additional attributes.

Estimate incremental costs of undertaking and completing the project, including the expected net present value of future considerations such as goodwill, plant closure, layoffs, overtime, and training costs.

Estimate the probabilities of being the successful bidder at each of several prices above incremental costs, and calculate the expected value of the project at each price level.

Apply your standard practice of marking up either incremental or fully allocated costs by the usual percentage to arrive at the "cost-plus standard markup" price level.

(a) Bid at the price that has the maximum E.V. if this type of decision is taken frequently and there are no aesthetic or political factors involved.

(b) Bid below the maximum E.V. price if indicated by certainty equivalent criterion or by aesthetic or political factors.

(c) Bid above the maximum E.V. price if indicated by the certainty equivalent criterion or by aesthetic or political factors.

(a) Bid the "cost-plus" price level if industry situation seems normal and this practice has kept your plant utilization and profitability at suitable levels.

(b) Bid below "cost-plus" level if industry conditions are tough, or if indicated by aesthetic or political factors.

(c) Bid above "cost-plus" if industry situation is exceptionally good, or if indicated by aesthetic or political factors.

past bidding situations does not ensure that all firms will act as anticipated in the next bidding situation.

## DISCUSSION QUESTIONS

12.1 Outline three situations in which you have recently been the buyer in a competitive bidding or price quote situation. (Even if you only received one quote in each instance.)

12.2 Make a list of those items that you would expect to enter the incremental cost calculation for a contract to remove the sea gulls from the vicinity of a major coastal airport.

12.3   In calculating the incremental costs of a particular project, how would you treat the possible future cost of a lawsuit that may occur as a result of this project, where the cost of such a lawsuit may range from $10,000 to $500,000 with an associated probability distribution?

12.4   How would you value the goodwill that is expected to be generated as a result of undertaking a particular contract? If there is expected goodwill, does this mean you would be prepared to bid lower than otherwise? Why?

12.5   Explain why the strategy of choosing the bid price with the highest expected value is likely to generate the greatest contribution to overheads and profits over a large number of successful and unsuccessful bids.

12.6   Explain how the strategy of marking up incremental costs by a standard percentage (and subsequently winning some contracts and losing some contracts) may over a period of time give equivalent results as compared with the maximum expected value strategy.

12.7   Explain the logic of the declining success probability as more and more rival firms submit bids on a particular contract.

12.8   Outline the factors that would cause you to use a lower markup on incremental costs (as compared with your usual markup) in a particular bidding situation.

12.9   Explain the logic behind value analysis. What is the relationship between value analysis and attribute analysis of consumer choice behavior?

12.10   Why is collusive bidding illegal? Does it hurt the customer? The competing firms? Other firms?

## PROBLEMS

12.1   In the text it was shown that the success probabilities decline as the number of firms submitting bids increases. Using the data from Table 12.3, find the optimal bid price level

(a)   When there is one other firm bidding

(b)   When there are two other firms bidding

(c)   When there are three other firms bidding

(d)   When there are four other firms bidding

12.2   Your company is one of several companies manufacturing a special reflecting paint used for traffic signs. Your two major customers are the state and the federal Department of Transport. The federal Department of Transport has recently called for tenders for 10,000 gallons of this special paint in a light blue, to be delivered within two months after signing the contract. You can foresee being able to fit in a production run of 10,000 gallons of the blue paint and have decided to bid on the job. This particular contract is absolutely standard, similar in all respects to hundreds of contracts you have bid on in the past two years. Being government departments, the buyers always release the details of the bids received to demonstrate that no patronage is being practiced. You have collected the data on the bid prices of your competitors and have assembled these data for each of the competing firms as a ratio of your own incremental cost on each particular job. You have then calculated the percentage of the total that each firm bid less than 10 percent above your costs, less than 15 percent above, and so on, as shown in the table.

| Ratio of Rival's Bid to Your Incremental Cost | Percentage of Total Contracts on Which Rival's Bid Was Lower Than the Ratio Indicated (but higher than the preceding ratio) | | | |
|---|---|---|---|---|
| | *Rival A* | *Rival B* | *Rival C* | *Rival D* |
| 1.00 | 0.0 | 1.5 | 2.6 | 0.0 |
| 1.10 | 2.5 | 4.0 | 5.4 | 0.0 |
| 1.15 | 6.2 | 7.1 | 10.1 | 0.0 |
| 1.20 | 8.0 | 10.8 | 16.8 | 0.5 |
| 1.25 | 11.1 | 18.2 | 27.2 | 1.5 |
| 1.30 | 17.5 | 26.1 | 19.3 | 8.0 |
| 1.35 | 30.6 | 17.4 | 8.5 | 21.3 |
| 1.40 | 13.4 | 7.0 | 5.1 | 32.2 |
| 1.45 | 7.5 | 3.2 | 3.5 | 20.6 |
| 1.50 | 2.2 | 2.7 | 1.5 | 9.1 |
| 1.75 | 1.0 | 1.6 | 0.0 | 5.8 |
| 2.00 | 0.0 | 0.4 | 0.0 | 1.0 |
| | 100.0 | 100.0 | 100.0 | 100.0 |

Your incremental cost on this project has been calculated to be $76,200.

(a) Use the above information to calculate the success probabilities at markups of 10 percent, 15 percent, etc., as indicated in the first column of the table, when all four rivals are expected to submit bids.

(b) Which bid price maximizes expected contribution to overheads and profits?

(c) How would your optimal bid price be modified if only one of the firms, identity unknown, is rumored to have tendered a bid?

12.3   Tenders have been called for the fabrication of a steel watergate, and you are in the process of preparing to bid on this contract. The practice in your company has been to charge each contract with preparation costs of $2,000, which is actually about three times the actual value of time and office supplies spent on each bid but is costed this way because the company is the successful bidder only once in every three times it bids, on average. The bidding policy in the past has been to add a 15 percent margin to the incremental and allocated costs, and hence your colleague, a recent M.B.A. graduate from a rival university, insists that the appropriate bid price is $138,230 calculated as follows:

| | |
|---|---|
| Bid preparation costs | $   2,000 |
| Direct materials | 18,600 |
| Direct labor | 33,200 |
| Variable overhead | 14,400 |
| Fixed overhead | 52,000 |
| Profit margin | 18,030 |
| Suggested bid price | $138,230 |

You are a little worried that conditions in the industry have deteriorated recently. You are aware that some of your competitors have been operating below capacity, and you suspect that demand for steel-fabricated products is likely to be depressed for the coming twelve months.

(a)   What is the absolute minimum price you would bid on this contract? Explain and defend your answer.

(b)   On the basis of the information given, what bid price would you recommend?

(c)   What factors would you wish to investigate and evaluate before choosing the actual bid price?

12.4   A large department store has called for tenders for the following contracts: a truck plus its driver must be available, given one day's notice, whenever the store's own trucks are fully utilized, to deliver goods to suburban households. The expected number of days for which a truck will be required is 20, and the number of miles is expected to be 4,000, for the coming year.

You are the manager of the Clark Rent-A-Truck Company and have a number of trucks which you rent out on a day-to-day basis. One truck is a little older than the others and is always the last to be rented out because it does less for public relations than the newer trucks. In the absence of a contract with the department store, you expect this older truck to be rented out two-thirds of the 300 "rental days" this coming year. Your normal rental charge is $25.00 per day plus $0.35 per mile.

You estimate the costs of operating the older truck to be as follows, assuming 10,000 miles of rental over the coming year:

| | |
|---|---:|
| Depreciation | $ 800 |
| Interest on investment in truck | 360 |
| License fees and taxes | 125 |
| Insurance | 440 |
| Parking fees (permanently rented space) | 300 |
| Gasoline | 1,367 |
| Oil, grease, and preventive maintenance | 600 |
| Repairs | 1,450 |
| Allocated overheads | 1,650 |

You can hire a driver on one day's notice for $50 per day. A one-time cost of $400 will be involved in fitting the truck with a special loading ramp required by the contract. This ramp will not interfere with the normal use of the truck.

(a)   On the basis of this information, and making whatever assumptions you feel are necessary and reasonable, calculate the incremental cost that would be involved in accepting this contract.

(b)   What price would you bid, assuming that you wish to maximize profits and that you have no knowledge of who else will bid for this job, nor of the "going rate" for this type of job? (Outline the considerations involved and choose a bid price that would reflect *your* certainty equivalent for this gamble.)

12.5   Your company has decided to bid on a government contract to build a bridge fifty miles from the city during the coming winter. The bridge is to be of standard government design and hence should contain no unexpected in-process costs. Your present capacity utilization rate allows sufficient scope to undertake the contract if awarded. You calculate your incremental costs to be $268,000 and your fully allocated costs to be $440,000. You expect three other companies to bid on this contract, and you have assembled the following information concerning these companies.

| Consideration | Rival A | Rival B | Rival C |
|---|---|---|---|
| Capacity utilization | Near full | Sufficient slack | Very low |
| Goodwill consideration | Very concerned | Moderately concerned | Not concerned |
| Type of plant | Small and inefficient | Medium sized and efficient | Large and efficient |
| Previous bidding pattern | Incremental cost plus 35%-50% | Full cost plus 8%-12% | Full cost plus 10%-15% |
| Cost Structure | Incremental costs exceed yours by about 10% | Similar cost structure to yours | Incremental costs 20% lower but full costs similar to yours |
| Aesthetic factors | Likes to fully utilize capacity | Doesn't like "dirty" jobs | Likes creative projects |
| Political factors | Decision maker has friends in government | Decision maker is seeking a new job | None known |

Your usual bidding practice is to add between 60 percent and 80 percent to your incremental costs, depending upon capacity utilization rate and other factors. What price will you bid (a) if you *must* win the contract, or (b) if you wish to maximize the expected value of the contract? Defend your answers with discussion, making any assumptions you feel are supported by the information given and/or are otherwise reasonable.

12.6    Tenders have been called for the construction of a turbine generator for the Caughnawaga Power Station. Your company accountant has examined the specifications and has established the following costs associated with the contract:

| | |
|---|---|
| Bid preparation costs | $      750 |
| Direct materials | 115,000 |
| Direct labor | 252,500 |
| Specialized equipment required* | 27,500 |
| Variable overhead | 42,000 |
| Allocated overhead | 86,750 |

*This equipment will not be purchased unless the contract is won. It will last for the fabrication of two more generators, should such contracts be forthcoming in the future, although there is no indication at this time that there will be a demand for any more generators like this one.

You are aware of three other companies who are likely to bid on this project. Relevant details are as follows:

| Detail | Company A | Company B | Company C |
|---|---|---|---|
| Cost structure | Similar to yours | 10% higher | 10% lower |
| Previous bidding pattern | Incremental cost plus 60% | Full cost plus 15% | Full cost plus 40% |
| Current capacity utilization | Moderate | Very low | Near full |

Your current capacity utilization is moderate, leaving sufficient capacity to handle this project. Your previous bidding practice has been to add 25 percent to full costs.

    (a)    What is the absolute *minimum* price you would bid on this contract?

    (b)    What is your *actual* bid price, on the basis of the information given?

    (c)    What other factors would you wish to consider or investigate before making your bid?

12.7    Fact Finders Limited, a marketing research company, has been asked by the marketing director of a large food-processing company to submit a proposal for a small market research project aimed at determining consumers' probable responses to several planned changes in marketing strategy. The proposal should outline the procedures planned and quote a price. The marketing director is not binding himself to accepting the proposal, since he is still formulating his plan of action. It would cost Fact Finders about $200 to prepare the proposal.

Fact Finders' president, Ms. Denise Jutasi, designs each project to fit individual requirements. Furthermore, the nature of the research industry is such that in general the client depends on only one or two research firms, since a certain familiarity with the client's problems is needed in the designing of the project. In addition, although price is important to the client, it is the research house's reputation for doing high-quality work that will largely influence the client's choice of research supplier. This particular client has used Fact Finders' services several times in the past, although it has also adopted other proposals in some cases in preference to the proposals suggested by Fact Finders.

Ms. Jutasi has designed a project which she believes best fulfills the client's needs, and she estimates that the incremental cost of the project could vary between $1,500 and $2,500. The wide variation in cost estimation is due to the many situational difficulties that are part of market research, including snowstorms, respondents not being home, difficulty in obtaining field staff, and unforeseen complications in other projects already in progress which could affect the one in question (for example, cause delays in starting).

The marketing director of the food-processing firm has indicated that he has allocated a budget in the vicinity of $2,500 for this project. At the top of this range, however, and dependent on the type of information the research firm will be able to obtain for him (outlined in the proposal), he might consider other methods of obtaining needed information or go with what information he has.

As a rule of thumb in calculating prices, Fact Finders uses cost plus 10 percent as a regular policy. Following are its best estimates of the probabilities with respect to the cost of the project and its chance of obtaining an acceptance by the client.

| *Incremental Cost of Project* | *Probability* | *Price (cost +10%)* | *Probability of Acceptance* |
|---|---|---|---|
| $1,500 | 0.2 | $1,650 | 0.99 |
| 2,000 | 0.5 | 2,200 | 0.70 |
| 2,500 | 0.3 | 2,750 | 0.10 |

    (a)    Find the expected value of the proposal to Fact Finders at each of the three prices stated.

(b)   Interpolate between the three prices shown to estimate the probability of acceptance when price is varied by $50 increments above $1,650. Would one of these price quotes be preferable to the initial three prices?

(c)   How would you recommend that Ms. Jutasi deal with the risk that costs might exceed the asking price?

12.8   Prentice Plumbing and Pipes Limited specializes in household plumbing installation and repairs. The sales manager received a call this morning to provide a written price quotation for the installation of the entire plumbing system in a new house being built by the owner (with the aid of contractors for the plumbing and electrical work). The owner has called for three or four quotes on each of the plumbing and electrical jobs.

The sales manager, David Katz, sent his estimator to the job site and has since received the following cost estimate:

| | |
|---|---:|
| Materials | $2,422 |
| Direct labor | 2,760 |
| Standard charge for detailed quotation | 100 |
| Variable overhead (estimated incremental) | 650 |
| Allocated overhead | 1,380 |
| Estimated total cost | $7,312 |

Prentice's usual pricing policy is to mark up its estimated (full) costs by 12½ percent to 25 percent, depending upon (a) how badly it needs the work to avoid employee layoffs, (b) whether or not the buyer is considering one or more other quotations, and (c) whether or not it expects the job to provide an introduction to a client who will have more jobs to be done in the future. The present demand situation for Prentice Plumbing and Pipes is quite pleasing, although Prentice does have sufficient operating capacity to handle the job under consideration. Mr. Katz intends to quote $8,775, which is approximately equal to full cost plus 20 percent markup.

Suppose that you have ascertained that the expected value of the bid price for each of the three other firms also submitting quotes on this job is $8,592, with a standard deviation of $1,032. Assuming the probability distribution of each rival's bid price to be normally distributed around the mean (expected value), find the bid price that maximizes the expected value of the contribution to overheads and profits for Prentice.

(a)   Is the sales manager's price quote close enough for maximization of expected profits?

(b)   What would you advise Mr. Katz, and why?

## SUGGESTED REFERENCES AND FURTHER READING

ALPERT, M. I., *Pricing Decisions,* Chap. 3. Glenview, Ill.: Scott, Foresman, 1971.

CHRISTENSON, C. J., R. F. VANCIL, and P. W. MARSHALL, *Managerial Economics,* rev. ed., Chap. 8. Homewood, Ill.: Richard D. Irwin, 1973.

EDELMAN, R., "Art and Science of Competitive Bidding," *Harvard Business Review,* 43 (1965), 53-66.

LAPIN, L. L., *Statistics for Modern Business Decision,* New York: Harcourt Brace Jovanovich, 1973.

LIVESEY, F., *Pricing,* Chap. 10. London: Macmillan, 1976.

MILLER, E. M., "Oral and Sealed Bidding: Efficiency versus Equity," *Natural Resources Journal,* 12 (July 1972), 330-53.

OREN, M. E., and A. C. WILLIAMS, "On Competitive Bidding," *Operations Research,* 23 (November-December 1975), 1072-79.

ROBERGE, M. D., "Pricing for Government Contractors," *Management Accounting,* June 1973, pp. 28-34.

WALKER, A. W., "How to Price Industrial Products," *Harvard Business Review,* 45 (1967), 125-32.

part **V**

# Topics
# in Managerial
# Economics

# 13
# Linear-Programming Analysis

### 13.1 Introduction

The Linearity Assumptions.

### 13.2 Graphical Solution of a Linear-Programming Problem

Representation of the Constraints.   Isoprofit Lines.
Confirming the Solution Algebraically.

### 13.3 Algebraic Solution of the Linear-Programming Problem

Introduction of Slack Variables.
Response to a Change in the Parameters of the Problem.
Shadow Prices of the Constraints.

### 13.4 The Dual Problem

The Primal Problem Restated.   Solving the Dual Problem.

### 13.5 The Simplex Technique

The Simplex Tableau.   Rules of Pivoting.   Method of Solution.
Other Applications of Linear Programming.

### 13.6 Summary

## 13.1   INTRODUCTION

Linear programming is a mathematical technique that is of considerable use in decision-making problems. It is applicable to a variety of short-run decision problems in managerial economics, since it deals with absolute constraints on certain processes where the decision maker's problem is to optimize some variable within the confines of those constraints. A situation of great applicability in managerial economics is that where a firm produces two or more products by applying labor and raw materials to fixed inputs of certain capital facilities and wishes to find the profit-maximizing product mix. For example, a lathe and a drill press may be used to produce a number of products, each of which requires differing amounts of lathe and drill press time and makes differing contributions to the firm's overheads and profits. Alternatively, a firm producing paint may produce paints of various types and colors, in various-sized cans, which take more or less of the available equipment time, have different levels of variable cost per gallon, and have differing contributions per gallon. The problem in such a situation is to find the optimal product mix that can be produced subject to the constraints imposed by the limited availability of certain inputs.

If the problem can be expressed in linear form, then linear programming can be applied to find a solution. Linear programming is a special case of the more general (and much more complex) field of mathematical programming. We confine our attention here to simple linear programming, since it is a widely applicable technique in business situations, and since an examination of nonlinear programming would go beyond the level and scope of this text.

### The Linearity Assumptions

To apply linear programming to a particular problem, both the decision maker's objective function and the constraints that confine the decision must be linear (or sufficiently approximated by linearity) over the range of outputs to which the decision applies. Supposing the firm's objective function to be the maximization of contribution to overheads and profits, this implies that the profit contribution per unit of output must be constant in order for total contribution to be a linear function of output. For profit contribution per unit to be constant, this in turn requires either that both price and average variable costs are constant over the range of outputs affected by the decision or that, if the demand curve is negatively sloping, the average variable cost curve and the demand curve are parallel over the relevant range of outputs.

Under what circumstances would prices be constant over a range of output levels? We know from Chapter 9 that this situation applies in markets characterized by pure competition, or situations approaching that extreme, in which the individual firm supplies such a small proportion of total industry output that it may presume that its output decision will not influence the market price. In such cases the individual firm may assume that the market price for the various products in question will remain constant regardless of the product mix chosen by the firm. Clearly, as we consider progressively larger firms this assumption becomes more tenuous unless the range of outputs being considered is correspondingly reduced. Thus a relatively large firm may consider that for small variations in its output level it will not cause a change in the price level.

Constant average variable costs imply a situation of constant returns to the variable factor, as we saw in Chapter 6; and as indicated by the empirical studies referred to in Chapter 7, this may be a common experience within limited ranges of operation of many business firms. Moreover, constant average variable costs require that factor prices remain constant regardless of the level of demand we place upon these factors. Again this is probably a reasonable assumption for most short-run decision-making situations.

Where price is influenced by variations in the firm's output of a particular product, the demand curve will be negatively sloping rather than horizontal. In order for the contribution per unit to be constant in such a situation, the average variable cost must be similarly negatively sloping and parallel to the demand curve. Such situations may occur in some production processes if increasing output levels are accompanied by increasing returns in production to the variable factors. In order for linear programming to be applicable, however, the reduction in per unit variable cost as output is increased must be of a similar magnitude to the reduction in price that is required to cause the higher output levels to be demanded. In many business situations the linearity requirement of profit contribution is either satisfied or sufficiently approximated such that linear programming can be applied to product-mix problems.

The second linearity requirement is that each of the possible outputs use each of the constraints as a linear function of the output of each product. If, for example, the first unit of Product X uses twenty minutes of machine time,[1] so

---

[1] This should be interpreted as the first unit in the "relevant range" of outputs, rather than the very first unit produced. All we require is that, over the range of output levels likely to contain the optimal output level, the relationship between input usage and output rate is constant.

must all subsequent units of Product X. Thus the efficiency of the fixed re-sources is constant and does not depend on the output level of each particular product to be produced. In any particular machine or plant facility, therefore, there will be a constant trade-off between Product X and Product Y, or more generally between any two products that may be produced by that machine.

In the following sections the emphasis will be upon understanding the technique of linear programming so that it can be correctly applied to decision problems. Simple linear-programming problems may be solved either graphically or algebraically, but more complex problems demand the assistance of computer programs designed to search for the optimal solution. In managerial economics our concern is largely to make sure that the problem is accurately set up for linear-programming solution and then to correctly interpret the results of the analysis.

## 13.2   GRAPHICAL SOLUTION OF A LINEAR-PROGRAMMING PROBLEM

We shall explain the process of linear programming in the context of the following simple problem. Suppose a small firm is in the business of making chromed shelf display units for city stores and boutiques. It has the necessary plant and equipment plus a small work force whose members belong to a militant union and therefore regard their labor input as being fixed at certain weekly maximum levels. The firm has tapped a market for two particular shelf units and has found that demand exceeds its capacity to produce either product. The firm is considering expansion of its facilities, but it is not convinced that demand will be sustained over a long enough period to justify this expansion. In the meantime, the firm is investigating the question of the optimal output mix between its two products. It is considering specialization in either Product X or Product Y, or some combination of the two products.

Suppose that Product X involves a more complex design and has a constant per unit cost of $300 and that any feasible output of the firm can be sold at the current market price of $600 per unit. Product Y is a more simple design, has constant variable per unit costs of $200, and can be sold within the range of feasible outputs at a market price of $400. The firm has three processes which have limited capacity to produce both Product X and Product Y. The first process consists of cutting the material to the appropriate size and configurations on the firm's power hacksaw. The power hacksaw is available for only thirty-two hours weekly, since the operator of this machine is available for this period only. The second process consists of welding the materials to construct the shelf units, and the availability of the welding equipment and its operator is limited to thirty hours per week. The third process involves immersing the units in the chrome bath, and this facility and its operator are available for forty hours a week only.

### Representation of the Constraints

Product X requires eight hours per unit in the first process, six hours per unit in the welding process, and five hours per unit in the chrome bath. Product Y requires four hours of the hacksaw time per unit, five hours of the welding time, and eight hours of the chrome bath time per unit. It can be seen that while Product Y contributes less per unit, its demands on two of the processes are less than the demands of Product X. Alternatively, Product X demands more time per unit for two of the three processes yet has a significantly higher contribution than does Product Y. Thus it is not obvious that the firm should specialize in either Product X or Product Y, and in fact we shall see that a combination of the two products will allow a maximum contribution to overheads and profits. The linear-programming problem is to find the output mix that will achieve the maximum contribution, given the constraints imposed upon the production of these two products.

Let us state the linear-programming problem in symbolic form. Supposing the firm wishes to maximize the total contribution of its operations, it thus wishes to maximize an objective function of the form:

$$\pi = AX + BY \tag{13.1}$$

where $\pi$ represents the total contribution to overheads and profits, $X$ and $Y$ are the number of units of each product to be produced, and the coefficients $A$ and $B$ represent the per unit contribution expected from each of the two products. Using the per unit price and average variable cost data outlined above, we can deduce that the contribution per unit of Product X is $300, and for Product Y is $200. Thus we can express the objective function as

$$\pi = 300X + 200Y \tag{13.2}$$

The constraints upon the maximization of contribution can be expressed as follows:

*Process 1:* $\quad 8X + 4Y \leqslant 32$                                           (13.3)

*Process 2:* $\quad 6X + 5Y \leqslant 30$                                           (13.4)

*Process 3:* $\quad 5X + 8Y \leqslant 40$                                           (13.5)

Equation (13.3) says in effect that the sum of the time utilized by the production of both Product X and Product Y must not exceed the time available in the first process. Since each unit of Product X demands eight hours of the power hacksaw's time, and each unit of Product Y demands four hours, the number of units of Products X and Y produced are constrained to that which can be produced within thirty-two hours' utilization of the power hacksaw and its operator. Similarly for the welding process, where each unit of Product X requires six hours and each unit of Product Y requires five hours, the sum must not exceed thirty hours in total. Finally, for the chrome bath process, each unit of Product X requires five hours and each unit of Product Y requires eight hours, and the total utilization of this process must be less than or equal to forty hours weekly.

Since linear programming is a mathematical procedure, it is likely to assign both positive and negative values to the variables $X$ and $Y$ unless we instruct it otherwise. Since negative values of output for Product X and Product Y make economic nonsense, we must add the condition that

$$X \geqslant 0, Y \geqslant 0$$

These are known as the nonnegativity requirements of linear-programming analysis.

The problem to be solved is thus to maximize profit contribution as shown by Eq.(13.2) subject to the constraints indicated by Eqs.(13.3) through (13.5), and the nonnegativity requirements on the variables $X$ and $Y$. Thus we wish to choose values of $X$ and $Y$ such that none of the constraints are broken and $\pi$ is maximized. We can solve this problem graphically by expressing the constraints and the objective function on a specific graph and finding the output level for which profits are maximized. To find the feasible combinations of $X$ and $Y$, that is, those that it is possible to produce without violating one or more of the constraints, we must delineate between those combinations that are possible on each process and those that are impossible to produce given the total time available in each process. Beginning with the first process, it is clear that the limits of possible combinations will be achieved where all of the available thirty-two hours weekly are used in the production of $X$ and $Y$. Thus we can remove the inequality from Eq.(13.3) and state that

$$8X + 4Y = 32$$

or in terms of $Y$:
$$4Y = 32 - 8X$$
$$Y = \ 8 - 2X \tag{13.6}$$

We now have an expression that shows $Y$ as a linear function of $X$. In a graph with Product Y on the vertical axis and Product X on the horizontal axis, it is clear that the first term is the intercept on the $Y$ axis, and the coefficient to the $X$ term represents the slope of the line relating Products Y and X. In Figure 13.1 we show the first constraint graphed against Products Y and X. Those combinations of $Y$ and $X$ that lie outside the line are clearly unobtainable, since they would demand more than thirty-two hours of the time available in Process 1.

To find the feasible output combinations under the other two processes we proceed similarly. Thus for the second constraint:

$$6X + 5Y = 30$$
$$5Y = 30 - 6X$$
$$Y = \ 6 - 1.2X \tag{13.7}$$

and for the third process:

$$5X + 8Y = 40$$

$$8Y = 40 - 5X$$

$$Y = 5 - 0.625X \qquad (13.8)$$

As shown in Figure 13.1, the second constraint has an intercept value of 6 and a slope of $-1.2$, while the third constraint has an intercept value of 5 and a slope of $-0.625$.

**FIGURE 13.1**
**Feasible region of production problem**

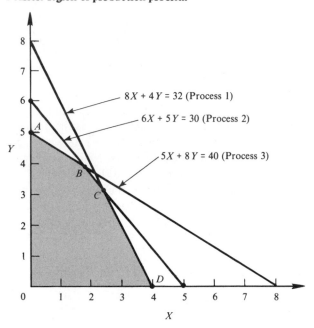

The irregular area encompassing all combinations of $X$ and $Y$ that lie below all the constraint lines is known as the *feasible region* of the production problem and is shown as the shaded area $0ABCD$ in Figure 13.1. The feasible region has several linear facets at its outer boundary, each corresponding to a particular constraint that is binding on the feasible combinations of $X$ and $Y$.

### Isoprofit Lines

To find which of the feasible combinations allows the highest profit contribution we introduce the concept of isoprofit lines, which are analogous to the iso-cost lines discussed in Chapter 6. An isoprofit line is a locus of the combinations of Products X and Y that allow the same total profit to be derived. Expressing the profit function, Eq.(13.2), in terms of Product Y, we have

$$Y = \frac{\pi}{200} - \frac{300}{200}X$$

or

$$Y = \frac{\pi}{200} - 1.5X \qquad (13.9)$$

Thus we have represented the isoprofit function in terms of $Y$ and $X$. On any given isoprofit line the value of $\pi$ will be known, and hence we may find the combinations of $X$ and $Y$ that preserve the equality shown in Eq.(13.9). Suppose we wish to find the combinations of $X$ and $Y$ that allow a profit level of $1,000. Substituting in Eq.(13.9), we have

$$Y = \frac{1,000}{200} - 1.5X$$

$$Y = 5 - 1.5X \qquad (13.10)$$

Hence Eq.(13.10) represents the equation for the isoprofit line along which profits are $1,000. We note that the intercept of this line on the $Y$ axis must be at five units, and the slope of this line is $-1.5$ as the production of $X$ is increased in one-unit increments. This isoprofit line is shown in Figure 13.2, along with two other arbitrarily chosen profit levels. Notice that higher levels of profits are represented by higher isoprofit lines, and that all isoprofit lines are parallel, since the slope of the isoprofit function is unchanged by variations in the value of $\pi$.

By superimposing the relevant isoprofit map upon the relevant feasible region, we are able to ascertain which of the combinations of $X$ and $Y$ allows the

**FIGURE 13.2**
**Isoprofit map for production problem**

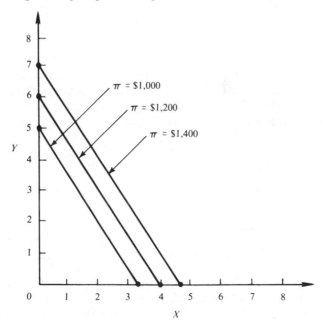

**FIGURE 13.3**
**Solution to production problem**

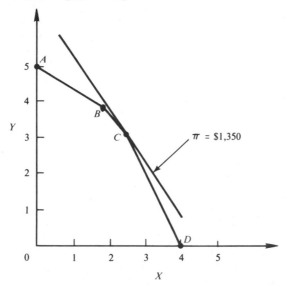

attainment of the highest possible isoprofit line. In Figure 13.3 we reproduce the feasible region of the production problem from Figure 13.1 and show that the highest isoprofit line that can be obtained is the line representing $1,350, which just touches the point $C$ on the feasible region. Any other point on the feasible region must lie on lower isoprofit lines, and any higher isoprofit lines will not touch the feasible region. Thus the optimal combination of $Y$ and $X$ is three units of $Y$ and two and one-half units of $X$ per week. (The fractional value of $X$ does not worry us: every two weeks five complete units of Product X will be produced.)

Note that the solution occurs at one of the corners of the feasible region. Since the isoprofit lines are linear, and the constraints are linear, this must always be the case. In the event that the isoprofit line has the same slope as one of the constraint lines, the highest attainable isoprofit line would coincide with the facet of the feasible region that represents that particular constraint. In Figure 13.4 we show such a situation. In this case the highest attainable isoprofit line coincides with the section $CD$ of the feasible region. Note that any output combination of $X$ and $Y$ along the facet $CD$ allows the same level of profits to be attained. Thus the earlier statement that the solution will always occur at a corner of the feasible region is vindicated, since the corners represented by the points $C$ and $D$ represent equivalent levels of profit contribution when compared with any point on the facet of the feasible region, and thus either one will be an optimal solution.

A second interesting point depicted in Figure 13.4 is the horizontal facet of the feasible region, labeled $AB$. This indicates a constraint that operates only on the production of Product Y. It is thus a process that is not needed for the output of Product X, and which when utilized fully by Product Y allows $OA$ units

FIGURE 13.4
Isoprofit line coinciding with a facet of the feasible region

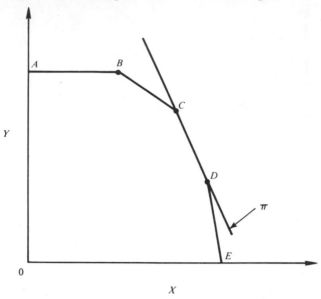

of $Y$ to be produced. Similarly, a process that is utilized by Product X would give rise to a vertical section on the feasible region (if it is a binding constraint).

### Confirming the Solution Algebraically

The above discussion indicates that the slope of the constraint equations, in comparison with the slope of the isoprofit line, can be used to find the solution values for $X$ and $Y$. Referring back to Figure 13.3, notice that the slope of the isoprofit curve is greater than the slope of the third constraint (shown by the section $AB$ of the feasible region), and is greater than the slope of the second constraint (shown by the segment $BC$), but is less than the slope of the first constraint (shown by the segment $CD$). Thus we might have simply compared the slopes of the profit function with the slopes of the constraint lines to find, in comparison with the profit function, the next-steepest constraint line and the next-flattest constraint line. The intersection of these two constraint lines will thus define the point at which profit contribution is maximized, unless one of these constraints lies outside the feasible region. The comparison of the slopes of the objective function and the constraint functions that bound the feasible region thus acts as a check upon our graphical procedures.

Since the solution line lies at the intersection of the first and second constraint lines, we are able to confirm the graphical results by simultaneous solution of those two equations for the values of $X$ and $Y$, as follows:

$$8X + 4Y = 32 \qquad\qquad (13.11)$$

$$6X + 5Y = 30 \qquad\qquad (13.12)$$

We proceed to eliminate $Y$ by multiplying Eq.(13.11) by 5 and Eq.(13.12) by 4:

$$40X + 20Y = 160 \qquad \textbf{(13.13)}$$

$$24X + 20Y = 120 \qquad \textbf{(13.14)}$$

and subtracting Eq.(13.14) from Eq.(13.13), we have

$$16X = 40$$

or

$$X = 2.5$$

Substituting for $X$ in Eq.(13.11) to find $Y$:

$$8(2.5) + 4Y = 32$$

$$4Y = 12$$

$$Y = 3$$

To find the profit level, we substitute for $X$ and $Y$ in the isoprofit function, Eq.(13.2):

$$\pi = 300(2.5) + 200(3)$$

$$= 750 + 600$$

$$= 1,350$$

It is clear that Process 1 and Process 2 are fully utilized by the production of the three units of $Y$ and the two and a half units of $X$ per week. Process 3, however, is not fully utilized, since this output combination requires less than forty hours of the third process. To confirm this, let us substitute the optimal values for $X$ and $Y$ into the constraint inequality given by Eq.(13.3):

$$5X + 8Y \leqslant 40$$

$$5(2.5) + 8(3) \leqslant 40$$

$$12.5 + 24 \leqslant 40$$

$$36.5 \leqslant 40$$

Thus there are 3.5 units (hours) of the third process remaining unutilized at the optimal output combinations.

## 13.3   ALGEBRAIC SOLUTION OF THE LINEAR-PROGRAMMING PROBLEM

### Introduction of Slack Variables

Given the knowledge that the solution to linear-programming programs will occur at one of the corners, we could solve for the values of $X$ and $Y$ at each of the corners, substitute these values into the objective function, and choose that pair of values that generates the greatest value in the objective function. To solve the problem algebraically, however, all constraints must be expressed as equations rather than inequalities. To cause all constraints to be expressed as equalities, we insert what are known as "slack variables" in each of the constraint expressions. The slack variables take up the slack if the constraint is not binding and are thus valued at the amount of idle capacity remaining in a particular process. Obviously, if a constraint is binding, the value of the slack variable is zero.

Algebraic solution of the linear-programming problem offers two main advantages over the graphical solution. First, it allows us to handle problems in which there are three or more variables; and second, the values of the slack variables provide information that is extremely useful for decision-making purposes. To demonstrate the algebraic solution of a linear-programming problem, suppose that the small firm making the shelf display units discovers that a market exists for a third product, Product Z, which is essentially a smaller version of Product X. Suppose that its price is expected to remain constant at $250 per unit, and that its per unit costs will be $150 per unit, such that the contribution will be $100 per unit. It will require two hours of hacksaw time, four hours of welding time, and three hours of the chrome bath time to produce each unit of Product Z. Modifying the earlier objective function and constraints by the addition of the information relevant to Product Z, and inserting slack variables, we may state the linear-programming problem algebraically as follows:

Maximize

$$\pi = 300X + 200Y + 100Z \tag{13.15}$$

Subject to

$$8X + 4Y + 2Z + S_1 = 32 \tag{13.16}$$

$$6X + 5Y + 4Z + S_2 = 30 \tag{13.17}$$

$$5X + 8Y + 3Z + S_3 = 40 \tag{13.18}$$

with the nonnegativity requirements

$$X \geqslant 0, Y \geqslant 0, Z \geqslant 0, S_1 \geqslant 0, S_2 \geqslant 0, S_3 \geqslant 0$$

We wish to find the values of $X$, $Y$, and $Z$ at each of the corners or peaks of a three-dimensional feasible region. The constraint equations (13.16) to (13.18) provide a system of three equations in six unknowns, and the system is therefore underdetermined. We know, however, that at each of the corners or peaks of the feasible region the values of some of the variables will be zero. In the three-dimensional case, three variables will be zero at each corner. This may be verified in Figure 13.5 where the feasible region of production possibilities is shown by the irregular three-dimensional surface. Points $0ABCD$ are the same as in Figure 13.1, and points $EFG$ are added by the introduction of a third variable, $Z$.

**FIGURE 13.5**
**Feasible region with three variables**

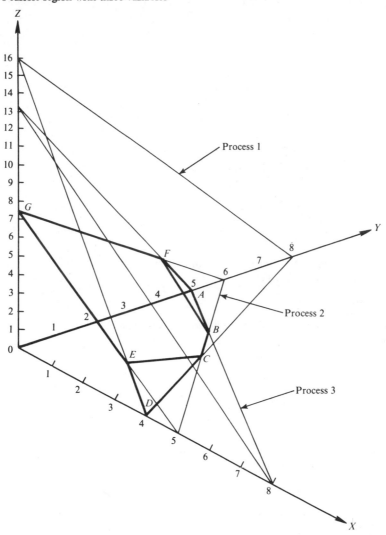

In Table 13.1 we show the value of each of the variables at each of the corners of the three-dimensional feasible region. It is clear that at the origin output of the three products is zero, and the slack variables must take the maximum values. At corner $A$, the values of $X$ and $Z$ are zero and the third constraint is binding, such that the slack variable $S_3$ is also zero. At this corner the value of $Y$ is 5, and we find the values of $S_1$ and $S_2$ by substitution of $Y = 5$ in the equations (13.16) and (13.17). Since $X$ and $Z$ are zero in each of these expressions, and $Y$ is known, it is a simple matter to find $S_1 = 12$, and $S_2 = 5$. At corner $B$ we know that $Z = 0$, $S_2 = 0$, and $S_3 = 0$. This collapses equations (13.17) and (13.18) into the following system of two equations in two unknowns:

**401**

$$6X + 5Y = 30 \qquad (13.19)$$

$$5X + 8Y = 40 \qquad (13.20)$$

By simultaneous solution of equations (13.19) and (13.20) we find $X = 1.74$, and $Y = 3.91$. Substituting these values into Eq.(13.16), we find the missing value of slack variable $S_1$, which is 0.44. Substituting the calculated values for $X$ and $Y$ into the objective function (13.15), we find the total profit contribution at this corner to be $1,304. Corner $C$ is familiar to us from the earlier example, and the values of the variables and the objective function at the other corners are calculated in similar fashion. The values of the objective function at the corners of the feasible region are calculated by substitution of the values of $X$, $Y$, and $Z$ in the objective function Eq.(13.15) and are shown in the next to the last column of Table 13.1. It can be seen that contribution is maximized at corner $C$, as it was in the earlier two-dimensional case. The addition of Product Z does not change the optimality of the earlier solution, since the contribution of Product Z relative to its use of the constrained processes is lower than for the original two products. Thus the firm would maximize total product contribution by producing 2.5 units of $X$, 3.0 units of $Y$, and ignoring the market opportunity for Product Z.

**TABLE 13.1**
**Algebraic solution of a linear-programming problem**

| | | Value of Variables | | | | | Value of Objective Function | |
|---|---|---|---|---|---|---|---|---|
| | $X$ | $Y$ | $Z$ | $S_1$ | $S_3$ | $S_3$ | Initial | Later |
| 0 | 0 | 0 | 0 | 32 | 30 | 40 | $ 0 | 0 |
| A | 0 | 5 | 0 | 12 | 5 | 0 | 1,000 | 500 |
| B | 1.74 | 3.91 | 0 | 0.44 | 0 | 0 | 1,304 | 870 |
| C | 2.5 | 3 | 0 | 0 | 0 | 3.5 | 1,350* | 988 |
| D | 4 | 0 | 0 | 0 | 6 | 20 | 1,200 | 1,100 |
| E | 3.4 | 0 | 2.4 | 0 | 0 | 15.8 | 1,260 | 1,115* |
| F | 0 | 4.12 | 2.35 | 10.8 | 0 | 0 | 1,059 | 588 |
| G | 0 | 0 | 7.5 | 17.0 | 0 | 17.5 | 750 | 563 |

*Maximum.

### Response to a Change
### in the Parameters of the Problem

The above optimal combination of the three products depends upon their relative contributions to overheads and profits, and their relative use of the three production processes. If either of these factors changes, or we were able to relax one of the constraints, we should expect a new combination of the three products to be optimal. To illustrate, let us suppose that market conditions change and the relative contributions of the three products change. Suppose a new firm begins making these units in direct competition with Product Y, but causing the prices of Products X and Z to also be reduced, such that the new objective function becomes

$$\pi = 275X + 100Y + 75Z \qquad (13.21)$$

Note that there has been no change in the availability of any of the production processes, or in the usage rates of these processes by any of the products. Thus the corner solutions found earlier are still applicable. Inserting these values for the variables into the new objective function, we find the value of the objective function at each corner as shown in the last column in Table 13.1. Note that profit contribution is now greatest at corner $E$ rather than at corner $C$: under the new market conditions it is now more profitable to drop Product Y and increase the production of both Products X and Z. This result comes about because the isoprofit plane has shifted due to the change in the relative contributions of the three products, and the highest-attainable isoprofit plane now touches the feasible region at the corner $E$, whereas previously the highest-attainable isoprofit plane rested on point $C$.

If the capacity of a particular process could be increased, that is, if the constraint could be relaxed, would we expect this to change the optimal combination of outputs, and the total profit contribution? The answer to this question is yes to both issues if the constraint is binding, while it is no if slack exists in the particular constraint. In order for additional availability of a constraint process to cause the solution to change, availability of additional capacity must cause the frontier of the feasible region to move outward and poke through the previously highest attainable isoprofit line or surface, such that a new higher isoprofit line or surface can be attained. This is demonstrated in the two-variable case in Figure 13.6. Here the constraint represented by the facet $BC$ has been re-

**FIGURE 13.6**
**Relaxation of a constraint and its impact on profit contribution**

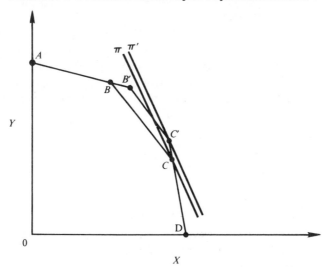

laxed by a certain amount to cause the feasible region to expand to the area bounded by $0AB'C'D'$. Whereas the previously highest attainable isoprofit curve was that shown by $\pi$, tangent at point $C$, the new feasible region allows the higher isoprofit line $\pi'$ to be attained at point $C'$.

Note that relaxation of the other constraint that was binding at point $C$—the constraint represented by the section $CD$ of the feasible region—would similarly cause the feasible region to extend beyond the highest-attainable isoprofit line. At the initial solution point $C$, one of the constraints was not binding. This constraint, represented by the facet $AB$ on the initial feasible region, could be relaxed without causing the feasible region to pierce the isoprofit line, since the new feasible region would expand in a direction away from the direction of greater profitability.

The question arises, by how much will profit contribution increase when we relax each of the constraints? If the increase in profit contribution could be foreseen to exceed the capital expenditures necessary to expand facilities, the decision maker would wish to spend the funds to expand facilities, since the consequent net addition to profits would be positive. Some linear-programming solution techniques are able to generate the information concerning the change in profit contribution due to the relaxation of each constraint by one unit. This value is known as the shadow price of the constraint.

### Shadow Prices of the Constraints

The *shadow price* of a constraint is defined as the increment to the value of the objective function that results from that constraint being relaxed by one unit. From the above discussion it is clear that only those constraints that are binding will have positive shadow prices, since those constraints with slack remaining will add nothing to profit contribution if increased further.

Graphically we could find the shadow price of each constraint by expanding the frontier for each constraint, finding the new highest-attainable isoprofit line, and calculating the value of this level of profit from the intercept value of this isoprofit line. Algebraically, the procedure is similar. We would expand one constraint by one unit, e.g., $8X + 4Y + 2Z + S_1 = 33$, and solve for the optimal combinations of $X$, $Y$, and $Z$ in conjunction with the other two constraint equations in their original form. We would then substitute the solution values for $X$, $Y$, and $Z$ in the objective function to find the new profit-contribution level. A simple subtraction of the earlier maximum profit contribution from the new maximum profit contribution would generate the shadow price of the constraint that was augmented.

An alternative algebraic method of obtaining the shadow prices is to solve the "dual" of the linear-programming problem.

## 13.4    THE DUAL PROBLEM

In the above we have worked with what is by convention called the "primal" problem. A primal problem may be to maximize some variable subject to various constraints, as in the above example, or it may be to minimize a variable subject to several constraints in a different problem. Every primal linear-programming problem has a dual problem associated with it. For every maximization problem there is an associated (dual) minimization problem, and for every minimization problem there is an associated (dual) maximization problem. This relationship derives from the mathematical nature of the linear-programming technique. Although it may not be intuitively obvious, for every problem in which a particular variable is to be maximized (or minimized) subject to certain constraints, there is another variable that, if minimized (or maximized) subject to another set of constraints, will derive the same values for the crucial variables. In the case discussed above, we maximized profit contribution subject to the limited availability of three production processes, by choosing the optimal output mix of Products X, Y, and Z. The dual to this problem is to minimize the value of these three production processes subject to the constraints that the value of the production processes used in the production of each unit of output do not exceed the contribution generated by each unit of each output. When this minimization problem is solved, the output mix of Products X, Y, and Z will be the same as it would have been in the primal maximization problem. The virtue of solving the dual problem is that the solution imputes a value to the marginal units of each of the constraints, which of course are the shadow prices we seek.

Let us now return to the simple two-variable problem discussed above.

### The Primal Problem Restated

Maximize

$$\pi = 300X + 200Y$$

subject to

$$8X + 4Y + S_1 = 32$$
$$6X + 5Y + S_2 = 30$$
$$5X + 8Y + S_3 = 40$$

with the nonnegativity requirements that $X, Y, S_1$, and $S_2$ are all $\geqslant 0$.

To establish the dual problem, we must define a number of new variables as follows:

$V$ = the total value of the three production processes.

$W_1$ = the shadow price of the first process,

$W_2$ = the shadow price of the second process,

$W_3$ = the shadow price of the third process,

$R_1$ = slack variable in the constraint that the value of the resources used in production of a unit of $X$ should not exceed the contribution from a unit of $X$, and

$R_2$ = the slack variable in the constraint pertaining to Product Y.

We can now state the dual problem:

Minimize

$$V = 32W_1 + 30W_2 + 40W_3 \qquad (13.22)$$

subject to

$$8W_1 + 6W_2 + 5W_3 + R_1 = 300 \qquad (13.23)$$

$$4W_1 + 5W_2 + 8W_3 + R_2 = 200 \qquad (13.24)$$

with the nonnegativity requirements that $W_1$, $W_2$, $W_3$, $R_1$, and $R_2$ are all $\geqslant 0$.

### Solving the Dual Problem

The objective function of the dual problem is thus to minimize the total value of the firm's fixed resources, measured in terms of the shadow prices of each resource times the availability of that resource in units. The constraints are that the total cost of the firm's resources involved in the production of each product should be less than or equal to the contribution from each of the products. We insert the slack variables to allow the constraints to be represented as equalities.

The dual problem could be represented in a three-dimensional figure with the three shadow prices on the axes. Think how it would appear graphically. The feasible region would be inverted as compared with the primal problem discussed above but would have corners or points due to the linearity of the constraints. The objective function will be a plane in $W_1$, $W_2$, and $W_3$, and the solution will be the combination of $W_1$, $W_2$, and $W_3$ that allows the lowest plane to be achieved. Clearly, it must be the lowest plane that still touches some point of the feasible region and therefore must touch one of the corners of the feasible region, or possibly coincide with a facet of the feasible region, and hence touch two or more corners of the feasible region.

Equations (13.23) and (13.24) are a system of two equations in five unknowns, and this system is thus underdetermined. However, our knowledge of the nature of the solution to the linear-programming problem allows us to predict that at each corner of the feasible region three of the variables will take zero values, and hence we may iteratively assign zero values to combinations of three variables and find the combination that provides the minimum value of the objective function. There will be five factorial combinations of the five variables, but some of these combinations will not represent corners on the feasible region. Some of the combinations will give rise to values for the variables that violate the nonnegativity requirements and are hence ruled out. We could array the values of the variables and the objective function in a table, as we did for the primal problem in Table 13.1, where each line would represent the values of the variables and the objective function at one of the corners. That corner that meets all the nonnegativity requirements and shows the minimum value for $V$ will represent the optimal solution. At that corner the values of the variables $W_1$, $W_2$, and $W_3$ will represent the shadow price of each of the constraints.

Rather than follow the above procedure, however, we shall use the knowledge gained from the solution of the primal problem to assign zero values to three of the variables in the system of equations (13.23) and (13.24) such that we may solve for the values of the shadow prices at the optimal solution. We know that in the primal problem the first and second constraints were binding. Thus $W_1$ and $W_2$ in the dual problem will have positive values, while $W_3$, $R_1$, and $R_2$ must take zero values. Eliminating the latter three variables from equations (13.23) and (13.24), we have

$$8W_1 + 6W_2 = 300 \qquad (13.25)$$

$$4W_1 + 5W_2 = 200 \qquad (13.26)$$

which is a system of two equations in two unknowns and can thus be solved by simultaneous solution. Multiplying Eq.(13.26) by 2, we have

$$8W_1 + 10W_2 = 400 \qquad (13.27)$$

Subtracting Eq.(13.25) from (13.27) to eliminate $W_1$, we have

$$4W_2 = 100$$

or

$$W_2 = 25$$

Substituting into Eq.(13.25) to find $W_1$:

$$8W_1 + 6(25) = 300$$

$$8W_1 = 150$$

$$W_1 = 18.75$$

Thus the shadow prices of the two constraints that are binding are $25 for the hacksaw process, and $18.75 for the welding process. That is to say, an extra hour of utilization of either process would add those amounts to the total contribution to overheads and profits. If an additional hour of the hacksaw operator's time plus associated expenses could be employed for less than $25, the decision maker would wish to do so. Similarly, if an additional hour of the welding equipment's utilization could be employed for less than $18.75, the decision maker would be advised to do so, since there would result a net increase in the contribution to overheads and profits.

Can the time input of these processes be increased by additional hours for continued increases in profits to the firm? We can expect the relaxation of one constraint by one-unit increments to continue to add the shadow price value to the objective function until a second or third constraint becomes binding. In Figure 13.7 we show the limit to which the constraint represented by the intermediate facet of the feasible region can be relaxed before the other two constraints become binding. Clearly, at point $E$ additional units of the intermediate

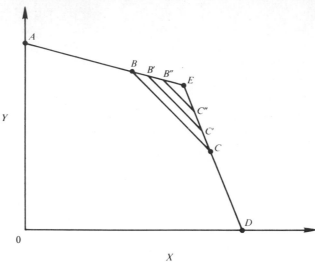

constraint will add nothing to the objective function due to one of the other constraints becoming effective at that point. As a general rule we must recalculate the shadow prices at new levels of the constraints rather than continue to use the earlier figures, since in more complex cases it will not be obvious when this additional constraint will become binding.

## 13.5   THE SIMPLEX TECHNIQUE

An alternate method that finds both the optimal values of the variables and the shadow prices of the constraints is the simplex method.[2] Essentially, the simplex method uses the knowledge that the solution must occur at a corner of the feasible region, and that at each corner the number of nonzero variables is exactly equal to the number of constraints in the problem, to search for the solution. The simplex method starts at the origin of the feasible region and proceeds to compare the profitability of that corner point with an adjacent corner point. If the adjacent corner yields a greater profit, the next corner point is evaluated and compared. When the adjacent corner yields a lower profit, the procedure ceases, and the previous highest profit point is taken to be the optimal solution.[3]

In the two-dimensional case this procedure is easy to visualize and is relatively simple, but in the *n*-dimensional case a great deal of effort would be needed to identify the location of adjacent corners. The simplex method has been developed to facilitate this problem.

[2] The simplex method is attributed to the mathematician George M. Dantzig. See Dantzig, *A Procedure for Maximizing a Linear Function Subject to Linear Inequalities* (Washington, D.C.: Headquarters U.S. Air Force, Comptroller, 1948).

[3] Although the word *simplex* might imply simplicity, a simplex is the *n*-dimensional analogue of a triangle. The simplex technique is named for its procedure of systematically evaluating the objective function at the simplexes of the feasible region.

### The Simplex Tableau

We begin by expressing the objective function and the constraints in terms of the $X$ and $Y$ variables and the real numbers. Thus we will rewrite the primal problem as follows:

Maximize

$$\pi = 0 + 300X + 200Y \qquad\qquad (13.28)$$

subject to

$$S_1 = 32 - 8X - 4Y \qquad\qquad (13.29)$$

$$S_2 = 30 - 6X - 5Y \qquad\qquad (13.30)$$

$$S_3 = 40 - 5X - 8Y \qquad\qquad (13.31)$$

and $S_1$, $S_2$, $X$, and $Y$ are all $\geqslant 0$.

We put the equations in this form in order to facilitate the construction of the simplex tableau, which is the matrix of the real numbers and the coefficients to the $X$ and $Y$ variables, as shown in Table 13.2.

The first column of the Simplex Tableau shows the values of the variables down the left-hand side of the tableau when $X$ and $Y$ are zero. The second and third columns of the tableau show the impact upon the first column, and hence the profit level or slack variables, when $X$ and $Y$ are increased by one unit, respectively. Thus if the coefficients for $X$ and $Y$ in the first row of the tableau are positive, this indicates that an increase in the production of $X$ or $Y$ will contribute to the profit level and should therefore be undertaken. The simplex method allows units of the slack variables to be used up in the production of $X$ or $Y$ until the coefficients are negative in the second and third column in the first row of the tableau. This result ensues through a process of "pivoting" two of the slack variables with the $X$ and $Y$ variables. When the pivoting procedure is completed, the $X$ and $Y$ variables will be on the left-hand side of the tableau and two of the constraints will be on the top of the tableau in the place of $X$ and $Y$ in Table 13.2. The values in column 1 upon completion of the procedure will show the optimum profit level in the first row, the optimal output levels of $X$ and $Y$ and the amount of slack remaining in the constraint that is not binding in the other three rows. The values in the top row of the second and

**TABLE 13.2**
**Simplex tableau for the production problem**

|       | 1 ,<br>(1) | X<br>(2) | Y<br>(3) |
|-------|-----------|----------|----------|
| $\pi$   | 0         | 300      | 200      |
| $S_1$ | 32        | $-8$     | $-4$     |
| $S_2$ | 30        | $-6$     | $-5$     |
| $S_3$ | 40        | $-5$     | $-8$     |

third columns will be the shadow prices of the constraints that are binding. Let us proceed to demonstrate this using the following pivoting rules.

### Rules of Pivoting

In the following paragraphs we shall simply state the rules for the operation of the simplex method in order to demonstrate how the solution and the shadow prices can be attained, and the reader is referred to Professor Baumol's comprehensive treatment of the theory underlying these rules of manipulation.[4]

*Choice of the Pivot Element.* To find the starting point for the pivoting process, we first choose the column (other than the first column) with the largest positive top element and call this the pivot column. To find the pivot row (and hence the pivot element), we then take each negative element in the pivot column and, for each row, divide the element in the first column by the element in the pivot column. Finally, we compare these quotients and choose as the pivot the quotient that is the smallest in absolute value. In terms of Table 13.2 we choose $X$ as the entering variable, since its value in the first row is greatest. Thus the pivot column is the second column, and it remains to calculate the quotients to find which element in the pivot column is the pivot element. The quotient of the second row of the second column is $-4$, it is $-5$ for the third row, and it is $-8$ for the fourth row. The smallest of these quotients in absolute terms is that relating to the second row, and hence the pivot element is the coefficient $-8$ at the intersection of the second row and the second column, which is shown circled in Table 13.2.

This procedure for choosing the pivot element ensures that the product that contributes most to the profit function will enter the analysis first, and it will enter via the constraint process that is in relatively shortest supply. Thus the variables $X$ and $S_1$ will be pivoted and will change places on the Simplex Tableau. This will cause a complete transformation of the tableau, and the following rules allow a relatively simple method of finding the new values.

*Rule 1, Treatment of the Pivot Element.* The new element that replaces the pivot element is simply the reciprocal of the pivot element.

*Rule 2, Other Pivot Row Elements.* These elements are transformed by changing the sign of the element and dividing by the old pivot element.

*Rule 3, Other Pivot Column Elements.* These elements are transformed by dividing each element by the pivot element.

*Rule 4, All Other Elements.* All elements not in the pivot column or the pivot row must be transformed by subtracting from the existing element the ratio of the product of the two "corner elements" to the initial pivot element. The corner elements of an element are those that make up the square or rectangle with the element in question and the pivot element. For example, the value $-5$ in the third row of the third column forms a diagonal with the pivot element

[4] W. J. Baumol, *Economic Theory and Operations Analysis,* 4th ed. (Englewood Cliffs, N.J.: Prentice-Hall, 1977), pp. 84-99.

−8 in Table 13.2. The corresponding corner elements are thus −6 and −4, which form a square with the element in question and the pivot element. Similarly for the element in the third column, fourth row, the corner elements are −4 and −5.

## Method of Solution

Let us now utilize the above rules in solving the earlier decision problem using the simplex method. The column with the largest top element is that under $X$, and the row that allows the smallest quotient with the first column is that opposite $S_1$. Hence the variables to be pivoted, or interchanged, are $X$ and $S_1$, and we show the pivot element by circling the element that is common to the $X$ column and the $S_1$ row in Table 13.2. Following the rules outlined above we begin the pivoting process by taking the reciprocal of the pivot—that is, $1/-8$, or −0.125— and inserting this in the pivot position in the new Simplex Tableau shown as Table 13.3. Following the rule for other pivot row elements, we change the sign of those elements in Table 13.2, divide by the old pivot, and arrive at the new

**TABLE 13.3**
**Revised tableau after first pivoting process**

|       | 1<br>(1) | $S_1$<br>(2) | Y<br>(3) |
|-------|----------|--------------|----------|
| $\pi$ | 1,200    | −37.5        | 50       |
| $X$   | 4        | − 0.125      | −0.5     |
| $S_2$ | 6        | 0.75         | ⊂−2⊃     |
| $S_3$ | 20       | 0.625        | −5.5     |

values as shown in Table 13.3. Following Rule 3 for other elements in the pivot column, we divide the old element by the old pivot to find the values shown under the second column in Table 13.3 which is now identified under $S_1$. The reader should be convinced that the −37.5 value shown in the top row of the second column in Table 13.3 is the quotient of the initial element in that position (viz., 300), divided by the initial pivot value −8. To find the remaining values in the revised tableau we follow Rule 4. To demonstrate with regard to the upper-left-hand element, we take the initial value and subtract from it the product of the corner elements (viz., 300 and 32), and divide this by the initial pivot value. Hence

$$\text{New element} = \text{Old element} - \frac{\text{Product of corner elements}}{\text{Old pivot element}}$$

$$= 0 - \left(\frac{300 \times 32}{-8}\right)$$

$$= 0 - (-1,200)$$

$$= 1,200$$

The other elements that remain to be added to the revised tableau are obtained by applying the same process to each of the other elements remaining to be transformed, making sure to use the appropriate corner elements for each element.

In Table 13.3 it can be seen that the top element in the third column is positive. This indicates that an increase in the production of $Y$ would add to the level of profit contribution. The third column now becomes the pivot column, and to find the pivot row we divide the elements in the first column of the second, third, and fourth rows by the elements in the corresponding rows of the third column. These quotients are $-8$, $-3$, and $-3.64$, respectively. The smallest of these in absolute terms is $-3$, and hence the third row becomes the pivot row and the circled element $-2$ becomes the pivot element for the second pivoting process.

To begin the pivoting process we take the reciprocal of the pivot, viz., $-0.5$, and insert this in the pivot position in a new Simplex Tableau which we show as Table 13.4. Following Rule 2 we complete the other elements of the pivot row. In the first column we have $-6$ divided by $-2 = 3$, and in the second column we have $-0.75$ divided by $-2 = 0.375$. Following Rule 3 we find the elements of the new pivot column, being the old elements from Table 13.3 divided by the pivot value in that table. Following Rule 4 we find the values of the elements that are neither in the pivot column nor in the pivot row. The element at the top-left-hand corner will be:

$$\text{New element} = 1{,}200 - \left(\frac{50 \times 6}{-2}\right)$$

$$= 1{,}200 - (-150)$$

$$= 1{,}350$$

Note that this is the level of profit contribution that we found from the previous algebraic analysis to be the maximum level. To find the element in the top row of the second column, we calculate:

$$\text{New element} = -37.5 - \left(\frac{50 \times 0.75}{-2}\right)$$

$$= -37.5 - (-18.75)$$

$$= -18.75$$

**TABLE 13.4**
**Revised tableau after second pivoting process**

|       | 1<br>(1) | $S_1$<br>(2) | $S_2$<br>(3) |
|-------|---------|-------------|-------------|
| $\pi$ | 1,350   | $-18.75$    | $-25$       |
| $X$   | 2.5     | $-0.3125$   | 0.25        |
| $Y$   | 3       | 0.375       | $-0.5$      |
| $S_3$ | 3.5     | $-2.6875$   | 2.75        |

Note that this was the shadow price of the first process as calculated earlier. Similarly, the −25 figure in the first row of the third column is the shadow price of the second process, as calculated earlier. To find the value for $X$ that will be indicated in the first column of the revised tableau, we calculate:

$$\text{New element} = 4 - \left(\frac{6 \times -0.5}{-2}\right)$$

$$= 4 - (1.5)$$

$$= 2.5$$

Note that this is the optimal value of $X$ as calculated earlier and that the optimal value of $Y$ is 3 units, also as calculated in the algebraic treatment of the problem. The remaining element of any interest to us is the value for $S_3$ in the fourth row of the first column. This value will indicate the number of units of that constraint that remained unutilized. It is calculated as follows:

$$\text{New element} = 20 - \left(\frac{6 \times -5.5}{-2}\right)$$

$$= 20 - (16.5)$$

$$= 3.5$$

Thus 3.5 hours of the chrome-bath process remain unutilized at the optimal output-mix solution, confirming our earlier algebraic result.

Note that the simplex method of solving the linear-programming problem in effect solves the primal and the dual problem simultaneously. In the first column it shows the maximum attainable level of the objective function, the optimal levels of each of the variables $X$ and $Y$ and, as a bonus, the amount of slack remaining in any of the processes that are not fully utilized. In the first row of the second and subsequent columns it shows the shadow prices of those processes that are fully utilized. It thus gives the decision maker all the information necessary for the current decision as to the optimal output mix and profit level to be earned, as well as the contribution to be gained by increasing each of the binding constraints by one unit each, *ceteris paribus*.

The above discussion and trial run of the simplex method have served to indicate how this method may generate all the desired information with a series of relatively simple calculations. More complicated problems, of course, would preferably be solved using the computerized simplex method, as the computer is easily instructed to follow the simple rules of the simplex method. Simple problems with a relatively small number of variables and constraints can be solved without undue effort using the simplex method with the aid of a hand calculator. After a few iterations, the four rules of pivoting will be memorized and you should have little difficulty with this method of solution.

### Other Applications of Linear Programming

In this chapter we have confined our attention to the solution of a product-mix problem. Linear-programming analysis is applicable to a wide variety of decision problems that arise in the business firm or institutional environment. Linear programming is commonly used to solve transportation problems in which the shortest route must be found between a number of delivery points, subject to the constraints imposed by the highway or railroad system.[5] The classic diet problem involves minimizing the cost of supplying patients in a hospital with the minimum required amounts of certain vitamins and other nutrients which are contained in differing quantities in various foodstuffs, which in turn cost differing amounts.[6] This is analogous to a firm wishing to minimize the cost of meeting all specifications on a particular project when there is more than one way to meet each specification. In marketing, linear programming may be used to find the minimum costs of obtaining a certain level of advertising exposure given the different costs and availabilities of the various media. These examples serve to indicate the range of applications of linear-programming analysis. As long as the objective function and the constraints can be expressed linearly in terms of the variables, linear programming will serve as a valid solution procedure. Some of the problems at the end of this chapter will test your understanding of linear-programming analysis in the context of other types of business problems.

## 13.6   SUMMARY

In this chapter we have outlined the application of linear programming to the product-mix problem. Linear programming allows the optimal combinations to be found, given the presence of certain absolute constraints. Simple two-variable cases can be solved graphically by graphing the constraints in the two-variable space and finding the corner solution that supports the highest-attainable isoprofit line. At this corner solution two of the constraints will be equalities and thus can be solved for the values of the two variables at the optimal combination point, and the optimal level of profits will be found by substituting the solution values of the variables in the objective function equation.

More complex cases can be solved algebraically on the basis of the knowledge that the nature of the solution is such that the number of nonzero variables will equal the number of constraints at the solution point. Thus, if we have $n$ constraints and $m$ variables, we could set $m - n$ variables equal to zero and solve for the remaining $n$ variables in the $n$ equations provided by the constraints. We would do this for all combinations of the variables. For each of the $m - n$ zero-valued variables and $n$ positively valued variables that would result, we would evaluate the objective function and choose as a solution that combination that gave the optimal value to the objective function. The solution of the dual prob-

[5] See, for example, W. J. Fabrycky and G. J. Thuesen, *Economic Decision Analysis* (Englewood Cliffs, N.J.: Prentice-Hall, 1974), pp. 324-32.

[6] See R. Dorfman, P. A. Samuelson, and R. M. Solow, *Linear Programming and Economic Analysis* (New York: McGraw-Hill, 1958), Chap. 2.

lem may be easier than solving the primal problem, but in any case it provides values for the shadow prices of each constraint, which provide valuable information for the decision maker.

The simplex method of solution effectively solves the primal and dual problems simultaneously. A number of iterations of a few simple steps will allow the optimal combinations of the variables, the value of the objective function, the shadow prices, and the slack variables to be evaluated. The mechanistic nature of the linear-programming solution lends itself to computer programming, such that this technique is able to handle extremely complex decision problems. It has wide applicability in business situations, but the decision maker must be assured that the problem to be solved can be fairly represented by linear constraints and a linear objective function.

## DISCUSSION QUESTIONS

13.1 Outline the features necessary to make a problem suitable for solution by linear-programming analysis.

13.2 Why is linear programming a technique suitable for short-run production problems rather than for long-run production problems?

13.3 If a firm produces two products, both of which make exactly the same demands on resources and contribute the same to profits, how is the optimal product mix determined?

13.4 What is the logic behind changing the inequality to an equality in order to depict each constraint graphically?

13.5 For algebraic solution of the linear-programming problem, we insert slack variables in order to express the constraints as equalities. Why?

13.6 Outline the process involved in the algebraic solution of the linear-programming problem. Why are we able to confine our attention to the corner solutions?

13.7 What happens to the shape of the feasible region if a production process suddenly becomes more efficient in terms of the output of one product?

13.8 What should the decision maker do after having ascertained the shadow prices of each constraint?

13.9 Outline the relationship between the primal problem and its dual problem in linear-programming analysis.

13.10 How does the simplex method of solution ensure that the optimal solution is found by comparison of increasingly more profitable corner solutions?

## PROBLEMS

13.1 Frank's Fish Packing Company produces two items, fish cakes (for human consumption) and fish meal (for animal consumption). The light-meat parts of the fish are separated from the rest of the fish for the fish cakes, while the rest of the fish is used for the fish meal. The ratio of fish cakes output to fish meal output can vary as more or less of the lighter meat is separated from the rest of the fish. As the fresh fish comes into the plant it goes through four processes: separating, shredding, packing, and canning. Each of these processes has a maximum input available due to the labor available with the required training for each process, and these workers' prior agreements with management as to the length of their workweek. The total time available in each process, and the time required in each process per 1,000 pounds of output for each of the products, is as follows:

| | Total Time Available | Hours Required (per 1,000 lb) | |
|---|---|---|---|
| Process | (hours weekly) | Fishcakes | Fishmeal |
| Separating | 205 | 22.78 | 13.67 |
| Shredding | 106 | 10.60 | 8.83 |
| Packing | 188 | 14.46 | 17.09 |
| Canning | 65 | 5.00 | 5.00 |

Frank's sells the fish cakes for $0.80 per pound and the fish meal for $0.70 per pound. All costs, including the fresh fish, are joint costs, and hence these revenue figures can be treated as the per unit contribution to joint (overhead) costs and profits.

Solve this product-mix problem using graphical analysis. Confirm your answers algebraically.

(a)    What is the contribution-maximizing product mix?

(b)    What is the maximum contribution attainable?

(c)    Which processes are at full capacity?

13.2    The Munchies Cake Company wishes to minimize the materials cost for its "Jumbo" fruit-and-nut cakes. The company has found that market acceptance of these cakes is maximized when they contain at least 250 grams of currants, 375 grams of sultanas, 150 grams of citrus peel, and 225 grams of nuts, and it consequently wishes to maintain at least these levels of these components in each cake. Neither of the two commercially available fruit and nut mixes comes in exactly these proportions, however, and Munchies combines these two mixes to achieve a mix that meets the above constraints on the minimum weight of each component. Brand A fruit-and-nut mix costs $2.15 per kilogram, and Brand B fruit-and-nut mix costs $2.35 per kilogram. Each kilogram of these two mixes contains the following percentage breakdown of the four components:

| | Currants | Sultanas | Peel | Nuts |
|---|---|---|---|---|
| Brand A | 30% | 40% | 10% | 20% |
| Brand B | 15% | 35% | 25% | 25% |

(a)    Using graphical analysis, find the combination of Brand A and Brand B fruit-and-nut mix that minimizes cost subject to the minimum weights being achieved for each of the four components. Confirm your answers algebraically.

(b)    What is the minimum fruit-and-nut mix cost per Jumbo cake?

(c)    Which constraints are binding? What would you suggest Munchies do? Why?

13.3    Mr. C. Slicker has recently purchased a 250-acre dairy farm, complete with all necessary buildings. He is now contemplating the purchase of a herd of cattle and wishes to know which breed(s) of cattle he should buy in order to maximize his sales revenue from the venture. He is considering Jersey cows, a breed known for the relatively high butterfat content (BFC) in its milk, although the cows' actual milk output is relatively low. He knows he can buy Jersey cows from a nearby farm, and that these cows have an average milk output of 38 pounds per day and an average BFC of 5 percent over their lactation period of 300 days. His contract with the milk-processing company will be for $0.075 per pound for all milk with a minimum BFC of 3.5 percent. This lower limit on BFC makes Mr. Slicker start thinking about Holsteins, a breed known for its relatively high milk output with relatively low BFC. He knows he can purchase Holstein cows nearby which average 65 pounds of milk daily with average BFC of 2.8 percent over their 300-day lactation period. With a mixed herd of Jerseys and Holsteins, he reasons that he could increase milk output while still meeting the BFC constraint.

Holstein cows are considerably larger than Jerseys, however, and as a consequence they require more acreage for grazing and eat more hay and cattle meal during the winter. Whereas Jerseys need about 1.75 acres per cow in this area, Holsteins need about 2.5 acres per cow. For winter feed Jerseys require 8.8 pounds of hay and 3.2 pounds of meal per cow daily, compared with the Holsteins' requirements of 10.2 pounds of hay and 5.1 pounds of meal per cow. The limits on hay and meal storage above the cattle stalls are 1,200 pounds of hay and 500 pounds of meal, and it is not feasible to replenish this stock more frequently than once daily. The Holstein cows, moreover, cost $750 each as compared with the Jerseys at $550 each. Mr. Slicker expects to be able to borrow up to $80,000 for the purchase of his herd.

Please advise Mr. Slicker, using graphical analysis and confirming your answers algebraically, as to

(a) The maximum ratio of Holsteins to Jerseys that will allow the 3.5 percent BFC minimum to be attained.

(b) The revenue-maximizing composition of his dairy herd, given that all constraints are satisfied.

(c) The maximum revenue obtainable from milk sales over the 300-day lactation period.

13.4 The Grimes Gravel Company produces three mixtures of sand, pebbles, and rocks for eventual sale in 20-kg. bags to the home handyperson for use in cement work. The sandy mixture is composed of 10 kg. sand, 7 kg. pebbles, and 3 kg. rocks. The pebbly mixture is composed of 6 kg. sand, 10 kg. pebbles, and 4 kg. rocks. The rocky mixture is composed of 2 kg. sand, 8 kg. pebbles, and 10 kg. rocks. The market prices prevailing are $2.75 for the sandy mixture, $2.50 for the pebbly mixture, and $2.25 for the rocky mixture. Grimes Gravel feels that the market prices will hold regardless of the volume of each product it supplies.

Grimes Gravel wishes to maximize sales revenue from its present plant and equipment. The constraints on output are the limited size of the storage bins for the sand, pebbles, and rocks. These bins hold 2,000, 3,000, and 2,000 kilograms, respectively, and replenishment of supplies can only be made once weekly.

(a) Use the algebraic approach to find the optimal output of each of the three products.

(b) What is the maximum weekly revenue that Grimes Gravel can obtain?

(c) Which constraints are binding?

13.5 Corpulent Foods Inc. wishes to minimize the ingredient cost of its Krunchy-Karamel chocolate bar. This chocolate bar has become its major seller over the past year, but increasing costs have reduced the contribution margin below acceptable levels. The Krunchy-Karamel bar is now comprised of 45 percent chocolate, 35 percent caramel, and 20 percent nuts. It weighs 100 grams, and Corpulent Foods wholesales the bar at ten cents apiece (in bulk) and expects to continue paying $1.25 per kilogram for chocolate, $0.85 per kilogram for caramel, and $0.50 per kilogram for nuts.

Corpulent Foods' marketing research department has been conducting tests with experimental compositions of the Krunchy-Karamel bar. Using bars with various combinations of chocolate, caramel, and nuts, it has ascertained that as long as the bars contain at least 30 grams of chocolate, 15 grams of caramel, and 10 grams of nuts, and score at least 150 on the "crunch" index and 300 on the "flavor" index, all consumers who initially preferred the (regular) Krunchy-Karamel bar over the rival bars will still prefer the (modified) Krunchy-Karamel bar. The score on the crunch and flavor indices reflects the average subjective evaluation given by the consumer-participants to each experimental bar, on a scale of zero to 500. Regressing these average crunch and flavor scores against the contents of the various experimental bars, it was found that chocolate gives 2 units of crunch and 3.3 units of flavor per gram, caramel gives 1 unit of crunch and 5 units of flavor per gram, and nuts give 7 units of crunch and 2 units of flavor per gram.

(a) Formalize the above problem by expressing its objective function and six constraints algebraically.

(b) Solve for that minimum cost combination of ingredients that satisfies all constraints by systematically assigning zero values to some variables and evaluating the objective function at each of the feasible corner solutions.

(c) Should Corpulent Foods change the present composition of its Krunchy-Karamel bar? Why?

13.6 The P.M.D. Light Company produces and sells three standing lamps. The contribution to overheads and profit for these lamps is constant at the following levels regardless of output level: Model A, $8.75; Model B, $13.25, and Model C, $16.80. All three models go through the basic assembly process, then Models A and B go through the fabric installation process while Model C goes through the antique-bronzing process. The requirements of each model in each process and the weekly availability of these processes are as follows:

| Process | Hours Available | Hours Required per Unit | | |
|---------|:-------:|:----:|:----:|:----:|
| | | A | B | C |
| Assembly | 800 | 0.2 | 0.3 | 0.35 |
| Fabric | 480 | 0.1 | 0.12 | – |
| Bronzing | 160 | – | – | 0.8 |

Using the simplex method, solve for the contribution-maximizing output mix, the maximum contribution available, and the shadow prices of the constraints.

(a) Should P.M.D. Light continue to produce all three models? Why?

(b) Suppose overtime labor was available in each process at a cost of $12 per hour compared with the regular $8 per hour. Would you advise P.M.D. Light to employ this overtime labor? Explain.

13.7 The Sooflin Engineering Works fabricates small metal products for household usage. It is currently set up to make four products: a lantern, a flower pot, a trash can, and a wall ornament. It holds contracts with a major chain store to supply to the chain each week 500, 400, 600, and 300 units, respectively, of these four products. While it could not handle any new products, the firm has additional capacity available for more units of the same four products. Sooflin feels that it can obtain the same contribution margins per unit, namely, $1.15, $1.80, $2.05, and $3.60, respectively, from other buyers for any extra units it makes of these four products.

The constraints upon Sooflin's maximum output levels are the availability of the metal (which is common to all four products), the availability of time on the cutting and stamping machine, and the availability of labor time for assembling and finishing the products. The resources available and the requirements of each product are as follows:

| Input | Units | Total Available Weekly | Requirements per Unit. | | | |
|---|---|---|---|---|---|---|
| | | | Lantern | Pot | Can | Ornament |
| Metal | Kilograms | 1,000 | 0.15 | 0.25 | 0.42 | 0.63 |
| Machine | Hours | 160 | 0.08 | 0.03 | 0.05 | 0.10 |
| Labor | Hours | 960 | 0.10 | 0.12 | 0.18 | 0.25 |

(a) Using the simplex method, find the output combination that maximizes contribution to profits, the maximum contribution available, and the shadow prices of the constraints.

(b) What would you advise Sooflin as to future strategy?

## SUGGESTED REFERENCES AND FURTHER READING

BAUMOL, W. J., *Economic Theory and Operations Analysis,* 4th ed., Chaps. 5 and 6. Englewood Cliffs, N.J.: Prentice-Hall, 1977.

BRIGHAM, E. F., and J. L. PAPPAS, *Managerial Economics,* 2nd ed., Chap. 7. Hinsdale, Ill.: Dryden, 1976.

CHARNES, A., and W. W. COOPER, *Management Models and Industrial Applications of Linear Programming,* Vols. I and II. New York: John Wiley, 1961.

DANO, S., *Linear Programming in Industry: Theory and Applications.* Wien, Austria: Springer-Verlag, 1960.

DANTZIG, G. B., *Linear Programming and Extensions,* esp. Chaps. 1-5. Princeton, N.J.: Princeton University Press, 1963.

DORFMAN, R., "Mathematical, or Linear, Programming: A Nonmathematical Exposition," *American Economic Review,* 63 (December 1953), 797-825.

DORFMAN, R., P. A. SAMUELSON, and R. M. SOLOW, *Linear Programming and Economic Analysis,* Chaps. 1-7. New York: McGraw-Hill, 1958.

FABRYCKY, W. J., and G. J. THUESEN, *Economic Decision Analysis,* Chap. 15. Englewood Cliffs, N.J.: Prentice-Hall, 1974.

HEINEKE, J. M., *Microeconomics for Business Decisions: Theory and Applications,* Chaps. 4 and 5. Englewood Cliffs, N.J.: Prentice-Hall, 1976.

NAYLOR, T. H. and J. M. VERNON, *Microeconomics and Decision Models of the Firm,* Chaps. 6-8. New York: Harcourt, Brace & World, 1969.

# 14

# Advertising
# and Promotional
# Decisions

## 14.1 INTRODUCTION

In earlier chapters we considered the firm's strategic variable to be the price level, and we discussed the implications of differing price levels for the attainment of the firm's objectives. In some market situations, however, price competition may be virtually absent because of the nature of the product and/or the market. In some market situations we find that, for the most part, firms leave the price level alone and engage in active competition through advertising and promotional expenditures, due primarily to the costs associated with price wars. In other market situations we should expect to find firms adjusting both price and advertising expenditures simultaneously to obtain their objectives. Monopolistic competitors and oligopolists gain control over the price level as a result of the differentiation of their product: advertising and promotional expenditures are likely to increase this differentiation and hence increase the control these firms have over their market price, and increase the price that might be obtained for any given output level.

In the monopolistically competitive market situation the firm may presume that its actions will have an insignificant effect on each of its competitors and hence may presume that there will be no reaction from competitors to its actions. Thus we may analyze the monopolistically competitive firm's advertising and promotional decisions under the assumption of *ceteris paribus*. The same applies to the monopolist, since this firm has no existing competition to expect reactions from. The oligopolist, however, operating in an environment of strong interdependence of action, must expect its advertising and promotional expenditures to have a noticeable impact on competitors' sales and hence must expect these rivals to react to its advertising and promotional expenditures.

In the following sections we shall consider first the firm's optimal adjustment of its advertising and promotional expenditures under conditions of *ceteris paribus*, (1) given a particular price level and (2) under a situation where both price and advertising may be adjusted simultaneously to their optimal levels. We then turn to the advertising and promotional decision under conditions of oligopoly where the reaction of rivals must be taken into account. Finally, we address the issue of the uncertainty as to the impact of advertising upon the level of sales and profits.

Throughout this chapter the emphasis will be on the economics of the advertising and promotional decision, and we leave to our confreres in the discipline of marketing the more specialized problems of media selection, message composition, promotional mix, timing, and pattern of promotional campaigns. Throughout this chapter we shall, for simplicity of exposition, use the term *advertising* to include all elements of the promotional mix.

## 14.2 OPTIMAL ADVERTISING EXPENDITURES UNDER *CETERIS PARIBUS* CONDITIONS

In Chapter 4 we saw that the firm's sales or demand level was a function of several controllable variables and a variety of uncontrollable variables. The controllable variables were later termed the firm's strategic variables and may be familiar to you as the "marketing mix" of price, promotion, product design, and distribution. Since the firm's sales are a function of these variables, it follows that the firm's profits are a function of these variables, and if the firm wishes to maximize profits it should adjust these controllable variables to the point where further adjustment would make no positive contribution to profits.

### The Advertising-Sales Relationship

In Chapter 4 we held all other variables in the demand function constant while varying the level of price to find the influence on demand. Analogously, we shall now examine the effect of holding all other variables (including price) constant while varying the level of advertising. Thus demand will be equal to a constant (which represents the effect of all the other variables), plus some function of advertising expenditures. In the simple linear case:

$$Q = \alpha + \beta A \tag{14.1}$$

where $Q$ is the quantity demanded, $\alpha$ and $\beta$ are parameters, and $A$ is the level of advertising expenditure. Note that this implies that the marginal impact on sales for additional units of advertising expenditure (i.e., the parameter $\beta$) will be constant regardless of the level of advertising expenditure. More likely we would expect diminishing returns to advertising expenditures at higher advertising levels. Thus the advertising function may be quadratic in form, such as

$$Q = \alpha + \beta_1 A - \beta_2 A^2 \tag{14.2}$$

It might be argued that initial levels of advertising may benefit from increasing returns, since certain threshold levels of advertising expenditure must be reached in order to afford certain types of media and to penetrate the buyer's consciousness. However, we would expect that these thresholds would be soon overcome and that diminishing returns would be expected to set in for higher levels of advertising expenditure. Thus the general form of the advertising function for all levels of advertising might be expected to be cubic, such as

$$Q = \alpha + \beta_1 A + \beta_2 A^2 - \beta_3 A^3 \tag{14.3}$$

These three types of advertising relationship are shown in Figure 14.1. Note that in all cases quantity demanded has some positive value (viz., the parameter $\alpha$)

**FIGURE 14.1**
**Possible functional forms of the advertising/sales relationship**

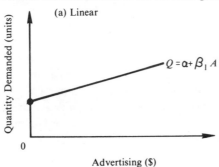

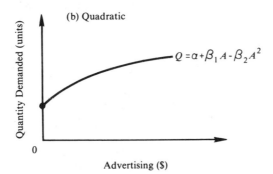

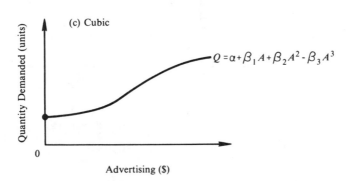

when advertising is zero, and that the general relationship between advertising and quantity demanded is positive. Clearly, we should not expect the relationship to be linear over a wide range of advertising levels, since this neglects the probable occurrence of diminishing returns to advertising expenditures. Nevertheless, a linear advertising function may be a sufficient approximation of both the quadratic and the cubic functions over a limited range of advertising expenditures.

The appropriate functional form of the advertising sales relationship is of course the one that provides the best statistical fit to the data in a particular case. If a firm could be assured that *ceteris paribus* held for all other significant variables, and was able to vary its level of advertising over a period and observe the variations in demand, it could apply regression analysis to the data generated to find which form of the regression equation best fits the observed data.[1]

### The Optimal Level of Advertising for a Given Price Level

You will recall from Chapter 4 that advertising expenditures are one of the variables that are held constant while a particular demand curve is being discussed. Changes in advertising expenditures cause a shift in the demand curve, causing it to move to the right when advertising expenditures are increased, or to the left when expenditures are reduced. In Figure 14.2 we show the initial price and quantity coordinates as $P_0$ and $Q_0$ on demand curve $D_0$. Suppose now that

**FIGURE 14.2**
**Impact of increasing advertising expenditures on the demand curve**

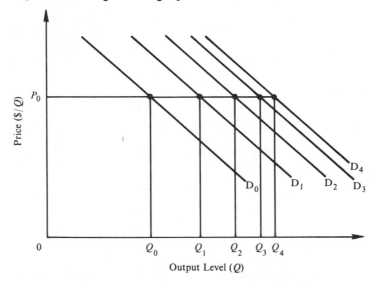

[1] See, for example, V. R. Rao, "Alternative Econometric Models of Sales-Advertising Relationships," *Journal of Marketing Research,* 9 (May 1972), 177-81; and D. G. Clarke, "Sales-Advertising Cross-Elasticities and Advertising Competition," *Journal of Marketing Research,* 10 (August 1973), 250-61.

advertising expenditures are increased from their previous level by a given amount, and that this causes the demand curve to shift to the right to that shown as $D_1$. Subsequent increases in advertising expenditures would be expected to shift the demand curve farther to the right, but if there are diminishing returns to advertising expenditures we should expect these subsequent shifts of the demand curve to become progressively smaller as advertising expenditures are increased by equal increments.

As advertising expenses are increased, total revenues derived are also increased, since at the given price level progressively larger quantities are demanded. If total revenues increase by more than the incremental cost of production and the increase in advertising expenditures, we must consider the increased advertising as beneficial if the firm's objective function is concerned with either profits and/or sales levels. That is, increased profits will have been derived by virtue of the increased advertising expenditure, and the sales level will have been increased. Supposing the objective to be maximization of contribution, the decision maker's problem is to increase advertising up to the point where the increase in total revenue just covers the increase in both the production and the selling costs that occasioned that increase in total revenues.

To demonstrate this, let us suppose that the advertising function for a particular firm has been estimated as follows:

$$Q = 10,000 + 25.2A - 0.8A^2 \qquad (14.4)$$

where $A$ represents advertising expenditures in thousands of dollars. The optimal level of advertising, using the marginalist approach, will be that level at which the last dollar spent on advertising contributes just one dollar toward overheads and profits. Thus the maximizing condition is

$$\frac{d\pi}{dA} = 1 \qquad (14.5)$$

where $\pi$ represents "contribution to overheads and profits" (considering only the variable production costs and not the selling costs). If we consider $dA$ in one-dollar increments, the requirement for profit maximization, that is, $d\pi$, equals one dollar in order to cover the last dollar of advertising expenditure incurred. Note that to find $d\pi/dA$ we must first find how quantity demanded varies with advertising, and then how profits vary with quantity demanded. That is, $d\pi/dA$ expands to

$$\frac{d\pi}{dA} = \frac{dQ}{dA} \cdot \frac{d\pi}{dQ} \qquad (14.6)$$

From Eq.(14.4) we can find $dQ/dA$ by taking the first derivative of the estimated advertising function with respect to the level of advertising expenditures. Hence

$$\frac{dQ}{dA} = 25.2 - 1.6A \qquad (14.7)$$

The second element on the right-hand side of Eq.(14.6), namely, the marginal contribution to overheads and profits, is in fact the contribution on the last unit produced. Supposing a simple case where both market price and per unit variable production costs are constant, we can express Eq.(14.6) as follows:

$$\frac{d\pi}{dA} = \frac{dQ}{dA} \circ CM \tag{14.8}$$

Since the maximizing condition is to set $d\pi/dA$ equal to one, we may restate the maximization condition as

$$\frac{dQ}{dA} = \frac{1}{CM} \tag{14.9}$$

Supposing the contribution margin to be constant at $6 per unit, by substitution from (14.7) into (14.9) we can solve for the optimal level of advertising as follows:

$$25.2 - 1.6A = \frac{1}{6}$$

$$151.2 - 9.6A = 1$$

$$-9.6A = -150.2$$

$$A = 15.646$$

Thus in the case where the advertising function is represented by Eq.(14.4) and the contribution margin is constant at $6 per unit, the profit-maximizing level of advertising is 15.646 units, or $15,646.

Where there are diminishing returns in production, or a downward-sloping demand curve, we cannot expect contribution margin per unit to remain constant regardless of output level, and hence we must specify the profit function in terms of total revenue and total costs such that we may accurately define the $d\pi/dQ$ term over all values of $Q$. A second problem arises where the advertising coefficient $(dQ/dA)$ is estimated from a linear multiple-regression equation, in which case it will be the average of the marginal impact of advertising over the range of the data observations. Since we expect the marginal impact of advertising to decline as the level of advertising increases, this coefficient will overstate the effect of additional advertising at the upper end of the observations (where our interest will probably be) and should be used with caution for decision-making purposes.

### Simultaneous Adjustment of Price and Advertising Levels

Where the firm is able to adjust both price and advertising, we should not expect the firm to wish to be constrained to a particular price level. The monopolistic competitor, for example, is able to adjust price without expecting retaliation from rival firms, and the monopolist has no rival firm's reactions to consider. Thus the *ceteris paribus* assumptions are appropriate for these market situations.

Advertising expenditures must be regarded as a fixed cost, since they are typically independent of the current level of output and sales. Thus the average advertising expenditures, or, more broadly, average selling costs, will be graphed as a rectangular hyperbola against the output level. In Figure 14.3 we show the average selling cost curve for a particular level of advertising expenditures, and given a particular demand and production situation.[2] The intersection of the

**FIGURE 14.3**
**The average selling cost curve**

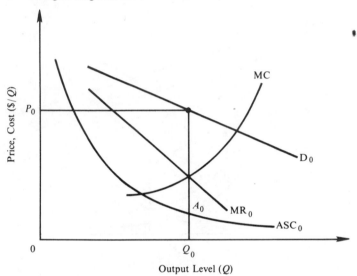

marginal cost and marginal revenue curve indicates that the profit- or contribution-maximizing output level is $Q_0$, to be sold at price $P_0$. The relevant point on the average selling cost curve ($ASC_0$) is the point labeled $A_0$, since this is the average selling cost level at output level $Q_0$. There is nothing in Figure 14.3 to indicate that $ASC_0$ is the optimal level of advertising expenditure. Larger advertising budgets will cause the demand curve to shift to the right but will also cause the average selling cost curve to move upward and to the right. To find the optimal level of advertising expenditure and the profit-maximizing price, we must know to what extent additional advertising expenditures will shift the demand curve.

[2] This analysis follows N. S. Buchanan, "Advertising Expenditures: A Suggested Treatment," *Journal of Political Economy,* August 1942, pp. 537-57. An alternate methodology is given by R. Dorfman and P. O. Steiner, "Optimal Advertising and Optimal Quality," *American Economic Review,* 44 (December 1954), 826-36.

In Figure 14.4 we show the results of increasing the level of advertising expenditure by two distinct steps. Starting from the initial advertising level, $ASC_0$, which gave rise to the optimal quantity and price levels $Q_0$ and $P_0$, we investigate the impact of increased advertising expenditures. Suppose that advertising expenditure is increased to the level indicated by the hyperbola $ASC_1$. This causes the demand curve to shift from $D_0$ to $D_1$. The marginal cost curve remains in the same place, of course, and intersects the new marginal revenue curve $MR_1$ at the output level $Q_1$, indicating a new profit-maximizing price level shown by the point $P_1$. At this output level, $A_1$ indicates the average selling cost per unit.

**FIGURE 14.4**
**Optimal prices for successive levels of advertising expenditure**

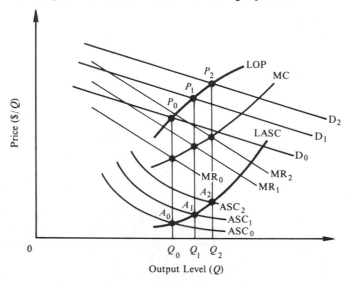

Suppose now that advertising expenditures are again increased, to the level shown by $ASC_2$. This in turn causes the demand curve to shift to $D_2$ and the related marginal revenue, $MR_2$, to intersect the marginal cost curve at output level $Q_2$. The profit-maximizing price for this output level is shown by $P_2$, and the average selling cost at this output level is shown by the point $A_2$. Clearly, by continuing this process we could trace a series of optimal price points and a series of average selling cost points. The locus of optimal prices for various levels of advertising expenditure is shown as the curve *LOP* in Figure 14.4, and the locus of the average selling costs for various advertising and demand levels is shown as the curve *LASC*. Note that the general shape of these curves reflects the presence of diminishing returns to advertising expenditures.

The LOP curve and the LASC curve in Figure 14.4 are both loci of a variable that represents an average—viz., average revenue (or price) and average selling cost. Each of these average curves will have a curve that is marginal to it. In Figure 14.5 we show the LMR curve (locus of marginal revenue) as the curve

**FIGURE 14.5**
Establishing the optimal price and advertising levels

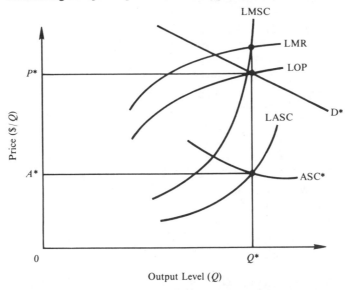

Output Level ($Q$)

that is marginal to the locus of optimal prices curve, and the LMSC curve (locus of marginal selling costs) as the curve that is marginal to the LASC curve. Note that the shape and placement of these marginal curves follow the general principles of the relationships between average and marginal curves. The decision maker's problem is to have the marginal increase in selling costs just equal to the marginal change in revenues. Thus the intersection of the LMSC curve with the LMR curve will indicate the output level at which the increment to revenues will be just equal to the increment to selling costs. The optimal output level is shown as $Q^*$ in Figure 14.5. The point on the LOP curve at that output level must lie on the optimal demand curve, which we show as $D^*$, and the optimal price level is thus $P^*$. The optimal level of advertising can be found from the LASC curve to be $ASC^*$, which represents $A^*$ dollars per unit of output at the optimal output level.

The above approach assumes knowledge of the cost and revenue curves shown in the figures, and the underlying production, demand, and advertising functions. In practice, of course, it may be extremely difficult and/or expensive to ascertain the actual shape and placement of these curves. The model is nevertheless useful for its pedagogical and explanatory value, since it incorporates the notions of simultaneous adjustment of price and advertising levels, with the subsequent interaction of the "law" of demand and the "law" of diminishing returns to advertising. Note that in effect this model sets the same optimizing condition as in the earlier simple case where price was held constant—viz., the advertising is carried to the point where the increment to the total advertising cost is just covered by the increment to the total revenue derived from the sale of the marginal unit.

## 14.3  ADVERTISING AND PROMOTIONAL EXPENDITURES WHEN MUTUAL DEPENDENCE IS RECOGNIZED

Under conditions of oligopoly the firm should be expected to recognize that its advertising and other marketing strategies would have a noticeable impact on the sales and profits of rivals unless the other firms are simultaneously carrying out new promotional campaigns. Unlike price adjustments, however, promotional campaigns require a significant lead time in which they must be planned and coordinated with the availability of time and space from the various advertising agencies and media channels. This means that if a firm is caught napping by a competitor's new advertising campaign there will be a significant lag before it can produce its own retaliatory campaign, during which time it may have lost a significant share of its market, which in turn may prove difficult or impossible to retrieve. The existence of this lag thus motivates firms to have an ongoing involvement in promotional activity. If there is always a new campaign in the pipeline, the firm does not expect to be caught napping to the extent that it would be if it waited until a competitor initiated advertising or promotional competition.

### Advertising Interdependence

Given that firms tend to have continual advertising and promotional strategies, changes in market shares should only be expected to occur when the relative advertising and promotional effectiveness of firms is suddenly made different by an increase in the relative size of an individual firm's advertising budget, and/ or in the relative effectiveness of a firm's advertising expenditures. Suppose two large firms share the major part of a particular market and each budgets approximately $4 million toward promotional expenditures each year. In Table 14.1 we show the payoff matrix for the interaction of the firms' advertising strategies. When both firms spend $4 million, the net profits to each firm are $10 million. By convention, A's payoffs are shown first (followed by B's payoffs) for each combination of promotional expenditure strategies. Suppose now that Firm A contemplates increasing the promotional budget level to $6 million. If Firm B maintains its promotional budget at $4 million, this will cause A's profits to rise to $12 million while B's profits will fall to $6 million. This indicates of course that the result of A's additional $2 million promotional expenditures will be to cause a substantial proportion of the market to switch from Firm B's products to Firm A's products, with associated changes in the firm's relative profitabilities.

**TABLE 14.1**
**Payoff matrix for advertising strategies**

|  |  | Firm B's Advertising Budget | |
|---|---|---|---|
|  |  | $4 m. | $6 m. |
| Firm A's | $4 m. | 10.0,   10.0 | 6.0,   12.0 |
| Advertising Budget | $6 m. | 12.0,   6.0 | 8.7,   8.7 |

Conversely, if Firm B considered increasing advertising levels to $6 million while Firm A held its advertising constant at $4 million, it would be Firm B that would benefit from the change in market share that resulted. If both firms increased advertising to the new higher advertising levels, the result would be as shown in the lower-right-hand quadrant of the payoff matrix, namely, that profits are reduced compared with the earlier levels of advertising expenditures. This may be rationalized in terms of the market becoming saturated by the products of the two firms, and/or that the firms' competing messages to consumers tend to offset each other's effectiveness by creating "noise" in the communication process.

In the above situation it is not unreasonable to expect each firm to follow a "maximin" strategy. Given that the firms are likely to be risk averters and that there will be a significant lag before the firm can retaliate to an increase in advertising expenditures by the other firm, we might expect each firm to wish to avoid the worst possible outcome. For each firm the worst outcome associated with the $4 million expenditure is $6 million profit, whereas the worst outcome associated with the $6 million promotional budget is $8.7 million profit. The best of these worst situations is the $8.7 million profit associated with the $6 million promotional expenditures. Thus the maximin strategy for each firm is to increase its promotional budget to the higher level.

### The Prisoner's Dilemma

In the above example the firms have independently increased their expenditures in pursuit of private gain, but instead they find that the result is inferior to that which was enjoyed at the earlier promotional levels. The firms are subject to what has become known as the "prisoner's dilemma." The prisoner's dilemma situation arises when two or more parties are motivated to behave in a self-serving manner, and they assume that their rivals or adversaries will act similarly. The result is that the outcome to all parties is inferior to that which could have been attained had the parties been able to to assume that their rivals would not act in a way detrimental to them.[3]

This situation is called the prisoner's dilemma after the supposed situation of two bank robbers caught with the proceeds of a robbery, but with no more than circumstantial evidence of being involved in that robbery. Interrogated in two separate rooms they are each told that if they confess and implicate the other, they will go free as a "state's witness" while the accomplice will receive a substantial term in prison. Each prisoner knows that if they both refuse to confess they will receive a short prison term for possession of stolen goods, while if both prisoners confess, neither will be allowed to turn state's witness, and both will receive relatively long jail sentences. Given the inability of the prisoners to communicate with each other (and since there is no honor among thieves), and given that each prisoner dislikes time spent in jail, each will be motivated to avoid the worst possible outcome. Since the worst possible outcome is that of not confess-

---

[3] See R. D. Luce and H. Raiffa, *Games and Decisions* (New York: John Wiley, 1957), pp 94-102; or F. M. Scherer, *Industrial Market Structure and Economic Performance* (Chicago: Rand McNally, 1970), pp. 142-45 and 335-37.

ing while the other does confess, the maximum strategy for each prisoner is to confess. Since each prisoner confesses, they each end up with a relatively long jail sentence, whereas if they had been able to communicate and coordinate their strategies they would have been sentenced to the relatively short prison term for possession of stolen goods.

The essence of the prisoner's dilemma thus applies to firms in situations of advertising rivalry. A lack of communication and coordination between parties with conflicting self-interest can lead to a situation in which both parties are worse off compared with the outcomes that would have been obtained had there been communication and coordination between those firms. Referring back to Table 14.1, had the firms agreed to limit their advertising expenditures to $4 million each, their net profits would have remained at the $10 million level. In pursuit of independent profit gains, however, and without knowing whether or not the other firm was simultaneously planning an increase in the promotional budget, both firms find themselves at a reduced level of profit.

Note that when both firms have increased their promotional budget to the $6 million level, there is no incentive for either firm to independently reduce the advertising budget, since this would lead to a loss of market share and net profits. Similarly, larger promotional budgets would promise increases in net profit levels if they were undertaken independently. When each firm fears that the other might undertake a further increase in promotional expenditures we have the prisoner's dilemma all over again, and both firms will be motivated to spend the additional amount on promotion so that they will not be left standing still when the other's promotional campaign is launched.

### Coordination of Advertising Expenditures

Is it reasonable to expect firms to coordinate their advertising and promotional expenditure levels? While firms may achieve an implicit agreement not to escalate advertising budgets beyond present levels, it is unlikely that they will achieve agreement to reduce budget levels to a point that would seem to be more efficient in terms of total profitability. In part this is undoubtedly due to the distrust that a firm might feel concerning the reduction of its own advertising expenditures while rivals may not in fact reduce theirs. Given the lead time required to prepare additional promotional campaigns, a firm that double-crosses its rivals could gain a market share advantage that might be impossible to regain.

A second factor militating against the coordination of advertising and promotional competition is that these activities are seen as an appropriate forum for the competitive instincts of rival firms, and that this avenue for civilized competition should not be closed to the firms. Promotional competition requires skill and planning and the services of talented people. Price competition, on the other hand, requires little planning and not much skill on the part of the instigator, yet the impact upon the profitabilies of all firms may be significantly adverse. To avoid active competition shifting to the price arena, firms may prefer to compete on a promotional level where gains in market shares and profits are the rewards for exceptional abilities on the promotional side.

In the above we have presumed that the firm can foresee the result of a given expenditure on advertising and promotion. In fact, $1,000 spent this month may be very effective in influencing the level of sales, whereas a similar amount spent next month may have virtually no impact. This may be the result of differences in the qualitative aspects of the advertising campaign, a different media mix, autonomous changes in consumer tastes and preferences, or similar changes induced by concurrent advertising campaigns of rival firms. Thus we must expect there to be a probability distribution of sales increases following an increase in the level of advertising and promotional expenditures.

### Predictability and Probabilities

Assigning the probabilities to the possible outcomes represents no small problem. The major issue is to predict the impact of the expenditures on the purchasing behavior of consumers, of course, but underlying this are the twin problems of understanding consumer needs and wants and predicting competitors' simultaneous offerings to satisfy these needs and wants. To increase the probabilities of increased sales levels for a given level of advertising, the firm should have a sound knowledge, through market research, of what tangible and intangible features the buyers want to see involved in the product. The firm's advertising and promotional expenditures should then be directed to informing the buyers of the availability of these attributes in this particular product, and to persuading the buyers that the desired attributes can be *best* obtained through purchase of this product.

Modern marketing theory emphasizes that products and promotion should be aimed at segments of the overall market, where each segment is defined in terms of a common set of attributes desired by the buyers in that segment. The attributes that may be perceived and appreciated by consumers may be physically incorporated into the product (tangibles such as strength, durability, and other performance characteristics), or may be intangibles that the consumer believes to exist (such as style, conferred status, and vicarious enjoyment of an agreeable lifestyle). Different attributes will be stressed (or invented) in the advertising campaigns for different segments, and some part of the persuasive element of advertising may relate to those tangible attributes that cannot be verified by the consumer, as well as to the intangibles.

Once the market research has been conducted to ascertain the attributes desired by consumers, and the perception of these attributes in our product vis-à-vis competitors' products, the choice of message and medium (or media mix) will be selected by specialists in the advertising area, and (it is hoped) will be confirmed by pretesting and posttesting upon representative potential buyers. In summary, the better that market research is able to identify the attributes desired by buyers, and the better that the product and the advertising campaign conform to the desires of the target segment(s), the more confident the decision maker can be in assigning probabilities to the various possible outcomes of a given advertising expenditure.

## Advertising as an Investment

The impact of an advertising campaign may not be felt simply in the period of that expenditure but should be expected to have a residual impact which gradually attenuates over subsequent periods. Potential buyers may be only partly convinced by a particular campaign, but this may build a necessary base for future persuasion. Alternatively, the campaign may convince consumers to switch to this product, but only after they deplete their personal inventories of rivals' products. Thus a dollar spent on advertising now may lead to revenues in the same period, plus a stream of revenues in future periods. In this respect advertising can be regarded as an investment project and should compete for funds within the firm on the same basis as other investment projects with multi-period revenue streams. The following chapter investigates the appropriate decision criteria to be applied when selecting investment projects to be undertaken, and advertising can be treated just like any other investment project.

The conditions for optimal advertising expenditure considered in the earlier sections of this chapter were generated under the implicit assumption that the total impact of the expenditure would be felt in the same period. This analysis remains sufficiently accurate if the residual impact of advertising expenditure is very low, or if the time period used for analysis is long enough to include the greater part of any residual impact. If there is a significant residual impact of advertising expenditures in subsequent periods, the present value of the future revenues generated must be included in the decision-making process. Current advertising expenditures may exceed the short-run profit-maximizing level to the extent of the present value of the future revenues generated, before we could say that the firm's longer-term objective of maximizing net worth was not being served.

## Advertising to Raise Barriers to Entry

It is widely supposed that advertising and promotional efforts operate to raise and/or maintain barriers to the entry of potential competition.[4] Repeated messages concerning existing firms and their products are said to increase consumer loyalty to existing products and cause consumers to be reluctant to switch to the products of new entrant firms.[5] To convince consumers that their products have comparable quality, reliability, and other desirable features, the entrant firms may need to spend more on advertising and promotion over at least the first few years, as compared with the existing firms. It has been argued that the prospect of these additional expenses in an uncertain market for their products causes potential entrants to decide against entry because of the low or negative level of expected profits.

[4] Following J. S. Bain, *Barriers to New Competition* (Cambridge: Harvard University Press, 1956), many economists have argued along these lines. For a recent view and a comprehensive bibliography, see D. Needham, "Entry Barriers and Non-Price Aspects of Firms' Behavior," *Journal of Industrial Economics,* 25 (September 1976), 29-43.

[5] Notice that this argument involves the residual effects of past advertising and promotional efforts. It is the sum of these residual effects that operates to enhance consumer loyalty to existing firms' products.

Thus high levels of advertising by existing firms in a particular industry might be expected to allow those firms to continue to earn higher than "normal" profits, since entry is not attempted (or successfully accomplished) due to the expectations (or actuality) of significantly higher cost structures for entrant firms. Various studies have been reported in which tests were made for the empirical relationship between levels of advertising and levels of profitability. The results of these tests tend to be ambiguous.[6] A more recent and probably much more fruitful avenue of inquiry concerns advertising's function of imparting price and quality information which can be expected to increase competition rather than inhibit competition.[7]

## 14.5 SUMMARY

Advertising and promotional decisions within the firm are an important adjunct to the firm's pricing decision, and in some cases they become the firm's primary strategic variable. Advertising and promotional expenditures are expected to shift the demand curve outward and cause the price elasticity of demand to be reduced at any given price level. The advertising function should be expected to exhibit diminishing returns to additional expenditures as the marginal consumer becomes increasingly more difficult to convince and the market approaches saturation.

The optimal level of advertising expenditures is that level at which the incremental cost of advertising is just equal to the incremental revenues associated with that expenditure. If these revenues extend beyond the current time period, they must be evaluated in present value terms for comparability with the current advertising expenditures. The general (marginalist) rule for optimality expressed above applies both to situations where price is held constant and to situations where price is adjusted simultaneously.

In practice several problems inhibit the application of the marginalist rule for optimal advertising. First, *ceteris paribus* is not likely to hold in many market situations as rival firms simultaneously adjust their pricing and/or advertising strategies. Second, the impact of advertising expenditures cannot easily be predicted with any great degree of accuracy. This in turn is due to the uncertainty as to what it is that potential buyers want, and whether or not the selected message and media will effectively inform and persuade the buyers that this particular product best provides the desired attributes.

In oligopoly situations the level of advertising and promotional expenditures may be taken to excess due to the uncertainty facing the decision maker concerning the simultaneous actions of rivals. Even when the future impact of advertising expenditures is taken into account, oligopolists unable or unwilling to coordinate their advertising strategies may be expected to spend beyond the point where profits (short- or long-term) are maximized. They must continue

[6] See the papers by Comanor and Wilson, Schmalensee, Peles, and Ayanian, which are listed under "Suggested References" at the end of this chapter.

[7] See "A New View of Advertising's Economic Impact," *Business Week,* December 22, 1975, pp. 49 and 54.

to run in order to stay in the same place, since any unilateral reduction in advertising expenditures would cause them to lose some part of their market share and would presumably reduce the present value of their future profit stream.

Advertising and promotional expenditures tend to generate a stream of future revenues as new customers finally purchase the product and current customers return to purchase more units in the future. Advertising and promotional expenditures thus may be considered as an investment in future revenues, and therefore they should compete with other investment projects for the funds available. This is the subject matter of the following chapter.

## DISCUSSION QUESTIONS

14.1 Under what conditions may a firm expect *ceteris paribus* conditions to hold for changes in its advertising and promotional expenditures?

14.2 Discuss the idea of a minimum threshold of advertising and promotional effectiveness. Is it reasonable to argue the existence of such a threshold?

14.3 Why should we expect diminishing returns to (eventually) apply to advertising and promotional efforts? Outline several reasons.

14.4 What is the rule for optimal advertising expenditure in the short run, given price and average variable cost levels? Explain.

14.5 Outline the process underlying the simultaneous selection of the optimal level of advertising and the optimal price.

14.6 Why do oligopolists face a "prisoner's dilemma" problem when it comes to deciding on the level of advertising expenditures?

14.7 If firms decided to limit their advertising expenditures to a given amount, would this mean that market shares would then remain stable at the present levels? Why or why not?

14.8 Outline the issues involved in attempting to predict the impact of an advertising or promotional campaign.

14.9 If there are residual impacts in future periods of this period's advertising expenditure, is it necessarily excessive to spend beyond the point where short-run incremental cost of advertising exceeds short-run incremental revenue from advertising?

14.10 Outline the issues involved in the argument that advertising and promotional expenditures raise the product differentiation barriers to entry. Would these barriers exist without advertising? Why?

## PROBLEMS

14.1 The Thompson Textile Company has asked you for advice as to the optimality of its advertising policy with respect to one of its products, Product X. The following data are supplied:

| | |
|---|---|
| Sales (units) | 282,500 |
| Advertising elasticity of demand | 2.50 |
| Price per unit | $ 2.00 |
| Marginal cost per unit is constant at | $ 1.00 |
| Advertising budget for Product X | $ 56,000 |

(a) Is Thompson's advertising budget for Product X at the profit-maximizing level?

(b) If not, can you say how much more or less it should spend on advertising? Discuss all relevant issues and/or qualifications you think are important.

14.2 The McWilliams Bottling Company bottles and markets under license a major brand-name soft drink. Prices of soft drinks are virtually dictated by the market and the preponderance of dispensing machines that require a time-consuming adjustment in order to allow price changes to be effected. In the regional market that it serves, McWilliams has noticed that quantity demanded responds to variations in the level of advertising and promotional expenditures. The firm has kept the following records of sales (units) and advertising and promotional expenditures over the past two years:

| Last year | Sales (units) | Advertising/Promotion ($) |
|---|---|---|
| 1st quarter | 96,000 | 3,400 |
| 2nd quarter | 103,000 | 4,350 |
| 3rd quarter | 93,000 | 3,750 |
| 4th quarter | 111,000 | 5,900 |
| *Preceding year* | | |
| 1st quarter | 90,000 | 2,600 |
| 2nd quarter | 76,000 | 1,850 |
| 3rd quarter | 104,000 | 5,200 |
| 4th quarter | 120,000 | 7,300 |

McWilliams's present advertising and sales (units) levels are $4,000 and 99,500 units. Contribution margin (per unit) is considered to be constant at $0.22. The marketing department at McWilliams feels that there were no significant changes in any factors that would prevent the above data from being used to reliably estimate the firm's sales/advertising function.

(a) Plot the sales data against the advertising expenditures and sketch in what appears to be the line of best fit to the data.

(b) Please advise McWilliams as to the estimated optimal level of its advertising and promotional expenditutes. Explain and defend your recommendation.

14.3 Flintrock Fixtures is a small partnership that produces and markets a variety of kitchen and bathroom fixtures in ceramics, metal, and marble. The market for these products in Flintrock's area is not highly competitive, since the rival firms tend to compete in separate market segments of the fixtures market. Over the past year, one of the major partners, Charles Flint, has been experimenting with advertising and promotional levels in order to ascertain the impact of this variable on sales. Regressing monthly sales revenue against monthly advertising and promotional expenditures, Mr. Flint has obtained the following regression equation: $TR = 110,482.5 + 2318.6A - 103.2A^2$, where $TR$ represents sales revenue in dollars and $A$ represents advertising and promotional expenditures in thousands of dollars. This equation was derived from data ranging from $1,000 to $8,500 spent per month on advertising and promotion. ($R^2 = 0.99$, significant at 1 percent level.) The present level of advertising and promotional expenditure is $6,000 per month, and Mr. Flint, who wishes to maximize sales revenue, wishes to increase this to $7,500 per month, which is the maximum that Rocky Spinelli, the other major partner, will agree to.

A minor partner in the enterprise, Peter Pebble, is concerned with the short-term profits of the enterprise. He argues that given the firm's pricing policy of marking up average variable costs by 100 percent, monthly profits would be increased significantly by reducing advertising and promotional expenditures. Mr. Pebble argues that a reduction of at least $2,000 per month would augment profits considerably.

Another minor partner, John Stone, argues that the longer-term profitability of the enterprise is the appropriate objective to pursue and that he supports Mr. Flint.

(a)   What level of expenditure on advertising and promotion would maximize monthly sales revenue, given no limit on this level? How confident are you about the accuracy of this prediction? Explain.

(b)   What level of expenditure on advertising and promotion would maximize monthly profits? Explain.

(c)   Make an argument to support Mr. Stone's position.

(d)   Presuming Mr. Stone to be correct in his reasoning, and Mr. Pebble to be outvoted, what do you suggest Flintrock do?

14.4   Record Breakers is a downtown store selling phono records and tapes. Its nearest competitor is about six blocks away, and its clientele is almost entirely composed of downtown office workers and other personnel from nearby buildings. Record Breakers has found that the sales of phono records vary with the number of records it places on special at $3.99 (compared with the regular price of $6.99) and with the space purchased in the city's morning newspaper for advertising these specials. The specials are intended to attract customers into the store where they will (it is hoped) also purchase one or more other records at the regular price. The greater the number of specials offered, the lower the total revenue per record, or average price of the records sold. Given any specific number of records on special, the store finds that record sales vary positively, but with diminishing returns, with the area devoted to advertising these particular records in the newspaper. Regression analysis indicates that

$$Q = 624.3 - 216.52P + 481.8S - 35.85S^2$$

where $Q$ represents the weekly sales (units) of albums, $P$ is average price in dollars, and $S$ is space units (100 square inches daily for five days) in the morning newspaper. This regression equation is highly significant and explains virtually all the variation in weekly record sales.

The average variable cost per record is constant at $3 and space units in the newspaper cost $300, and this space is available in continuously variable fractions of a unit. The "average" situation is that Record Breakers will place six records on special and buy 2.5 units of advertising space, each week. This causes the average price to be $5.75 over all records sold. The relationship between average price and number of records on special has been estimated as Av.P = 6.93 − 0.19 NS (with $R^2 = 0.97$, significant at the 5 percent level) over the range of from one to fifteen records on special. This relationship holds independently of the units of advertising space purchased, although the latter does influence volume as indicated by the earlier regression equation.

(a)   Using graphical analysis, find the level of average price and the level of advertising space purchased that allow short-run profit contribution to be maximized.

(b)   How many records should be put on special each week? Explain.

14.5  Vincenzo Pizzaria Limited operates the only pizza place in town, although there are several other fast-food outlets in peripheral competition with Vincenzo. The manager, Vincenzo Fiorelli, feels that he has a virtual monopoly, since his clientele is largely comprised of fervent pizza lovers, and that selling more pizzas is just a matter of inducing people to "eat out" more often. Consequently Mr. Fiorelli holds prices constant and advertises in local newspapers and on a local television. His pizzas come in three sizes and with a variety of dressings, from "plain" (tomato paste and cheese) all the way up to "all dressed" (mushrooms, peppers, olives, ground beef, pepperoni sausage, and heaps of mozzarella cheese).

Mr. Firoelli's son Paolo has recently obtained his business degree and has joined the family business as marketing manager. Paolo is interested in maximizing profits of the enterprise, since his father has promised him half of any extra profits generated as a bonus. Paolo decides to conduct an analysis of the cost and demand conditions facing the firm. First he examines the cost structure. Given the three different sizes of pizza and the various combinations of dressings, the firm is in effect offering a very broad product line. Paolo's first task is to convert all the product offerings into the terms of a common denominator, which he calls a medium-pizza equivalent (MPE). The weights attached to each product reflect the relative variable costs of that product. Thus a medium-all-dressed pizza is equal to 1 MPE, a small-all-dressed is equal to .75 MPEs and a large-all-dressed is equal to 1.5 MPEs, with lower weights given in each size category where the pizza is less than all-dressed. The average variable cost of an MPE is $2.65, and Paolo finds this to be constant in the relevant output range. The first major decision Paolo makes is to standardize prices on all pizzas by marking up the average variable cost by 50 percent.

The marketing manager then undertakes a study of demand conditions. After examining past records and interviewing a random sample of five hundred customers and potential customers, Paolo generates the following demand function for Vincenzo's pizzas:

$$Q = 28105.1 - 5842.2P + 1061.6A - 22.5A^2$$

where $Q$ is the number of MPEs demanded per month, $P$ is the price of an MPE in dollars, and $A$ is the advertising and promotional expenditures per month in thousands of dollars.

At present, prices are as indicated by the above markup-pricing policy, and advertising and promotional expenditures are running at the rate of $8,000 per month.

(a)  Using graphical analysis (with algebraic confirmation of results), find the optimal price and advertising/promotional levels.

(b)  How much will Paolo's monthly bonus be? (State all qualifications and assumptions, if any, underlying your answers.)

14.6  The Silk Purse Cosmetics Company operates in close competition with several other major suppliers of cosmetics and toiletries. In this market consumers do not seem to be very price conscious: if they believe a product will help them, they tend to buy that product as long as its price lies below a limit that the consumer considers intolerable. Consequently, Silk Purse and its rivals tend to compete via their advertising and promotional expenditures, which are typically aimed at informing consumers of the virtues of their new and established products. Silk Purse's advertising and promotion budget is $25 million for this year, and it estimates that its rivals will collectively spend about $100 million this year. Silk Purse's net profits are projected to be $2.8 million this year.

The vice president of finance is worried that the expected profits this year will not be high enough to support the continuation of Silk Purse's research and development program, given that dividends, taxes, and managerial bonuses must be paid out of profits. He suggests that a reduction of advertising to around $20 million would cause the profit situation to improve.

The vice president of marketing argues that a reduction in the advertising budget to $20 million would cause sales to drop by $10 million, meaning a $1.7 million dollar reduction in net profits. On the contrary, she says, Silk Purse should increase advertising and promotional expenditures to $30 million. This will increase sales by $8.5 million and net profits by $1.2 million.

The president of Silk Purse, M. C. Hogg, fears that an increase in advertising and promotional expenditures of this magnitude will very likely cause a competitive reaction from the major rivals. You are called in to advise Mr. Hogg.

(a) With the aid of a payoff matrix, explain the vice-president of marketing's argument to Mr. Hogg.

(b) How does Mr. Hogg's assessment of the situation differ from that of the marketing vice-president?

(c) What information would you encourage Mr. Hogg to obtain before making his decision?

14.7   The automobile-manufacturing industry has three major domestic producers, one minor and several miniscule domestic producers, and several major foreign producers, each supplying vehicles to the North American market. Advertising and promotional expenditures constitute a large part of the competitive effort in this industry, once the product design and price levels have been determined for each model year. With a major purchase like an automobile, the potential purchaser must feel confident about the quality of the vehicle, the efficacy of after-sales service, and the future value of the automobile at trade-in time. Advertising campaigns typically stress these factors and are also aimed at reducing post-purchase dissonance and building brand loyalty.

Suppose you are the advertising manager of one of the very small domestic auto producers. Your company's sales have been hovering perilously around one-fortieth of one percent of the entire market. Your advertising budget is $1.5 million, and your projected net profits before taxes are less than $0.5 million. Your advertising budget represents 10 percent of sales revenue, compared with an industry average of 7.5 percent. Net profits are low, largely because of your relatively short production runs, which do not allow overheads to be amortized over large output levels.

(a) Prepare an argument to convince the marketing vice-president that your advertising budget should be increased. Include counterarguments to his probable objections in your proposal.

(b) Outline the information you would want the marketing research department to obtain before planning your major campaigns for this year.

## SUGGESTED REFERENCES AND FURTHER READING

AYANIAN, R., "Advertising and Rate of Return," *Journal of Law and Economics,* 18 (October 1975), 479-506.

BLAIR, J. M., *Economic Concentration: Structure, Behavior and Public Policy,* Chap. 13. New York: Harcourt Brace Jovanovich, 1972.

BRUSH, B. C., "The Influence of Market Structure on Industry Advertising Intensity," *Journal of Industrial Economics,* 25 (September 1976), 55-67.

BUCHANAN, N. S., "Advertising Expenditures: A Suggested Treatment," *Journal of Political Economy,* August 1942, pp. 537-57. Reprinted in *Readings in Microeconimics,* ed. W. Breit and H. M. Hochman, pp. 267-79. New York: Holt, Rinehart & Winston, 1968.

CLARKE, D. G., "Sales-Advertising Cross-Elasticities and Advertising Competition," *Journal of Marketing Research,* 10 (August 1973), 250-61.

COMANOR, W. S., and T. A. WILSON, "Advertising, Market Structure, and Performance," *Review of Economics and Statistics,* 49 (November 1971), 423-40.

DORFMAN, R., and P. O. STEINER, "Optimal Advertising and Optimal Quality," *American Economic Review,* 44 (December 1954), 826-36.

KOTLER, P., *Marketing Management,* 3rd ed., Chaps. 7, 15, and 16. Englewood Cliffs, N.J.: Prentice-Hall, 1976.

NEEDHAM, D., "Entry Barriers and Non-Price Aspects of Firms' Behavior," *Journal of Industrial Economics,* 25 (September 1976), 29-43.

NERLOVE, M., and K. J. ARROW, "Optimal Advertising Policy under Dynamic Conditions," *Economica,* May 1962, pp. 129-42.

PELES, Y., "Rates of Amortization of Advertising Expenditures," *Journal of Political Economy,* 79 (September-October 1971), 1032-58.

RAO, V. R., "Alternative Econometric Models of Sales-Advertising Relationships," *Journal of Marketing Research,* 9 (May 1972), 177-81.

SCHERER, F. M., *Industrial Market Structure and Economic Performance,* Chap. 14. Chicago: Rand McNally, 1970.

SCHMALENSEE, R., "Advertising and Profitability: Further Implications of the Null Hypothesis," *Journal of Industrial Economics,* 25 (September 1976), 45-54.

——, *The Economics of Advertising.* Amsterdam: North-Holland Publishing, 1972.

SIMON, J. L., *Applied Managerial Economics,* Chap. 7. Englewood Cliffs, N.J.: Prentice-Hall, 1975.

SPENCER, M. H., K. K. SEO, and M. G. SIMKIN, *Managerial Economics,* 4th ed., Chap. 11. Homewood, Ill.: Richard D. Irwin, 1975.

TELSER, L., "Advertising and Competition," *Journal of Political Economy,* December 1964, pp. 537.

# 15

# Capital Budgeting and Investment Decisions

**15.1 Introduction**

**15.2 Capital Budgeting with Unlimited Availability of Funds**

The Net Present Value Criterion.    The Internal Rate of Return Criterion.
Relationship Between NPV and IRR.    The Profitability Index Criterion.
The Payback Period Criterion.    The Average Rate of Return Criterion.

**15.3 Mutually Exclusive Investments**

The Superiority of NPV over IRR for Mutually Exclusive Investments.
The Superiority of NPV over the Profitability Index.

**15.4 Capital Budgeting Given Limited Availability of Capital**

The Opportunity Costs of Investing.    The Profitability Index Criterion.
Some Qualifications.

**15.5 Summary**

## 15.1 INTRODUCTION

Capital budgeting is concerned with the firm's decision (1) whether or not to invest financial resources and (2) how to choose between and among the available investment projects. These projects may be to replace or expand existing plant and equipment, to diversify the firm's activities, to take over another firm, to mount an advertising campaign, to put funds into bonds, or simply to hold the funds in liquid form for future investment projects. In general, the available investment projects will involve either cost reduction or revenue generation, or some combination of the two. Pure cost reduction investments include replacement of existing assets that are now relatively inefficient due to physical depreciation and technological obsolesence. Pure revenue-generating projects may be the investment in new-product development or advertising campaigns where these are treated as an investment that leads to a future revenue stream. Expansion projects typically involve both cost reduction and revenue generation, since newer plant and equipment is typically technologically superior to that being replaced.

Where there are no limits on the availability of capital, the capital-budgeting decision is simply to accept or reject each particular project. The following section establishes a number of criteria that allow the accept/reject decision to be made. Where some investments are mutually exclusive, in that they are alternative ways of achieving the same end or are alternative uses of available space or other resources, the available investment projects must be ranked in order of preference. The third section of this chapter establishes the criterion for ranking mutually exclusive projects. When there are limits to the availability of capital, a criterion must be established which ensures that the available capital is efficiently allocated between and among the possible projects such that the firm's objectives are achieved. Capital budgeting as an allocation problem is examined in the final section of this chapter.

443

As stated above, when funds are unlimited the capital budgeting decision is whether to accept or reject each available investment project. This decision must be based upon whether or not each project contributes to the attainment of the firm's objectives. In the following paragraphs we shall take the standard view that the firm's objective is to maximize its long-term profitability, or its net worth in present value terms. In some cases, of course, the firm's time horizon may be somewhat shorter due to cash-flow or accounting profit considerations. In such cases a less profitable project may be undertaken if it promises a very short payback period or relatively large immediate gains, in preference to a more profitable project that generates its income over a longer period of time.

We shall consider five separate criteria for the accept/reject decision. We shall examine the relationships between these criteria and show why some of these criteria are superior to others.

### The Net Present Value Criterion

You will recall from Chapter 2 that *net present value* refers to the sum of the discounted value of the future stream of costs and revenues associated with a particular project. If the net present value of a project is positive, this indicates that the project adds more to revenues in present value terms than it adds to cost in present value terms and should therefore be accepted. Symbolically, we can express the net present value as follows:

$$\text{NPV} = \sum_{t=1}^{n} \frac{R_t}{(1 + k)^t} - C_0 \tag{15.1}$$

where $R_t$ signifies the contribution to overheads and profits in each future period; $C_0$ represents the initial cost of the project, including installation charges and any other expenses such as increases in working capital required by the investment; and $k$ is the opportunity rate of interest. Thus the revenue stream is discounted at the rate of interest that the firm could obtain in its next-best-alternative use of these investment funds at a similar level of risk.

The revenue stream referred to in Eq.(15.1) by $R_t$ should be considered as the net cash flow after taxes. *Net cash flow after taxes* can be defined as incremental revenues minus incremental costs, plus tax savings due to depreciation charges being deductible from taxable income, plus tax credits (if any) allowed against tax liability in connection with the particular investment project. If a tax credit (e.g., 15 percent of the initial cost) is available for net investment, this will be deducted directly from the tax liability, and it thus avoids an outflow of a certain amount. Although this is not an actual inflow of cash, the avoidance of what would otherwise be an outflow of cash in effect amounts to a cash inflow. Depreciation charges against revenues enter the cash-flow picture only indirectly and as a result of the tax saving that can be obtained by subtracting the depreciation charges from the income of the firm. To demonstrate this, suppose an investment project involves an initial cash outlay of $10,000 and will generate revenues for three years, after which time it has a salvage value of $1,000. The value of the investment project to be depreciated over the three-year life of the project is thus $9,000, and for simplicity we use the straight-line method of depreciation to allocate $3,000 to each of the three years of the project's life. In Table 15.1 we show the calculation of the cash flow after taxes, given the contribution stream indicated.

**TABLE 15.1**
**Calculation of NPV of cash flow after taxes**

| Year | Contribution | Depreciation | Tax Saving | Cash Flow After Taxes | Discount Factors | Net Present Value |
|------|--------------|--------------|------------|-----------------------|------------------|-------------------|
| 0 | $-10,000 | – | – | $-10,000 | 1.000 | $-10,000.00 |
| 1 | 5,000 | $3,000 | $1,440 | 6,440 | 0.909 | 5,853.96 |
| 2 | 3,000 | 3,000 | 1,440 | 4,440 | 0.826 | 3,667.44 |
| 3 | 3,000 | 3,000 | 1,440 | 3,440 | 0.751 | 2,583.44 |
| | | | | | | $2,104.84 |

We assume that the firm is subject to the tax rate of 48 percent (that is, we assume that its taxable income exceeds $50,000, given the existing tax laws), and the tax saving shown as $1,440 in each of the three years represents 48 percent of the depreciation figure. The cash flow after taxes (CFAT) column shows the sum of the contribution and tax saving for each year. The next column shows the discount factors at an assumed opportunity rate of 10 percent, and the final column shows the net present value of the cash flow after taxes in each year, and in total.

Note that the sum of the net present value of the cash flow after taxes is positive, and hence this investment project adds to the net present value, or net worth, of the firm. It should therefore be accepted and the firm should continue accepting projects for implementation until it is left with only those projects that have zero or negative net present value at the appropriate opportunity rate of discount.

The *method* of depreciation employed has important implications for the NPV of the investment project. In the above example we used the straight-line method of depreciation, in which the difference between the initial cost of the asset and its salvage value is allocated equally to each year of the asset's life. Alternatively, we might have used a method of depreciation that accelerates the recovery of the difference between the initial cost and the salvage value, such that the depreciation expense is largest in the first year and declines each year until the asset is fully depreciated. Two such methods are the sum-of-years-digits method and the double-declining-balance method.

The sum-of-years-digits method, as implied by its name, sums the digits of the years that the asset will last, and each year depreciates a proportion of the amount to be recovered equal to the ratio of the number of years remaining to the sum of the digits. In the above example the asset is expected to last for three years, so the sum of the years' digits is $1 + 2 + 3 = 6$. Thus $\frac{3}{6}$, or half of the total depreciation expense, will be deducted in the first year; $\frac{2}{6}$, or one-third, will be deducted in the second year; and $\frac{1}{6}$ will be deducted in the final year.

The double-declining-balance method takes twice the depreciation rate implied by the straight-line method but applies it to the undepreciated balance remaining in each year. Thus, using this method we would recover two-thirds of $9,000 (i.e., $6,000) in the first year, two-thirds of the remaining $3,000 (i.e., $2,000) in the second year, and the remainder ($1,000) in the third year. Notice that both of these "accelerated" depreciation methods shift forward in time part of the net cash flow after taxes and thus increase the NPV of these dollars, since they will be subject to a larger discount factor when received earlier.

To demonstrate this effect, let us rework the above example using the sum-of-years-digits depreciation method. In Table 15.2 we show half of the depreciation (i.e., $4,500) being deducted in the first year, one-third being deducted in the

**TABLE 15.2**
**Impact of depreciation method upon net present value**

| Year | Contri-bution | Depre-ciation | Tax Saving | Cash Flow After Taxes | Discount Factors | Net Present Value |
|------|------|------|------|------|------|------|
| 0 | $-10,000 | – | – | $-10,000 | 1.000 | $-10,000.00 |
| 1 | 5,000 | $4,500 | $2,160 | 7,160 | 0.909 | 6,508.44 |
| 2 | 3,000 | 3,000 | 1,440 | 4,440 | 0.826 | 3,667.44 |
| 3 | 2,000 | 1,500 | 720 | 2,720 | 0.751 | 2,042.72 |
| | | | | | | $ 2,218.60 |

second year, and one-sixth being deducted in the third year. The tax saving is now weighted toward the earlier years, which in turn have larger discount factors. Hence the net present value of the same project with an accelerated depreciation method can be shown to be significantly higher than it was as calculated using straight-line depreciation. In fact, the accelerated depreciation provisions of the tax laws exist primarily to encourage firms to invest in new plant and facilities for the employment multiplier impact of such investment upon the economy.[1]

## The Internal Rate of Return Criterion

An alternative decision criterion that is related to the net present value criterion is the internal rate of return criterion. The internal rate of return (IRR) is that rate of discount that reduces the present value of the income stream to equality with the initial cost. It can be shown symbolically as

$$C_0 = \sum_{t=1}^{n} \frac{R_t}{(1+r)^t} \tag{15.2}$$

[1] See R. E. Hall and D. W. Jorgenson, "Tax Policy and Investment Behavior," *American Economic Review,* 57 (June 1967), 391-414.

where the only symbol different from Eq.(15.1) is $r$, which represents the internal rate of return.

We calculate the internal rate of return for a given project by a process of trial and error. (This beats attempting to solve a polynomial function of degree $n$.) Note that the internal rate of return will be that rate of discount that reduces the net present value of the income stream to zero. In the previous example we know that the internal rate of return exceeds 10 percent, since the net present value is positive at 10 percent. It will take a larger rate of discount to reduce the net present value to zero. In Table 15.3 we show the process of iteratively calculating the net present value at various discount rates, zeroing in on the rate of discount that reduces the net present value to zero. We start by testing for the value of net present value at the discount rate of 20 percent. This leaves a net present value of $437.64, indicating that it requires a larger discount rate to reduce net present value to zero. We then try a discount rate of 25 percent and find that the net present value at that discount rate is negative. Thus the internal rate of return lies between 20 percent and 25 percent. We try 23 percent and find that the net present value is $17.84. Clearly, a slightly larger internal rate of return is indicated, and we try 23.2 percent in the last column of the table to find a net present value of a mere −$7.88. Further iterations would show the internal rate of return to be precisely 23.1415873 percent.[2]

**TABLE 15.3**
**Calculation of the internal rate of return**

| Year | CFAT | NPV @ 20% | NPV @ 25% | NPV @ 23% | NPV @ 23.2% |
|------|------|-----------|-----------|-----------|-------------|
| 0 | $−10,000 | $−10,000.00 | $−10,000.00 | $−10,000.00 | $−10,000.00 |
| 1 | 6,440 | 5,364.52 | 5,152.00 | 5,235.72 | 5,227.27 |
| 2 | 4,440 | 3,081.36 | 2,841.60 | 2,934.84 | 2,925.24 |
| 3 | 3,440 | 1,991.76 | 1,761.28 | 1,847.28 | 1,839.61 |
| | | $ 437.64 | $− 245.12 | $ 17.84 | $− 7.88 |

The IRR *decision rule* is that projects with an internal rate of return greater than the opportunity rate of interest should be accepted and implemented by the firm. Given the availability of investment funds, investment in various projects should be taken to the point where the internal rate of return on the last project accepted just exceeds the cost of capital (the opportunity rate of interest for that project). Note that this decision rule is equivalent to the NPV rule that says to accept any project for which the NPV (when discounted at the opportunity rate) is above zero.

In Figure 15.1 we show a series of investment projects as the blocks A, B, C, D, E, and F. These investment projects are ranked in order of their internal rate of return, which represents the height of each block, and width of each

[2] In case you are wondering how many iterations it took to find that answer, I must confess I have a fancy calculator which is preprogrammed for the IRR calculation. Such calculators are becoming increasingly available at moderate cost and will, I think, soon be an essential part of the business student's tool kit.

**FIGURE 15.1**
**Determining the level of investment expenditure**

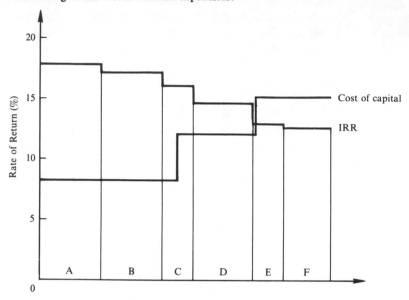

Level of Investment Expenditure

block represents the amount of capital required for the implementation of each project. The top of these blocks, shown as the heavy stepped line, is the curve relating the IRR to the level of investment expenditure.

The cost of capital to the firm is also likely to be a step function. Initially the firm will be able to utilize internal funds (undistributed profits), and the cost of these funds is their opportunity cost. That is, these could be invested elsewhere at a level of risk similar to that involved in holding the funds as un-distributed profits, and the firm would wish to receive at least that rate by utilizing these funds in the proposed investment projects. After a point, how-ever, the internal funds will be exhausted and the firm will need to borrow on the financial markets. We must expect the rate for such borrowing to exceed the opportunity cost of using internal funds, since the market will view the firm as involving at least some degree of risk. In Figure 15.1 we indicate that the firm's opportunity rate on internal funds is about 8 percent and that the firm can then borrow from the market (up to a point) at around 12 percent.

As the firm continues its borrowing in the financial market, however, the market will recognize the change in the financial structure of the firm and will at some point wish to impose a higher interest rate on loans to the firm. The greater debt/equity ratio (leverage) of the company as it continues to borrow in the market causes the firm to be a more risky proposition in the eyes of lenders. There is now a greater risk of default on the loans, and hence subse-quent borrowing by the firm will take place only at a higher rate of interest. In Figure 15.1 we show the higher rate of interest demanded by borrowers to be in the vicinity of 15 percent. The top line of the blocks, which represents the availability of funds, may thus be regarded as the cost-of-capital line. It can be seen that Projects A, B, C, and D promise an internal rate of return greater than the cost of capital, while Projects E and F promise lower rates of return which do not compensate for the cost of capital. Thus the firm in this particular situation would be advised to undertake Projects A to D only.

### Relationship between NPV and IRR

It should be firmly understood that if the internal rate of return exceeds the opportunity rate of interest, then the net present value of the proposed investment project will be positive. Using the example discussed earlier, we can plot the net present value of a project against all values that may be assigned to the rate of discount, as in Figure 15.2. To construct the net present value curve we have three points that are known to us. Point *A* in Figure 15.2 represents the net present value at a discount rate of zero. That is, when the future stream of profits is undiscounted (or discounted at zero percent), the project will have a net present value of $4,320, which we know from Table 15.1. The second point that is known to us, also from Table 15.1, is point *B*, which indicates the net present value of the project when discounted at an opportunity rate of 10 percent. The third point known to us is point *C*, which indicates the discount rate that reduces the net present value to zero. This is of course the internal rate of return, and we plot *C* at a discount rate of 23.14 percent.

Thus the NPV curve is a locus of the points representing the NPV of a project and the rate at which it was discounted, for all rates of discount between zero and the IRR. Note that the NPV curve is not a straight line but is slightly convex toward the origin. We shall return to the net present value curve later in the chapter.

**FIGURE 15.2**
**Net present value curve**

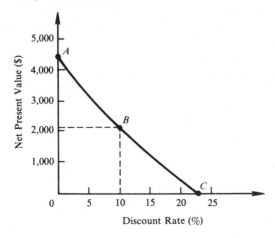

### The Profitability Index Criterion

The *profitability index* is defined as the ratio of the present value of the future stream of net cash flows to the initial cost of the investment project. Symbolically, it may be represented as

$$PI = \frac{\sum\limits_{t=1}^{n} \frac{R_t}{(1+k)^t}}{C_0} \tag{15.3}$$

Note the relationship of this criterion to the earlier formulas for the net present value and the internal rate of return. The profitability index is also called the *benefit/cost ratio* of an investment project or the *present value per dollar of outlay*. In the previous example with $k = 0.10$, the profitability index may be calculated as

$$PI = \frac{12,104.84}{10,000}$$

$$= 1.210484$$

The *decision rule* using the profitability criterion is to implement any investment project that promises a profitability index exceeding unity. Any such project will thus add more to the present value of revenues than it will cost. It will therefore add to the present value, or the net worth, of the firm.

There is no conflict between the net present value, internal rate of return, or profitability index for accept-reject decisions. If a project is acceptable under one criterion, then it will be acceptable under all three. Thus any one of these criteria could be employed alone for accepting or rejecting investment projects when capital availability is unlimited.

### The Payback Period Criterion

In practice firms commonly use an investment criterion known as the payback period.[3] In essence this criterion requires that the investment pay back the initial cost (in nominal dollars) before a specified period of time has elapsed. In Figure 15.3 we show graphically the determination of the payback period relating to the investment project we have been discussing. The initial cost of the project is shown at the $10,000 level and remains at that level over time. The undiscounted revenue stream reaches $6,440 at the end of the first year, $10,880 at the end of the second year, and $13,320 at the end of the third year. Interpolating between these points we are able to generate a curve showing the nominal dollar inflow as a function of time. This curve crosses the initial cost line at approximately 1.8 years, and this is thus the payback period.

Note that the payback period criterion in this form ignores the time value of

---

[3] For empirical evidence of the capital-budgeting techniques and criteria actually used in business practice, you are referred to the papers by Fremgen, Klammer, Mao, and Petty et al. which are listed in the "Suggested References" section at the end of this chapter.

**FIGURE 15.3**
**The payback period investment criterion**

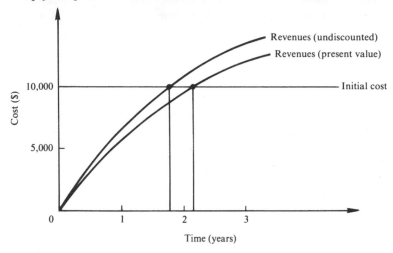

money. To avoid this fundamental shortcoming we could plot the present value of the revenue stream over time, and we have done so in Figure 15.3. In present value terms revenues amount to $5,853 in the first year, $9,521 in the second year, and $12,105 in the third year. The curve representing the present value of the revenue stream intersects the initial cost curve at approximately 2.18 years, and this is the payback period when determined by present values of the revenue stream. In either case the firm's decision rule will be to accept projects that have a payback period less than or equal to a specified period required by the firm.

A second problem is that the payback period criterion ignores the revenues that occur after the payback period of that investment. A decision is made based simply upon whether or not the investment pays back the initial cost before the elapse of a certain period. It would thus be unable to discriminate between two investment projects that had a payback period of, say, three years, but differed in that the net present value of one was substantially higher than the other due to a different or longer revenue stream.

The payback criterion may be appropriate for decision makers or firms with short time horizons, in which case managers are more concerned with short-term profitability. Projects that promise an early return of the outlay and hence will contribute well to accounting net income in the shorter term would be favored by decision makers under such an objective function. In a crude way the payback period criterion also acts as a screen against risky projects. Since uncertainty increases with the length of time into the future that cash flows must be estimated, the payback period selects the less risky projects at the expense of those that have longer gestation periods and longer revenue streams.

It can be shown that the payback period criterion may approximate the internal rate of return criterion under certain conditions.[4] If the original cost is the

---

[4] See M. H. Spencer, K. K. Seo, and M. G. Simkin, *Managerial Economics,* 4th ed. (Homewood, Ill.: Richard D. Irwin, 1975), pp. 449-56.

total cost, if projects are long lived, and if the revenue stream is uniform, we can show that the internal rate of return and the payback criteria would rank projects identically. Where the revenue stream is expected to be uniform in nominal dollars, we can express the sum of this revenue stream as

$$\sum_{t=1}^{n} R_t = \frac{U}{1+r} + \frac{U}{(1+r)^2} + \cdots + \frac{U}{(1+r)^n} \tag{15.4}$$

where $U$ is the uniform annual net cash flow after taxes. The sum of the geometric progression represented by Eq.(15.4) is

$$\sum_{t=1}^{n} R_t = \frac{U/1+r \ [1 - (1/1+r)^n]}{1 - (1/1+r)} \tag{15.5}$$

which simplifies to:

$$\sum_{t=1}^{n} R_t = \frac{U}{r} - \frac{U}{r} \left(\frac{1}{1+r}\right)^n \tag{15.6}$$

Or, in terms of the internal rate of return:

$$r = \frac{U}{\Sigma R_t} - \frac{U}{\Sigma R_t} \left(\frac{1}{1+r}\right)^n \tag{15.7}$$

The first term in the above expression is in fact the reciprocal of the payback period, since it is the uniform annual revenue stream divided by the total revenue stream. Where the project is long lived the second term will approach zero, since the exponent $n$ will be large. Hence the internal rate of return will approach the reciprocal of the payback period when projects are long lived and the revenue stream is uniform, and there are no other capital costs during the life of the investment project. Thus decision makers using the simple payback criterion may not be too far wrong in some cases.

### The Average Rate of Return Criterion

A second commonly used investment decision criterion is the *average rate of return,* which is defined as the average annual revenues (undiscounted) divided by the initial cost. Symbolically:

$$ARR = \frac{\left(\sum_{t=1}^{n} R_t\right)/n}{C_0} \tag{15.8}$$

In the example we have been using, the total (undiscounted) revenues from the project are $14,320 and the average annual revenues are $4,773. Hence

$$ARR = \frac{4,773}{10,000}$$

$$= .4773$$

or 4.77 percent. Note that this criterion ignores the time value of money and would therefore be unable to discriminate between two projects with the same initial cost and revenue totals, but with differing patterns of the receipts. If we modify the ARR criterion to include the discounted present value of the revenue stream, we have

$$ARR = \frac{(12,104.84)/3}{10,000}$$

$$= \frac{4,035}{10,000}$$

$$= .4035$$

Note that this result is exactly the profitability index divided by three, that is:

$$\frac{PI}{3} = \frac{1.210484}{3} = .4035$$

This should be no surprise, for the only difference between the PI formula and the ARR formula (using the present value of the revenue stream) is that the latter is divided by the number of years of the project's life. The additional step of averaging the income stream may obscure important cash-flow information, however. Thus the ARR criterion is seriously deficient in undiscounted form and can be regarded as inferior (or at least redundant) to the PI criterion even when the former is calculated using the present value of the revenue stream.[5]

## 15.3 MUTUALLY EXCLUSIVE INVESTMENTS

In many cases a firm will be considering investment projects that are mutually exclusive. For example, two or more projects may be able to perform the same function or will utilize the same space or other constrained resource, such as skilled labor within the firm. We defer discussion of investment projects that utilize the same funds to the next section, where limited availability of capital is discussed. Where investment projects are mutually exclusive, it is necessary for the firm to rank the investment projects in order of their desirability. It will then

[5] A variation of the ARR criterion is the accounting return on investment (AROI) criterion. The latter is calculated as the ratio of accounting net income (undiscounted) to the initial cost of the project. This criterion is clearly inferior to those discussed above, since it ignores the time value of money, is subject to ambiguity resulting from the several acceptable accounting methods of calculating net income (e.g., treatment of depreciation and allocation of overheads), and moreover allows sunk costs to enter the decision-making process.

choose the project that contributes the most toward the firm's objective function.

Suppose a firm is planning to introduce a new product and has called for tenders for the construction of the plant and physical facilities to manufacture that product. Let us consider two tenders, which we will call Plant A and Plant B. Plant A is more expensive but also more efficient in terms of cost per unit and maintenance requirements, as compared with Plant B. The relevant cash flows and net present values are shown in Table 15.4.

**TABLE 15.4**
**Comparison of costs and revenues from two
alternative investment projects**

| | Plant A | | Plant B | |
|---|---|---|---|---|
| *Cash Flow* | *($)* | *NPV at 15% ($)* | *($)* | *NPV at 15% ($)* |
| Initial cost | −100,000 | −100,000 | −60,000 | −60,000 |
| Year 1 | 45,000 | 39,150 | 30,000 | 26,100 |
| Year 2 | 55,000 | 41,580 | 37,000 | 27,972 |
| Year 3 | 50,000 | 32,900 | 28,000 | 18,424 |
| Net cash flow | 50,000 | 13,630 | 35,000 | 12,496 |

It can be seen that Plant A offers the greater net present value when discounted at 15 percent. If the firm's objective is to maximize the present value of its longer-term profitability, it should thus choose Plant A, since this contributes more in present value terms than does Plant B.

### The Superiority of NPV over IRR
### for Mutually Exclusive Investments

Let us now consider the relative internal rates of return of the two plants. Once again we need to find the internal rate of return by a trial-and-error procedure of zeroing in on the discount rate that reduces the net present value to zero. In Table 15.5 we perform this exercise for Plant A and see that the internal rate of return is slightly more than 22.8 percent.

**TABLE 15.5**
**Calculation of internal rate of return: plant A**

| Year | CFAT | NPV @ 25% | NPV @ 20% | NPV @ 23% | NPV @ 22.8% |
|---|---|---|---|---|---|
| 0 | $−100,000 | $−100,000 | $−100,000 | $−100,000 | $−100,000 |
| 1 | 45,000 | 36,000 | 37,485 | 36,585 | 36,360 |
| 2 | 55,000 | 35,200 | 38,170 | 36,355 | 36,465 |
| 3 | 50,000 | 25,600 | 28,950 | 26,850 | 27,000 |
| | | $− 3,200 | $ 4,605 | $− 210 | $ 95 |

**TABLE 15.6**
Calculation of internal rate of return: plant B

| Year | CFAT | NPV @ 25% | NPV @ 28% | NPV @ 27% | NPV @ 27.2% |
|---|---|---|---|---|---|
| 0 | $-60,000 | $-60,000 | $-60,000 | $-60,000 | $-60,000 |
| 1 | 30,000 | 24,000 | 23,430 | 23,622 | 23,580 |
| 2 | 37,000 | 23,680 | 22,570 | 22,940 | 22,866 |
| 3 | 28,000 | 14,336 | 13,356 | 13,670 | 13,608 |
| | | $ 2,016 | $- 644 | $ 232 | $ 54 |

In Table 15.6 we perform the search procedure for the internal rate of return to Plant B and find that the rate of discount that reduces the net present value to zero is slightly more than 27.2 percent. Thus the internal rate of return criterion would suggest that Plant B is preferable to Plant A, and it evidently conflicts with the judgment of the net present value criterion.

To see why this conflict arises, let us plot the net present value curves of both Plant A and Plant B, as shown in Figure 15.4. To plot the net present value curve for Plant A, we know that at a zero rate of discount the net present value will be equal to the net cash inflow (in nominal dollars) of $50,000. From Table 15.4 we know that at a discount rate of 15 percent, the net present value of Plant A is $13,630. Finally, we know that the rate of discount that reduces the net present value to zero is approximately 22.8 percent. Similarly for Plant B we can plot its present value curve, beginning at $35,000 when the discount rate is zero, passing through $12,496 when the discount rate is 15 percent, and terminating at 27.2 percent on the horizontal axis.

It is clear that the net present value curves for the two projects intersect at approximately the 18 percent rate of discount. For discount rates below 18 per-

**FIGURE 15.4**
Net present value curves

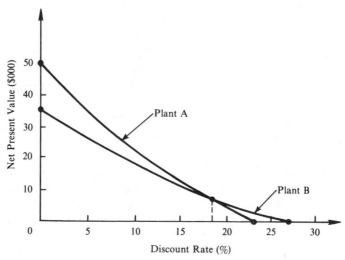

cent, the net present value criterion would suggest Project A, but above 18 percent the net present value criterion would suggest Project B. The internal rate of return criterion, since it looks at only one point on the net present value curve, would suggest Project B under all opportunity rates of discount up to 27.2 percent. However, for actual opportunity rates of discount less than about 18 percent, the internal rate of return criterion would be suggesting the investment project with the lower net present value and would thus lead decision makers to a suboptimal decision in terms of the addition to the firm's net worth, since Plant A clearly has the greater net present value at these lower opportunity rates of discount.

Why does this conflict arise between the net present value and the internal rate of return criteria? It arises because of the implicit assumption that the profit stream of each project could be reinvested at the internal rate of return. To see this, note that discounting a future stream of profits is the reverse of compounding a presently held sum over the same period of time at the same rate. At higher interest rates (namely, greater than 18 percent), the net present value of Plant B would compound to a greater value over the three years than would the net present value of Plant A at the same interest rates. The conflict with net present value arises because the calculation of net present value implicitly assumes the reinvestment of the profit stream at the opportunity discount rate rather than at the internal rate of return.

As a decision criterion, we need the criterion that will always indicate the project that adds the most toward the attainment of the firm's objective function. Hence the net present value criterion is superior to the internal rate of return criterion for situations where mutually exclusive projects must be evaluated.

### The Superiority of NPV over the Profitability Index

Let us now calculate the profitability indices for each of the projects under consideration. According to the profitability index criterion, the plant with the higher profitability index should be chosen for implementation. The calculations are as follows:

|                       | *Plant A*         | *Plant B*       |
| --------------------- | ----------------- | --------------- |
| PV of revenues        | 113,363           | 72,496          |
| Initial costs         | 100,000           | 60,000          |
| Profitability Index   | 1.13363           | 1.20826         |

Note that the profitability index supports the judgment of the internal rate of return criterion, by indicating that Project B is superior to Project A in this situation. However, it is inferior to the net present value criterion for the same reason that the IRR criterion is: namely, it would indicate acceptance of the project that contributes the lesser amount to the net worth of the firm in at least some cases and would therefore result in decisions that do not accord with the objectives of the firm.

The conflict between the profitability index criterion and the net present value criterion arises due to what is known as the "size disparity" problem. Where there is a difference in the size of the initial cost, or in the magnitude and time pattern of the revenue streams, the profitability index criterion and the net present value criterion may rank projects differently. If the firm's objective is to maximize its net worth, the net present value criterion must be used, since although the profitability index indicates which project is the most efficient at generating net present value, this is a "relative" consideration rather than the "absolute" consideration of maximizing the firm's net worth.

Thus, in general, it is preferable to use the net present value criterion for ranking mutually exclusive projects under situations of unlimited availability of capital. Both the internal rate of return and the profitability index may indicate the acceptance of projects that are not in the best interest of the firm's objective to maximize the present value of its longer-term earnings.

## 15.4 CAPITAL BUDGETING GIVEN LIMITED AVAILABILITY OF CAPITAL

The availability of investment funds should not, in theory, ever impose a constraint upon the level of investments. We saw in Figure 15.1 that although the cost of capital might increase as the level of investment is increased, the level of investment will be carried to the point where the marginal investment project has an internal rate of return at least equal to the cost of capital. Thus, if the internal rate of return exceeds the cost of capital, or the net present value at the opportunity rate is positive, or if the profitability index exceeds unity, the project should be implemented, since it will contribute to the enlargement of the firm's net present value. Where investment projects are mutually exclusive, the problem was to choose the one project of those available that would best serve the firm's objective function. The implicit assumption was that once this choice for this particular purpose was made, the firm would continue to consider other investment projects and/or groups of mutually exclusive investment projects and would implement those that met the acceptability criterion. In theory the funds are always available, although at progressively higher rates of interest perhaps, and if the net present value is positive at this higher cost of capital, the investment project under consideration should be undertaken.

In practice, however, we often find the situation of a decision maker facing a constraint upon investment funds. It is common business practice to set investment budgets for departments or divisions within the firm, such that the decision-making unit faces a constraint upon investment funds. Setting investment budgets for individual departments or decision-making units, and/or for the firm as a whole, may be a response to the reluctance of top management to take on additional debt, with its subsequent impact upon the leverage position and the market value of the firm's shares. In such situations the decision maker faces an allocation problem. That is, given an investment budget the decision maker will wish to maximize the return from that limited supply of investment funds. This changes the decision problem somewhat, since any investment project undertaken will use some of the available investment funds and may preclude another investment project. Hence we must examine quite carefully the opportunity costs associated with each particular investment project.

### The Opportunity Costs of Investing

To illustrate this, let us return to the previous example of Projects A and B. Suppose that the total budget is $100,000 and that the opportunity interest rate is 15 percent. Thus the entire $100,000 could earn 15 percent per annum if invested elsewhere. Recall that Project A uses the entire $100,000 and generates $13,630 net present value, while Project B uses only $60,000 and generates $12,496 net present value. Project B therefore leaves $40,000 remaining to be invested in another project, or bonds, or some other interest-earning asset. The implementation of Project A thus has an opportunity cost involved, which is the net present value of the funds remaining if Project B were to be implemented.

The $40,000 that remains if Plant B is constructed could be invested at 15 percent per annum and would therefore generate a stream of interest revenue of $6,000 per annum. Discounting this revenue stream at the appropriate rate of discount (that is, the opportunity rate of 15 percent) gives this interest revenue a present value of zero. Hence the net present value of the currently held $40,000 is indeed $40,000! The interest that it would earn over the period of the project is exactly offset by the discounting process using the same opportunity investment rate. This illustrates the reciprocity of the discounting and compounding processes.

Thus the net present value of the $100,000 spent on Project A is still $13,630, while the net present value of the $100,000 spent on Project B (with the remainder invested elsewhere) is $12,496 plus $40,000, giving a total net present value of the $100,000 budget of $52,496. Alternatively, using the same framework in the preceding section but now including the opportunity cost involved in the selection of Project A, we show the calculations in Table 15.7. Note that the net present value criterion, taking into account the opportunity costs, now indicates that Plant B is superior to Plant A. Plant B is superior because the returns to the total $100,000 budget are greater than when that $100,000 is invested simply in Plant A.

**TABLE 15.7**
**Comparison of NPV of plants A and B when opportunity costs are involved**

|  | Plant A | Plant B |
|---|---|---|
| Initial cost | $−100,000 | $−60,000 |
| Opportunity cost | − 40,000 | − |
| NPV Year 1 | 39,150 | 26,100 |
| NPV Year 2 | 41,580 | 27,972 |
| NPV Year 3 | 32,900 | 18,424 |
|  | $− 26,370 | $ 12,496 |

## The Profitability Index Criterion

When there is more than one project that can be afforded within the constraints set by the investment budget, the application of the net present value approach, using the opportunity costs associated with the funds left over, becomes quite difficult in practice. An alternate and considerably faster method of ranking projects for a limited capital budget is to use the profitability index. Recall that the profitability index shows the ratio of benefits to cost, or the efficiency of the investment project regarding the generation of net present value. The solution of constrained maximization problems generally involves the use of alternatives which allows the greatest return for the smallest outlay, and hence the benefit-cost ratio is a means of ranking projects in order to attain the constrained optimization solution. From the calculations in the preceding section we know that the profitability index for Project A is 1.13, whereas for Project B it is 1.21. The profitability index criterion thus agrees with the ranking established by the net present value criterion when the latter incorporates the opportunity cost involved under limited availability of funds.

Let us now demonstrate this in the context of more than one available project with limited investment resources. Suppose that the investment budget of the firm is $80,000 and that there are five investment projects competing for these funds. In Table 15.8 we show the five projects identified as Projects A to E with their initial costs, their net present values at an assumed opportunity rate of 12 percent (excluding the opportunity costs associated with each), their profitability indices, and their rankings based on the NPV and the PI values. It can be seen that the ranking by the net present value differs from the ranking by the profitability index. While the net present value criterion ranks the projects in order of the absolute contribution to net present value, the profitability index ranks the projects in terms of the relative efficiency with which they generate net present value dollars per dollar of initial outlay.

Since the total cost of the five projects exceeds $80,000, it is clear that all five cannot be implemented. Rather, we need to select the two or more projects that can be afforded and which best serve the firm's objectives. Considering the net present value criterion first, the project ranked first is Project B, which would immediately consume $40,000 of the investment budget. Project D, ranked second, would consume another $25,000, leaving $15,000 funds remain-

**TABLE 15.8**
Comparison of five competing investment projects

| Project | Initial Cost | NPV @ 12% | PI @ 12% | NPV Ranking | PI Ranking |
|---------|--------------|-----------|----------|-------------|------------|
| A | $20,000 | $10,000 | 1.5 | 4 | 3 |
| B | 40,000 | 18,000 | 1.45 | 1 | 4 |
| C | 30,000 | 12,000 | 1.4 | 3 | 5 |
| D | 25,000 | 17,500 | 1.7 | 2 | 1 |
| E | 10,000 | 6,000 | 1.6 | 5 | 2 |

ing. Both the third- and fourth-ranked projects cost more than $15,000, however, and the firm is forced to implement Project E because this project is the only one remaining that is affordable. It is worthwhile to implement Project E, of course, since its net present value at the opportunity interest rate is positive, or alternatively the internal rate of return of Project B exceeds the opportunity interest rate. Thus, under the net present value criterion the firm would select Projects B, D, and E, which in total exhausts $75,000 of the investment budget, leaving $5,000 funds remaining to be invested at the opportunity interest rate.

In Table 15.9 we show the projects that would be selected using the simple NPV criterion and the total cost of this combination of projects. The third column shows the net present values associated with each of the investment projects, and the sum of the net present values when the funds remaining are added in. Thus the application of the net present value criterion allows the investment budget to generate an income stream with a net present value of $46,500.

TABLE 15.9
Comparison of alternate investment criteria

| | NPV Criterion | | | PI Criterion | |
|---|---|---|---|---|---|
| Project | Initial Cost | NPV | Project | Initial Cost | NPV |
| B | $40,000 | $18,000 | D | $25,000 | $17,500 |
| D | 25,000 | 17,500 | E | 10,000 | 6,000 |
| E | 10,000 | 6,000 | A | 20,000 | 10,000 |
| | $75,000 | $41,500 | | $55,000 | $33,500 |
| Funds remaining | 5,000 | 5,000 | | 25,000 | 25,000 |
| Funds available | $80,000 | $46,500 | | $80,000 | $58,500 |

Alternatively, if we were to select the project on the basis of the profitability index, Projects D, E, and A would be selected. The next highest profitability index belongs to Project B, but this has an initial cost of $40,000 and there is only $25,000 remaining in the budget. Similarly, Project C, the fifth-ranked project under this criterion, costs $30,000 and is therefore not affordable. Thus there is $25,000 remaining to be invested at the opportunity interest rate. The final column of Table 15.9 sums the net present value of the three selected projects and the $25,000 remaining and indicates a total net present value of $58,500.

It is clear that the projects selected by the profitability index generate a greater net present value than the projects selected by the net present value criterion. Where the objective of the firm is to maximize the present value of its longer-term profitability, or its net worth, subject to a constraint upon the availability of total investment funds, the profitability index is clearly the superior criterion, since it considers the efficiency with which the projects generate dollars of net present value.[6]

[6] See J. H. Lorie and L. J. Savage, "Three Problems in Rationing Capital," *Journal of Business*, 2 (October 1955), 229-39.

### Some Qualifications

The estimation of the future cash flows associated with investment projects involves techniques discussed in Chapters 5 and 8. Initial costs should cause few estimation problems, since they are to be incurred in the very near future and thus should be determined with relative accuracy. Future costs and revenue streams, however, are subject to uncertainty and thus may be accompanied by a probability distribution. The above analysis would need to be modified by insertion of the expected values of the net cash flow after taxes for each project rather than the point estimates used in the above examples.

Use of probability distributions and the resultant expected value of net cash flows after taxes for each year in the future involves the law of averages and could therefore cause the net present value criterion to be an unsuitable decision criterion for some investment decisions. "One-shot" investment decisions may expose the investor to the risk of a very low outcome, which cannot be averaged upward by other similar projects having outcomes above their expected values. Thus we might expect the firm with a one-shot decision involving capital budgeting to apply the certainty equivalent criterion, which allows the decision maker to place his or her own evaluation upon the riskiness and other nonquantifiable aspects of the investment decision, as explained in Chapter 2.

Differing riskiness of differing investment projects is adjusted for by the use of differing opportunity rates of discount. Recall that the opportunity rate of discount for any project is what the investment funds involved in that project could earn elsewhere at a comparable degree of riskiness. Thus a firm considering a series of investment projects may discount these projects at differing opportunity discount rates if the degree of risk perceived to be associated with each project differs.[7]

## 15.5  SUMMARY

In this chapter we have considered the capital-budgeting decision, which is the decision to invest in plant, equipment, and other projects expected to generate a future stream of net cash flows. Given unlimited availability of capital, but typically with an increasing cost of capital, the firm should invest up to the point where the marginal investment project implemented has an internal rate of return at least equal to the cost of capital. This will mean that the project has a net present value that is nonnegative, or a profitability index of at least unity. When investment projects are mutually exclusive the three investment criteria mentioned above may give conflicting results, and we found the net present value criterion to be the only reliable guide if the firm wishes to maximize its net worth.

Where the investment funds available are constrained, the firm must consider the efficiency with which competing investment projects generate dollars of future revenue. The profitability index proves to be the superior criterion under

---

[7] An alternate means of adjusting for differing riskiness is to reduce the period over which you will recognize the revenues from the more risky projects. See J. C. Van Horne, "Variation of Project Life as a Means of Adjusting for Risk," *Engineering Economist,* 21 (Spring 1976), 151-58.

these circumstances, although the net present value criterion—if properly adjusted for the opportunity costs associated with choosing one particular project rather than another—would rank the projects in the same order. The projects are then implemented in order of their ranking up to the point where the next project cannot be afforded, and the remaining funds are invested at the opportunity rate of interest.

The techniques introduced in Chapter 2 regarding the decision-making process under conditions of risk and uncertainty must be applied to the capital-budgeting decision, since there will be a probability distribution surrounding the expected values of future cost and revenue streams. Similarly, the techniques outlined in Chapters 5 and 8 for demand and cost estimation and forecasting must be used to establish the future stream of net cash flow after taxes for each project under consideration. Finally, it should be noted that the appropriate decision criterion in any particular firm is the one that best pursues the firm's objective function. If the firm has a long time horizon and wishes to maximize the net present value of the firm, the net present value criterion is appropriate under most circumstances, and the profitability index is the preferred criterion given a constraint on available funds. On the other hand, if the firm's time horizon is relatively short, and management is concerned with accounting profitability, market value of outstanding shares, and other considerations involving immediate or short-term cash flow, the payback criterion or the average rate of return criterion may be the appropriate investment criteria in these cases.

## DISCUSSION QUESTIONS

15.1    Explain in three sentences why the NPV criterion and the IRR criterion must always agree on the accept/reject investment decision, given the availability of sufficient funds.

15.2    In calculating the expected net revenue stream associated with an investment project, what factors enter the calculation?

15.3    When comparing possible investment projects, why is it important to ensure that all projects have been evaluated using the same depreciation method?

15.4    Why is the cost of capital to the firm likely to be a step-function of the amount of funds demanded for investment purposes?

15.5    Under what circumstances is the use of the payback period investment criterion appropriate?

15.6    Why is the average rate of return criterion inferior to the other investment criteria discussed?

15.7    Where projects are mutually exclusive, the IRR criterion may rank projects in conflict with their ranking by the NPV criterion. Why? Does this invalidate the IRR criterion?

15.8    Under what circumstances might the profitability index disagree with the NPV criterion in the ranking of mutually exclusive projects? Explain.

15.9    Given limited funds, how must the NPV criterion be adjusted so that it will always rank projects in such a way that the NPV of the capital budget is maximized?

15.10 Why does the profitability index rank projects in the order that will maximize NPV of the capital budget, when capital funds are limited?

## PROBLEMS

15.1 The Omega Investment Corporation has over half a million dollars to invest as the result of a recent windfall gain due to revaluation of a foreign currency it was holding. Failing all else, these funds can be invested in government bonds, which are considered to be risk free, at 8 percent per annum. Omega is evaluating four other investment projects as well. These projects seem to be equally risky and Omega feels they should return at least 10 percent per annum in order to be considered an equivalent proposition to placing the funds in the risk-free bonds. The initial outlays and net cash flows after taxes for each year of each project's life are as follows:

| Project | A ($) | B ($) | C ($) | D ($) |
|---|---|---|---|---|
| Initial outlay | 100,000 | 135,000 | 85,000 | 122,000 |
| NCFAT–Yr. 1 | –12,200 | 26,300 | 56,000 | –25,000 |
| NCFAT–Yr. 2 | – 8,500 | 34,400 | 32,000 | 10,600 |
| NCFAT–Yr. 3 | 76,600 | 48,600 | 18,600 | 48,200 |
| NCFAT–Yr. 4 | 62,400 | 56,500 | 12,400 | 96,500 |
| NCFAT–Yr. 5 | 23,500 | 22,000 | 5,500 | 34,000 |
| NCFAT–Yr. 6 | 9,500 | 10,000 | 0 | 18,700 |

You are asked to advise Omega as to which of these projects, if any, it should undertake. Explain your reasoning.

15.2 The Anderson Electronics Company is considering investing $1 million in a major advertising campaign. This expenditure will be tax deductible at the end of the year in which it is incurred, and Anderson's tax rate is 48 percent. It will take a year to produce the campaign after the million dollars is spent, and the impact of the campaign on sales is expected to be felt over the following three years. The precise outcomes are uncertain, however. The marketing research department has generated the following estimates (and associated probabilities) of incremental net cash flows after taxes due to this campaign for each of the three years.

| Incremental NCFAT ($) | Probabilities | | |
|---|---|---|---|
| | Year 2 | Year 3 | Year 4 |
| 50,000 | 0.05 | 0.10 | 0.25 |
| 150,000 | 0.10 | 0.20 | 0.35 |
| 250,000 | 0.15 | 0.40 | 0.25 |
| 350,000 | 0.35 | 0.15 | 0.10 |
| 450,000 | 0.25 | 0.10 | 0.05 |
| 650,000 | 0.10 | 0.05 | 0.00 |

The probability distributions should be treated as being independent from year to year (hence no conditional probabilities), and the NCFAT figures should be regarded as arriving at the end of each year. Anderson considers this project to be about as risky as investing the funds in the bonds of a large trust company which would currently pay 12 percent per annum. Assume that Anderson's tax assessment will be finalized one year after the million is spent.

(a) What is the net present value of this investment project?

(b) What is the internal rate of return of the project?

(c) Sketch the NPV curve against various opportunity discount rates, and estimate from this the NPV if the appropriate discount rate is 10 percent.

15.3 Custy Canoe and Kayak Inc. is considering investing in a facility that would allow it to manufacture lightweight fiberglass sports kayaks. The proposed plant would involve an initial investment of $212,500 and would have an expected life of four years, after which time its expected scrap value would be $12,500. The marketing manager, Maureen Custy, expects these kayaks to become increasingly popular in future years, although other firms are likely to begin supplying competitive canoes within two or three years. Extensive market research and cost estimation studies have established the following (independent) probability distributions of the level of contribution to overheads and profits in each of the four years.

| Contributions ($) | Probabilities | | | |
| --- | --- | --- | --- | --- |
| | Year 1 | Year 2 | Year 3 | Year 4 |
| 10,000 | 0.05 | 0.05 | 0.10 | 0.20 |
| 25,000 | 0.20 | 0.15 | 0.20 | 0.30 |
| 50,000 | 0.40 | 0.20 | 0.35 | 0.25 |
| 75,000 | 0.25 | 0.35 | 0.20 | 0.15 |
| 100,000 | 0.10 | 0.15 | 0.10 | 0.10 |
| 125,000 | 0.00 | 0.10 | 0.05 | 0.00 |

Note that the contribution figures do not include consideration of the tax savings due to depreciation. For tax purposes, depreciation is calculated using the sum-of-years-digits method. The finance manager, Michael Gable, advises that the applicable tax rate is 48 percent, and that this project should be evaluated in terms of the alternative use of these funds to establish a camping resort area for canoe enthusiasts, which he considers to be of equal riskiness. The resort project has an expected internal rate of return of 15 percent.

Assume that the kayak plant can be purchased and installed at the start of this year, that tax payments or refunds become due at the end of each year, that the profit contributions are received continuously throughout each year, and that the expected scrap value is realized at the end of the fourth year.

(a) Calculate the expected net present value of the kayak project, taking care to use the appropriate discount factors.

(b) Using the same discount factors, find the approximate internal rate of return of the kayak project.

(c) Recalculate the expected net present value of the kayak project, assuming this time that all cash flows take place in lump sum at the start or end of each year.

(d) Explain why there is a difference between your answers to (a) and (c).

(e)  In which project (kayak or resort) should Custy Canoe and Kayak invest the funds? Explain.

15.4   Marilyn Monibaggs is considering investing in a small shop in the downtown area of a large city. Ms. Monibaggs has not been lax in her investigations but has found that only two locations are feasible. Ms. Monibaggs is considering establishing either a sportswear boutique or a sporting equipment store, and she could put either type of store at either location. Location A is initially more suitable for the sportswear boutique, but the profitability of this venture will decline in the future due to the planned establishment of a major department store and other shops nearby. After this event the sporting equipment shop would be more profitable than the sportswear shop at this location. Location B, on the other hand, is close to several competitors in both types of merchandise but is frequented by considerably more potential customers. The initial cash outlay will be $50,000 for the sportswear store versus $60,000 for the equipment store. These outlays are for the initial inventories required in each store, and Ms. Monibaggs will pay a monthly lease on the location chosen. The net cash flows after taxes for each of the four alternatives have been carefully estimated as follows:

| Year | Location A | | Location B | |
|---|---|---|---|---|
| | Sportswear | Equipment | Sportswear | Equipment |
| 1 | $-18,000 | $-24,000 | $-24,000 | $-30,000 |
| 2 | 37,400 | 26,000 | 32,000 | 28,600 |
| 3 | 26,200 | 28,400 | 33,500 | 30,800 |
| 4 | 22,400 | 29,800 | 34,300 | 36,400 |
| 5 | 20,800 | 30,200 | 35,000 | 38,900 |

These figures include the initial cash outlay for inventories which was incurred at the start of the first year. Treat the other net cash flows as arriving in a continuous stream throughout each year. Ms. Monibaggs is only interested in a time horizon of five years and considers the opportunity discount rates to be 14 percent and 15 percent for the sportswear and equipment stores, respectively, at location A; and 17 percent and 20 percent for the sportswear and equipment stores, respectively, at location B.

(a)  What is the net present value of each of the four projects?

(b)  Estimate the payback period for each of the four projects.

(c)  Supposing Ms. Monibaggs is interested in maximizing her net worth but at the same time wants to get her (undiscounted) money back quickly in order to be ready to invest elsewhere if an opportunity arises, which alternative should she choose? Explain.

15.5   A consortium of business professors at a high-quality university are thinking of investing in the takeout food industry. A location has been found which is considered to be highly suitable due to its proximity to thousands of downtown offices and stores, a major stadium, and two very large high schools. The professors are in the process of deciding whether they should go with hamburgers, chicken, or tacos as their product line. Extensive studies have provided the following estimated probabilities for various levels of net cash flow after taxes in each of the first three years for each of the three projects.

| NCFAT ($) | Probabilities | | |
|---|---|---|---|
| | Hamburgers | Chicken | Tacos |
| *Year 1* | | | |
| $-10,000 | 0.05 | 0.10 | 0.15 |
| 0 | 0.10 | 0.15 | 0.20 |
| 10,000 | 0.25 | 0.30 | 0.35 |
| 20,000 | 0.35 | 0.25 | 0.15 |
| 30,000 | 0.15 | 0.15 | 0.10 |
| 40,000 | 0.10 | 0.05 | 0.05 |
| *Year 2* | | | |
| $-10,000 | 0.00 | 0.05 | 0.05 |
| 0 | 0.05 | 0.05 | 0.10 |
| 10,000 | 0.15 | 0.10 | 0.15 |
| 20,000 | 0.20 | 0.25 | 0.20 |
| 30,000 | 0.30 | 0.35 | 0.30 |
| 40,000 | 0.20 | 0.15 | 0.15 |
| 50,000 | 0.10 | 0.05 | 0.05 |
| *Year 3* | | | |
| $ 0 | 0.00 | 0.05 | 0.00 |
| 10,000 | 0.15 | 0.10 | 0.05 |
| 20,000 | 0.20 | 0.30 | 0.10 |
| 30,000 | 0.30 | 0.35 | 0.40 |
| 40,000 | 0.20 | 0.15 | 0.25 |
| 50,000 | 0.10 | 0.05 | 0.15 |
| 60,000 | 0.05 | 0.00 | 0.05 |

The above net cash flows after taxes do not include the initial franchise fee of $50,000 for "Hamburgers," $40,000 for "Chicken," and $35,000 for "Tacos." They do allow for depreciation, however. The professors' time horizon is only three years, since they are all on three-year contracts at the university and expect their research and teaching efforts to suffer so badly that their contracts will not be renewed and they will have to go elsewhere for a job. Their collective judgment is that the opportunity discount rate is 15 percent for "Hamburgers," 13 percent for "Chicken," and 16 percent for "Tacos." Treat the expected net cash flows after taxes as arriving continuously throughout each year, and the probability distributions as being independent of each other.

(a) Calculate the expected net present value of each alternative, assuming that the franchise fee cannot be recovered at the end of the period.

(b) Estimate the payback period for each project, using the undiscounted net cash flows after taxes.

(c) Advise the professors as to which project, if any, to undertake. Support your recommendation.

15.6 You have recently been hired as an assistant investment analyst in a small corporation which promotes new products and inventions. Your boss has asked you to evaluate and rank four potential investment projects. He tells you that the capital budget for the year is $105,000, and that anything left over can be invested in government bonds at 8.5 percent per annum. The details of the four projects are as follows:

|  | Project | | | |
| --- | --- | --- | --- | --- |
|  | A | B | C | D |
| Initial Cost | $35,000 | $28,000 | $16,000 | $40,000 |
| Expected NCFAT | | | | |
| Year 1 | 12,681 | 9,650 | 8,480 | 22,680 |
| Year 2 | 28,323 | 25,462 | 12,624 | 51,070 |
| Year 3 | 36,084 | 31,836 | 28,970 | 28,218 |
| Year 4 | 20,880 | 42,420 | 14,381 | 8,440 |
| Salvage value | $10,000 | $ 8,000 | $ 2,000 | $12,000 |
| Opportunity discount rate | 12% | 10% | 14% | 15% |

Your boss tells you that it is "company policy" to consider the expected net cash flow stream up to and including the fourth year only. He says to treat flows as if they were to arrive in lump sum on the last day of each year.

(a) Calculate the expected net present value of each project, and rank the projects in descending order.

(b) Calculate the profitability index for each project, and rank them in descending order.

(c) Which projects do you recommend should be implemented if your boss wishes to maximize the expected net present value of the capital budget?

(d) What is the maximum expected net present value of the capital budget? Explain.

15.7 A large real estate firm has half a million dollars which it wishes to invest in urban-housing development projects. The available opportunities have been carefully evaluated and the four most promising projects have been thoroughly examined, with cost and demand estimates being supplied by a reliable group of consultants at a cost of $10,000. The projects are known as North, South, East, and West due to their locations relative to the firm's main office. The relevant details are as follows:

|  | North | South | East | West |
| --- | --- | --- | --- | --- |
| Initial cost | $120,000 | $180,000 | $250,000 | $285,000 |
| Expected NCFAT | | | | |
| Year 1 | $ 40,000 | $ 62,000 | $ 90,000 | $115,000 |
| Year 2 | 42,000 | 75,000 | 88,000 | 140,000 |
| Year 3 | 45,000 | 81,000 | 84,000 | 132,000 |
| Year 4 | 48,000 | 84,000 | 82,000 | 90,000 |
| Year 5 | 51,000 | 80,000 | 80,000 | 75,000 |
| Salvage value | $ 30,000 | $ 20,000 | $ 50,000 | $ 70,000 |
| Opportunity discount rate | 10% | 15% | 12% | 18% |

Each project would be developed in five yearly stages, with all accounts being paid and all revenues being received from sales on the last day of each year. The initial costs shown refer to the cost of purchasing each tract of land, and this must be paid before any activity can begin.

(a) Calculate the expected net present value of each project, and rank the projects in descending order.

(b) Calculate the profitability index for each project, and rank them in descending order.

(c) Which projects should be undertaken in order to maximize the net present value of the funds available?

(d) What is the maximum net present value of the funds available? Explain.

## SUGGESTED REFERENCES AND FURTHER READING

AHMED, S. B., "Optimal Equipment Replacement Policy," *Journal of Transport Economics and Policy,* 7 (January 1973), 71-79.

BAUMOL, W. J. *Economic Theory and Operations Analysis,* 4th ed., Chap. 25. Englewood Cliffs, N.J.: Prentice-Hall, 1977.

EISNER, R., "Components of Capital Expenditures: Replacement and Modernization versus Expansion," *Review of Economics and Statistics,* 54 (August 1972), 297-305.

FELDSTEIN, M. S., and D. K. FOOT, "The Other Half of Gross Investment: Replacement and Modernization Expenditures," *Review of Economics and Statistics,* 53 (February 1971), 49-58.

FREMGEN, J. M., "Capital Budgeting Practices: A Survey," *Management Accounting,* May 1973, pp. 19-25.

HALL, R. E., and D. W. JORGENSON, "Tax Policy and Investment Behavior," *American Economic Review,* 57 (June 1967), 391-414.

HIRSHLEIFER, J., "Investment Decision under Uncertainty: Choice-Theoretic Approaches," *Quarterly Journal of Economics,* 79 (November 1965), 509-36.

JORGENSON, D. W., "Econometric Studies of Investment Behavior: A Survey," *Journal of Economic Literature,* 9 (December 1971), 1111-47.

KLAMMER, T., "Empirical Evidence of the Adoption of Sophisticated Capital Budgeting Techniques," *Journal of Business,* July 1972, pp. 387-97.

LORIE, J. H., and L. J. SAVAGE, "Three Problems in Rationing Capital," *Journal of Business,* 28 (October 1955), 229-39.

MAO, J. C. T., "Survey of Capital Budgeting: Theory and Practice," *Journal·of Finance,* May 1970, pp. 349-60.

PETTY, J. W., D. F. SCOTT, Jr., and M. M. BIRD, "The Capital Expenditure Decision-Making Process of Large Corporations," *Engineering Economist,* 20 (Spring 1975), 159-72.

VAN HORNE, J. C., "Capital Budgeting under Conditions of Uncertainty as to Project Life," *Engineering Economist,* 17 (Spring 1972), 189-99.

————, *Financial Management and Policy,* 4th ed., Chaps. 4-8. Englewood Cliffs, N.J.: Prentice-Hall, 1977.

————, "Variation of Project Life as a Means of Adjusting for Risk," *Engineering Economist,* 21 (Spring 1976), 151-58.

WEINGARTNER, H. M., *Mathematical Programming and Analysis of Capital Budgeting Problems* Englewood Cliffs, N.J.: Prentice-Hall, 1963.

# appendix A

## Present Value Tables

**A.1.** Present Value of $1 Received at the End of $N$ Years

**A.2.** Present Value of $1 Received Continuously during the $N$th Year

**A.3.** Present Value of an Annuity of $1

I wish to express my thanks to Deena Eliosoff, who wrote the programs and generated the following tables, and to Brian Chernoff for his assistance with the conceptual issues underlying Table A.2.

**TABLE A.1**
**Present value of $1 received at the end of *N* years**

|  | Discount Rate | | | | | | | | | | | | | |
|---|---|---|---|---|---|---|---|---|---|---|---|---|---|---|
| Years Hence | 1% | 2% | 3% | 4% | 5% | 6% | 7% | 8% | 9% | 10% | 11% | 12% | 13% | 14% |
| 1 | .9901 | .9804 | .9709 | .9615 | .9524 | .9434 | .9346 | .9259 | .9174 | .9091 | .9009 | .8929 | .8850 | .8772 |
| 2 | .9803 | .9612 | .9426 | .9246 | .9070 | .8900 | .8734 | .8573 | .8417 | .8264 | .8116 | .7972 | .7831 | .7695 |
| 3 | .9706 | .9423 | .9151 | .8890 | .8638 | .8396 | .8163 | .7938 | .7722 | .7513 | .7312 | .7118 | .6931 | .6750 |
| 4 | .9610 | .9238 | .8885 | .8548 | .8227 | .7921 | .7629 | .7350 | .7084 | .6830 | .6587 | .6355 | .6133 | .5921 |
| 5 | .9515 | .9057 | .8626 | .8219 | .7835 | .7473 | .7130 | .6806 | .6499 | .6209 | .5935 | .5674 | .5428 | .5194 |
| 6 | .9420 | .8880 | .8375 | .7903 | .7462 | .7050 | .6663 | .6302 | .5963 | .5645 | .5346 | .5066 | .4803 | .4556 |
| 7 | .9327 | .8706 | .8131 | .7599 | .7107 | .6651 | .6227 | .5835 | .5470 | .5132 | .4817 | .4523 | .4251 | .3996 |
| 8 | .9235 | .8535 | .7894 | .7307 | .6768 | .6274 | .5820 | .5403 | .5019 | .4665 | .4339 | .4039 | .3762 | .3506 |
| 9 | .9143 | .8368 | .7664 | .7026 | .6446 | .5919 | .5439 | .5002 | .4604 | .4241 | .3909 | .3606 | .3329 | .3075 |
| 10 | .9053 | .8203 | .7441 | .6756 | .6139 | .5584 | .5083 | .4632 | .4224 | .3855 | .3522 | .3220 | .2946 | .2697 |
| 11 | .8963 | .8043 | .7224 | .6496 | .5847 | .5268 | .4751 | .4289 | .3875 | .3505 | .3173 | .2875 | .2607 | .2366 |
| 12 | .8874 | .7885 | .7014 | .6246 | .5568 | .4970 | .4440 | .3971 | .3555 | .3186 | .2858 | .2567 | .2307 | .2076 |
| 13 | .8787 | .7730 | .6810 | .6006 | .5303 | .4688 | .4150 | .3677 | .3262 | .2897 | .2575 | .2292 | .2042 | .1821 |
| 14 | .8700 | .7579 | .6611 | .5775 | .5051 | .4423 | .3878 | .3405 | .2992 | .2633 | .2320 | .2046 | .1807 | .1597 |
| 15 | .8613 | .7430 | .6419 | .5553 | .4810 | .4173 | .3624 | .3152 | .2745 | .2394 | .2090 | .1827 | .1599 | .1401 |
| 16 | .8528 | .7284 | .6232 | .5339 | .4581 | .3936 | .3387 | .2919 | .2519 | .2176 | .1883 | .1631 | .1415 | .1229 |
| 17 | .8444 | .7142 | .6050 | .5134 | .4363 | .3714 | .3166 | .2703 | .2311 | .1978 | .1696 | .1456 | .1252 | .1078 |
| 18 | .8360 | .7002 | .5874 | .4936 | .4155 | .3503 | .2959 | .2502 | .2120 | .1799 | .1528 | .1300 | .1108 | .0946 |
| 19 | .8277 | .6864 | .5703 | .4746 | .3957 | .3305 | .2765 | .2317 | .1945 | .1635 | .1377 | .1161 | .0981 | .0829 |
| 20 | .8195 | .6730 | .5537 | .4564 | .3769 | .3118 | .2584 | .2145 | .1784 | .1486 | .1240 | .1037 | .0868 | .0728 |
| 21 | .8114 | .6598 | .5375 | .4388 | .3589 | .2942 | .2415 | .1987 | .1637 | .1351 | .1117 | .0926 | .0768 | .0638 |
| 22 | .8034 | .6468 | .5219 | .4220 | .3418 | .2775 | .2257 | .1839 | .1502 | .1228 | .1007 | .0826 | .0680 | .0560 |
| 23 | .7954 | .6342 | .5067 | .4057 | .3256 | .2618 | .2109 | .1703 | .1378 | .1117 | .0907 | .0738 | .0601 | .0491 |
| 24 | .7876 | .6217 | .4919 | .3901 | .3101 | .2470 | .1971 | .1577 | .1264 | .1015 | .0817 | .0659 | .0532 | .0431 |
| 25 | .7798 | .6095 | .4776 | .3751 | .2953 | .2330 | .1842 | .1460 | .1160 | .0923 | .0736 | .0588 | .0471 | .0378 |

**TABLE A.1**–*Continued*

Discount Rate

| Years Hence | 15% | 16% | 17% | 18% | 19% | 20% | 21% | 22% | 23% | 24% | 25% | 26% | 27% | 28% |
|---|---|---|---|---|---|---|---|---|---|---|---|---|---|---|
| 1 | .8696 | .8621 | .8547 | .8475 | .8403 | .8333 | .8264 | .8197 | .8130 | .8065 | .8000 | .7937 | .7874 | .7813 |
| 2 | .7561 | .7432 | .7305 | .7182 | .7062 | .6944 | .6830 | .6719 | .6610 | .6504 | .6400 | .6299 | .6200 | .6104 |
| 3 | .6575 | .6407 | .6244 | .6086 | .5934 | .5787 | .5645 | .5507 | .5374 | .5245 | .5120 | .4999 | .4882 | .4768 |
| 4 | .5718 | .5523 | .5337 | .5158 | .4987 | .4823 | .4665 | .4514 | .4369 | .4230 | .4096 | .3968 | .3844 | .3725 |
| 5 | .4972 | .4761 | .4561 | .4371 | .4190 | .4019 | .3855 | .3700 | .3552 | .3411 | .3277 | .3149 | .3027 | .2910 |
| 6 | .4323 | .4104 | .3898 | .3704 | .3521 | .3349 | .3186 | .3033 | .2888 | .2751 | .2621 | .2499 | .2383 | .2274 |
| 7 | .3759 | .3538 | .3332 | .3139 | .2959 | .2791 | .2633 | .2486 | .2348 | .2218 | .2097 | .1983 | .1877 | .1776 |
| 8 | .3269 | .3050 | .2848 | .2660 | .2487 | .2326 | .2176 | .2038 | .1909 | .1789 | .1678 | .1574 | .1478 | .1388 |
| 9 | .2843 | .2630 | .2434 | .2255 | .2090 | .1938 | .1799 | .1670 | .1552 | .1443 | .1342 | .1249 | .1164 | .1084 |
| 10 | .2472 | .2267 | .2080 | .1911 | .1756 | .1615 | .1486 | .1369 | .1262 | .1164 | .1074 | .0992 | .0916 | .0847 |
| 11 | .2149 | .1954 | .1778 | .1619 | .1476 | .1346 | .1228 | .1122 | .1026 | .0938 | .0859 | .0787 | .0721 | .0662 |
| 12 | .1869 | .1685 | .1520 | .1372 | .1240 | .1122 | .1015 | .0920 | .0834 | .0757 | .0687 | .0625 | .0568 | .0517 |
| 13 | .1625 | .1452 | .1299 | .1163 | .1042 | .0935 | .0839 | .0754 | .0678 | .0610 | .0550 | .0496 | .0447 | .0404 |
| 14 | .1413 | .1252 | .1110 | .0985 | .0876 | .0779 | .0693 | .0618 | .0551 | .0492 | .0440 | .0393 | .0352 | .0316 |
| 15 | .1229 | .1079 | .0949 | .0835 | .0736 | .0649 | .0573 | .0507 | .0448 | .0397 | .0352 | .0312 | .0277 | .0247 |
| 16 | .1069 | .0930 | .0811 | .0708 | .0618 | .0541 | .0474 | .0415 | .0364 | .0320 | .0281 | .0248 | .0218 | .0193 |
| 17 | .0929 | .0802 | .0693 | .0600 | .0520 | .0451 | .0391 | .0340 | .0296 | .0258 | .0225 | .0197 | .0172 | .0150 |
| 18 | .0808 | .0691 | .0592 | .0508 | .0437 | .0376 | .0323 | .0279 | .0241 | .0208 | .0180 | .0156 | .0135 | .0118 |
| 19 | .0703 | .0596 | .0506 | .0431 | .0367 | .0313 | .0267 | .0229 | .0196 | .0168 | .0144 | .0124 | .0107 | .0092 |
| 20 | .0611 | .0514 | .0433 | .0365 | .0308 | .0261 | .0221 | .0187 | .0159 | .0135 | .0115 | .0098 | .0084 | .0072 |
| 21 | .0531 | .0443 | .0370 | .0309 | .0259 | .0217 | .0183 | .0154 | .0129 | .0109 | .0092 | .0078 | .0066 | .0056 |
| 22 | .0462 | .0382 | .0316 | .0262 | .0218 | .0181 | .0151 | .0126 | .0105 | .0088 | .0074 | .0062 | .0052 | .0044 |
| 23 | .0402 | .0329 | .0270 | .0222 | .0183 | .0151 | .0125 | .0103 | .0086 | .0071 | .0059 | .0049 | .0041 | .0034 |
| 24 | .0349 | .0284 | .0231 | .0188 | .0154 | .0126 | .0103 | .0085 | .0070 | .0057 | .0047 | .0039 | .0032 | .0027 |
| 25 | .0304 | .0245 | .0197 | .0160 | .0129 | .0105 | .0085 | .0069 | .0057 | .0046 | .0038 | .0031 | .0025 | .0021 |

**TABLE A.1**–*Continued*

Discount Rate

| Years Hence | 29% | 30% | 31% | 32% | 33% | 34% | 35% | 36% | 37% | 38% | 39% | 40% |
|---|---|---|---|---|---|---|---|---|---|---|---|---|
| 1 | .7752 | .7692 | .7634 | .7576 | .7519 | .7463 | .7407 | .7353 | .7299 | .7246 | .7194 | .7143 |
| 2 | .6009 | .5917 | .5827 | .5739 | .5653 | .5569 | .5487 | .5407 | .5328 | .5251 | .5176 | .5102 |
| 3 | .4658 | .4552 | .4448 | .4348 | .4251 | .4156 | .4064 | .3975 | .3889 | .3805 | .3724 | .3644 |
| 4 | .3611 | .3501 | .3396 | .3294 | .3196 | .3102 | .3011 | .2923 | .2839 | .2757 | .2679 | .2603 |
| 5 | .2799 | .2693 | .2592 | .2495 | .2403 | .2315 | .2230 | .2149 | .2072 | .1998 | .1927 | .1859 |
| 6 | .2170 | .2072 | .1979 | .1890 | .1807 | .1727 | .1652 | .1580 | .1512 | .1448 | .1386 | .1328 |
| 7 | .1682 | .1594 | .1510 | .1432 | .1358 | .1289 | .1224 | .1162 | .1104 | .1049 | .0997 | .0949 |
| 8 | .1304 | .1226 | .1153 | .1085 | .1021 | .0962 | .0906 | .0854 | .0806 | .0760 | .0718 | .0678 |
| 9 | .1011 | .0943 | .0880 | .0822 | .0768 | .0718 | .0671 | .0628 | .0588 | .0551 | .0516 | .0484 |
| 10 | .0784 | .0725 | .0672 | .0623 | .0577 | .0536 | .0497 | .0462 | .0429 | .0399 | .0371 | .0346 |
| 11 | .0607 | .0558 | .0513 | .0472 | .0434 | .0400 | .0368 | .0340 | .0313 | .0289 | .0267 | .0247 |
| 12 | .0471 | .0429 | .0392 | .0357 | .0326 | .0298 | .0273 | .0250 | .0229 | .0210 | .0192 | .0176 |
| 13 | .0365 | .0330 | .0299 | .0271 | .0245 | .0223 | .0202 | .0184 | .0167 | .0152 | .0138 | .0126 |
| 14 | .0283 | .0254 | .0228 | .0205 | .0185 | .0166 | .0150 | .0135 | .0122 | .0110 | .0099 | .0090 |
| 15 | .0219 | .0195 | .0174 | .0155 | .0139 | .0124 | .0111 | .0099 | .0089 | .0080 | .0072 | .0064 |
| 16 | .0170 | .0150 | .0133 | .0118 | .0104 | .0093 | .0082 | .0073 | .0065 | .0058 | .0051 | .0046 |
| 17 | .0132 | .0116 | .0101 | .0089 | .0078 | .0069 | .0061 | .0054 | .0047 | .0042 | .0037 | .0033 |
| 18 | .0102 | .0089 | .0077 | .0068 | .0059 | .0052 | .0045 | .0039 | .0035 | .0030 | .0027 | .0023 |
| 19 | .0079 | .0068 | .0059 | .0051 | .0044 | .0038 | .0033 | .0029 | .0025 | .0022 | .0019 | .0017 |
| 20 | .0061 | .0053 | .0045 | .0039 | .0033 | .0029 | .0025 | .0021 | .0018 | .0016 | .0014 | .0012 |
| 21 | .0048 | .0040 | .0034 | .0029 | .0025 | .0021 | .0018 | .0016 | .0013 | .0012 | .0010 | .0009 |
| 22 | .0037 | .0031 | .0026 | .0022 | .0019 | .0016 | .0014 | .0012 | .0010 | .0008 | .0007 | .0006 |
| 23 | .0029 | .0024 | .0020 | .0017 | .0014 | .0012 | .0010 | .0008 | .0007 | .0006 | .0005 | .0004 |
| 24 | .0022 | .0018 | .0015 | .0013 | .0011 | .0009 | .0007 | .0006 | .0005 | .0004 | .0004 | .0003 |
| 25 | .0017 | .0014 | .0012 | .0010 | .0008 | .0007 | .0006 | .0005 | .0004 | .0003 | .0003 | .0002 |

**TABLE A.2**
**Present value of $1 received continuously during the _N_th year**

| | | | | | | | Discount Rate | | | | | | |
|---|---|---|---|---|---|---|---|---|---|---|---|---|---|
| Years Hence | 1% | 2% | 3% | 4% | 5% | 6% | 7% | 8% | 9% | 10% | 11% | 12% | 13% | 14% |
| 1 | .9950 | .9902 | .9854 | .9806 | .9760 | .9714 | .9669 | .9625 | .9581 | .9538 | .9496 | .9454 | .9413 | .9373 |
| 2 | .9852 | .9707 | .9567 | .9429 | .9295 | .9164 | .9037 | .8912 | .8790 | .8671 | .8555 | .8441 | .8330 | .8222 |
| 3 | .9754 | .9517 | .9288 | .9067 | .8853 | .8646 | .8445 | .8252 | .8064 | .7883 | .7707 | .7537 | .7372 | .7212 |
| 4 | .9658 | .9331 | .9017 | .8718 | .8431 | .8156 | .7893 | .7641 | .7398 | .7166 | .6943 | .6729 | .6524 | .6326 |
| 5 | .9562 | .9148 | .8755 | .8383 | .8030 | .7695 | .7377 | .7075 | .6788 | .6515 | .6255 | .6008 | .5773 | .5549 |
| 6 | .9467 | .8968 | .8500 | .8060 | .7647 | .7259 | .6894 | .6551 | .6227 | .5922 | .5635 | .5365 | .5109 | .4868 |
| 7 | .9374 | .8792 | .8252 | .7750 | .7283 | .6848 | .6443 | .6065 | .5713 | .5384 | .5077 | .4790 | .4521 | .4270 |
| 8 | .9281 | .8620 | .8012 | .7452 | .6936 | .6461 | .6021 | .5616 | .5241 | .4895 | .4574 | .4277 | .4001 | .3746 |
| 9 | .9189 | .8451 | .7779 | .7165 | .6606 | .6095 | .5628 | .5200 | .4808 | .4450 | .4121 | .3818 | .3541 | .3286 |
| 10 | .9098 | .8285 | .7552 | .6890 | .6291 | .5750 | .5259 | .4815 | .4411 | .4045 | .3712 | .3409 | .3133 | .2882 |
| 11 | .9008 | .8123 | .7332 | .6625 | .5992 | .5424 | .4915 | .4458 | .4047 | .3677 | .3344 | .3044 | .2773 | .2528 |
| 12 | .8919 | .7964 | .7118 | .6370 | .5706 | .5117 | .4594 | .4128 | .3713 | .3343 | .3013 | .2718 | .2454 | .2218 |
| 13 | .8830 | .7807 | .6911 | .6125 | .5435 | .4828 | .4293 | .3822 | .3406 | .3039 | .2714 | .2427 | .2172 | .1945 |
| 14 | .8743 | .7654 | .6710 | .5889 | .5176 | .4554 | .4012 | .3539 | .3125 | .2763 | .2445 | .2167 | .1922 | .1706 |
| 15 | .8656 | .7504 | .6514 | .5663 | .4929 | .4297 | .3750 | .3277 | .2867 | .2512 | .2203 | .1935 | .1701 | .1497 |
| 16 | .8571 | .7357 | .6325 | .5445 | .4695 | .4053 | .3505 | .3034 | .2630 | .2283 | .1985 | .1727 | .1505 | .1313 |
| 17 | .8486 | .7213 | .6140 | .5236 | .4471 | .3824 | .3275 | .2809 | .2413 | .2076 | .1788 | .1542 | .1332 | .1152 |
| 18 | .8402 | .7071 | .5962 | .5034 | .4258 | .3608 | .3061 | .2601 | .2214 | .1887 | .1611 | .1377 | .1179 | .1010 |
| 19 | .8319 | .6933 | .5788 | .4841 | .4055 | .3403 | .2861 | .2409 | .2031 | .1716 | .1451 | .1229 | .1043 | .0886 |
| 20 | .8236 | .6797 | .5619 | .4655 | .3862 | .3211 | .2674 | .2230 | .1863 | .1560 | .1307 | .1098 | .0923 | .0777 |
| 21 | .8155 | .6664 | .5456 | .4476 | .3678 | .3029 | .2499 | .2065 | .1710 | .1418 | .1178 | .0980 | .0817 | .0682 |
| 22 | .8074 | .6533 | .5297 | .4303 | .3503 | .2857 | .2335 | .1912 | .1568 | .1289 | .1061 | .0875 | .0723 | .0598 |
| 23 | .7994 | .6405 | .5143 | .4138 | .3336 | .2696 | .2182 | .1770 | .1439 | .1172 | .0956 | .0781 | .0640 | .0525 |
| 24 | .7915 | .6279 | .4993 | .3979 | .3178 | .2543 | .2040 | .1639 | .1320 | .1065 | .0861 | .0698 | .0566 | .0460 |
| 25 | .7837 | .6156 | .4847 | .3826 | .3026 | .2399 | .1906 | .1518 | .1211 | .0968 | .0776 | .0623 | .0501 | .0404 |

**TABLE A.2**–*Continued*

| | | | | | | | Discount Rate | | | | | | | |
|---|---|---|---|---|---|---|---|---|---|---|---|---|---|---|
| Years Hence | 15% | 16% | 17% | 18% | 19% | 20% | 21% | 22% | 23% | 24% | 25% | 26% | 27% | 28% |
| 1 | .9333 | .9293 | .9255 | .9216 | .9179 | .9141 | .9105 | .9068 | .9033 | .8998 | .8963 | .8929 | .8895 | .8861 |
| 2 | .8115 | .8011 | .7910 | .7810 | .7713 | .7618 | .7525 | .7433 | .7344 | .7256 | .7170 | .7086 | .7004 | .6923 |
| 3 | .7057 | .6906 | .6761 | .6619 | .6482 | .6348 | .6219 | .6093 | .5971 | .5852 | .5736 | .5624 | .5515 | .5409 |
| 4 | .6136 | .5954 | .5778 | .5609 | .5447 | .5290 | .5139 | .4994 | .4854 | .4719 | .4589 | .4463 | .4342 | .4225 |
| 5 | .5336 | .5133 | .4939 | .4754 | .4577 | .4408 | .4247 | .4094 | .3946 | .3806 | .3671 | .3542 | .3419 | .3301 |
| 6 | .4640 | .4425 | .4221 | .4029 | .3846 | .3674 | .3510 | .3355 | .3208 | .3069 | .2937 | .2811 | .2692 | .2579 |
| 7 | .4035 | .3814 | .3608 | .3414 | .3232 | .3061 | .2901 | .2750 | .2609 | .2475 | .2350 | .2231 | .2120 | .2015 |
| 8 | .3508 | .3288 | .3084 | .2893 | .2716 | .2551 | .2398 | .2254 | .2121 | .1996 | .1880 | .1771 | .1669 | .1574 |
| 9 | .3051 | .2835 | .2636 | .2452 | .2282 | .2126 | .1981 | .1848 | .1724 | .1610 | .1504 | .1405 | .1314 | .1230 |
| 10 | .2653 | .2444 | .2253 | .2078 | .1918 | .1772 | .1638 | .1515 | .1402 | .1298 | .1203 | .1115 | .1035 | .0961 |
| 11 | .2307 | .2107 | .1925 | .1761 | .1612 | .1476 | .1353 | .1241 | .1140 | .1047 | .0962 | .0885 | .0815 | .0751 |
| 12 | .2006 | .1816 | .1646 | .1492 | .1354 | .1230 | .1118 | .1018 | .0927 | .0844 | .0770 | .0703 | .0642 | .0586 |
| 13 | .1744 | .1566 | .1406 | .1265 | .1138 | .1025 | .0924 | .0834 | .0753 | .0681 | .0616 | .0558 | .0505 | .0458 |
| 14 | .1517 | .1350 | .1202 | .1072 | .0956 | .0854 | .0764 | .0684 | .0612 | .0549 | .0493 | .0443 | .0398 | .0358 |
| 15 | .1319 | .1163 | .1027 | .0908 | .0804 | .0712 | .0631 | .0560 | .0498 | .0443 | .0394 | .0351 | .0313 | .0280 |
| 16 | .1147 | .1003 | .0878 | .0770 | .0675 | .0593 | .0522 | .0459 | .0405 | .0357 | .0315 | .0279 | .0247 | .0218 |
| 17 | .0997 | .0865 | .0751 | .0652 | .0568 | .0494 | .0431 | .0377 | .0329 | .0288 | .0252 | .0221 | .0194 | .0171 |
| 18 | .0867 | .0745 | .0641 | .0553 | .0477 | .0412 | .0356 | .0309 | .0268 | .0232 | .0202 | .0176 | .0153 | .0133 |
| 19 | .0754 | .0643 | .0548 | .0468 | .0401 | .0343 | .0295 | .0253 | .0218 | .0187 | .0161 | .0139 | .0120 | .0104 |
| 20 | .0656 | .0554 | .0469 | .0397 | .0337 | .0286 | .0243 | .0207 | .0177 | .0151 | .0129 | .0111 | .0095 | .0081 |
| 21 | .0570 | .0478 | .0401 | .0336 | .0283 | .0238 | .0201 | .0170 | .0144 | .0122 | .0103 | .0088 | .0075 | .0064 |
| 22 | .0496 | .0412 | .0342 | .0285 | .0238 | .0199 | .0166 | .0139 | .0117 | .0098 | .0083 | .0070 | .0059 | .0050 |
| 23 | .0431 | .0355 | .0293 | .0242 | .0200 | .0166 | .0137 | .0114 | .0095 | .0079 | .0066 | .0055 | .0046 | .0039 |
| 24 | .0375 | .0306 | .0250 | .0205 | .0168 | .0138 | .0114 | .0094 | .0077 | .0064 | .0053 | .0044 | .0036 | .0030 |
| 25 | .0326 | .0264 | .0214 | .0174 | .0141 | .0115 | .0094 | .0077 | .0063 | .0052 | .0042 | .0035 | .0029 | .0024 |

**TABLE A.2**–*Continued*

Discount Rate

| Years Hence | 29% | 30% | 31% | 32% | 33% | 34% | 35% | 36% | 37% | 38% | 39% | 40% |
|---|---|---|---|---|---|---|---|---|---|---|---|---|
| 1 | .8828 | .8796 | .8764 | .8732 | .8701 | .8670 | .8639 | .8609 | .8579 | .8549 | .8520 | .8491 |
| 2 | .6844 | .6766 | .6690 | .6615 | .6542 | .6470 | .6399 | .6330 | .6262 | .6195 | .6130 | .6065 |
| 3 | .5305 | .5205 | .5107 | .5011 | .4919 | .4828 | .4740 | .4654 | .4571 | .4489 | .4410 | .4332 |
| 4 | .4113 | .4004 | .3898 | .3797 | .3698 | .3603 | .3511 | .3422 | .3336 | .3253 | .3173 | .3095 |
| 5 | .3188 | .3080 | .2976 | .2876 | .2781 | .2689 | .2601 | .2516 | .2435 | .2357 | .2282 | .2210 |
| 6 | .2471 | .2369 | .2272 | .2179 | .2091 | .2007 | .1927 | .1850 | .1778 | .1708 | .1642 | .1579 |
| 7 | .1916 | .1822 | .1734 | .1651 | .1572 | .1498 | .1427 | .1361 | .1298 | .1238 | .1181 | .1128 |
| 8 | .1485 | .1402 | .1324 | .1251 | .1182 | .1118 | .1057 | .1000 | .0947 | .0897 | .0850 | .0806 |
| 9 | .1151 | .1078 | .1010 | .0947 | .0889 | .0834 | .0783 | .0736 | .0691 | .0650 | .0611 | .0575 |
| 10 | .0892 | .0829 | .0771 | .0718 | .0668 | .0622 | .0580 | .0541 | .0505 | .0471 | .0440 | .0411 |
| 11 | .0692 | .0638 | .0589 | .0544 | .0502 | .0464 | .0430 | .0398 | .0368 | .0341 | .0316 | .0294 |
| 12 | .0536 | .0491 | .0449 | .0412 | .0378 | .0347 | .0318 | .0292 | .0269 | .0247 | .0228 | .0210 |
| 13 | .0416 | .0378 | .0343 | .0312 | .0284 | .0259 | .0236 | .0215 | .0196 | .0179 | .0164 | .0150 |
| 14 | .0322 | .0290 | .0262 | .0236 | .0214 | .0193 | .0175 | .0158 | .0143 | .0130 | .0118 | .0107 |
| 15 | .0250 | .0223 | .0200 | .0179 | .0161 | .0144 | .0129 | .0116 | .0105 | .0094 | .0085 | .0076 |
| 16 | .0194 | .0172 | .0153 | .0136 | .0121 | .0108 | .0096 | .0085 | .0076 | .0068 | .0061 | .0055 |
| 17 | .0150 | .0132 | .0117 | .0103 | .0091 | .0080 | .0071 | .0063 | .0056 | .0049 | .0044 | .0039 |
| 18 | .0116 | .0102 | .0089 | .0078 | .0068 | .0060 | .0053 | .0046 | .0041 | .0036 | .0032 | .0028 |
| 19 | .0090 | .0078 | .0068 | .0059 | .0051 | .0045 | .0039 | .0034 | .0030 | .0026 | .0023 | .0020 |
| 20 | .0070 | .0060 | .0052 | .0045 | .0039 | .0033 | .0029 | .0025 | .0022 | .0019 | .0016 | .0014 |
| 21 | .0054 | .0046 | .0040 | .0034 | .0029 | .0025 | .0021 | .0018 | .0016 | .0014 | .0012 | .0010 |
| 22 | .0042 | .0036 | .0030 | .0026 | .0022 | .0019 | .0016 | .0014 | .0012 | .0010 | .0008 | .0007 |
| 23 | .0033 | .0027 | .0023 | .0019 | .0016 | .0014 | .0012 | .0010 | .0008 | .0007 | .0006 | .0005 |
| 24 | .0025 | .0021 | .0018 | .0015 | .0012 | .0010 | .0009 | .0007 | .0006 | .0005 | .0004 | .0004 |
| 25 | .0020 | .0016 | .0013 | .0011 | .0009 | .0008 | .0006 | .0005 | .0004 | .0004 | .0003 | .0003 |

**TABLE A.3**
**Present value of an annuity of $1**

|  | | | | | | | | Discount Rate | | | | | | |
|---|---|---|---|---|---|---|---|---|---|---|---|---|---|---|
| Years Hence | 1% | 2% | 3% | 4% | 5% | 6% | 7% | 8% | 9% | 10% | 11% | 12% | 13% | 14% |
| 1 | 0.9901 | 0.9804 | 0.9709 | 0.9615 | 0.9524 | 0.9434 | 0.9346 | 0.9259 | 0.9174 | 0.9091 | 0.9009 | 0.8929 | 0.8850 | 0.8772 |
| 2 | 1.9704 | 1.9416 | 1.9135 | 1.8861 | 1.8594 | 1.8334 | 1.8080 | 1.7833 | 1.7591 | 1.7355 | 1.7125 | 1.6901 | 1.6681 | 1.6467 |
| 3 | 2.9410 | 2.8839 | 2.8286 | 2.7751 | 2.7232 | 2.6730 | 2.6243 | 2.5771 | 2.5313 | 2.4869 | 2.4437 | 2.4018 | 2.3612 | 2.3216 |
| 4 | 3.9020 | 3.8077 | 3.7171 | 3.6299 | 3.5460 | 3.4651 | 3.3872 | 3.3121 | 3.2397 | 3.1699 | 3.1024 | 3.0373 | 2.9745 | 2.9137 |
| 5 | 4.8534 | 4.7135 | 4.5797 | 4.4518 | 4.3295 | 4.2124 | 4.1002 | 3.9927 | 3.8897 | 3.7908 | 3.6959 | 3.6048 | 3.5172 | 3.4331 |
| 6 | 5.7955 | 5.6014 | 5.4172 | 5.2421 | 5.0757 | 4.9173 | 4.7665 | 4.6229 | 4.4859 | 4.3553 | 4.2305 | 4.1114 | 3.9976 | 3.8887 |
| 7 | 6.7282 | 6.4720 | 6.2303 | 6.0021 | 5.7864 | 5.5824 | 5.3893 | 5.2064 | 5.0330 | 4.8684 | 4.7122 | 4.5638 | 4.4226 | 4.2883 |
| 8 | 7.6517 | 7.3255 | 7.0197 | 6.7327 | 6.4632 | 6.2098 | 5.9713 | 5.7466 | 5.5348 | 5.3349 | 5.1461 | 4.9676 | 4.7988 | 4.6389 |
| 9 | 8.5660 | 8.1622 | 7.7861 | 7.4353 | 7.1078 | 6.8017 | 6.5152 | 6.2469 | 5.9952 | 5.7590 | 5.5370 | 5.3282 | 5.1317 | 4.9464 |
| 10 | 9.4713 | 8.9826 | 8.5302 | 8.1109 | 7.7217 | 7.3601 | 7.0236 | 6.7101 | 6.4177 | 6.1446 | 5.8892 | 5.6502 | 5.4262 | 5.2161 |
| 11 | 10.3676 | 9.7869 | 9.2526 | 8.7605 | 8.3064 | 7.8869 | 7.4987 | 7.1390 | 6.8052 | 6.4951 | 6.2065 | 5.9377 | 5.6869 | 5.4527 |
| 12 | 11.2551 | 10.5753 | 9.9540 | 9.3851 | 8.8633 | 8.3838 | 7.9427 | 7.5361 | 7.1607 | 6.8137 | 6.4924 | 6.1944 | 5.9176 | 5.6603 |
| 13 | 12.1337 | 11.3484 | 10.6350 | 9.9856 | 9.3936 | 8.8527 | 8.3577 | 7.9038 | 7.4869 | 7.1034 | 6.7499 | 6.4235 | 6.1218 | 5.8424 |
| 14 | 13.0037 | 12.1063 | 11.2961 | 10.5631 | 9.8986 | 9.2950 | 8.7455 | 8.2442 | 7.7862 | 7.3667 | 6.9819 | 6.6282 | 6.3025 | 6.0021 |
| 15 | 13.8651 | 12.8493 | 11.9379 | 11.1184 | 10.3797 | 9.7122 | 9.1079 | 8.5595 | 8.0607 | 7.6061 | 7.1909 | 6.8109 | 6.4624 | 6.1422 |
| 16 | 14.7179 | 13.5777 | 12.5611 | 11.6523 | 10.8378 | 10.1059 | 9.4466 | 8.8514 | 8.3126 | 7.8237 | 7.3792 | 6.9740 | 6.6039 | 6.2651 |
| 17 | 15.5623 | 14.2919 | 13.1661 | 12.1657 | 11.2741 | 10.4773 | 9.7632 | 9.1216 | 8.5436 | 8.0216 | 7.5488 | 7.1196 | 6.7291 | 6.3729 |
| 18 | 16.3983 | 14.9920 | 13.7535 | 12.6593 | 11.6896 | 10.8276 | 10.0591 | 9.3719 | 8.7556 | 8.2014 | 7.7016 | 7.2497 | 6.8399 | 6.4674 |
| 19 | 17.2260 | 15.6785 | 14.3238 | 13.1339 | 12.0853 | 11.1581 | 10.3356 | 9.6036 | 8.9501 | 8.3649 | 7.8393 | 7.3658 | 6.9380 | 6.5504 |
| 20 | 18.0456 | 16.3514 | 14.8775 | 13.5903 | 12.4622 | 11.4699 | 10.5940 | 9.8181 | 9.1285 | 8.5136 | 7.9633 | 7.4694 | 7.0248 | 6.6231 |
| 21 | 18.8570 | 17.0112 | 15.4150 | 14.0292 | 12.8212 | 11.7641 | 10.8355 | 10.0168 | 9.2922 | 8.6487 | 8.0751 | 7.5620 | 7.1016 | 6.6870 |
| 22 | 19.6604 | 17.6581 | 15.9369 | 14.4511 | 13.1630 | 12.0416 | 11.0612 | 10.2007 | 9.4424 | 8.7715 | 8.1757 | 7.6446 | 7.1695 | 6.7429 |
| 23 | 20.4558 | 18.2922 | 16.4436 | 14.8568 | 13.4886 | 12.3034 | 11.2722 | 10.3711 | 9.5802 | 8.8832 | 8.2664 | 7.7184 | 7.2297 | 6.7921 |
| 24 | 21.2434 | 18.9139 | 16.9355 | 15.2470 | 13.7986 | 12.5504 | 11.4693 | 10.5288 | 9.7066 | 8.9847 | 8.3481 | 7.7843 | 7.2829 | 6.8351 |
| 25 | 22.0232 | 19.5235 | 17.4131 | 15.6221 | 14.0939 | 12.7834 | 11.6536 | 10.6748 | 9.8226 | 9.0770 | 8.4217 | 7.8431 | 7.3300 | 6.8729 |

**TABLE A.3**—*Continued*

*Discount Rate*

| Years Hence | 15% | 16% | 17% | 18% | 19% | 20% | 21% | 22% | 23% | 24% | 25% | 26% | 27% | 28% |
|---|---|---|---|---|---|---|---|---|---|---|---|---|---|---|
| 1 | 0.8696 | 0.8621 | 0.8547 | 0.8475 | 0.8403 | 0.8333 | 0.8264 | 0.8197 | 0.8130 | 0.8065 | 0.8000 | 0.7937 | 0.7874 | 0.7813 |
| 2 | 1.6257 | 1.6052 | 1.5852 | 1.5656 | 1.5465 | 1.5278 | 1.5095 | 1.4915 | 1.4740 | 1.4568 | 1.4400 | 1.4235 | 1.4074 | 1.3916 |
| 3 | 2.2832 | 2.2459 | 2.2096 | 2.1743 | 2.1399 | 2.1065 | 2.0739 | 2.0422 | 2.0114 | 1.9813 | 1.9520 | 1.9234 | 1.8956 | 1.8684 |
| 4 | 2.8550 | 2.7982 | 2.7432 | 2.6901 | 2.6386 | 2.5887 | 2.5404 | 2.4936 | 2.4483 | 2.4043 | 2.3616 | 2.3202 | 2.2800 | 2.2410 |
| 5 | 3.3522 | 3.2743 | 3.1993 | 3.1272 | 3.0576 | 2.9906 | 2.9260 | 2.8636 | 2.8035 | 2.7454 | 2.6893 | 2.6351 | 2.5827 | 2.5320 |
| 6 | 3.7845 | 3.6847 | 3.5892 | 3.4976 | 3.4098 | 3.3255 | 3.2446 | 3.1669 | 3.0923 | 3.0205 | 2.9514 | 2.8850 | 2.8210 | 2.7594 |
| 7 | 4.1604 | 4.0386 | 3.9224 | 3.8115 | 3.7057 | 3.6046 | 3.5079 | 3.4155 | 3.3270 | 3.2423 | 3.1611 | 3.0833 | 3.0087 | 2.9370 |
| 8 | 4.4873 | 4.3436 | 4.2072 | 4.0776 | 3.9544 | 3.8372 | 3.7256 | 3.6193 | 3.5179 | 3.4212 | 3.3289 | 3.2407 | 3.1564 | 3.0758 |
| 9 | 4.7716 | 4.6065 | 4.4506 | 4.3030 | 4.1633 | 4.0310 | 3.9054 | 3.7863 | 3.6731 | 3.5655 | 3.4631 | 3.3657 | 3.2728 | 3.1842 |
| 10 | 5.0188 | 4.8332 | 4.6586 | 4.4941 | 4.3389 | 4.1925 | 4.0541 | 3.9232 | 3.7993 | 3.6819 | 3.5705 | 3.4648 | 3.3644 | 3.2689 |
| 11 | 5.2337 | 5.0286 | 4.8364 | 4.6560 | 4.4865 | 4.3271 | 4.1769 | 4.0354 | 3.9018 | 3.7757 | 3.6564 | 3.5435 | 3.4365 | 3.3351 |
| 12 | 5.4206 | 5.1971 | 4.9884 | 4.7932 | 4.6105 | 4.4392 | 4.2784 | 4.1274 | 3.9852 | 3.8514 | 3.7251 | 3.6059 | 3.4933 | 3.3868 |
| 13 | 5.5831 | 5.3423 | 5.1183 | 4.9095 | 4.7147 | 4.5327 | 4.3624 | 4.2028 | 4.0530 | 3.9124 | 3.7801 | 3.6555 | 3.5381 | 3.4272 |
| 14 | 5.7245 | 5.4675 | 5.2293 | 5.0081 | 4.8023 | 4.6106 | 4.4317 | 4.2646 | 4.1082 | 3.9616 | 3.8241 | 3.6949 | 3.5733 | 3.4587 |
| 15 | 5.8474 | 5.5755 | 5.3242 | 5.0916 | 4.8759 | 4.6755 | 4.4890 | 4.3152 | 4.1530 | 4.0013 | 3.8593 | 3.7261 | 3.6010 | 3.4834 |
| 16 | 5.9542 | 5.6685 | 5.4053 | 5.1624 | 4.9377 | 4.7296 | 4.5364 | 4.3567 | 4.1894 | 4.0333 | 3.8874 | 3.7509 | 3.6228 | 3.5026 |
| 17 | 6.0472 | 5.7487 | 5.4746 | 5.2223 | 4.9897 | 4.7746 | 4.5755 | 4.3908 | 4.2190 | 4.0591 | 3.9099 | 3.7705 | 3.6400 | 3.5177 |
| 18 | 6.1280 | 5.8178 | 5.5339 | 5.2732 | 5.0333 | 4.8122 | 4.6079 | 4.4187 | 4.2431 | 4.0799 | 3.9279 | 3.7861 | 3.6536 | 3.5294 |
| 19 | 6.1982 | 5.8775 | 5.5845 | 5.3162 | 5.0700 | 4.8435 | 4.6346 | 4.4415 | 4.2627 | 4.0967 | 3.9424 | 3.7985 | 3.6642 | 3.5386 |
| 20 | 6.2593 | 5.9288 | 5.6278 | 5.3527 | 5.1009 | 4.8696 | 4.6567 | 4.4603 | 4.2786 | 4.1103 | 3.9539 | 3.8083 | 3.6726 | 3.5458 |
| 21 | 6.3125 | 5.9731 | 5.6648 | 5.3837 | 5.1268 | 4.8913 | 4.6750 | 4.4756 | 4.2916 | 4.1212 | 3.9631 | 3.8161 | 3.6792 | 3.5514 |
| 22 | 6.3587 | 6.0113 | 5.6964 | 5.4099 | 5.1486 | 4.9094 | 4.6900 | 4.4882 | 4.3021 | 4.1300 | 3.9705 | 3.8223 | 3.6844 | 3.5558 |
| 23 | 6.3988 | 6.0442 | 5.7234 | 5.4321 | 5.1668 | 4.9245 | 4.7025 | 4.4985 | 4.3106 | 4.1371 | 3.9764 | 3.8273 | 3.6885 | 3.5592 |
| 24 | 6.4338 | 6.0726 | 5.7465 | 5.4509 | 5.1822 | 4.9371 | 4.7128 | 4.5070 | 4.3176 | 4.1428 | 3.9811 | 3.8312 | 3.6918 | 3.5619 |
| 25 | 6.4641 | 6.0971 | 5.7662 | 5.4669 | 5.1951 | 4.9476 | 4.7213 | 4.5139 | 4.3232 | 4.1474 | 3.9849 | 3.8342 | 3.6943 | 3.5640 |

Discount Rate

| Years Hence | 29% | 30% | 31% | 32% | 33% | 34% | 35% | 36% | 37% | 38% | 39% | 40% |
|---|---|---|---|---|---|---|---|---|---|---|---|---|
| 1 | 0.7752 | 0.7692 | 0.7634 | 0.7576 | 0.7519 | 0.7463 | 0.7407 | 0.7353 | 0.7299 | 0.7246 | 0.7194 | 0.7143 |
| 2 | 1.3761 | 1.3609 | 1.3461 | 1.3315 | 1.3172 | 1.3032 | 1.2894 | 1.2760 | 1.2627 | 1.2497 | 1.2370 | 1.2245 |
| 3 | 1.8420 | 1.8161 | 1.7909 | 1.7663 | 1.7423 | 1.7188 | 1.6959 | 1.6735 | 1.6516 | 1.6302 | 1.6093 | 1.5889 |
| 4 | 2.2031 | 2.1662 | 2.1305 | 2.0957 | 2.0618 | 2.0290 | 1.9969 | 1.9658 | 1.9355 | 1.9060 | 1.8772 | 1.8492 |
| 5 | 2.4830 | 2.4356 | 2.3897 | 2.3452 | 2.3021 | 2.2604 | 2.2200 | 2.1807 | 2.1427 | 2.1058 | 2.0699 | 2.0352 |
| 6 | 2.7000 | 2.6427 | 2.5875 | 2.5342 | 2.4828 | 2.4331 | 2.3852 | 2.3388 | 2.2939 | 2.2506 | 2.2086 | 2.1680 |
| 7 | 2.8682 | 2.8021 | 2.7386 | 2.6775 | 2.6187 | 2.5620 | 2.5075 | 2.4550 | 2.4043 | 2.3555 | 2.3083 | 2.2628 |
| 8 | 2.9986 | 2.9247 | 2.8539 | 2.7860 | 2.7208 | 2.6582 | 2.5982 | 2.5404 | 2.4849 | 2.4315 | 2.3801 | 2.3306 |
| 9 | 3.0997 | 3.0190 | 2.9419 | 2.8681 | 2.7976 | 2.7300 | 2.6653 | 2.6033 | 2.5437 | 2.4866 | 2.4317 | 2.3790 |
| 10 | 3.1781 | 3.0915 | 3.0091 | 2.9304 | 2.8553 | 2.7836 | 2.7150 | 2.6495 | 2.5867 | 2.5265 | 2.4689 | 2.4136 |
| 11 | 3.2388 | 3.1473 | 3.0604 | 2.9776 | 2.8987 | 2.8236 | 2.7519 | 2.6834 | 2.6180 | 2.5555 | 2.4956 | 2.4383 |
| 12 | 3.2859 | 3.1903 | 3.0995 | 3.0133 | 2.9314 | 2.8534 | 2.7792 | 2.7084 | 2.6409 | 2.5764 | 2.5148 | 2.4559 |
| 13 | 3.3224 | 3.2233 | 3.1294 | 3.0404 | 2.9559 | 2.8757 | 2.7994 | 2.7268 | 2.6576 | 2.5916 | 2.5286 | 2.4685 |
| 14 | 3.3507 | 3.2487 | 3.1522 | 3.0609 | 2.9744 | 2.8923 | 2.8144 | 2.7403 | 2.6698 | 2.6026 | 2.5386 | 2.4775 |
| 15 | 3.3726 | 3.2682 | 3.1696 | 3.0764 | 2.9883 | 2.9047 | 2.8255 | 2.7502 | 2.6787 | 2.6106 | 2.5457 | 2.4839 |
| 16 | 3.3896 | 3.2832 | 3.1829 | 3.0882 | 2.9987 | 2.9140 | 2.8337 | 2.7575 | 2.6852 | 2.6164 | 2.5509 | 2.4885 |
| 17 | 3.4028 | 3.2948 | 3.1931 | 3.0971 | 3.0065 | 2.9209 | 2.8398 | 2.7629 | 2.6899 | 2.6206 | 2.5546 | 2.4918 |
| 18 | 3.4130 | 3.3037 | 3.2008 | 3.1039 | 3.0124 | 2.9260 | 2.8443 | 2.7668 | 2.6934 | 2.6236 | 2.5573 | 2.4941 |
| 19 | 3.4210 | 3.3105 | 3.2067 | 3.1090 | 3.0169 | 2.9299 | 2.8476 | 2.7697 | 2.6959 | 2.6258 | 2.5592 | 2.4958 |
| 20 | 3.4271 | 3.3158 | 3.2112 | 3.1129 | 3.0202 | 2.9327 | 2.8501 | 2.7718 | 2.6977 | 2.6274 | 2.5606 | 2.4970 |
| 21 | 3.4319 | 3.3198 | 3.2147 | 3.1158 | 3.0227 | 2.9349 | 2.8519 | 2.7734 | 2.6991 | 2.6285 | 2.5616 | 2.4979 |
| 22 | 3.4356 | 3.3230 | 3.2173 | 3.1180 | 3.0246 | 2.9365 | 2.8533 | 2.7746 | 2.7000 | 2.6294 | 2.5623 | 2.4985 |
| 23 | 3.4384 | 3.3254 | 3.2193 | 3.1197 | 3.0260 | 2.9377 | 2.8543 | 2.7754 | 2.7008 | 2.6300 | 2.5628 | 2.4989 |
| 24 | 3.4406 | 3.3272 | 3.2209 | 3.1210 | 3.0271 | 2.9386 | 2.8550 | 2.7760 | 2.7013 | 2.6304 | 2.5632 | 2.4992 |
| 25 | 3.4423 | 3.3286 | 3.2220 | 3.1220 | 3.0279 | 2.9392 | 2.8556 | 2.7765 | 2.7017 | 2.6307 | 2.5634 | 2.4994 |

# Short Answers to Odd-Numbered Problems

# SHORT ANSWERS TO ODD-NUMBERED PROBLEMS

## Chapter 1

1.1    (a)    $Y = a + bX$

       (b)    $Y = a + bX^2$ or $Y = a + bX + cX^2$

       (c)    $Y = a + bX^3$ etc.

       (d)    $Y = ae^{bX}$ or $Y = a + b^X$

       (e)    $Y = aX^b$

       (f)    $Y = a/X^b$ or $Y = aX^{-b}$

       (g)    $Y = a \log bX$

1.3    (a)    $Y = -27.5$ is a maximum

       (b)    $Y = 12$ is a minimum

       (c)    $A = -15,245.25$ is a minimum

       (d)    $K = 244.667$ is a maximum

1.5    (a)    Mean = 4.076

       (b)    Mode = 5.0

       (c)    Median = 4.0

       (d)    SD = 1.498

       (e)    Negatively skewed.

## Chapter 2

2.1    (a)    SD = 5395.7 for the Large plant and 2903.6 for the Small plant

       (b)    CV = 0.8429 for the Large plant and 0.4575 for the Small plant

2.3    (a)    Outright purchase costs \$1,186,196.50, while the lease option costs \$1,419,100, both in present value terms.

       (b)    Plan A—outright purchase has net present value of \$420,153.50.

483

2.5    (a)    Medium-price strategy ENPV = $3806.30

        (b)    No. ENPV of Bonds alternative is zero.

        (c)    High, Low, Medium

        (d)    Medium, Low, High

2.7    (a)    Regular-sized store, ENPV = $327,650

## Chapter 3

There are no numerical answers involved in problems 3.1, 3.3, and 3.5.

3.6    (a)    Approximately 97 cents per bottle.

        (b)    No one will buy brand A, and only those with high MRS will buy brand B.

3.7    (a)    Sportscar B

        (b)    Sportscar A

        (c)    Sportscar A

## Chapter 4

4.1    (c)    Demand is elastic down to about $4.78, unitary elasticity at $4.77, and is inelastic below about $4.76.

4.3    (a)    Price elasticity = 1.89

        (b)    Advertising elasticity = 2.675

        (c)    Profit maximizing price is approximately $8.12.

4.5    (a)    No, since MR exceeds MC

        (b)    Profit maximizing price is approximately $1.81.

4.7    (a)    Sales maximizing price is $750.

        (b)    Advertising expenditures should be $18,800,000.

## Chapter 5

5.1    (a)    160; 335; 500; 640; 800.

        (c)    MC = $4.00 and all estimates are accurate.

5.3    (b)    Sales = 5283.74 + 4.15 per thousand households.

        (c)    Demand in 1980 is forecast as 11,488 units.

5.5    (b)    $P = 39.859 - 0.48254Q$, with $R^2 = 0.95$

        (c)    Approximately 35 hours flying instruction per day will be demanded.

        (d)    Strictly, the optimal price is $24.93.

5.7    (a)    These exceed expected sales due to company practice of printing 2-3 per cent more than expected demand.

        (b)    Your answer will depend upon assumptions made. My assumptions gave me the following:

| *Campaign* | *Estimated Sales* |
| --- | --- |
| 10 | 1059.98 |
| 11 | 1044.03 |
| 12 | 1028.08 |

## Chapter 6

6.1　(a)　Increasing returns up to 5, constant returns from 6 to 12, and diminishing returns for the 13th and subsequent divers employed.

　　　(b)　5

　　　(c)　14

6.3　(a)

| L | 1 | 2 | 3 | 4 | 5 | 6 |
|---|---|---|---|---|---|---|
| TP | 66.2 | 85.0 | 99.1 | 103.6 | 93.2 | 63.0 |
| MP | 66.2 | 18.8 | 14.1 | 4.5 | −10.4 | −30.2 |

　　　(b)　Diminishing returns to labor throughout.

　　　(c)　TP is maximized at approximately 385 hours of labor input.

6.5　(b)

| Q | 10 | 15 | 20 | 25 | 30 |
|---|----|----|----|----|----|
| TVC | $7.29 | 12.30 | 17.99 | 23.91 | 30.75 |

　　　(c)　The production function is homogeneous to degree less than one, implying decreasing returns to scale. At each level of the fixed input there are diminishing returns to the variable input.

6.7　(b)　Economies of plant size up to and including Plant 4. Constant returns to plant size between Plants 4 and 5. Diseconomies of plant size for Plant 6.

　　　(c)　Plant 3.

## Chapter 7

7.1　(a)　Buy, since incremental cost of this option ($4,930) is less than the incremental cost ($6,105) of making the assemblies.

　　　(b)　Are incremental costs per unit equal to average variable costs? Is Fenton's quality and reliability of delivery acceptable?

7.3　Take the order, since contribution is enhanced by doing so (under reasonable assumptions. The exact amount of contribution will depend upon the actual assumptions you made.)

7.5　Incremental cost is $3,105.67, assuming that three cost categories are fully variable and the rest are fixed, and including the opportunity costs of $338.87.

7.7　Yes, since the proposal is expected to contribute $738 to overheads and profits, assuming no subsequent goodwill or illwill effects, price competition from rivals, etc.

## Chapter 8

8.1　(c)　Estimated incremental cost is $4,000.

　　　(d)　Estimated incremental cost is $16,000.

　　　(e)　*Ceteris paribus* is assumed to prevail over period of observations and prediction period. Above answers assume that freehand line of best fit is the true relationship and that deviations from this line are due to random influences.

8.3　(a)　For the proposed plant:

| Q | 400 | 800 | 1200 | 1600 | 2000 |
|---|-----|-----|------|------|------|
| AVC($) | 1.21 | 0.87 | 0.65 | 0.70 | 1.08 |
| MC($) | | 0.54 | 0.21 | 0.85 | 2.60 |

For the present plant:

| Q | 100 | 300 | 500 | 700 | 900 | 1000 |
|---|-----|-----|-----|-----|-----|------|
| AVC($) | 1.05 | 0.77 | 0.72 | 0.80 | 0.89 | 1.17 |
| MC($) | | 0.63 | 0.65 | 1.00 | 1.21 | 3.68 |

(b)  No, Beaudet should not invest in the new plant, according to the expected value, maximin, and coefficient of variation criteria. The expected value of profits in the proposed plant is $104,990 compared to $593,360 in the present plant. (Some cost data was obtained by interpolation, and thus these results are approximate.)

8.5  (a)  Yes, since contribution with the special order is $14,060 greater than without the order. It should be produced as follows: 1000 in Plant A in January, 2000 in Plant B in January, 5000 in Plant A in February, and 7000 in Plant B in February.

(b)  Will cost trends continue until full capacity? Can January production achieve full capacity this late in the month? Is there any impact on goodwill, illwill, labor relations, etc.?

8.7  Autorollers should have built the new plant in Ohio, since it was expected to increase total profit by $1,493,000 in 1980 dollars. (Approximately, since a cost extrapolation is involved.)

## Chapter 9

9.1  (a)  The price falls to clear the market.

(b)  Each firm reduces output to point where MC = MR, or ceases production if P < AVC.

(c)  No firms will exit the industry unless the temporary reduction of demand lasts longer than the short run.

9.3  (a)  The firms probably envision a kinked demand curve for their products.

(b)  The auto firms traditionally set prices at the start of each model year, and a situation of conscious parallelism probably applies, giving rise to an envisioned *mutatis mutandis* demand curve for price increases.

9.5  Fluctuating demand and supply conditions cause entry in response to pure profits and exit in response to losses.

## Chapter 10

10.1  Each firm's *mutatis mutandis* demand curve has the same intercept and three times the slope of the market demand curve. The price followers face kinked demand curves at the price leader's profit-maximizing price.

10.3  (a)  Where $\Sigma MR = \Sigma MC$

(b)  Where each MC rises to the level of $\Sigma MR = \Sigma MC$

(c)  Where each MR falls to the level of $\Sigma MR = \Sigma MC$

(d)  The price in each market is the market clearing price for the quantity assigned to that market.

10.5  (a)  New entrants undercut Prangle's price and enjoyed an elastic demand response, eroding Prangle's market share at a rate faster than the market was expanding.

(b)  Demand curve is apparently kinked at $8.

(c)  $8 to retailers, where contribution will be $2.2 million.

10.7  (a)  The firms should practice limit pricing if the ENPV of profits out to their time horizon is greater under this option compared to the ENPV of profits under the present price (with subsequent changes). The limit price is probably close to $30 per ton.

(b)  A price of $106 per ton would maximize the joint profits of the six firms presuming no further entry is possible or that time horizons are very short. Since these two conditions are probably not met, the firms will more likely set a considerably lower price.

## Chapter 11

11.1  (a)  The firm's cost and revenue curves can be plotted by interpolation from the following data:

| Q | 20,500 | 29,000 | 32,500 |
|---|--------|--------|--------|
| TR($) | 184,500 | 203,000 | 195,000 |
| TC($) | 121,915 | 138,359 | 162,795 |

(b)  It appears that the profit target can (barely) be attained in the area of 26,000 units. Thus the firm should charge approximately $7.66 per unit.

11.3  Management should implement the new policy since it is expected to contribute $1,708.59 per week. Assumptions include no price competition from rivals and no adverse reaction by regular customers.

11.5  (a)  Price between $110 and $115 for the typical bag, given apparently inelastic demand for these bags and conscious parallelism of rivals.

(b)  Product diversification and promotional efforts, to mention the most obvious.

11.7  (a)  To maximize contribution, price should be set at $5.38, at which 18,494 units would be sold (and 6,507 units would be left over) for a maximum contribution of $49,495.72.

(b)  To maximize sales volume subject to a $40,000 contribution, price should be $3.72.

11.9  (a)  $17.75, $17.50, and $14.50 approximately.

(b)  If entry of other firms is expected to be relatively quick, and/or if product is highly differentiable with prospects of repeat sales and sales of accessory items.

## Chapter 12

12.1  By interpolating between the expected value points for each situation, the following (approximate) optimal bid prices can be found:

(a)  $65,000

(b)  $61,500

(c)  $58,750 and

(d)  $56,500.

12.3  (a)  Incremental costs are $66,200.

(b)  Somewhere between incremental costs and full costs plus 15 percent, with the actual price depending on your judgment of the situation.

(c)  Both the likely bids of rivals and the future demand situation bear investigation.

12.5  (a)  To be assured of a success probability of one, you would need to bid in the vicinity of $396,500.

(b)  $428,000, although your answer will depend upon the assumptions you make.

12.7  (a)  $-396.00, $105.00, and $70.00.

(b)  $2,450 bid price has the highest expected value.

(c)  Tender a bid of (audited) costs plus 10 percent, for example.

## Chapter 13

13.1  (a)  2,822 pounds of fish cakes and 8,612 pounds of fish meal.

(b)  $8,286.00

(c)  Shredding and Packing.

13.3  (a)  1.25 Holsteins per Jersey

(b)  51 Jerseys and 64 Holsteins

(c)  $137,205.00

13.5  (a)  Minimize TC = 0.125A + 0.085B + 0.05C
subject to
$$\begin{aligned}
A + B + C - S_1 &= 100 \\
2A + B + 7C - S_2 &= 150 \\
3.3A + 5B + 2C - S_3 &= 300 \\
A - S_4 &= 30 \\
B - S_5 &= 15 \\
C - S_6 &= 10
\end{aligned}$$

(b)  30 grams of chocolate; 20.33 grams of caramel; and 49.67 grams of nuts.

(c)  Yes. Contribution is currently $0.004 per bar and would rise to $0.020384 per bar, which represents a more than five-fold increase.

13.7  (a)  Lantern, 530.97 units; Pot, 1,917.42 units; Can, 600 units; Ornament, 300 units. Maximum contribution, $6,371.97. Shadow price of metal input, $7.06 per kg. Shadow price of machine input, $1.13 per hour.

(b)  Investigate the expansion of the two constrained inputs, and do so if the incremental cost per unit is less than the shadow price for each input.

## Chapter 14

14.1  (a)  No, since $dQ/dA = 12.61$ exceeds the reciprocal of the contribution per unit.

(b)  We cannot say with certainty, since the slope of the advertising function is likely to diminish as advertising increases, and *ceteris paribus* may not hold with respect to rivals, for example.

14.3  (a)  $11,233.53. Although the relationship is highly significant, this represents a substantial extrapolation outside the data base.

(b)  Approximately $3,750.

(c)  The impact of advertising expenditures may not accrue totally in the current period. Thus current advertising expenditures may not be too high.

(d)  Maintain advertising expenditure at $6,000 per month and investigate the residual impact of this advertising.

14.5  (a)  Optimal advertising expenditure is approximately $11,000 per month. Optimal price for the MPE is $4.50. (This represents a 70 percent markup on AVC, which may be applied to all pizzas in the product line, presuming that information on demand for specific sizes and types of pizza is not available.)

(b)  Approximately $563.26.

14.7 (a) Your argument would be based on the proposition that rivals are unlikely to react to your increased advertising, and that the incremental revenue would exceed the incremental cost.

(b) The information required would pertain to the attributes desired by consumers and their likely response to your increased advertising.

## Chapter 15

15.1 NPV's are $2,007.26 for A, $11,744.97 for B, $18,212.73 for C and −$2,178.78 for D. Therefore invest in Projects A, B and C only, and invest remainder at 8 percent opportunity interest rate.

15.3 (a) NPV is $49,416.53

(b) IRR is almost 30 percent

(c) NPV is $37,031.18

(d) Latter method underestimates the NPV by ignoring the interest that may be earned by funds that arrive before the end of the year.

(e) The kayak project.

15.5 (a) The NPV's are $10,172.85 for hamburgers, $12,283.25 for chicken, and $16,488.75 for tacos.

(b) The payback periods are two years and 60 days for hamburgers, two years and 28 days for chicken, and two years and 26 days for tacos.

(c) The professors should invest in the taco franchise, since the NPV is highest and the payback period lowest for this venture, assuming their time horizon to be only three years.

15.7 (a)

| Project | NPV | Rank |
|---------|-----|------|
| West | $103,144.56 | 1 |
| East | 86,177.72 | 2 |
| South | 81,627.58 | 3 |
| North | 67,962.82 | 4 |

(b)

| Project | PI | Rank |
|---------|-----|------|
| North | 1.566 | 1 |
| South | 1.453 | 2 |
| West | 1.362 | 3 |
| East | 1,345 | 4 |

(c) North and South, with the remaining $200,000 invested at the opportunity interest rates.

(d) $349,590.40, being the NPV of North and South plus the remaining $200,000.

# Author Index

# Subject Index